THE
CLANDESTINAUTS

PUBLISHERS TOM KACZYNSKI AND JORDAN SHIVELEY
DESIGN BY TOM KACZYNSKI
PRODUCTION BY JORDAN SHIVELEY

UNCIVILIZED BOOKS
P.O. BOX 6534
MINNEAPOLIS, MN 55406
USA
UNCIVILIZEDBOOKS.COM

ISBN: 9781941250259

FIRST EDITION, 2018

10 9 8 7 6 5 4 3 2 1

PRINTED IN CHINA

THE CLANDES

TIM SIEVERT

FORTRESS OF THE CRIMSON WIZARD

LOW VOLGSBERG

SOURFOOT CAVERNS

safest travels

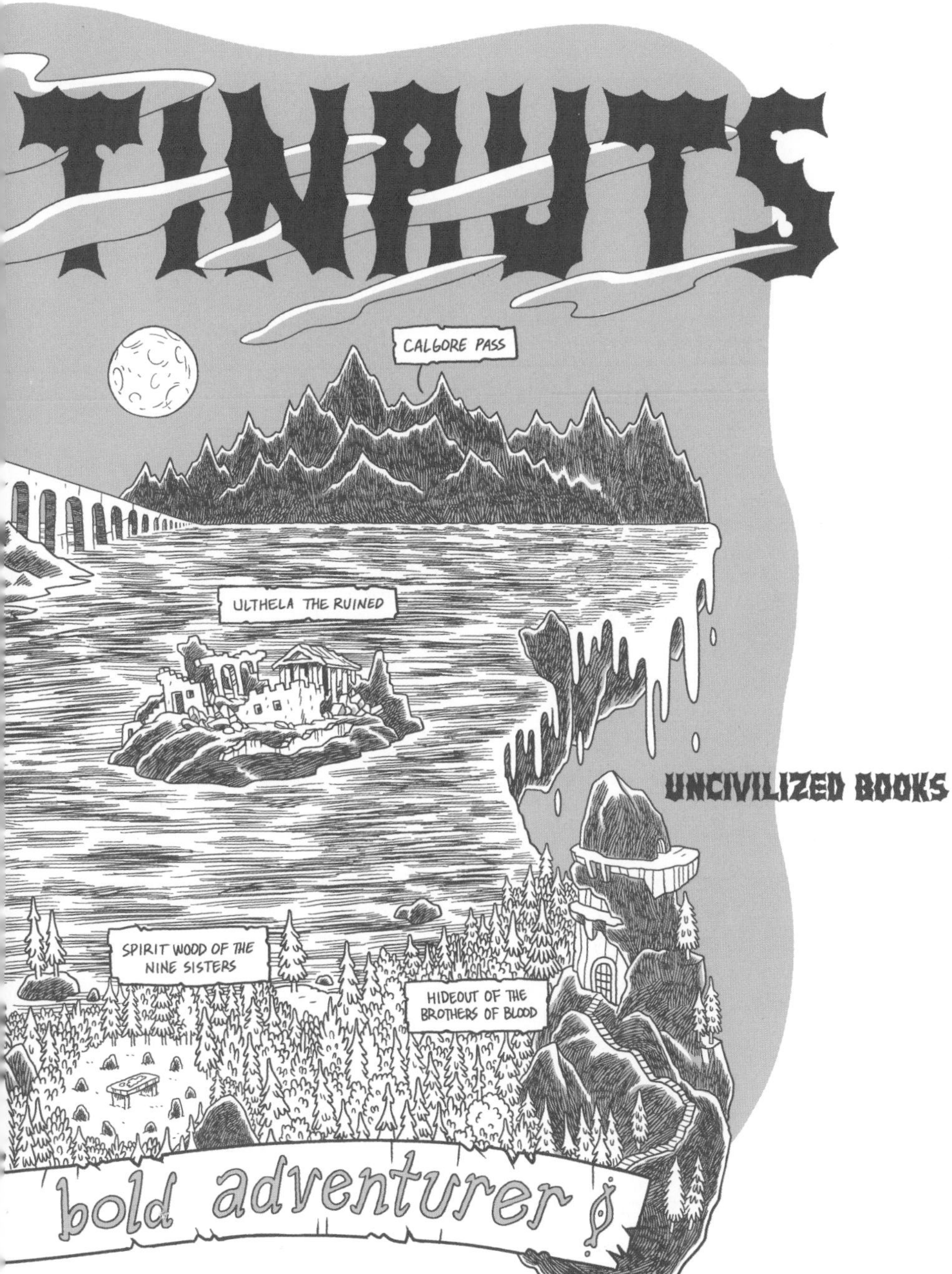
TINAUTS
CALGORE PASS
ULTHELA THE RUINED
UNCIVILIZED BOOKS
SPIRIT WOOD OF THE NINE SISTERS
HIDEOUT OF THE BROTHERS OF BLOOD
bold adventurers

the CLANDESTINAUTS

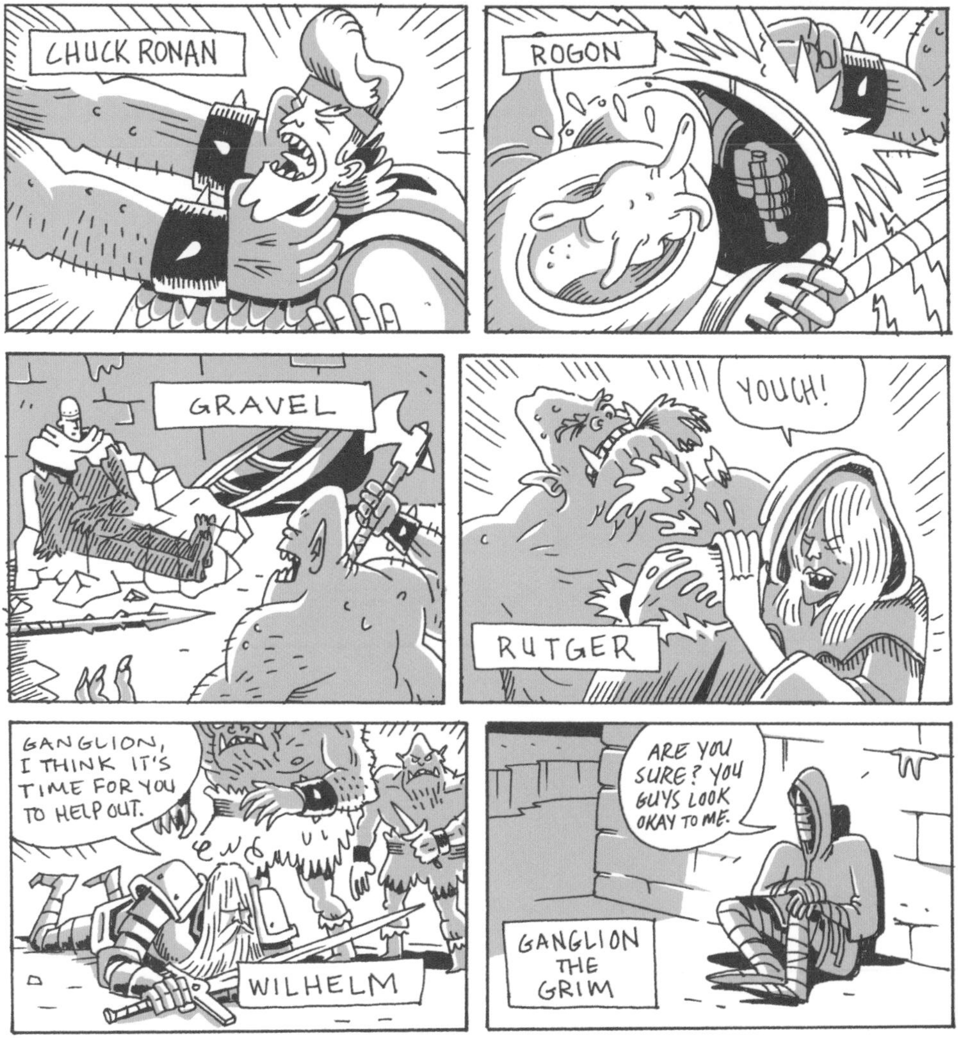
CHUCK RONAN
ROGON
GRAVEL
YOUCH!
RUTGER
GANGLION, I THINK IT'S TIME FOR YOU TO HELP OUT.
WILHELM
ARE YOU SURE? YOU GUYS LOOK OKAY TO ME.
GANGLION THE GRIM

WHAT? NO! LEAVE THIS TO A TRUE WARLOCK!
WATCH AND LEARN CHILD, JUST YOU WATCH AND LEARN.
I'VE GOT FRIENDS WHO'LL EAT THEIR EYELIDS BEFORE YOU COULD PULL YOUR ROD OUT.
SWOOP!
BUT I'VE GOT MY ROD OUT!
HA!
YOU SOLD YOUR SOUL FOR THAT WITHERED OLD WAND OF YOURS.
I'VE SWORN MY FLESH...
...AND BLOOD...
...FOR TRUE POWER!
AH, THERE YOU ARE.
CLANDESTINAUTS, WE'D BETTER CLEAR OUT OF HERE!

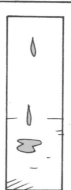

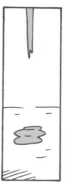

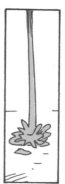

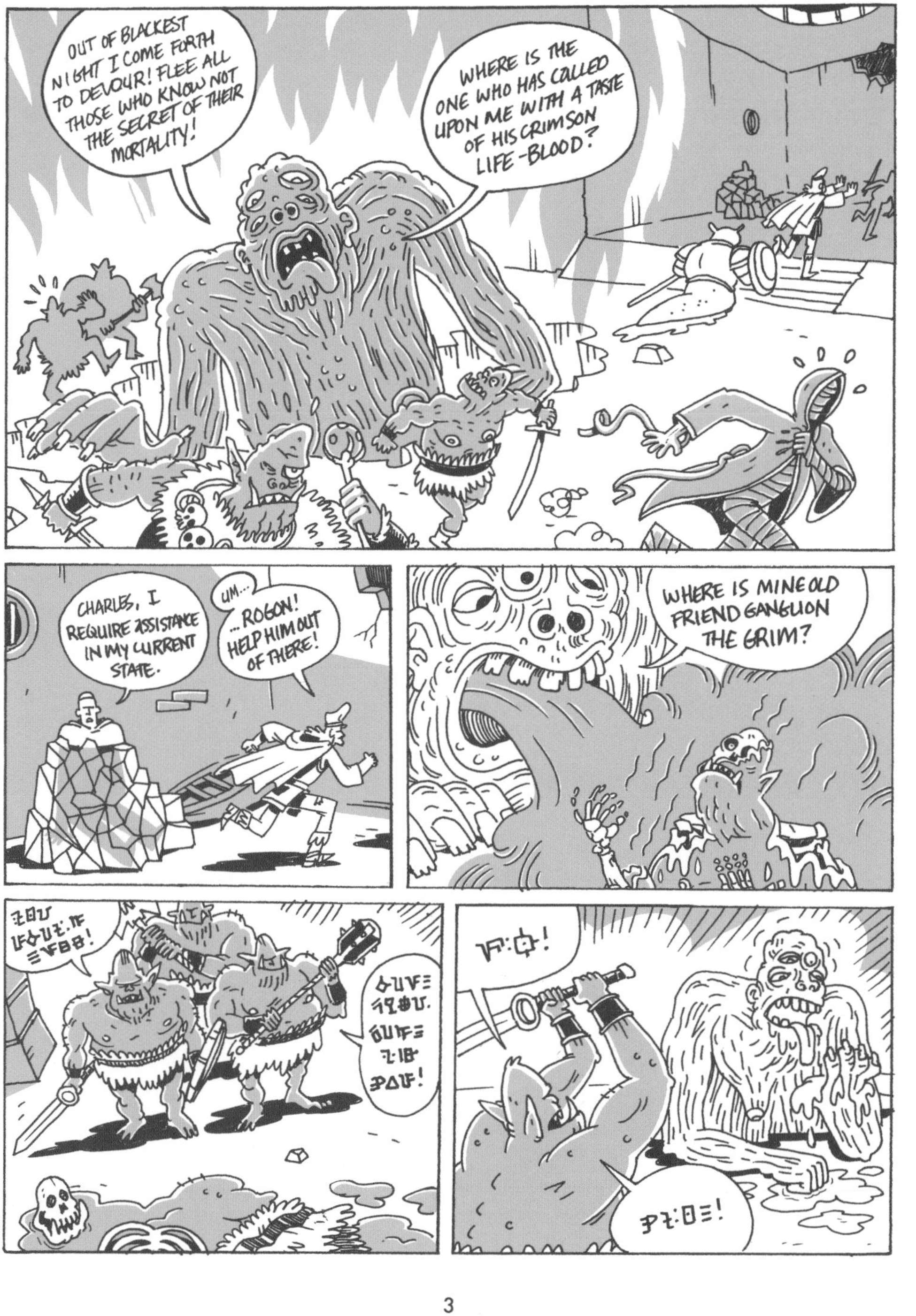

OUT OF BLACKEST NIGHT I COME FORTH TO DEVOUR! FLEE ALL THOSE WHO KNOW NOT THE SECRET OF THEIR MORTALITY!
WHERE IS THE ONE WHO HAS CALLED UPON ME WITH A TASTE OF HIS CRIMSON LIFE-BLOOD?
CHARLES, I REQUIRE ASSISTANCE IN MY CURRENT STATE.
UM... ...ROGON! HELP HIM OUT OF THERE!
WHERE IS MINE OLD FRIEND GANGLION THE GRIM?

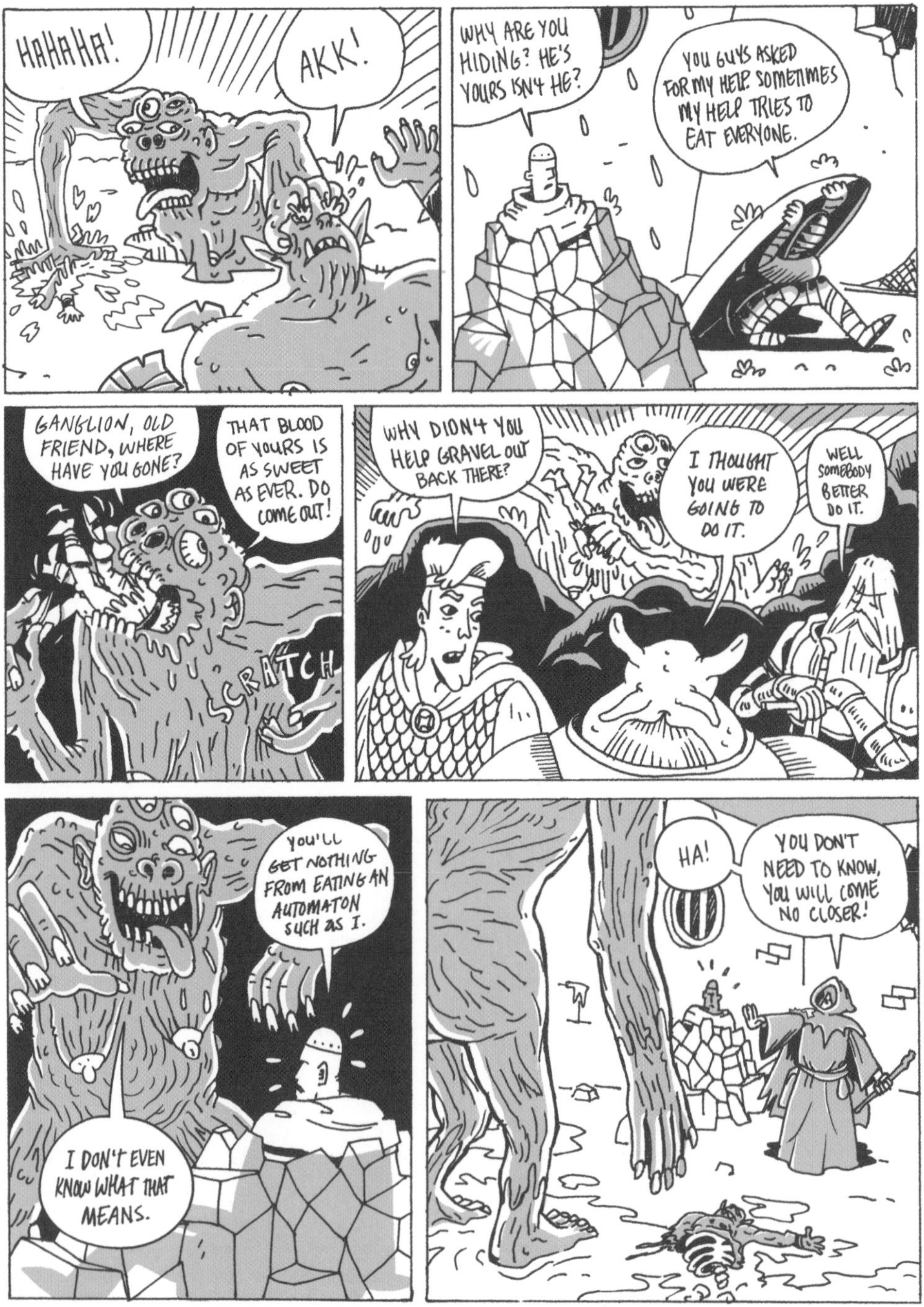
HAHAHA!
AKK!
WHY ARE YOU HIDING? HE'S YOURS ISN'T HE?
YOU GUYS ASKED FOR MY HELP. SOMETIMES MY HELP TRIES TO EAT EVERYONE.
GANGLION, OLD FRIEND, WHERE HAVE YOU GONE?
THAT BLOOD OF YOURS IS AS SWEET AS EVER. DO COME OUT!
SCRATCH
WHY DIDN'T YOU HELP GRAVEL OUT BACK THERE?
I THOUGHT YOU WERE GOING TO DO IT.
WELL SOMEBODY BETTER DO IT.
YOU'LL GET NOTHING FROM EATING AN AUTOMATON SUCH AS I.
I DON'T EVEN KNOW WHAT THAT MEANS.
HA!
YOU DON'T NEED TO KNOW, YOU WILL COME NO CLOSER!

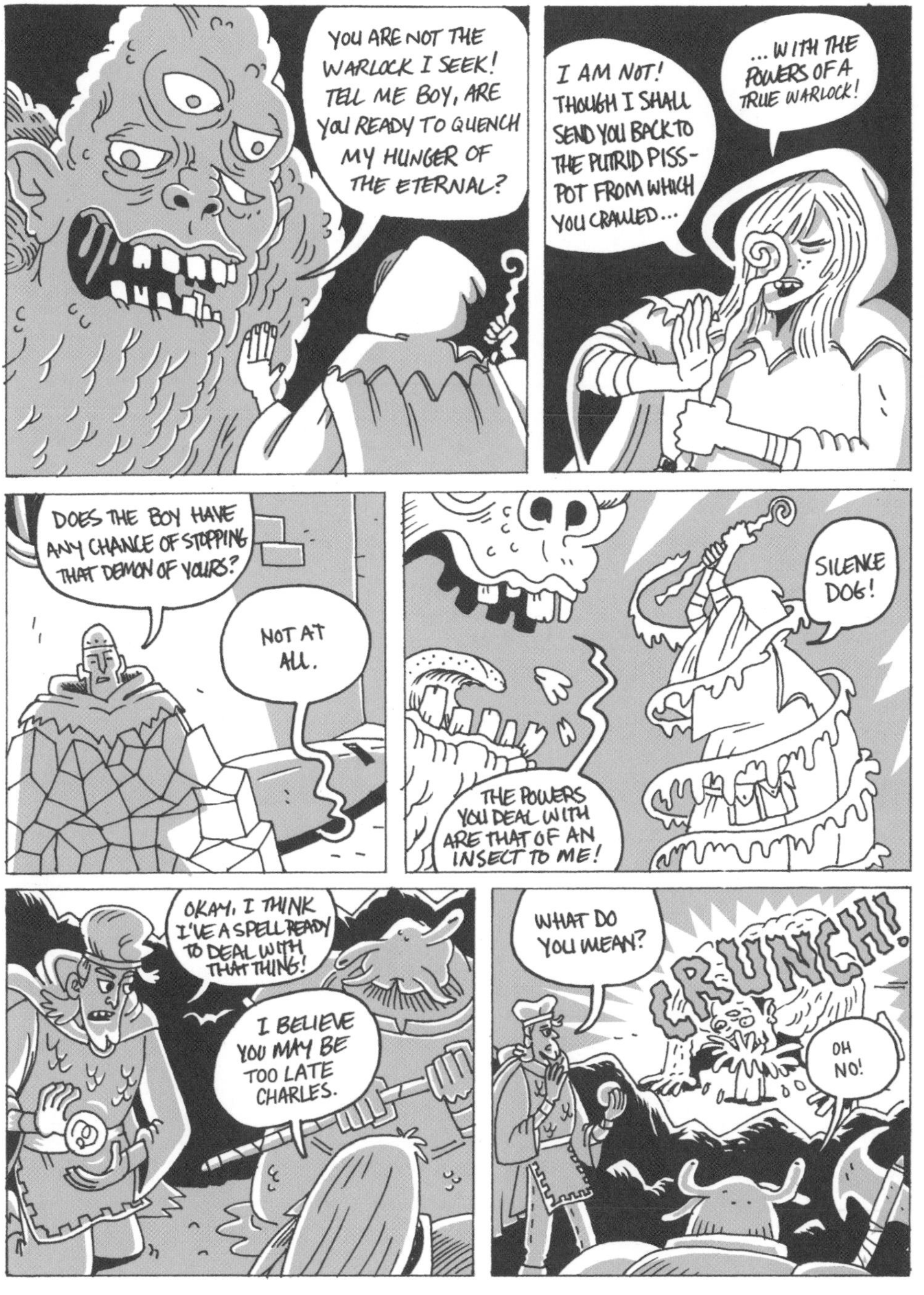
YOU ARE NOT THE WARLOCK I SEEK! TELL ME BOY, ARE YOU READY TO QUENCH MY HUNGER OF THE ETERNAL?
I AM NOT! THOUGH I SHALL SEND YOU BACK TO THE PUTRID PISS-POT FROM WHICH YOU CRAWLED...
...WITH THE POWERS OF A TRUE WARLOCK!
DOES THE BOY HAVE ANY CHANCE OF STOPPING THAT DEMON OF YOURS?
NOT AT ALL.
SILENCE DOG!
THE POWERS YOU DEAL WITH ARE THAT OF AN INSECT TO ME!
OKAY, I THINK I'VE A SPELL READY TO DEAL WITH THAT THING!
I BELIEVE YOU MAY BE TOO LATE CHARLES.
WHAT DO YOU MEAN?
CRUNCH!
OH NO!

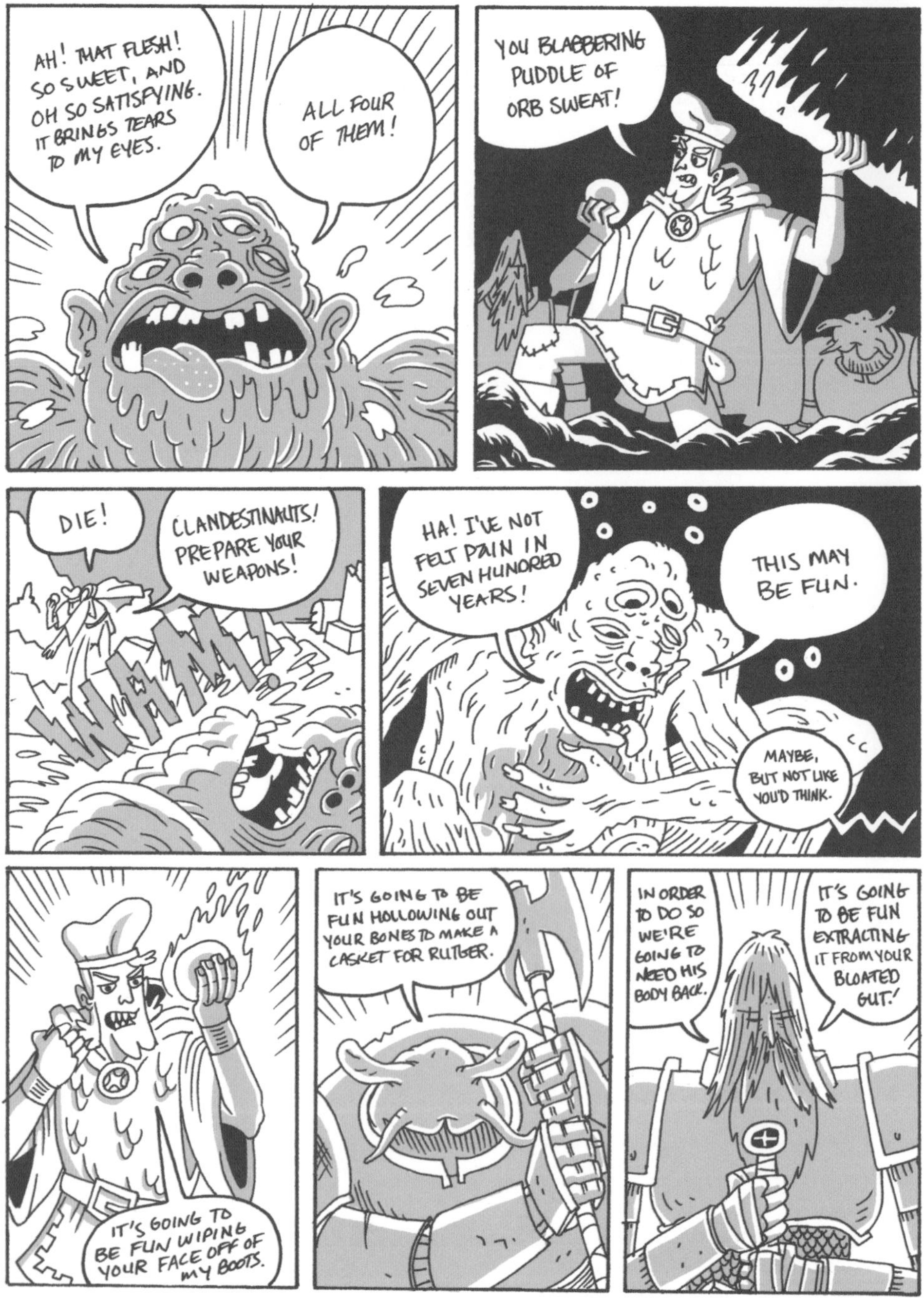
AH! THAT FLESH! SO SWEET, AND OH SO SATISFYING. IT BRINGS TEARS TO MY EYES.
ALL FOUR OF THEM!
YOU BLABBERING PUDDLE OF ORB SWEAT!
DIE!
CLANDESTINAUTS! PREPARE YOUR WEAPONS!
WAM!
HA! I'VE NOT FELT PAIN IN SEVEN HUNDRED YEARS!
THIS MAY BE FUN.
MAYBE, BUT NOT LIKE YOU'D THINK.
IT'S GOING TO BE FUN WIPING YOUR FACE OFF OF MY BOOTS.
IT'S GOING TO BE FUN HOLLOWING OUT YOUR BONES TO MAKE A CASKET FOR RUTGER.
IN ORDER TO DO SO WE'RE GOING TO NEED HIS BODY BACK.
IT'S GOING TO BE FUN EXTRACTING IT FROM YOUR BLOATED GUT!

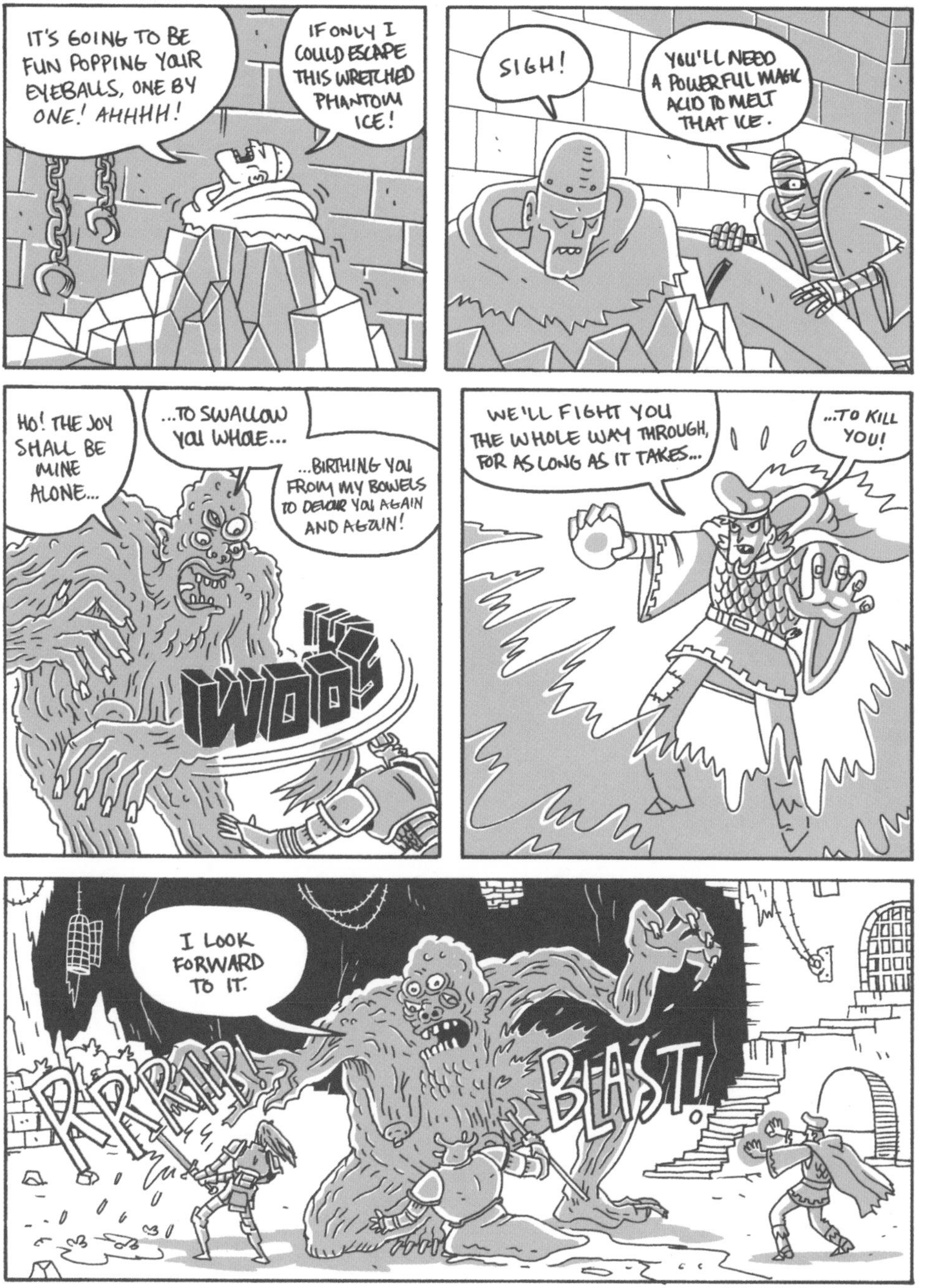

IT'S GOING TO BE FUN POPPING YOUR EYEBALLS, ONE BY ONE! AHHHH!
IF ONLY I COULD ESCAPE THIS WRETCHED PHANTOM ICE!
SIGH!
YOU'LL NEED A POWERFUL MAGIC ACID TO MELT THAT ICE.
HO! THE JOY SHALL BE MINE ALONE...
...TO SWALLOW YOU WHOLE...
...BIRTHING YOU FROM MY BOWELS TO DEVOUR YOU AGAIN AND AGAIN!
WOOSH
WE'LL FIGHT YOU THE WHOLE WAY THROUGH, FOR AS LONG AS IT TAKES...
...TO KILL YOU!
I LOOK FORWARD TO IT.
RRRRIP!
BLAST!

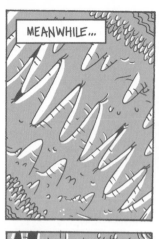

MEANWHILE...

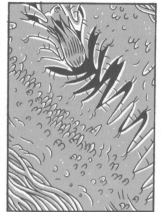

GRUMBLE!

HURRY UP YOU SWINE! BEFORE IT MOVES AGAIN!

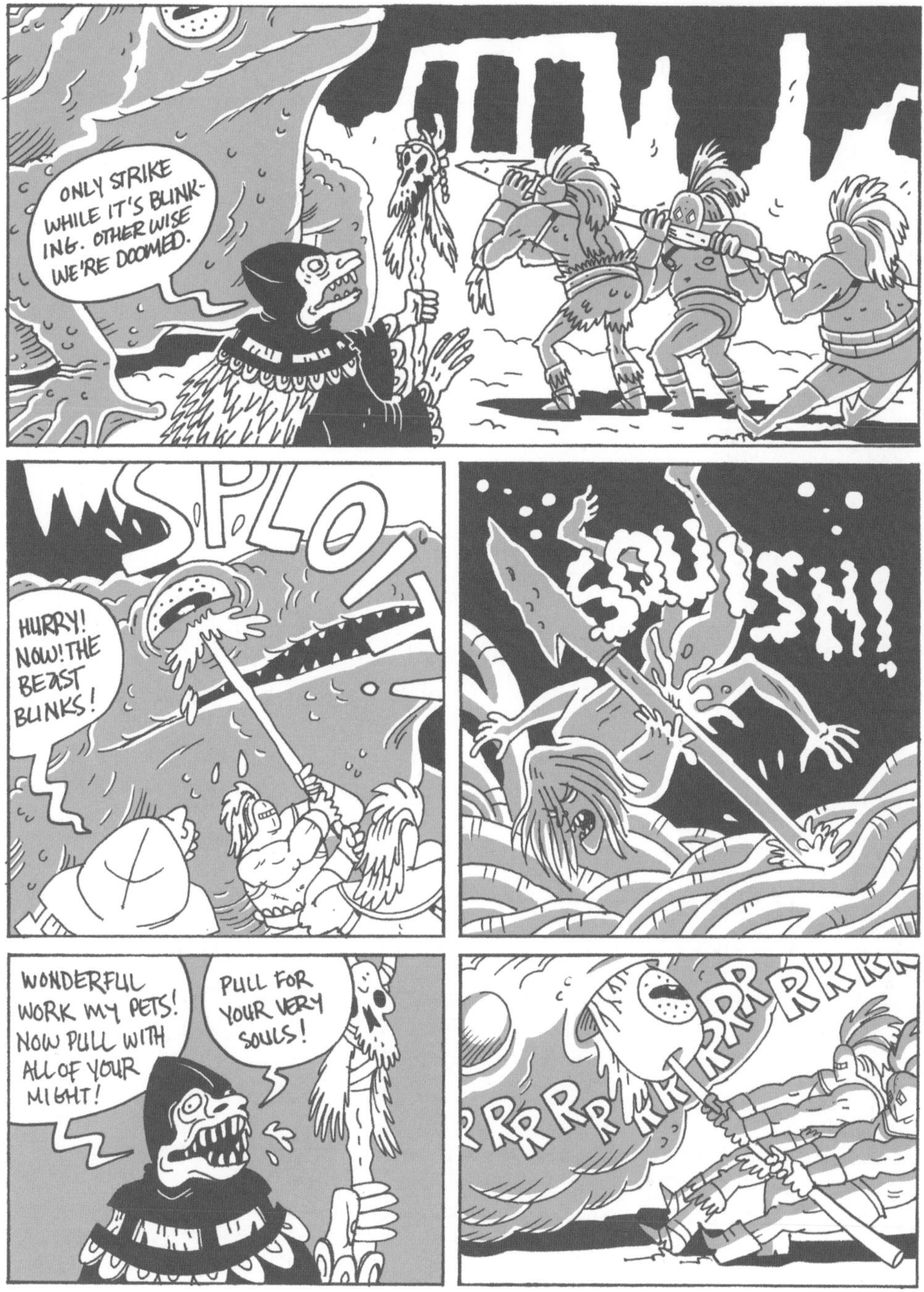
ONLY STRIKE WHILE IT'S BLINK-ING. OTHERWISE WE'RE DOOMED.
SPLOIT
HURRY! NOW! THE BEAST BLINKS!
SQUISH!
WONDERFUL WORK MY PETS! NOW PULL WITH ALL OF YOUR MIGHT!
PULL FOR YOUR VERY SOULS!

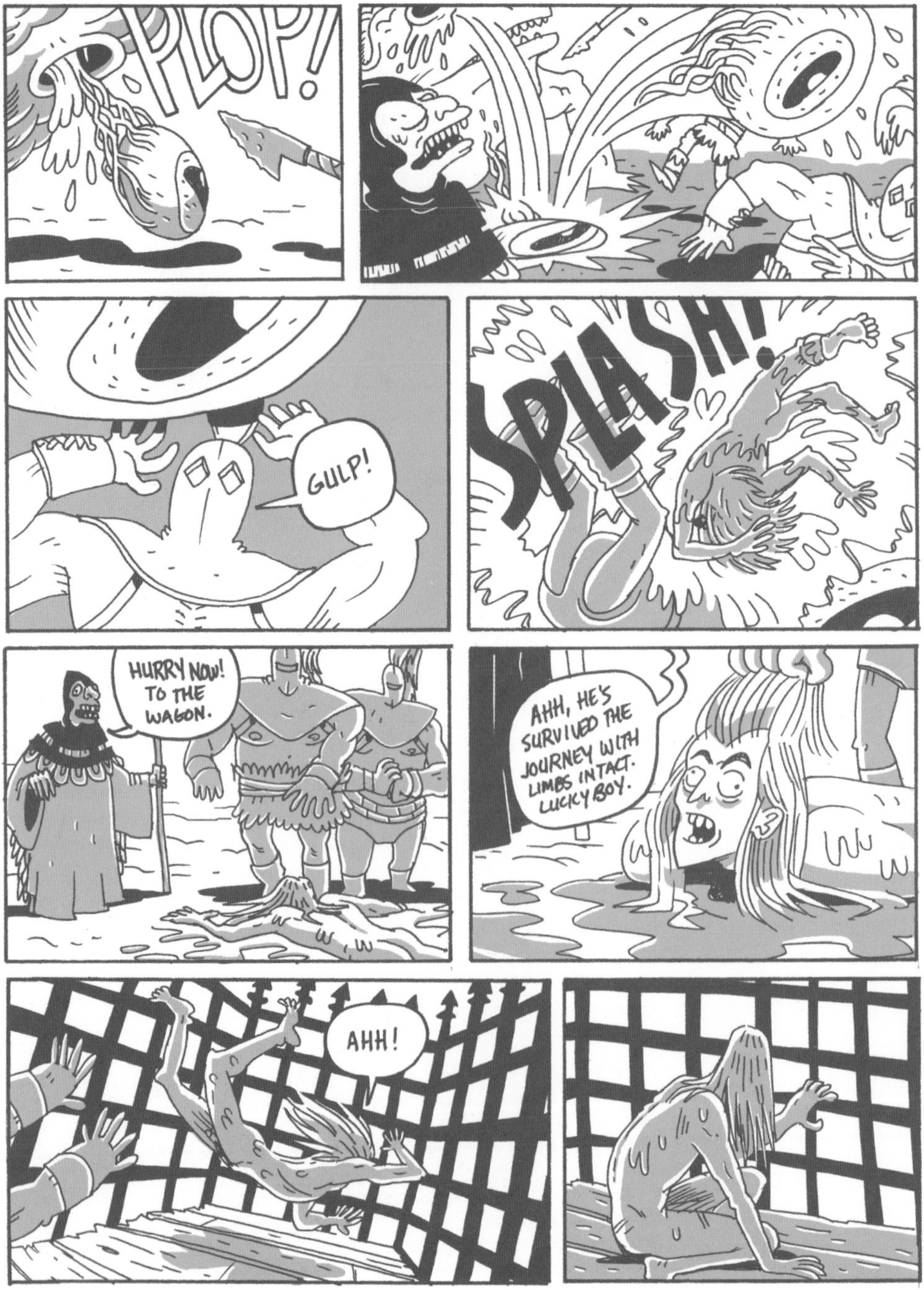
PLOP!
GULP!
SPLASH!
HURRY NOW! TO THE WAGON.
AHH, HE'S SURVIVED THE JOURNEY WITH LIMBS INTACT. LUCKY BOY.
AHH!

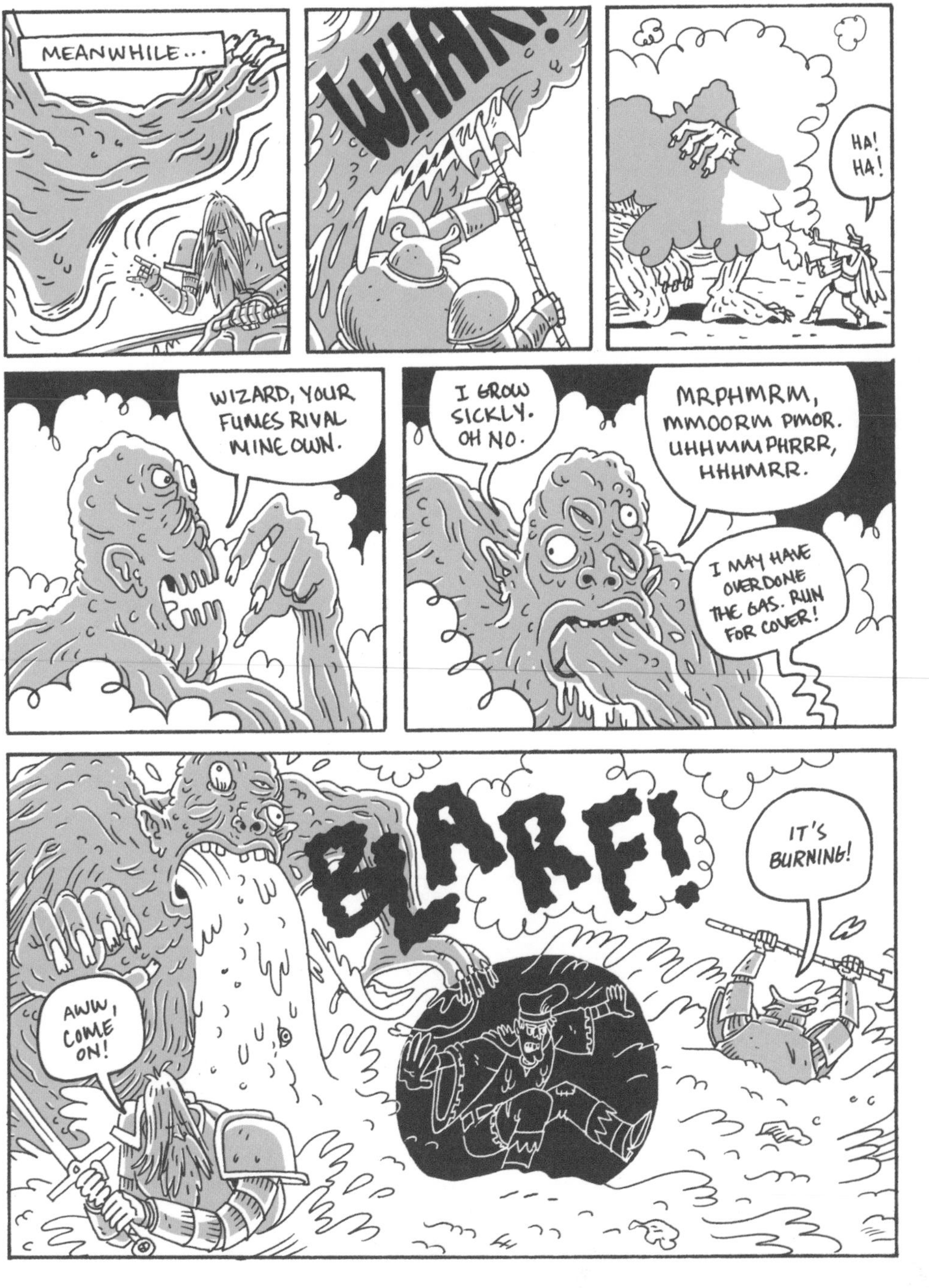
MEANWHILE...
WHAR!
HA! HA!
WIZARD, YOUR FUMES RIVAL MINE OWN.
I GROW SICKLY. OH NO.
MRPHMRM, MMOORM PMOR. UHHMMPHRRR, HHHMRR.
I MAY HAVE OVERDONE THE GAS. RUN FOR COVER!
BLARF!
IT'S BURNING!
AWW, COME ON!

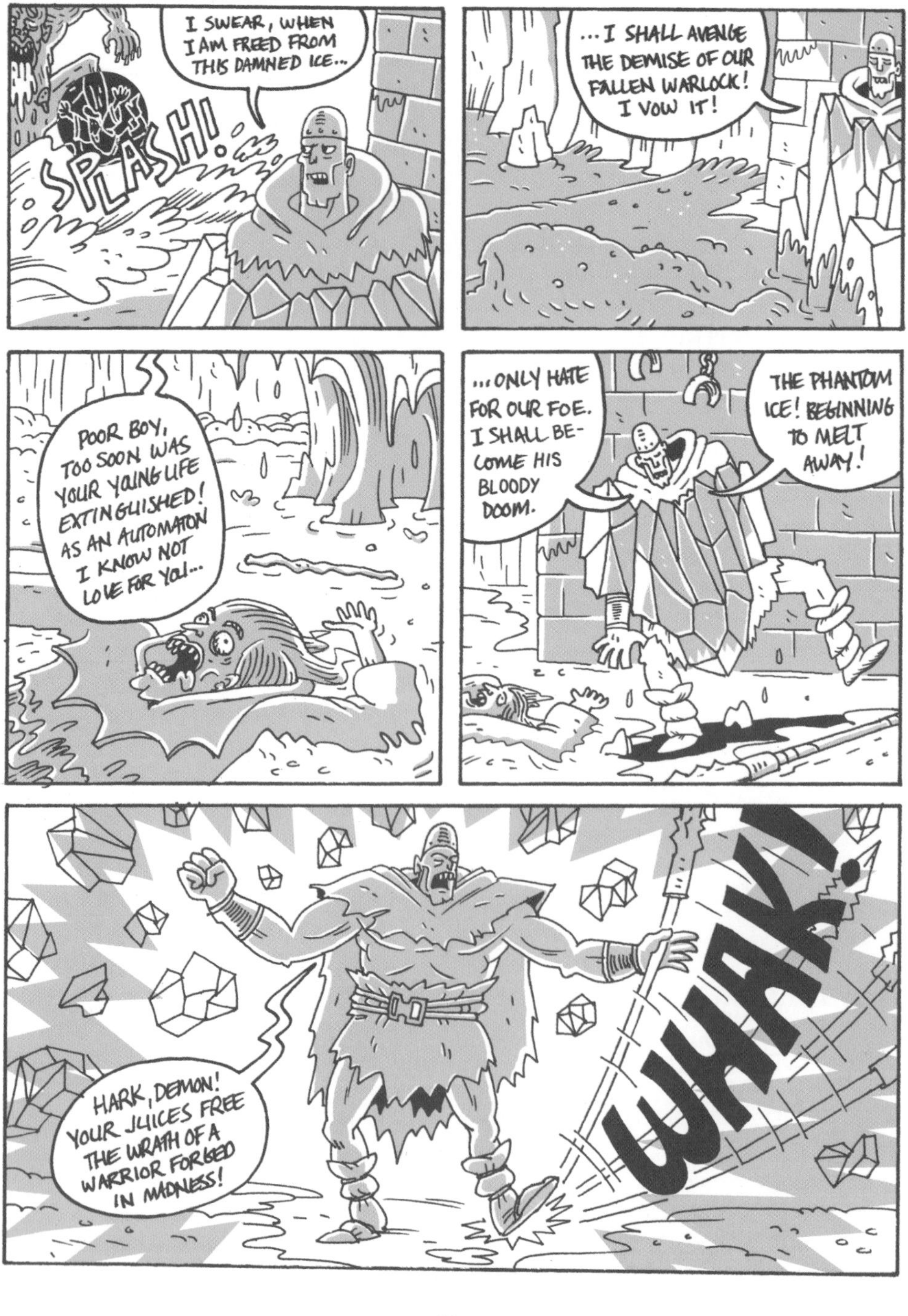
I SWEAR, WHEN I AM FREED FROM THIS DAMNED ICE...
SPLASH!
...I SHALL AVENGE THE DEMISE OF OUR FALLEN WARLOCK! I VOW IT!
POOR BOY, TOO SOON WAS YOUR YOUNG LIFE EXTINGUISHED! AS AN AUTOMATON I KNOW NOT LOVE FOR YOU...
...ONLY HATE FOR OUR FOE. I SHALL BECOME HIS BLOODY DOOM.
THE PHANTOM ICE! BEGINNING TO MELT AWAY!
HARK, DEMON! YOUR JUICES FREE THE WRATH OF A WARRIOR FORGED IN MADNESS!
WHAK!

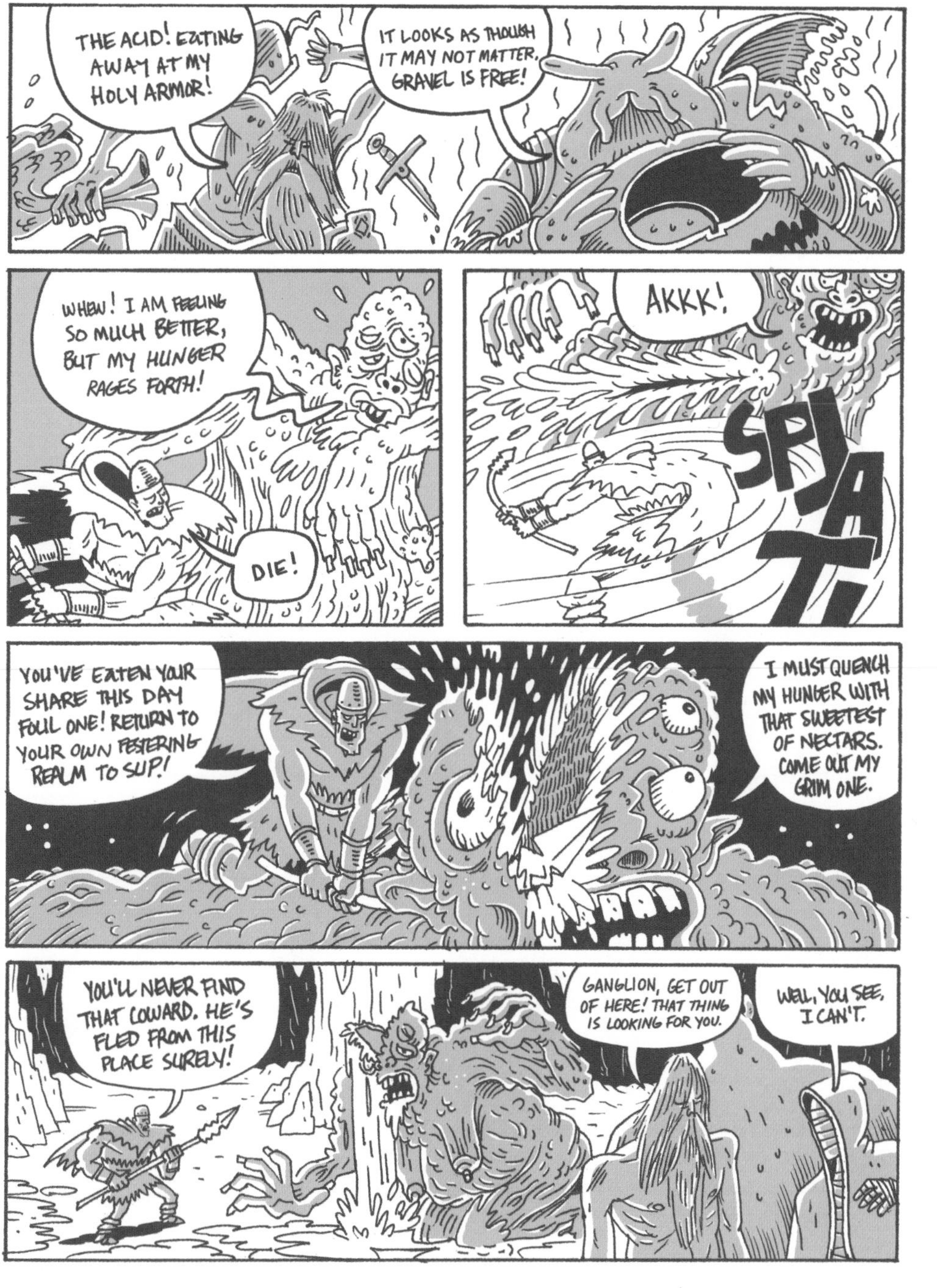
THE ACID! EATING AWAY AT MY HOLY ARMOR!
IT LOOKS AS THOUGH IT MAY NOT MATTER, GRAVEL IS FREE!
WHEW! I AM FEELING SO MUCH BETTER, BUT MY HUNGER RAGES FORTH!
DIE!
AKKK!
SPLATT
YOU'VE EATEN YOUR SHARE THIS DAY FOUL ONE! RETURN TO YOUR OWN FESTERING REALM TO SUP!
I MUST QUENCH MY HUNGER WITH THAT SWEETEST OF NECTARS. COME OUT MY GRIM ONE.
YOU'LL NEVER FIND THAT COWARD. HE'S FLED FROM THIS PLACE SURELY!
GANGLION, GET OUT OF HERE! THAT THING IS LOOKING FOR YOU.
WELL, YOU SEE, I CAN'T.

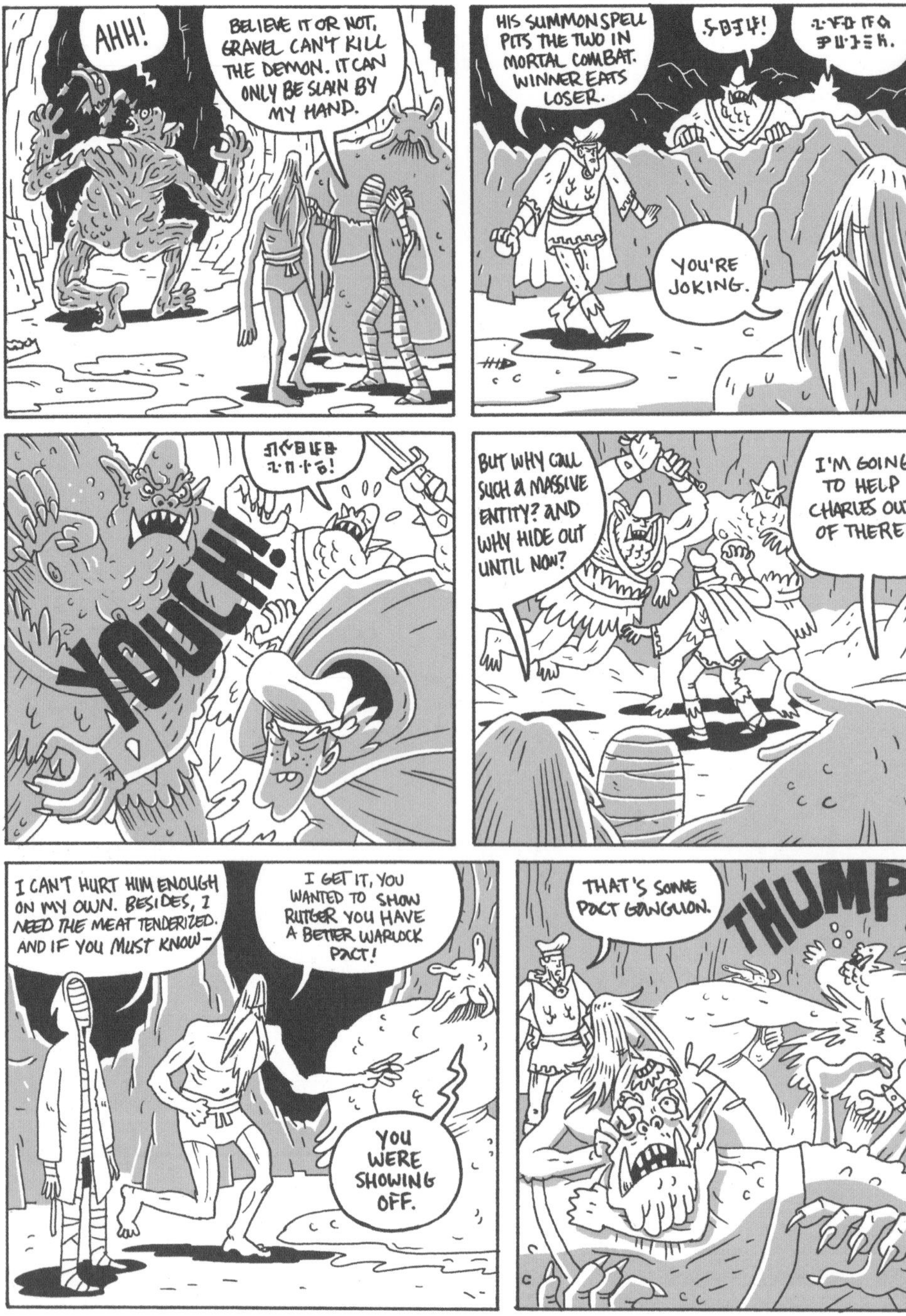
AHH!
BELIEVE IT OR NOT, GRAVEL CAN'T KILL THE DEMON. IT CAN ONLY BE SLAIN BY MY HAND.
HIS SUMMON SPELL PITS THE TWO IN MORTAL COMBAT. WINNER EATS LOSER.
YOU'RE JOKING.
YOUCH!
BUT WHY CALL SUCH A MASSIVE ENTITY? AND WHY HIDE OUT UNTIL NOW?
I'M GOING TO HELP CHARLES OUT OF THERE.
I CAN'T HURT HIM ENOUGH ON MY OWN. BESIDES, I NEED THE MEAT TENDERIZED. AND IF YOU MUST KNOW—
I GET IT, YOU WANTED TO SHOW RUTGER YOU HAVE A BETTER WARLOCK PACT!
YOU WERE SHOWING OFF.
THAT'S SOME PACT GANGLION.
THUMP!

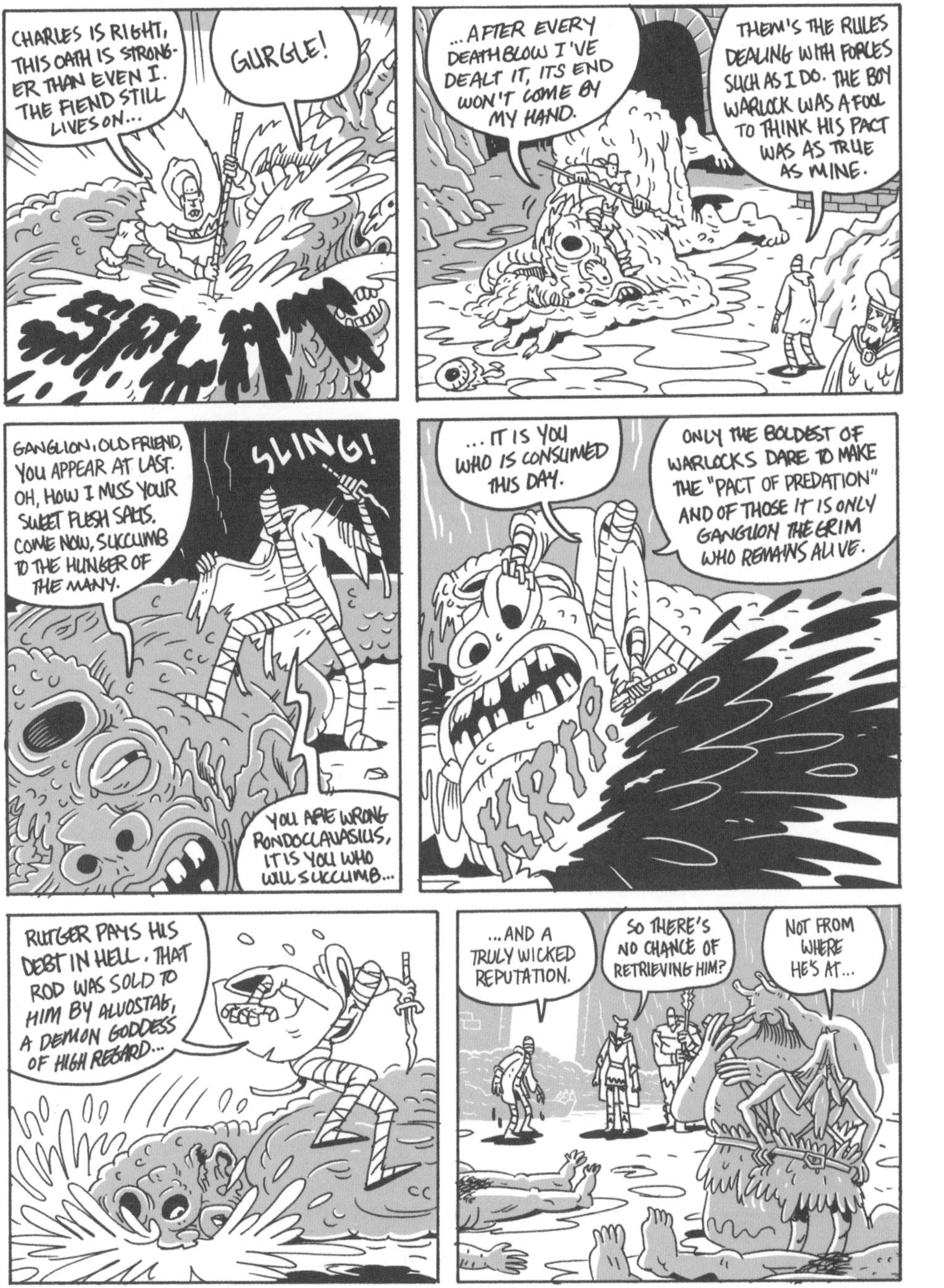

CHARLES IS RIGHT, THIS OATH IS STRONGER THAN EVEN I. THE FIEND STILL LIVES ON...
GURGLE!
SPLAT
...AFTER EVERY DEATHBLOW I'VE DEALT IT, ITS END WON'T COME BY MY HAND.
THEM'S THE RULES DEALING WITH FORCES SUCH AS I DO. THE BOY WARLOCK WAS A FOOL TO THINK HIS PACT WAS AS TRUE AS MINE.
GANGLION, OLD FRIEND, YOU APPEAR AT LAST. OH, HOW I MISS YOUR SWEET FLESH SALTS. COME NOW, SUCCUMB TO THE HUNGER OF THE MANY.
SLING!
YOU ARE WRONG RONDOCLAVASIUS, IT IS YOU WHO WILL SUCCUMB...
...IT IS YOU WHO IS CONSUMED THIS DAY.
ONLY THE BOLDEST OF WARLOCKS DARE TO MAKE THE "PACT OF PREDATION" AND OF THOSE IT IS ONLY GANGLION THE GRIM WHO REMAINS ALIVE.
KRIP.
RUTGER PAYS HIS DEBT IN HELL. THAT ROD WAS SOLD TO HIM BY ALVOSTAG, A DEMON GODDESS OF HIGH REGARD...
...AND A TRULY WICKED REPUTATION.
SO THERE'S NO CHANCE OF RETRIEVING HIM?
NOT FROM WHERE HE'S AT...

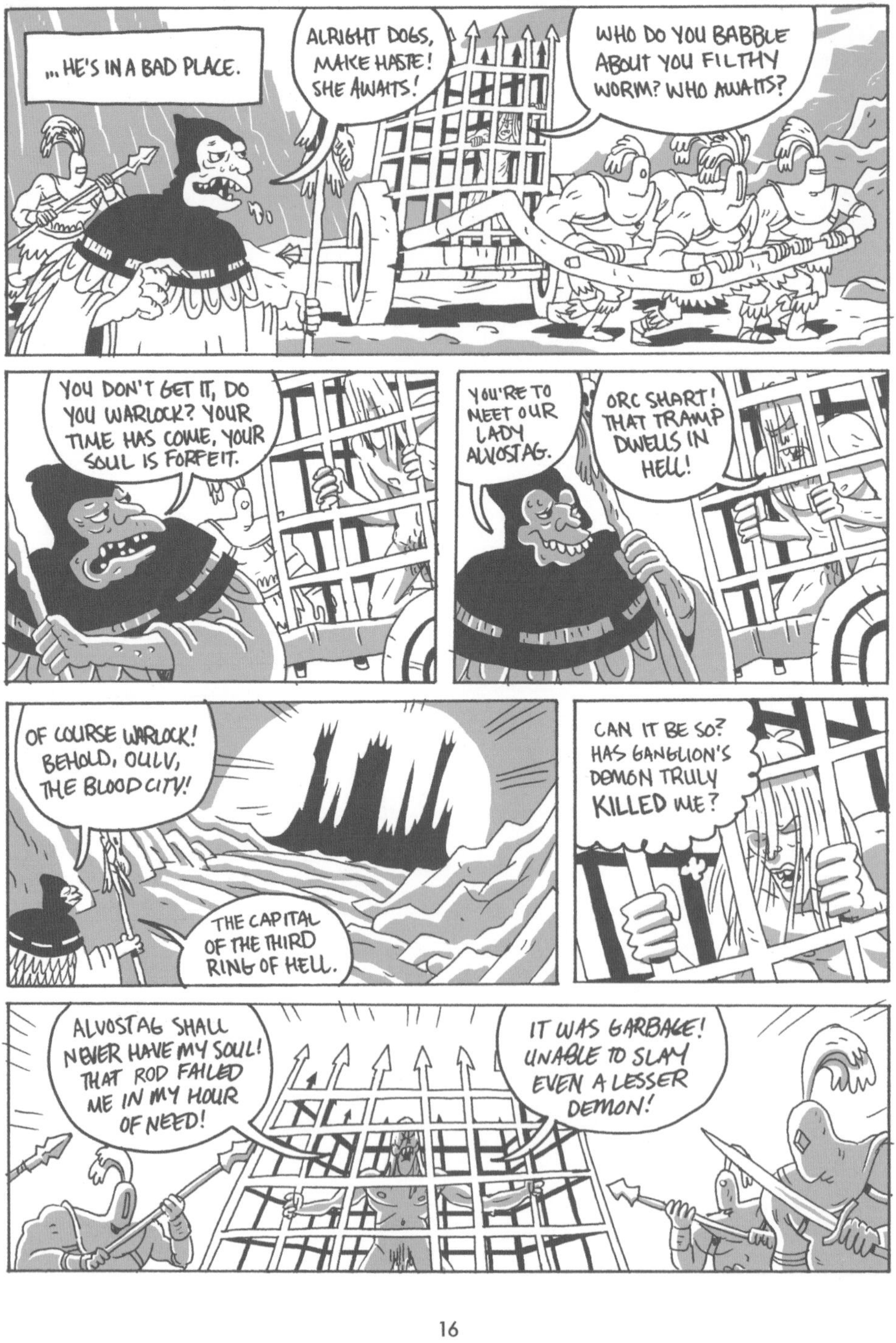
... HE'S IN A BAD PLACE.
ALRIGHT DOGS, MAKE HASTE! SHE AWAITS!
WHO DO YOU BABBLE ABOUT YOU FILTHY WORM? WHO AWAITS?
YOU DON'T GET IT, DO YOU WARLOCK? YOUR TIME HAS COME, YOUR SOUL IS FORFEIT.
YOU'RE TO MEET OUR LADY ALVOSTAG.
ORC SHART! THAT TRAMP DWELLS IN HELL!
OF COURSE WARLOCK! BEHOLD, OULV, THE BLOOD CITY!
THE CAPITAL OF THE THIRD RING OF HELL.
CAN IT BE SO? HAS GANGLION'S DEMON TRULY KILLED ME?
ALVOSTAG SHALL NEVER HAVE MY SOUL! THAT ROD FAILED ME IN MY HOUR OF NEED!
IT WAS GARBAGE! UNABLE TO SLAY EVEN A LESSER DEMON!

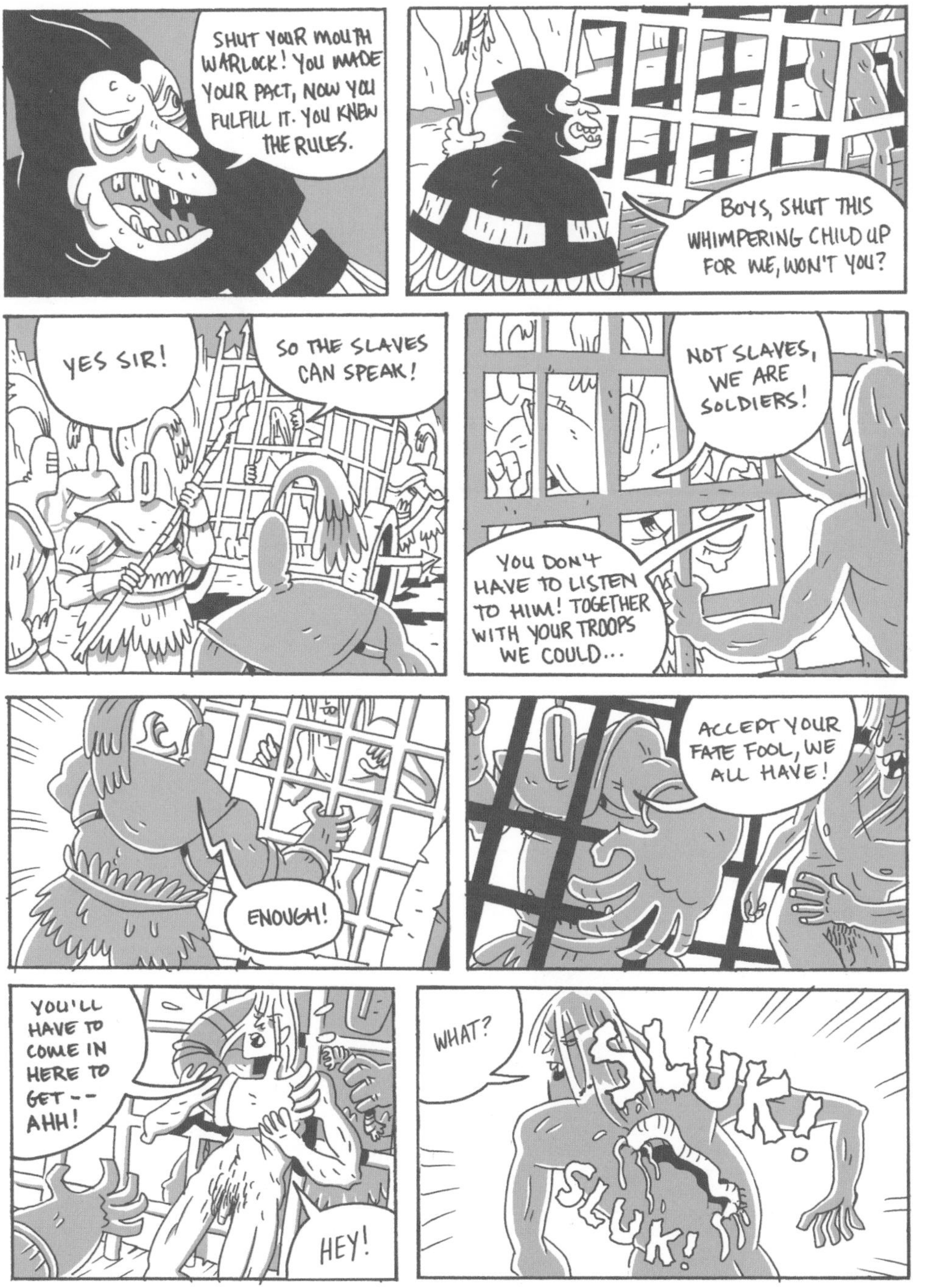
SHUT YOUR MOUTH WARLOCK! YOU MADE YOUR PACT, NOW YOU FULFILL IT. YOU KNEW THE RULES.
BOYS, SHUT THIS WHIMPERING CHILD UP FOR ME, WON'T YOU?
YES SIR!
SO THE SLAVES CAN SPEAK!
NOT SLAVES, WE ARE SOLDIERS!
YOU DON'T HAVE TO LISTEN TO HIM! TOGETHER WITH YOUR TROOPS WE COULD...
ENOUGH!
ACCEPT YOUR FATE FOOL, WE ALL HAVE!
YOU'LL HAVE TO COME IN HERE TO GET -- AHH!
HEY!
WHAT?
SLUK!
SLUK!

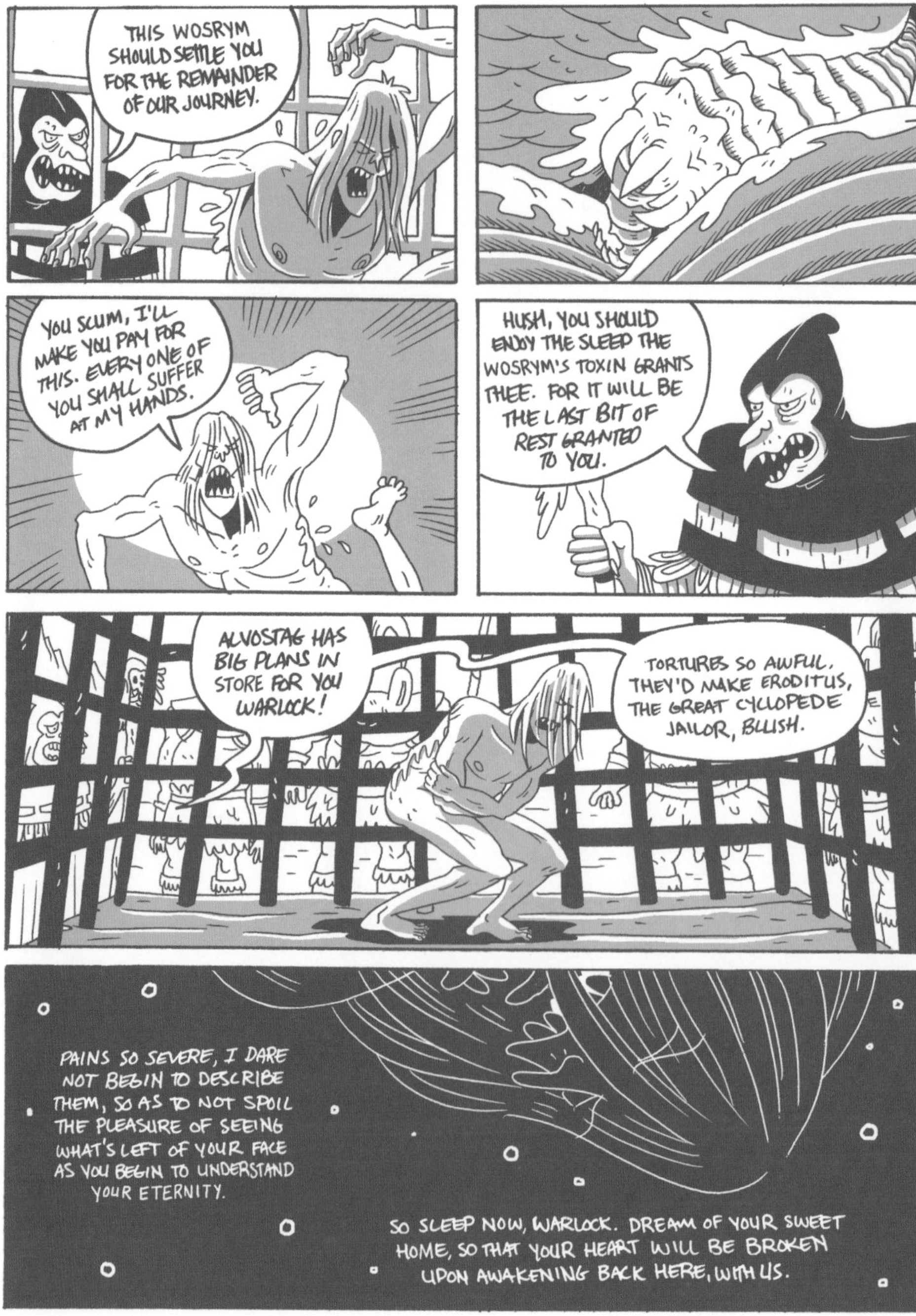
THIS WOSRYM SHOULD SETTLE YOU FOR THE REMAINDER OF OUR JOURNEY.
YOU SCUM, I'LL MAKE YOU PAY FOR THIS. EVERY ONE OF YOU SHALL SUFFER AT MY HANDS.
HUSH, YOU SHOULD ENJOY THE SLEEP THE WOSRYM'S TOXIN GRANTS THEE. FOR IT WILL BE THE LAST BIT OF REST GRANTED TO YOU.
ALVOSTAG HAS BIG PLANS IN STORE FOR YOU WARLOCK!
TORTURES SO AWFUL, THEY'D MAKE ERODITUS, THE GREAT CYCLOPEDE JAILOR, BLUSH.
PAINS SO SEVERE, I DARE NOT BEGIN TO DESCRIBE THEM, SO AS TO NOT SPOIL THE PLEASURE OF SEEING WHAT'S LEFT OF YOUR FACE AS YOU BEGIN TO UNDERSTAND YOUR ETERNITY.
SO SLEEP NOW, WARLOCK. DREAM OF YOUR SWEET HOME, SO THAT YOUR HEART WILL BE BROKEN UPON AWAKENING BACK HERE, WITH US.

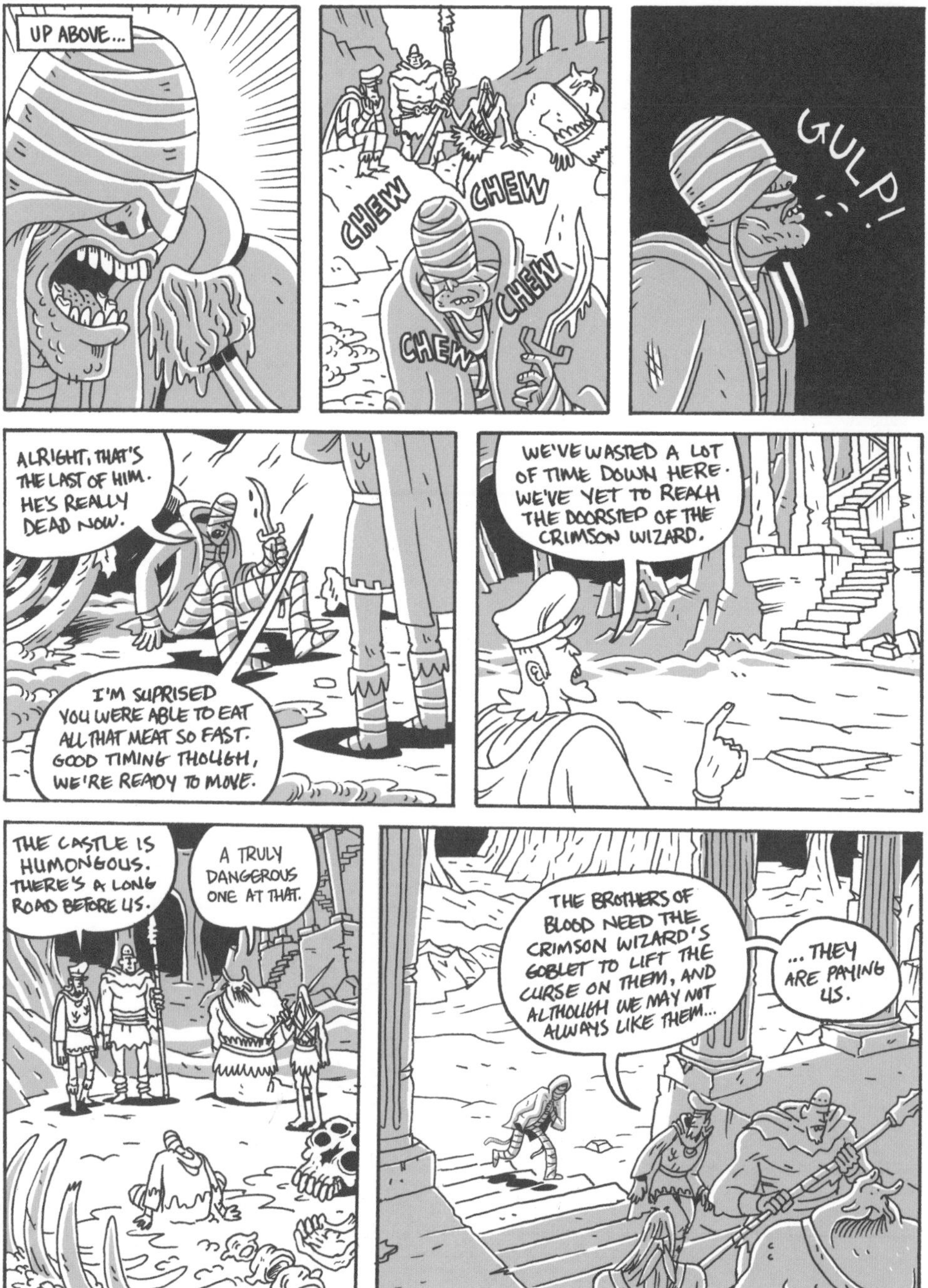
UP ABOVE...
CHEW
CHEW
CHEW
CHEW
CHEW
GULP!
ALRIGHT, THAT'S THE LAST OF HIM. HE'S REALLY DEAD NOW.
I'M SUPRISED YOU WERE ABLE TO EAT ALL THAT MEAT SO FAST. GOOD TIMING THOUGH, WE'RE READY TO MOVE.
WE'VE WASTED A LOT OF TIME DOWN HERE. WE'VE YET TO REACH THE DOORSTEP OF THE CRIMSON WIZARD.
THE CASTLE IS HUMONGOUS. THERE'S A LONG ROAD BEFORE US.
A TRULY DANGEROUS ONE AT THAT.
THE BROTHERS OF BLOOD NEED THE CRIMSON WIZARD'S GOBLET TO LIFT THE CURSE ON THEM, AND ALTHOUGH WE MAY NOT ALWAYS LIKE THEM...
...THEY ARE PAYING US.

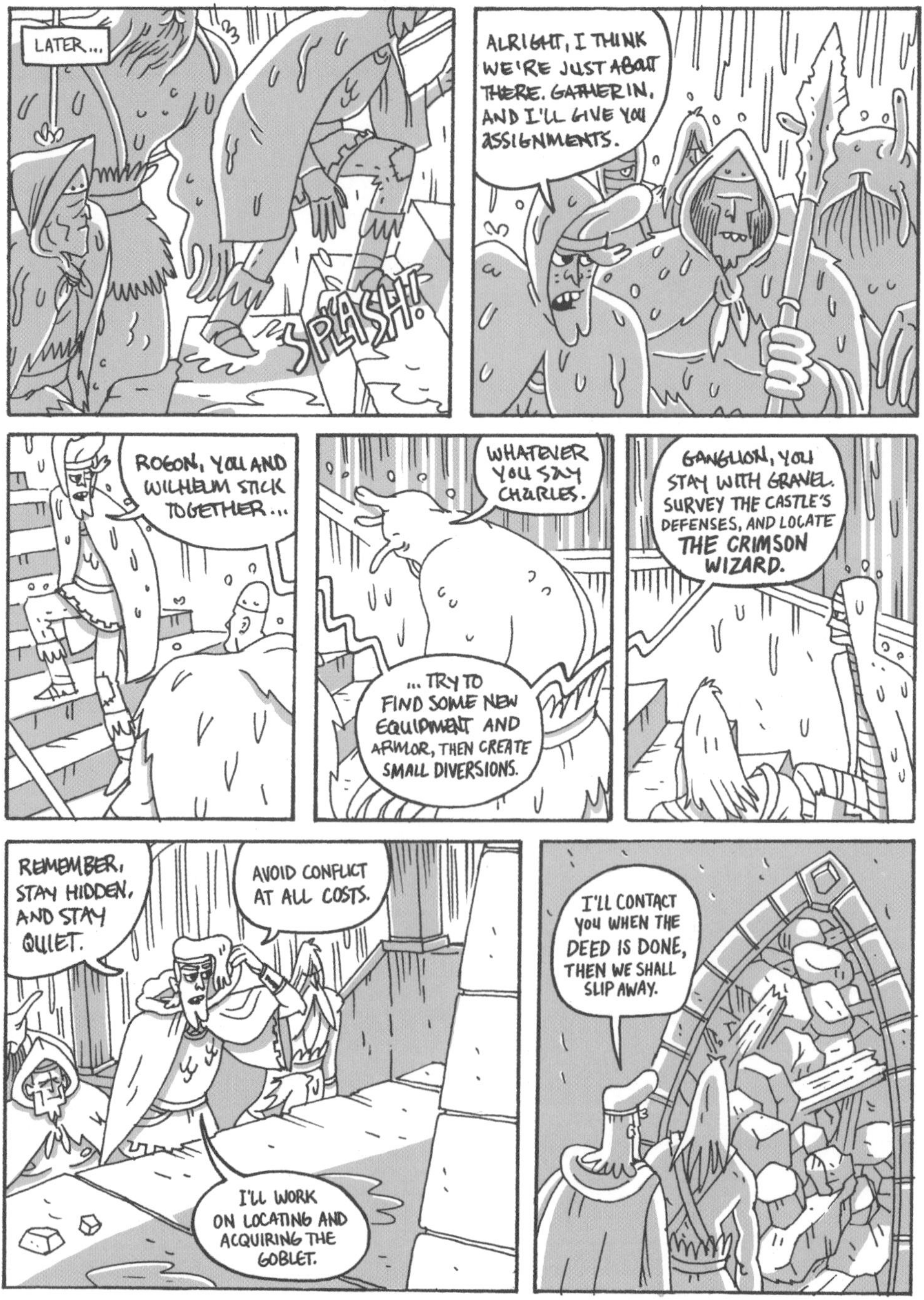
LATER...
SPLASH!
ALRIGHT, I THINK WE'RE JUST ABOUT THERE. GATHER IN, AND I'LL GIVE YOU ASSIGNMENTS.
ROGON, YOU AND WILHELM STICK TOGETHER...
...TRY TO FIND SOME NEW EQUIPMENT AND ARMOR, THEN CREATE SMALL DIVERSIONS.
WHATEVER YOU SAY CHARLES.
GANGLION, YOU STAY WITH GRAVEL. SURVEY THE CASTLE'S DEFENSES, AND LOCATE THE CRIMSON WIZARD.
REMEMBER, STAY HIDDEN, AND STAY QUIET.
AVOID CONFLICT AT ALL COSTS.
I'LL WORK ON LOCATING AND ACQUIRING THE GOBLET.
I'LL CONTACT YOU WHEN THE DEED IS DONE, THEN WE SHALL SLIP AWAY.

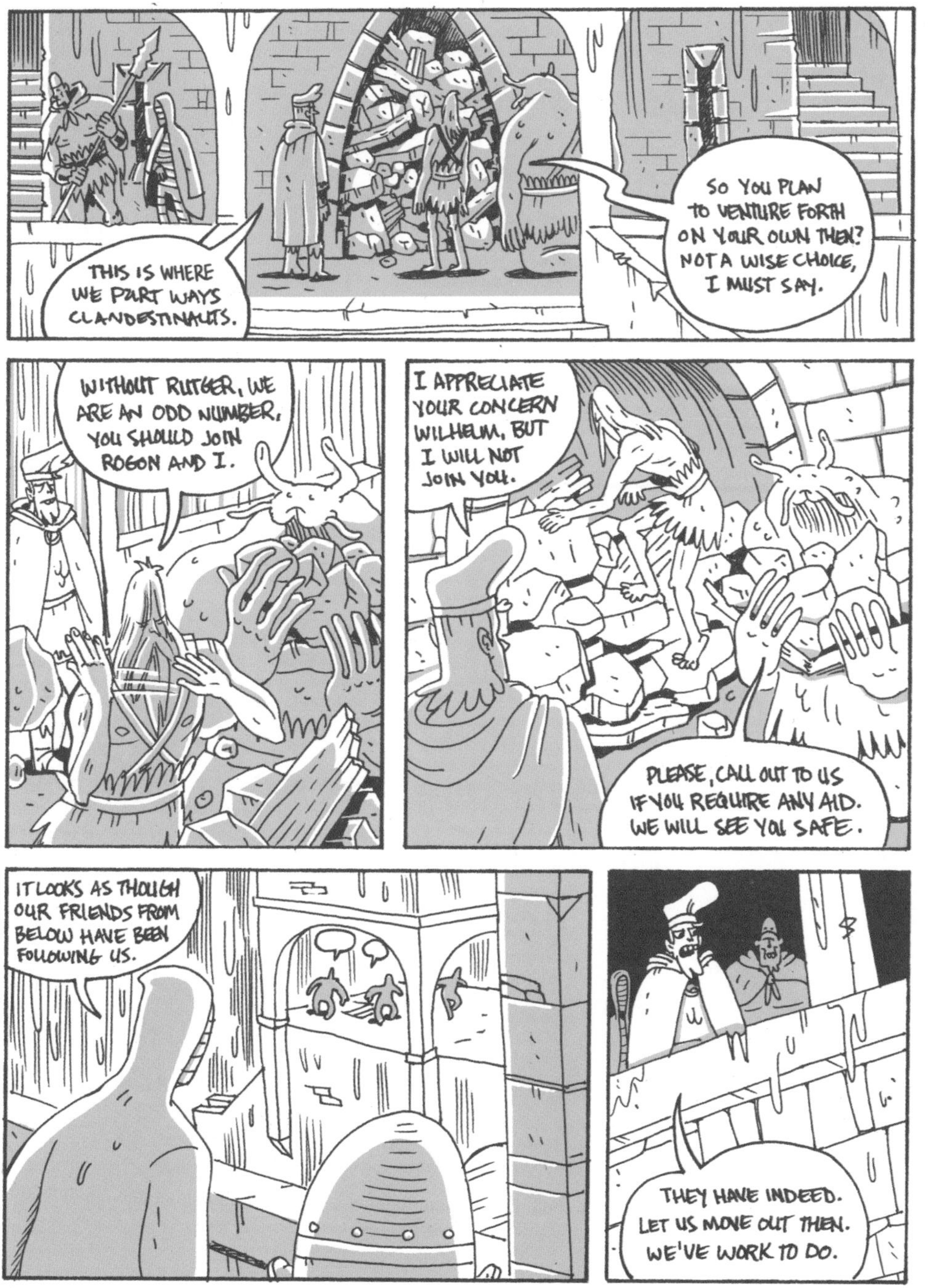
THIS IS WHERE WE PART WAYS CLANDESTINAUTS.
SO YOU PLAN TO VENTURE FORTH ON YOUR OWN THEN? NOT A WISE CHOICE, I MUST SAY.
WITHOUT RUTGER, WE ARE AN ODD NUMBER. YOU SHOULD JOIN ROGON AND I.
I APPRECIATE YOUR CONCERN WILHELM, BUT I WILL NOT JOIN YOU.
PLEASE, CALL OUT TO US IF YOU REQUIRE ANY AID. WE WILL SEE YOU SAFE.
IT LOOKS AS THOUGH OUR FRIENDS FROM BELOW HAVE BEEN FOLLOWING US.
THEY HAVE INDEED. LET US MOVE OUT THEN. WE'VE WORK TO DO.

WE LEAVE TO IT THEN. CHARLES, WE SHALL AWAIT YOUR WORD.

GOOD FORTUNE TO YOU FRIENDS, MAY YOUR GODS PROTECT YOU.

IT'S HARD, BUT TRY NOT TO THINK ABOUT RUTGER.

HE KNEW WHAT HE WAS GETTING HIMSELF INTO.

HELLO THERE BOYS.

ᗒᒐᖴᕲᘿᗡ ᗰᘿᕓᙏᕼᗺ ᖰᘜᙏᖴᐃ.

ᗡᒐᗺᗐ!

22

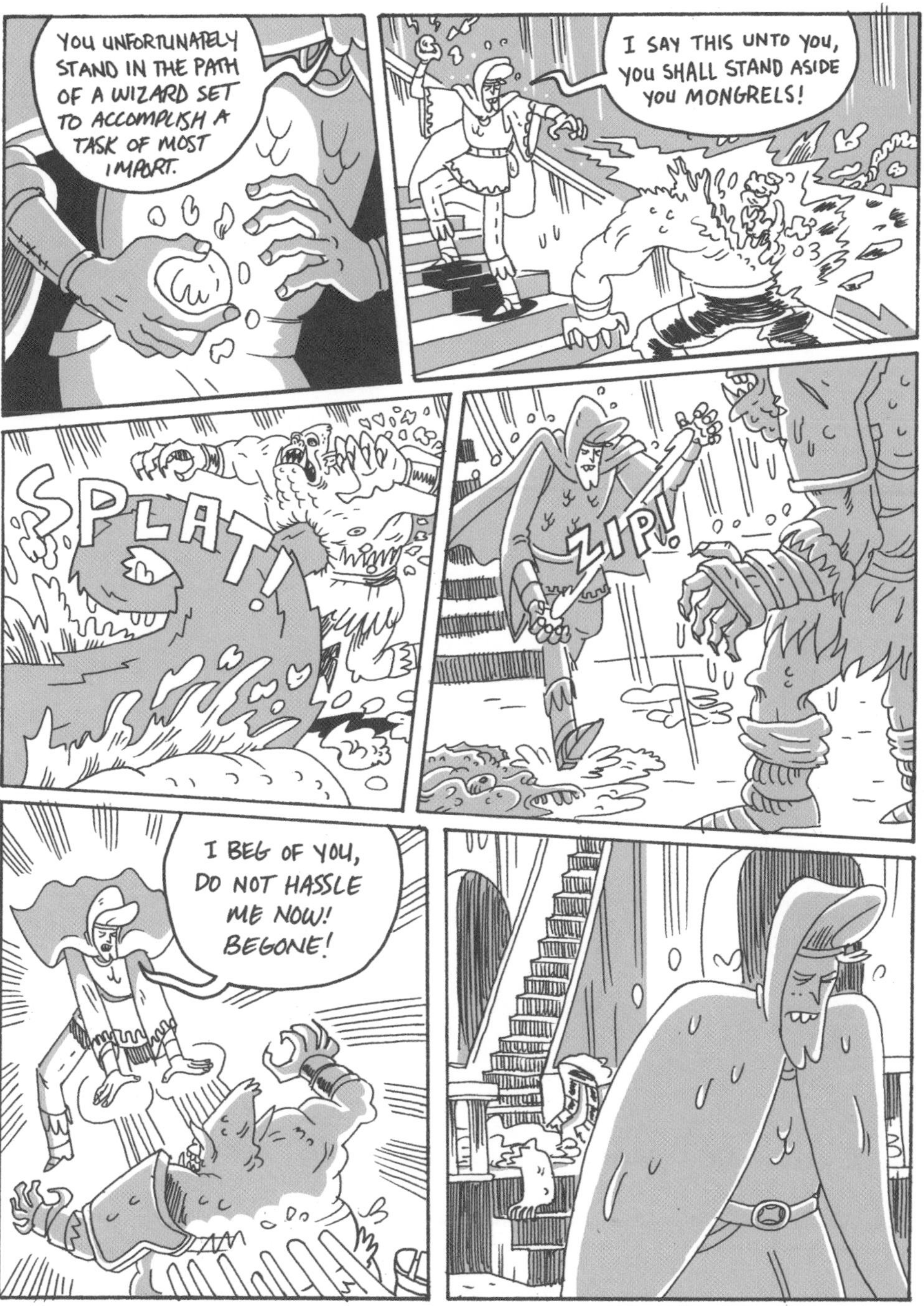
YOU UNFORTUNATELY STAND IN THE PATH OF A WIZARD SET TO ACCOMPLISH A TASK OF MOST IMPORT.
I SAY THIS UNTO YOU, YOU SHALL STAND ASIDE YOU MONGRELS!
SPLAT!
ZIP!
I BEG OF YOU, DO NOT HASSLE ME NOW! BEGONE!

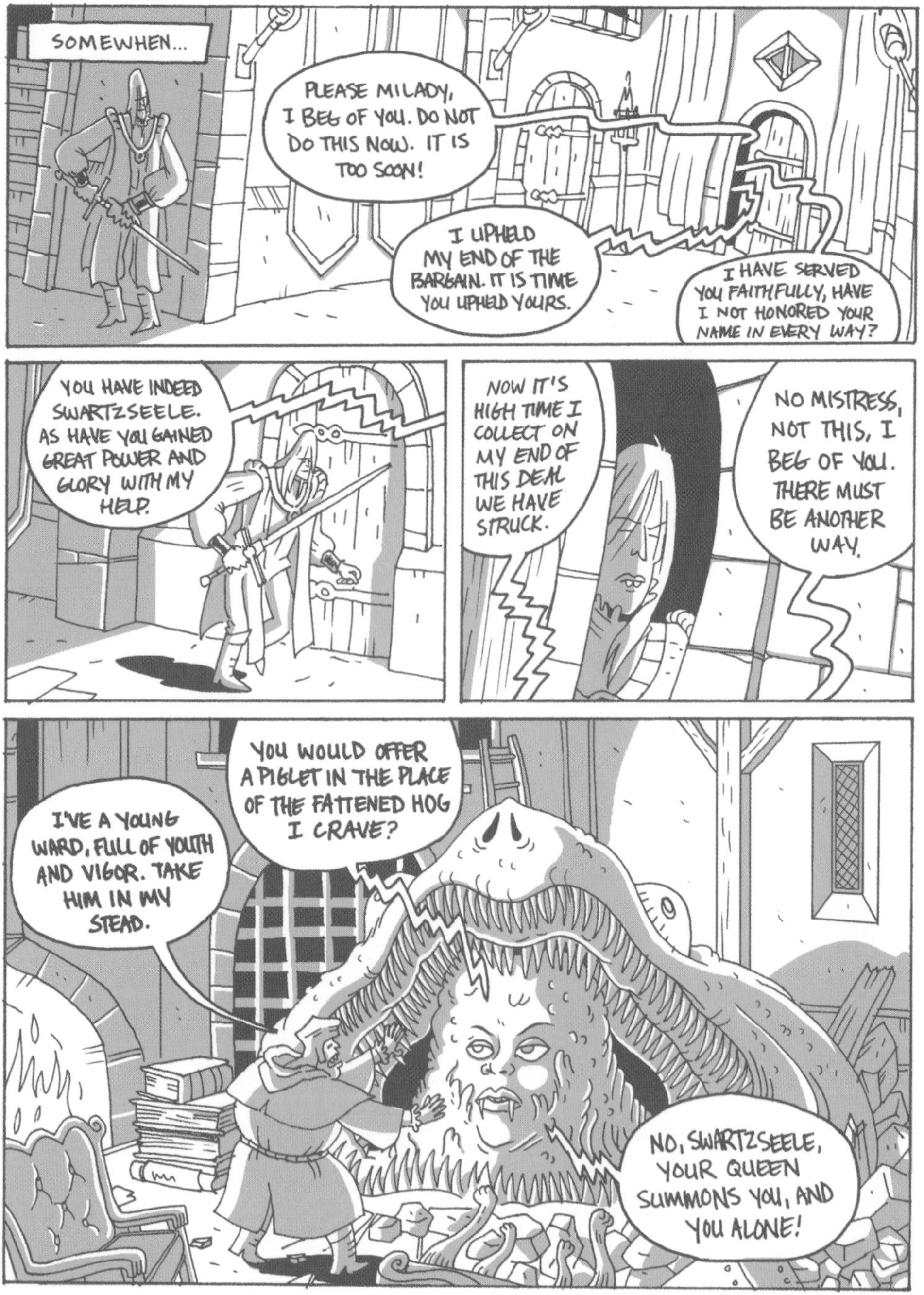
SOMEWHEN...
PLEASE MILADY, I BEG OF YOU. DO NOT DO THIS NOW. IT IS TOO SOON!
I UPHELD MY END OF THE BARGAIN. IT IS TIME YOU UPHELD YOURS.
I HAVE SERVED YOU FAITHFULLY, HAVE I NOT HONORED YOUR NAME IN EVERY WAY?
YOU HAVE INDEED SWARTZSEELE. AS HAVE YOU GAINED GREAT POWER AND GLORY WITH MY HELP.
NOW IT'S HIGH TIME I COLLECT ON MY END OF THIS DEAL WE HAVE STRUCK.
NO MISTRESS, NOT THIS, I BEG OF YOU. THERE MUST BE ANOTHER WAY.
I'VE A YOUNG WARD, FULL OF YOUTH AND VIGOR. TAKE HIM IN MY STEAD.
YOU WOULD OFFER A PIGLET IN THE PLACE OF THE FATTENED HOG I CRAVE?
NO, SWARTZSEELE, YOUR QUEEN SUMMONS YOU, AND YOU ALONE!

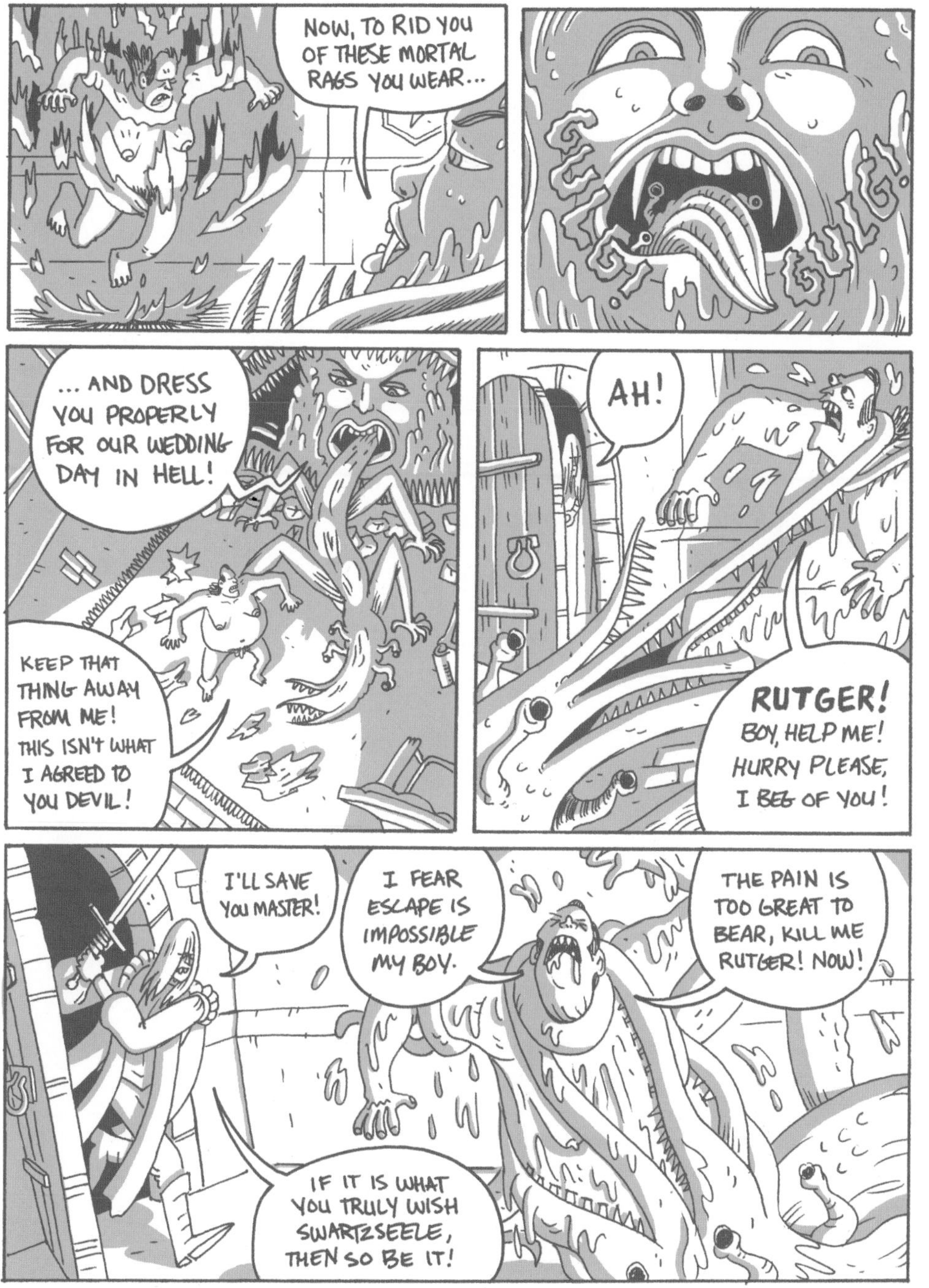
NOW, TO RID YOU OF THESE MORTAL RAGS YOU WEAR...
GLUG! GULG!
... AND DRESS YOU PROPERLY FOR OUR WEDDING DAY IN HELL!
KEEP THAT THING AWAY FROM ME! THIS ISN'T WHAT I AGREED TO YOU DEVIL!
AH!
RUTGER! BOY, HELP ME! HURRY PLEASE, I BEG OF YOU!
I'LL SAVE YOU MASTER!
I FEAR ESCAPE IS IMPOSSIBLE MY BOY.
THE PAIN IS TOO GREAT TO BEAR, KILL ME RUTGER! NOW!
IF IT IS WHAT YOU TRULY WISH SWARTZSEELE, THEN SO BE IT!

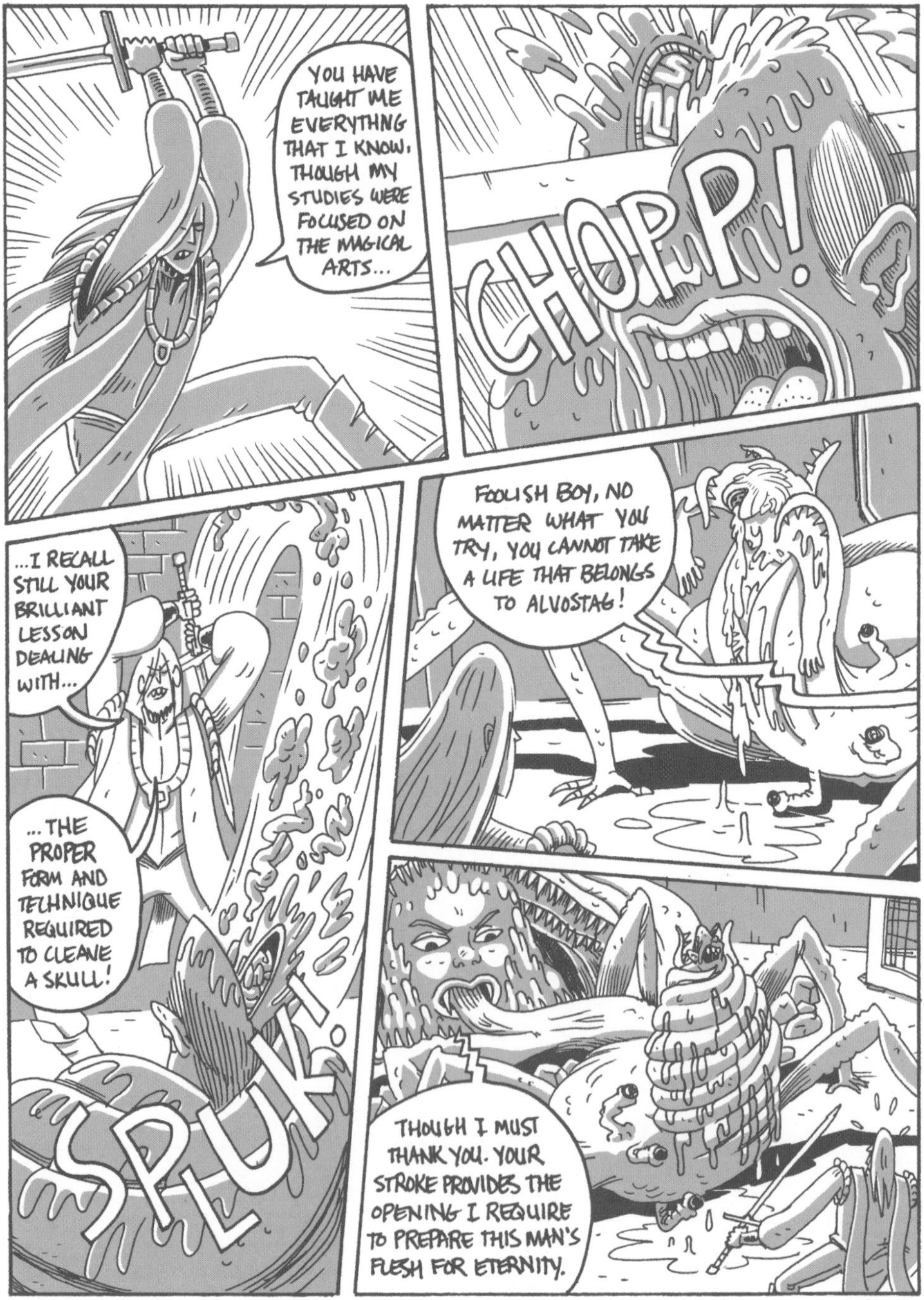
YOU HAVE TAUGHT ME EVERYTHING THAT I KNOW, THOUGH MY STUDIES WERE FOCUSED ON THE MAGICAL ARTS...
CHOPP!
...I RECALL STILL YOUR BRILLIANT LESSON DEALING WITH...
...THE PROPER FORM AND TECHNIQUE REQUIRED TO CLEAVE A SKULL!
SPLUK!
FOOLISH BOY, NO MATTER WHAT YOU TRY, YOU CANNOT TAKE A LIFE THAT BELONGS TO ALVOSTAG!
THOUGH I MUST THANK YOU. YOUR STROKE PROVIDES THE OPENING I REQUIRE TO PREPARE THIS MAN'S FLESH FOR ETERNITY.

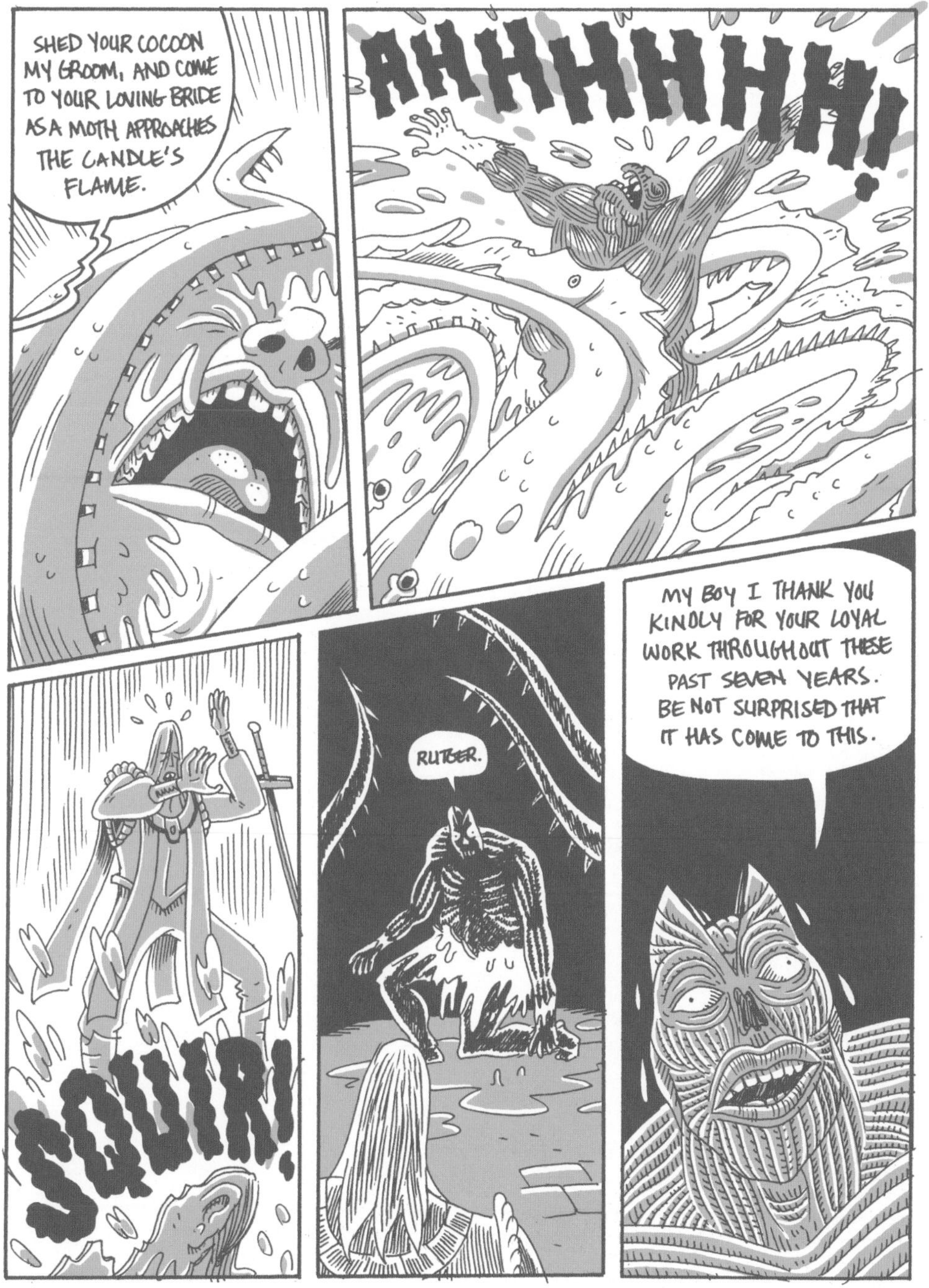
SHED YOUR COCOON MY GROOM, AND COME TO YOUR LOVING BRIDE AS A MOTH APPROACHES THE CANDLE'S FLAME.
AHHHHHHH!
SQUIR!
RUTGER.
MY BOY I THANK YOU KINDLY FOR YOUR LOYAL WORK THROUGHOUT THESE PAST SEVEN YEARS. BE NOT SURPRISED THAT IT HAS COME TO THIS.

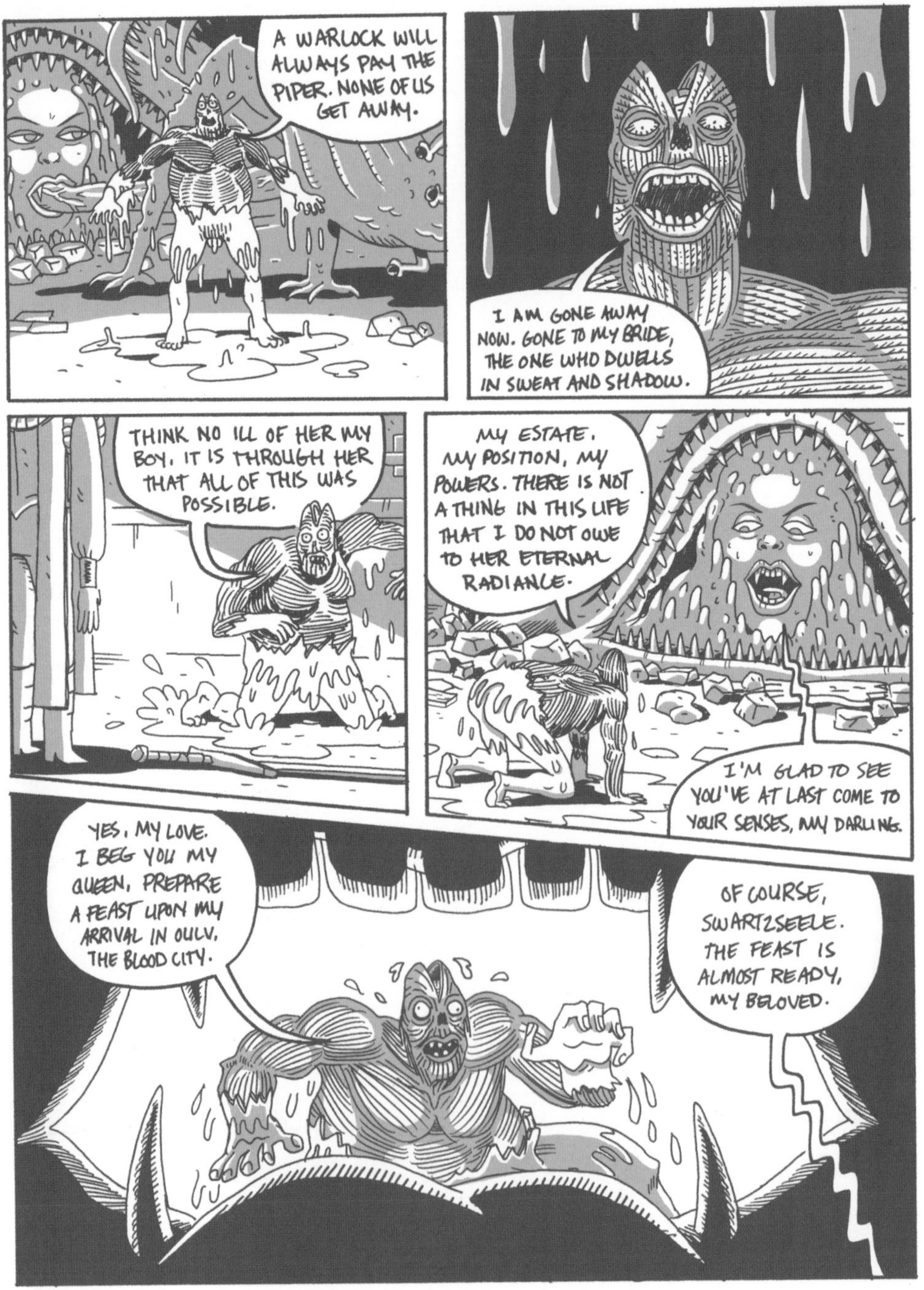
A WARLOCK WILL ALWAYS PAY THE PIPER. NONE OF US GET AWAY.
I AM GONE AWAY NOW. GONE TO MY BRIDE, THE ONE WHO DWELLS IN SWEAT AND SHADOW.
THINK NO ILL OF HER MY BOY. IT IS THROUGH HER THAT ALL OF THIS WAS POSSIBLE.
MY ESTATE. MY POSITION, MY POWERS. THERE IS NOT A THING IN THIS LIFE THAT I DO NOT OWE TO HER ETERNAL RADIANCE.
I'M GLAD TO SEE YOU'VE AT LAST COME TO YOUR SENSES, MY DARLING.
YES, MY LOVE. I BEG YOU MY QUEEN, PREPARE A FEAST UPON MY ARRIVAL IN OULV, THE BLOOD CITY.
OF COURSE, SWARTZSEELE. THE FEAST IS ALMOST READY, MY BELOVED.

IT'S JUST A SHAME YOU WILL NOT BE ATTENDING MY DARLING. **CHOMP!**

AND WHAT OF I, MILADY? WHAT IS TO BECOME OF RUTGER?

AM I TO PERISH ALONGSIDE MY MASTER? TO BE DEVOURED AND DIGESTED THROUGH THE BOWELS OF HELL ITSELF?

BOY, I'VE NO CLAIM TO YOUR SOUL, NO DESIRE FOR YOUR FLESH. THERE IS NO PACT BETWEEN US.

THE POWERS OF A WARLOCK WOULD ONLY BORE A YOUNG MAGE SUCH AS YOURSELF.

YOU'VE NO DESIRE FOR ABSOLUTE POWER, SO I SHALL TAKE MY LEAVE OF YOUR PRESENCE.

FORGET ALL YOU HAVE WITNESSED FOR THE SAKE OF YOUR OWN SANITY.

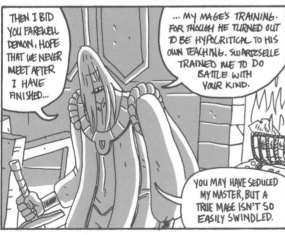

THEN I BID YOU FAREWELL DEMON, HOPE THAT WE NEVER MEET AFTER I HAVE FINISHED...

... MY MAGE'S TRAINING. FOR THOUGH HE TURNED OUT TO BE HYPOCRITICAL TO HIS OWN TEACHING. SWARTZSELLE TRAINED ME TO DO BATTLE WITH YOUR KIND.

YOU MAY HAVE SEDUCED MY MASTER, BUT A TRUE MAGE ISN'T SO EASILY SWINDLED.

HA!

YOU SOUND LIKE A LAD THAT HAS NEVER BEEN OFFERED A WARLOCK'S PACT!

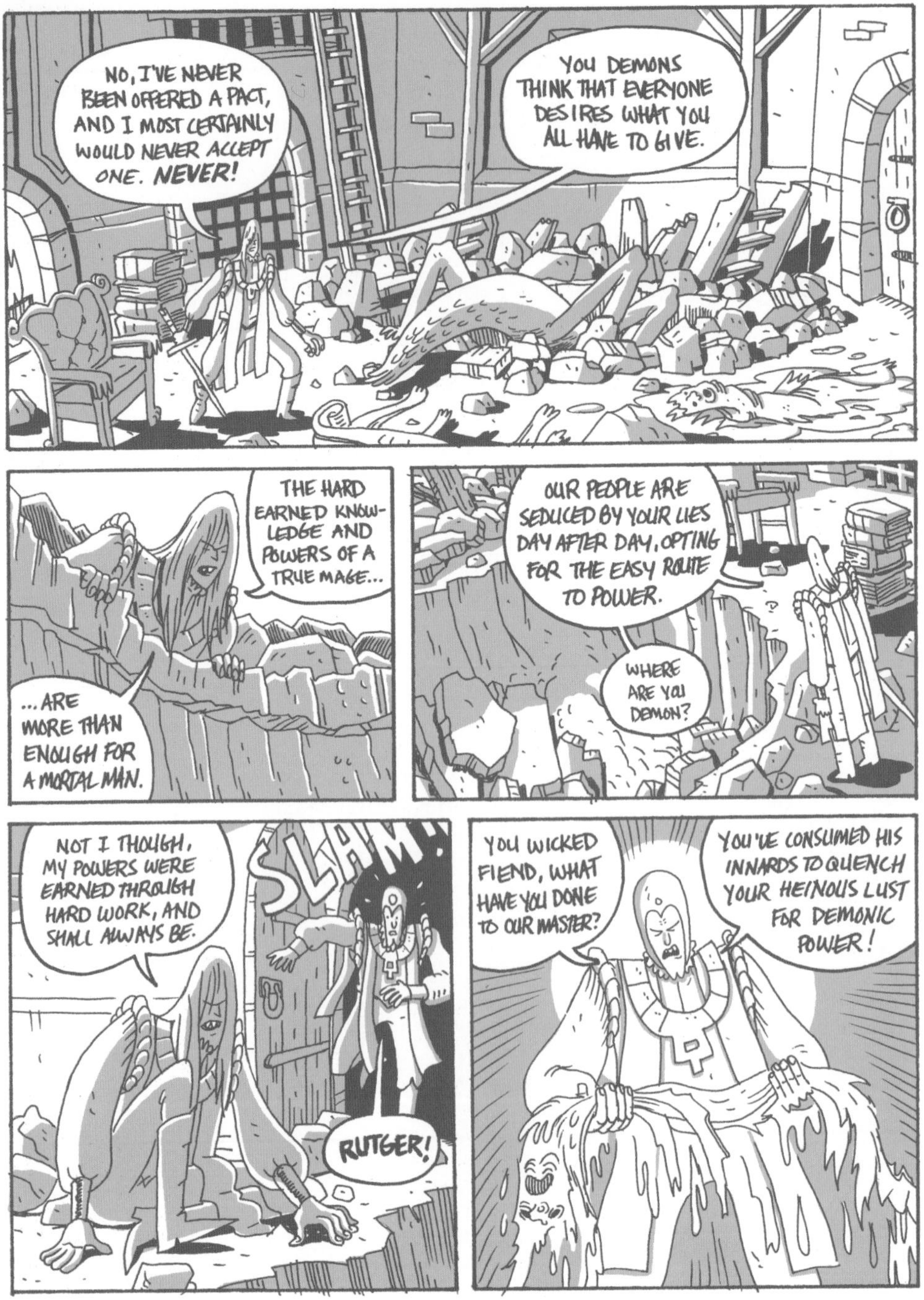
NO, I'VE NEVER BEEN OFFERED A PACT, AND I MOST CERTAINLY WOULD NEVER ACCEPT ONE. NEVER!
YOU DEMONS THINK THAT EVERYONE DESIRES WHAT YOU ALL HAVE TO GIVE.
THE HARD EARNED KNOW-LEDGE AND POWERS OF A TRUE MAGE...
...ARE MORE THAN ENOUGH FOR A MORTAL MAN.
OUR PEOPLE ARE SEDUCED BY YOUR LIES DAY AFTER DAY, OPTING FOR THE EASY ROUTE TO POWER.
WHERE ARE YOU DEMON?
NOT I THOUGH, MY POWERS WERE EARNED THROUGH HARD WORK, AND SHALL ALWAYS BE.
SLAM!
RUTGER!
YOU WICKED FIEND, WHAT HAVE YOU DONE TO OUR MASTER?
YOU'VE CONSUMED HIS INNARDS TO QUENCH YOUR HEINOUS LUST FOR DEMONIC POWER!

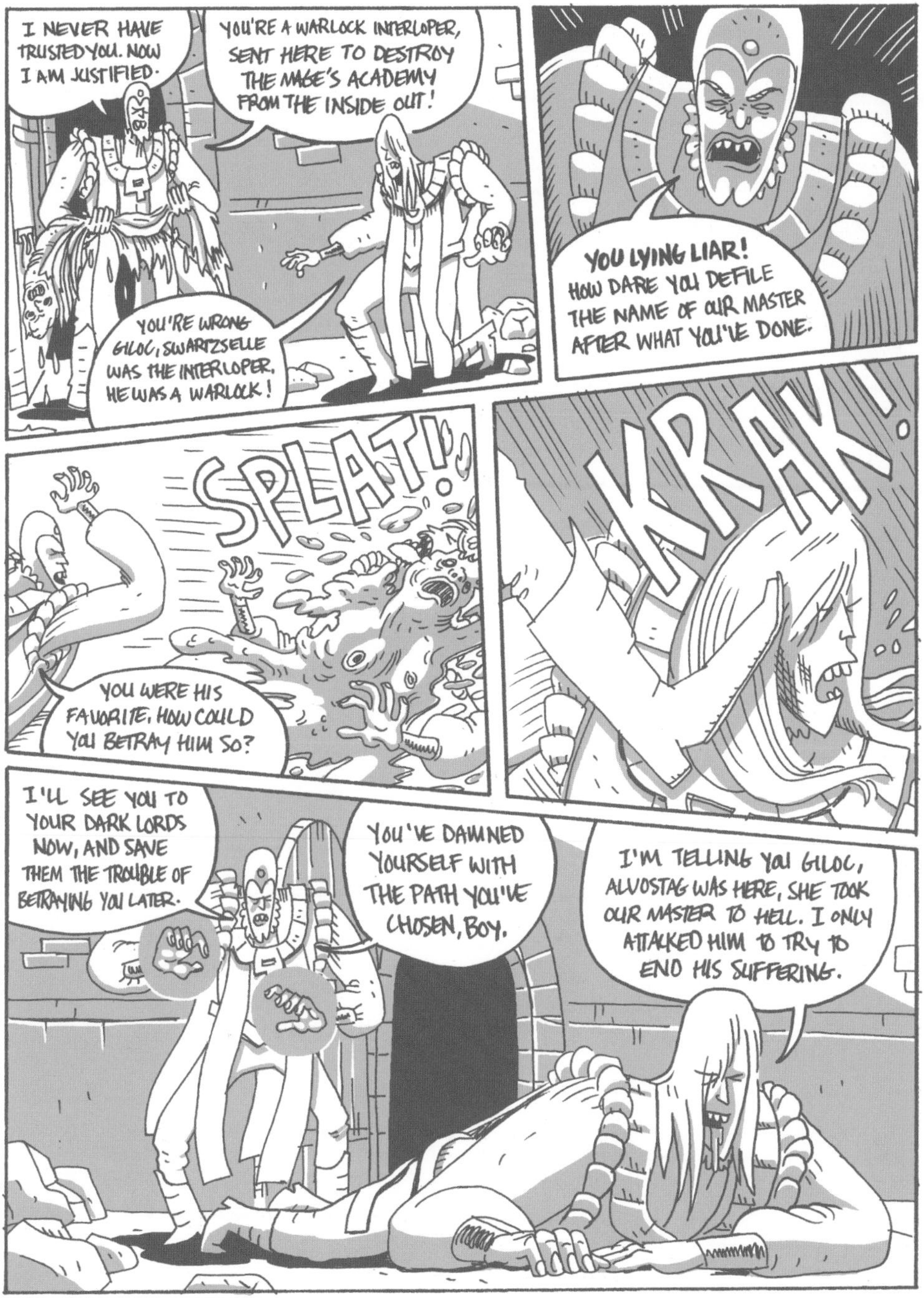
I NEVER HAVE TRUSTED YOU. NOW I AM JUSTIFIED.
YOU'RE A WARLOCK INTERLOPER, SENT HERE TO DESTROY THE MAGE'S ACADEMY FROM THE INSIDE OUT!
YOU'RE WRONG GILOC, SWARTZSELLE WAS THE INTERLOPER. HE WAS A WARLOCK!
YOU LYING LIAR! HOW DARE YOU DEFILE THE NAME OF OUR MASTER AFTER WHAT YOU'VE DONE.
SPLAT!
YOU WERE HIS FAVORITE. HOW COULD YOU BETRAY HIM SO?
KRAK!
I'LL SEE YOU TO YOUR DARK LORDS NOW, AND SAVE THEM THE TROUBLE OF BETRAYING YOU LATER.
YOU'VE DAMNED YOURSELF WITH THE PATH YOU'VE CHOSEN, BOY.
I'M TELLING YOU GILOC, ALVOSTAG WAS HERE, SHE TOOK OUR MASTER TO HELL. I ONLY ATTACKED HIM TO TRY TO END HIS SUFFERING.

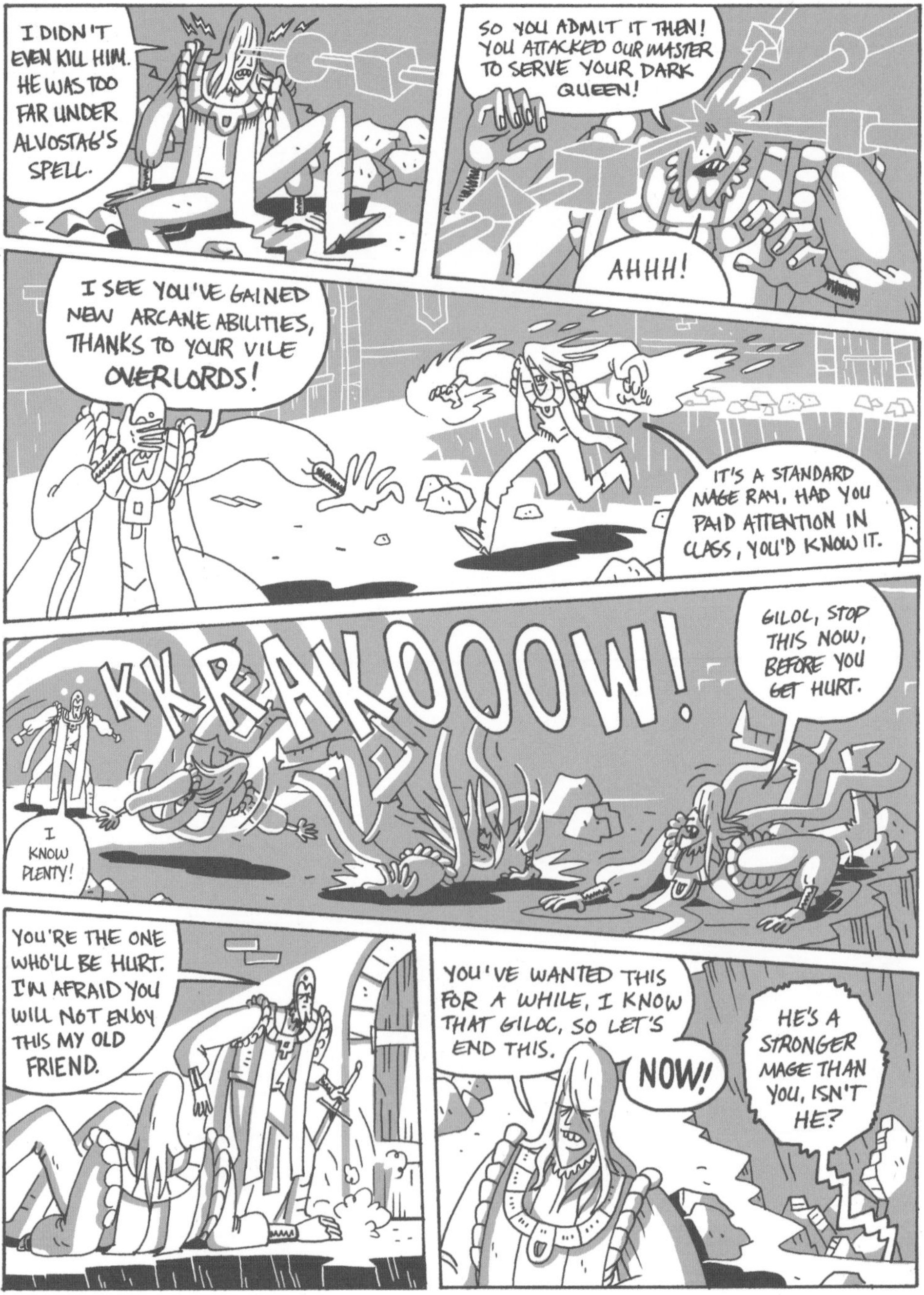
I DIDN'T EVEN KILL HIM. HE WAS TOO FAR UNDER ALVOSTAG'S SPELL.
SO YOU ADMIT IT THEN! YOU ATTACKED OUR MASTER TO SERVE YOUR DARK QUEEN!
AHHH!
I SEE YOU'VE GAINED NEW ARCANE ABILITIES, THANKS TO YOUR VILE OVERLORDS!
IT'S A STANDARD MAGE RAY. HAD YOU PAID ATTENTION IN CLASS, YOU'D KNOW IT.
KKRAKOOOOW!
I KNOW PLENTY!
GILOC, STOP THIS NOW, BEFORE YOU GET HURT.
YOU'RE THE ONE WHO'LL BE HURT. I'M AFRAID YOU WILL NOT ENJOY THIS MY OLD FRIEND.
YOU'VE WANTED THIS FOR A WHILE, I KNOW THAT GILOC, SO LET'S END THIS.
NOW!
HE'S A STRONGER MAGE THAN YOU, ISN'T HE?

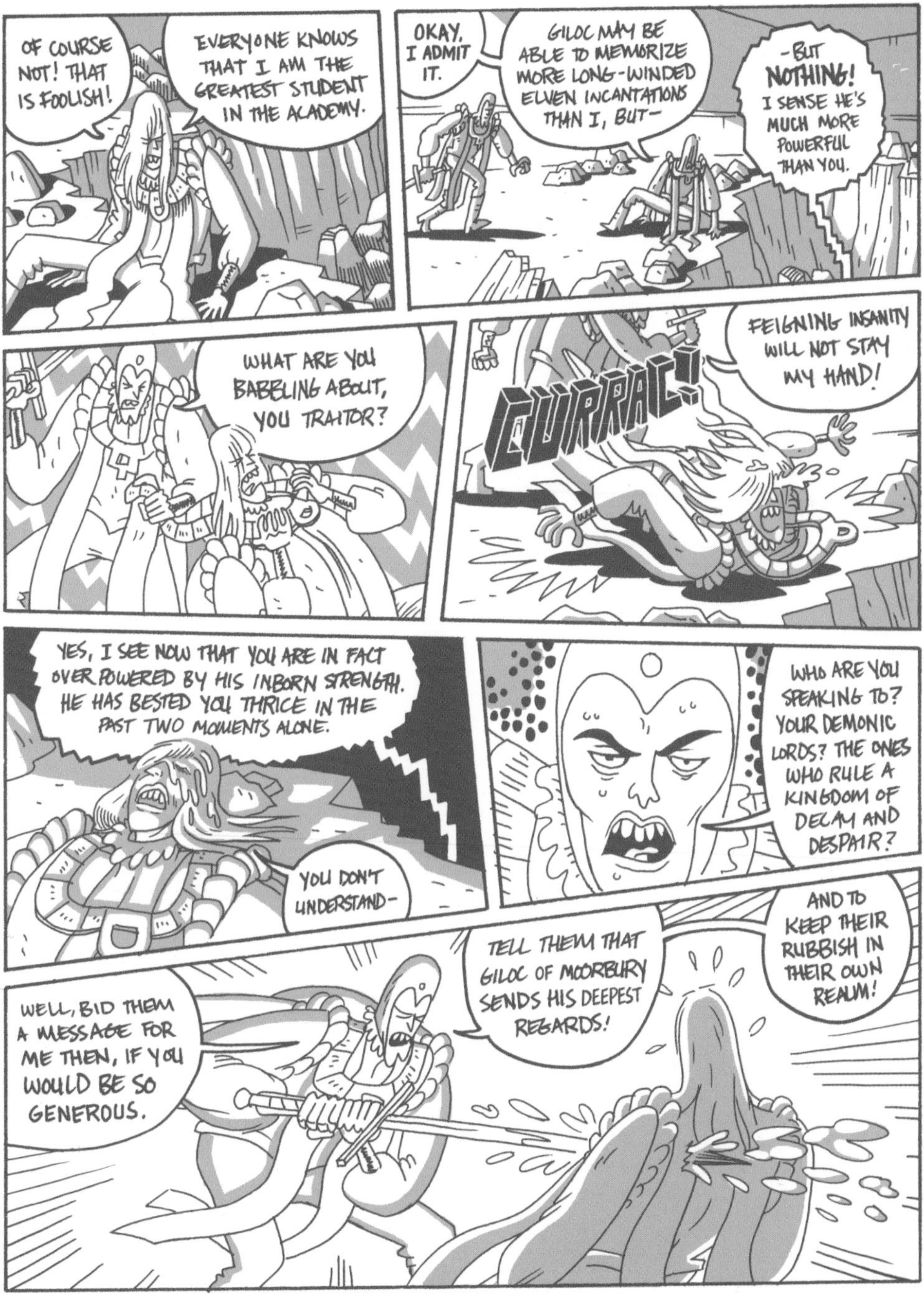

OF COURSE NOT! THAT IS FOOLISH!
EVERYONE KNOWS THAT I AM THE GREATEST STUDENT IN THE ACADEMY.
OKAY, I ADMIT IT.
GILOC MAY BE ABLE TO MEMORIZE MORE LONG-WINDED ELVEN INCANTATIONS THAN I, BUT—
—BUT NOTHING! I SENSE HE'S MUCH MORE POWERFUL THAN YOU.
WHAT ARE YOU BABBLING ABOUT, YOU TRAITOR?
CURRAC!
FEIGNING INSANITY WILL NOT STAY MY HAND!
YES, I SEE NOW THAT YOU ARE IN FACT OVERPOWERED BY HIS INBORN STRENGTH. HE HAS BESTED YOU THRICE IN THE PAST TWO MOMENTS ALONE.
YOU DON'T UNDERSTAND—
WHO ARE YOU SPEAKING TO? YOUR DEMONIC LORDS? THE ONES WHO RULE A KINGDOM OF DECAY AND DESPAIR?
WELL, BID THEM A MESSAGE FOR ME THEN, IF YOU WOULD BE SO GENEROUS.
TELL THEM THAT GILOC OF MOORBURY SENDS HIS DEEPEST REGARDS!
AND TO KEEP THEIR RUBBISH IN THEIR OWN REALM!

AKKK!

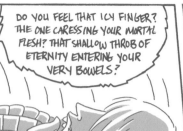
DO YOU FEEL THAT ICY FINGER? THE ONE CARESSING YOUR MORTAL FLESH? THAT SHALLOW THROB OF ETERNITY ENTERING YOUR VERY BOWELS?

THAT IS DEATH!

I'VE KNOW HIM SINCE HE WAS BUT A FLEDGLING IDEA, A TWINKLE IN THE EYE OF THE UNIVERSE.

I KNOW THAT YOU ARE ABOUT TO BE BROKEN DOWN INTO YOUR BASE MATERIALS, STRIPPED OF YOUR VERY SELF.

SOON, YOU SHALL LOSE YOUR VERY SENSE OF BEING. SHATTERED BEYOND ALL MATTER, YOU WILL DISOLVE INTO THE VOID OF NOTHINGNESS.

PITIFUL.

I ALONE COULD SEE YOU FOR WHAT YOU TRULY WERE, RUTGER!

THERE IS A WAY TO AVOID ALL OF THIS MY FRIEND. A SIMPLE SOLUTION, A CURE FOR YOUR CURRENT STATE.

HHH.

ACCEPT THIS SMALL GIFT FROM ME. JUST REACH OUT YOUR HAND, AND TAKE YOUR LIFE BACK FROM NOTHINGNESS.

SQUARR!

ARG!

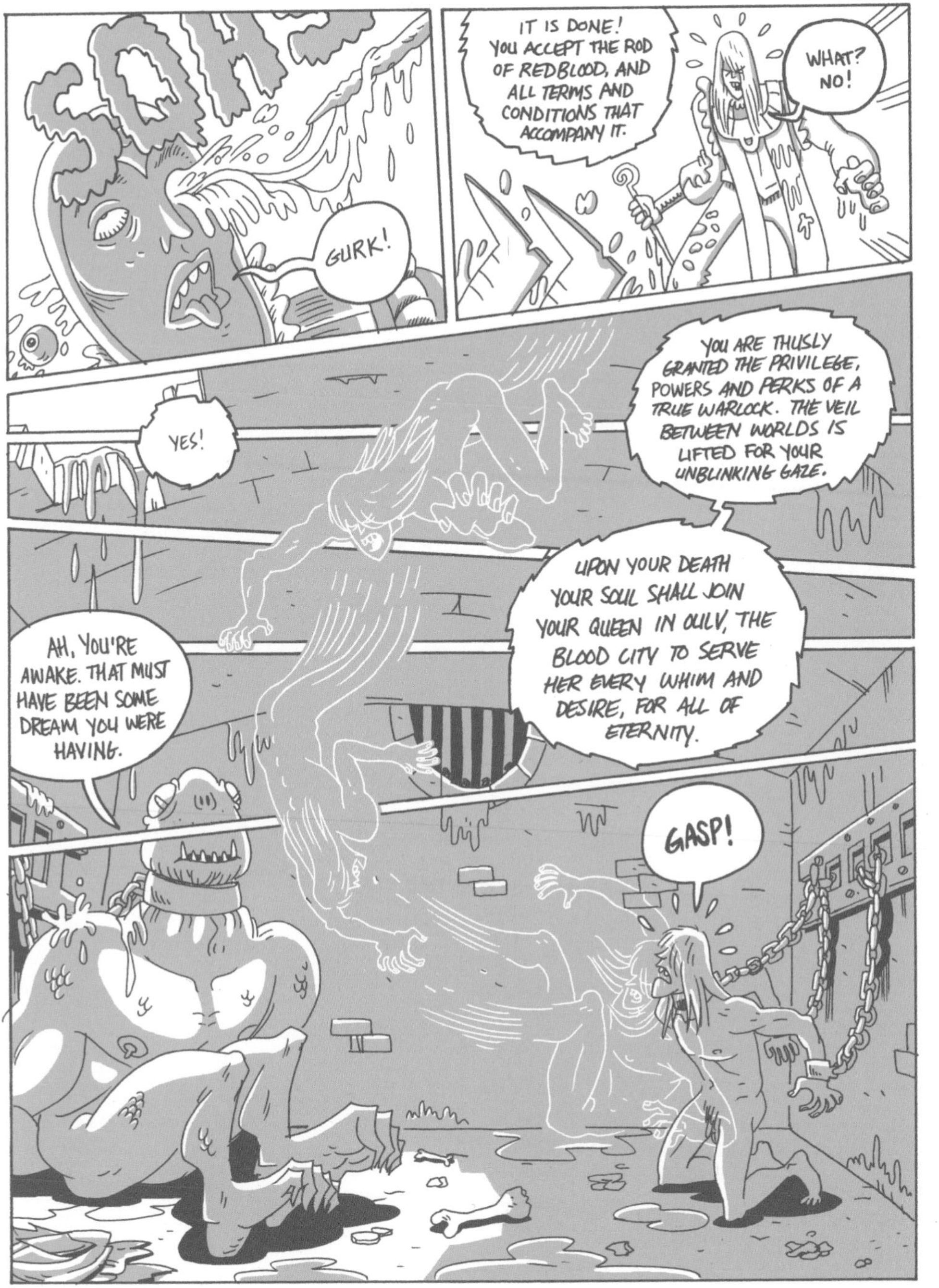
SQAS
GURK!
IT IS DONE! YOU ACCEPT THE ROD OF REDBLOOD, AND ALL TERMS AND CONDITIONS THAT ACCOMPANY IT.
WHAT? NO!
YES!
YOU ARE THUSLY GRANTED THE PRIVILEGE, POWERS AND PERKS OF A TRUE WARLOCK. THE VEIL BETWEEN WORLDS IS LIFTED FOR YOUR UNBLINKING GAZE.
UPON YOUR DEATH YOUR SOUL SHALL JOIN YOUR QUEEN IN OULV, THE BLOOD CITY TO SERVE HER EVERY WHIM AND DESIRE, FOR ALL OF ETERNITY.
AH, YOU'RE AWAKE. THAT MUST HAVE BEEN SOME DREAM YOU WERE HAVING.
GASP!

YOU'RE LUCKY IN A WAY. I'VE NOT DREAMED IN YEARS.

IT WAS NOT A DREAM WORTH HAVING.

THE WOSRYM'S VENOM HAD ME UNDER FOR A MONTH. I RELIVED MY LIFE'S JOYS OVER AND OVER AGAIN, ONLY TO WAKE CHAINED TO THIS DAMNED WALL.

THAT **WAS** PART OF YOUR BARGAIN, TURDOLON. WASN'T IT?

YOU TRADED YOUR SOUL FOR A FEMALE IF I'M NOT MISTAKEN. TRULY A FOOL'S CHOICE.

I WAS TRICKED! TRICKED!

RUMBLE!

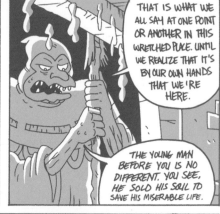

THAT IS WHAT WE ALL SAY AT ONE POINT OR ANOTHER IN THIS WRETCHED PLACE. UNTIL WE REALIZE THAT IT'S BY OUR OWN HANDS THAT WE'RE HERE.

THE YOUNG MAN BEFORE YOU IS NO DIFFERENT. YOU SEE, HE SOLD HIS SOUL TO SAVE HIS MISERABLE LIFE.

HIS LIFE, AND THE POWERS OF A WARLOCK THROUGH THAT UNHOLY INSTRUMENT, THE ROD OF REDBLOOD!

I'LL KILL YOU!

CLINK!

CLINK!

THE ROD OF RED-BLOOD WAS USELESS. IT DIDN'T EVEN WORK! I'VE MORE INBORN MAGIC THAN THAT PIECE OF PECKER-WOOD!

AIR YOUR GRIEV-ANCES TO URAC, WHEN HE COMES TO COLLECT YOU. EXPECT HIM IN ABOUT SIX THOUSAND YEARS. THE QUEUE'S A LITTLE BACKED UP.

GRUMBLE!

END PART ONE.

MEANWHILE...

DO I DROP THE EAVES CORRECTLY? DO I HEAR YOU TWO SEEK THE ARMORY OF THE CRIMSON WIZARD?

A CASTLE THIS BIG'S GOT TO HAVE AN ARM...

UM, YES BROTHER, WE SEEK ARMS AND ARMOR.

FOR THE WAR. YES, I KNOW.

HEAD AROUND THE CORNER, AND THROUGH YONDER PASSAGE. THE OTHERS ARE ALREADY GATHERED TOGETHER.

THE WAR? WHAT IS THAT FOOL TALKING ABOUT?

THE CRIMSON WIZARD HAS NOT RAISED AN ARMY IN FIVE HUNDRED YEARS...

...SINCE BEFORE HE BECAME THE CRIMSON WIZARD.

WHAT DOES A GRAND MASTER WIZARD WANT WITH AN ARMY ANYWAY?

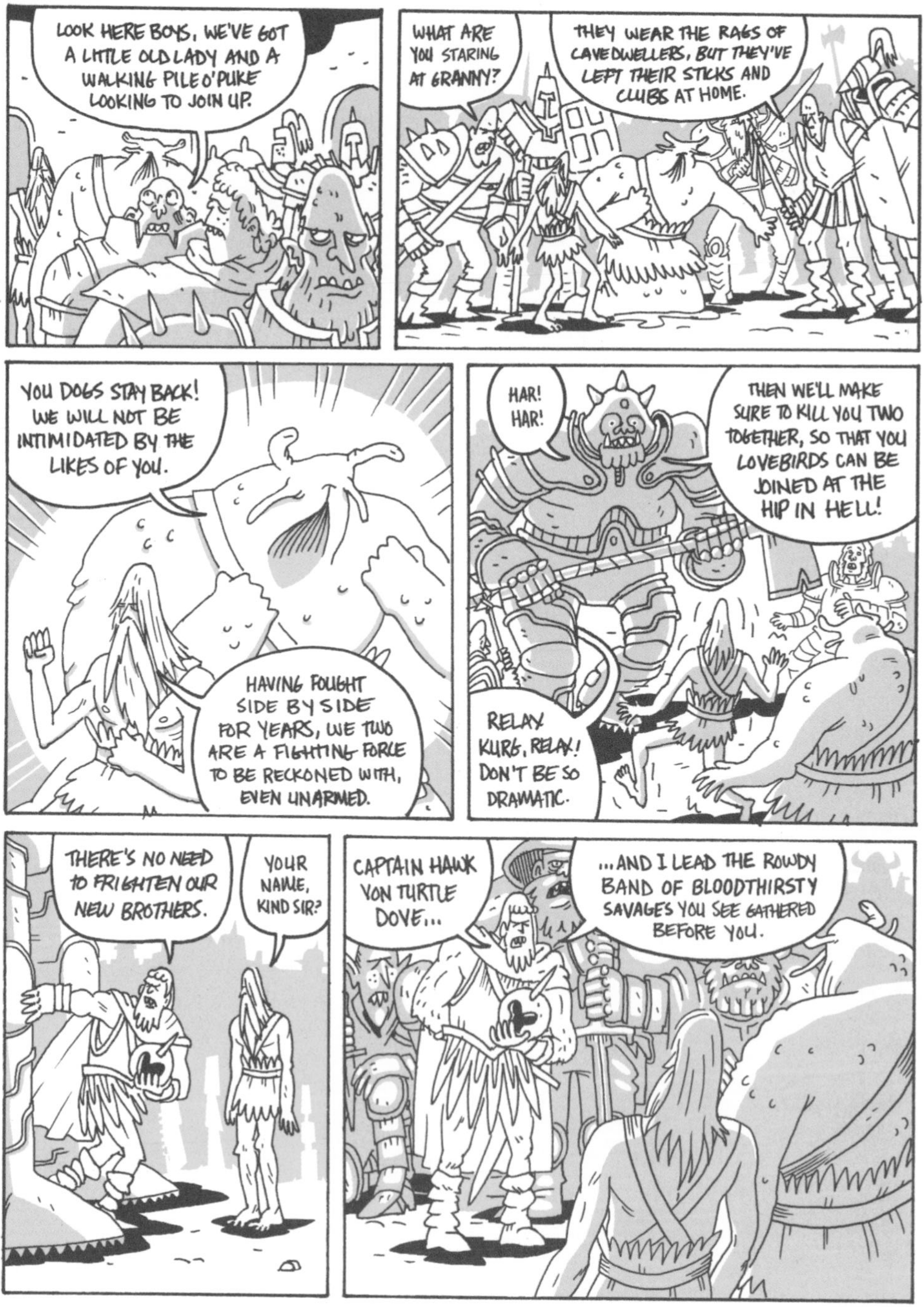
LOOK HERE BOYS, WE'VE GOT A LITTLE OLD LADY AND A WALKING PILE O'PUKE LOOKING TO JOIN UP.
WHAT ARE YOU STARING AT GRANNY?
THEY WEAR THE RAGS OF CAVEDWELLERS, BUT THEY'VE LEFT THEIR STICKS AND CLUBS AT HOME.
YOU DOGS STAY BACK! WE WILL NOT BE INTIMIDATED BY THE LIKES OF YOU.
HAVING FOUGHT SIDE BY SIDE FOR YEARS, WE TWO ARE A FIGHTING FORCE TO BE RECKONED WITH, EVEN UNARMED.
HAR! HAR!
THEN WE'LL MAKE SURE TO KILL YOU TWO TOGETHER, SO THAT YOU LOVEBIRDS CAN BE JOINED AT THE HIP IN HELL!
RELAX KURG, RELAX! DON'T BE SO DRAMATIC.
THERE'S NO NEED TO FRIGHTEN OUR NEW BROTHERS.
YOUR NAME, KIND SIR?
CAPTAIN HAWK VON TURTLE DOVE...
...AND I LEAD THE ROWDY BAND OF BLOODTHIRSTY SAVAGES YOU SEE GATHERED BEFORE YOU.

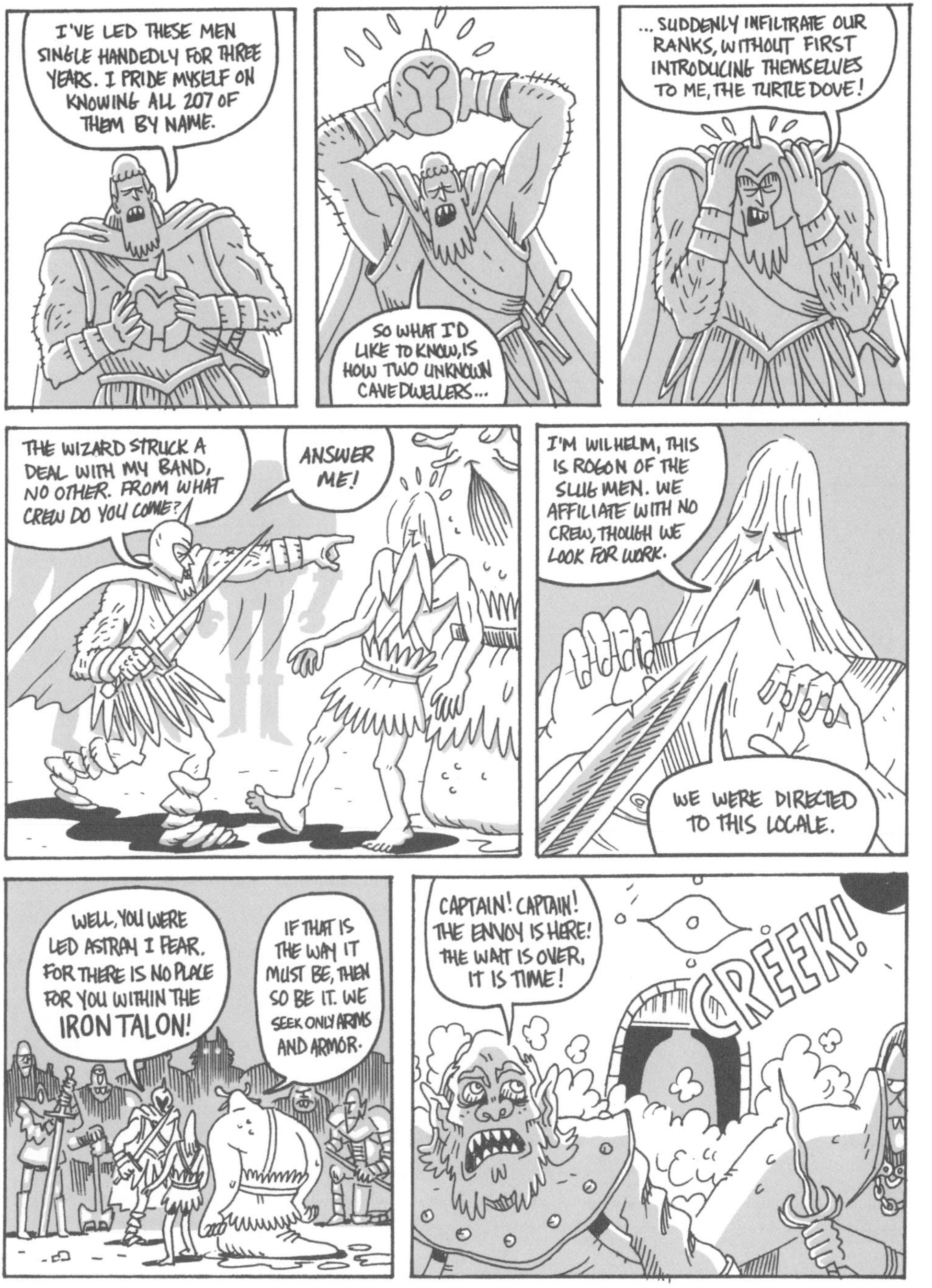

I'VE LED THESE MEN SINGLE HANDEDLY FOR THREE YEARS. I PRIDE MYSELF ON KNOWING ALL 207 OF THEM BY NAME.
SO WHAT I'D LIKE TO KNOW, IS HOW TWO UNKNOWN CAVE DWELLERS...
... SUDDENLY INFILTRATE OUR RANKS, WITHOUT FIRST INTRODUCING THEMSELVES TO ME, THE TURTLE DOVE!
THE WIZARD STRUCK A DEAL WITH MY BAND, NO OTHER. FROM WHAT CREW DO YOU COME?
ANSWER ME!
I'M WILHELM, THIS IS ROGON OF THE SLUG MEN. WE AFFILIATE WITH NO CREW, THOUGH WE LOOK FOR WORK.
WE WERE DIRECTED TO THIS LOCALE.
WELL, YOU WERE LED ASTRAY I FEAR. FOR THERE IS NO PLACE FOR YOU WITHIN THE IRON TALON!
IF THAT IS THE WAY IT MUST BE, THEN SO BE IT. WE SEEK ONLY ARMS AND ARMOR.
CAPTAIN! CAPTAIN! THE ENVOY IS HERE! THE WAIT IS OVER, IT IS TIME!
CREEK!

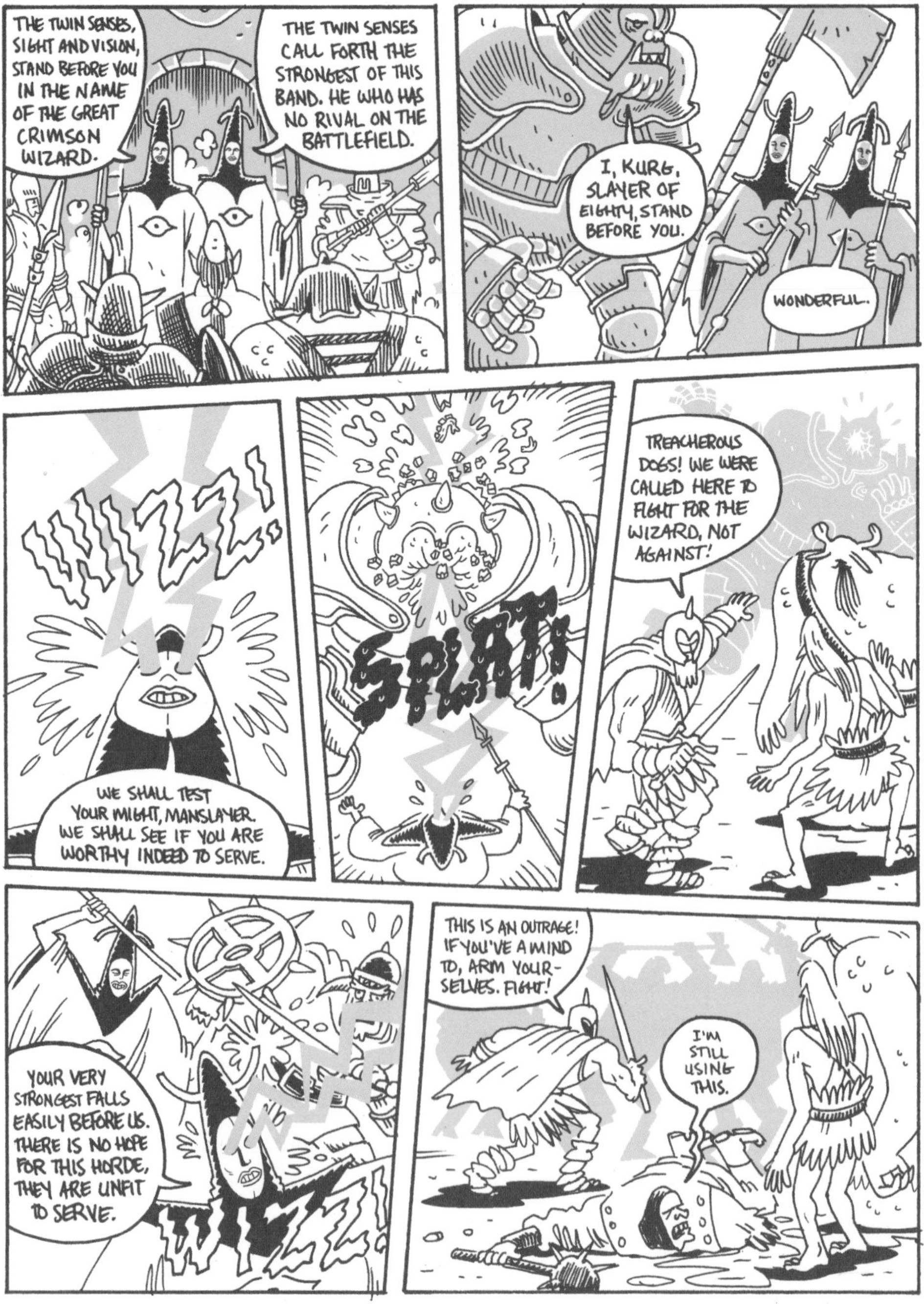
THE TWIN SENSES, SIGHT AND VISION, STAND BEFORE YOU IN THE NAME OF THE GREAT CRIMSON WIZARD.
THE TWIN SENSES CALL FORTH THE STRONGEST OF THIS BAND. HE WHO HAS NO RIVAL ON THE BATTLEFIELD.
I, KURG, SLAYER OF EIGHTY, STAND BEFORE YOU.
WONDERFUL.
WHIZZ!
WE SHALL TEST YOUR MIGHT, MANSLAYER. WE SHALL SEE IF YOU ARE WORTHY INDEED TO SERVE.
SPLAT!
TREACHEROUS DOGS! WE WERE CALLED HERE TO FIGHT FOR THE WIZARD, NOT AGAINST!
YOUR VERY STRONGEST FALLS EASILY BEFORE US. THERE IS NO HOPE FOR THIS HORDE, THEY ARE UNFIT TO SERVE.
THIS IS AN OUTRAGE! IF YOU'VE A MIND TO, ARM YOURSELVES. FIGHT!
I'M STILL USING THIS.

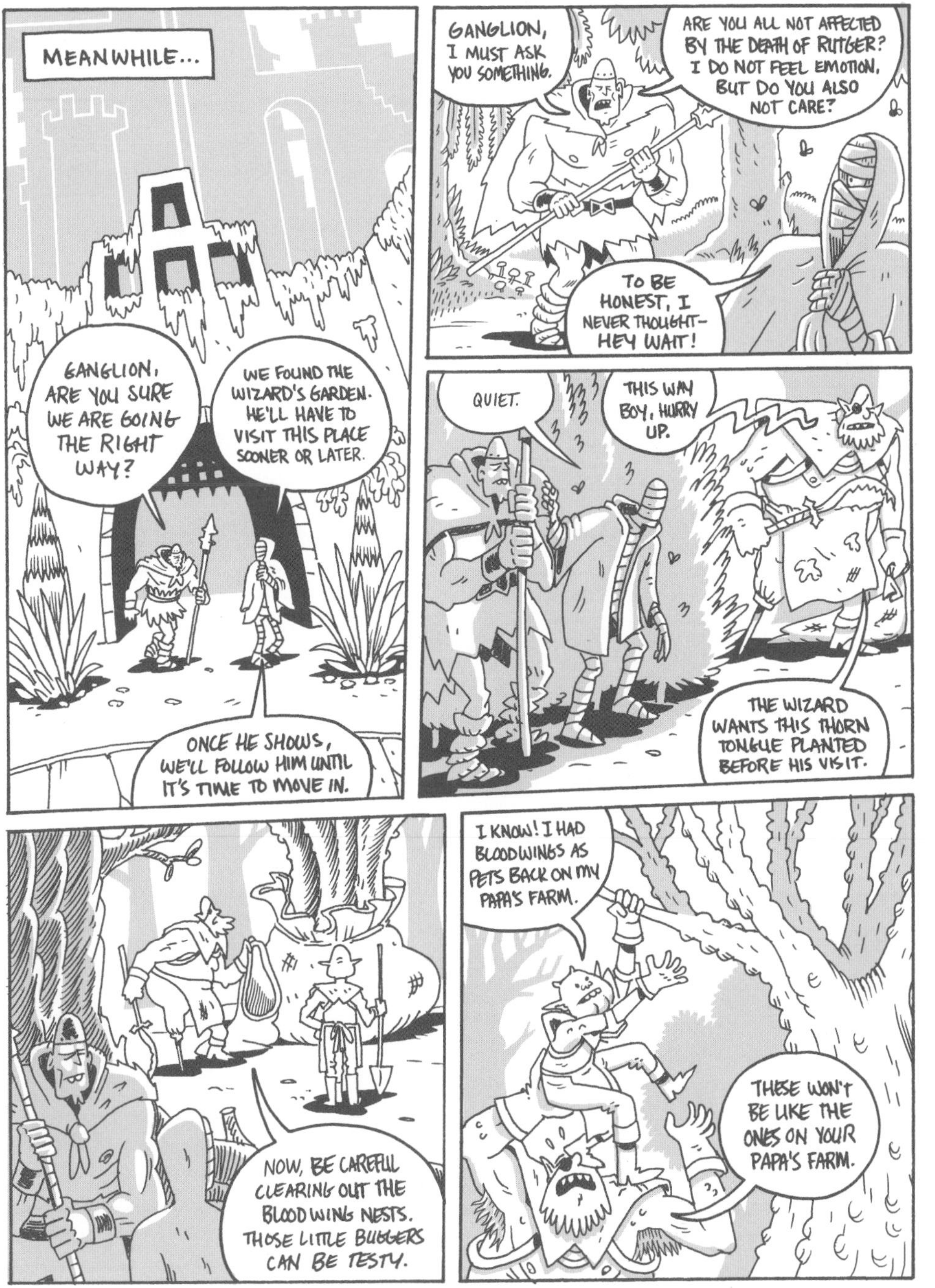
MEANWHILE...
GANGLION, ARE YOU SURE WE ARE GOING THE RIGHT WAY?
WE FOUND THE WIZARD'S GARDEN. HE'LL HAVE TO VISIT THIS PLACE SOONER OR LATER.
ONCE HE SHOWS, WE'LL FOLLOW HIM UNTIL IT'S TIME TO MOVE IN.
GANGLION, I MUST ASK YOU SOMETHING.
ARE YOU ALL NOT AFFECTED BY THE DEATH OF RUTGER? I DO NOT FEEL EMOTION, BUT DO YOU ALSO NOT CARE?
TO BE HONEST, I NEVER THOUGHT— HEY WAIT!
QUIET.
THIS WAY BOY, HURRY UP.
THE WIZARD WANTS THIS THORN TONGUE PLANTED BEFORE HIS VISIT.
NOW, BE CAREFUL CLEARING OUT THE BLOODWING NESTS. THOSE LITTLE BUGGERS CAN BE TESTY.
I KNOW! I HAD BLOODWINGS AS PETS BACK ON MY PAPA'S FARM.
THESE WON'T BE LIKE THE ONES ON YOUR PAPA'S FARM.

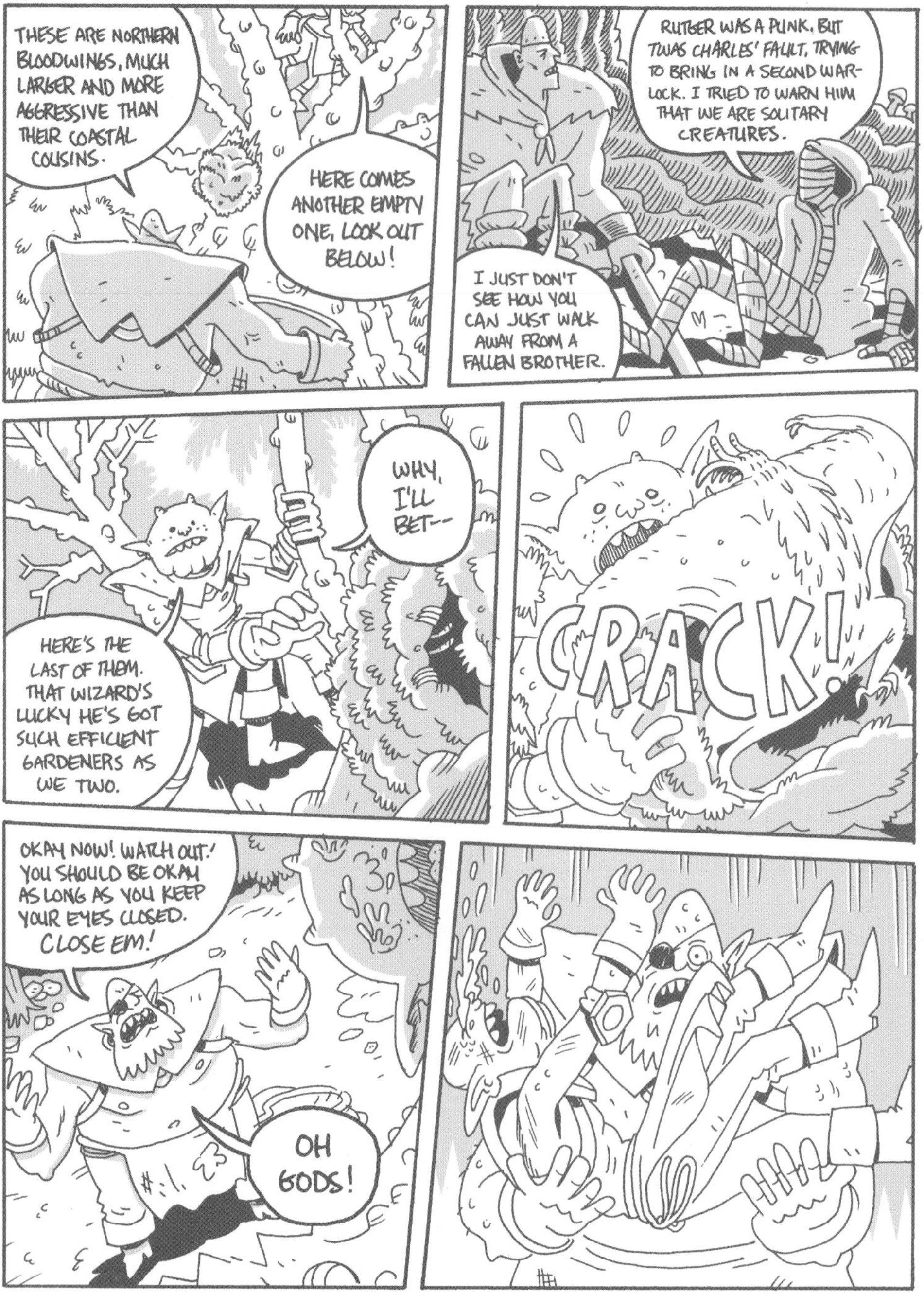
THESE ARE NORTHERN BLOODWINGS, MUCH LARGER AND MORE AGGRESSIVE THAN THEIR COASTAL COUSINS.
HERE COMES ANOTHER EMPTY ONE, LOOK OUT BELOW!
RUTGER WAS A PUNK, BUT TWAS CHARLES' FAULT, TRYING TO BRING IN A SECOND WARLOCK. I TRIED TO WARN HIM THAT WE ARE SOLITARY CREATURES.
I JUST DON'T SEE HOW YOU CAN JUST WALK AWAY FROM A FALLEN BROTHER.
WHY, I'LL BET--
HERE'S THE LAST OF THEM. THAT WIZARD'S LUCKY HE'S GOT SUCH EFFICIENT GARDENERS AS WE TWO.
CRACK!
OKAY NOW! WATCH OUT! YOU SHOULD BE OKAY AS LONG AS YOU KEEP YOUR EYES CLOSED. CLOSE EM!
OH GODS!

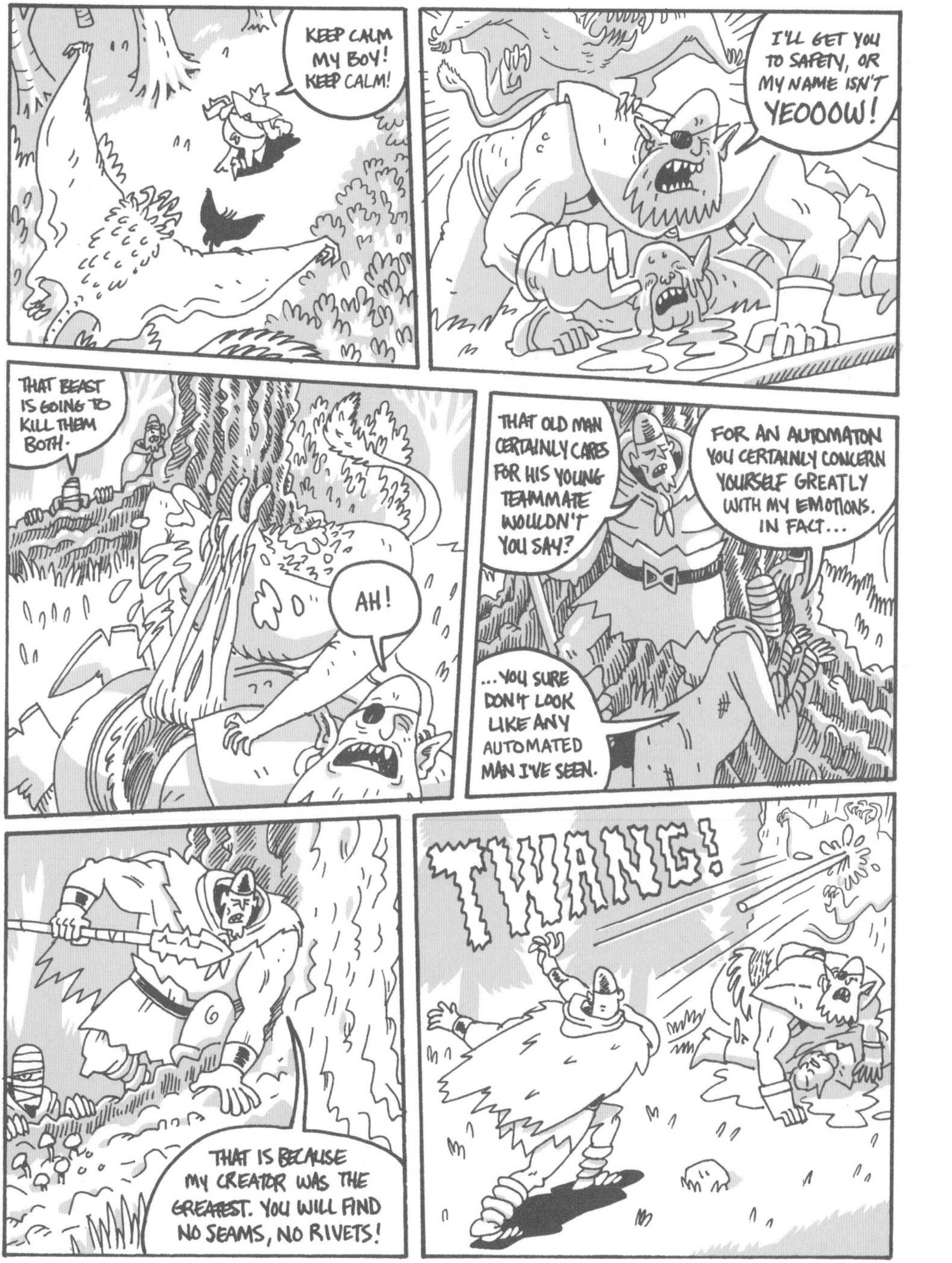
KEEP CALM MY BOY! KEEP CALM!
I'LL GET YOU TO SAFETY, OR MY NAME ISN'T YEOOOW!
THAT BEAST IS GOING TO KILL THEM BOTH.
AH!
THAT OLD MAN CERTAINLY CARES FOR HIS YOUNG TEAMMATE WOULDN'T YOU SAY?
FOR AN AUTOMATON YOU CERTAINLY CONCERN YOURSELF GREATLY WITH MY EMOTIONS. IN FACT...
...YOU SURE DON'T LOOK LIKE ANY AUTOMATED MAN I'VE SEEN.
THAT IS BECAUSE MY CREATOR WAS THE GREATEST. YOU WILL FIND NO SEAMS, NO RIVETS!
TWANG!

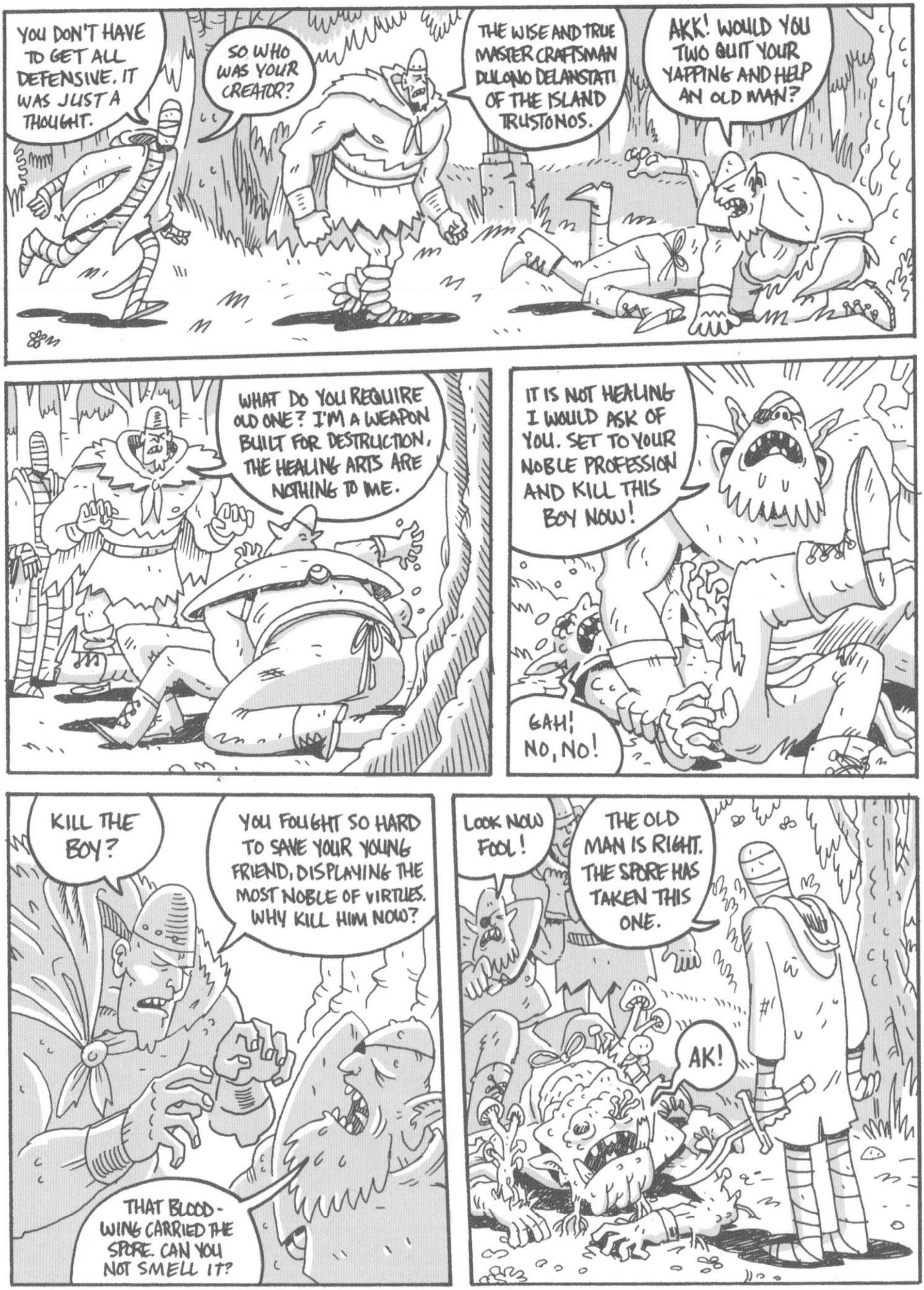
YOU DON'T HAVE TO GET ALL DEFENSIVE. IT WAS JUST A THOUGHT.
SO WHO WAS YOUR CREATOR?
THE WISE AND TRUE MASTER CRAFTSMAN DULONO DELANSTATI OF THE ISLAND TRUSTONOS.
AKK! WOULD YOU TWO QUIT YOUR YAPPING AND HELP AN OLD MAN?
WHAT DO YOU REQUIRE OLD ONE? I'M A WEAPON BUILT FOR DESTRUCTION, THE HEALING ARTS ARE NOTHING TO ME.
IT IS NOT HEALING I WOULD ASK OF YOU. SET TO YOUR NOBLE PROFESSION AND KILL THIS BOY NOW!
GAH! NO, NO!
KILL THE BOY?
YOU FOUGHT SO HARD TO SAVE YOUR YOUNG FRIEND, DISPLAYING THE MOST NOBLE OF VIRTUES. WHY KILL HIM NOW?
THAT BLOOD-WING CARRIED THE SPORE. CAN YOU NOT SMELL IT?
LOOK NOW FOOL!
THE OLD MAN IS RIGHT. THE SPORE HAS TAKEN THIS ONE.
AK!

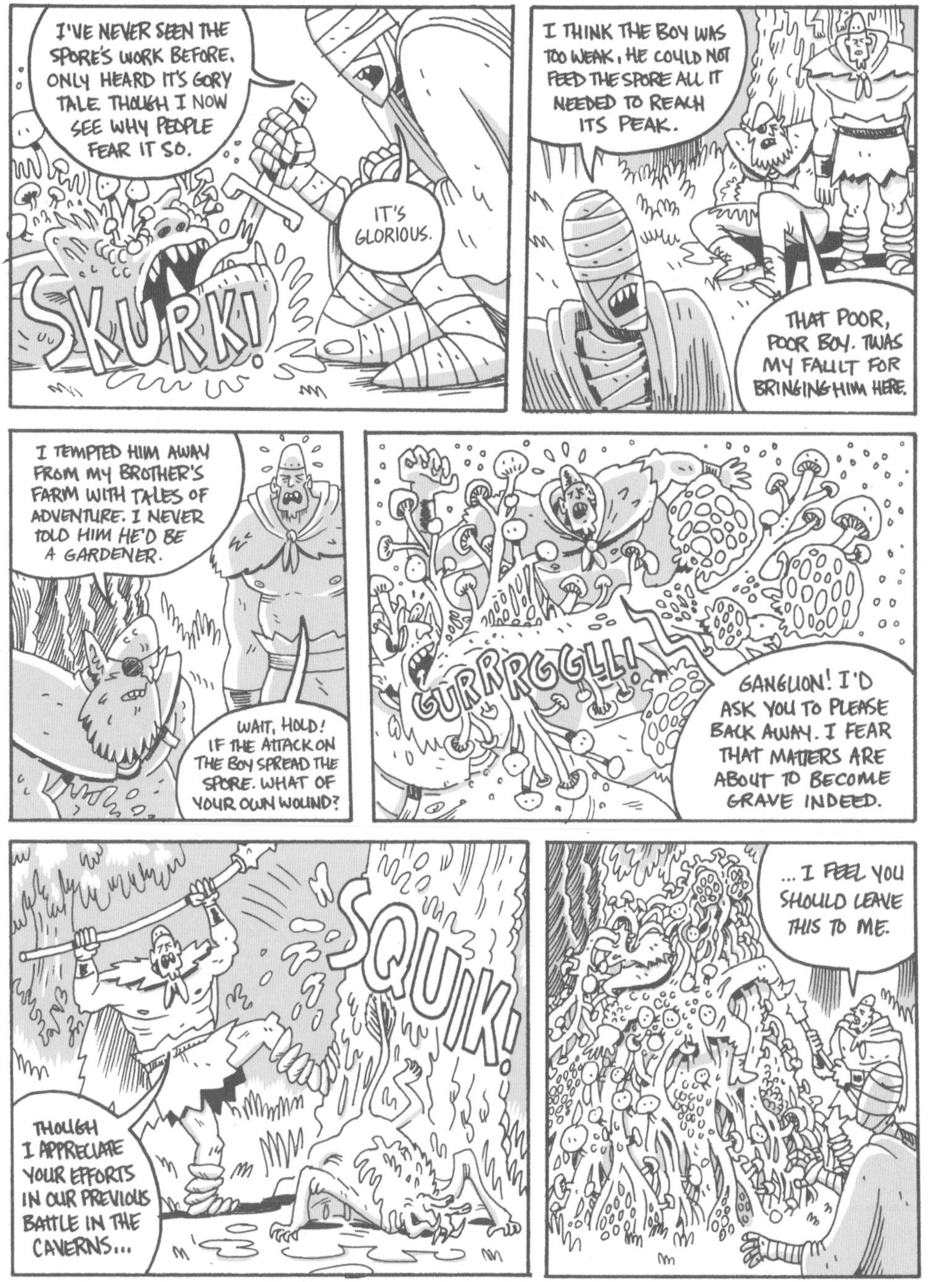
I'VE NEVER SEEN THE SPORE'S WORK BEFORE. ONLY HEARD IT'S GORY TALE. THOUGH I NOW SEE WHY PEOPLE FEAR IT SO.
SKURK!
IT'S GLORIOUS.
I THINK THE BOY WAS TOO WEAK. HE COULD NOT FEED THE SPORE ALL IT NEEDED TO REACH ITS PEAK.
THAT POOR, POOR BOY. TWAS MY FAULT FOR BRINGING HIM HERE.
I TEMPTED HIM AWAY FROM MY BROTHER'S FARM WITH TALES OF ADVENTURE. I NEVER TOLD HIM HE'D BE A GARDENER.
WAIT, HOLD! IF THE ATTACK ON THE BOY SPREAD THE SPORE. WHAT OF YOUR OWN WOUND?
GURRRGGLL!
GANGLION! I'D ASK YOU TO PLEASE BACK AWAY. I FEAR THAT MATTERS ARE ABOUT TO BECOME GRAVE INDEED.
SQUIK!
THOUGH I APPRECIATE YOUR EFFORTS IN OUR PREVIOUS BATTLE IN THE CAVERNS...
... I FEEL YOU SHOULD LEAVE THIS TO ME.

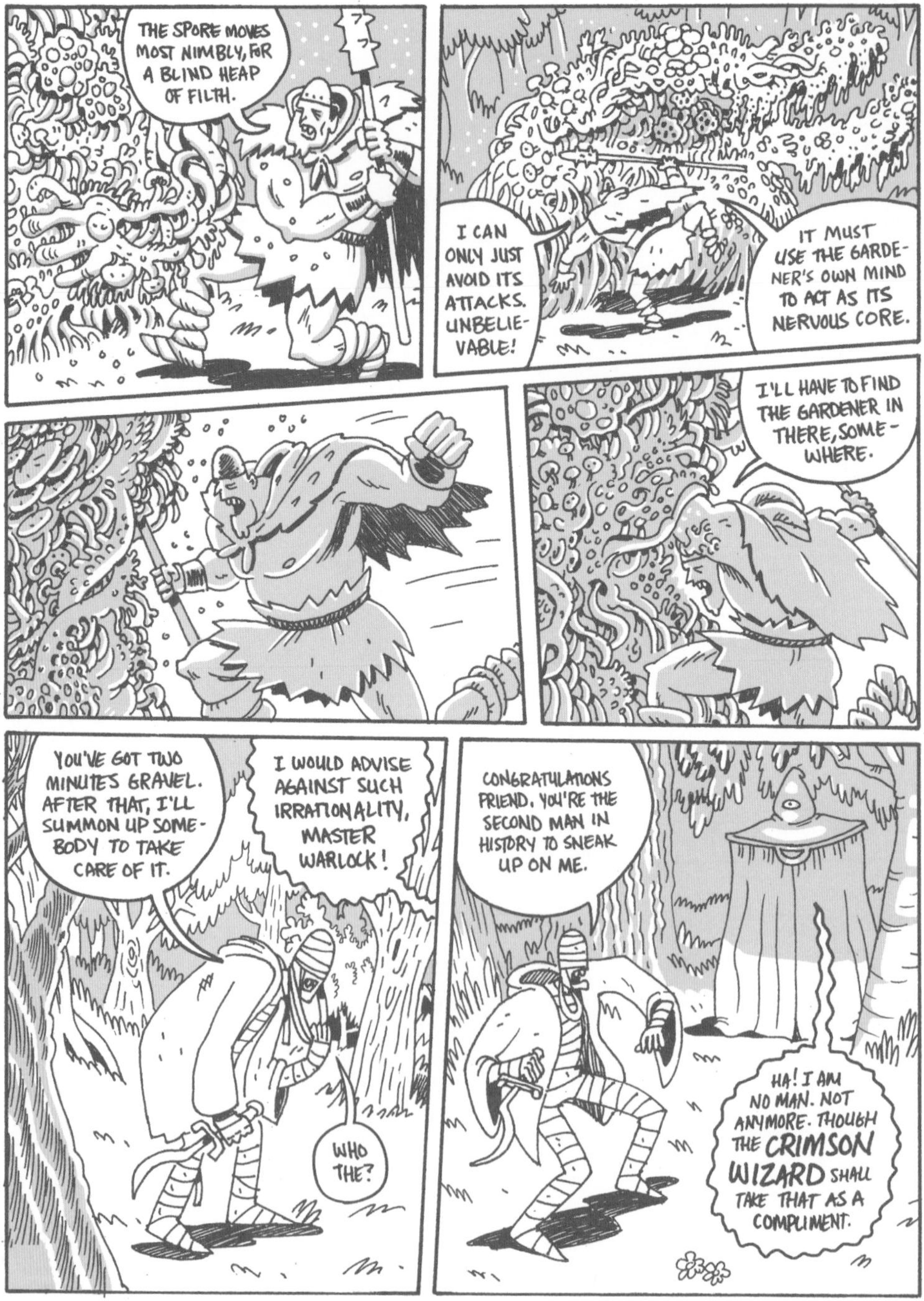
THE SPORE MOVES MOST NIMBLY, FOR A BLIND HEAP OF FILTH.
I CAN ONLY JUST AVOID ITS ATTACKS. UNBELIEVABLE!
IT MUST USE THE GARDENER'S OWN MIND TO ACT AS ITS NERVOUS CORE.
I'LL HAVE TO FIND THE GARDENER IN THERE, SOMEWHERE.
YOU'VE GOT TWO MINUTES GRAVEL. AFTER THAT, I'LL SUMMON UP SOMEBODY TO TAKE CARE OF IT.
I WOULD ADVISE AGAINST SUCH IRRATIONALITY, MASTER WARLOCK!
WHO THE?
CONGRATULATIONS FRIEND. YOU'RE THE SECOND MAN IN HISTORY TO SNEAK UP ON ME.
HA! I AM NO MAN. NOT ANYMORE. THOUGH THE CRIMSON WIZARD SHALL TAKE THAT AS A COMPLIMENT.

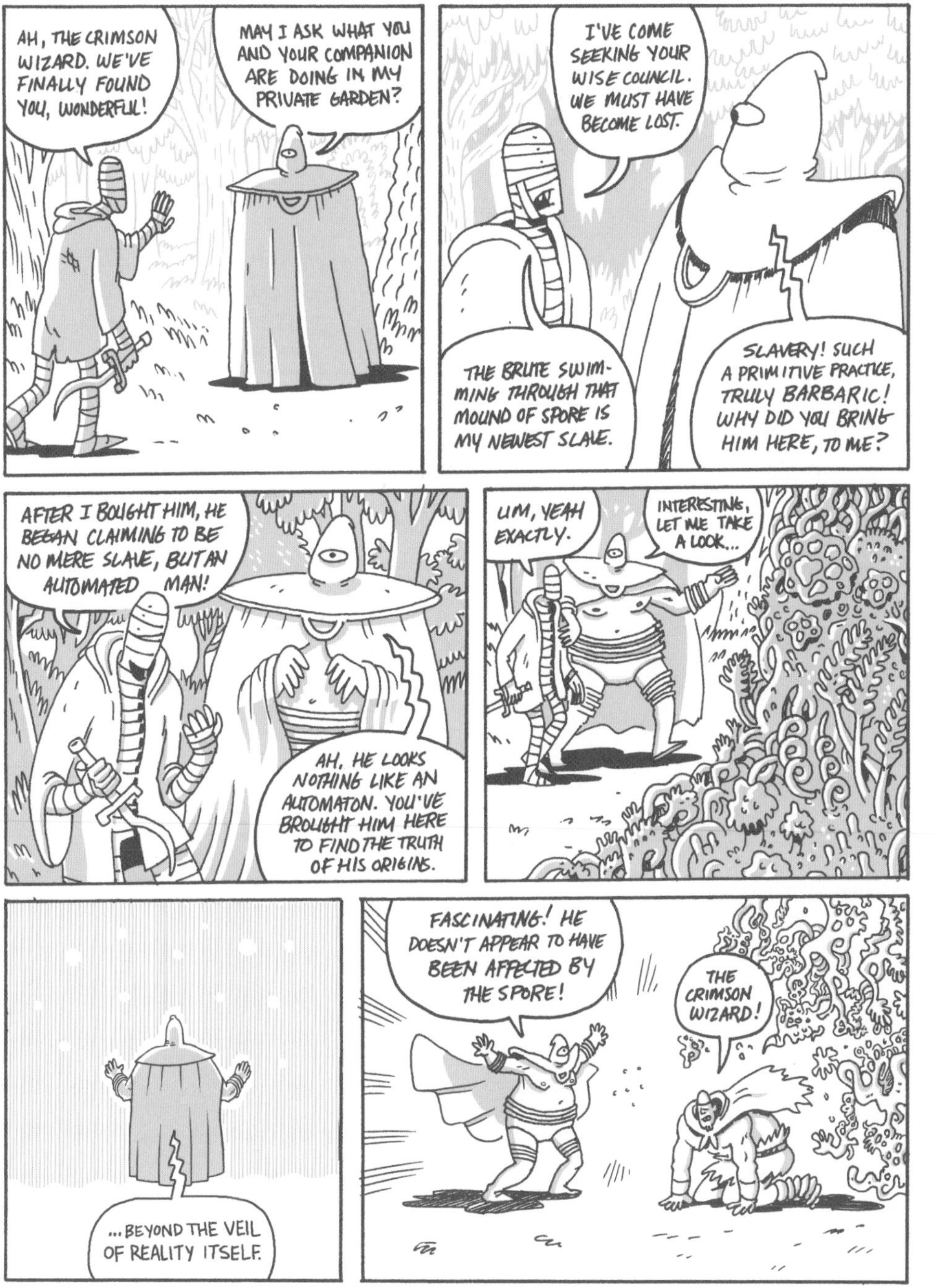
AH, THE CRIMSON WIZARD. WE'VE FINALLY FOUND YOU, WONDERFUL!
MAY I ASK WHAT YOU AND YOUR COMPANION ARE DOING IN MY PRIVATE GARDEN?
I'VE COME SEEKING YOUR WISE COUNCIL. WE MUST HAVE BECOME LOST.
THE BRUTE SWIMMING THROUGH THAT MOUND OF SPORE IS MY NEWEST SLAVE.
SLAVERY! SUCH A PRIMITIVE PRACTICE, TRULY BARBARIC! WHY DID YOU BRING HIM HERE, TO ME?
AFTER I BOUGHT HIM, HE BEGAN CLAIMING TO BE NO MERE SLAVE, BUT AN AUTOMATED MAN!
AH, HE LOOKS NOTHING LIKE AN AUTOMATON. YOU'VE BROUGHT HIM HERE TO FIND THE TRUTH OF HIS ORIGINS.
UM, YEAH EXACTLY.
INTERESTING, LET ME TAKE A LOOK...
...BEYOND THE VEIL OF REALITY ITSELF.
FASCINATING! HE DOESN'T APPEAR TO HAVE BEEN AFFECTED BY THE SPORE!
THE CRIMSON WIZARD!

YES, HE'S UNHARMED! ANOTHER STRANGE OCCURRENCE ADDING CREDENCE TO HIS UNBELIEVABLE CLAIM OF MECHANICAL IMMORTALITY.

GANGLION? WHAT ARE YOU DOING? LET GO OF ME!

SILENCE SLAVE! YOU DARE COMMAND YOUR MASTER?

HA! THERE WILL BE TIME FOR SUCH DOMESTIC SQUABBLES LATER. THIS MYSTERY HAS NOW MY FULL AND UNDIVIDED ATTENTION. QUICKLY! TO THE WORKSHOP!

I MUST CONFESS, I'M MOST EXCITED.

THE CHANCE TO STUDY AN AUTOMATED MAN OF SUCH QUALITY, COMES NOT EVERY DAY.

WHAT HAVE YOU DONE GRIM ONE?

I TINKERED WITH A FEW IN MY YOUTH, BUT COULD NEVER GET THE HANG OF THEM.

SURE, THANKS.

PLEASE, RIGHT THIS WAY.

KEEP YOUR MOUTH SHUT! I TOLD HIM YOU WERE MY SLAVE, JUST PLAY ALONG. HE'S GONNA LEAD US TO THAT GOBLET!

THIS WIZARD IS NOT ONE TO BE FOOLED EASILY. OUR MISSION IS OVER IF YOUR LIE IS UNCOVERED.

CHARLES TOLD US TO OBSERVE, NOT ENGAGE.

YOU ENGAGED ON BEHALF OF THAT GARDENER, REMEMBER?

WELCOME SLAYER. I DULRONKIN, SHALL BEGIN INITIAL TESTING ON THE MECHANISM, AS THE WIZARD PREPARES HIS CHAMBER.

48

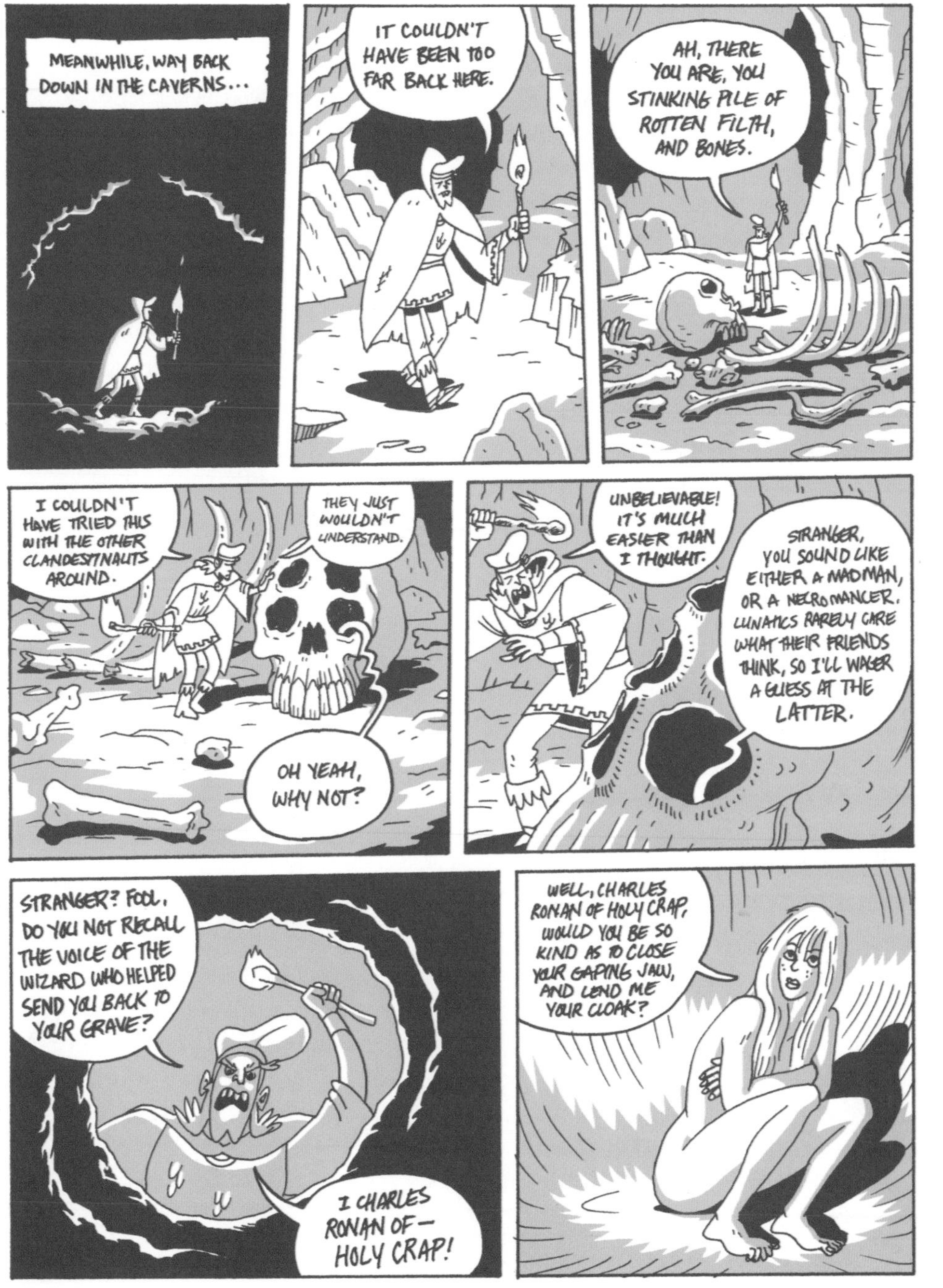
MEANWHILE, WAY BACK DOWN IN THE CAVERNS...
IT COULDN'T HAVE BEEN TOO FAR BACK HERE.
AH, THERE YOU ARE, YOU STINKING PILE OF ROTTEN FILTH, AND BONES.
I COULDN'T HAVE TRIED THIS WITH THE OTHER CLANDESTINAUTS AROUND.
THEY JUST WOULDN'T UNDERSTAND.
OH YEAH, WHY NOT?
UNBELIEVABLE! IT'S MUCH EASIER THAN I THOUGHT.
STRANGER, YOU SOUND LIKE EITHER A MADMAN, OR A NECROMANCER. LUNATICS RARELY CARE WHAT THEIR FRIENDS THINK, SO I'LL WAGER A GUESS AT THE LATTER.
STRANGER? FOOL. DO YOU NOT RECALL THE VOICE OF THE WIZARD WHO HELPED SEND YOU BACK TO YOUR GRAVE?
I CHARLES RONAN OF— HOLY CRAP!
WELL, CHARLES RONAN OF HOLY CRAP, WOULD YOU BE SO KIND AS TO CLOSE YOUR GAPING JAW, AND LEND ME YOUR CLOAK?

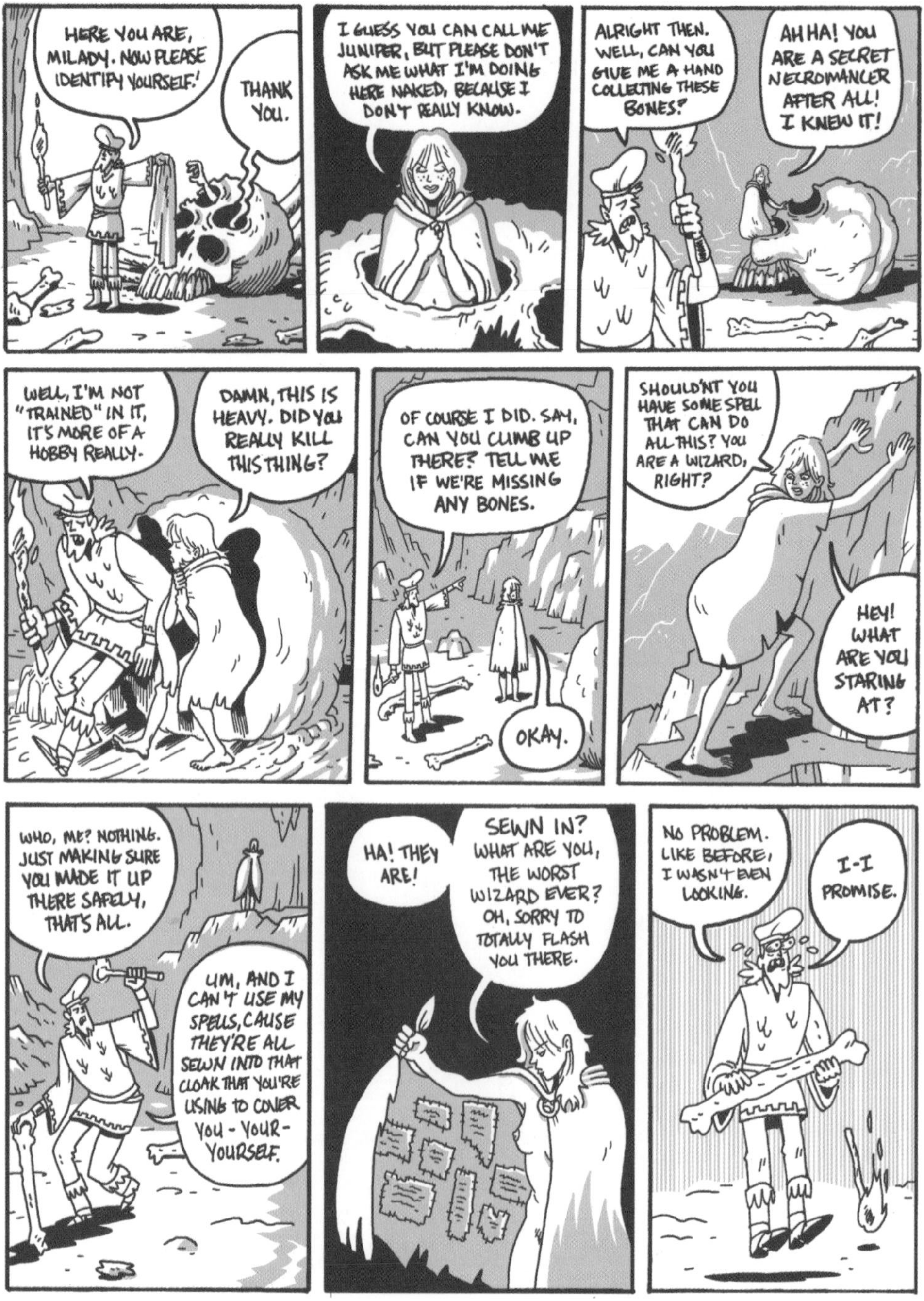
HERE YOU ARE, MILADY. NOW PLEASE IDENTIFY YOURSELF!
THANK YOU.
I GUESS YOU CAN CALL ME JUNIPER, BUT PLEASE DON'T ASK ME WHAT I'M DOING HERE NAKED, BECAUSE I DON'T REALLY KNOW.
ALRIGHT THEN. WELL, CAN YOU GIVE ME A HAND COLLECTING THESE BONES?
AH HA! YOU ARE A SECRET NECROMANCER AFTER ALL! I KNEW IT!
WELL, I'M NOT "TRAINED" IN IT, IT'S MORE OF A HOBBY REALLY.
DAMN, THIS IS HEAVY. DID YOU REALLY KILL THIS THING?
OF COURSE I DID. SAY, CAN YOU CLIMB UP THERE? TELL ME IF WE'RE MISSING ANY BONES.
OKAY.
SHOULDN'T YOU HAVE SOME SPELL THAT CAN DO ALL THIS? YOU ARE A WIZARD, RIGHT?
HEY! WHAT ARE YOU STARING AT?
WHO, ME? NOTHING. JUST MAKING SURE YOU MADE IT UP THERE SAFELY, THAT'S ALL.
UM, AND I CAN'T USE MY SPELLS, CAUSE THEY'RE ALL SEWN INTO THAT CLOAK THAT YOU'RE USING TO COVER YOU - YOUR- YOURSELF.
HA! THEY ARE!
SEWN IN? WHAT ARE YOU, THE WORST WIZARD EVER? OH, SORRY TO TOTALLY FLASH YOU THERE.
NO PROBLEM. LIKE BEFORE, I WASN'T EVEN LOOKING.
I-I PROMISE.

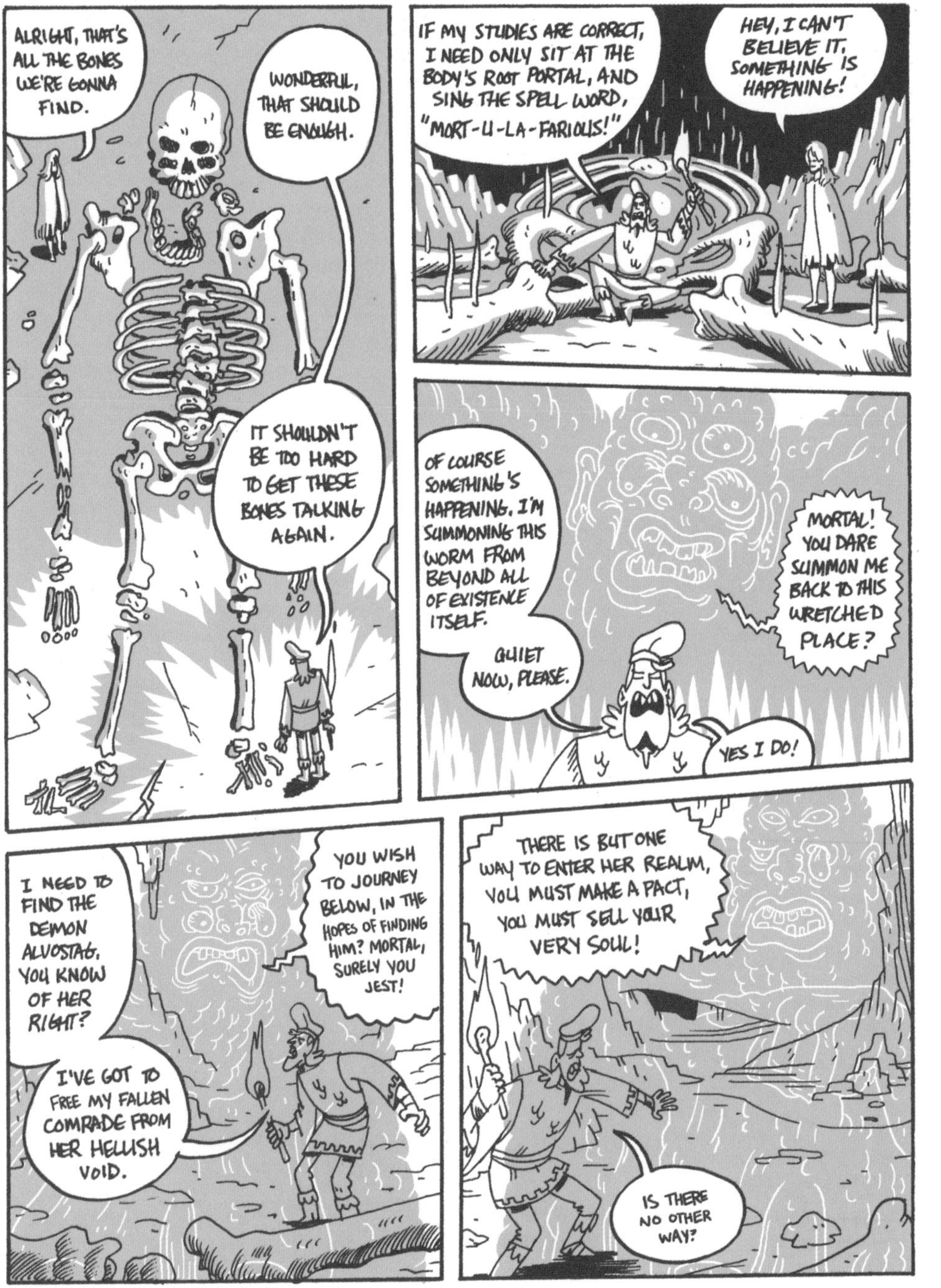
ALRIGHT, THAT'S ALL THE BONES WE'RE GONNA FIND.
WONDERFUL, THAT SHOULD BE ENOUGH.
IT SHOULDN'T BE TOO HARD TO GET THESE BONES TALKING AGAIN.
IF MY STUDIES ARE CORRECT, I NEED ONLY SIT AT THE BODY'S ROOT PORTAL, AND SING THE SPELL WORD, "MORT-U-LA-FARIOUS!"
HEY, I CAN'T BELIEVE IT. SOMETHING IS HAPPENING!
OF COURSE SOMETHING'S HAPPENING. I'M SUMMONING THIS WORM FROM BEYOND ALL OF EXISTENCE ITSELF.
MORTAL! YOU DARE SUMMON ME BACK TO THIS WRETCHED PLACE?
QUIET NOW, PLEASE.
YES I DO!
I NEED TO FIND THE DEMON ALVOSTAG. YOU KNOW OF HER RIGHT?
YOU WISH TO JOURNEY BELOW, IN THE HOPES OF FINDING HIM? MORTAL, SURELY YOU JEST!
I'VE GOT TO FREE MY FALLEN COMRADE FROM HER HELLISH VOID.
THERE IS BUT ONE WAY TO ENTER HER REALM, YOU MUST MAKE A PACT, YOU MUST SELL YOUR VERY SOUL!
IS THERE NO OTHER WAY?

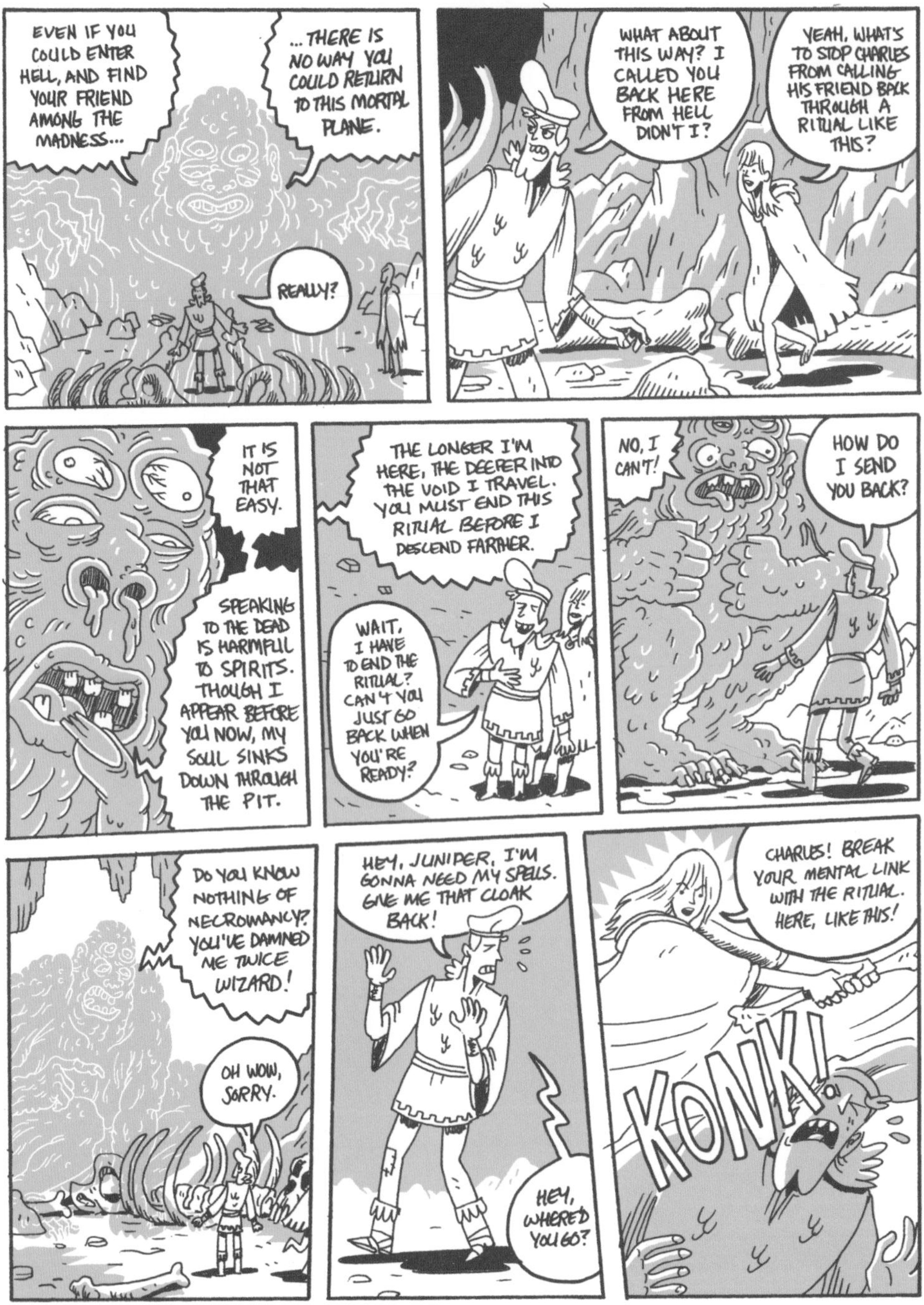

EVEN IF YOU COULD ENTER HELL, AND FIND YOUR FRIEND AMONG THE MADNESS...
...THERE IS NO WAY YOU COULD RETURN TO THIS MORTAL PLANE.
REALLY?
WHAT ABOUT THIS WAY? I CALLED YOU BACK HERE FROM HELL DIDN'T I?
YEAH, WHAT'S TO STOP CHARLES FROM CALLING HIS FRIEND BACK THROUGH A RITUAL LIKE THIS?
IT IS NOT THAT EASY.
SPEAKING TO THE DEAD IS HARMFUL TO SPIRITS. THOUGH I APPEAR BEFORE YOU NOW, MY SOUL SINKS DOWN THROUGH THE PIT.
THE LONGER I'M HERE, THE DEEPER INTO THE VOID I TRAVEL. YOU MUST END THIS RITUAL BEFORE I DESCEND FARTHER.
WAIT, I HAVE TO END THE RITUAL? CAN'T YOU JUST GO BACK WHEN YOU'RE READY?
HOW DO I SEND YOU BACK?
NO, I CAN'T!
DO YOU KNOW NOTHING OF NECROMANCY? YOU'VE DAMNED ME TWICE WIZARD!
OH WOW, SORRY.
HEY, JUNIPER, I'M GONNA NEED MY SPELLS. GIVE ME THAT CLOAK BACK!
HEY, WHERE'D YOU GO?
CHARLES! BREAK YOUR MENTAL LINK WITH THE RITUAL. HERE, LIKE THIS!
KONK!

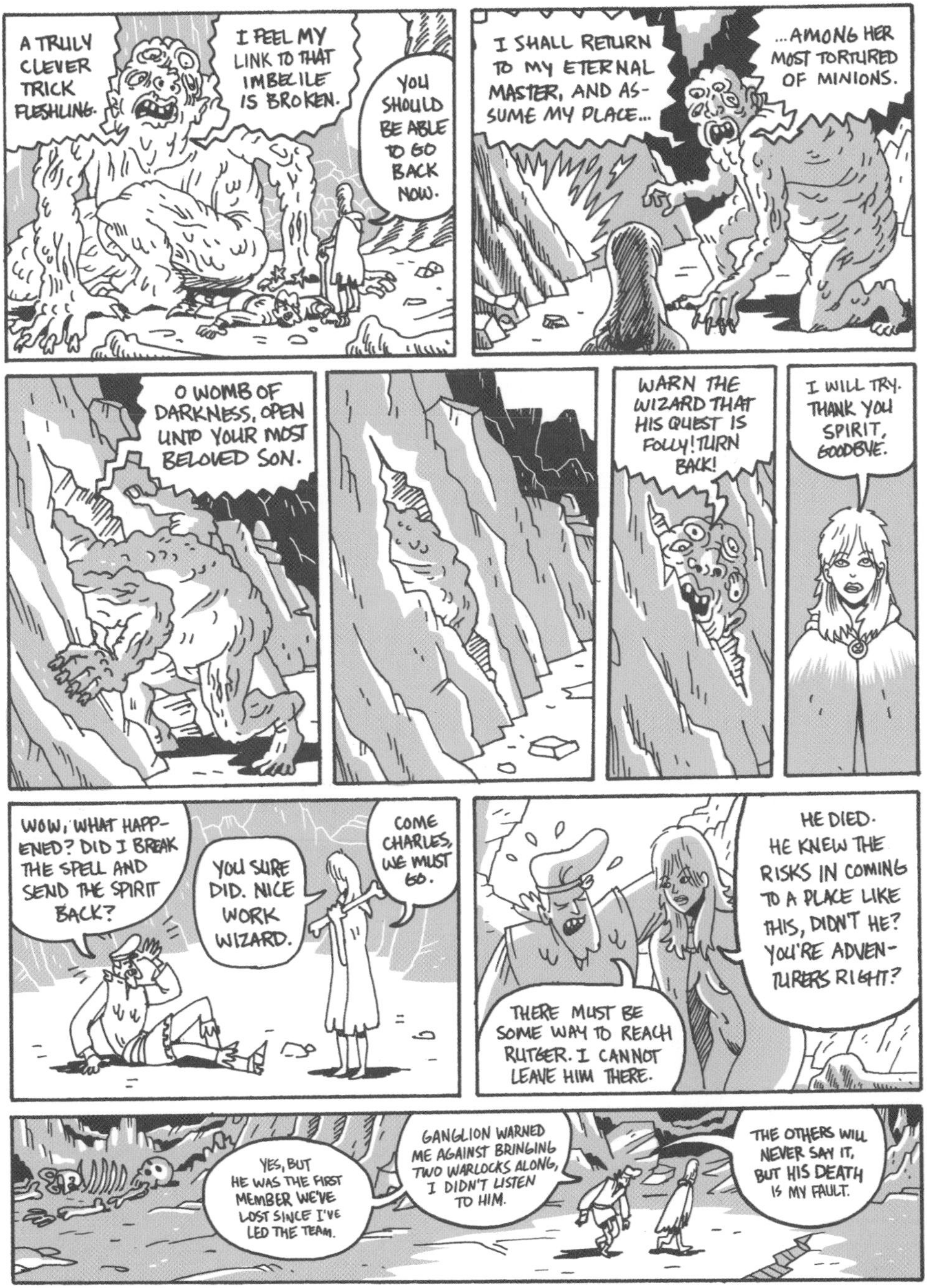
A TRULY CLEVER TRICK FLESHLING.
I FEEL MY LINK TO THAT IMBECILE IS BROKEN.
YOU SHOULD BE ABLE TO GO BACK NOW.
I SHALL RETURN TO MY ETERNAL MASTER, AND ASSUME MY PLACE...
...AMONG HER MOST TORTURED OF MINIONS.
O WOMB OF DARKNESS, OPEN UNTO YOUR MOST BELOVED SON.
WARN THE WIZARD THAT HIS QUEST IS FOLLY! TURN BACK!
I WILL TRY. THANK YOU SPIRIT, GOODBYE.
WOW, WHAT HAPPENED? DID I BREAK THE SPELL AND SEND THE SPIRIT BACK?
YOU SURE DID. NICE WORK WIZARD.
COME CHARLES, WE MUST GO.
HE DIED. HE KNEW THE RISKS IN COMING TO A PLACE LIKE THIS, DIDN'T HE? YOU'RE ADVENTURERS RIGHT?
THERE MUST BE SOME WAY TO REACH RUTGER. I CANNOT LEAVE HIM THERE.
YES, BUT HE WAS THE FIRST MEMBER WE'VE LOST SINCE I'VE LED THE TEAM.
GANGLION WARNED ME AGAINST BRINGING TWO WARLOCKS ALONG, I DIDN'T LISTEN TO HIM.
THE OTHERS WILL NEVER SAY IT, BUT HIS DEATH IS MY FAULT.

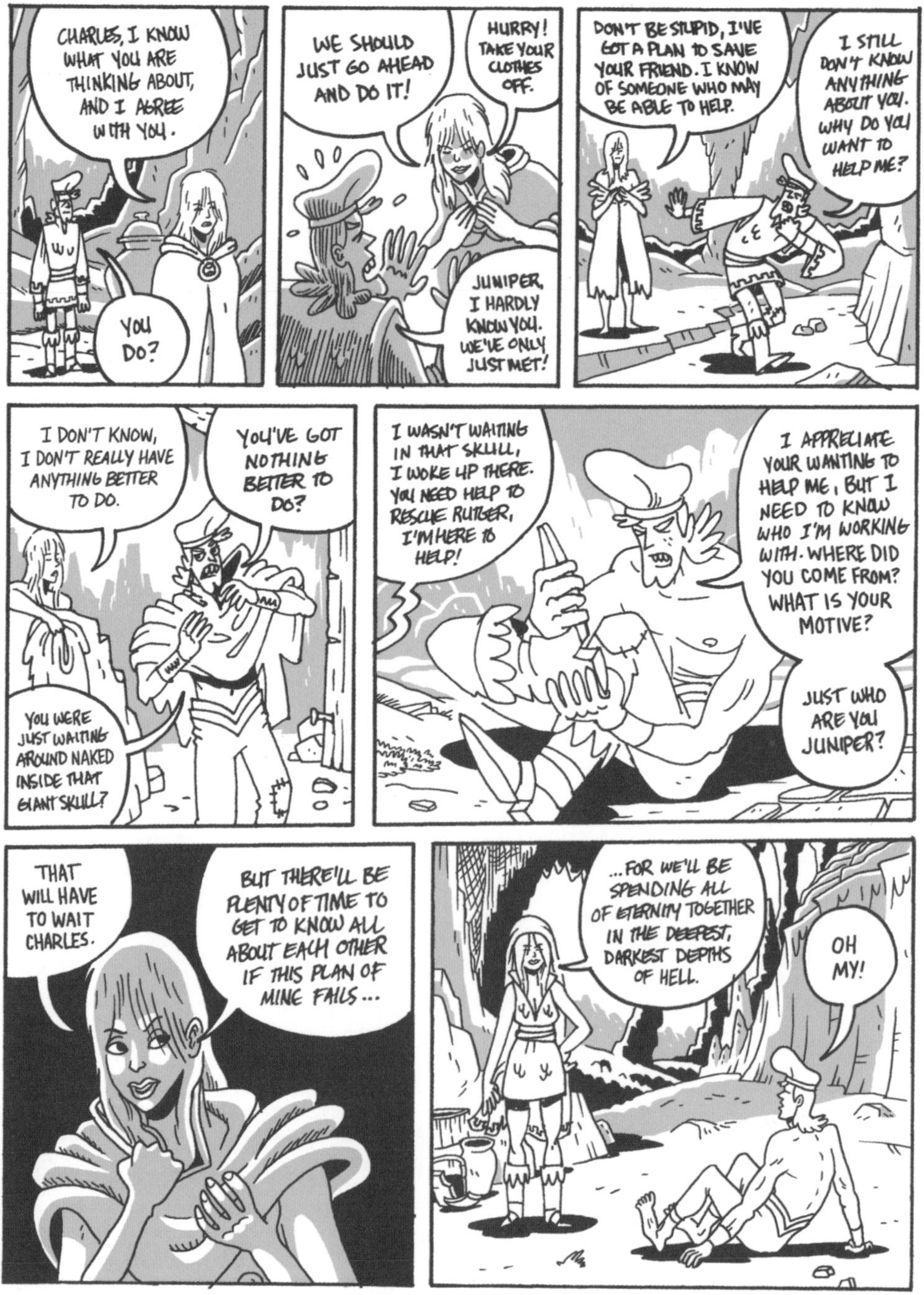
CHARLES, I KNOW WHAT YOU ARE THINKING ABOUT, AND I AGREE WITH YOU.
YOU DO?
WE SHOULD JUST GO AHEAD AND DO IT!
HURRY! TAKE YOUR CLOTHES OFF.
JUNIPER, I HARDLY KNOW YOU. WE'VE ONLY JUST MET!
DON'T BE STUPID, I'VE GOT A PLAN TO SAVE YOUR FRIEND. I KNOW OF SOMEONE WHO MAY BE ABLE TO HELP.
I STILL DON'T KNOW ANYTHING ABOUT YOU. WHY DO YOU WANT TO HELP ME?
I DON'T KNOW, I DON'T REALLY HAVE ANYTHING BETTER TO DO.
YOU'VE GOT NOTHING BETTER TO DO?
YOU WERE JUST WAITING AROUND NAKED INSIDE THAT GIANT SKULL?
I WASN'T WAITING IN THAT SKULL, I WOKE UP THERE. YOU NEED HELP TO RESCUE RUTGER, I'M HERE TO HELP!
I APPRECIATE YOUR WANTING TO HELP ME, BUT I NEED TO KNOW WHO I'M WORKING WITH. WHERE DID YOU COME FROM? WHAT IS YOUR MOTIVE?
JUST WHO ARE YOU JUNIPER?
THAT WILL HAVE TO WAIT CHARLES.
BUT THERE'LL BE PLENTY OF TIME TO GET TO KNOW ALL ABOUT EACH OTHER IF THIS PLAN OF MINE FAILS...
...FOR WE'LL BE SPENDING ALL OF ETERNITY TOGETHER IN THE DEEPEST, DARKEST DEPTHS OF HELL.
OH MY!

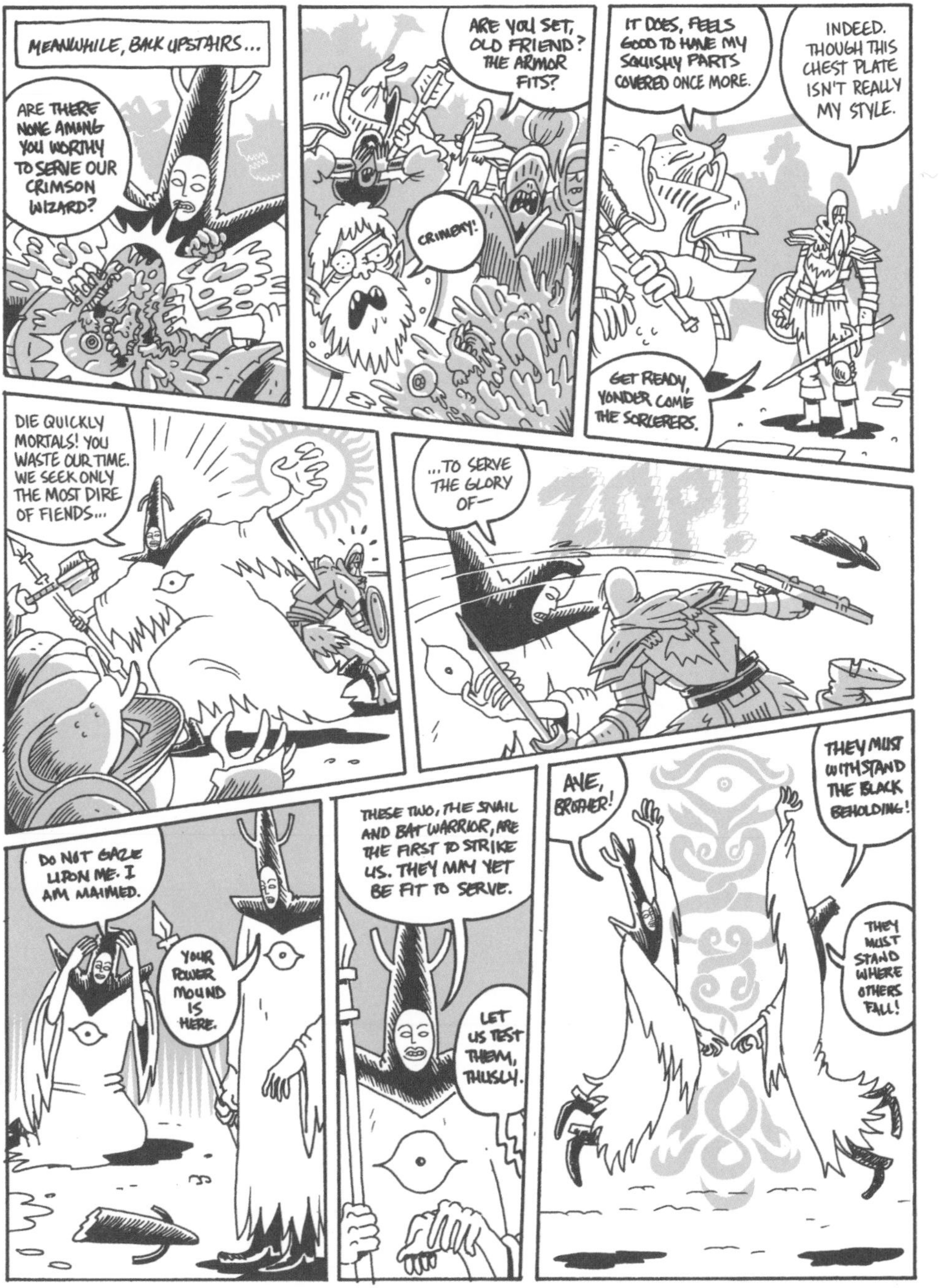
MEANWHILE, BACK UPSTAIRS...
ARE THERE NONE AMONG YOU WORTHY TO SERVE OUR CRIMSON WIZARD?
ARE YOU SET, OLD FRIEND? THE ARMOR FITS?
CRIMENY!
IT DOES, FEELS GOOD TO HAVE MY SQUISHY PARTS COVERED ONCE MORE.
INDEED. THOUGH THIS CHEST PLATE ISN'T REALLY MY STYLE.
GET READY, YONDER COME THE SORCERERS.
DIE QUICKLY MORTALS! YOU WASTE OUR TIME. WE SEEK ONLY THE MOST DIRE OF FIENDS...
...TO SERVE THE GLORY OF—
ZOP!
DO NOT GAZE UPON ME. I AM MAIMED.
YOUR POWER MOUND IS HERE.
THESE TWO, THE SNAIL AND BAT WARRIOR, ARE THE FIRST TO STRIKE US. THEY MAY YET BE FIT TO SERVE.
LET US TEST THEM, THUSLY.
AYE, BROTHER!
THEY MUST WITHSTAND THE BLACK BEHOLDING!
THEY MUST STAND WHERE OTHERS FALL!

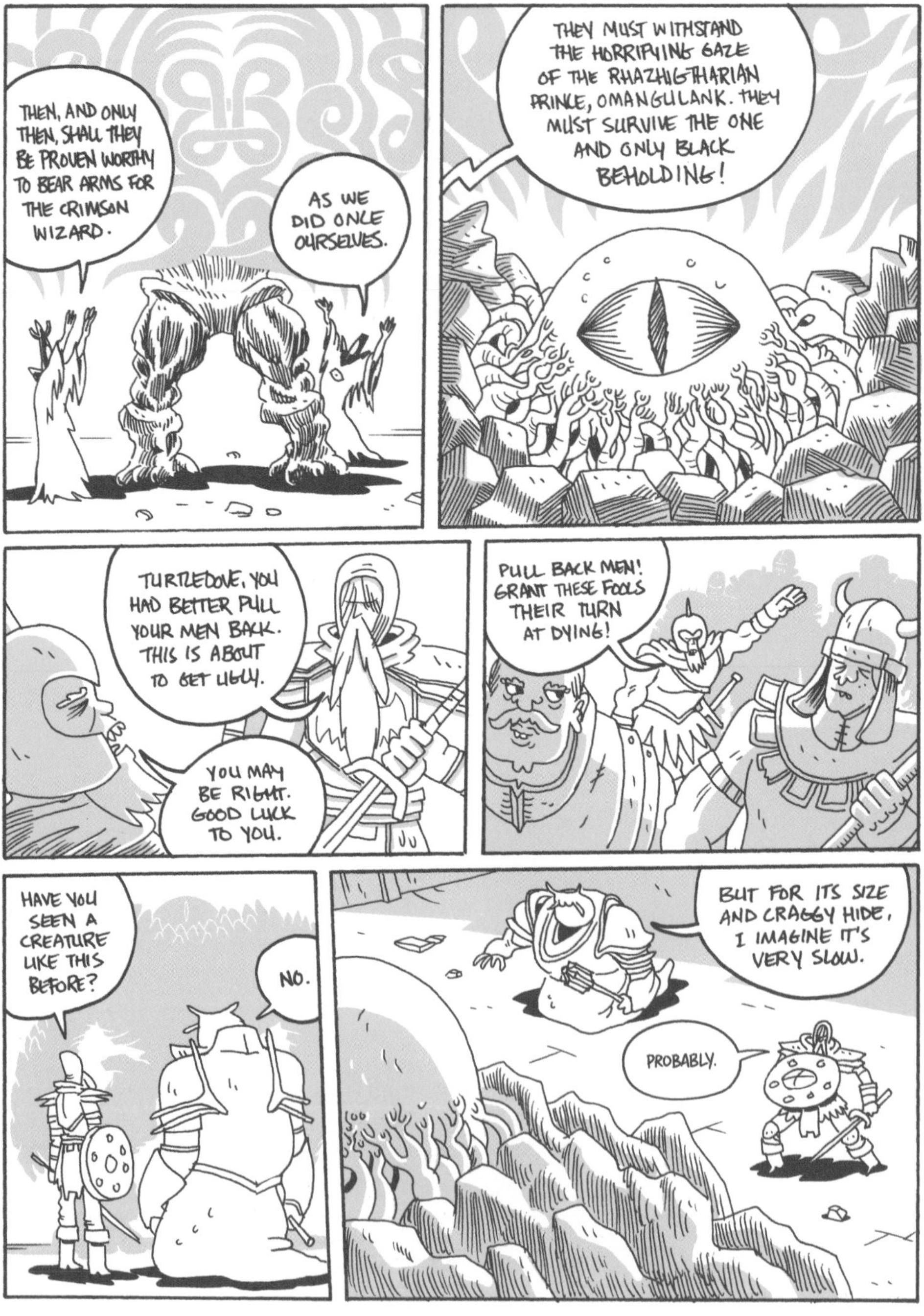
THEN, AND ONLY THEN, SHALL THEY BE PROVEN WORTHY TO BEAR ARMS FOR THE CRIMSON WIZARD.
AS WE DID ONCE OURSELVES.
THEY MUST WITHSTAND THE HORRIFYING GAZE OF THE RHAZHIGTHARIAN PRINCE, OMANGULANK. THEY MUST SURVIVE THE ONE AND ONLY BLACK BEHOLDING!
TURTLEDOVE, YOU HAD BETTER PULL YOUR MEN BACK. THIS IS ABOUT TO GET UGLY.
YOU MAY BE RIGHT. GOOD LUCK TO YOU.
PULL BACK MEN! GRANT THESE FOOLS THEIR TURN AT DYING!
HAVE YOU SEEN A CREATURE LIKE THIS BEFORE?
NO.
BUT FOR ITS SIZE AND CRAGGY HIDE, I IMAGINE IT'S VERY SLOW.
PROBABLY.

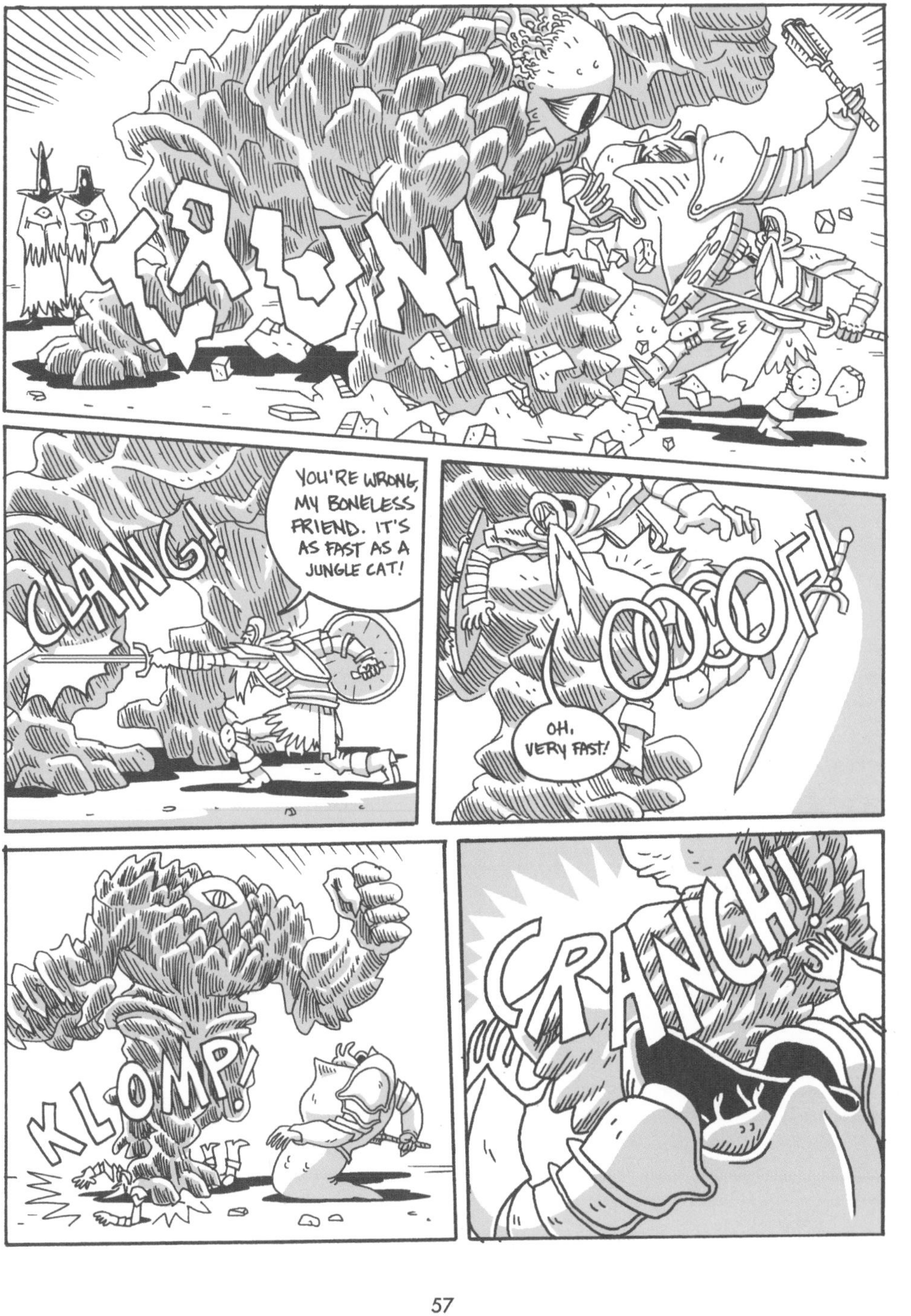
CRUNK!
CLANG!
YOU'RE WRONG, MY BONELESS FRIEND. IT'S AS FAST AS A JUNGLE CAT!
OOOOF!
OH, VERY FAST!
KLOMP!
CRANCH!

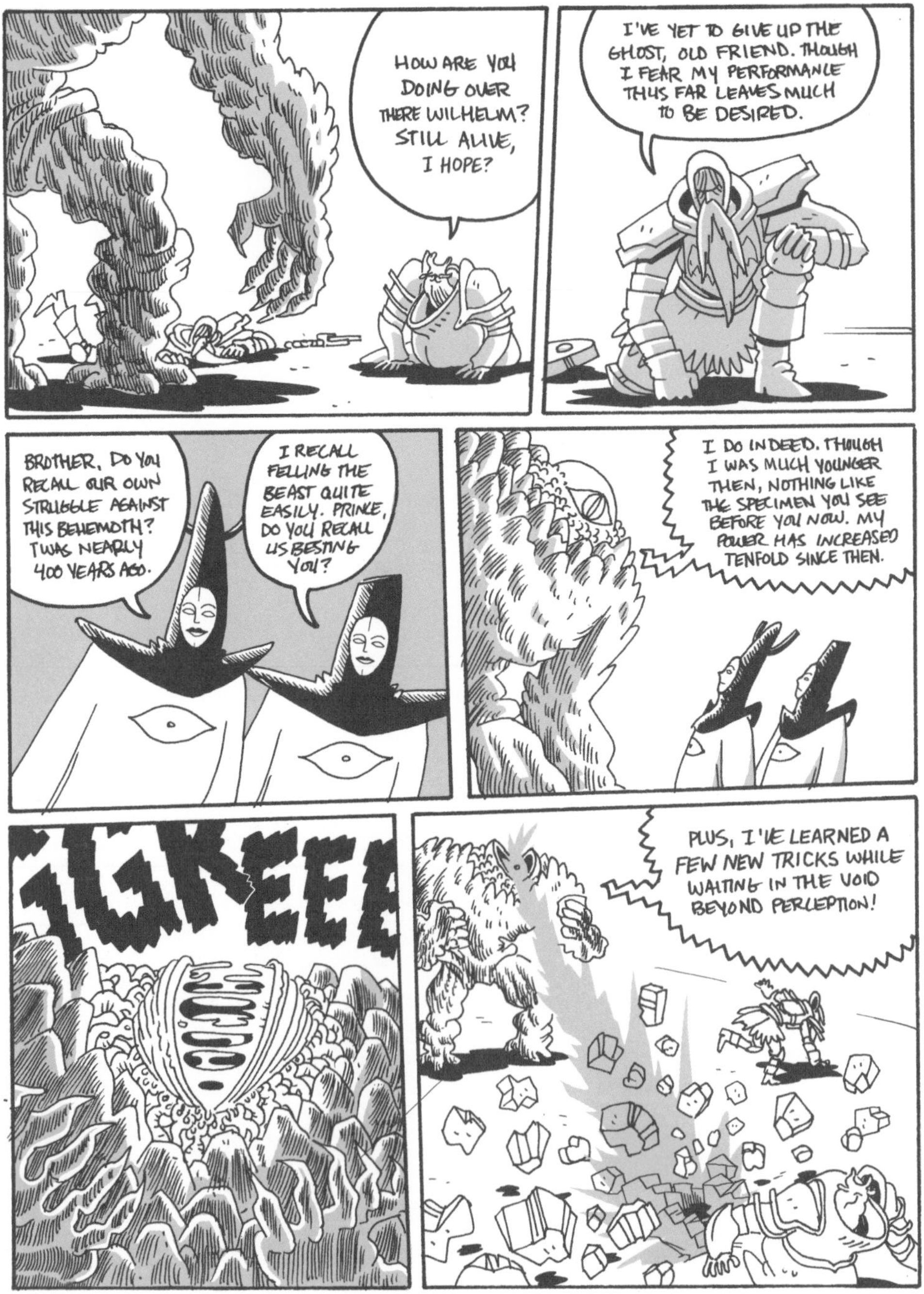
HOW ARE YOU DOING OVER THERE WILHELM? STILL ALIVE, I HOPE?
I'VE YET TO GIVE UP THE GHOST, OLD FRIEND. THOUGH I FEAR MY PERFORMANCE THUS FAR LEAVES MUCH TO BE DESIRED.
BROTHER, DO YOU RECALL OUR OWN STRUGGLE AGAINST THIS BEHEMOTH? TWAS NEARLY 400 YEARS AGO.
I RECALL FELLING THE BEAST QUITE EASILY. PRINCE, DO YOU RECALL US BESTING YOU?
I DO INDEED. THOUGH I WAS MUCH YOUNGER THEN, NOTHING LIKE THE SPECIMEN YOU SEE BEFORE YOU NOW. MY POWER HAS INCREASED TENFOLD SINCE THEN.
IGREEE
PLUS, I'VE LEARNED A FEW NEW TRICKS WHILE WAITING IN THE VOID BEYOND PERCEPTION!

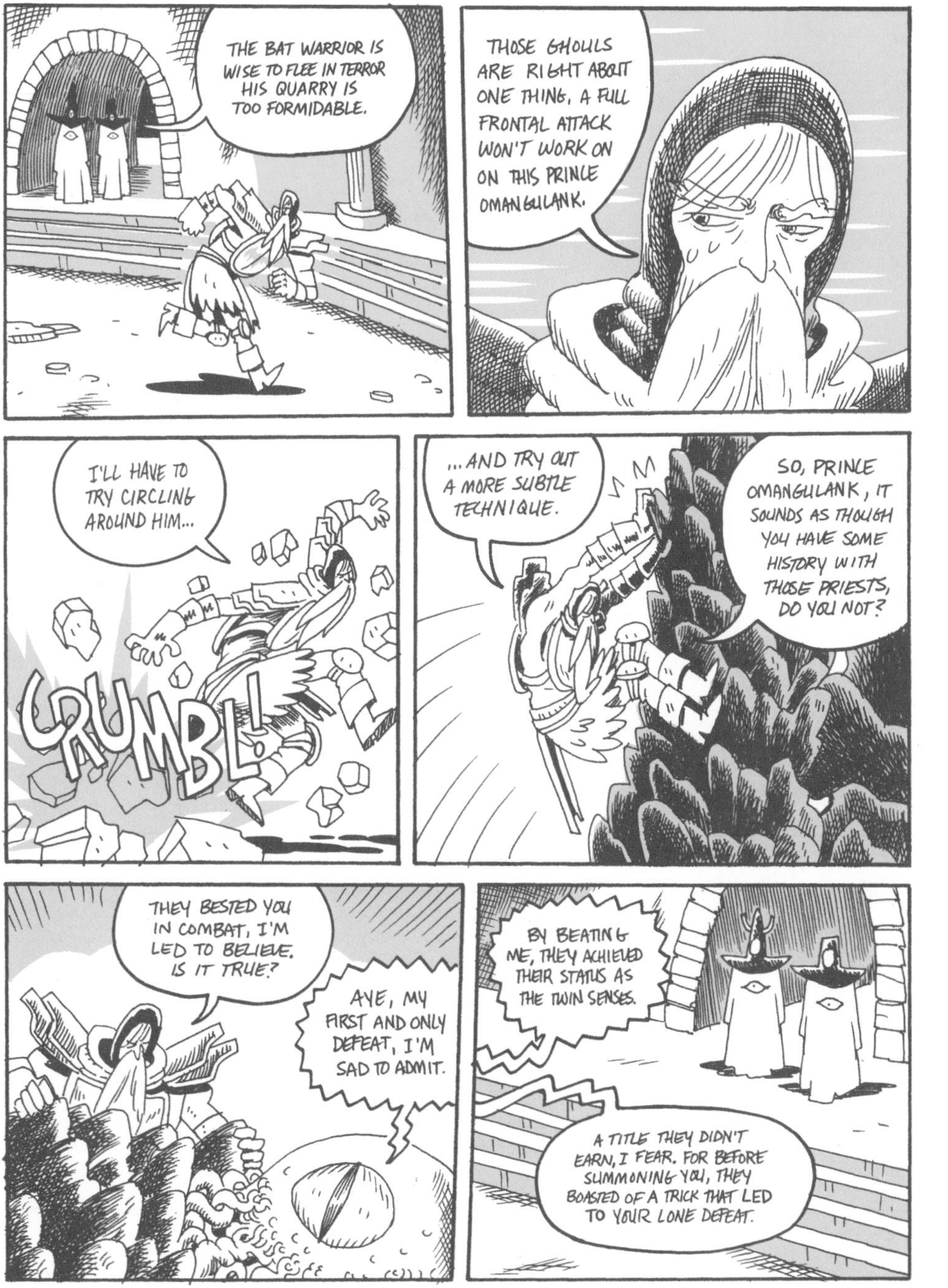
THE BAT WARRIOR IS WISE TO FLEE IN TERROR HIS QUARRY IS TOO FORMIDABLE.
THOSE GHOULS ARE RIGHT ABOUT ONE THING, A FULL FRONTAL ATTACK WON'T WORK ON ON THIS PRINCE OMANGULANK.
I'LL HAVE TO TRY CIRCLING AROUND HIM...
CRUMBL!
...AND TRY OUT A MORE SUBTLE TECHNIQUE.
SO, PRINCE OMANGULANK, IT SOUNDS AS THOUGH YOU HAVE SOME HISTORY WITH THOSE PRIESTS, DO YOU NOT?
THEY BESTED YOU IN COMBAT, I'M LED TO BELIEVE. IS IT TRUE?
AYE, MY FIRST AND ONLY DEFEAT, I'M SAD TO ADMIT.
BY BEATING ME, THEY ACHIEVED THEIR STATUS AS THE TWIN SENSES.
A TITLE THEY DIDN'T EARN, I FEAR. FOR BEFORE SUMMONING YOU, THEY BOASTED OF A TRICK THAT LED TO YOUR LONE DEFEAT.

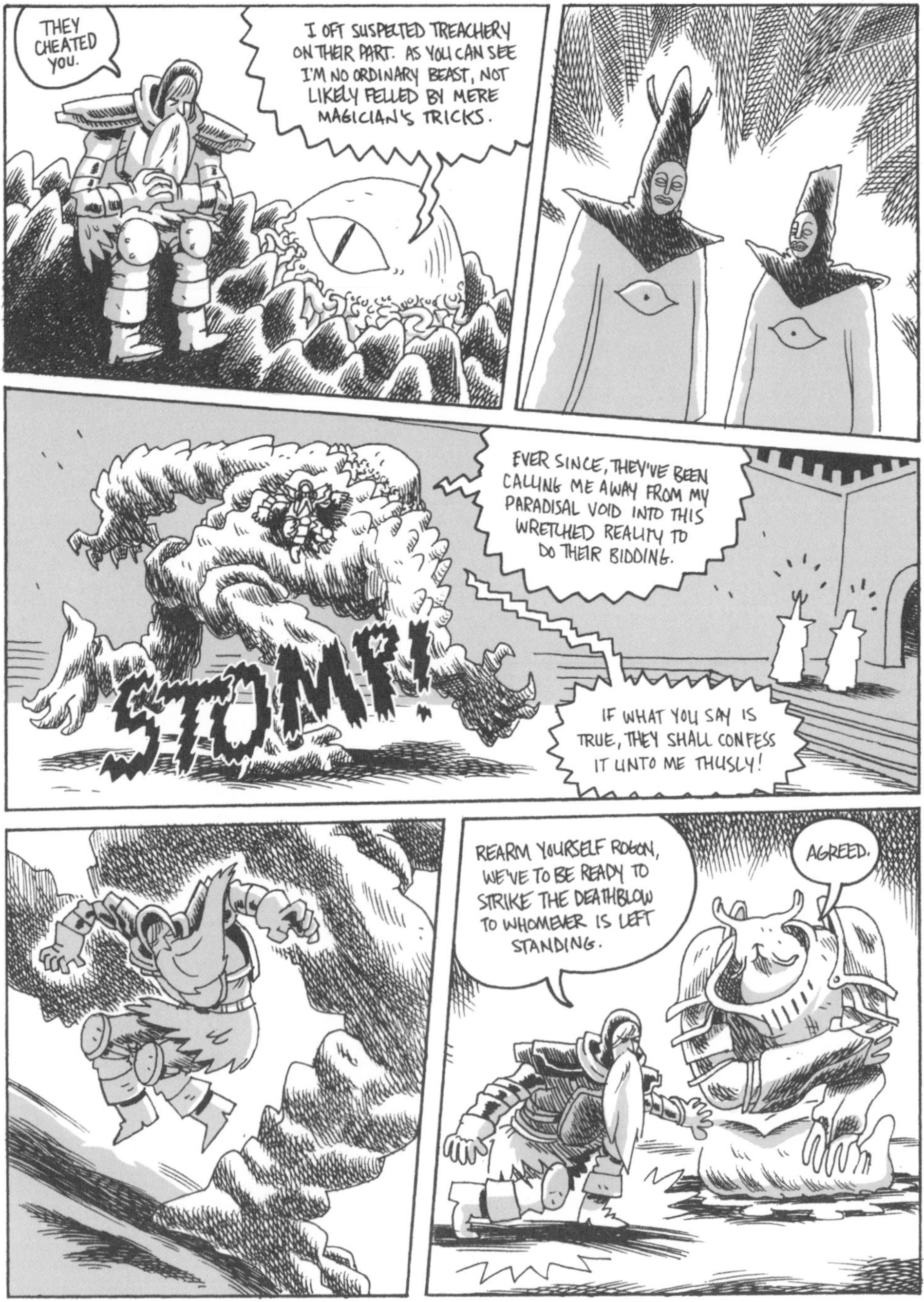
THEY CHEATED YOU.
I OFT SUSPECTED TREACHERY ON THEIR PART. AS YOU CAN SEE I'M NO ORDINARY BEAST, NOT LIKELY FELLED BY MERE MAGICIAN'S TRICKS.
EVER SINCE, THEY'VE BEEN CALLING ME AWAY FROM MY PARADISAL VOID INTO THIS WRETCHED REALITY TO DO THEIR BIDDING.
STOMP!
IF WHAT YOU SAY IS TRUE, THEY SHALL CONFESS IT UNTO ME THUSLY!
REARM YOURSELF ROGON, WE'VE TO BE READY TO STRIKE THE DEATHBLOW TO WHOMEVER IS LEFT STANDING.
AGREED.

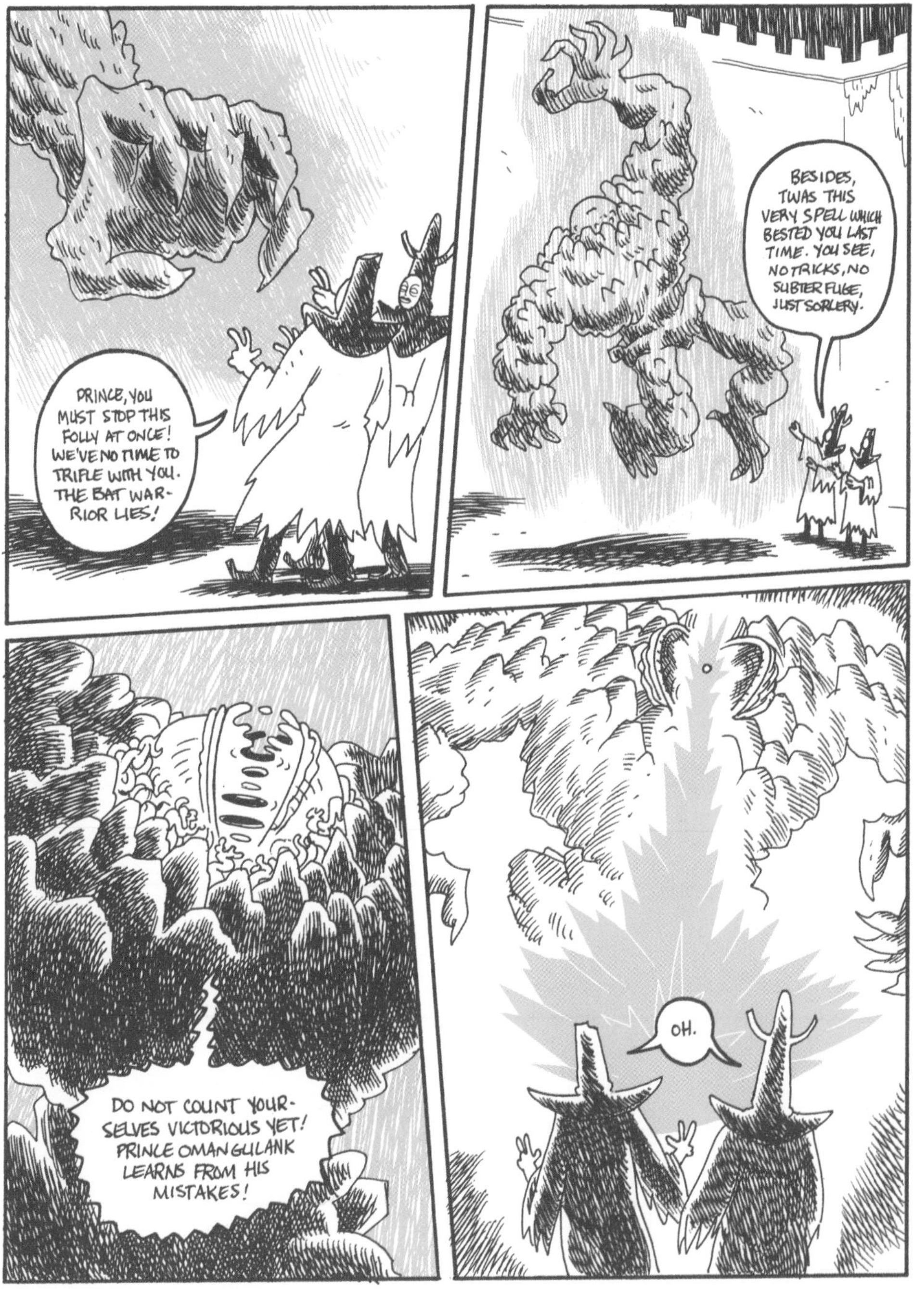
PRINCE, YOU MUST STOP THIS FOLLY AT ONCE! WE'VE NO TIME TO TRIFLE WITH YOU. THE BAT WARRIOR LIES!
BESIDES, TWAS THIS VERY SPELL WHICH BESTED YOU LAST TIME. YOU SEE, NO TRICKS, NO SUBTERFUGE, JUST SORCERY.
DO NOT COUNT YOURSELVES VICTORIOUS YET! PRINCE OMANGULANK LEARNS FROM HIS MISTAKES!
OH.

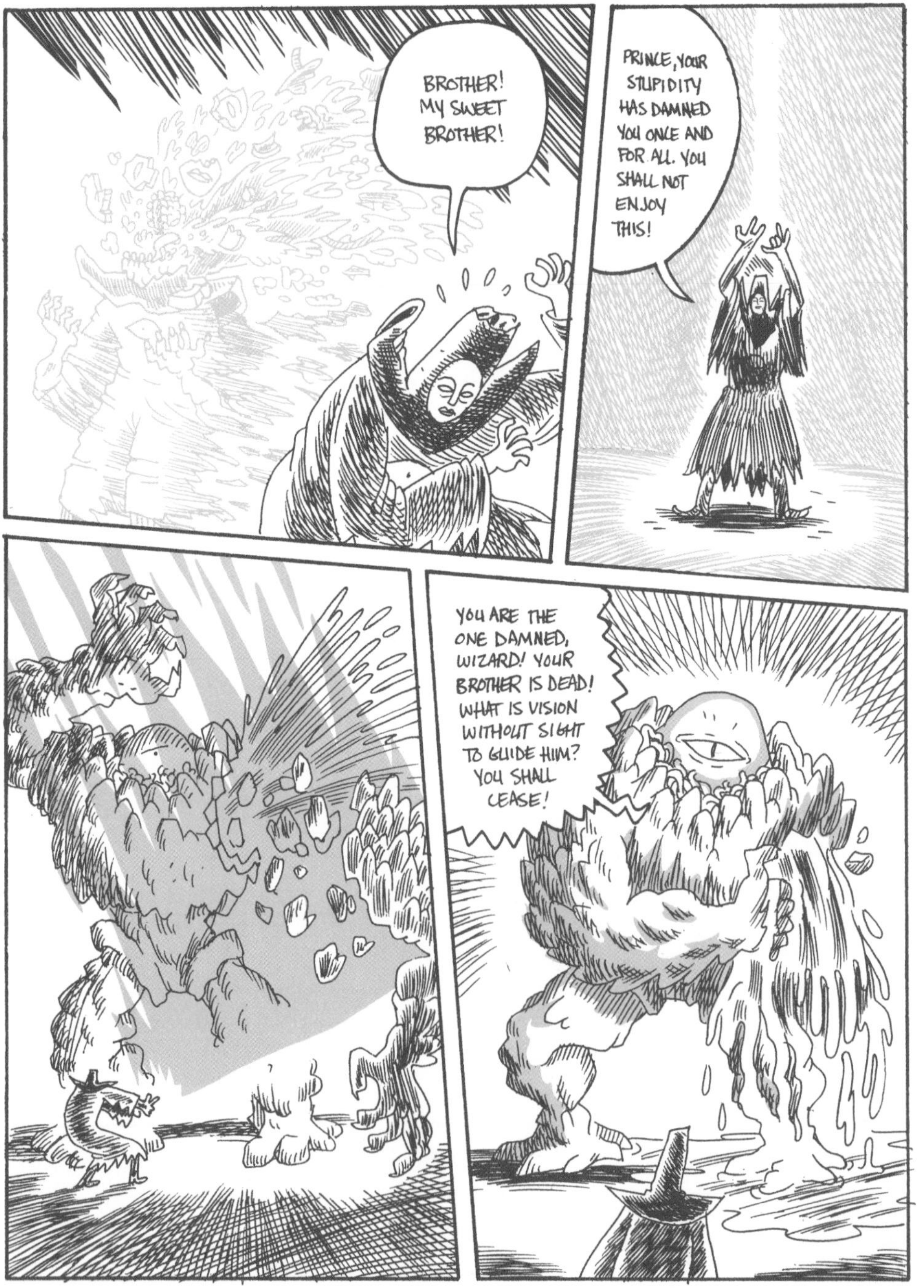
BROTHER! MY SWEET BROTHER!
PRINCE, YOUR STUPIDITY HAS DAMNED YOU ONCE AND FOR ALL. YOU SHALL NOT ENJOY THIS!
YOU ARE THE ONE DAMNED, WIZARD! YOUR BROTHER IS DEAD! WHAT IS VISION WITHOUT SIGHT TO GUIDE HIM? YOU SHALL CEASE!

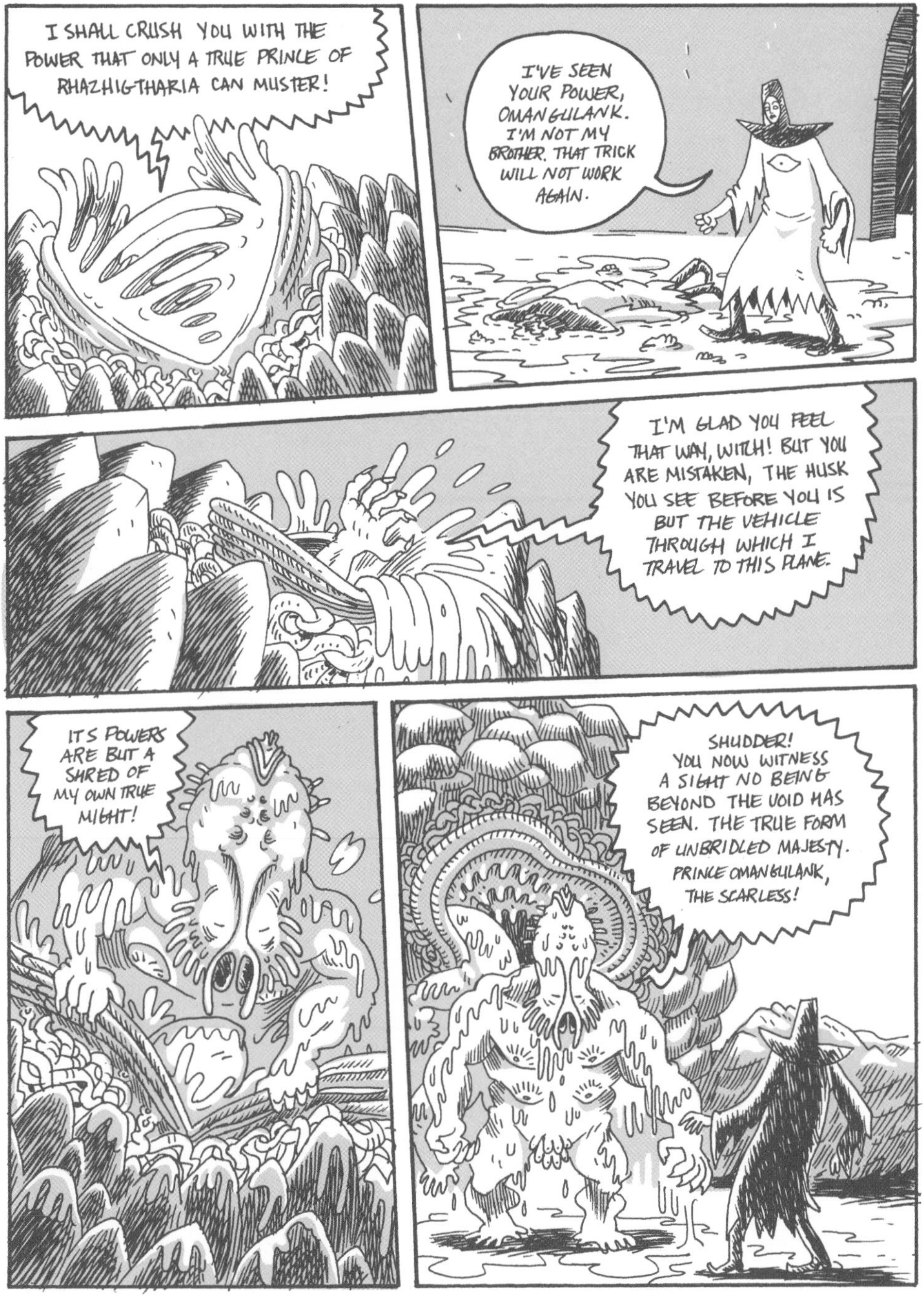
I SHALL CRUSH YOU WITH THE POWER THAT ONLY A TRUE PRINCE OF RHAZHIGTHARIA CAN MUSTER!
I'VE SEEN YOUR POWER, OMANGULANK. I'M NOT MY BROTHER. THAT TRICK WILL NOT WORK AGAIN.
I'M GLAD YOU FEEL THAT WAY, WITCH! BUT YOU ARE MISTAKEN, THE HUSK YOU SEE BEFORE YOU IS BUT THE VEHICLE THROUGH WHICH I TRAVEL TO THIS PLANE.
ITS POWERS ARE BUT A SHRED OF MY OWN TRUE MIGHT!
SHUDDER! YOU NOW WITNESS A SIGHT NO BEING BEYOND THE VOID HAS SEEN. THE TRUE FORM OF UNBRIDLED MAJESTY. PRINCE OMANGULANK, THE SCARLESS!

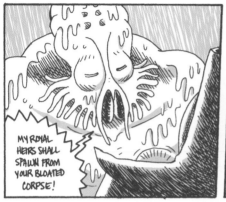

MY ROYAL HEIRS SHALL SPAWN FROM YOUR BLOATED CORPSE!

BY THE GODS!

I TIRE GREATLY OF THIS DEBACLE.

THE IRON TALON HAS NO TIME TO AWAIT THE SETTLEMENT OF YOUR DISPUTE.

I'VE SAVED YOU, NOW HIRE US!

I THANK YOU KINDLY, CAPTAIN HAWK VON TURTLEDOVE. YOUR ASSISTANCE IS APPRECIATED.

THOUGH I COULD HAVE SURELY HANDLED HIM ON MY OWN...

...GIVEN JUST A MOMENT MORE. UNFORTUNATELY, I MUST STAND BY MY PREVIOUS JUDGEMENT...

WHACK!

GRKK!

YEAH, WE GET IT. WE'RE ALL STILL UNWORTHY TO SERVE THE MAGNIFICENCE OF THE CRIMSON WIZARD.

TOO BAD YOU CAN'T TELL HIM THAT.

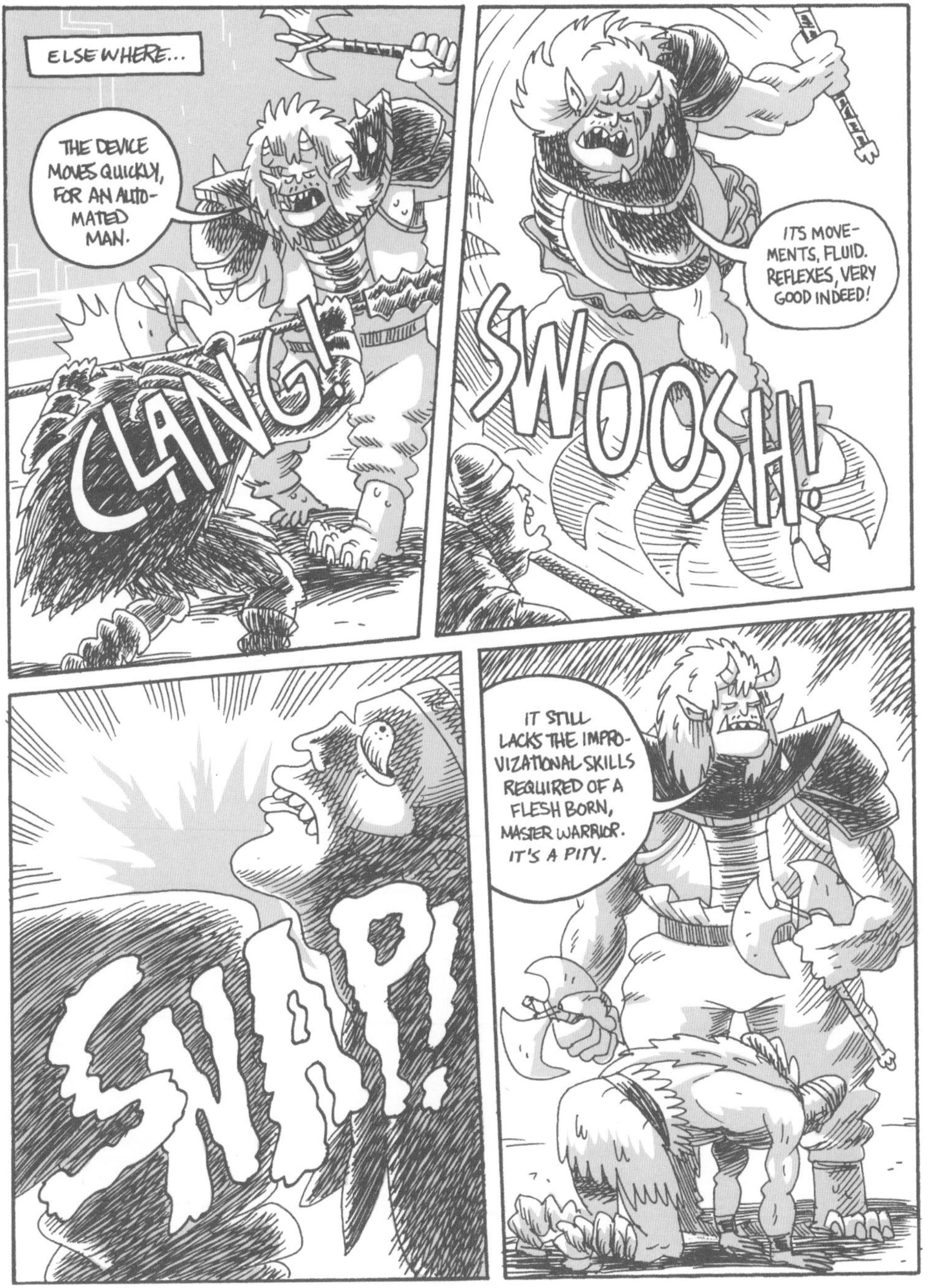
ELSEWHERE...
THE DEVICE MOVES QUICKLY, FOR AN AUTO-MATED MAN.
CLANG!
ITS MOVE-MENTS, FLUID. REFLEXES, VERY GOOD INDEED!
SWOOSH!
SNAP!
IT STILL LACKS THE IMPRO-VIZATIONAL SKILLS REQUIRED OF A FLESH BORN, MASTER WARRIOR. IT'S A PITY.

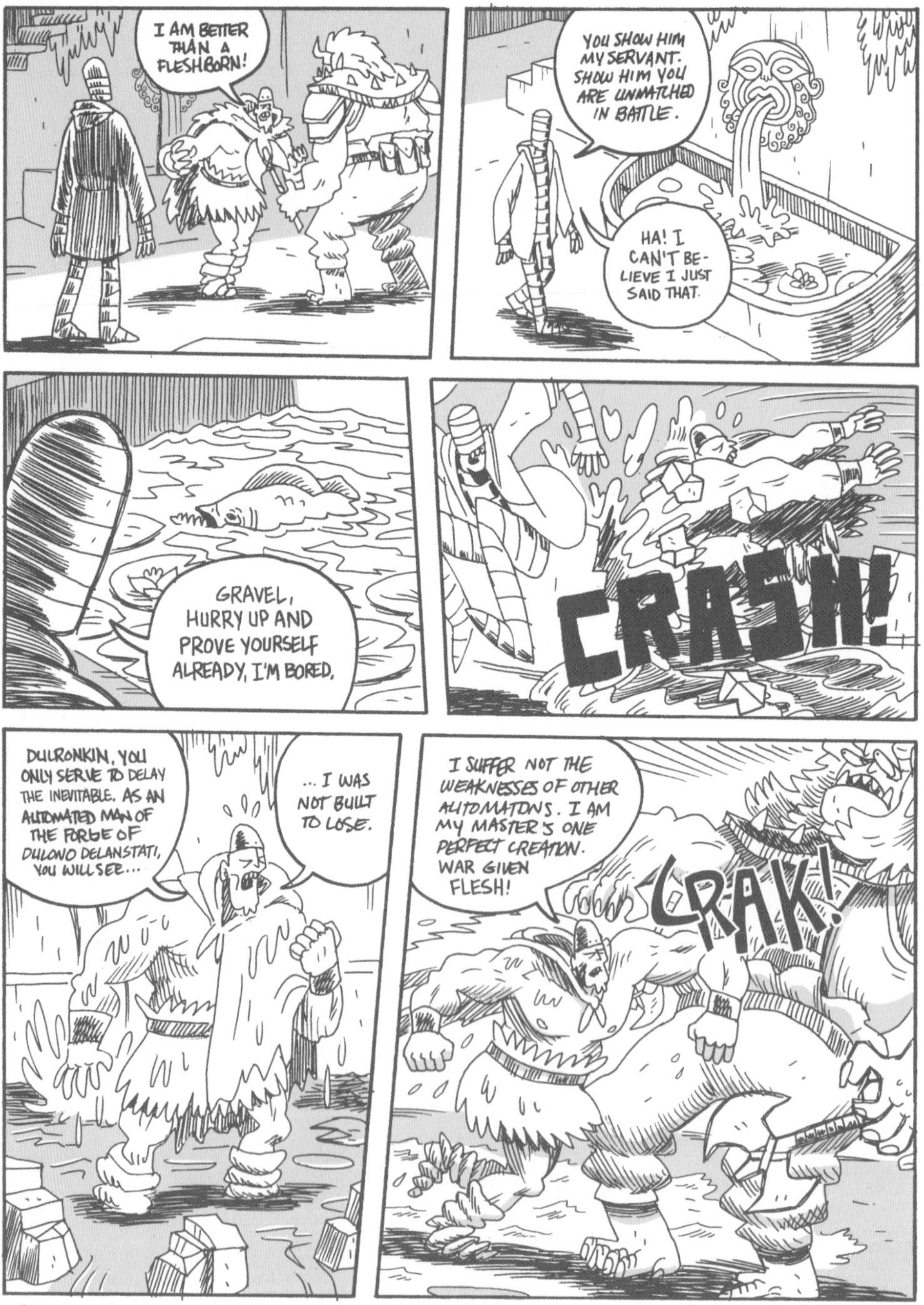
I AM BETTER THAN A FLESHBORN!
YOU SHOW HIM MY SERVANT. SHOW HIM YOU ARE UNMATCHED IN BATTLE.
HA! I CAN'T BE-LIEVE I JUST SAID THAT.
GRAVEL, HURRY UP AND PROVE YOURSELF ALREADY, I'M BORED.
CRASH!
DULRONKIN, YOU ONLY SERVE TO DELAY THE INEVITABLE. AS AN AUTOMATED MAN OF THE FORGE OF DULONO DELANSTATI, YOU WILL SEE...
...I WAS NOT BUILT TO LOSE.
I SUFFER NOT THE WEAKNESSES OF OTHER AUTOMATONS. I AM MY MASTER'S ONE PERFECT CREATION. WAR GIVEN FLESH!
CRAK!

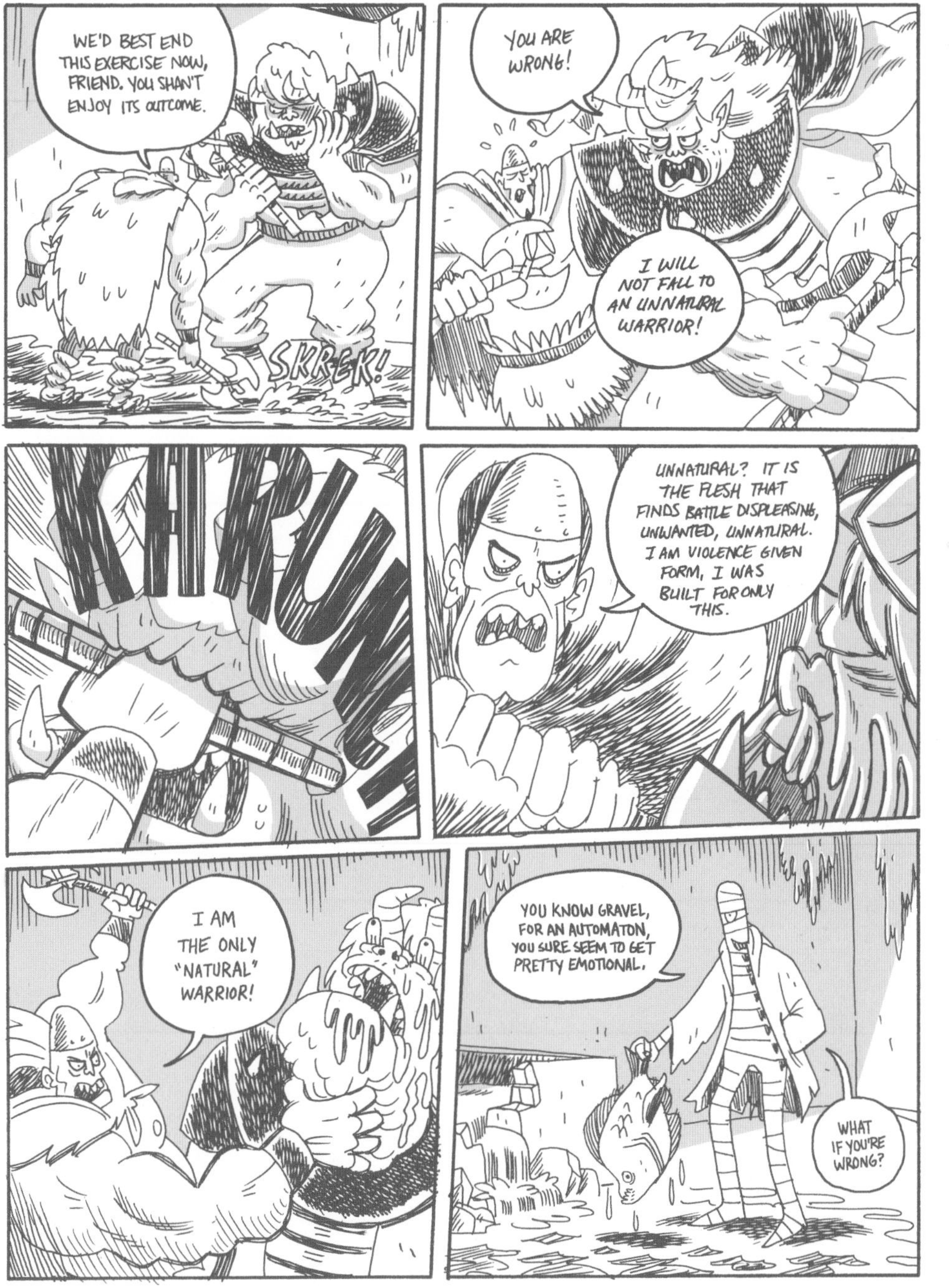
WE'D BEST END THIS EXERCISE NOW, FRIEND. YOU SHAN'T ENJOY ITS OUTCOME.
SKREEK!
YOU ARE WRONG!
I WILL NOT FALL TO AN UNNATURAL WARRIOR!
KARUNCH!
UNNATURAL? IT IS THE FLESH THAT FINDS BATTLE DISPLEASING, UNWANTED, UNNATURAL. I AM VIOLENCE GIVEN FORM, I WAS BUILT FOR ONLY THIS.
I AM THE ONLY "NATURAL" WARRIOR!
YOU KNOW GRAVEL, FOR AN AUTOMATON, YOU SURE SEEM TO GET PRETTY EMOTIONAL.
WHAT IF YOU'RE WRONG?

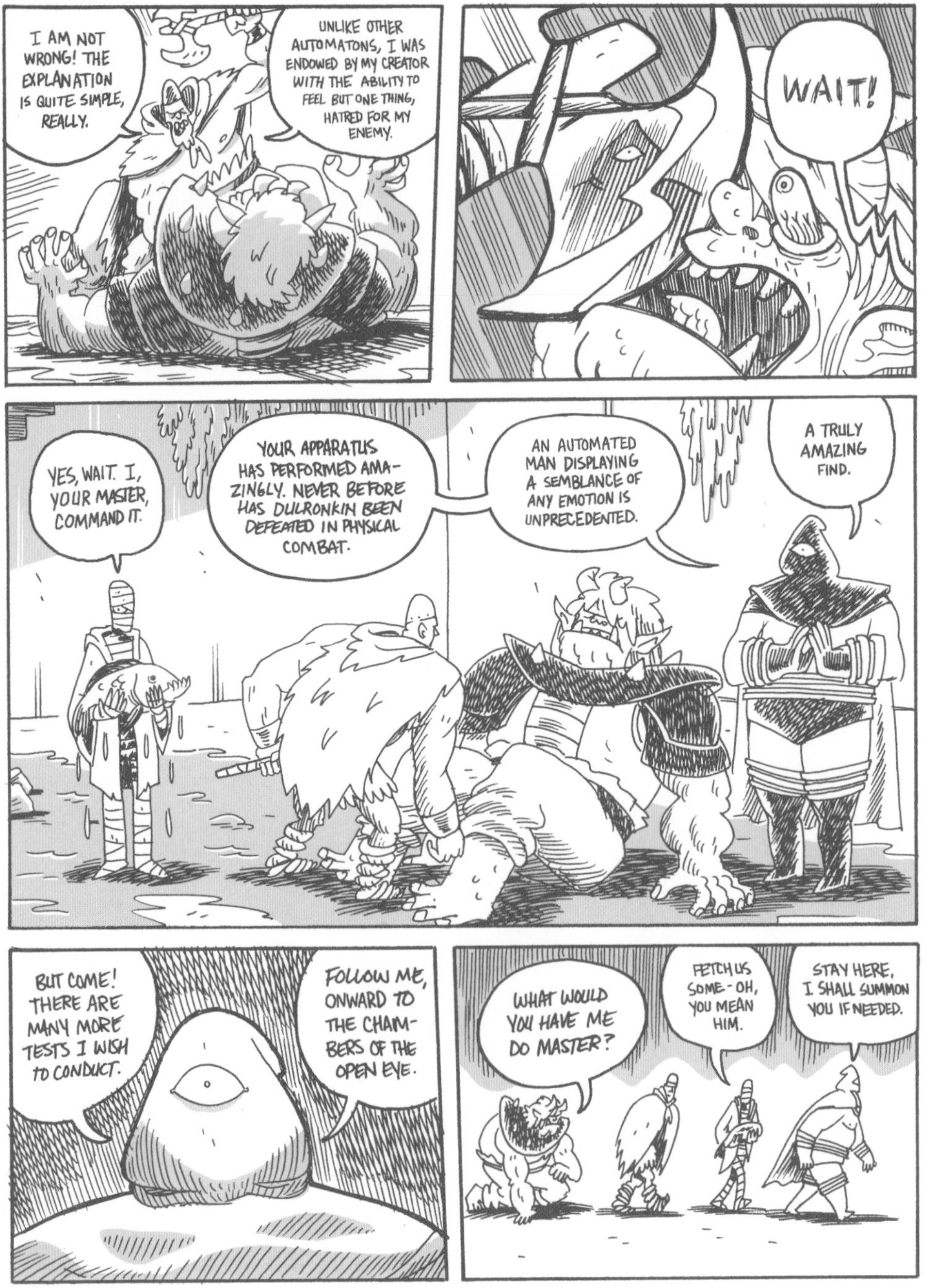

I AM NOT WRONG! THE EXPLANATION IS QUITE SIMPLE, REALLY.
UNLIKE OTHER AUTOMATONS, I WAS ENDOWED BY MY CREATOR WITH THE ABILITY TO FEEL BUT ONE THING, HATRED FOR MY ENEMY.
WAIT!
YES, WAIT. I, YOUR MASTER, COMMAND IT.
YOUR APPARATUS HAS PERFORMED AMA-ZINGLY. NEVER BEFORE HAS DULRONKIN BEEN DEFEATED IN PHYSICAL COMBAT.
AN AUTOMATED MAN DISPLAYING A SEMBLANCE OF ANY EMOTION IS UNPRECEDENTED.
A TRULY AMAZING FIND.
BUT COME! THERE ARE MANY MORE TESTS I WISH TO CONDUCT.
FOLLOW ME, ONWARD TO THE CHAM-BERS OF THE OPEN EYE.
WHAT WOULD YOU HAVE ME DO MASTER?
FETCH US SOME- OH, YOU MEAN HIM.
STAY HERE, I SHALL SUMMON YOU IF NEEDED.

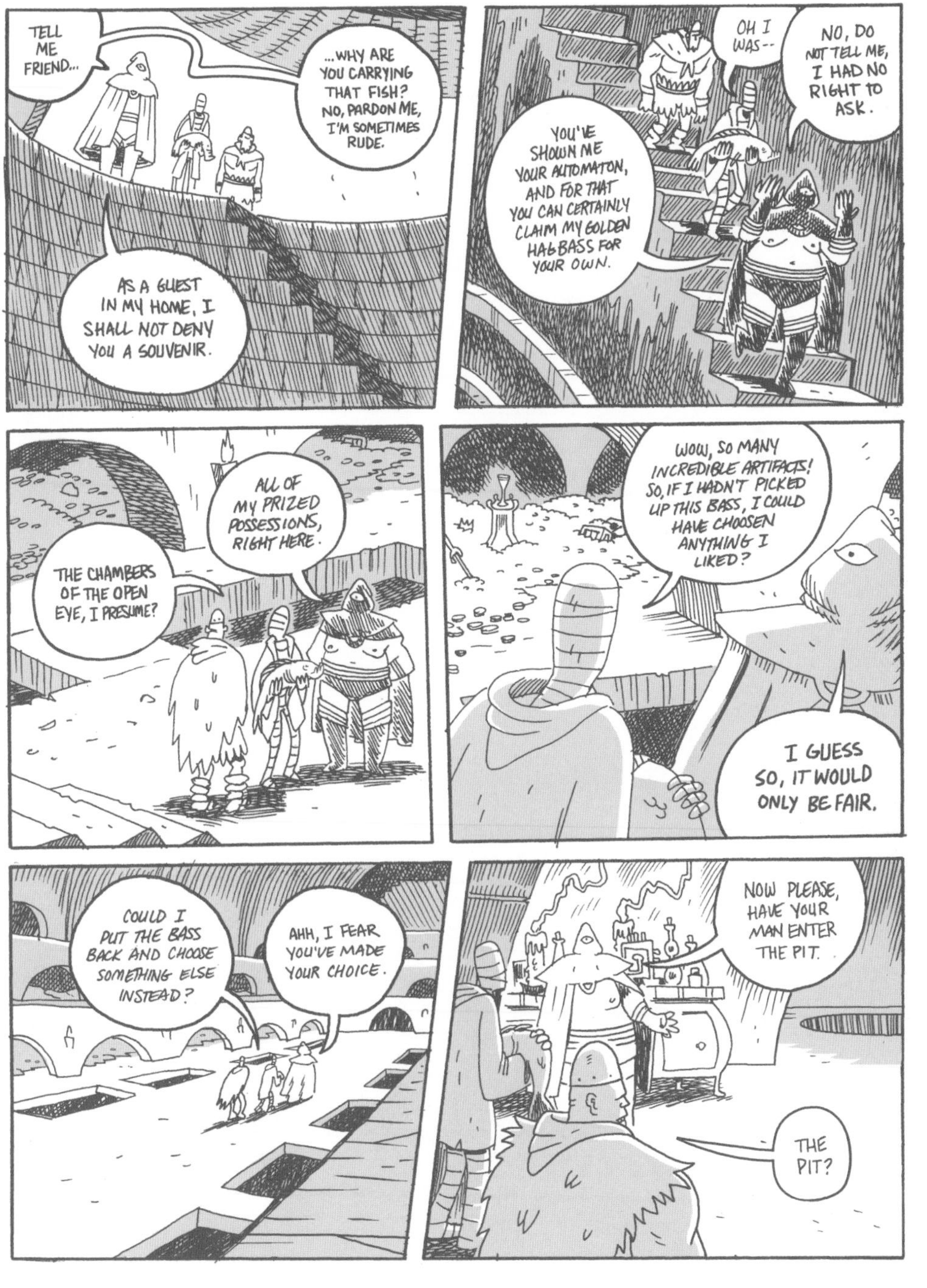
TELL ME FRIEND...
...WHY ARE YOU CARRYING THAT FISH? NO, PARDON ME, I'M SOMETIMES RUDE.
AS A GUEST IN MY HOME, I SHALL NOT DENY YOU A SOUVENIR.
OH I WAS--
NO, DO NOT TELL ME, I HAD NO RIGHT TO ASK.
YOU'VE SHOWN ME YOUR AUTOMATON, AND FOR THAT YOU CAN CERTAINLY CLAIM MY GOLDEN HAGBASS FOR YOUR OWN.
ALL OF MY PRIZED POSSESSIONS, RIGHT HERE.
THE CHAMBERS OF THE OPEN EYE, I PRESUME?
WOW, SO MANY INCREDIBLE ARTIFACTS! SO, IF I HADN'T PICKED UP THIS BASS, I COULD HAVE CHOOSEN ANYTHING I LIKED?
I GUESS SO, IT WOULD ONLY BE FAIR.
COULD I PUT THE BASS BACK AND CHOOSE SOMETHING ELSE INSTEAD?
AHH, I FEAR YOU'VE MADE YOUR CHOICE.
NOW PLEASE, HAVE YOUR MAN ENTER THE PIT.
THE PIT?

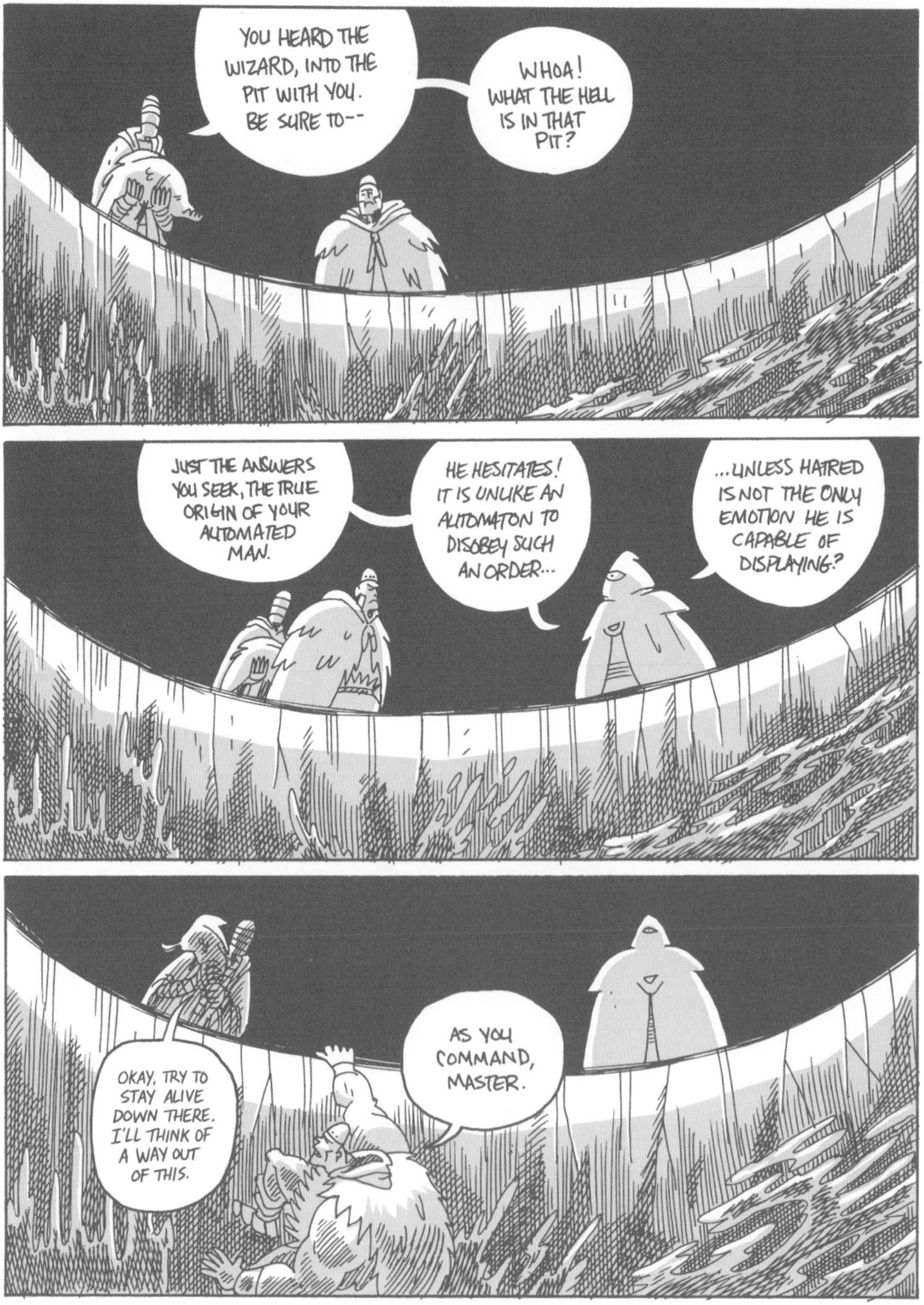
YOU HEARD THE WIZARD, INTO THE PIT WITH YOU. BE SURE TO--
WHOA! WHAT THE HELL IS IN THAT PIT?
JUST THE ANSWERS YOU SEEK, THE TRUE ORIGIN OF YOUR AUTOMATED MAN.
HE HESITATES! IT IS UNLIKE AN AUTOMATON TO DISOBEY SUCH AN ORDER...
...UNLESS HATRED IS NOT THE ONLY EMOTION HE IS CAPABLE OF DISPLAYING?
OKAY, TRY TO STAY ALIVE DOWN THERE. I'LL THINK OF A WAY OUT OF THIS.
AS YOU COMMAND, MASTER.

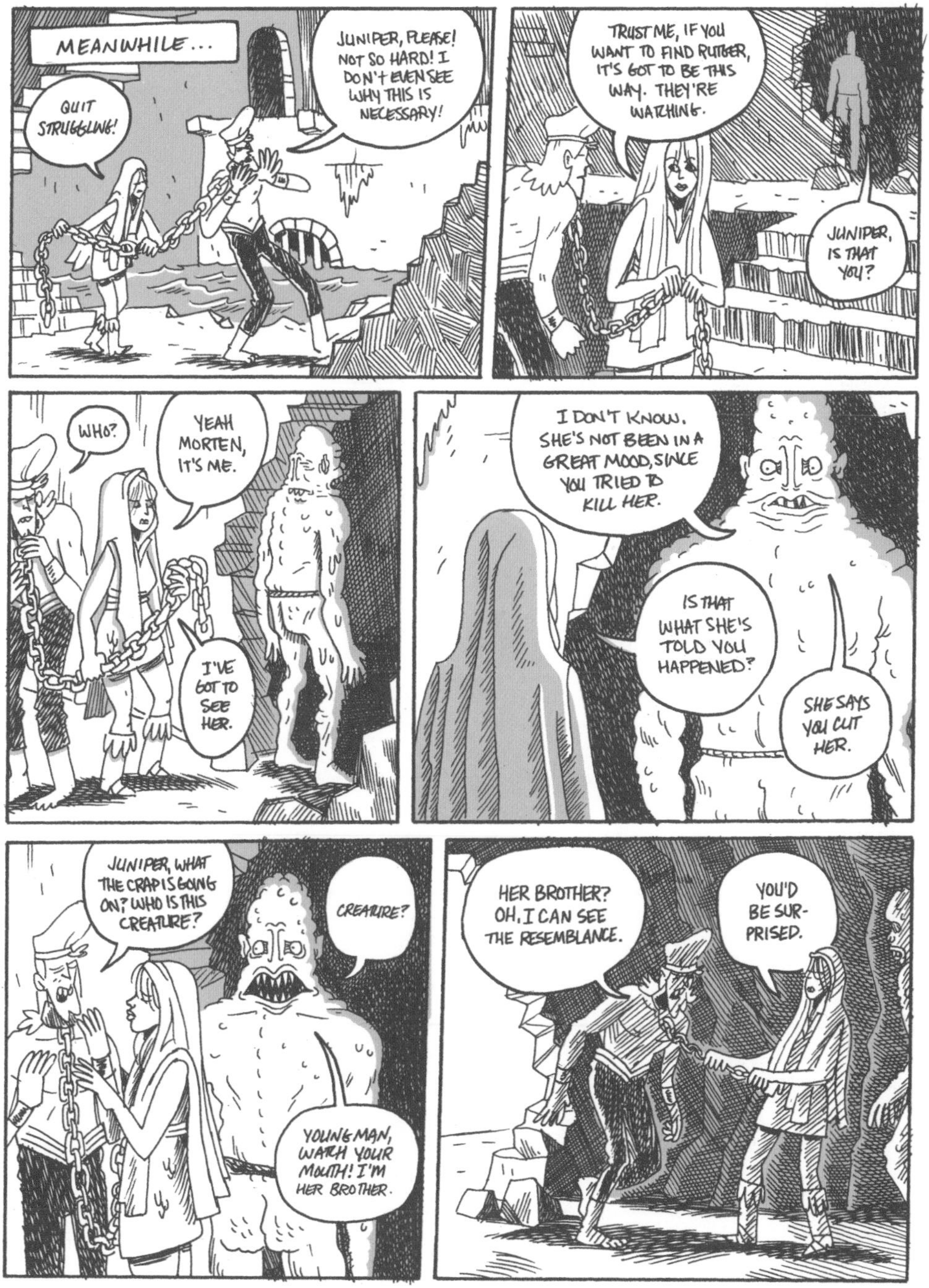
MEANWHILE...
QUIT STRUGGLING!
JUNIPER, PLEASE! NOT SO HARD! I DON'T EVEN SEE WHY THIS IS NECESSARY!
TRUST ME, IF YOU WANT TO FIND RUTGER, IT'S GOT TO BE THIS WAY. THEY'RE WATCHING.
JUNIPER, IS THAT YOU?
WHO?
YEAH MORTEN, IT'S ME.
I'VE GOT TO SEE HER.
I DON'T KNOW. SHE'S NOT BEEN IN A GREAT MOOD, SINCE YOU TRIED TO KILL HER.
IS THAT WHAT SHE'S TOLD YOU HAPPENED?
SHE SAYS YOU CUT HER.
JUNIPER, WHAT THE CRAP IS GOING ON? WHO IS THIS CREATURE?
CREATURE?
YOUNG MAN, WATCH YOUR MOUTH! I'M HER BROTHER.
HER BROTHER? OH, I CAN SEE THE RESEMBLANCE.
YOU'D BE SUR-PRISED.

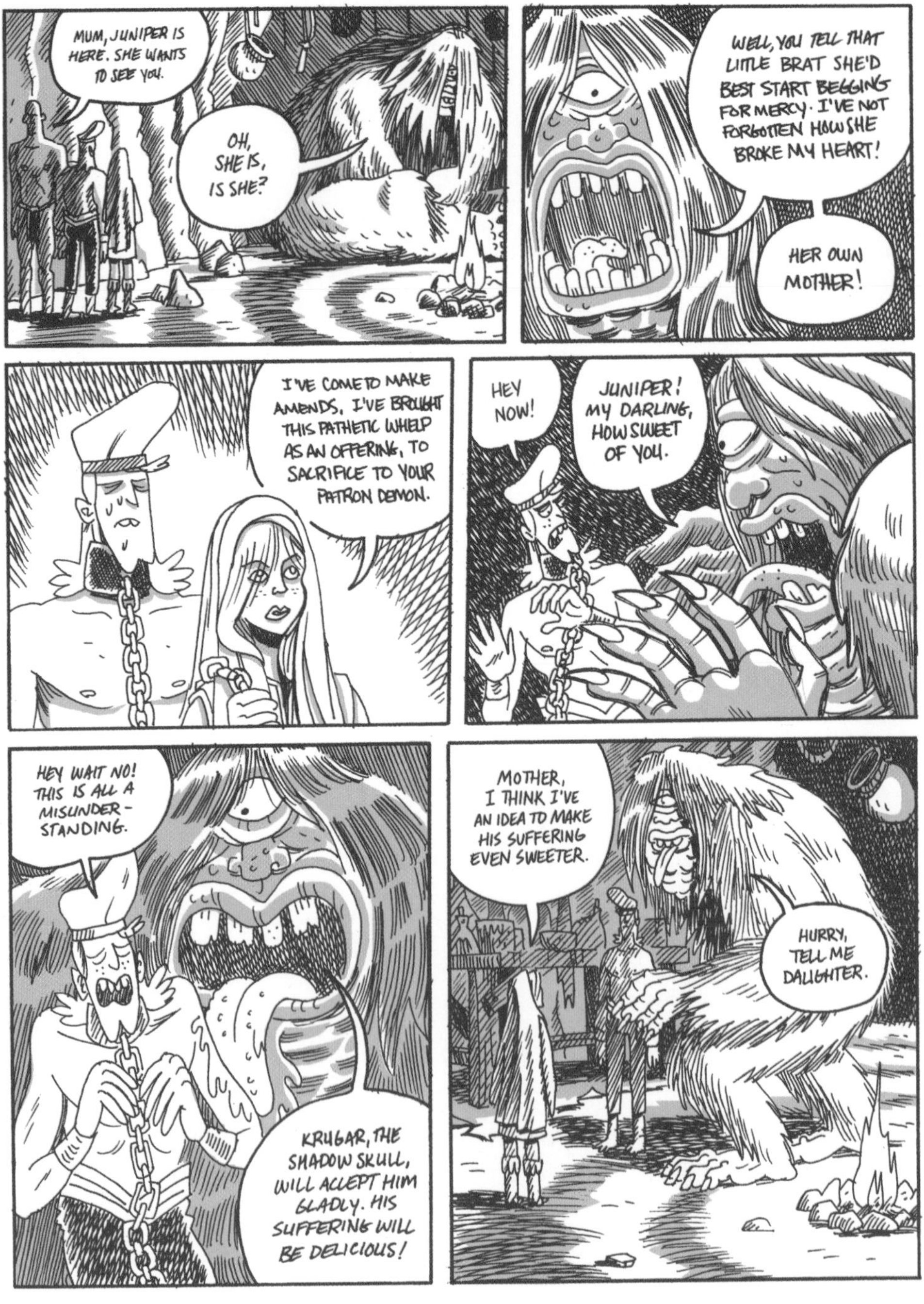
MUM, JUNIPER IS HERE. SHE WANTS TO SEE YOU.
OH, SHE IS, IS SHE?
WELL, YOU TELL THAT LITTLE BRAT SHE'D BEST START BEGGING FOR MERCY. I'VE NOT FORGOTTEN HOW SHE BROKE MY HEART!
HER OWN MOTHER!
I'VE COME TO MAKE AMENDS. I'VE BROUGHT THIS PATHETIC WHELP AS AN OFFERING, TO SACRIFICE TO YOUR PATRON DEMON.
HEY NOW!
JUNIPER! MY DARLING, HOW SWEET OF YOU.
HEY WAIT NO! THIS IS ALL A MISUNDER-STANDING.
KRUGAR, THE SHADOW SKULL, WILL ACCEPT HIM GLADLY. HIS SUFFERING WILL BE DELICIOUS!
MOTHER, I THINK I'VE AN IDEA TO MAKE HIS SUFFERING EVEN SWEETER.
HURRY, TELL ME DAUGHTER.

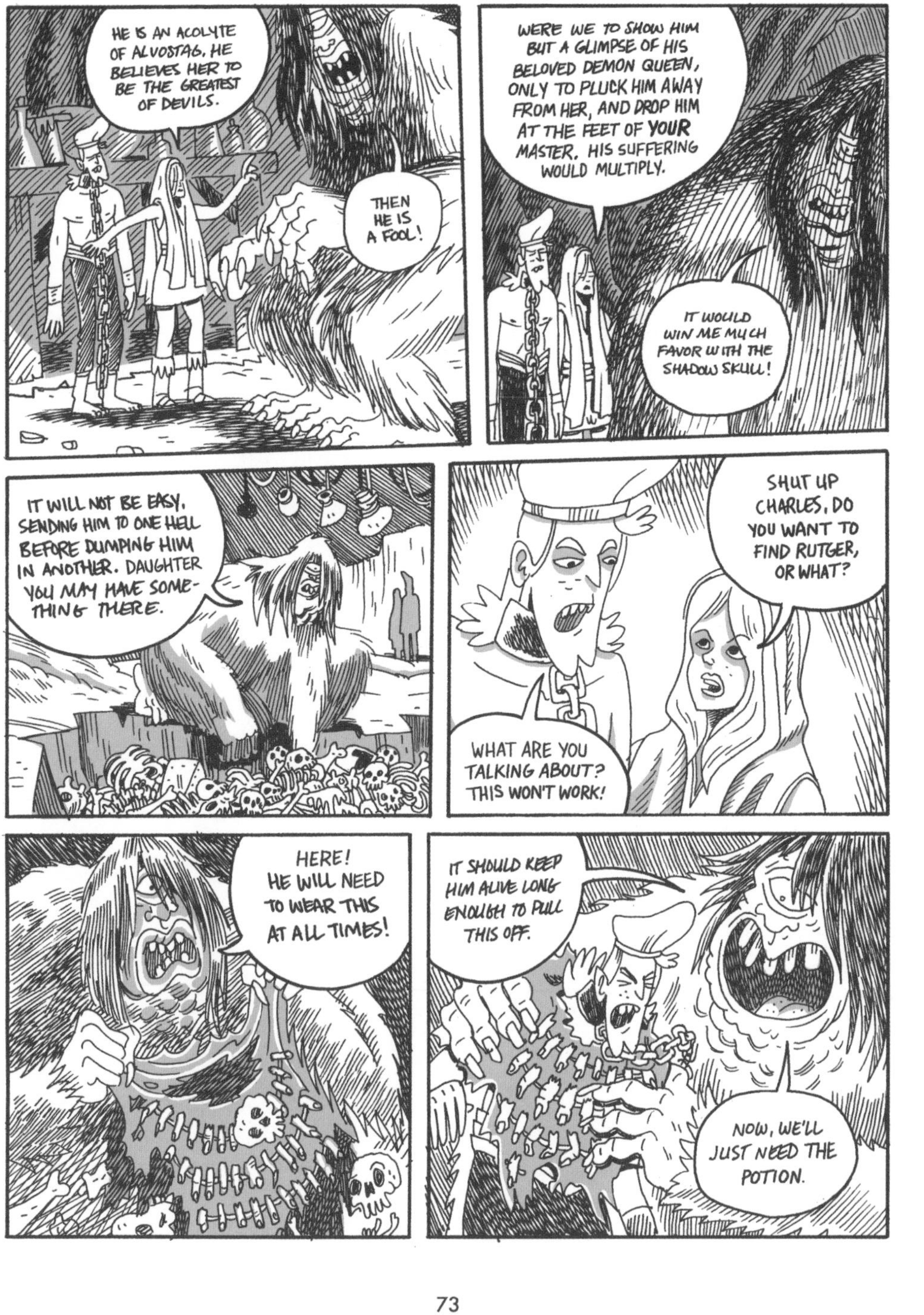

HE IS AN ACOLYTE OF ALVOSTAG. HE BELIEVES HER TO BE THE GREATEST OF DEVILS.
THEN HE IS A FOOL!
WERE WE TO SHOW HIM BUT A GLIMPSE OF HIS BELOVED DEMON QUEEN, ONLY TO PLUCK HIM AWAY FROM HER, AND DROP HIM AT THE FEET OF YOUR MASTER. HIS SUFFERING WOULD MULTIPLY.
IT WOULD WIN ME MUCH FAVOR WITH THE SHADOW SKULL!
IT WILL NOT BE EASY, SENDING HIM TO ONE HELL BEFORE DUMPING HIM IN ANOTHER. DAUGHTER YOU MAY HAVE SOME-THING THERE.
WHAT ARE YOU TALKING ABOUT? THIS WON'T WORK!
SHUT UP CHARLES, DO YOU WANT TO FIND RUTGER, OR WHAT?
HERE! HE WILL NEED TO WEAR THIS AT ALL TIMES!
IT SHOULD KEEP HIM ALIVE LONG ENOUGH TO PULL THIS OFF.
NOW, WE'LL JUST NEED THE POTION.

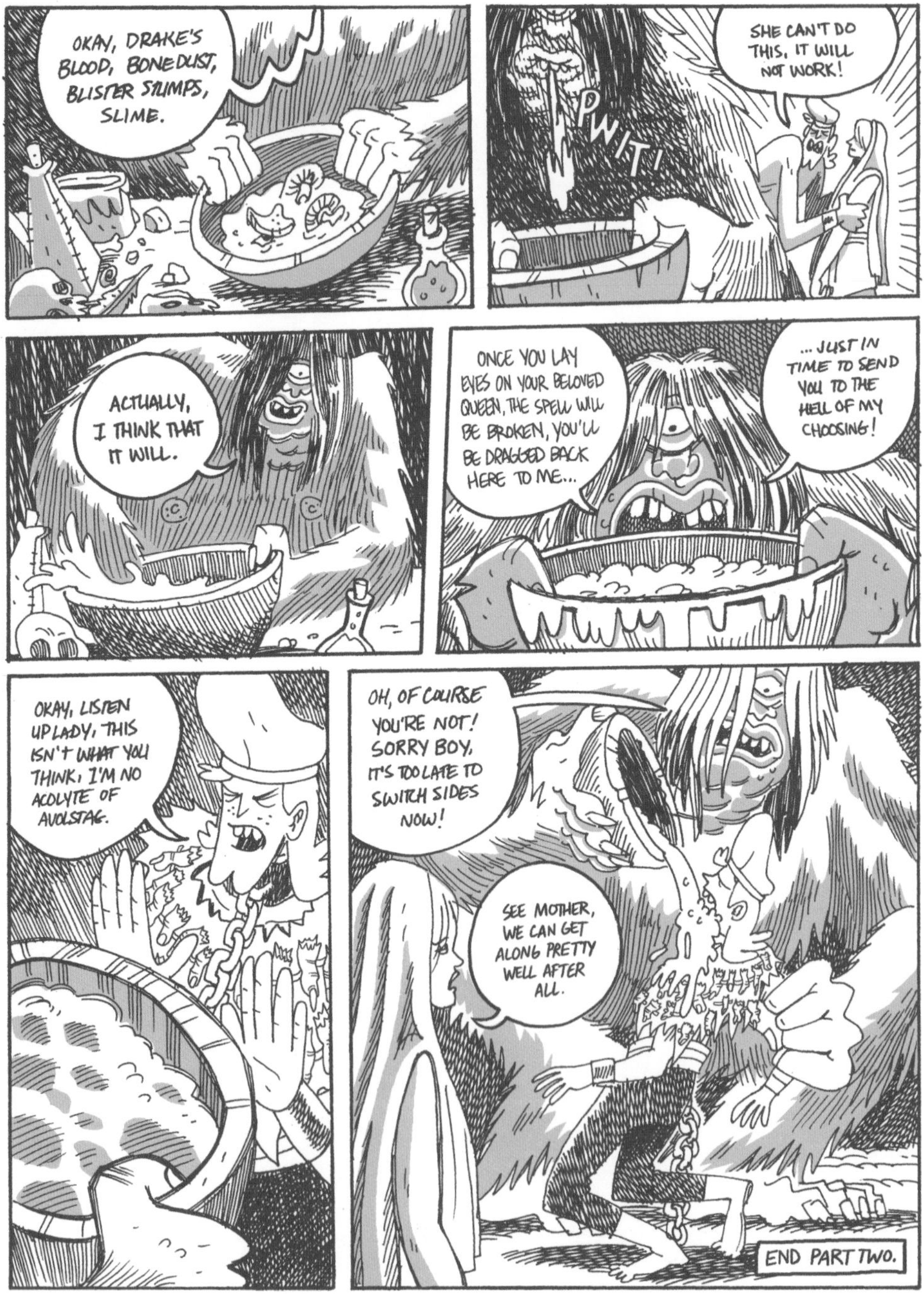
OKAY, DRAKE'S BLOOD, BONEDUST, BLISTER STUMPS, SLIME.
PWIT!
SHE CAN'T DO THIS, IT WILL NOT WORK!
ACTUALLY, I THINK THAT IT WILL.
ONCE YOU LAY EYES ON YOUR BELOVED QUEEN, THE SPELL WILL BE BROKEN, YOU'LL BE DRAGGED BACK HERE TO ME...
...JUST IN TIME TO SEND YOU TO THE HELL OF MY CHOOSING!
OKAY, LISTEN UP LADY, THIS ISN'T WHAT YOU THINK, I'M NO ACOLYTE OF AVOLSTAG.
OH, OF COURSE YOU'RE NOT! SORRY BOY, IT'S TOO LATE TO SWITCH SIDES NOW!
SEE MOTHER, WE CAN GET ALONG PRETTY WELL AFTER ALL.
END PART TWO.

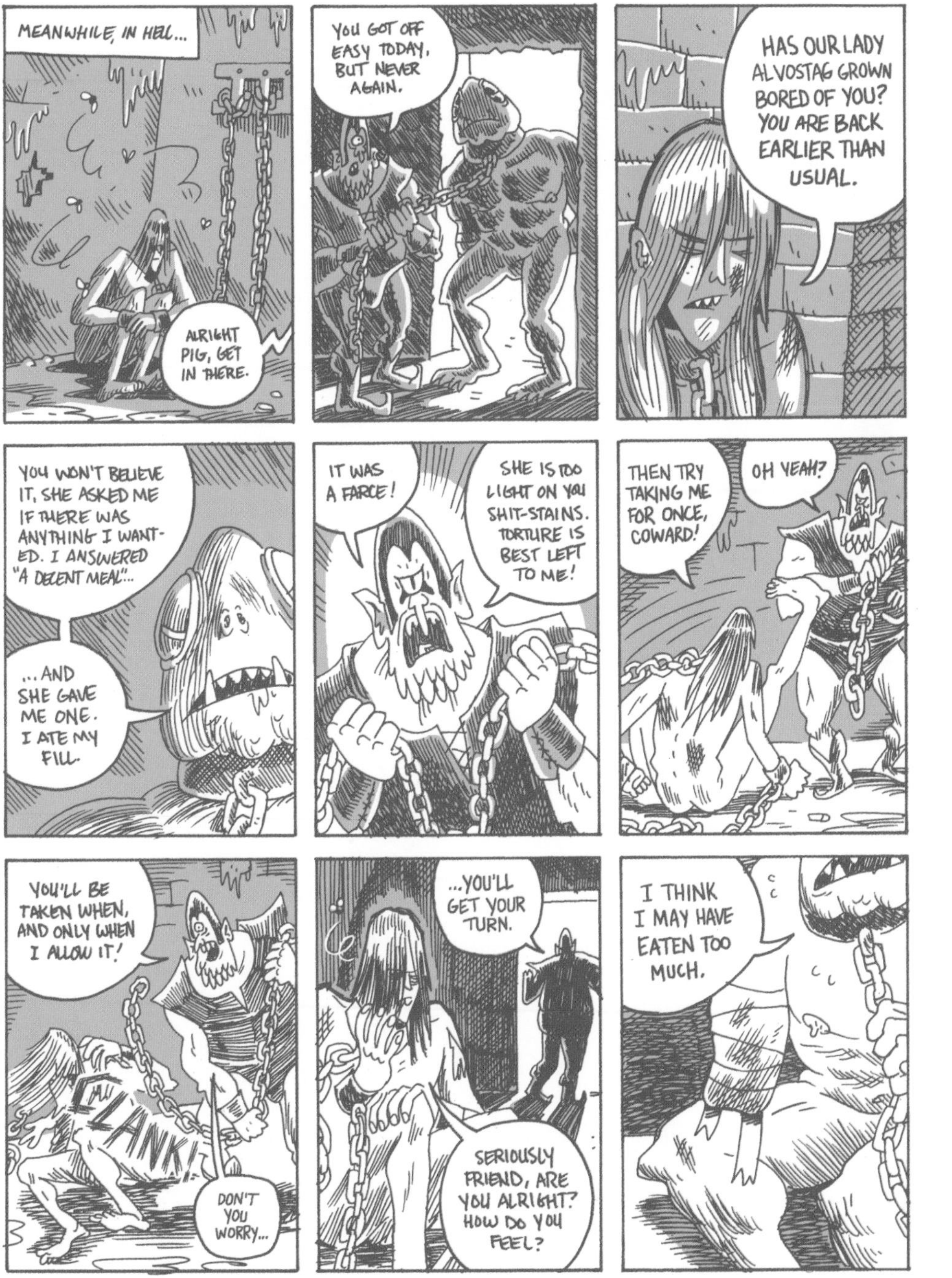
MEANWHILE, IN HELL...
ALRIGHT PIG, GET IN THERE.
YOU GOT OFF EASY TODAY, BUT NEVER AGAIN.
HAS OUR LADY ALVOSTAG GROWN BORED OF YOU? YOU ARE BACK EARLIER THAN USUAL.
YOU WON'T BELIEVE IT, SHE ASKED ME IF THERE WAS ANYTHING I WANTED. I ANSWERED "A DECENT MEAL"...
...AND SHE GAVE ME ONE. I ATE MY FILL.
IT WAS A FARCE!
SHE IS TOO LIGHT ON YOU SHIT-STAINS. TORTURE IS BEST LEFT TO ME!
THEN TRY TAKING ME FOR ONCE, COWARD!
OH YEAH?
YOU'LL BE TAKEN WHEN, AND ONLY WHEN I ALLOW IT!
CLANK!
DON'T YOU WORRY...
...YOU'LL GET YOUR TURN.
SERIOUSLY FRIEND, ARE YOU ALRIGHT? HOW DO YOU FEEL?
I THINK I MAY HAVE EATEN TOO MUCH.

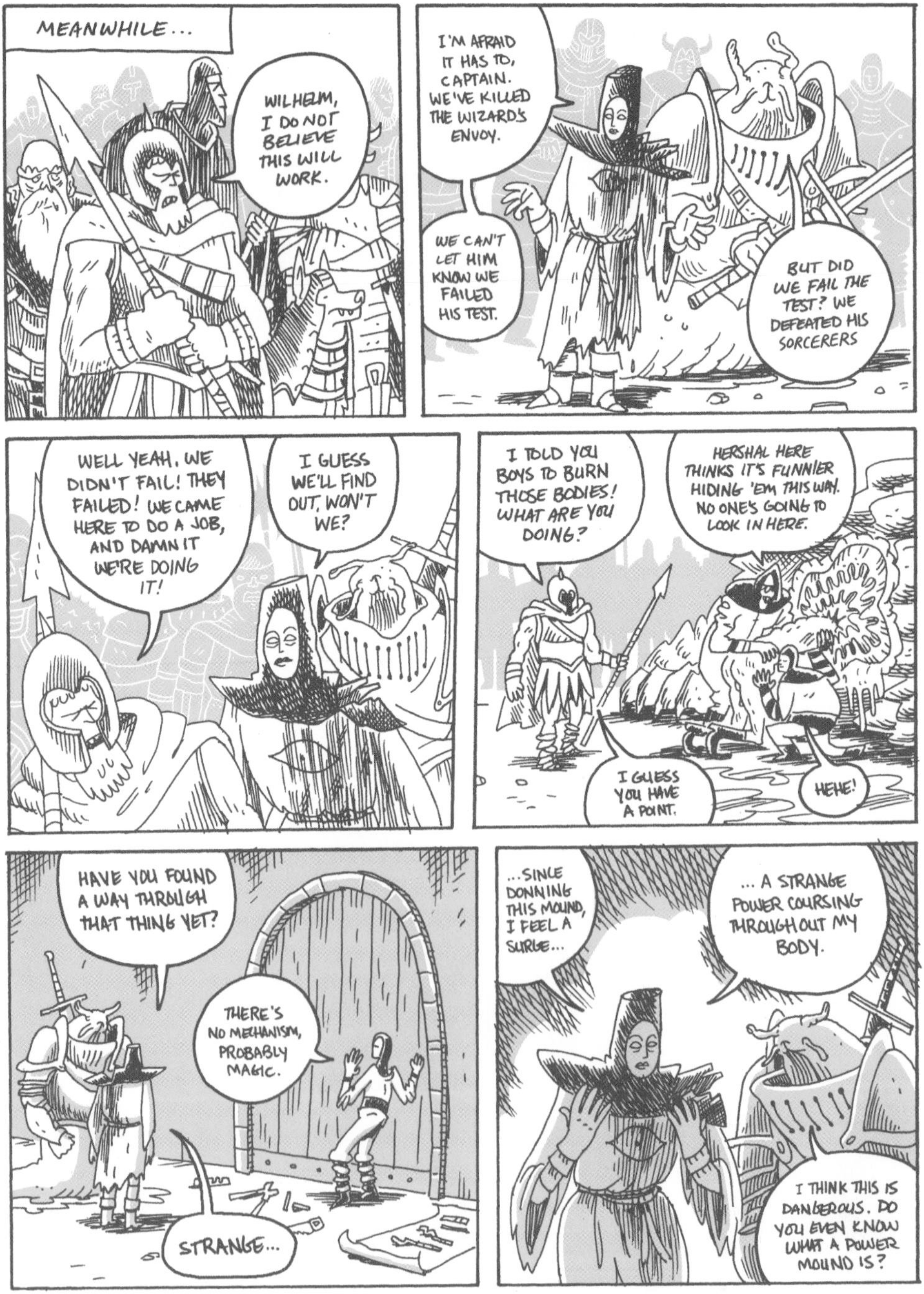

MEANWHILE...
WILHELM, I DO NOT BELIEVE THIS WILL WORK.
I'M AFRAID IT HAS TO, CAPTAIN. WE'VE KILLED THE WIZARD'S ENVOY.
WE CAN'T LET HIM KNOW WE FAILED HIS TEST.
BUT DID WE FAIL THE TEST? WE DEFEATED HIS SORCERERS
WELL YEAH, WE DIDN'T FAIL! THEY FAILED! WE CAME HERE TO DO A JOB, AND DAMN IT WE'RE DOING IT!
I GUESS WE'LL FIND OUT, WON'T WE?
I TOLD YOU BOYS TO BURN THOSE BODIES! WHAT ARE YOU DOING?
HERSHAL HERE THINKS IT'S FUNNIER HIDING 'EM THIS WAY. NO ONE'S GOING TO LOOK IN HERE.
I GUESS YOU HAVE A POINT.
HEHE!
HAVE YOU FOUND A WAY THROUGH THAT THING YET?
THERE'S NO MECHANISM, PROBABLY MAGIC.
STRANGE...
...SINCE DONNING THIS MOUND, I FEEL A SURGE...
... A STRANGE POWER COURSING THROUGHOUT MY BODY.
I THINK THIS IS DANGEROUS. DO YOU EVEN KNOW WHAT A POWER MOUND IS?

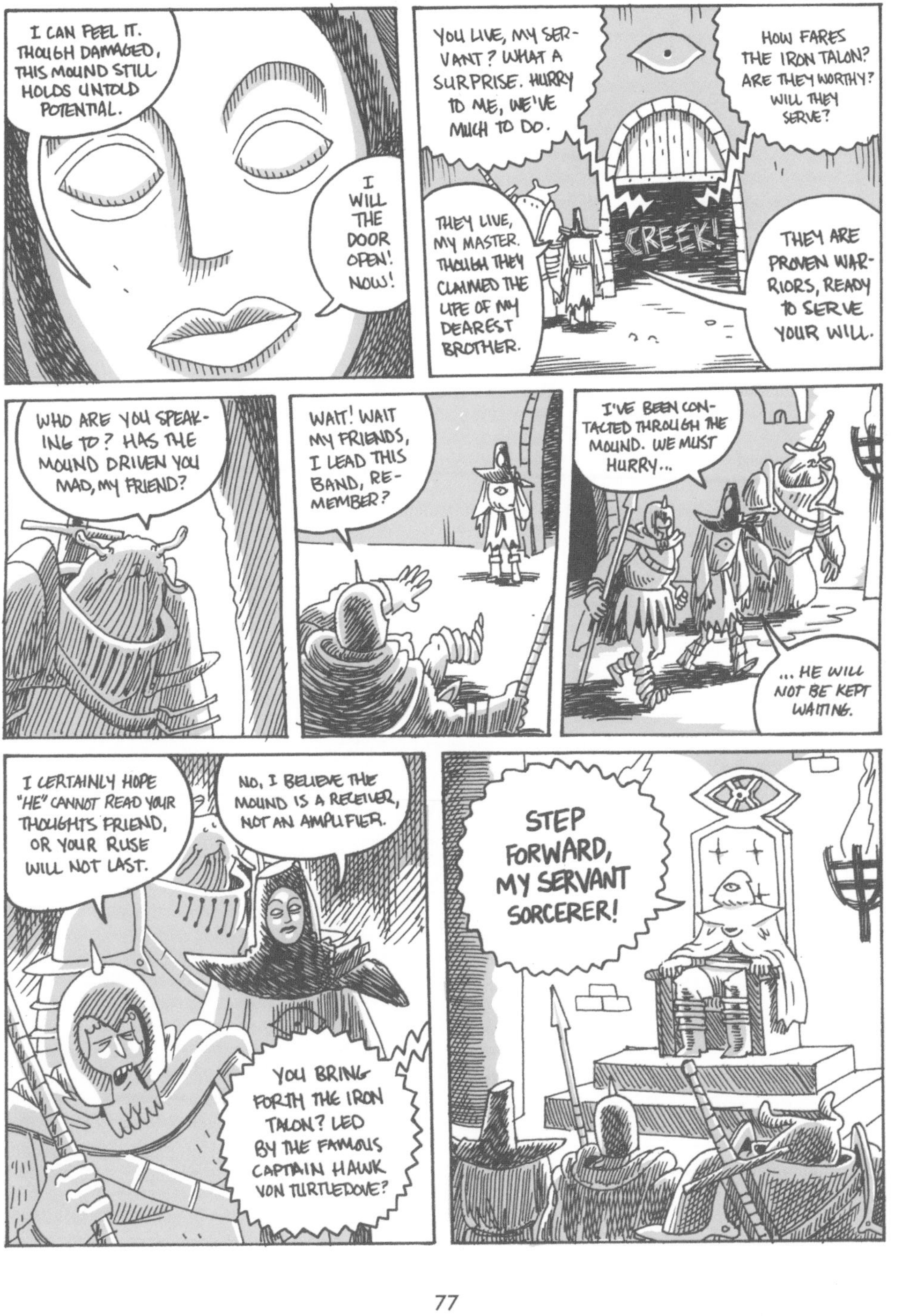
I CAN FEEL IT. THOUGH DAMAGED, THIS MOUND STILL HOLDS UNTOLD POTENTIAL.
I WILL THE DOOR OPEN! NOW!
YOU LIVE, MY SERVANT? WHAT A SURPRISE. HURRY TO ME, WE'VE MUCH TO DO.
HOW FARES THE IRON TALON? ARE THEY WORTHY? WILL THEY SERVE?
CREEK!
THEY LIVE, MY MASTER. THOUGH THEY CLAIMED THE LIFE OF MY DEAREST BROTHER.
THEY ARE PROVEN WARRIORS, READY TO SERVE YOUR WILL.
WHO ARE YOU SPEAKING TO? HAS THE MOUND DRIVEN YOU MAD, MY FRIEND?
WAIT! WAIT MY FRIENDS, I LEAD THIS BAND, REMEMBER?
I'VE BEEN CONTACTED THROUGH THE MOUND. WE MUST HURRY...
...HE WILL NOT BE KEPT WAITING.
I CERTAINLY HOPE "HE" CANNOT READ YOUR THOUGHTS FRIEND, OR YOUR RUSE WILL NOT LAST.
NO, I BELIEVE THE MOUND IS A RECEIVER, NOT AN AMPLIFIER.
YOU BRING FORTH THE IRON TALON? LED BY THE FAMOUS CAPTAIN HAWK VON TURTLEDOVE?
STEP FORWARD, MY SERVANT SORCERER!

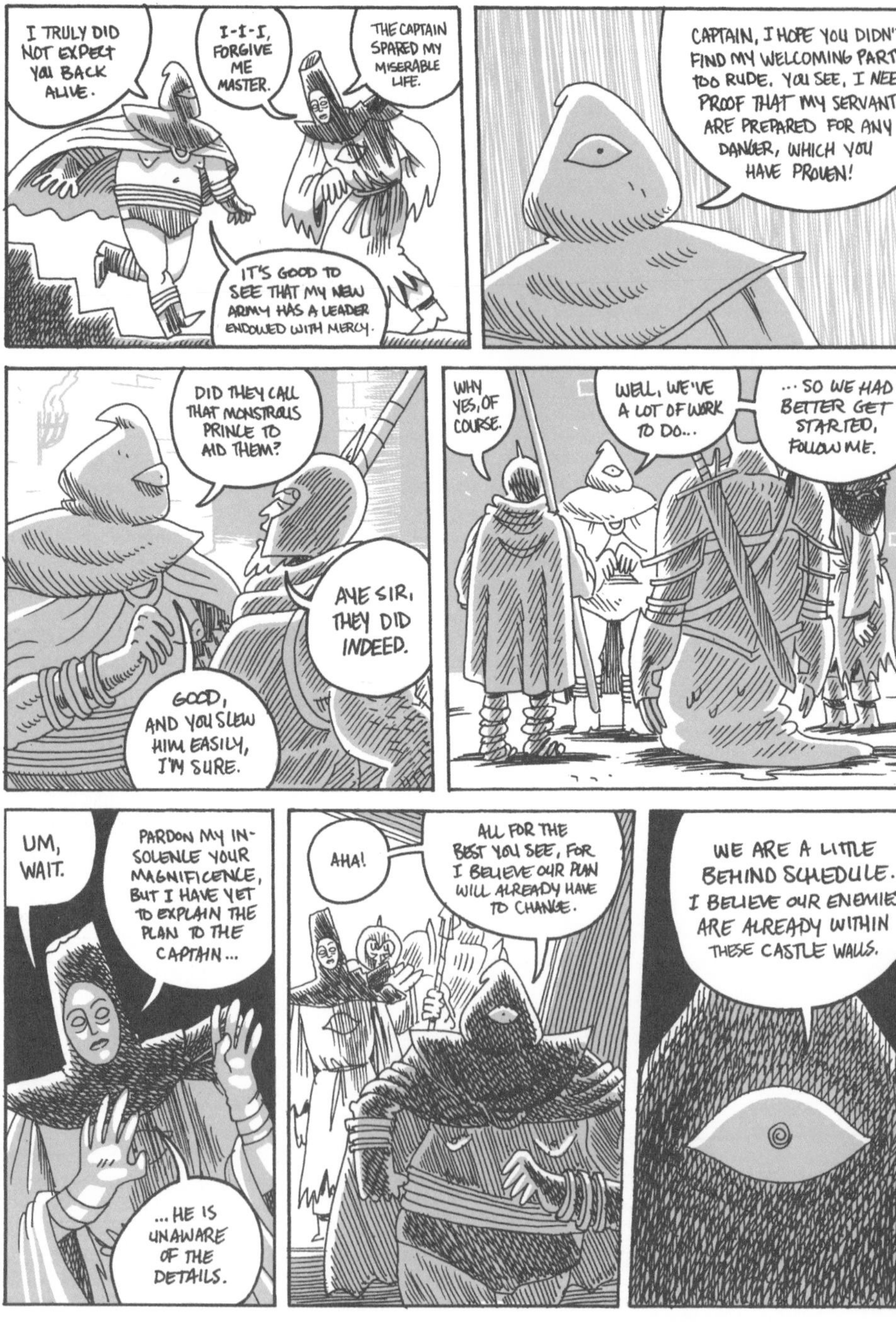
I TRULY DID NOT EXPECT YOU BACK ALIVE.
I-I-I, FORGIVE ME MASTER.
THE CAPTAIN SPARED MY MISERABLE LIFE.
IT'S GOOD TO SEE THAT MY NEW ARMY HAS A LEADER ENDOWED WITH MERCY.
CAPTAIN, I HOPE YOU DIDN'T FIND MY WELCOMING PARTY TOO RUDE. YOU SEE, I NEED PROOF THAT MY SERVANTS ARE PREPARED FOR ANY DANGER, WHICH YOU HAVE PROVEN!
DID THEY CALL THAT MONSTROUS PRINCE TO AID THEM?
AYE SIR, THEY DID INDEED.
GOOD, AND YOU SLEW HIM EASILY, I'M SURE.
WHY YES, OF COURSE.
WELL, WE'VE A LOT OF WORK TO DO...
... SO WE HAD BETTER GET STARTED, FOLLOW ME.
UM, WAIT.
PARDON MY IN-SOLENCE YOUR MAGNIFICENCE, BUT I HAVE YET TO EXPLAIN THE PLAN TO THE CAPTAIN...
... HE IS UNAWARE OF THE DETAILS.
AHA!
ALL FOR THE BEST YOU SEE, FOR I BELIEVE OUR PLAN WILL ALREADY HAVE TO CHANGE.
WE ARE A LITTLE BEHIND SCHEDULE. I BELIEVE OUR ENEMIES ARE ALREADY WITHIN THESE CASTLE WALLS.

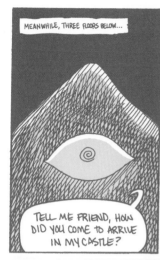

MEANWHILE, THREE FLOORS BELOW...

TELL ME FRIEND, HOW DID YOU COME TO ARRIVE IN MY CASTLE?

WORD OF AN AUTOMATED MAN AT THE MAIN GATES WOULD SURELY HAVE REACHED ME, YET YOU TWO WERE IN MY GARDEN.

THERE WAS A QUEUE SEVENTEEN DAYS LONG AT THE MAIN GATE.

WE FOUND A DIFFERENT WAY IN.

AH, A TRIP THROUGH THE CAVERNS THEN? THOUGH SURELY TWAS A TRIP TOO DANGEROUS.

I DOUBT IT COULD HAVE SAVED YOU MUCH TIME.

FOR I HAVE GIVEN CONTROL OF THOSE CAVES TO THE ORC TRIBES. QUITE A TREK FOR A LOWLY MERCHANT...

...EVEN ONE ACCOMPANIED BY AN AUTOMATED MAN.

YET, HERE YOU ARE...

...A SINGULAR MAN, POISED FOR DESTINY.

79

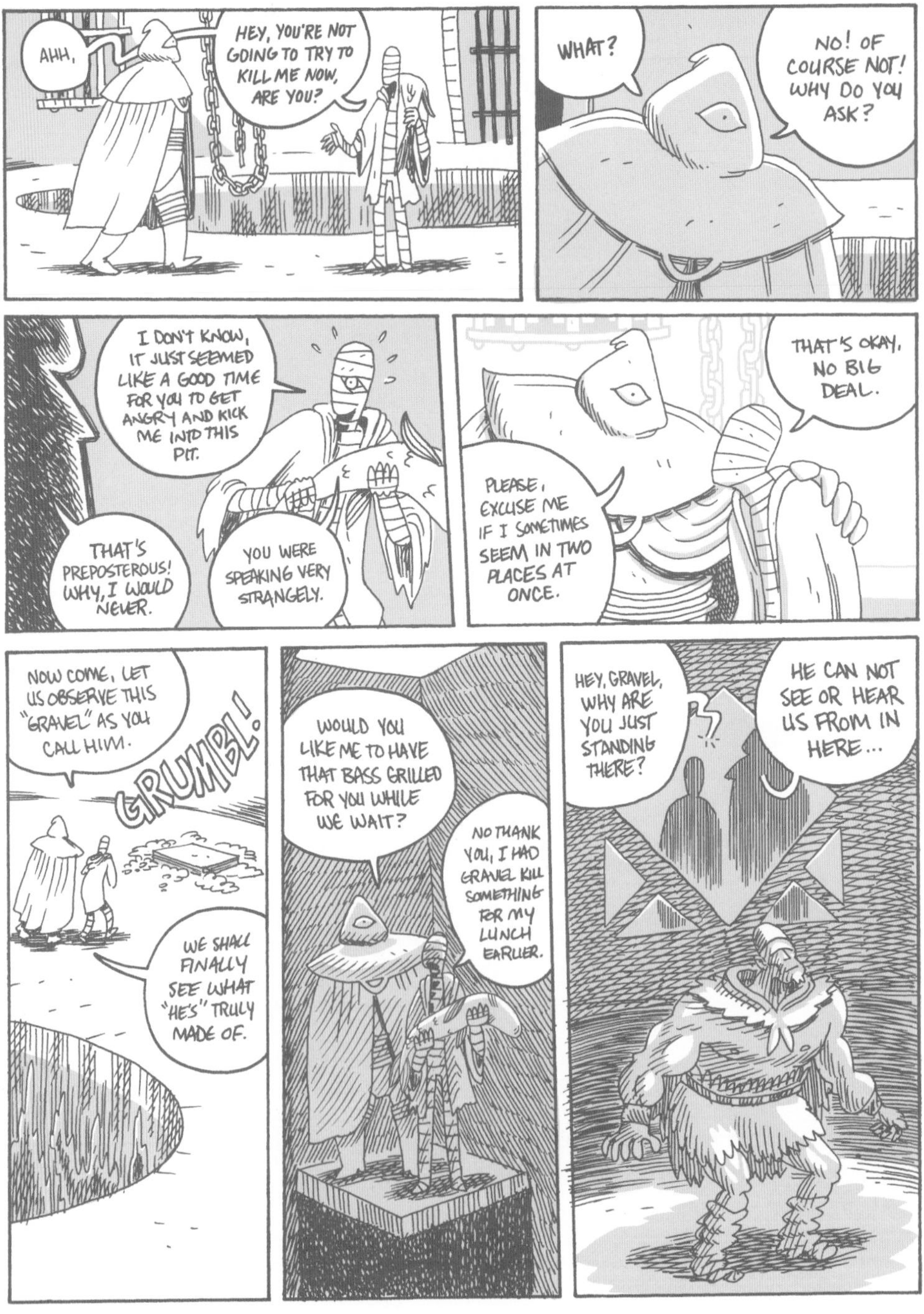
AHH,
HEY, YOU'RE NOT GOING TO TRY TO KILL ME NOW, ARE YOU?
WHAT?
NO! OF COURSE NOT! WHY DO YOU ASK?
I DON'T KNOW, IT JUST SEEMED LIKE A GOOD TIME FOR YOU TO GET ANGRY AND KICK ME INTO THIS PIT.
THAT'S PREPOSTEROUS! WHY, I WOULD NEVER.
YOU WERE SPEAKING VERY STRANGELY.
THAT'S OKAY. NO BIG DEAL.
PLEASE, EXCUSE ME IF I SOMETIMES SEEM IN TWO PLACES AT ONCE.
NOW COME, LET US OBSERVE THIS "GRAVEL" AS YOU CALL HIM.
GRUMBL!
WE SHALL FINALLY SEE WHAT "HE'S" TRULY MADE OF.
WOULD YOU LIKE ME TO HAVE THAT BASS GRILLED FOR YOU WHILE WE WAIT?
NO THANK YOU, I HAD GRAVEL KILL SOMETHING FOR MY LUNCH EARLIER.
HEY, GRAVEL, WHY ARE YOU JUST STANDING THERE?
HE CAN NOT SEE OR HEAR US FROM IN HERE...

...THOUGH HE IS NOT ALONE.

HUH?

CRUMBLE!

HEY, TURDOLON, WAKE UP, I'VE FOUND A HOLE IN THIS WALL.

THIS PLACE IS BUILT PRETTY POORLY. WE MIGHT FIND A WAY OUT OF HERE.

HUH, WHAT'S THAT?

WHO SPEAKS LIKE A FOOL? BOY, THERE'S NO WAY OUT OF THIS PLACE FOR YOU, IT'S HELL!

WELL, ONE OF THEM ANYWAY. ACCEPT IT!

YOU KNOW, IT COULD BE WORSE FOR YOU, REALLY.

HOW COULD IT POSSIBLY BE WORSE?

SNIFF!

SNIFF!

WE'RE DAMNED FOR ETERNITY!

HA! THIS HELL IS NOTHING REALLY. LOCKED UP, TORTURED, THAT'S ABOUT AS BAD AS IT GETS.

YOU'LL GET USED TO IT.

YOUR FRIEND ON THE OTHER HAND, HE'S IN A BAD WAY.

HE'S IN TROUBLE.

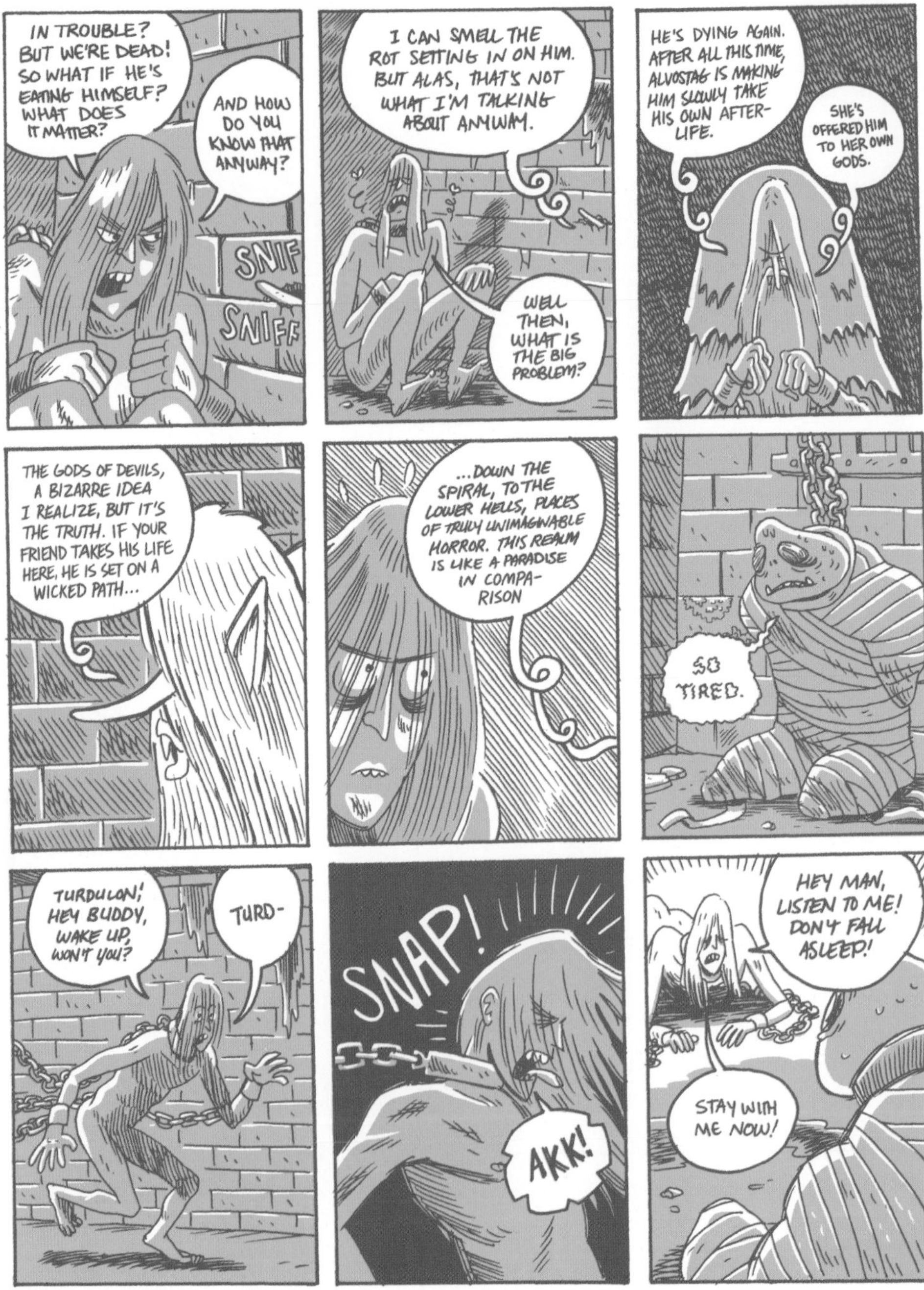
IN TROUBLE? BUT WE'RE DEAD! SO WHAT IF HE'S EATING HIMSELF? WHAT DOES IT MATTER?
AND HOW DO YOU KNOW THAT ANYWAY?
SNIF
SNIFF
I CAN SMELL THE ROT SETTING IN ON HIM. BUT ALAS, THAT'S NOT WHAT I'M TALKING ABOUT ANYWAY.
WELL THEN, WHAT IS THE BIG PROBLEM?
HE'S DYING AGAIN. AFTER ALL THIS TIME, ALVOSTAG IS MAKING HIM SLOWLY TAKE HIS OWN AFTER-LIFE.
SHE'S OFFERED HIM TO HER OWN GODS.
THE GODS OF DEVILS, A BIZARRE IDEA I REALIZE, BUT IT'S THE TRUTH. IF YOUR FRIEND TAKES HIS LIFE HERE, HE IS SET ON A WICKED PATH...
...DOWN THE SPIRAL, TO THE LOWER HELLS, PLACES OF TRULY UNIMAGINABLE HORROR. THIS REALM IS LIKE A PARADISE IN COMPA-RISON
SO TIRED.
TURDULON! HEY BUDDY, WAKE UP, WON'T YOU?
TURD-
SNAP!
AKK!
HEY MAN, LISTEN TO ME! DON'T FALL ASLEEP!
STAY WITH ME NOW!

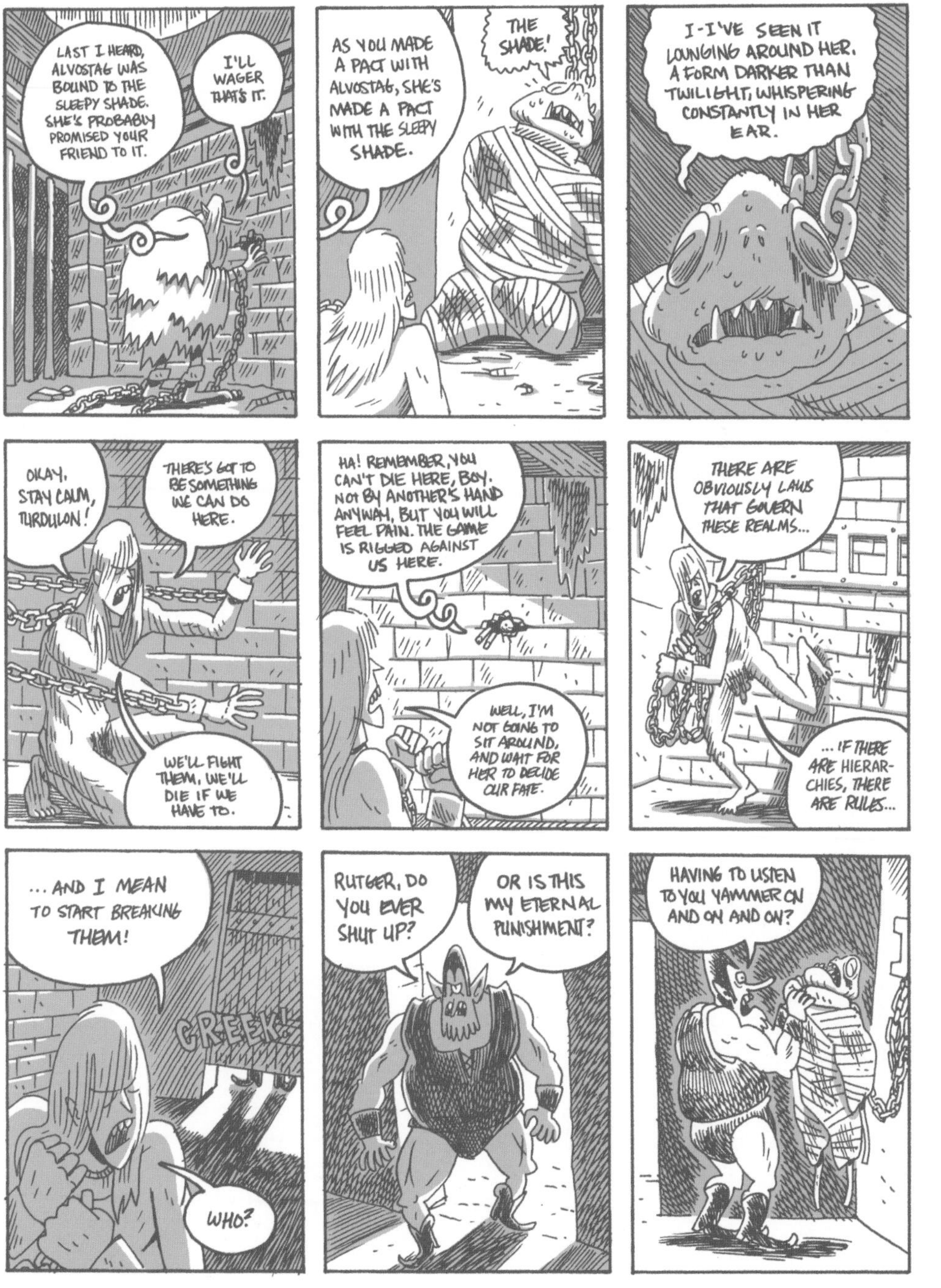
LAST I HEARD, ALVOSTAG WAS BOUND TO THE SLEEPY SHADE. SHE'S PROBABLY PROMISED YOUR FRIEND TO IT.
I'LL WAGER THAT'S IT.
AS YOU MADE A PACT WITH ALVOSTAG, SHE'S MADE A PACT WITH THE SLEEPY SHADE.
THE SHADE!
I-I'VE SEEN IT LOUNGING AROUND HER. A FORM DARKER THAN TWILIGHT, WHISPERING CONSTANTLY IN HER EAR.
OKAY. STAY CALM, TURDULON!
THERE'S GOT TO BE SOMETHING WE CAN DO HERE.
WE'LL FIGHT THEM. WE'LL DIE IF WE HAVE TO.
HA! REMEMBER, YOU CAN'T DIE HERE, BOY. NOT BY ANOTHER'S HAND ANYWAY. BUT YOU WILL FEEL PAIN. THE GAME IS RIGGED AGAINST US HERE.
WELL, I'M NOT GOING TO SIT AROUND, AND WAIT FOR HER TO DECIDE OUR FATE.
THERE ARE OBVIOUSLY LAWS THAT GOVERN THESE REALMS...
... IF THERE ARE HIERARCHIES, THERE ARE RULES...
... AND I MEAN TO START BREAKING THEM!
CREEK!
WHO?
RUTGER, DO YOU EVER SHUT UP?
OR IS THIS MY ETERNAL PUNISHMENT?
HAVING TO LISTEN TO YOU YAMMER ON AND ON AND ON?

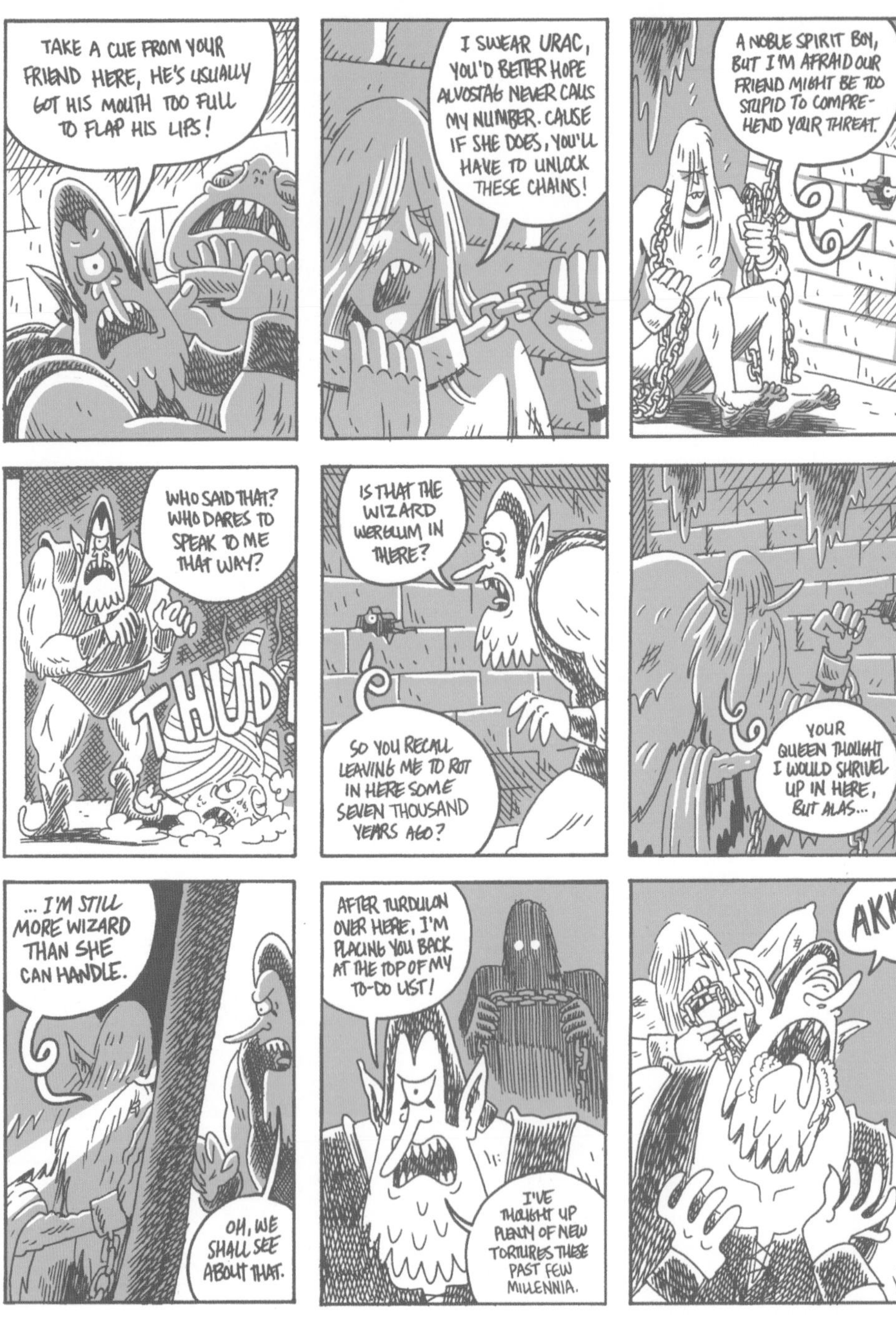
TAKE A CUE FROM YOUR FRIEND HERE, HE'S USUALLY GOT HIS MOUTH TOO FULL TO FLAP HIS LIPS!
I SWEAR URAC, YOU'D BETTER HOPE ALVOSTAG NEVER CALLS MY NUMBER. CAUSE IF SHE DOES, YOU'LL HAVE TO UNLOCK THESE CHAINS!
A NOBLE SPIRIT BOY, BUT I'M AFRAID OUR FRIEND MIGHT BE TOO STUPID TO COMPRE-HEND YOUR THREAT.
WHO SAID THAT? WHO DARES TO SPEAK TO ME THAT WAY?
THUD!
IS THAT THE WIZARD WERGLUM IN THERE?
SO YOU RECALL LEAVING ME TO ROT IN HERE SOME SEVEN THOUSAND YEARS AGO?
YOUR QUEEN THOUGHT I WOULD SHRIVEL UP IN HERE, BUT ALAS...
... I'M STILL MORE WIZARD THAN SHE CAN HANDLE.
OH, WE SHALL SEE ABOUT THAT.
AFTER TURDULON OVER HERE, I'M PLACING YOU BACK AT THE TOP OF MY TO-DO LIST!
I'VE THOUGHT UP PLENTY OF NEW TORTURES THESE PAST FEW MILLENNIA.
AKK!

NOT TOO FAR AWAY...

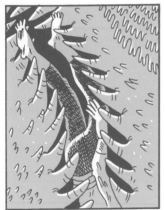

GRUMBLE!

ALRIGHT, HERE COMES ANOTHER ONE. GET IN POSITION, HURRY!

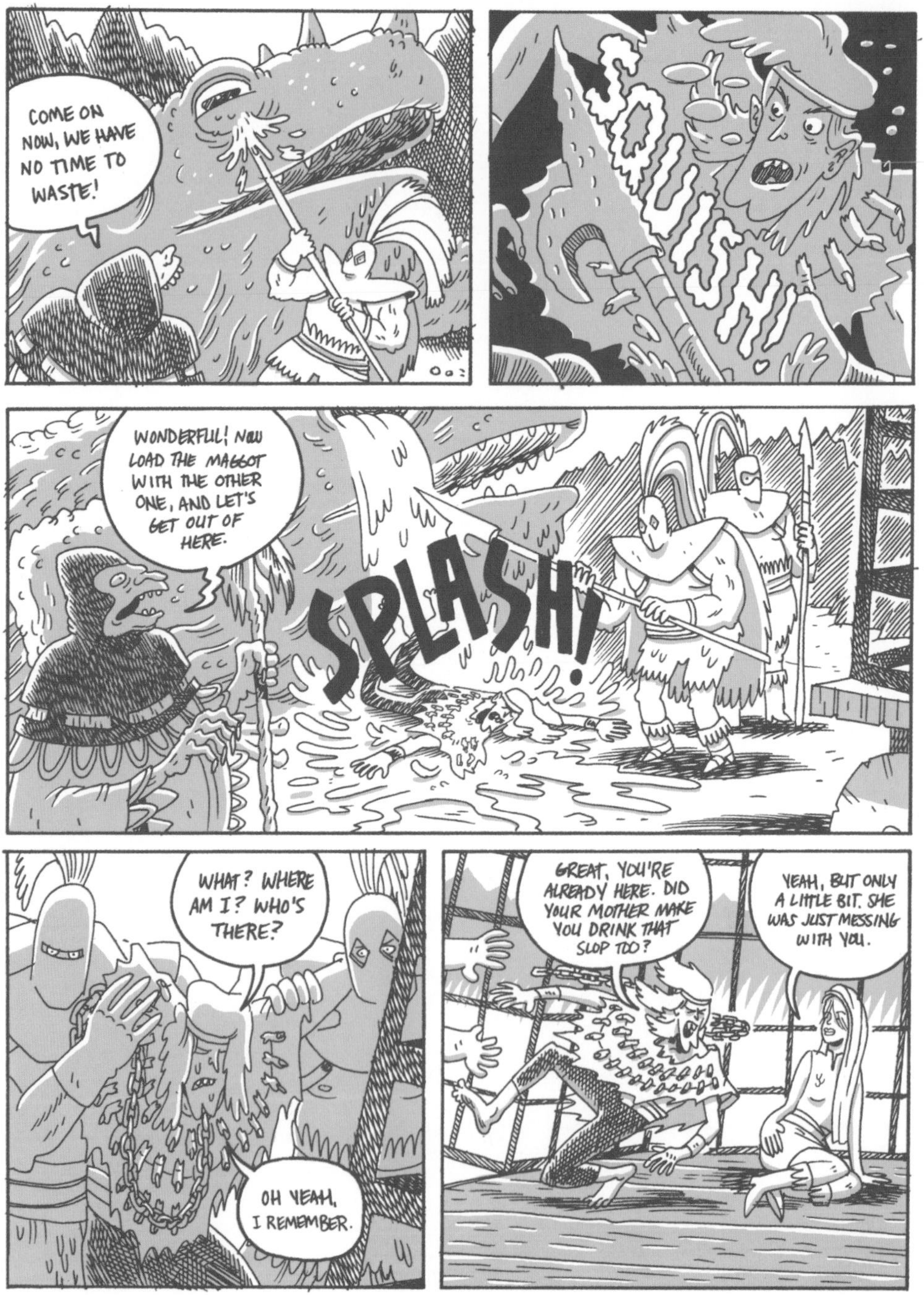
COME ON NOW, WE HAVE NO TIME TO WASTE!
SQUISH!
WONDERFUL! NOW LOAD THE MAGGOT WITH THE OTHER ONE, AND LET'S GET OUT OF HERE.
SPLASH!
WHAT? WHERE AM I? WHO'S THERE?
OH YEAH, I REMEMBER.
GREAT, YOU'RE ALREADY HERE. DID YOUR MOTHER MAKE YOU DRINK THAT SLOP TOO?
YEAH, BUT ONLY A LITTLE BIT. SHE WAS JUST MESSING WITH YOU.

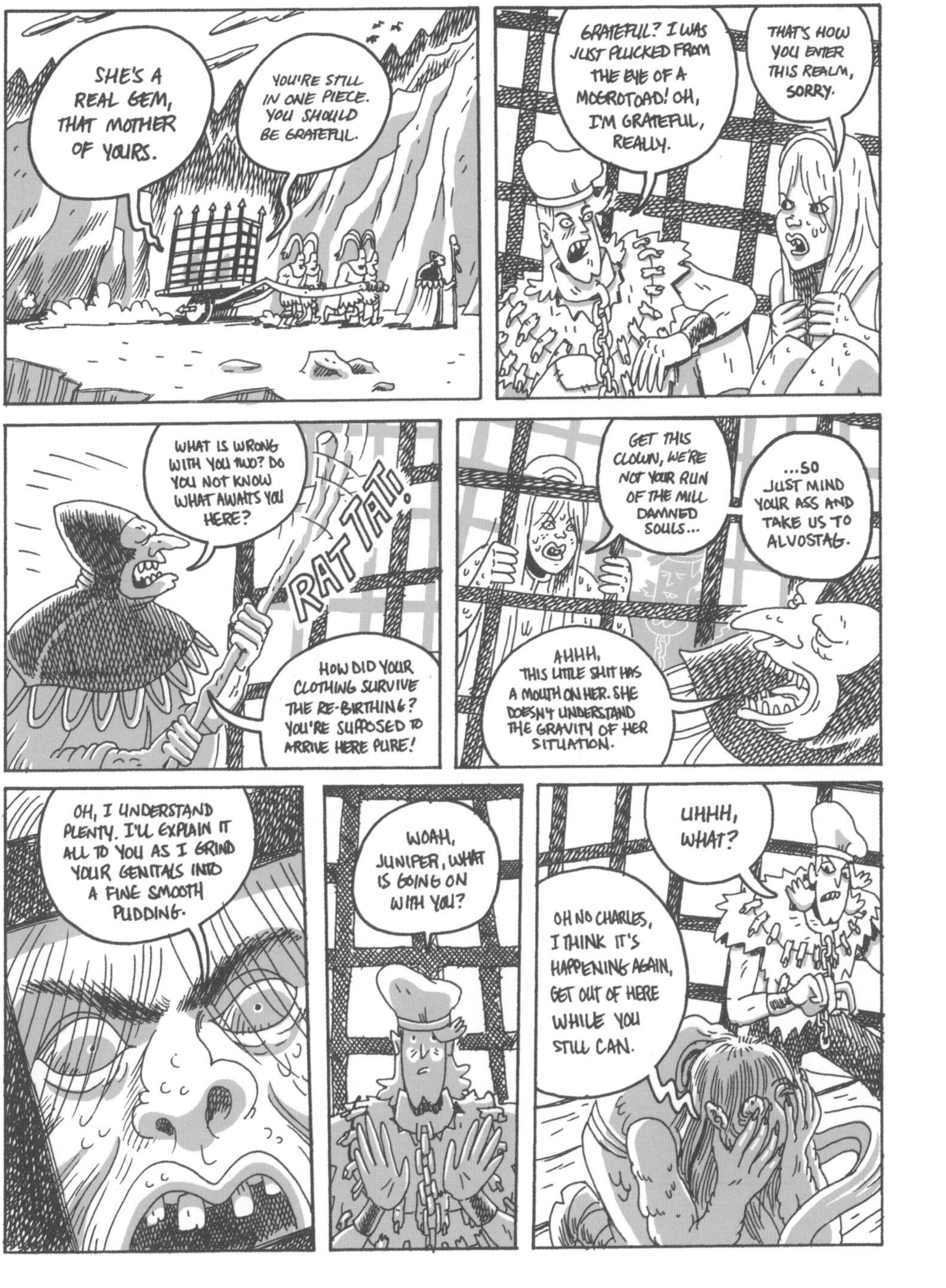
SHE'S A REAL GEM, THAT MOTHER OF YOURS.
YOU'RE STILL IN ONE PIECE. YOU SHOULD BE GRATEFUL.
GRATEFUL? I WAS JUST PLUCKED FROM THE EYE OF A MOGROTOAD! OH, I'M GRATEFUL, REALLY.
THAT'S HOW YOU ENTER THIS REALM, SORRY.
WHAT IS WRONG WITH YOU TWO? DO YOU NOT KNOW WHAT AWAITS YOU HERE?
RAT TAT!
HOW DID YOUR CLOTHING SURVIVE THE RE-BIRTHING? YOU'RE SUPPOSED TO ARRIVE HERE PURE!
GET THIS CLOWN, WE'RE NOT YOUR RUN OF THE MILL DAMNED SOULS...
...SO JUST MIND YOUR ASS AND TAKE US TO ALVOSTAG.
AHHH, THIS LITTLE SHIT HAS A MOUTH ON HER. SHE DOESN'T UNDERSTAND THE GRAVITY OF HER SITUATION.
OH, I UNDERSTAND PLENTY. I'LL EXPLAIN IT ALL TO YOU AS I GRIND YOUR GENITALS INTO A FINE SMOOTH PUDDING.
WOAH, JUNIPER, WHAT IS GOING ON WITH YOU?
UHHH, WHAT?
OH NO CHARLES, I THINK IT'S HAPPENING AGAIN, GET OUT OF HERE WHILE YOU STILL CAN.

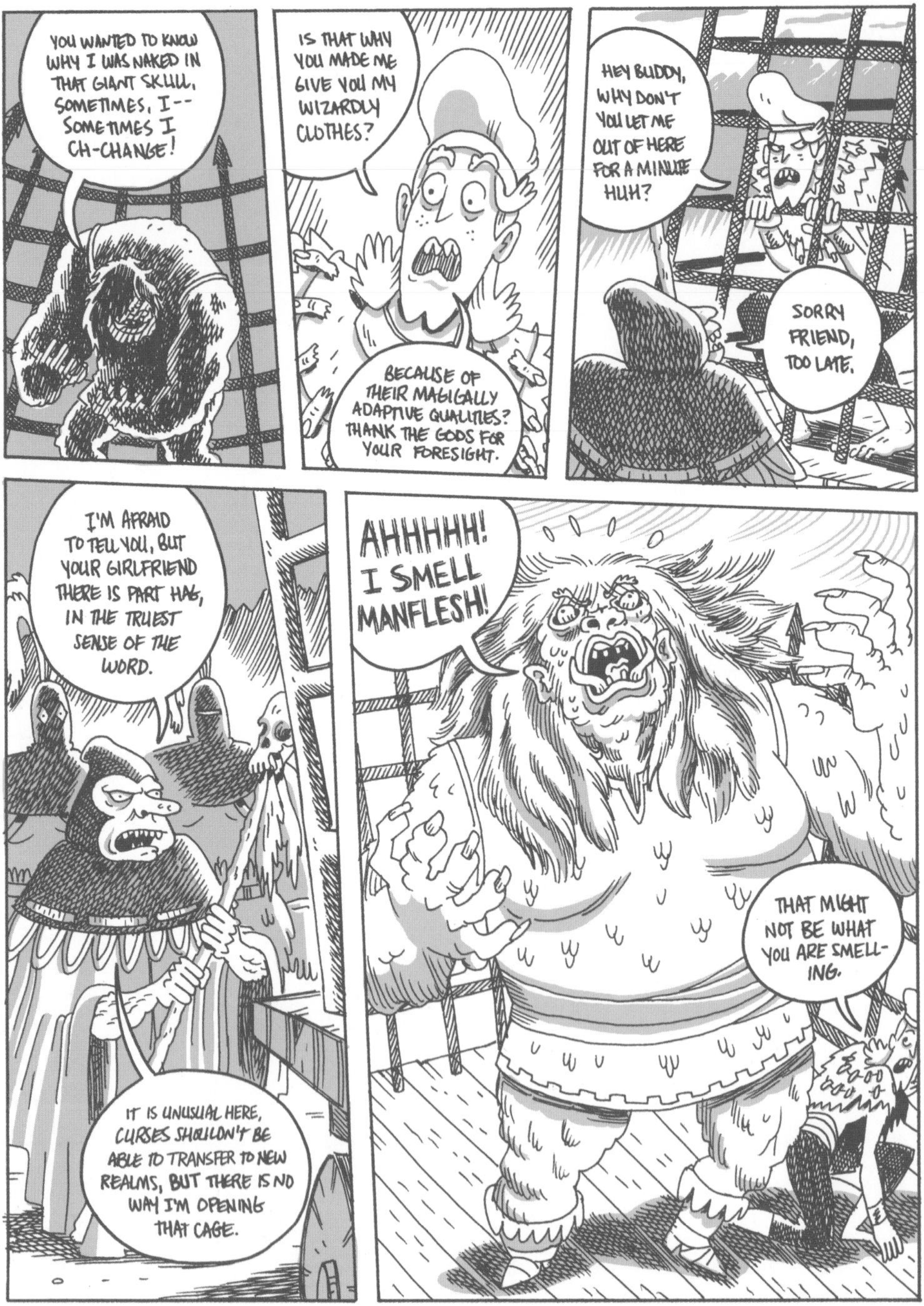
YOU WANTED TO KNOW WHY I WAS NAKED IN THAT GIANT SKULL. SOMETIMES, I-- SOMETIMES I CH-CHANGE!
IS THAT WHY YOU MADE ME GIVE YOU MY WIZARDLY CLOTHES?
BECAUSE OF THEIR MAGICALLY ADAPTIVE QUALITIES? THANK THE GODS FOR YOUR FORESIGHT.
HEY BUDDY, WHY DON'T YOU LET ME OUT OF HERE FOR A MINUTE HUH?
SORRY FRIEND, TOO LATE.
I'M AFRAID TO TELL YOU, BUT YOUR GIRLFRIEND THERE IS PART HAG, IN THE TRUEST SENSE OF THE WORD.
IT IS UNUSUAL HERE, CURSES SHOULDN'T BE ABLE TO TRANSFER TO NEW REALMS, BUT THERE IS NO WAY I'M OPENING THAT CAGE.
AHHHHH! I SMELL MANFLESH!
THAT MIGHT NOT BE WHAT YOU ARE SMELL-ING.

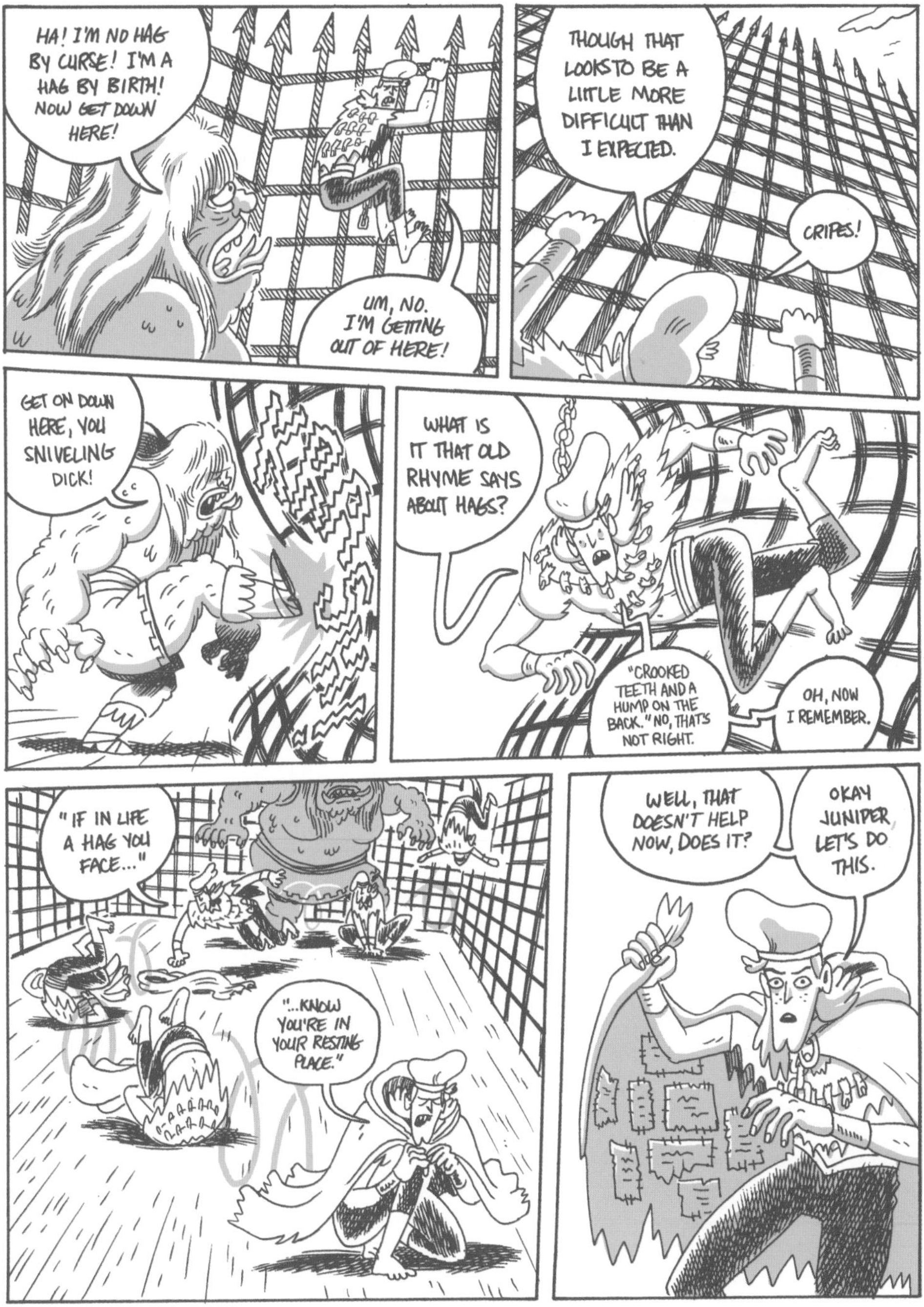
HA! I'M NO HAG BY CURSE! I'M A HAG BY BIRTH! NOW GET DOWN HERE!
UM, NO. I'M GETTING OUT OF HERE!
THOUGH THAT LOOKS TO BE A LITTLE MORE DIFFICULT THAN I EXPECTED.
CRIPES!
GET ON DOWN HERE, YOU SNIVELING DICK!
WHAT IS IT THAT OLD RHYME SAYS ABOUT HAGS?
"CROOKED TEETH AND A HUMP ON THE BACK." NO, THAT'S NOT RIGHT.
OH, NOW I REMEMBER.
"IF IN LIFE A HAG YOU FACE..."
"...KNOW YOU'RE IN YOUR RESTING PLACE."
WELL, THAT DOESN'T HELP NOW, DOES IT?
OKAY JUNIPER, LET'S DO THIS.

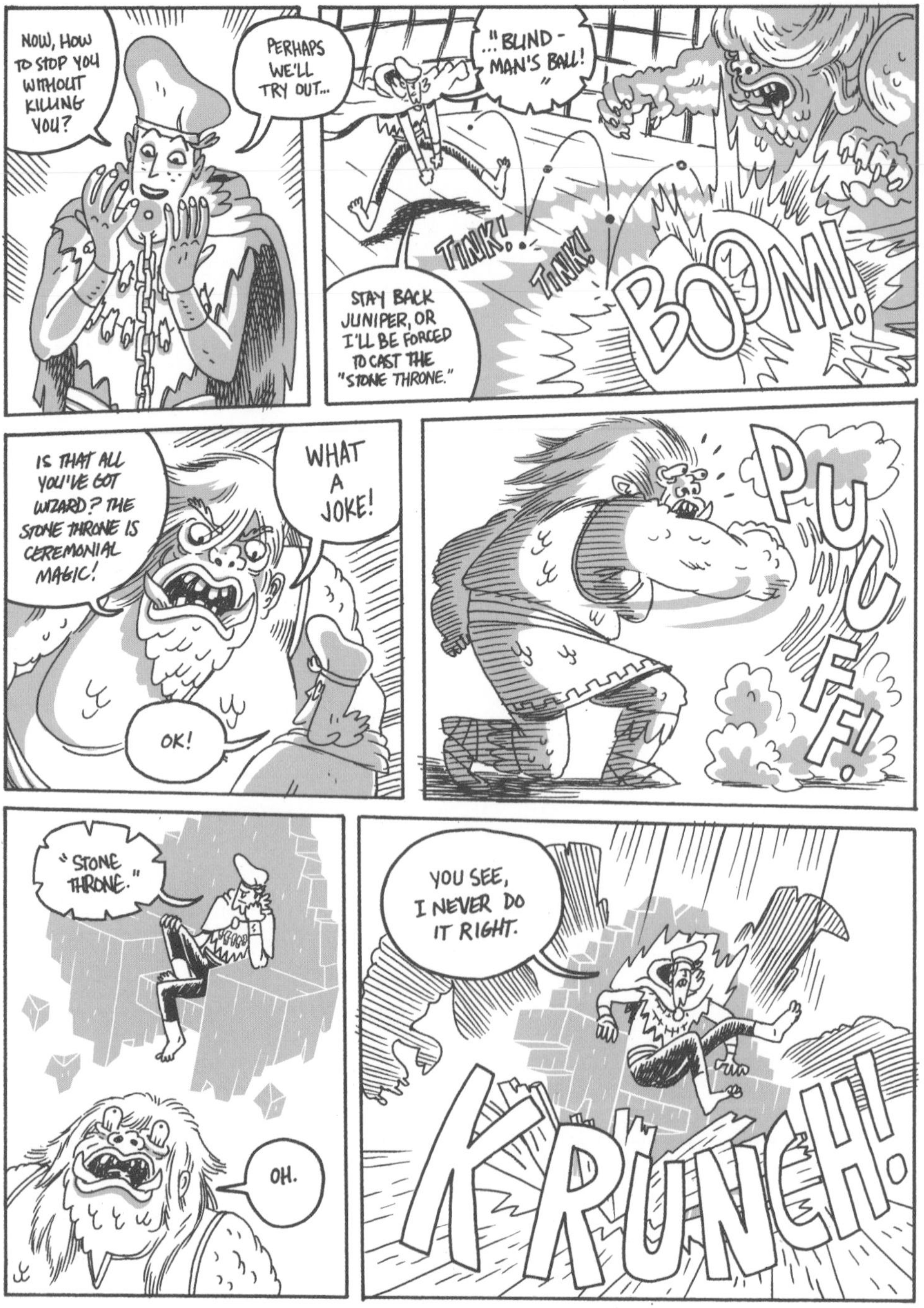
NOW, HOW TO STOP YOU WITHOUT KILLING YOU?
PERHAPS WE'LL TRY OUT...
..."BLIND-MAN'S BALL!"
STAY BACK JUNIPER, OR I'LL BE FORCED TO CAST THE "STONE THRONE."
TINK!
TINK!
BOOM!
IS THAT ALL YOU'VE GOT WIZARD? THE STONE THRONE IS CEREMONIAL MAGIC!
WHAT A JOKE!
OK!
PUUFFF!
"STONE THRONE."
OH.
YOU SEE, I NEVER DO IT RIGHT.
KRUNCH!

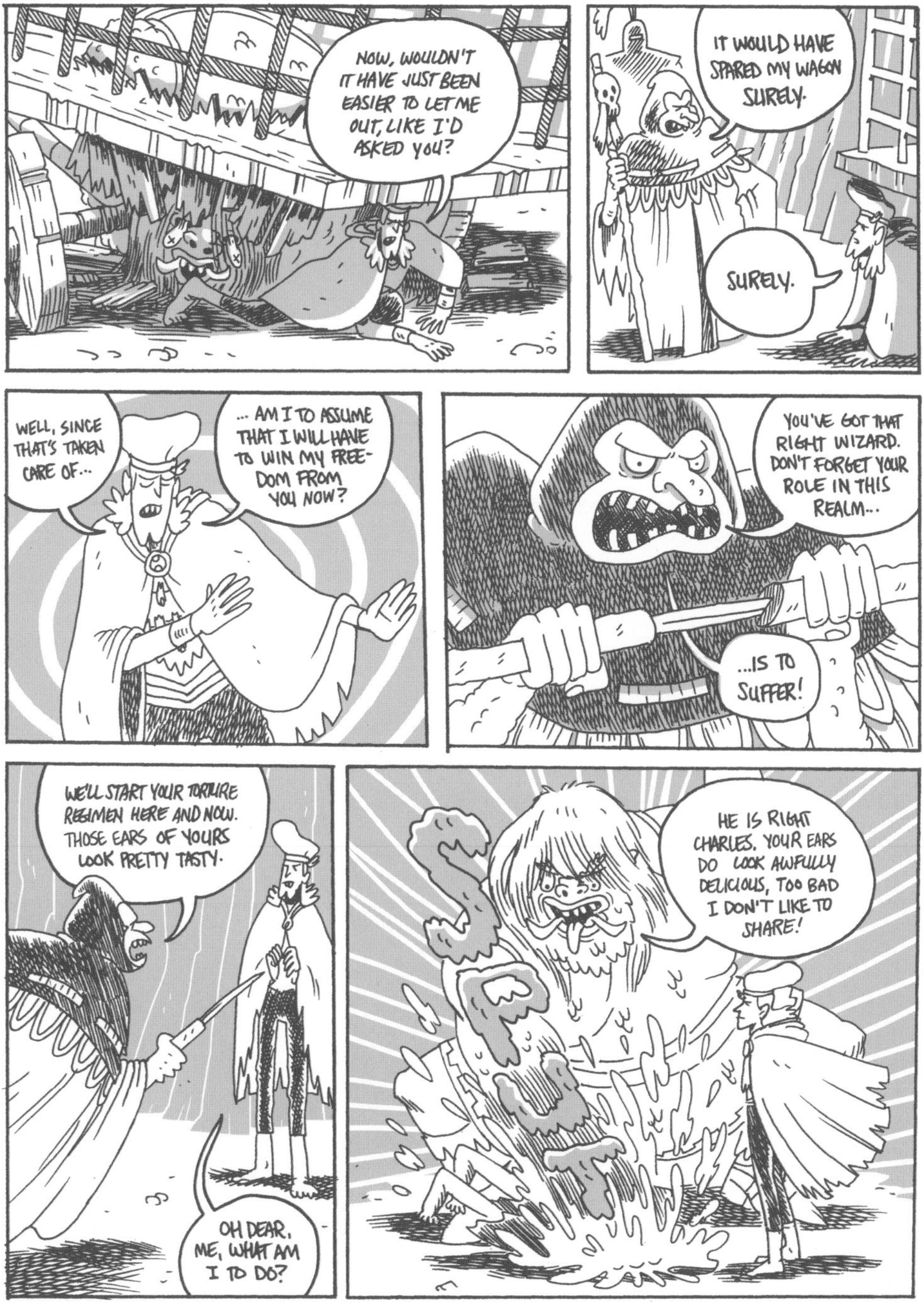

NOW, WOULDN'T IT HAVE JUST BEEN EASIER TO LET ME OUT, LIKE I'D ASKED YOU?
IT WOULD HAVE SPARED MY WAGON SURELY.
SURELY.
WELL, SINCE THAT'S TAKEN CARE OF...
... AM I TO ASSUME THAT I WILL HAVE TO WIN MY FREE-DOM FROM YOU NOW?
YOU'VE GOT THAT RIGHT WIZARD. DON'T FORGET YOUR ROLE IN THIS REALM...
...IS TO SUFFER!
WE'LL START YOUR TORTURE REGIMEN HERE AND NOW. THOSE EARS OF YOURS LOOK PRETTY TASTY.
OH DEAR. ME, WHAT AM I TO DO?
HE IS RIGHT CHARLES. YOUR EARS DO LOOK AWFULLY DELICIOUS, TOO BAD I DON'T LIKE TO SHARE!

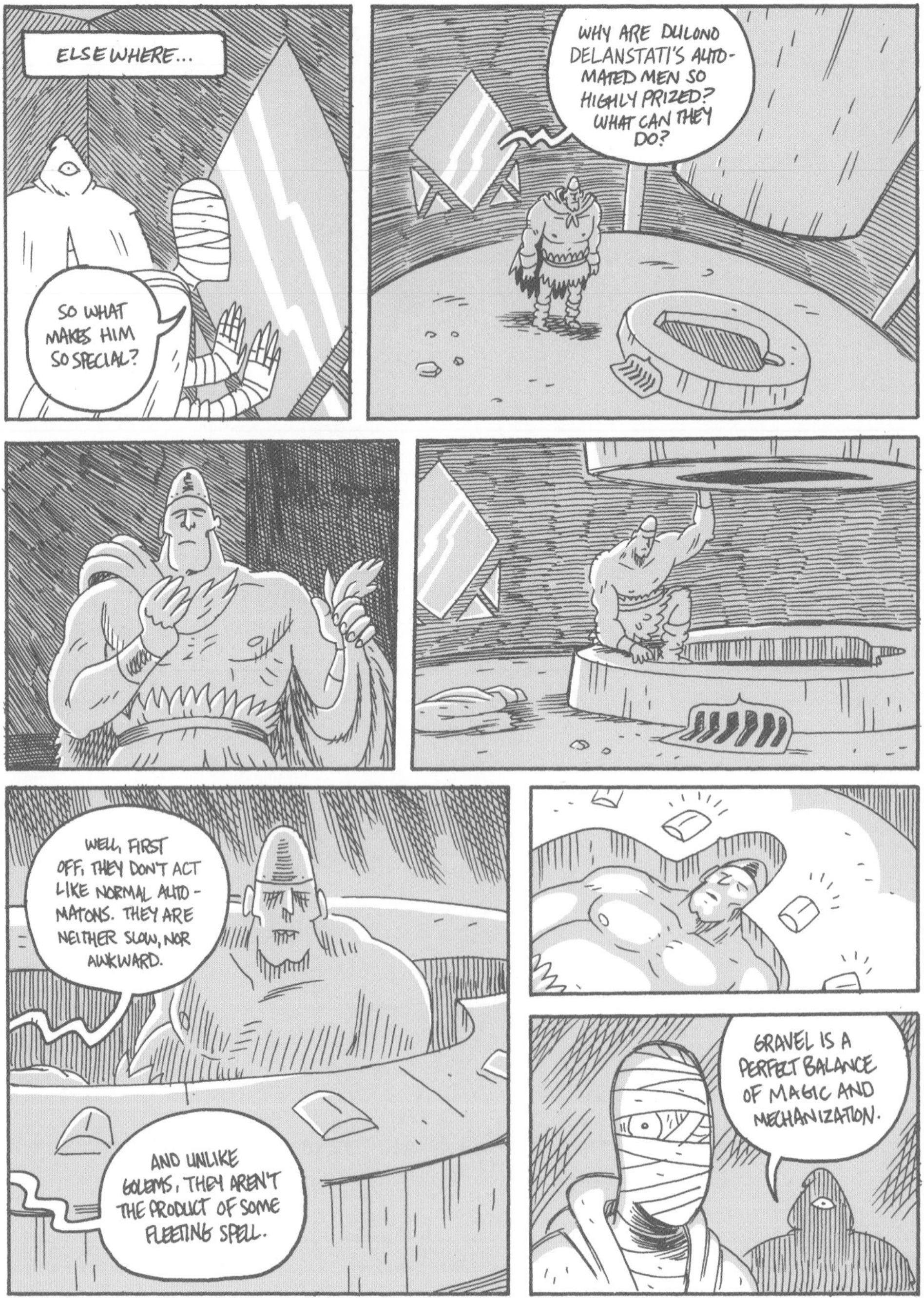

ELSEWHERE...
SO WHAT MAKES HIM SO SPECIAL?
WHY ARE DULONO DELANSTATI'S AUTOMATED MEN SO HIGHLY PRIZED? WHAT CAN THEY DO?
WELL, FIRST OFF, THEY DON'T ACT LIKE NORMAL AUTOMATONS. THEY ARE NEITHER SLOW, NOR AWKWARD.
AND UNLIKE GOLEMS, THEY AREN'T THE PRODUCT OF SOME FLEETING SPELL.
GRAVEL IS A PERFECT BALANCE OF MAGIC AND MECHANIZATION.

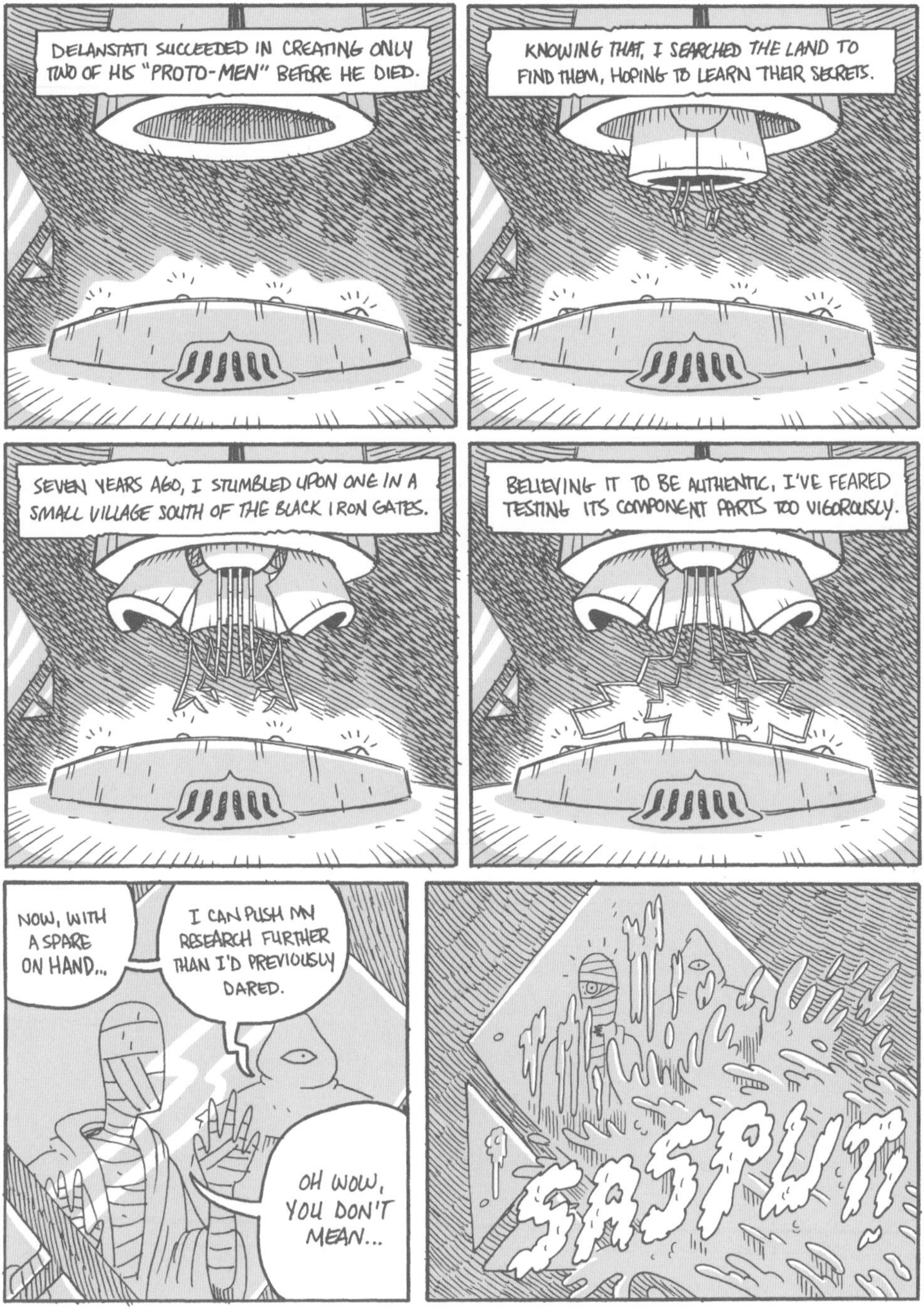
DELANSTATI SUCCEEDED IN CREATING ONLY TWO OF HIS "PROTO-MEN" BEFORE HE DIED.
KNOWING THAT, I SEARCHED THE LAND TO FIND THEM, HOPING TO LEARN THEIR SECRETS.
SEVEN YEARS AGO, I STUMBLED UPON ONE IN A SMALL VILLAGE SOUTH OF THE BLACK IRON GATES.
BELIEVING IT TO BE AUTHENTIC, I'VE FEARED TESTING ITS COMPONENT PARTS TOO VIGOROUSLY.
NOW, WITH A SPARE ON HAND...
I CAN PUSH MY RESEARCH FURTHER THAN I'D PREVIOUSLY DARED.
OH WOW, YOU DON'T MEAN...
SASPLUT!

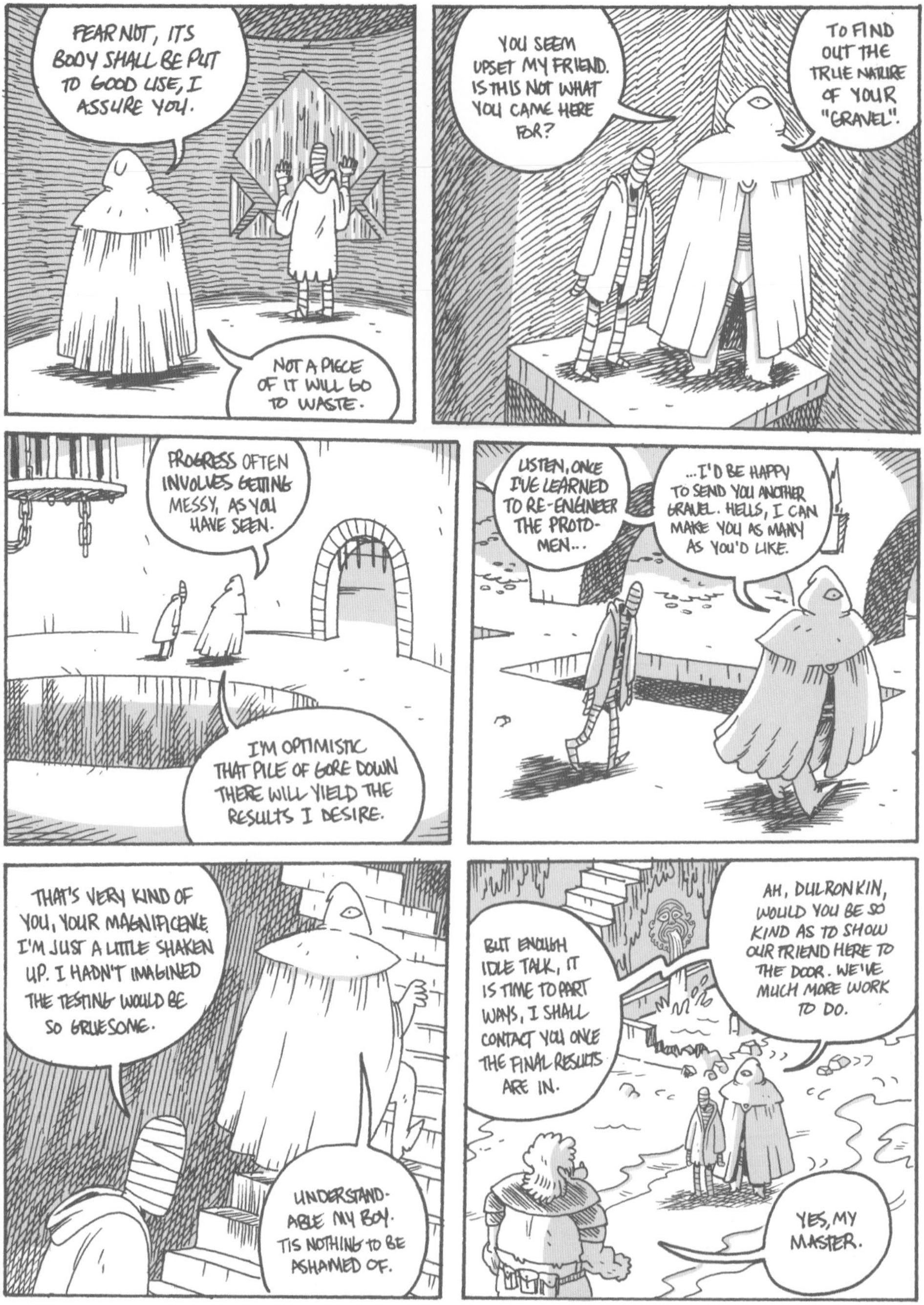
FEAR NOT, ITS BODY SHALL BE PUT TO GOOD USE, I ASSURE YOU.
NOT A PIECE OF IT WILL GO TO WASTE.
YOU SEEM UPSET MY FRIEND. IS THIS NOT WHAT YOU CAME HERE FOR?
TO FIND OUT THE TRUE NATURE OF YOUR "GRAVEL".
PROGRESS OFTEN INVOLVES GETTING MESSY, AS YOU HAVE SEEN.
I'M OPTIMISTIC THAT PILE OF GORE DOWN THERE WILL YIELD THE RESULTS I DESIRE.
LISTEN, ONCE I'VE LEARNED TO RE-ENGINEER THE PROTO-MEN...
...I'D BE HAPPY TO SEND YOU ANOTHER GRAVEL. HELLS, I CAN MAKE YOU AS MANY AS YOU'D LIKE.
THAT'S VERY KIND OF YOU, YOUR MAGNIFICENCE. I'M JUST A LITTLE SHAKEN UP. I HADN'T IMAGINED THE TESTING WOULD BE SO GRUESOME.
UNDERSTAND-ABLE MY BOY. TIS NOTHING TO BE ASHAMED OF.
BUT ENOUGH IDLE TALK, IT IS TIME TO PART WAYS, I SHALL CONTACT YOU ONCE THE FINAL RESULTS ARE IN.
AH, DULRONKIN, WOULD YOU BE SO KIND AS TO SHOW OUR FRIEND HERE TO THE DOOR. WE'VE MUCH MORE WORK TO DO.
YES, MY MASTER.

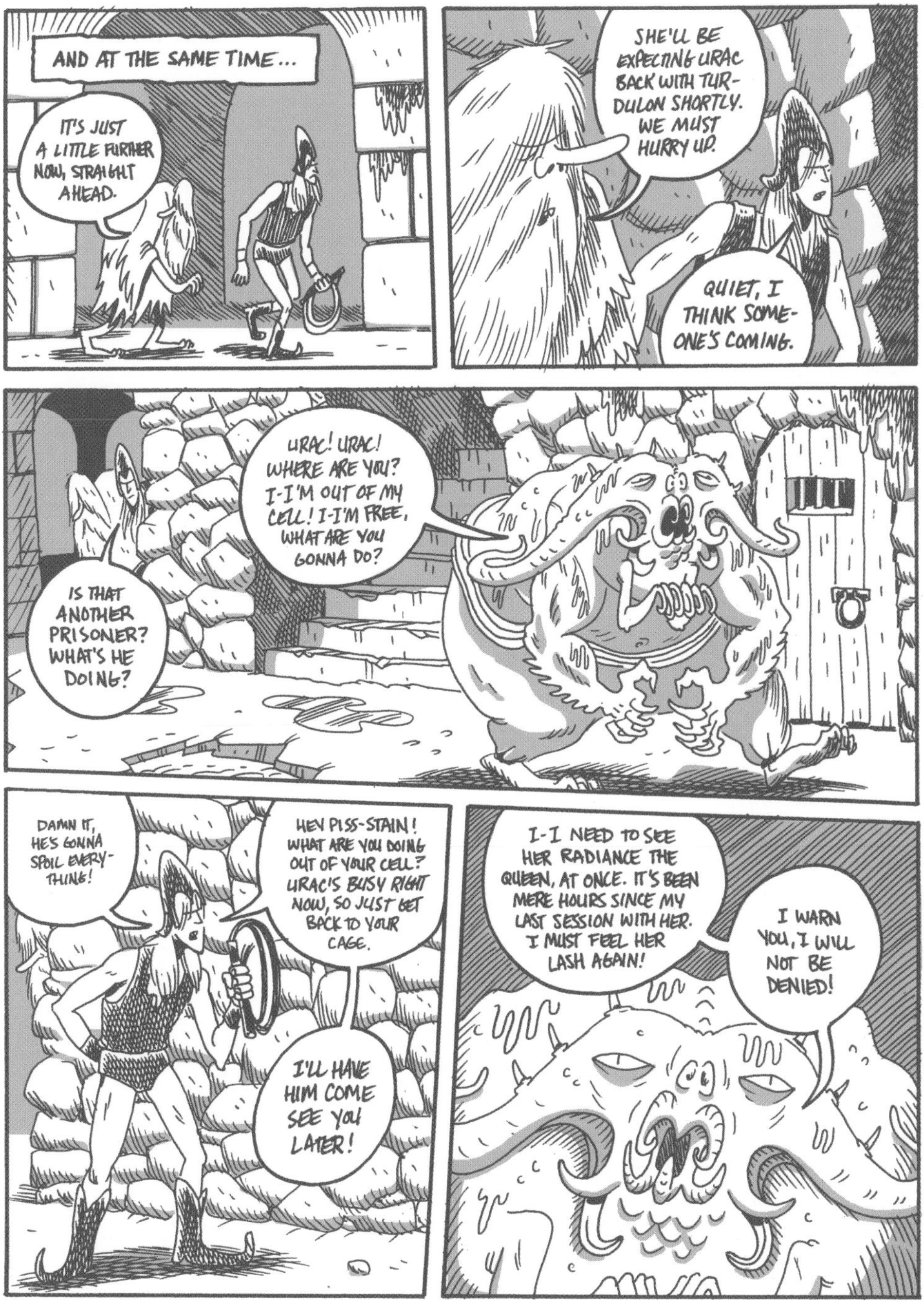
AND AT THE SAME TIME...
IT'S JUST A LITTLE FURTHER NOW, STRAIGHT AHEAD.
SHE'LL BE EXPECTING URAC BACK WITH TURDULON SHORTLY. WE MUST HURRY UP.
QUIET, I THINK SOMEONE'S COMING.
URAC! URAC! WHERE ARE YOU? I-I'M OUT OF MY CELL! I-I'M FREE, WHAT ARE YOU GONNA DO?
IS THAT ANOTHER PRISONER? WHAT'S HE DOING?
DAMN IT, HE'S GONNA SPOIL EVERYTHING!
HEY PISS-STAIN! WHAT ARE YOU DOING OUT OF YOUR CELL? URAC'S BUSY RIGHT NOW, SO JUST GET BACK TO YOUR CAGE.
I'LL HAVE HIM COME SEE YOU LATER!
I-I NEED TO SEE HER RADIANCE THE QUEEN, AT ONCE. IT'S BEEN MERE HOURS SINCE MY LAST SESSION WITH HER. I MUST FEEL HER LASH AGAIN!
I WARN YOU, I WILL NOT BE DENIED!

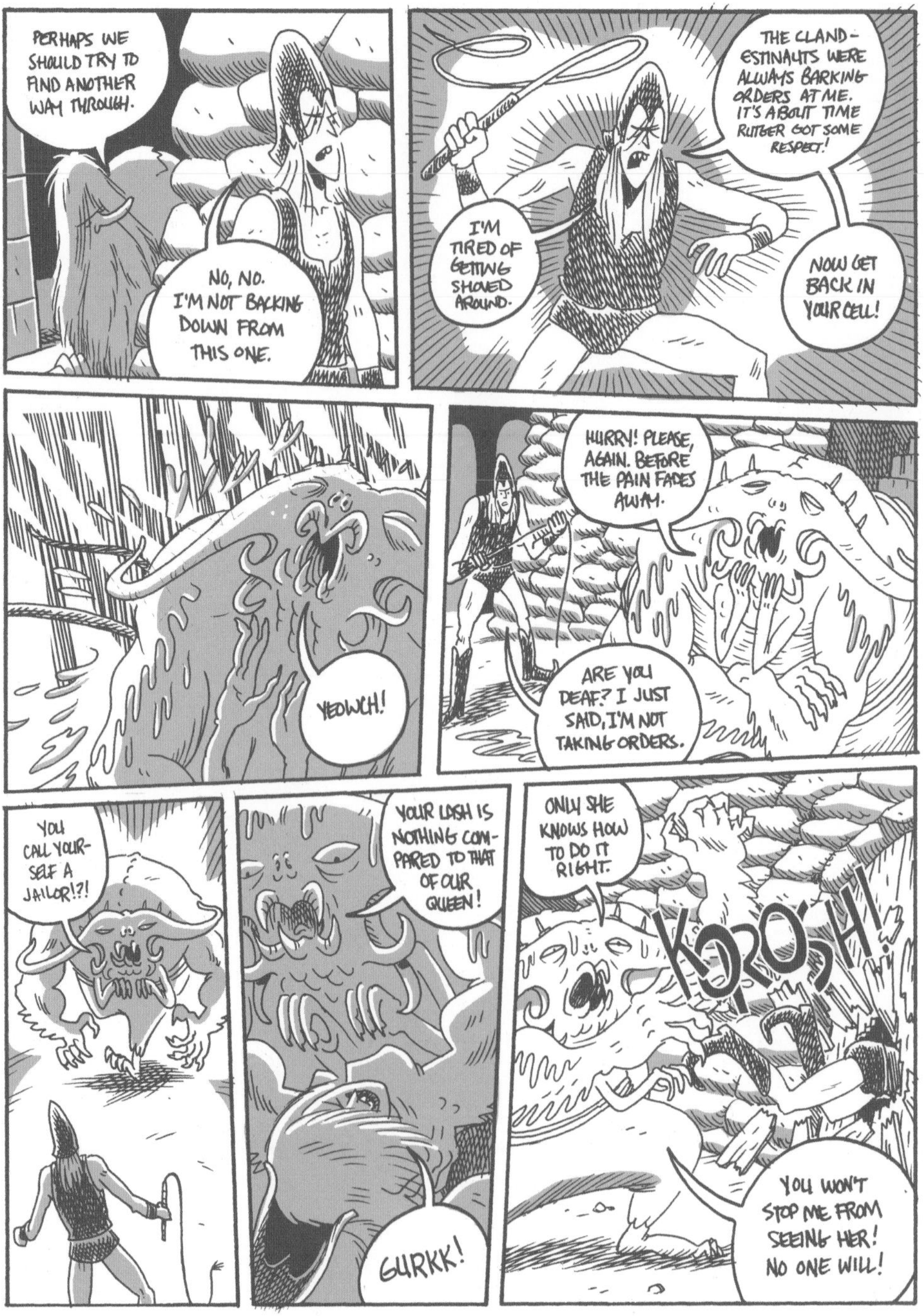
PERHAPS WE SHOULD TRY TO FIND ANOTHER WAY THROUGH.
NO, NO. I'M NOT BACKING DOWN FROM THIS ONE.
THE CLAND-ESTINAUTS WERE ALWAYS BARKING ORDERS AT ME. IT'S ABOUT TIME RUTGER GOT SOME RESPECT!
I'M TIRED OF GETTING SHOVED AROUND.
NOW GET BACK IN YOUR CELL!
YEOWCH!
HURRY! PLEASE, AGAIN. BEFORE THE PAIN FADES AWAY.
ARE YOU DEAF? I JUST SAID, I'M NOT TAKING ORDERS.
YOU CALL YOURSELF A JAILOR!?!
YOUR LASH IS NOTHING COMPARED TO THAT OF OUR QUEEN!
GURKK!
ONLY SHE KNOWS HOW TO DO IT RIGHT.
KOROSH!
YOU WON'T STOP ME FROM SEEING HER! NO ONE WILL!

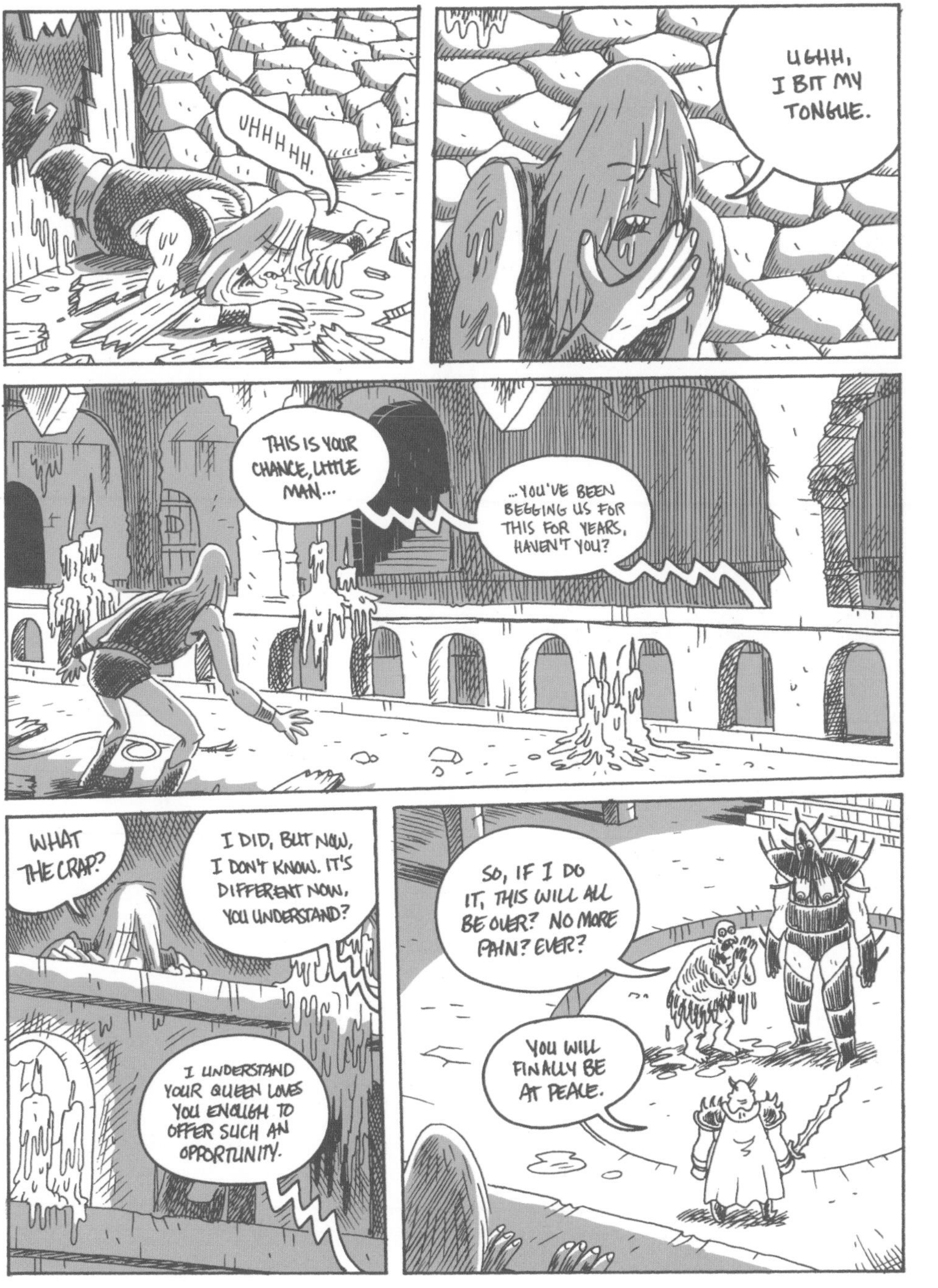

UHHHHHH.
UGHH, I BIT MY TONGUE.
THIS IS YOUR CHANCE, LITTLE MAN...
...YOU'VE BEEN BEGGING US FOR THIS FOR YEARS, HAVEN'T YOU?
WHAT THE CRAP?
I DID, BUT NOW, I DON'T KNOW. IT'S DIFFERENT NOW, YOU UNDERSTAND?
I UNDERSTAND YOUR QUEEN LOVES YOU ENOUGH TO OFFER SUCH AN OPPORTUNITY.
SO, IF I DO IT, THIS WILL ALL BE OVER? NO MORE PAIN? EVER?
YOU WILL FINALLY BE AT PEACE.

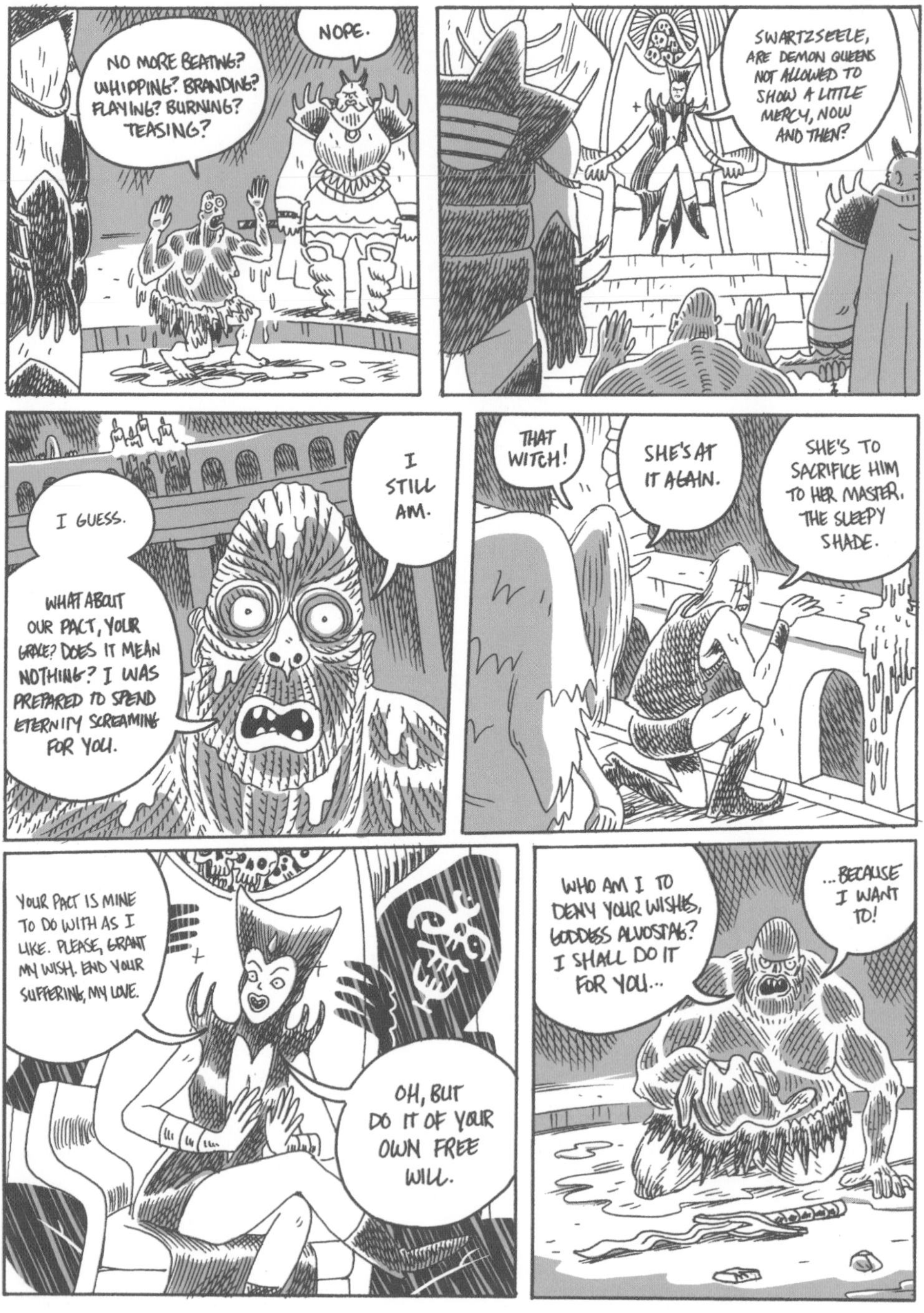
NO MORE BEATING? WHIPPING? BRANDING? FLAYING? BURNING? TEASING?
NOPE.
SWARTZSEELE, ARE DEMON QUEENS NOT ALLOWED TO SHOW A LITTLE MERCY, NOW AND THEN?
I GUESS.
WHAT ABOUT OUR PACT, YOUR GRACE? DOES IT MEAN NOTHING? I WAS PREPARED TO SPEND ETERNITY SCREAMING FOR YOU.
I STILL AM.
THAT WITCH!
SHE'S AT IT AGAIN.
SHE'S TO SACRIFICE HIM TO HER MASTER, THE SLEEPY SHADE.
YOUR PACT IS MINE TO DO WITH AS I LIKE. PLEASE, GRANT MY WISH. END YOUR SUFFERING, MY LOVE.
OH, BUT DO IT OF YOUR OWN FREE WILL.
WHO AM I TO DENY YOUR WISHES, GODDESS ALVOSTAG? I SHALL DO IT FOR YOU...
...BECAUSE I WANT TO!

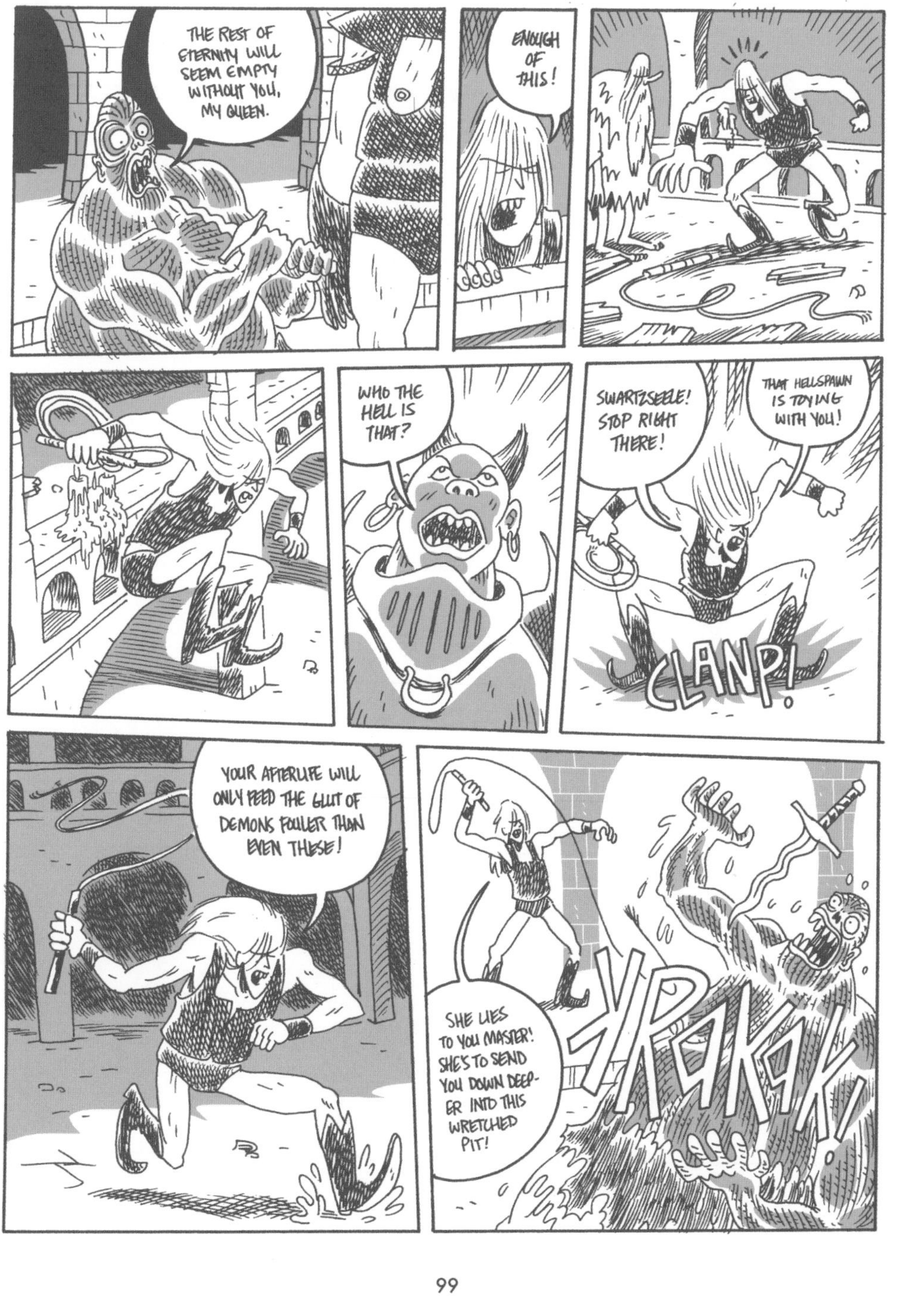
THE REST OF ETERNITY WILL SEEM EMPTY WITHOUT YOU, MY QUEEN.
ENOUGH OF THIS!
WHO THE HELL IS THAT?
SWARTZSEELE! STOP RIGHT THERE!
THAT HELLSPAWN IS TOYING WITH YOU!
CLANP!
YOUR AFTERLIFE WILL ONLY FEED THE GLUT OF DEMONS FOULER THAN EVEN THESE!
SHE LIES TO YOU MASTER! SHE'S TO SEND YOU DOWN DEEP-ER INTO THIS WRETCHED PIT!
YRAKAK!

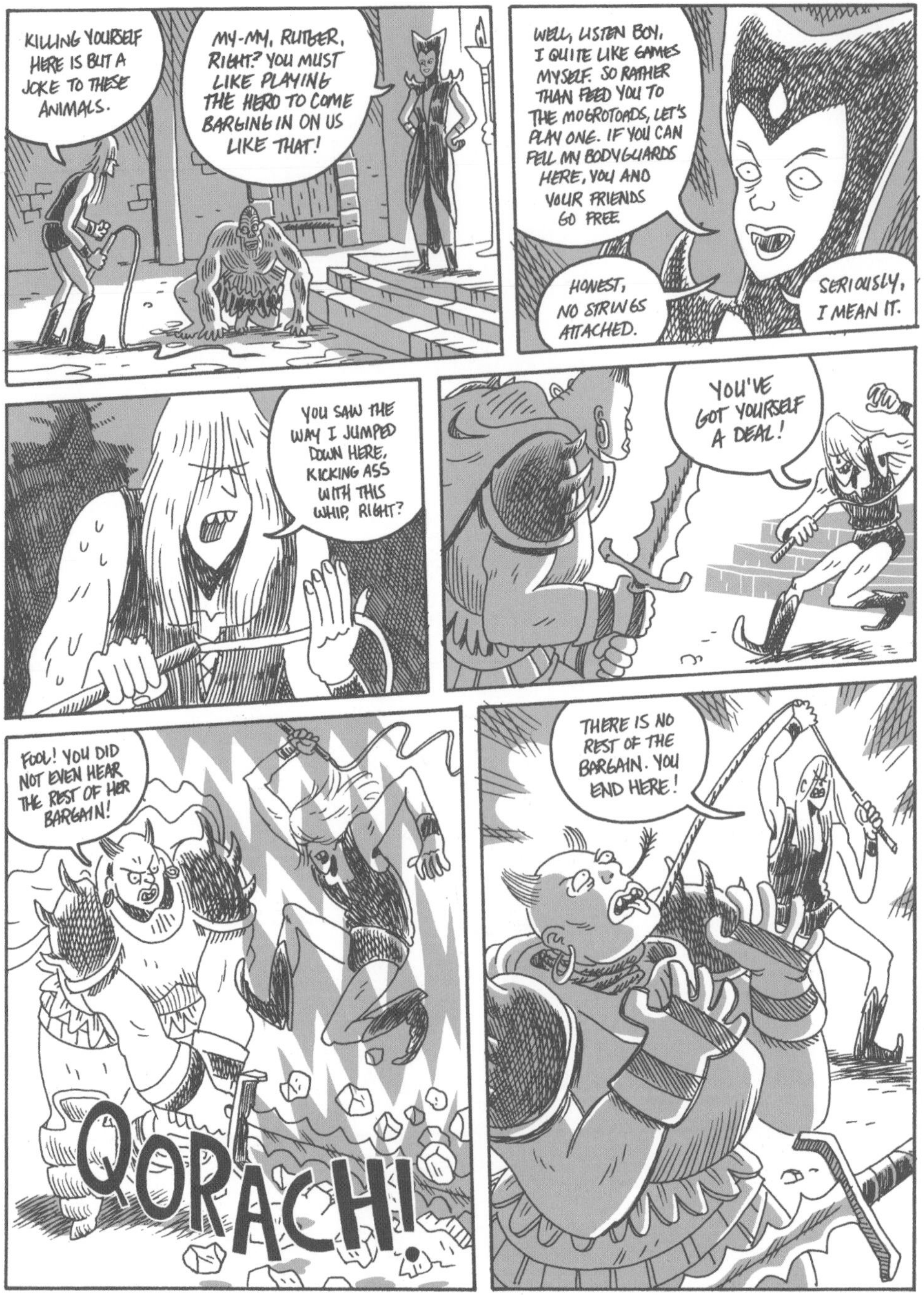
KILLING YOURSELF HERE IS BUT A JOKE TO THESE ANIMALS.
MY-MY, RUTGER, RIGHT? YOU MUST LIKE PLAYING THE HERO TO COME BARGING IN ON US LIKE THAT!
WELL, LISTEN BOY, I QUITE LIKE GAMES MYSELF. SO RATHER THAN FEED YOU TO THE MOGROTOADS, LET'S PLAY ONE. IF YOU CAN FELL MY BODYGUARDS HERE, YOU AND YOUR FRIENDS GO FREE.
HONEST, NO STRINGS ATTACHED.
SERIOUSLY, I MEAN IT.
YOU SAW THE WAY I JUMPED DOWN HERE, KICKING ASS WITH THIS WHIP, RIGHT?
YOU'VE GOT YOURSELF A DEAL!
FOOL! YOU DID NOT EVEN HEAR THE REST OF HER BARGAIN!
QORACH!
THERE IS NO REST OF THE BARGAIN. YOU END HERE!

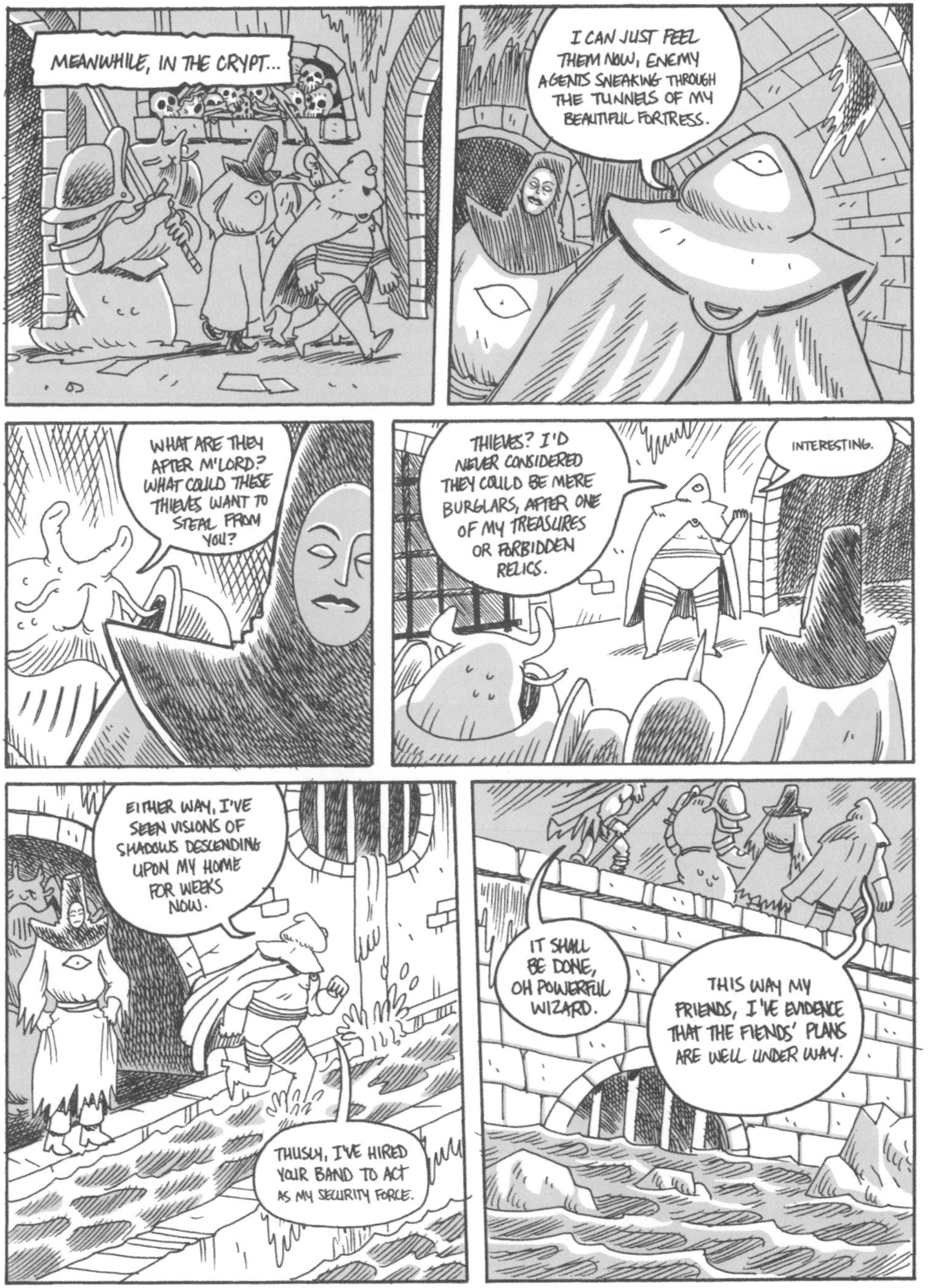
MEANWHILE, IN THE CRYPT...
I CAN JUST FEEL THEM NOW, ENEMY AGENTS SNEAKING THROUGH THE TUNNELS OF MY BEAUTIFUL FORTRESS.
WHAT ARE THEY AFTER M'LORD? WHAT COULD THESE THIEVES WANT TO STEAL FROM YOU?
THIEVES? I'D NEVER CONSIDERED THEY COULD BE MERE BURGLARS, AFTER ONE OF MY TREASURES OR FORBIDDEN RELICS.
INTERESTING.
EITHER WAY, I'VE SEEN VISIONS OF SHADOWS DESCENDING UPON MY HOME FOR WEEKS NOW.
THUSLY, I'VE HIRED YOUR BAND TO ACT AS MY SECURITY FORCE.
IT SHALL BE DONE, OH POWERFUL WIZARD.
THIS WAY MY FRIENDS, I'VE EVIDENCE THAT THE FIENDS' PLANS ARE WELL UNDER WAY.

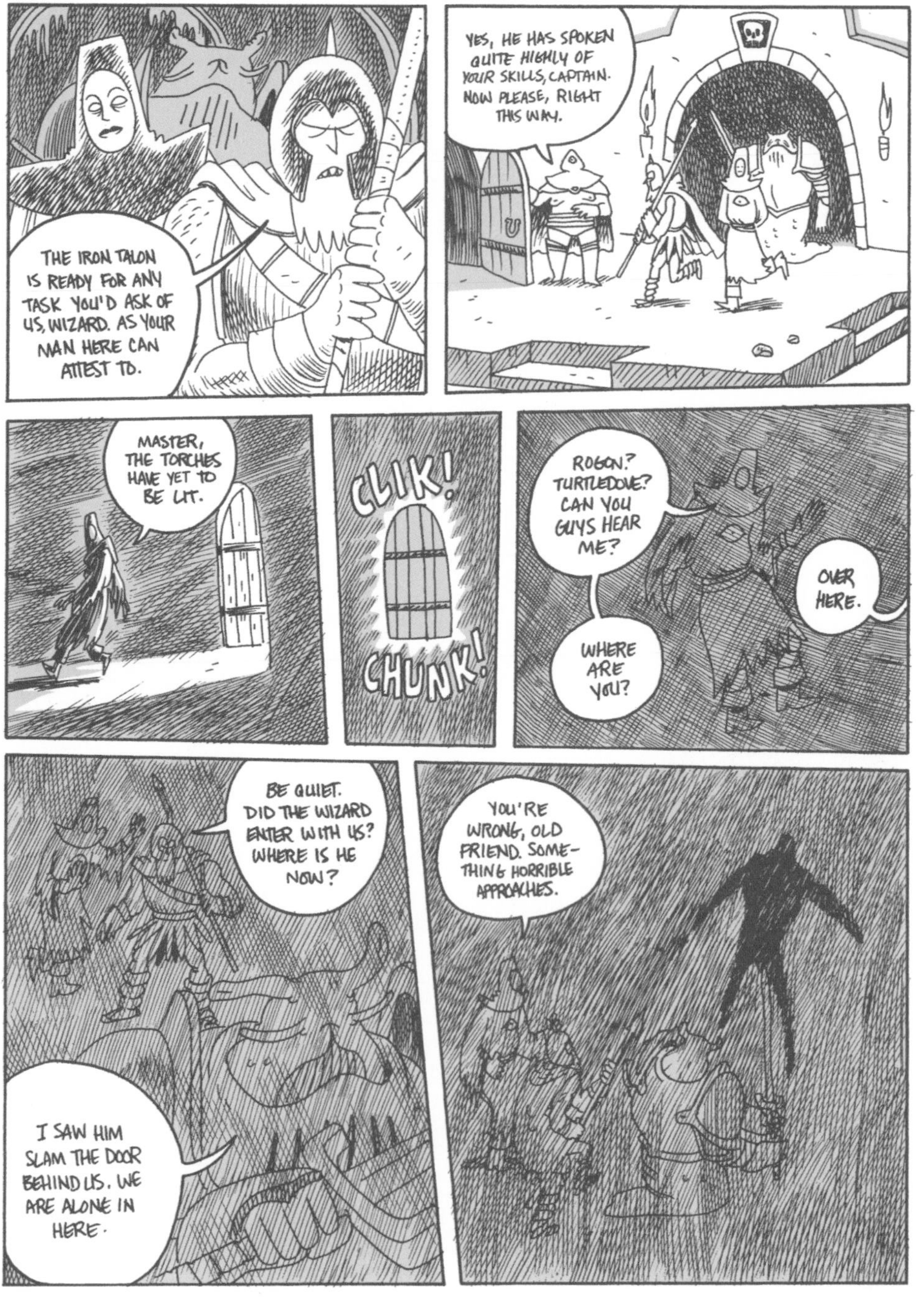
THE IRON TALON IS READY FOR ANY TASK YOU'D ASK OF US, WIZARD. AS YOUR MAN HERE CAN ATTEST TO.
YES, HE HAS SPOKEN QUITE HIGHLY OF YOUR SKILLS, CAPTAIN. NOW PLEASE, RIGHT THIS WAY.
MASTER, THE TORCHES HAVE YET TO BE LIT.
CLIK!
CHUNK!
ROGON? TURTLEDOVE? CAN YOU GUYS HEAR ME?
WHERE ARE YOU?
OVER HERE.
BE QUIET. DID THE WIZARD ENTER WITH US? WHERE IS HE NOW?
I SAW HIM SLAM THE DOOR BEHIND US. WE ARE ALONE IN HERE.
YOU'RE WRONG, OLD FRIEND. SOME-THING HORRIBLE APPROACHES.

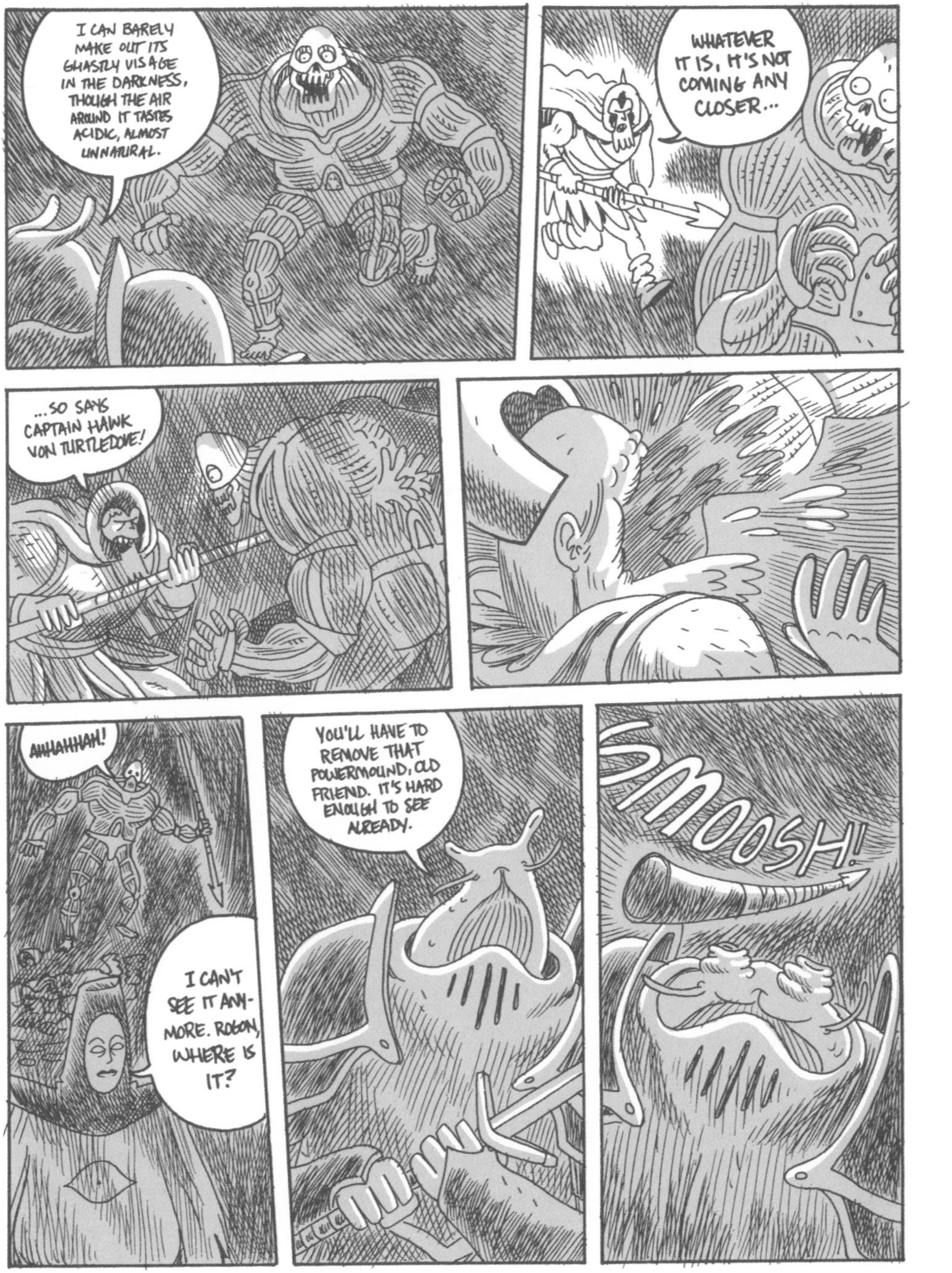
I CAN BARELY MAKE OUT ITS GHASTLY VISAGE IN THE DARKNESS, THOUGH THE AIR AROUND IT TASTES ACIDIC, ALMOST UNNATURAL.
WHATEVER IT IS, IT'S NOT COMING ANY CLOSER...
...SO SAYS CAPTAIN HAWK VON TURTLEDOVE!
AAAHAHHAH!
I CAN'T SEE IT ANY-MORE. ROGON, WHERE IS IT?
YOU'LL HAVE TO REMOVE THAT POWERMOUND, OLD FRIEND. IT'S HARD ENOUGH TO SEE ALREADY.
SMOOSH!

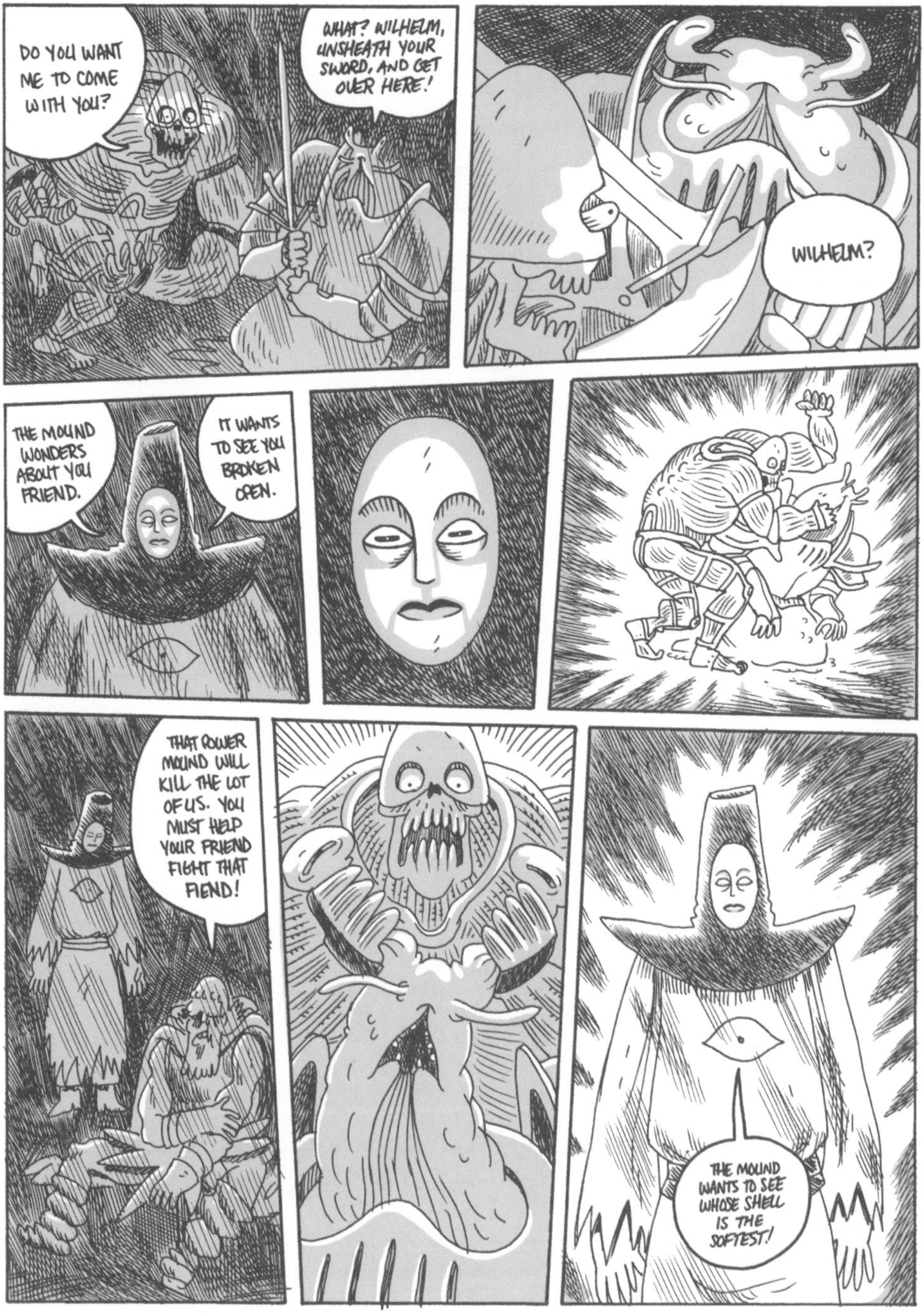
DO YOU WANT ME TO COME WITH YOU?
WHAT? WILHELM, UNSHEATH YOUR SWORD, AND GET OVER HERE!
WILHELM?
THE MOUND WONDERS ABOUT YOU FRIEND.
IT WANTS TO SEE YOU BROKEN OPEN.
THAT POWER MOUND WILL KILL THE LOT OF US. YOU MUST HELP YOUR FRIEND FIGHT THAT FIEND!
THE MOUND WANTS TO SEE WHOSE SHELL IS THE SOFTEST!

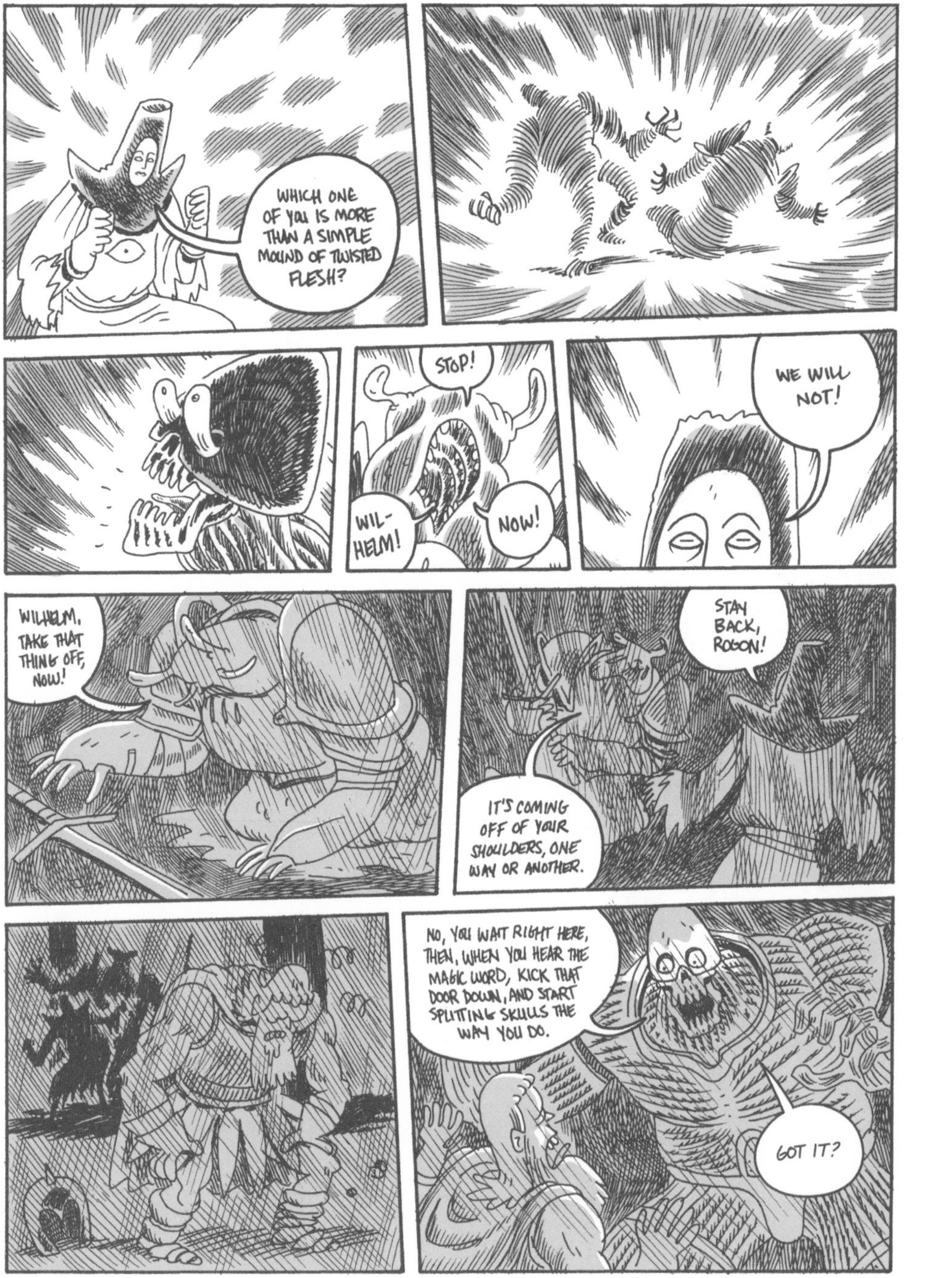
WHICH ONE OF YOU IS MORE THAN A SIMPLE MOUND OF TWISTED FLESH?
STOP!
WIL-HELM!
NOW!
WE WILL NOT!
WILHELM, TAKE THAT THING OFF, NOW!
STAY BACK, ROGON!
IT'S COMING OFF OF YOUR SHOULDERS, ONE WAY OR ANOTHER.
NO, YOU WAIT RIGHT HERE, THEN, WHEN YOU HEAR THE MAGIC WORD, KICK THAT DOOR DOWN, AND START SPLITTING SKULLS THE WAY YOU DO.
GOT IT?

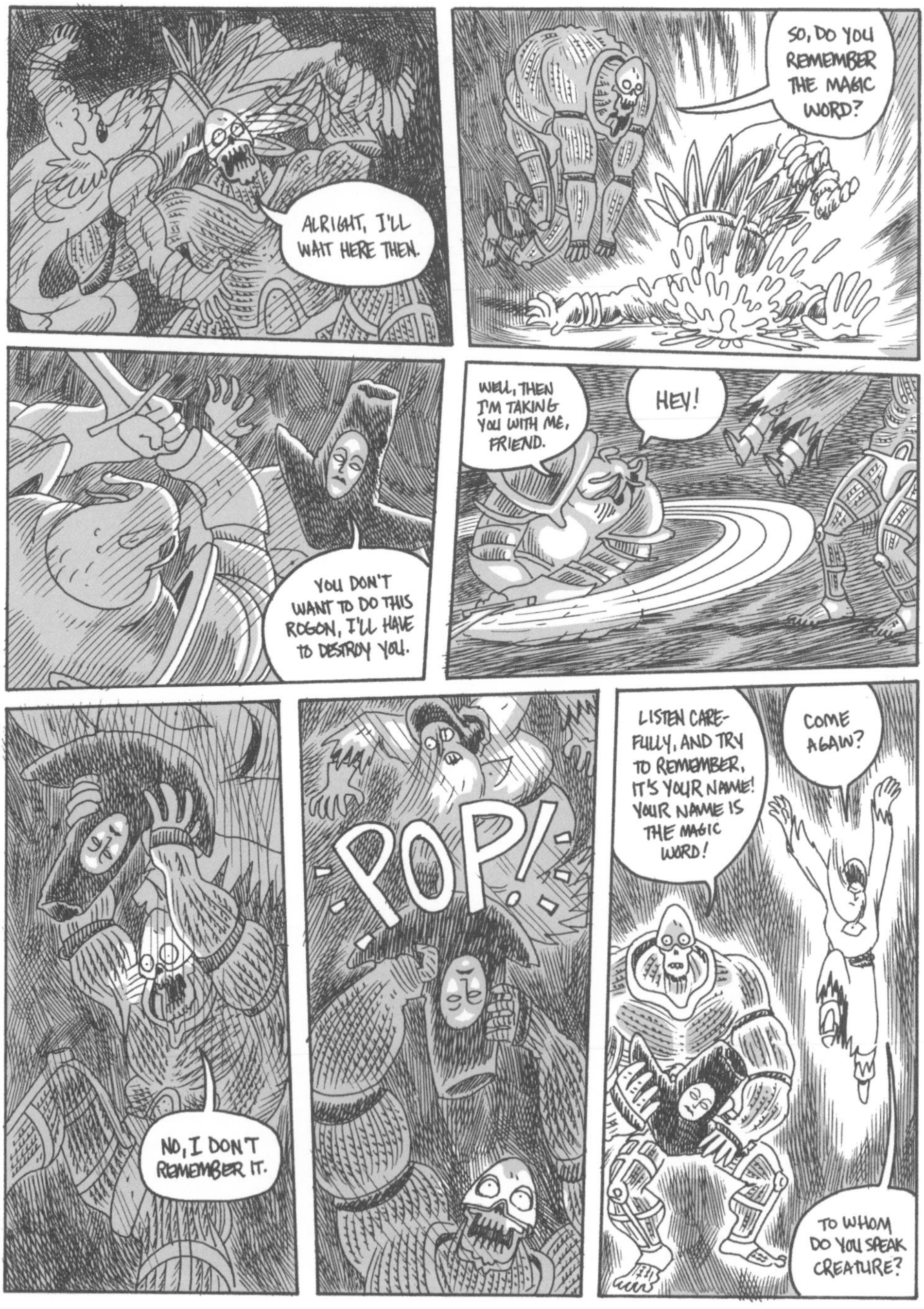
ALRIGHT, I'LL WAIT HERE THEN.
SO, DO YOU REMEMBER THE MAGIC WORD?
YOU DON'T WANT TO DO THIS ROGON, I'LL HAVE TO DESTROY YOU.
WELL, THEN I'M TAKING YOU WITH ME, FRIEND.
HEY!
NO, I DON'T REMEMBER IT.
POP!
LISTEN CARE-FULLY, AND TRY TO REMEMBER, IT'S YOUR NAME! YOUR NAME IS THE MAGIC WORD!
COME AGAIN?
TO WHOM DO YOU SPEAK CREATURE?

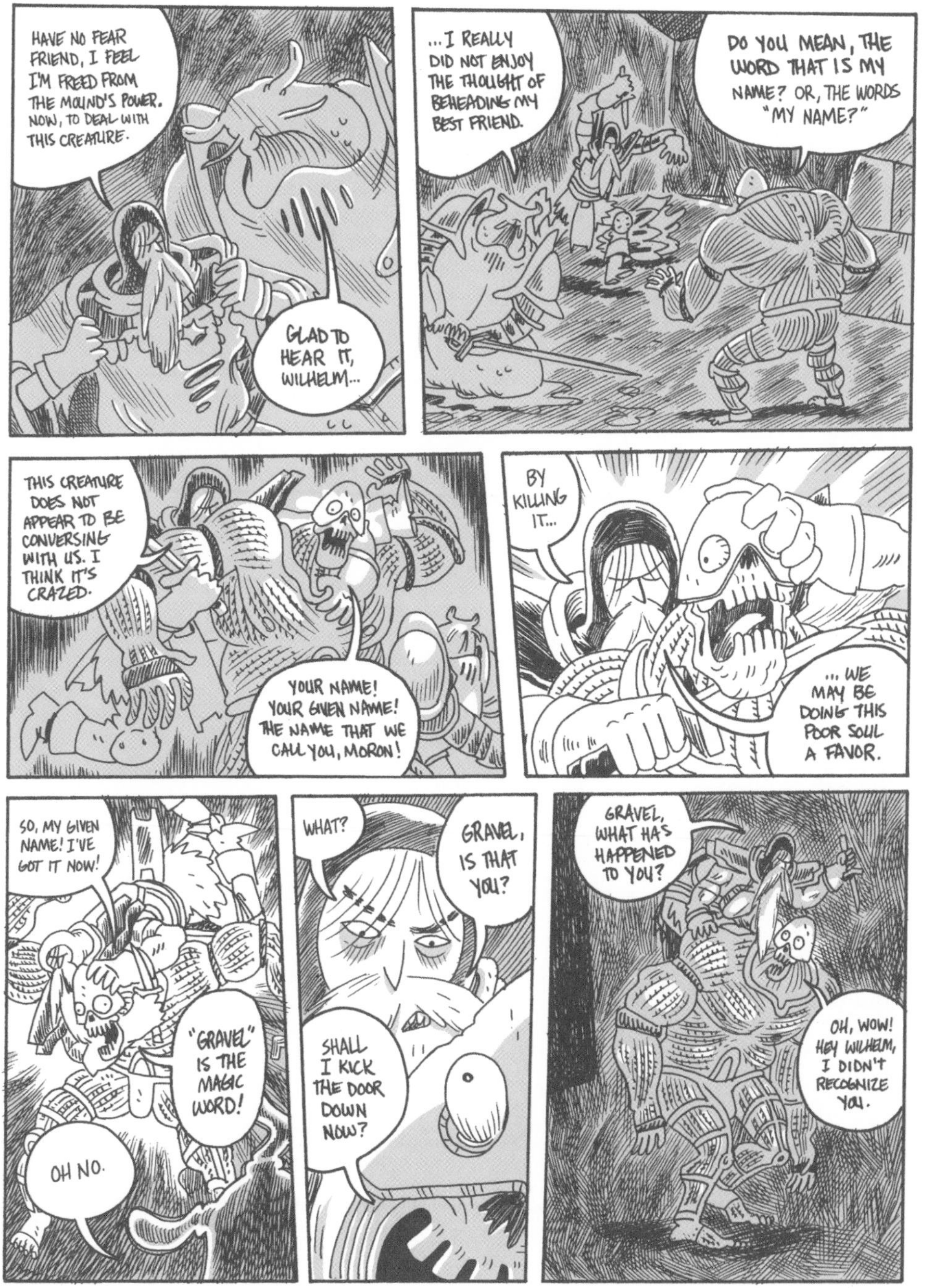
HAVE NO FEAR FRIEND, I FEEL I'M FREED FROM THE MOUND'S POWER. NOW, TO DEAL WITH THIS CREATURE.
GLAD TO HEAR IT, WILHELM...
...I REALLY DID NOT ENJOY THE THOUGHT OF BEHEADING MY BEST FRIEND.
DO YOU MEAN, THE WORD THAT IS MY NAME? OR, THE WORDS "MY NAME?"
THIS CREATURE DOES NOT APPEAR TO BE CONVERSING WITH US. I THINK IT'S CRAZED.
YOUR NAME! YOUR GIVEN NAME! THE NAME THAT WE CALL YOU, MORON!
BY KILLING IT...
...WE MAY BE DOING THIS POOR SOUL A FAVOR.
SO, MY GIVEN NAME! I'VE GOT IT NOW!
"GRAVEL" IS THE MAGIC WORD!
OH NO.
WHAT?
GRAVEL, IS THAT YOU?
SHALL I KICK THE DOOR DOWN NOW?
GRAVEL, WHAT HAS HAPPENED TO YOU?
OH, WOW! HEY WILHELM, I DIDN'T RECOGNIZE YOU.

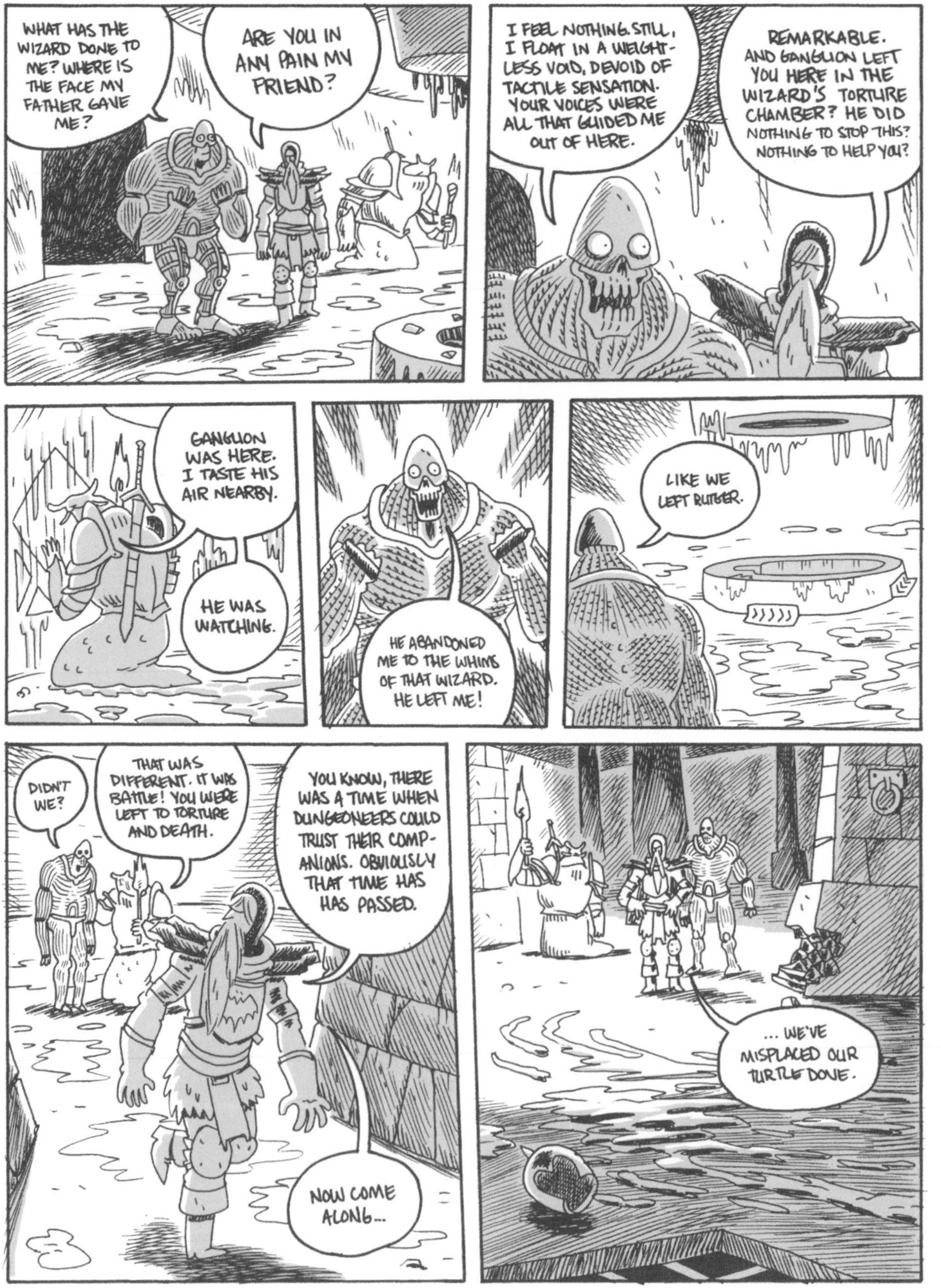
WHAT HAS THE WIZARD DONE TO ME? WHERE IS THE FACE MY FATHER GAVE ME?
ARE YOU IN ANY PAIN MY FRIEND?
I FEEL NOTHING. STILL, I FLOAT IN A WEIGHTLESS VOID, DEVOID OF TACTILE SENSATION. YOUR VOICES WERE ALL THAT GUIDED ME OUT OF HERE.
REMARKABLE. AND GANGLION LEFT YOU HERE IN THE WIZARD'S TORTURE CHAMBER? HE DID NOTHING TO STOP THIS? NOTHING TO HELP YOU?
GANGLION WAS HERE. I TASTE HIS AIR NEARBY.
HE WAS WATCHING.
HE ABANDONED ME TO THE WHIMS OF THAT WIZARD. HE LEFT ME!
LIKE WE LEFT RUTGER.
DIDN'T WE?
THAT WAS DIFFERENT. IT WAS BATTLE! YOU WERE LEFT TO TORTURE AND DEATH.
YOU KNOW, THERE WAS A TIME WHEN DUNGEONEERS COULD TRUST THEIR COMPANIONS. OBVIOUSLY THAT TIME HAS HAS PASSED.
NOW COME ALONG...
... WE'VE MISPLACED OUR TURTLE DOVE.

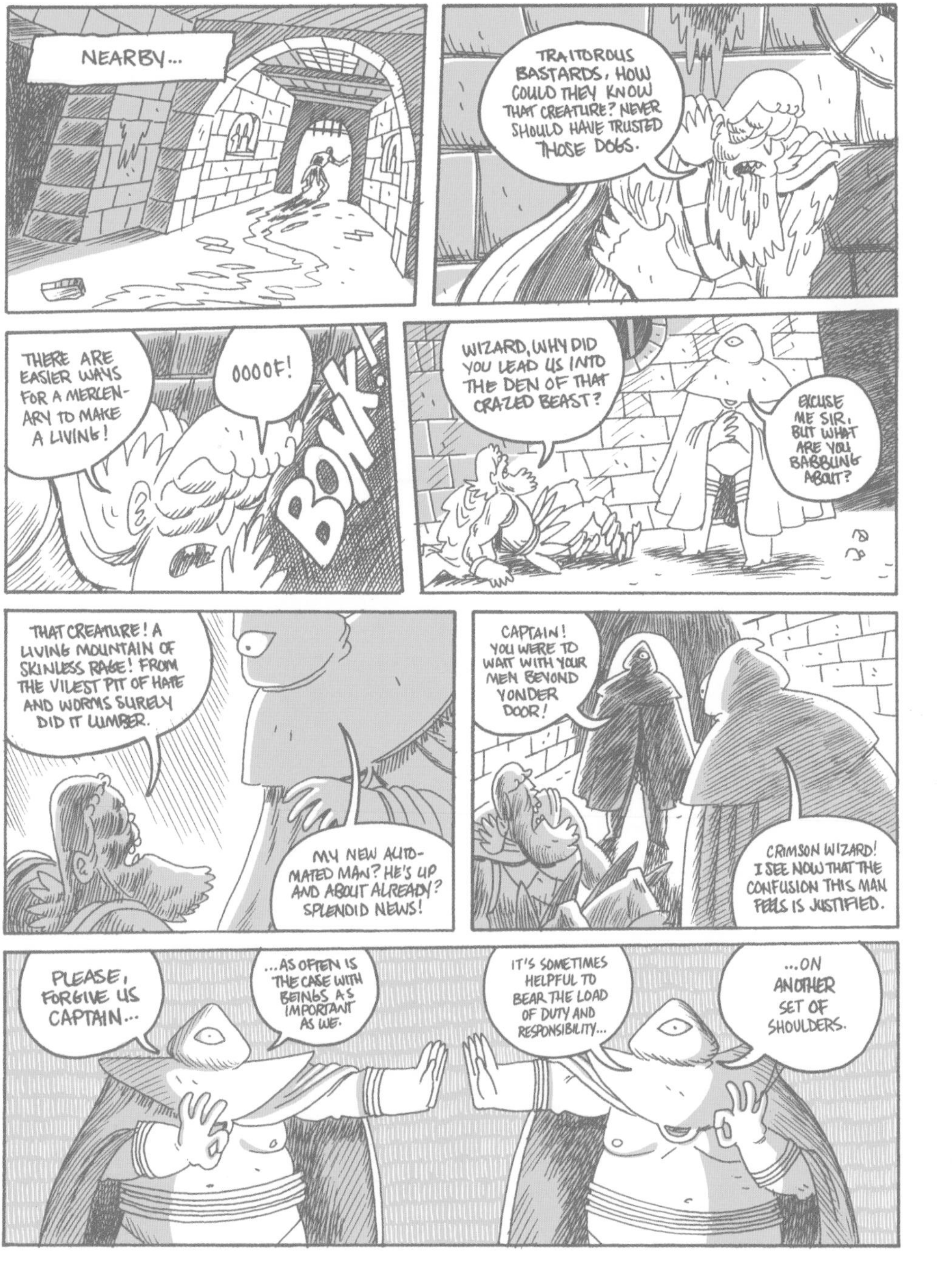
NEARBY...
TRAITOROUS BASTARDS, HOW COULD THEY KNOW THAT CREATURE? NEVER SHOULD HAVE TRUSTED THOSE DOGS.
THERE ARE EASIER WAYS FOR A MERCENARY TO MAKE A LIVING!
OOOOF!
BONK!
WIZARD, WHY DID YOU LEAD US INTO THE DEN OF THAT CRAZED BEAST?
EXCUSE ME SIR, BUT WHAT ARE YOU BABBLING ABOUT?
THAT CREATURE! A LIVING MOUNTAIN OF SKINLESS RAGE! FROM THE VILEST PIT OF HATE AND WORMS SURELY DID IT LUMBER.
MY NEW AUTOMATED MAN? HE'S UP AND ABOUT ALREADY? SPLENDID NEWS!
CAPTAIN! YOU WERE TO WAIT WITH YOUR MEN BEYOND YONDER DOOR!
CRIMSON WIZARD! I SEE NOW THAT THE CONFUSION THIS MAN FEELS IS JUSTIFIED.
PLEASE, FORGIVE US CAPTAIN...
...AS OFTEN IS THE CASE WITH BEINGS AS IMPORTANT AS WE.
IT'S SOMETIMES HELPFUL TO BEAR THE LOAD OF DUTY AND RESPONSIBILITY...
...ON ANOTHER SET OF SHOULDERS.

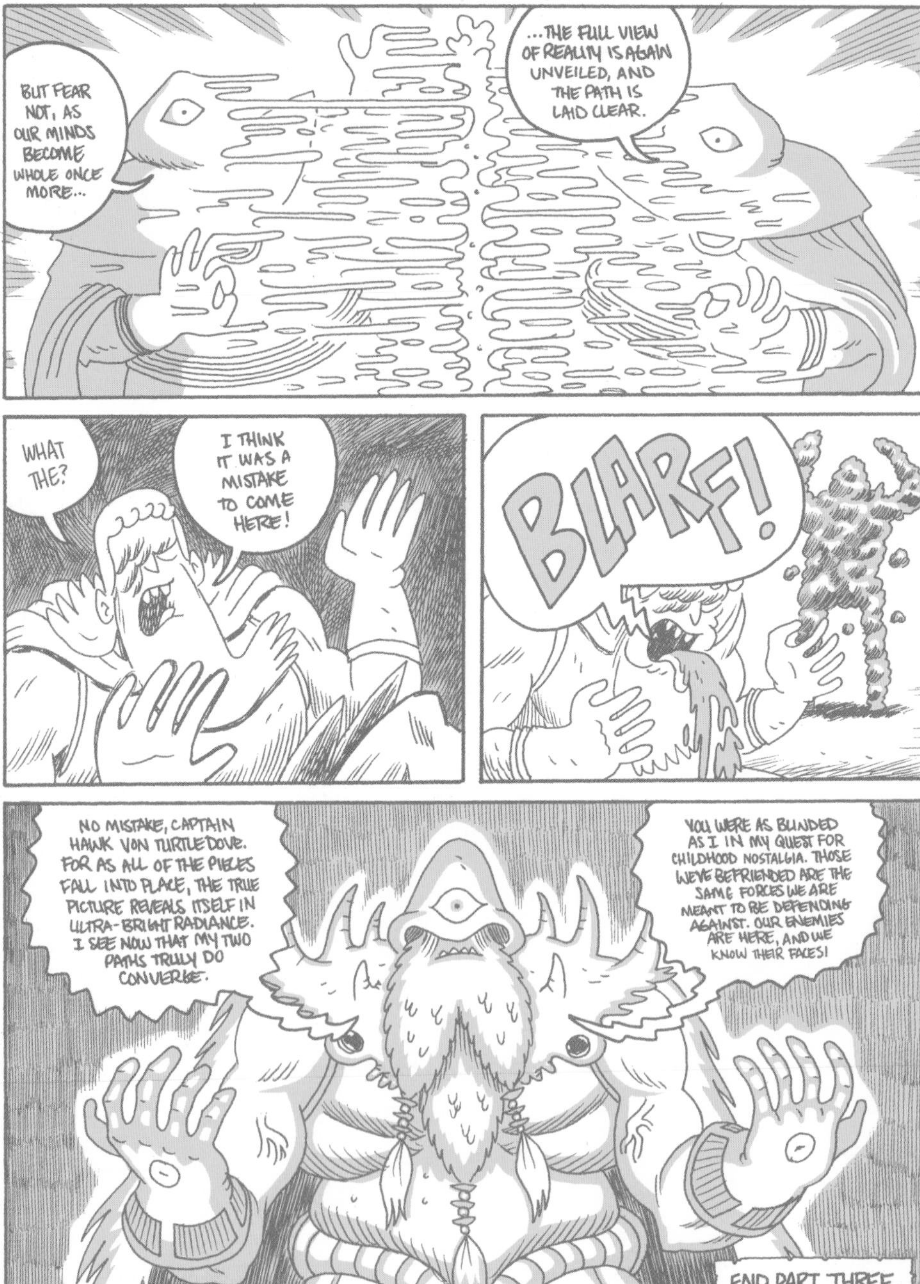
BUT FEAR NOT, AS OUR MINDS BECOME WHOLE ONCE MORE...
...THE FULL VIEW OF REALITY IS AGAIN UNVEILED, AND THE PATH IS LAID CLEAR.
WHAT THE?
I THINK IT WAS A MISTAKE TO COME HERE!
BLARF!
NO MISTAKE, CAPTAIN HAWK VON TURTLEDOVE. FOR AS ALL OF THE PIECES FALL INTO PLACE, THE TRUE PICTURE REVEALS ITSELF IN ULTRA-BRIGHT RADIANCE. I SEE NOW THAT MY TWO PATHS TRULY DO CONVERGE.
YOU WERE AS BLINDED AS I IN MY QUEST FOR CHILDHOOD NOSTALGIA. THOSE WE'VE BEFRIENDED ARE THE SAME FORCES WE ARE MEANT TO BE DEFENDING AGAINST. OUR ENEMIES ARE HERE, AND WE KNOW THEIR FACES!
END PART THREE.

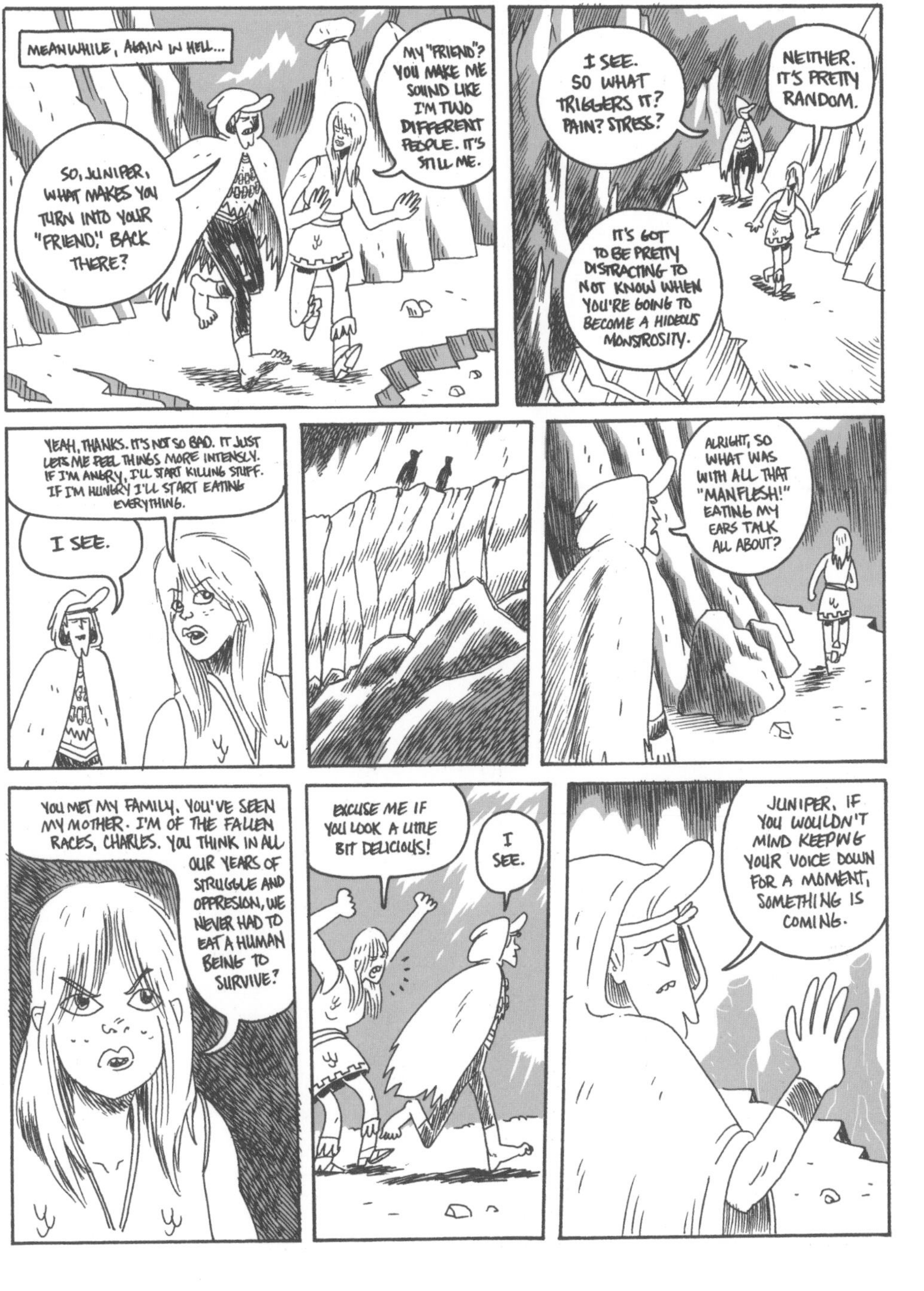

MEANWHILE, AGAIN IN HELL...
SO, JUNIPER, WHAT MAKES YOU TURN INTO YOUR "FRIEND," BACK THERE?
MY "FRIEND"? YOU MAKE ME SOUND LIKE I'M TWO DIFFERENT PEOPLE. IT'S STILL ME.
I SEE. SO WHAT TRIGGERS IT? PAIN? STRESS?
NEITHER. IT'S PRETTY RANDOM.
IT'S GOT TO BE PRETTY DISTRACTING TO NOT KNOW WHEN YOU'RE GOING TO BECOME A HIDEOUS MONSTROSITY.
YEAH, THANKS. IT'S NOT SO BAD. IT JUST LETS ME FEEL THINGS MORE INTENSLY. IF I'M ANGRY, I'LL START KILLING STUFF. IF I'M HUNGRY I'LL START EATING EVERYTHING.
I SEE.
ALRIGHT, SO WHAT WAS WITH ALL THAT "MANFLESH!" EATING MY EARS TALK ALL ABOUT?
YOU MET MY FAMILY. YOU'VE SEEN MY MOTHER. I'M OF THE FALLEN RACES, CHARLES. YOU THINK IN ALL OUR YEARS OF STRUGGLE AND OPPRESION, WE NEVER HAD TO EAT A HUMAN BEING TO SURVIVE?
EXCUSE ME IF YOU LOOK A LITTLE BIT DELICIOUS!
I SEE.
JUNIPER, IF YOU WOULDN'T MIND KEEPING YOUR VOICE DOWN FOR A MOMENT, SOMETHING IS COMING.

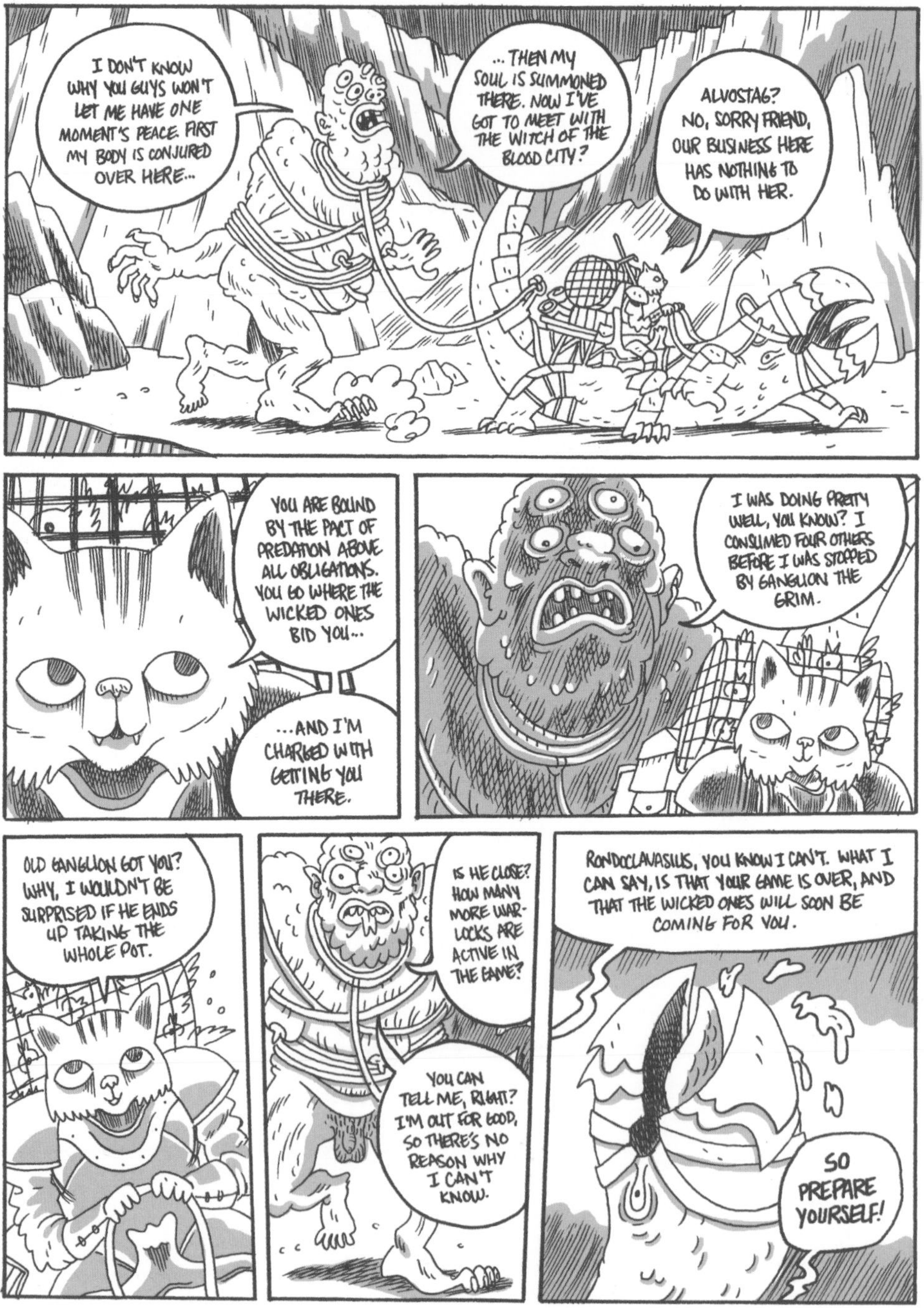
I DON'T KNOW WHY YOU GUYS WON'T LET ME HAVE ONE MOMENT'S PEACE. FIRST MY BODY IS CONJURED OVER HERE...
...THEN MY SOUL IS SUMMONED THERE. NOW I'VE GOT TO MEET WITH THE WITCH OF THE BLOOD CITY?
ALVOSTAG? NO, SORRY FRIEND, OUR BUSINESS HERE HAS NOTHING TO DO WITH HER.
YOU ARE BOUND BY THE PACT OF PREDATION ABOVE ALL OBLIGATIONS. YOU GO WHERE THE WICKED ONES BID YOU...
...AND I'M CHARGED WITH GETTING YOU THERE.
I WAS DOING PRETTY WELL, YOU KNOW? I CONSUMED FOUR OTHERS BEFORE I WAS STOPPED BY GANGLION THE GRIM.
OLD GANGLION GOT YOU? WHY, I WOULDN'T BE SURPRISED IF HE ENDS UP TAKING THE WHOLE POT.
IS HE CLOSE? HOW MANY MORE WAR-LOCKS ARE ACTIVE IN THE GAME?
YOU CAN TELL ME, RIGHT? I'M OUT FOR GOOD, SO THERE'S NO REASON WHY I CAN'T KNOW.
RONDOCLAVASILUS, YOU KNOW I CAN'T. WHAT I CAN SAY, IS THAT YOUR GAME IS OVER, AND THAT THE WICKED ONES WILL SOON BE COMING FOR YOU.
SO PREPARE YOURSELF!

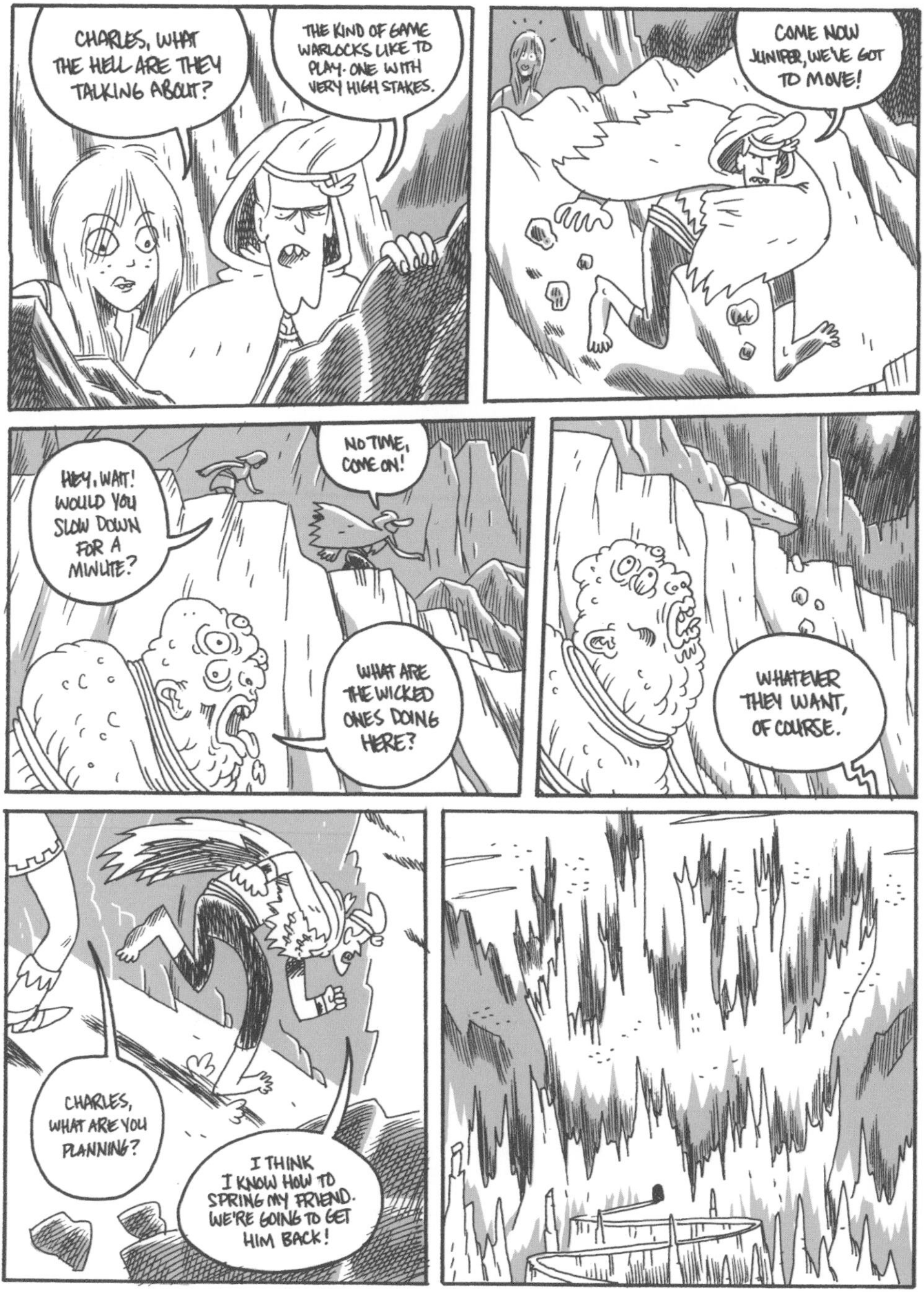
CHARLES, WHAT THE HELL ARE THEY TALKING ABOUT?
THE KIND OF GAME WARLOCKS LIKE TO PLAY. ONE WITH VERY HIGH STAKES.
COME NOW JUNIPER, WE'VE GOT TO MOVE!
HEY, WAIT! WOULD YOU SLOW DOWN FOR A MINUTE?
NO TIME, COME ON!
WHAT ARE THE WICKED ONES DOING HERE?
WHATEVER THEY WANT, OF COURSE.
CHARLES, WHAT ARE YOU PLANNING?
I THINK I KNOW HOW TO SPRING MY FRIEND. WE'RE GOING TO GET HIM BACK!

IN THE GARDEN...

THE TREES BLOOM BEAUTIFULLY THIS SEASON. OUR GARDENER WAS A REAL MIRACLE WORKER, DON'T YOU THINK?

ARE YOU EVEN LISTENING TO ME? IT IS NOT POLITE TO TREAT ME WITH SUCH SILENCE!

OH, I'M SORRY, I AM JUST A BIT DISTRACTED IS ALL.

MY STOMACH IS GROWLING LIKE A CALEBEAR.

WE WILL SOON BE OUTSIDE, FOOD VENDORS CAN BE FOUND THERE.

I KNOW, BUT THE THOUGHT OF A HOT MEAL ONLY MAKES MY GUTS BURN EVEN MORE.

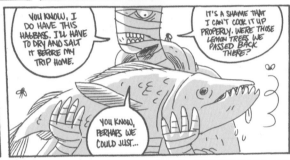

YOU KNOW, I DO HAVE THIS HAGBASS. I'LL HAVE TO DRY AND SALT IT BEFORE MY TRIP HOME.

IT'S A SHAME THAT I CAN'T COOK IT UP PROPERLY. WERE THOSE LEMON TREES WE PASSED BACK THERE?

YOU KNOW, PERHAPS WE COULD JUST...

WE COULD JUST ROAST IT UP HERE, IN THE GARDEN. THE WIZARD WON'T BE PASSING BACK THROUGH HERE FOR A FEW HOURS.

HE DOESN'T EVEN NEED TO KNOW.

WHAT A GREAT IDEA! WE CAN— OOPS! CLUMSY ME.

SPLAT!

WHY DON'T YOU START THE FIRE, AND I'LL PICK SOME OF THOSE LEMONS, AND LOOK FOR A FEW SAVORY HERBS.

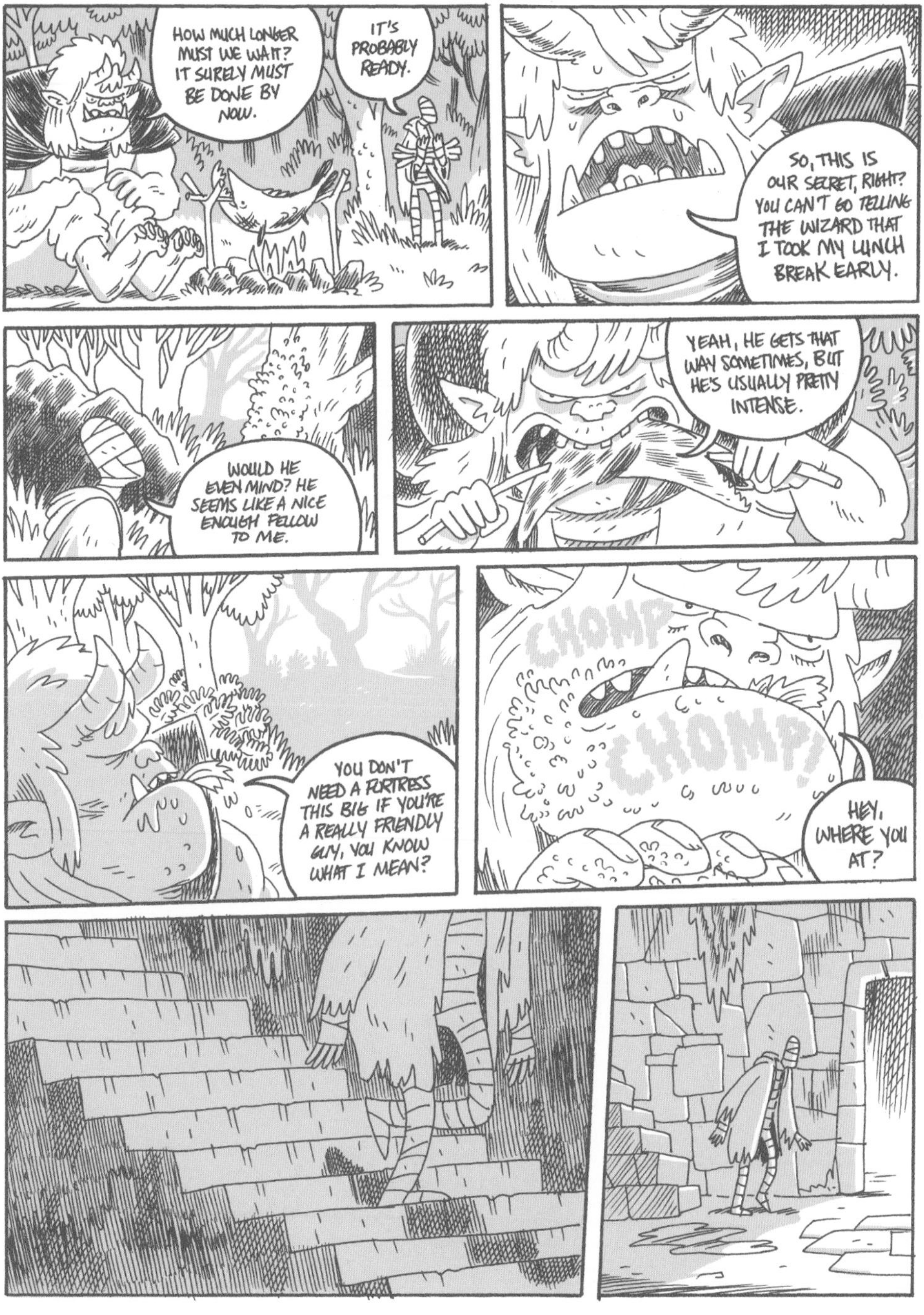
HOW MUCH LONGER MUST WE WAIT? IT SURELY MUST BE DONE BY NOW.
IT'S PROBABLY READY.
SO, THIS IS OUR SECRET, RIGHT? YOU CAN'T GO TELLING THE WIZARD THAT I TOOK MY LUNCH BREAK EARLY.
WOULD HE EVEN MIND? HE SEEMS LIKE A NICE ENOUGH FELLOW TO ME.
YEAH, HE GETS THAT WAY SOMETIMES, BUT HE'S USUALLY PRETTY INTENSE.
YOU DON'T NEED A FORTRESS THIS BIG IF YOU'RE A REALLY FRIENDLY GUY, YOU KNOW WHAT I MEAN?
CHOMP
CHOMP!
HEY, WHERE YOU AT?

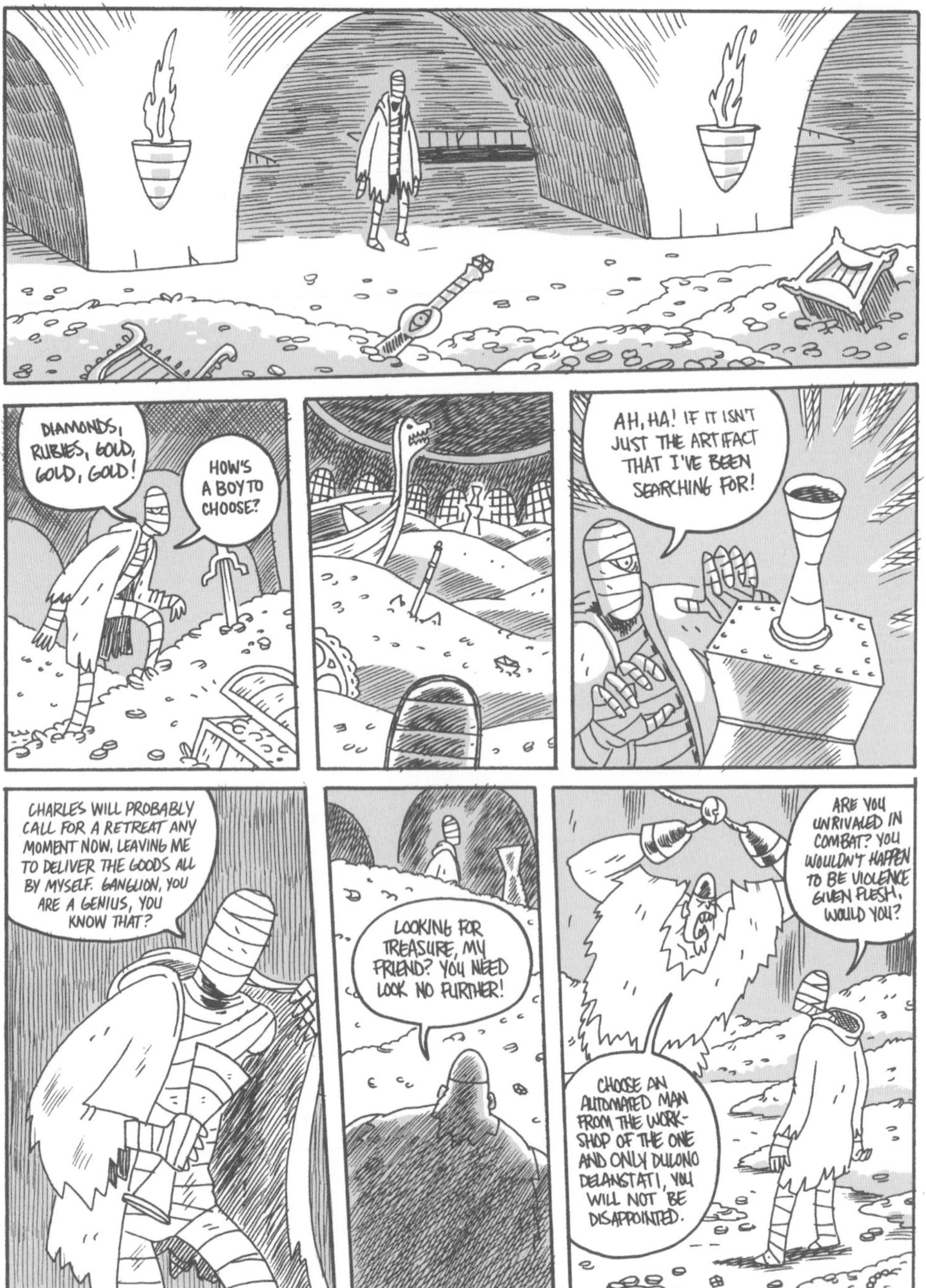
DIAMONDS, RUBIES, GOLD, GOLD, GOLD!
HOW'S A BOY TO CHOOSE?
AH, HA! IF IT ISN'T JUST THE ARTIFACT THAT I'VE BEEN SEARCHING FOR!
CHARLES WILL PROBABLY CALL FOR A RETREAT ANY MOMENT NOW, LEAVING ME TO DELIVER THE GOODS ALL BY MYSELF. GANGLION, YOU ARE A GENIUS, YOU KNOW THAT?
LOOKING FOR TREASURE, MY FRIEND? YOU NEED LOOK NO FURTHER!
ARE YOU UNRIVALED IN COMBAT? YOU WOULDN'T HAPPEN TO BE VIOLENCE GIVEN FLESH, WOULD YOU?
CHOOSE AN AUTOMATED MAN FROM THE WORKSHOP OF THE ONE AND ONLY DULONO DELANSTATI, YOU WILL NOT BE DISAPPOINTED.

I AM INDEED. HOW ON EARTH DID YOU KNOW THAT?
I KNOW A LOT.
I KNOW YOU ARE THE AUTOMATED MAN FOUND SOUTH OF THE BLACK IRON GATES.
I AM BORAL. AS YOU CAN SEE, MY TALENTS ARE WASTED IN THE SERVICE OF THE WIZARD.
HE BELIEVES ME TOO RARE AN ASSET TO UTILIZE. I'VE BEEN LOCKED UP HERE FOR COUNTLESS YEARS.
YEAH, I FIGURED AS MUCH.
YOU SEE, I SAVED HIS LIFE, SO THE WIZARD GRANTED ME ALL OF THE TREASURE I CAN CARRY.
THAT MEANS WHATEVER YOU CAN CARRY TOO.
CLANK
MY HANDS, THEY FEEL SO SMALL.
NOT MY PROBLEM. AS YOUR NEW MASTER, I DECREE YOUR NAME TO NOW BE GRAVEL. YOU SERVE ME, BUT ARE NEVER TO SPEAK OF IT.
WHOM WOULD I SPEAK IT TO?
OUR GROUP, THE CLANDESTINAUTS. YOU'VE BEEN A MEMBER FOR TWO YEARS. YOU ARE OUR MUSCLE. YOU HAVE A KIND HEART, AND ONCE SLEW THE BOAR OF CALGORE PASS.
GOT IT?
I KILLED THE LEGENDARY BOAR OF CALGORE PASS? NO ONE IS GOING TO BELIEVE THAT!
YOU DID. I WAS THERE, IT WAS PRETTY AMAZING.

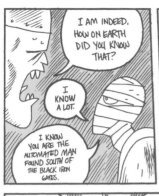

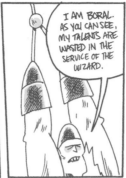

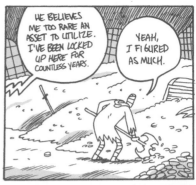

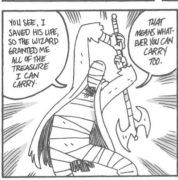

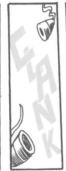

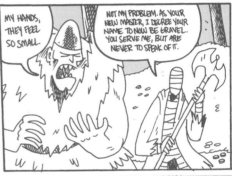

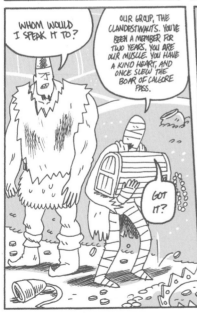

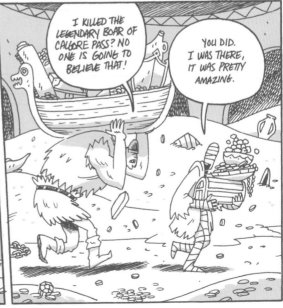

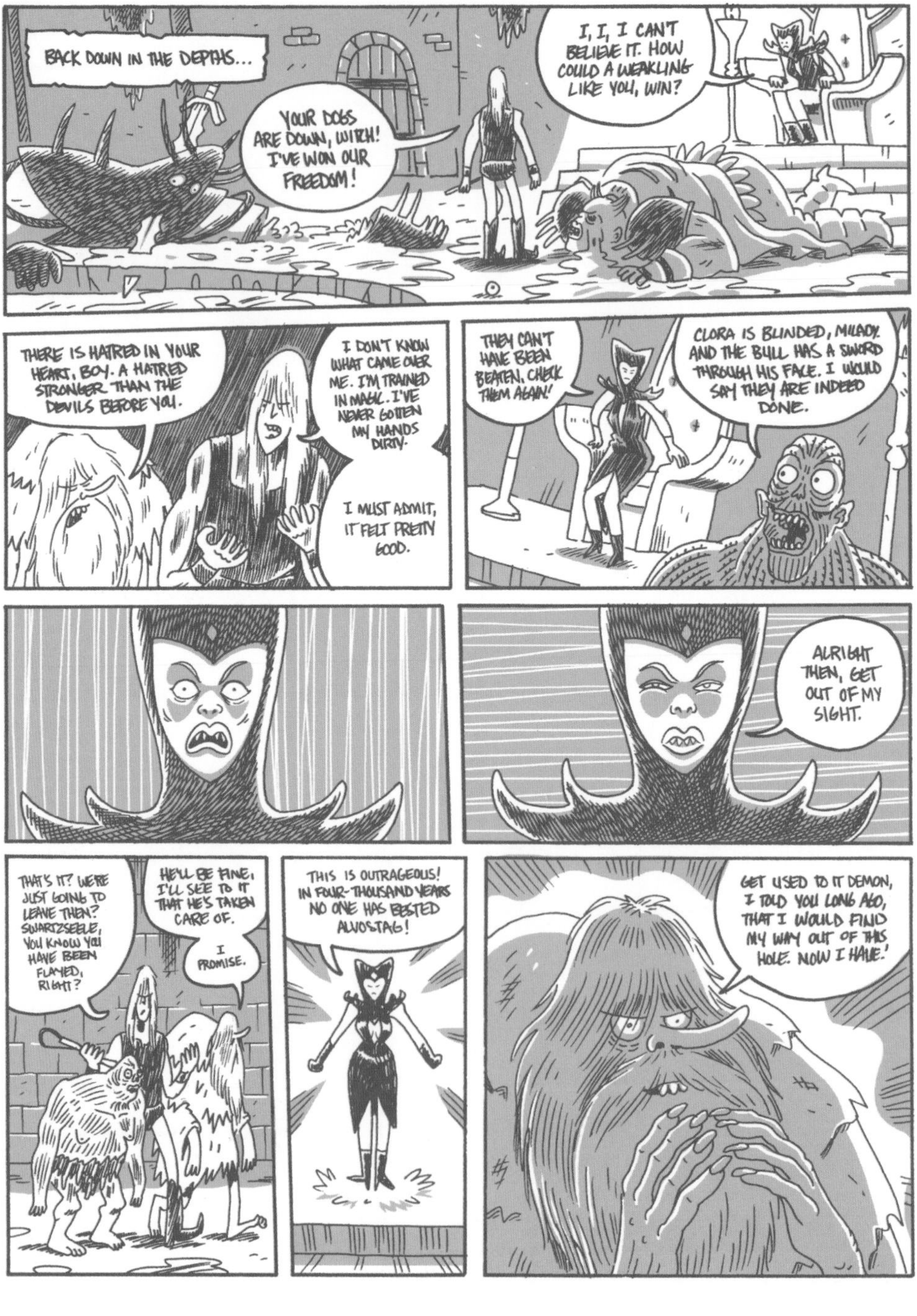
BACK DOWN IN THE DEPTHS...
YOUR DOGS ARE DOWN, WITCH! I'VE WON OUR FREEDOM!
I, I, I CAN'T BELIEVE IT. HOW COULD A WEAKLING LIKE YOU, WIN?
THERE IS HATRED IN YOUR HEART, BOY. A HATRED STRONGER THAN THE DEVILS BEFORE YOU.
I DON'T KNOW WHAT CAME OVER ME. I'M TRAINED IN MAGIC. I'VE NEVER GOTTEN MY HANDS DIRTY.
I MUST ADMIT, IT FELT PRETTY GOOD.
THEY CAN'T HAVE BEEN BEATEN. CHECK THEM AGAIN!
CLORA IS BLINDED, MILADY. AND THE BULL HAS A SWORD THROUGH HIS FACE. I WOULD SAY THEY ARE INDEED DONE.
ALRIGHT THEN, GET OUT OF MY SIGHT.
THAT'S IT? WE'RE JUST GOING TO LEAVE THEN? SWARTZSEELE, YOU KNOW YOU HAVE BEEN FLAYED, RIGHT?
HE'LL BE FINE, I'LL SEE TO IT THAT HE'S TAKEN CARE OF.
I PROMISE.
THIS IS OUTRAGEOUS! IN FOUR-THOUSAND YEARS NO ONE HAS BESTED ALVOSTAG!
GET USED TO IT DEMON, I TOLD YOU LONG AGO, THAT I WOULD FIND MY WAY OUT OF THIS HOLE. NOW I HAVE.

SHE'S RIGHT, THIS IS INSANE. I THOUGHT I WAS DAMNED FOR ETERNITY, BUT HERE I AM, ABOUT TO WALK OUT OF HELL, BACK TO MY OLD LIFE.

HEY, WHAT'S GOING TO HAPPEN TO TURDULON?

HEY! WHAT ARE YOU DOING?

YOUR PAL TURDULON IS BUSY JOINING THE SLEEPY SHADE, WHERE YOU WILL SOON BE.

URAL, YOU MORON! YOUR MASTER JUST LET US GO, WE'RE FREE MEN, TELL HIM ALVOSTAG!

POOR, NAIVE, RUTGER HERE DEFEATED MY BODYGUARDS, AND FOR SOME REASON TAKES A DEVIL-QUEEN AT HER WORD!

CAN YOU BELIEVE IT?

IT'S A TRICK, DUMMY! ONE PLAYED ON ME A FEW TIMES IN MY DAY.

THERE IS NO ESCAPE!

YOU WITCH! WHY, I'LL N—

BRAK!

CHARLES, IS THAT HIM? YOUR RUTGER? HE DOESN'T LOOK LIKE ANY POWERFUL WARLOCK!

THAT'S HIM ALRIGHT.

I TAKE IT THAT SCARY CHICK OVER THERE, IS THE QUEEN YOU CAN'T LOOK AT? THE OTHERS JUST LOOK LIKE GARBAGE TO ME.

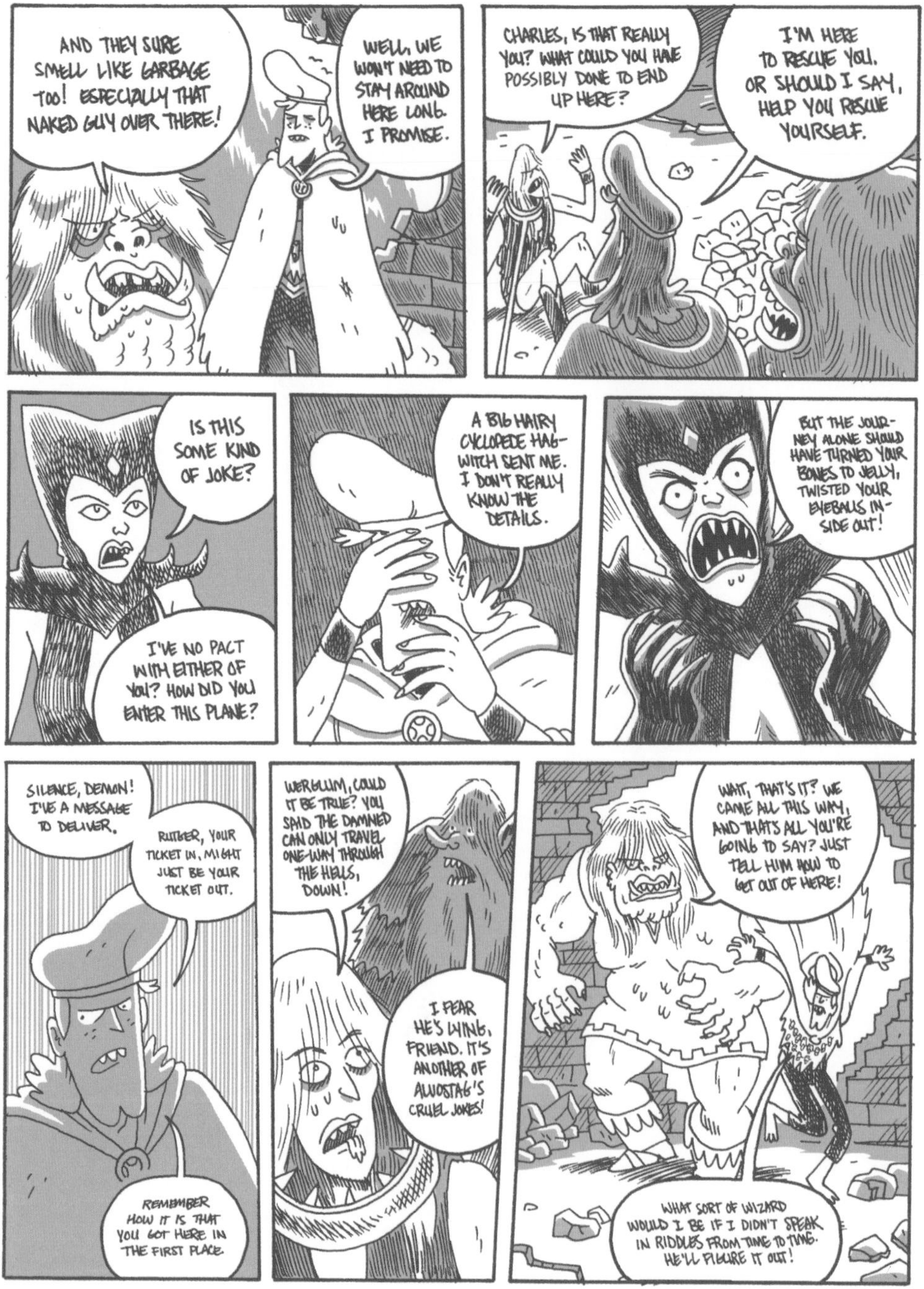
AND THEY SURE SMELL LIKE GARBAGE TOO! ESPECIALLY THAT NAKED GUY OVER THERE!
WELL, WE WON'T NEED TO STAY AROUND HERE LONG. I PROMISE.
CHARLES, IS THAT REALLY YOU? WHAT COULD YOU HAVE POSSIBLY DONE TO END UP HERE?
I'M HERE TO RESCUE YOU. OR SHOULD I SAY, HELP YOU RESCUE YOURSELF.
IS THIS SOME KIND OF JOKE?
I'VE NO PACT WITH EITHER OF YOU? HOW DID YOU ENTER THIS PLANE?
A BIG HAIRY CYCLOPEDE HAG-WITCH SENT ME. I DON'T REALLY KNOW THE DETAILS.
BUT THE JOURNEY ALONE SHOULD HAVE TURNED YOUR BONES TO JELLY, TWISTED YOUR EYEBALLS INSIDE OUT!
SILENCE, DEMON! I'VE A MESSAGE TO DELIVER.
RUTGER, YOUR TICKET IN, MIGHT JUST BE YOUR TICKET OUT.
REMEMBER HOW IT IS THAT YOU GOT HERE IN THE FIRST PLACE.
WERGLUM, COULD IT BE TRUE? YOU SAID THE DAMNED CAN ONLY TRAVEL ONE WAY THROUGH THE HELLS, DOWN!
I FEAR HE'S LYING, FRIEND. IT'S ANOTHER OF ALLOSTAG'S CRUEL JOKES!
WAIT, THAT'S IT? WE CAME ALL THIS WAY, AND THAT'S ALL YOU'RE GOING TO SAY? JUST TELL HIM HOW TO GET OUT OF HERE!
WHAT SORT OF WIZARD WOULD I BE IF I DIDN'T SPEAK IN RIDDLES FROM TIME TO TIME. HE'LL FIGURE IT OUT!

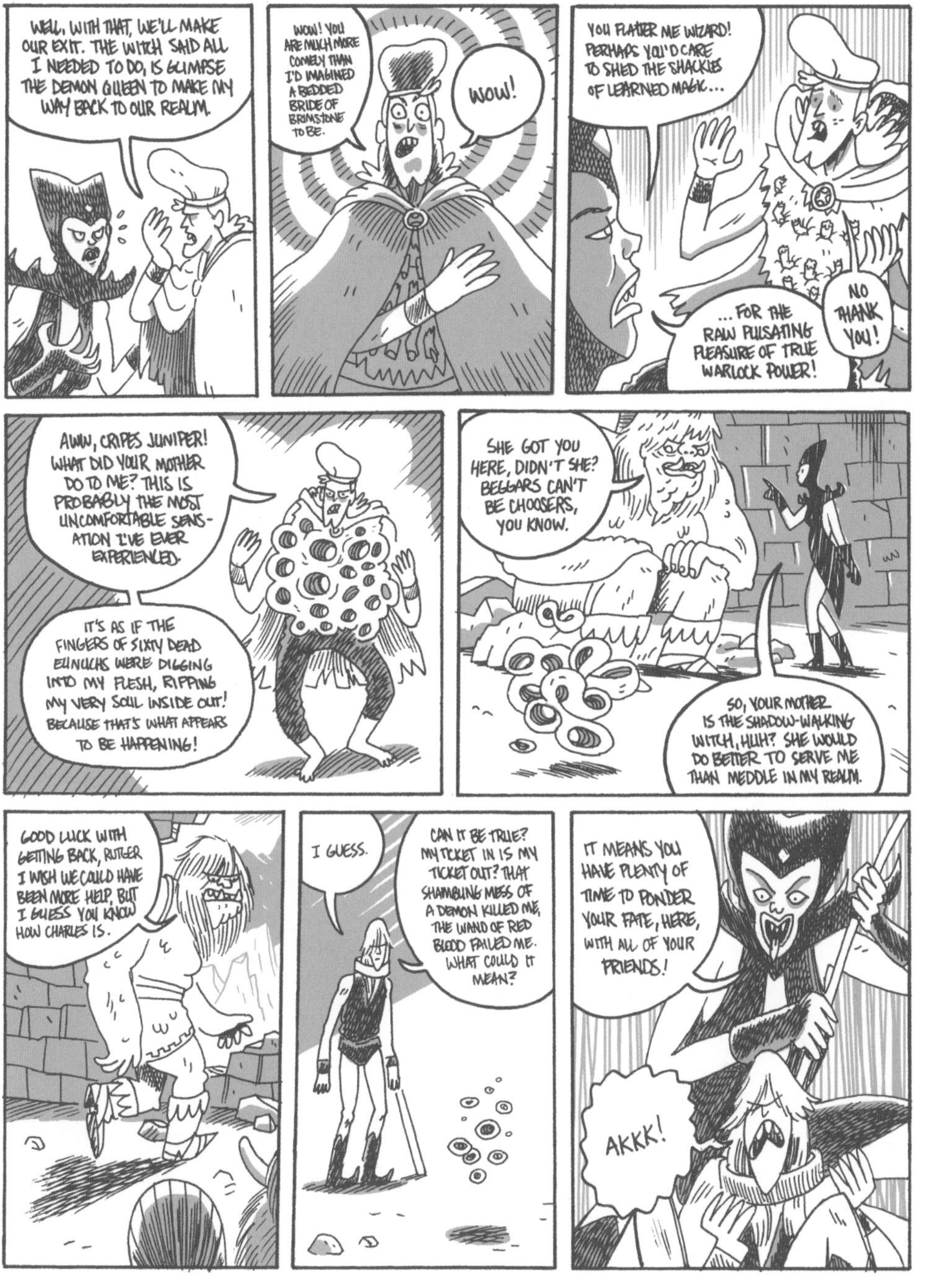
WELL, WITH THAT, WE'LL MAKE OUR EXIT. THE WITCH SAID ALL I NEEDED TO DO, IS GLIMPSE THE DEMON QUEEN TO MAKE MY WAY BACK TO OUR REALM.
WOW! YOU ARE MUCH MORE COMELY THAN I'D IMAGINED A BEDDED BRIDE OF BRIMSTONE TO BE.
WOW!
YOU FLATTER ME WIZARD! PERHAPS YOU'D CARE TO SHED THE SHACKLES OF LEARNED MAGIC...
...FOR THE RAW PULSATING PLEASURE OF TRUE WARLOCK POWER!
NO THANK YOU!
AWW, CRIPES JUNIPER! WHAT DID YOUR MOTHER DO TO ME? THIS IS PROBABLY THE MOST UNCOMFORTABLE SENSATION I'VE EVER EXPERIENCED.
IT'S AS IF THE FINGERS OF SIXTY DEAD EUNUCHS WERE DIGGING INTO MY FLESH, RIPPING MY VERY SOUL INSIDE OUT! BECAUSE THAT'S WHAT APPEARS TO BE HAPPENING!
SHE GOT YOU HERE, DIDN'T SHE? BEGGARS CAN'T BE CHOOSERS, YOU KNOW.
SO, YOUR MOTHER IS THE SHADOW-WALKING WITCH, HUH? SHE WOULD DO BETTER TO SERVE ME THAN MEDDLE IN MY REALM.
GOOD LUCK WITH GETTING BACK, RUTGER I WISH WE COULD HAVE BEEN MORE HELP, BUT I GUESS YOU KNOW HOW CHARLES IS.
I GUESS.
CAN IT BE TRUE? MY TICKET IN IS MY TICKET OUT? THAT SHAMBLING MESS OF A DEMON KILLED ME, THE WAND OF RED BLOOD FAILED ME. WHAT COULD IT MEAN?
IT MEANS YOU HAVE PLENTY OF TIME TO PONDER YOUR FATE, HERE, WITH ALL OF YOUR FRIENDS!
AKKK!

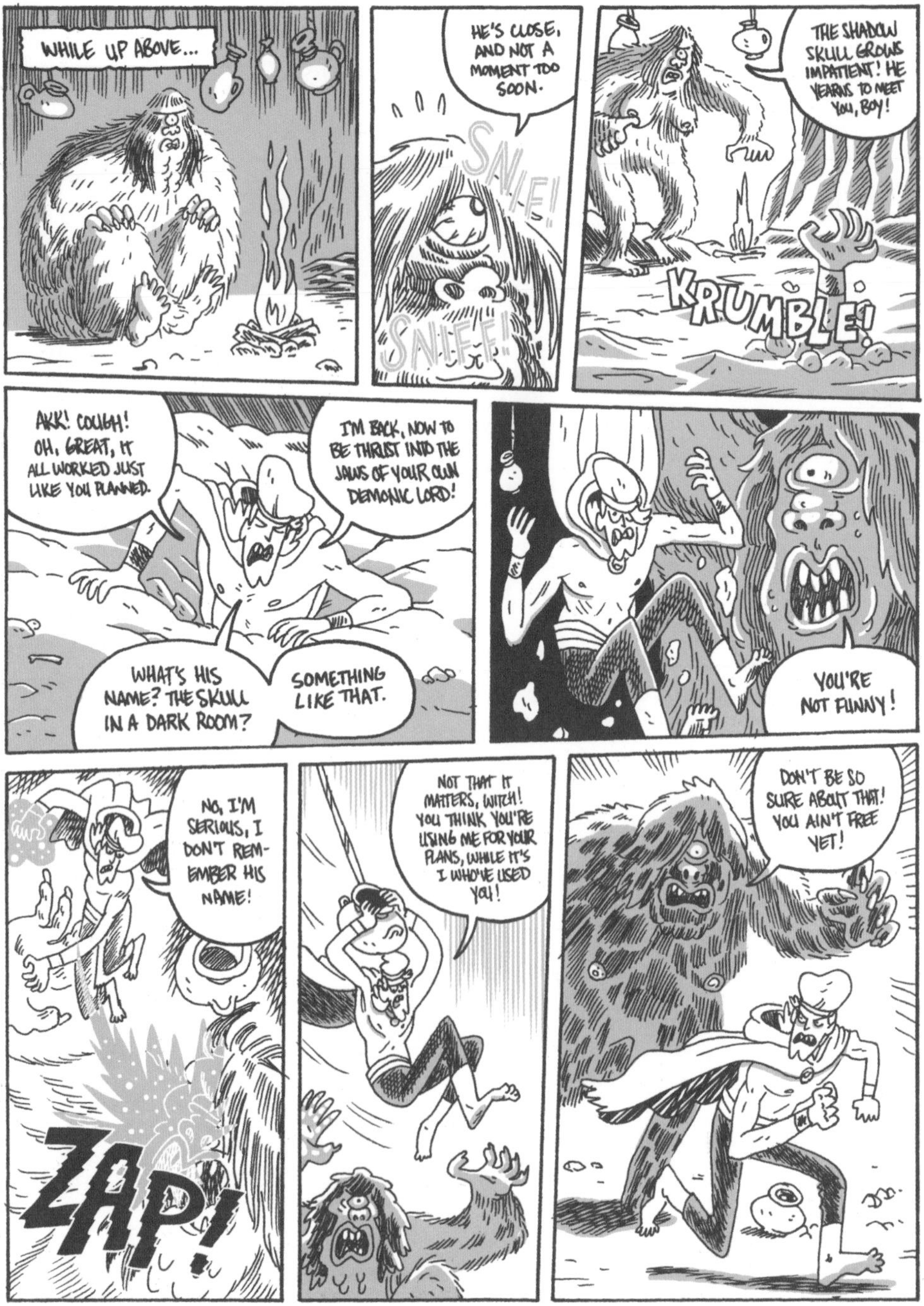

WHILE UP ABOVE...
HE'S CLOSE, AND NOT A MOMENT TOO SOON.
SNIFF!
SNIFF!
THE SHADOW SKULL GROWS IMPATIENT! HE YEARNS TO MEET YOU, BOY!
KRUMBLE!
AKK! COUGH! OH, GREAT, IT ALL WORKED JUST LIKE YOU PLANNED.
I'M BACK, NOW TO BE THRUST INTO THE JAWS OF YOUR OWN DEMONIC LORD!
WHAT'S HIS NAME? THE SKULL IN A DARK ROOM?
SOMETHING LIKE THAT.
YOU'RE NOT FUNNY!
NO, I'M SERIOUS, I DON'T REMEMBER HIS NAME!
ZAP!
NOT THAT IT MATTERS, WITCH! YOU THINK YOU'RE USING ME FOR YOUR PLANS, WHILE IT'S I WHO'VE USED YOU!
DON'T BE SO SURE ABOUT THAT! YOU AIN'T FREE YET!

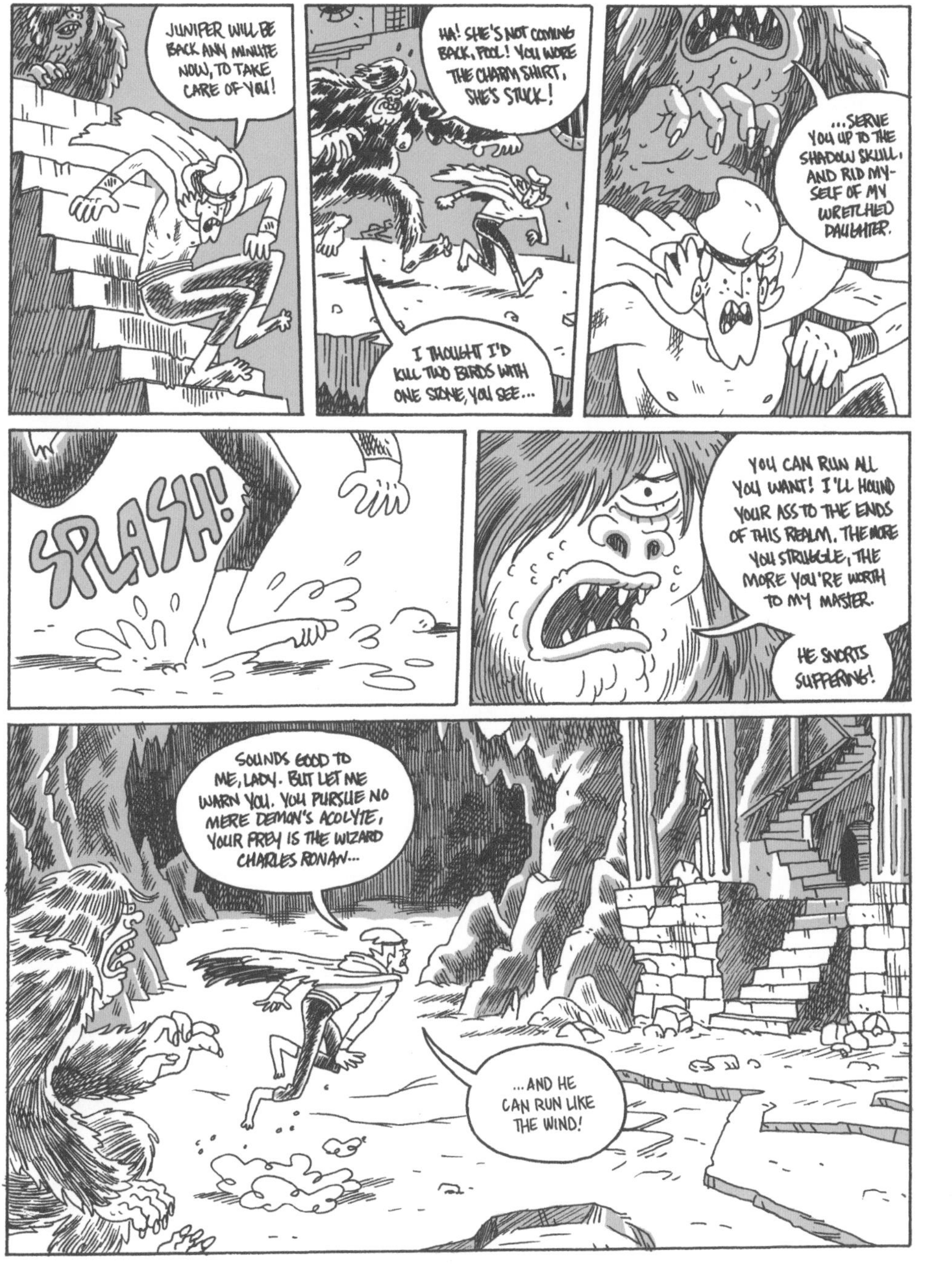
JUNIPER WILL BE BACK ANY MINUTE NOW, TO TAKE CARE OF YOU!
HA! SHE'S NOT COMING BACK, FOOL! YOU WORE THE CHARM SHIRT, SHE'S STUCK!
I THOUGHT I'D KILL TWO BIRDS WITH ONE STONE, YOU SEE...
...SERVE YOU UP TO THE SHADOW SKULL, AND RID MY-SELF OF MY WRETCHED DAUGHTER.
SPLASH!
YOU CAN RUN ALL YOU WANT! I'LL HOUND YOUR ASS TO THE ENDS OF THIS REALM. THE MORE YOU STRUGGLE, THE MORE YOU'RE WORTH TO MY MASTER.
HE SNORTS SUFFERING!
SOUNDS GOOD TO ME, LADY. BUT LET ME WARN YOU. YOU PURSUE NO MERE DEMON'S ACOLYTE, YOUR PREY IS THE WIZARD CHARLES RONAN...
...AND HE CAN RUN LIKE THE WIND!

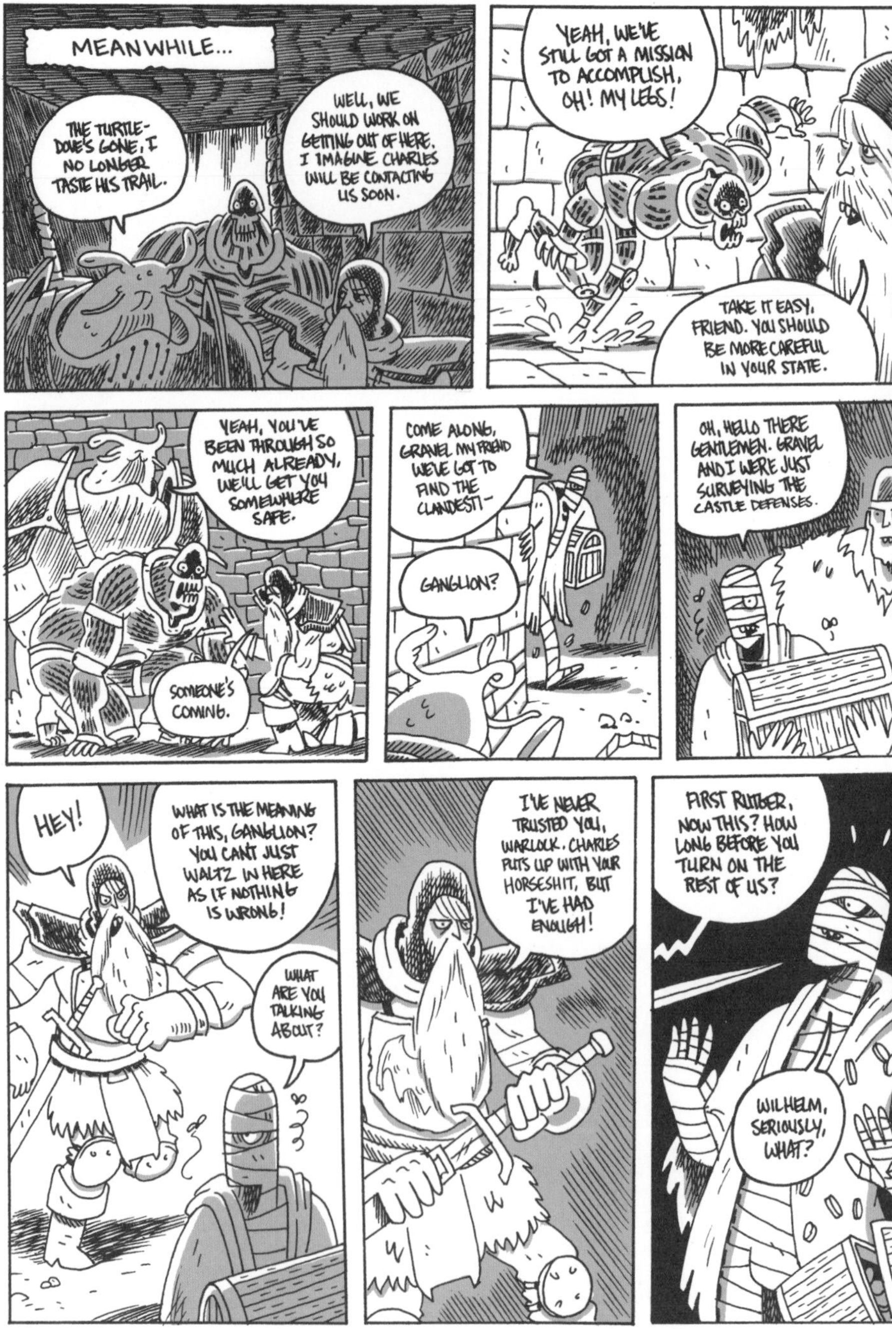

MEANWHILE...
THE TURTLE-DOVE'S GONE, I NO LONGER TASTE HIS TRAIL.
WELL, WE SHOULD WORK ON GETTING OUT OF HERE. I IMAGINE CHARLES WILL BE CONTACTING US SOON.
YEAH, WE'VE STILL GOT A MISSION TO ACCOMPLISH, OH! MY LEGS!
TAKE IT EASY, FRIEND. YOU SHOULD BE MORE CAREFUL IN YOUR STATE.
YEAH, YOU'VE BEEN THROUGH SO MUCH ALREADY, WE'LL GET YOU SOMEWHERE SAFE.
SOMEONE'S COMING.
COME ALONG, GRAVEL MY FRIEND WE'VE GOT TO FIND THE CLANDESTI-
GANGLION?
OH, HELLO THERE GENTLEMEN. GRAVEL AND I WERE JUST SURVEYING THE CASTLE DEFENSES.
HEY!
WHAT IS THE MEANING OF THIS, GANGLION? YOU CAN'T JUST WALTZ IN HERE AS IF NOTHING IS WRONG!
WHAT ARE YOU TALKING ABOUT?
I'VE NEVER TRUSTED YOU, WARLOCK. CHARLES PUTS UP WITH YOUR HORSESHIT, BUT I'VE HAD ENOUGH!
FIRST RUTGER, NOW THIS? HOW LONG BEFORE YOU TURN ON THE REST OF US?
WILHELM, SERIOUSLY, WHAT?

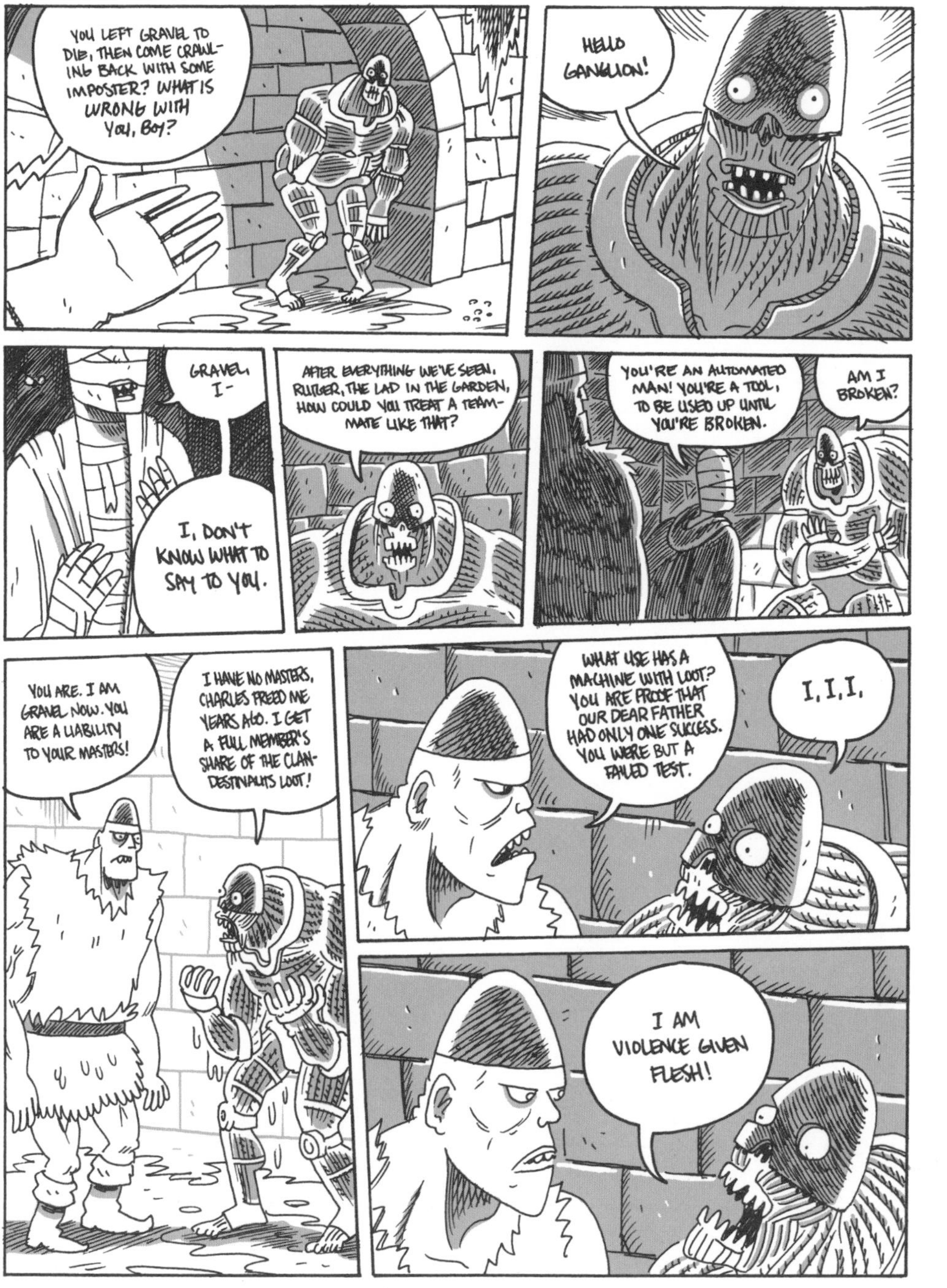
YOU LEFT GRAVEL TO DIE, THEN COME CRAWLING BACK WITH SOME IMPOSTER? WHAT IS WRONG WITH YOU, BOY?
HELLO GANGLION!
GRAVEL, I-
I, DON'T KNOW WHAT TO SAY TO YOU.
AFTER EVERYTHING WE'VE SEEN, RUTGER, THE LAD IN THE GARDEN, HOW COULD YOU TREAT A TEAM-MATE LIKE THAT?
YOU'RE AN AUTOMATED MAN! YOU'RE A TOOL, TO BE USED UP UNTIL YOU'RE BROKEN.
AM I BROKEN?
YOU ARE. I AM GRAVEL NOW. YOU ARE A LIABILITY TO YOUR MASTERS!
I HAVE NO MASTERS. CHARLES FREED ME YEARS AGO. I GET A FULL MEMBER'S SHARE OF THE CLAN-DESTINAUTS LOOT!
WHAT USE HAS A MACHINE WITH LOOT? YOU ARE PROOF THAT OUR DEAR FATHER HAD ONLY ONE SUCCESS. YOU WERE BUT A FAILED TEST.
I, I, I.
I AM VIOLENCE GIVEN FLESH!

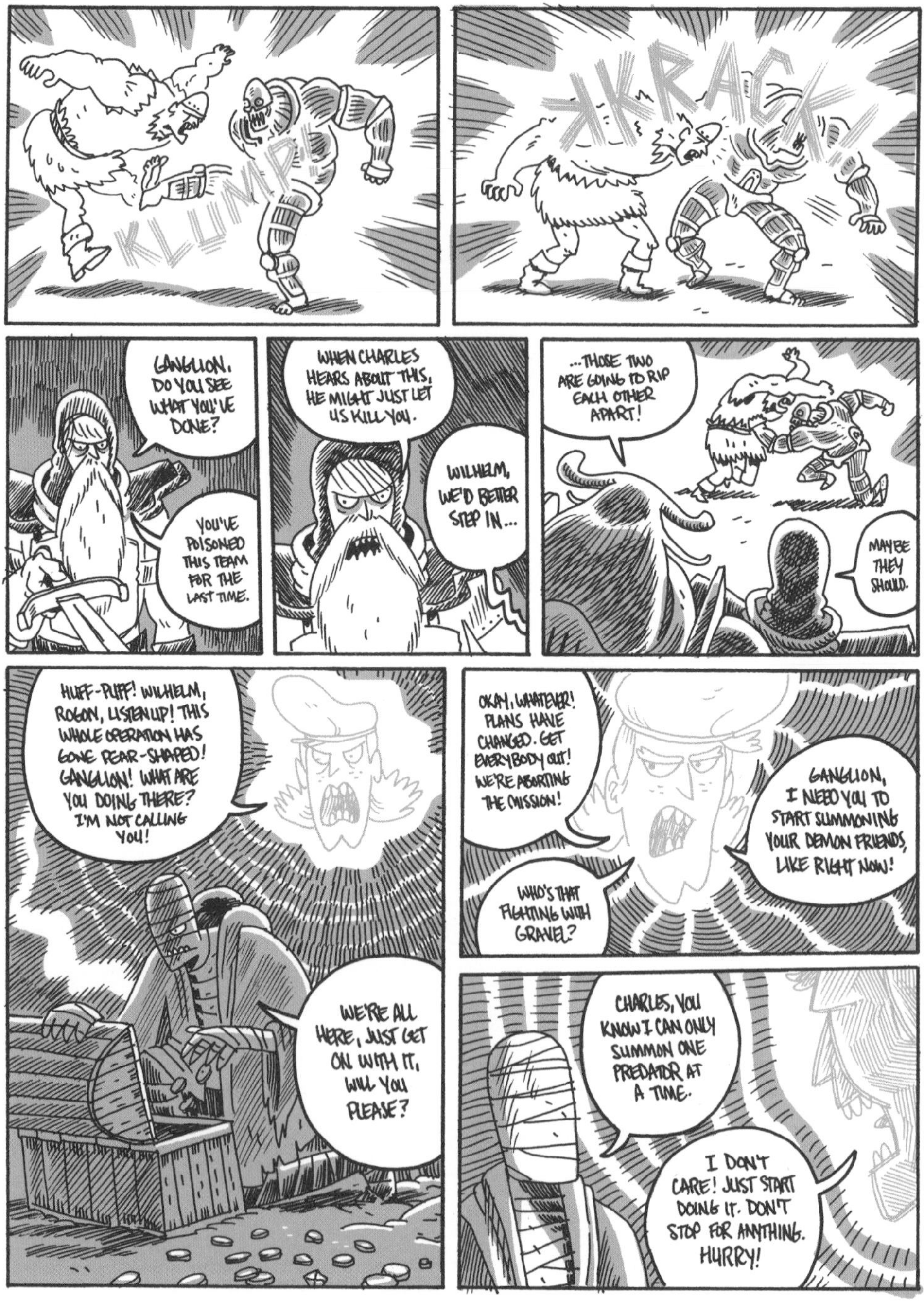
KLUMP!
KKRACK!
GANGLION. DO YOU SEE WHAT YOU'VE DONE?
YOU'VE POISONED THIS TEAM FOR THE LAST TIME.
WHEN CHARLES HEARS ABOUT THIS, HE MIGHT JUST LET US KILL YOU.
WILHELM, WE'D BETTER STEP IN...
...THOSE TWO ARE GOING TO RIP EACH OTHER APART!
MAYBE THEY SHOULD.
HUFF-PUFF! WILHELM, ROGON, LISTEN UP! THIS WHOLE OPERATION HAS GONE PEAR-SHAPED! GANGLION! WHAT ARE YOU DOING THERE? I'M NOT CALLING YOU!
WE'RE ALL HERE, JUST GET ON WITH IT, WILL YOU PLEASE?
OKAY, WHATEVER! PLANS HAVE CHANGED. GET EVERYBODY OUT! WE'RE ABORTING THE MISSION!
WHO'S THAT FIGHTING WITH GRAVEL?
GANGLION, I NEED YOU TO START SUMMONING YOUR DEMON FRIENDS, LIKE RIGHT NOW!
CHARLES, YOU KNOW I CAN ONLY SUMMON ONE PREDATOR AT A TIME.
I DON'T CARE! JUST START DOING IT. DON'T STOP FOR ANYTHING. HURRY!

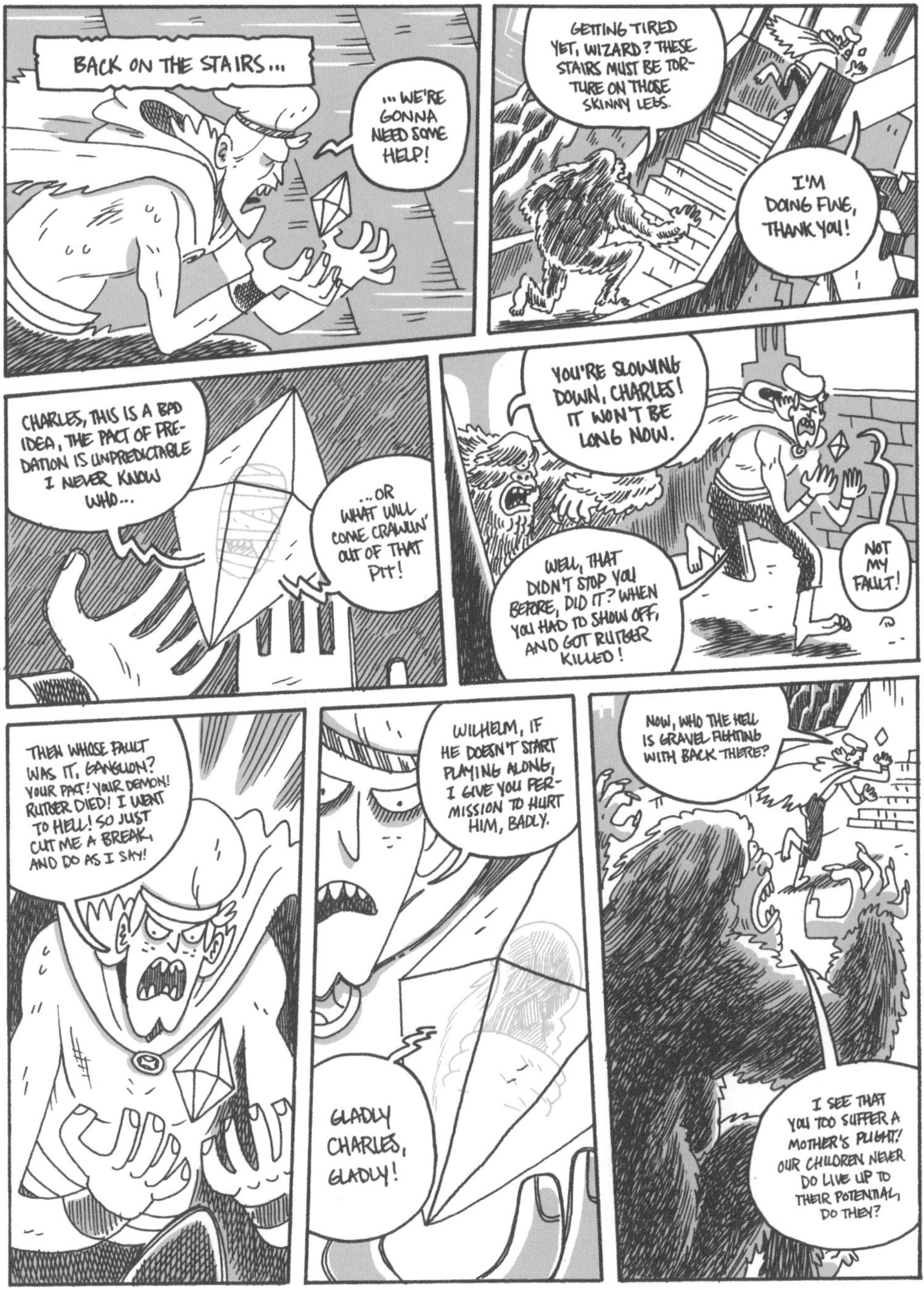
BACK ON THE STAIRS...
...WE'RE GONNA NEED SOME HELP!
GETTING TIRED YET, WIZARD? THESE STAIRS MUST BE TORTURE ON THOSE SKINNY LEGS.
I'M DOING FINE, THANK YOU!
CHARLES, THIS IS A BAD IDEA, THE PACT OF PREDATION IS UNPREDICTABLE I NEVER KNOW WHO...
...OR WHAT WILL COME CRAWLIN' OUT OF THAT PIT!
YOU'RE SLOWING DOWN, CHARLES! IT WON'T BE LONG NOW.
WELL, THAT DIDN'T STOP YOU BEFORE, DID IT? WHEN YOU HAD TO SHOW OFF, AND GOT RUTGER KILLED!
NOT MY FAULT!
THEN WHOSE FAULT WAS IT, GANGLION? YOUR PACT! YOUR DEMON! RUTGER DIED! I WENT TO HELL! SO JUST CUT ME A BREAK, AND DO AS I SAY!
WILHELM, IF HE DOESN'T START PLAYING ALONG, I GIVE YOU PERMISSION TO HURT HIM, BADLY.
GLADLY CHARLES, GLADLY!
NOW, WHO THE HELL IS GRAVEL FIGHTING WITH BACK THERE?
I SEE THAT YOU TOO SUFFER A MOTHER'S PLIGHT! OUR CHILDREN NEVER DO LIVE UP TO THEIR POTENTIAL, DO THEY?

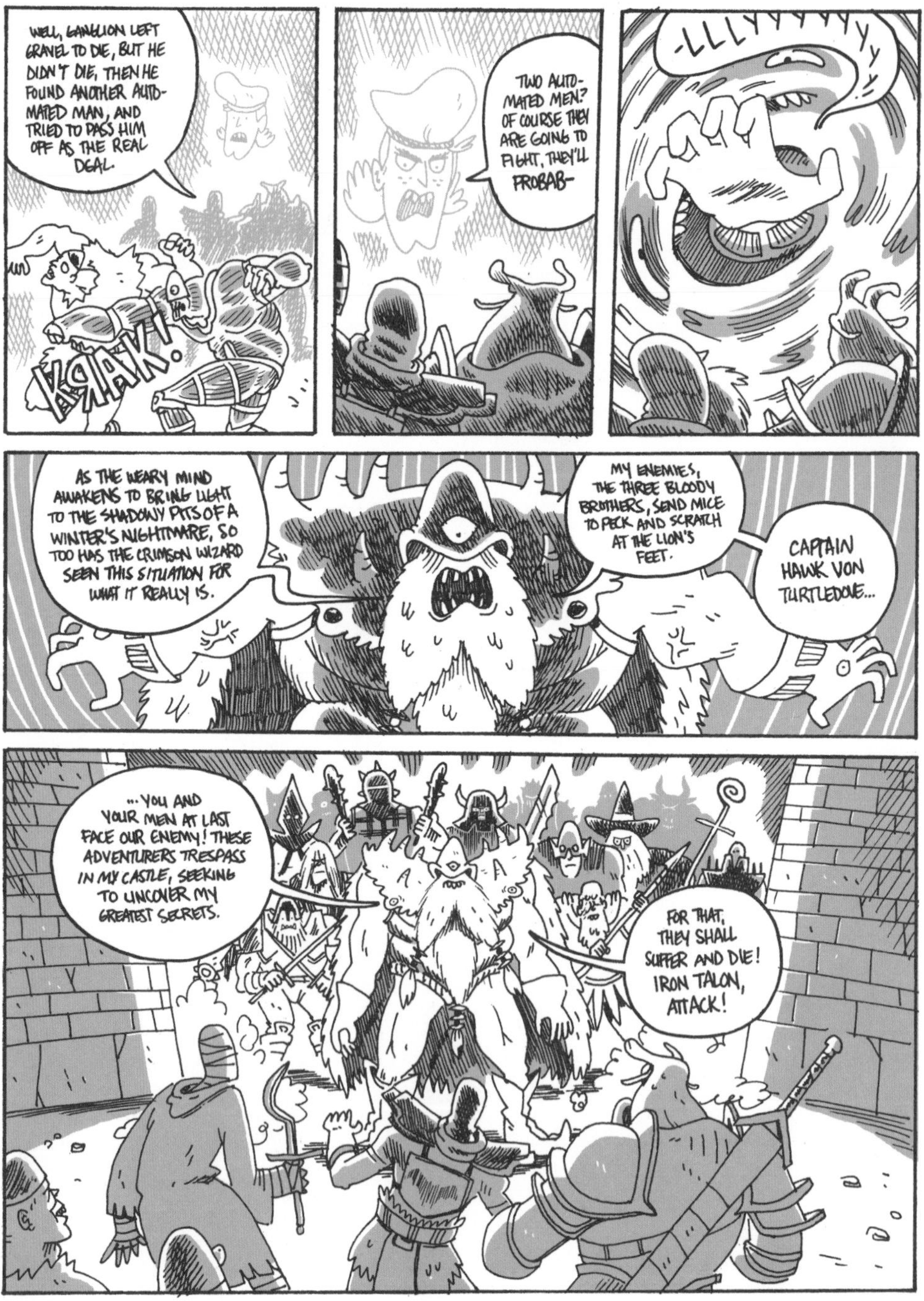
WELL, GANGLION LEFT GRAVEL TO DIE, BUT HE DIDN'T DIE, THEN HE FOUND ANOTHER AUTO-MATED MAN, AND TRIED TO PASS HIM OFF AS THE REAL DEAL.
KRAAK!
TWO AUTO-MATED MEN? OF COURSE THEY ARE GOING TO FIGHT, THEY'LL PROBAB-
-LLLYYYYYYy
AS THE WEARY MIND AWAKENS TO BRING LIGHT TO THE SHADOWY PITS OF A WINTER'S NIGHTMARE, SO TOO HAS THE CRIMSON WIZARD SEEN THIS SITUATION FOR WHAT IT REALLY IS.
MY ENEMIES, THE THREE BLOODY BROTHERS, SEND MICE TO PECK AND SCRATCH AT THE LION'S FEET.
CAPTAIN HAWK VON TURTLEDOVE...
...YOU AND YOUR MEN AT LAST FACE OUR ENEMY! THESE ADVENTURERS TRESPASS IN MY CASTLE, SEEKING TO UNCOVER MY GREATEST SECRETS.
FOR THAT, THEY SHALL SUFFER AND DIE! IRON TALON, ATTACK!

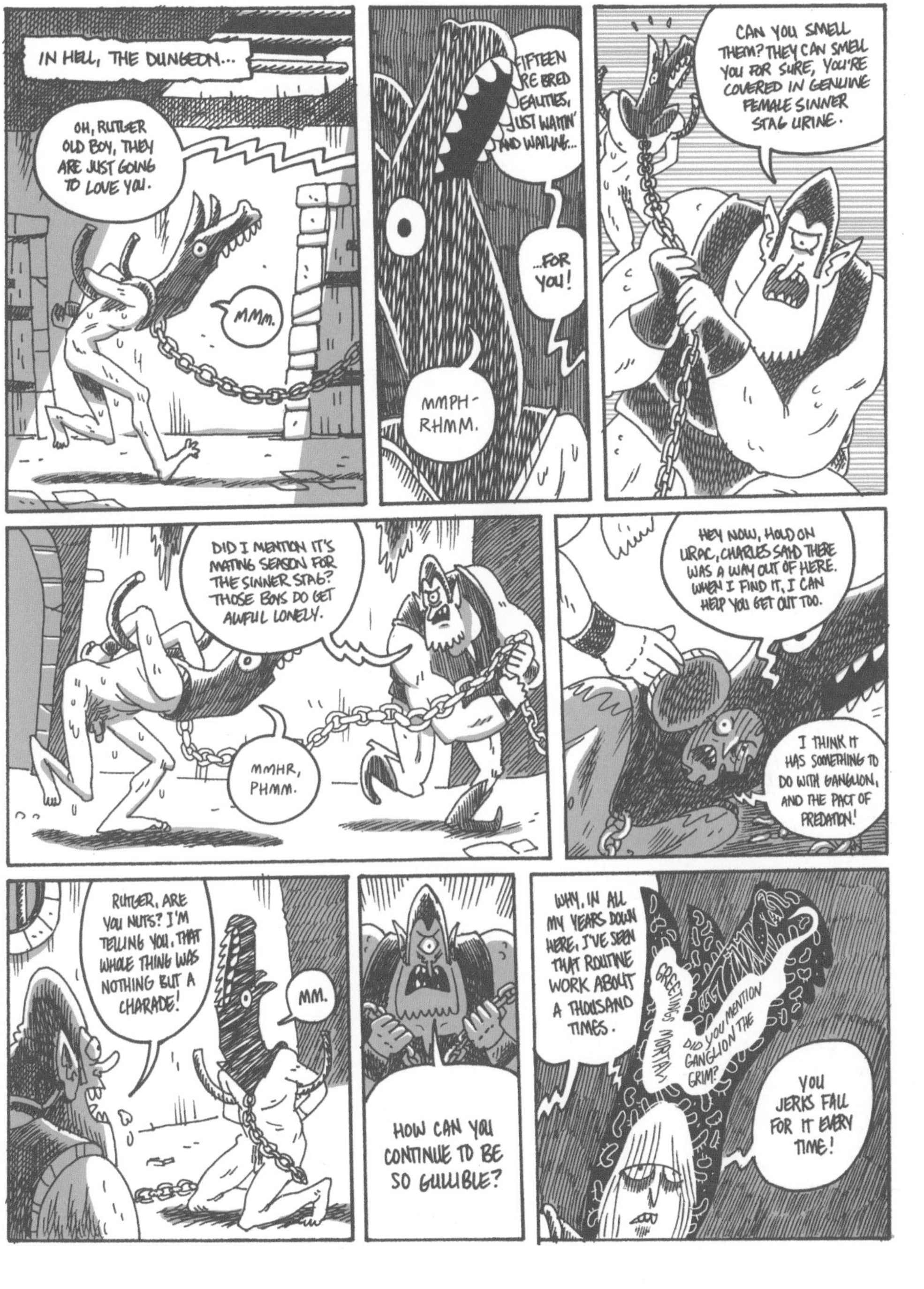

IN HELL, THE DUNGEON...
OH, RUTGER OLD BOY, THEY ARE JUST GOING TO LOVE YOU.
MMM.
FIFTEEN PURE BRED BEAUTIES, JUST WAITIN' AND WAILING...
...FOR YOU!
MMPH-RHMM.
CAN YOU SMELL THEM? THEY CAN SMELL YOU FOR SURE, YOU'RE COVERED IN GENUINE FEMALE SINNER STAG URINE.
DID I MENTION IT'S MATING SEASON FOR THE SINNER STAG? THOSE BOYS DO GET AWFUL LONELY.
MMHR, PHMM.
HEY NOW, HOLD ON URAC, CHARLES SAID THERE WAS A WAY OUT OF HERE. WHEN I FIND IT, I CAN HELP YOU GET OUT TOO.
I THINK IT HAS SOMETHING TO DO WITH GANGLION, AND THE PACT OF PREDATION!
RUTGER, ARE YOU NUTS? I'M TELLING YOU, THAT WHOLE THING WAS NOTHING BUT A CHARADE!
MM.
HOW CAN YOU CONTINUE TO BE SO GULLIBLE?
WHY, IN ALL MY YEARS DOWN HERE, I'VE SEEN THAT ROUTINE WORK ABOUT A THOUSAND TIMES.
GREETINGS MORTAL,
DID YOU MENTION GANGLION THE GRIM?
YOU JERKS FALL FOR IT EVERY TIME!

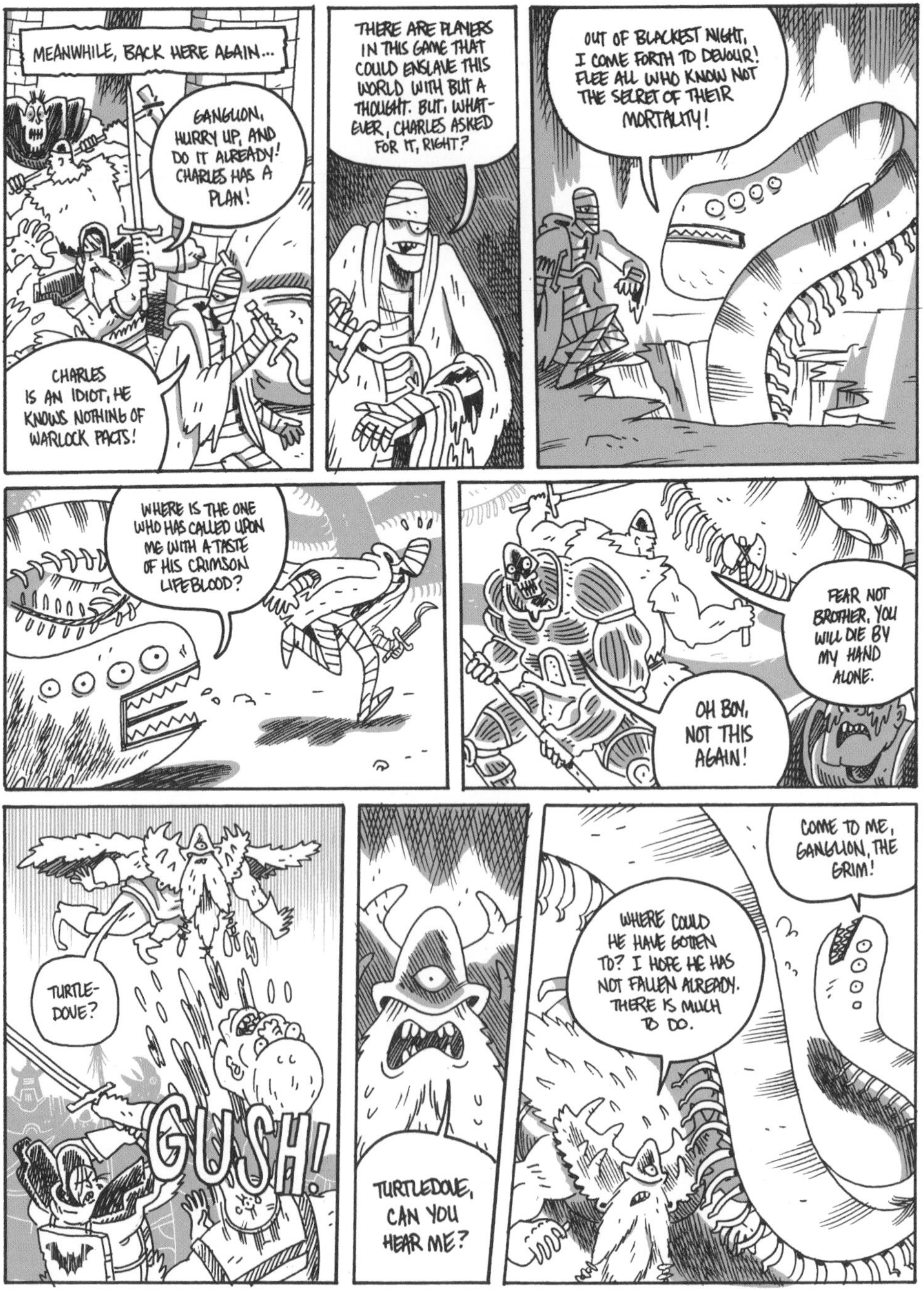
MEANWHILE, BACK HERE AGAIN...
GANGLION, HURRY UP, AND DO IT ALREADY! CHARLES HAS A PLAN!
CHARLES IS AN IDIOT, HE KNOWS NOTHING OF WARLOCK PACTS!
THERE ARE PLAYERS IN THIS GAME THAT COULD ENSLAVE THIS WORLD WITH BUT A THOUGHT. BUT, WHATEVER, CHARLES ASKED FOR IT, RIGHT?
OUT OF BLACKEST NIGHT, I COME FORTH TO DEVOUR! FLEE ALL WHO KNOW NOT THE SECRET OF THEIR MORTALITY!
WHERE IS THE ONE WHO HAS CALLED UPON ME WITH A TASTE OF HIS CRIMSON LIFEBLOOD?
FEAR NOT BROTHER. YOU WILL DIE BY MY HAND ALONE.
OH BOY, NOT THIS AGAIN!
TURTLE-DOVE?
GUSH!
TURTLEDOVE, CAN YOU HEAR ME?
COME TO ME, GANGLION, THE GRIM!
WHERE COULD HE HAVE GOTTEN TO? I HOPE HE HAS NOT FALLEN ALREADY. THERE IS MUCH TO DO.

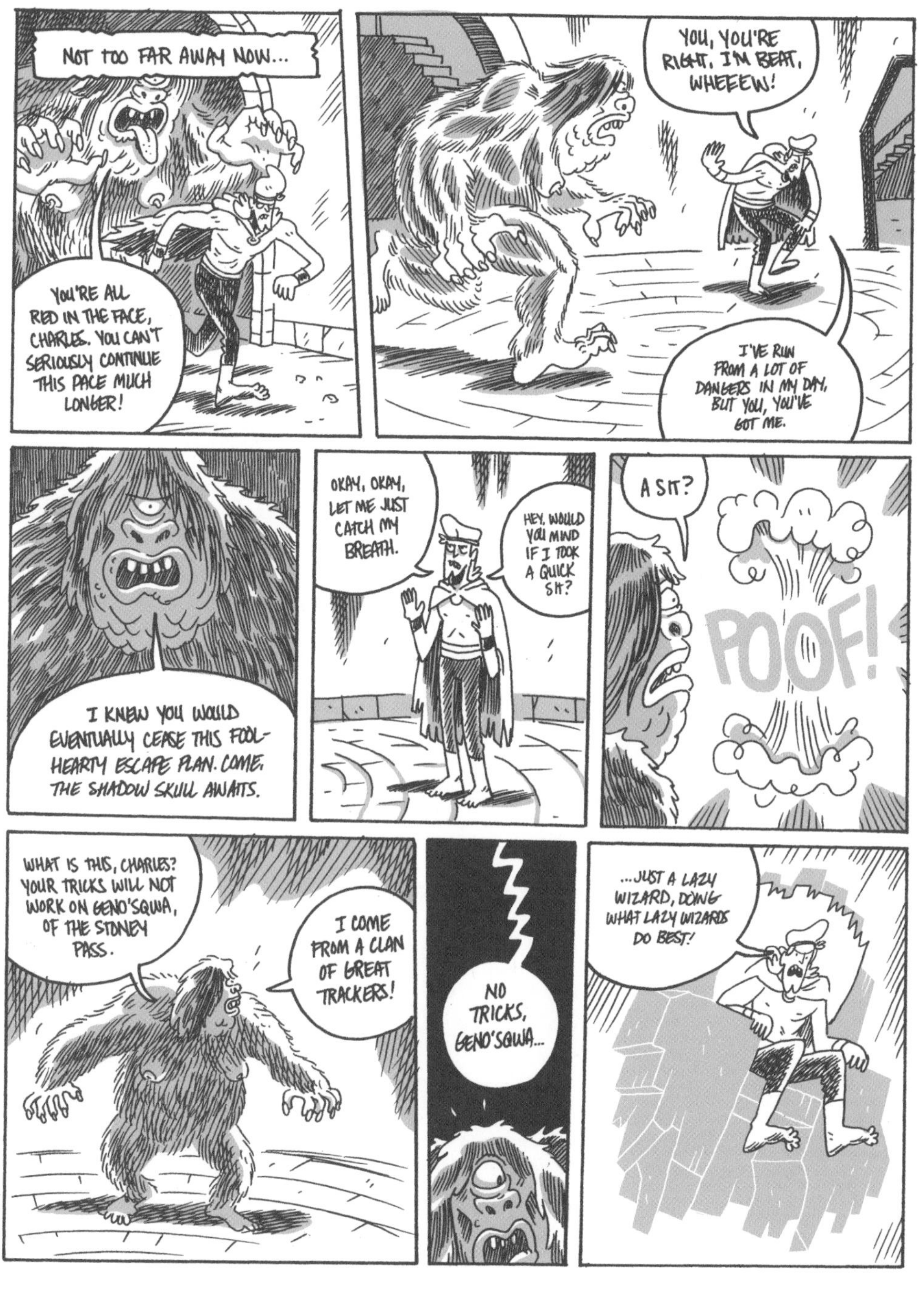
NOT TOO FAR AWAY NOW...
YOU'RE ALL RED IN THE FACE, CHARLES. YOU CAN'T SERIOUSLY CONTINUE THIS PACE MUCH LONGER!
YOU, YOU'RE RIGHT. I'M BEAT. WHEEEW!
I'VE RUN FROM A LOT OF DANGERS IN MY DAY, BUT YOU, YOU'VE GOT ME.
I KNEW YOU WOULD EVENTUALLY CEASE THIS FOOL-HEARTY ESCAPE PLAN. COME. THE SHADOW SKULL AWAITS.
OKAY, OKAY, LET ME JUST CATCH MY BREATH.
HEY, WOULD YOU MIND IF I TOOK A QUICK SIT?
A SIT?
POOF!
WHAT IS THIS, CHARLES? YOUR TRICKS WILL NOT WORK ON GENO'SQWA, OF THE STONEY PASS.
I COME FROM A CLAN OF GREAT TRACKERS!
NO TRICKS, GENO'SQWA...
...JUST A LAZY WIZARD, DOING WHAT LAZY WIZARDS DO BEST!

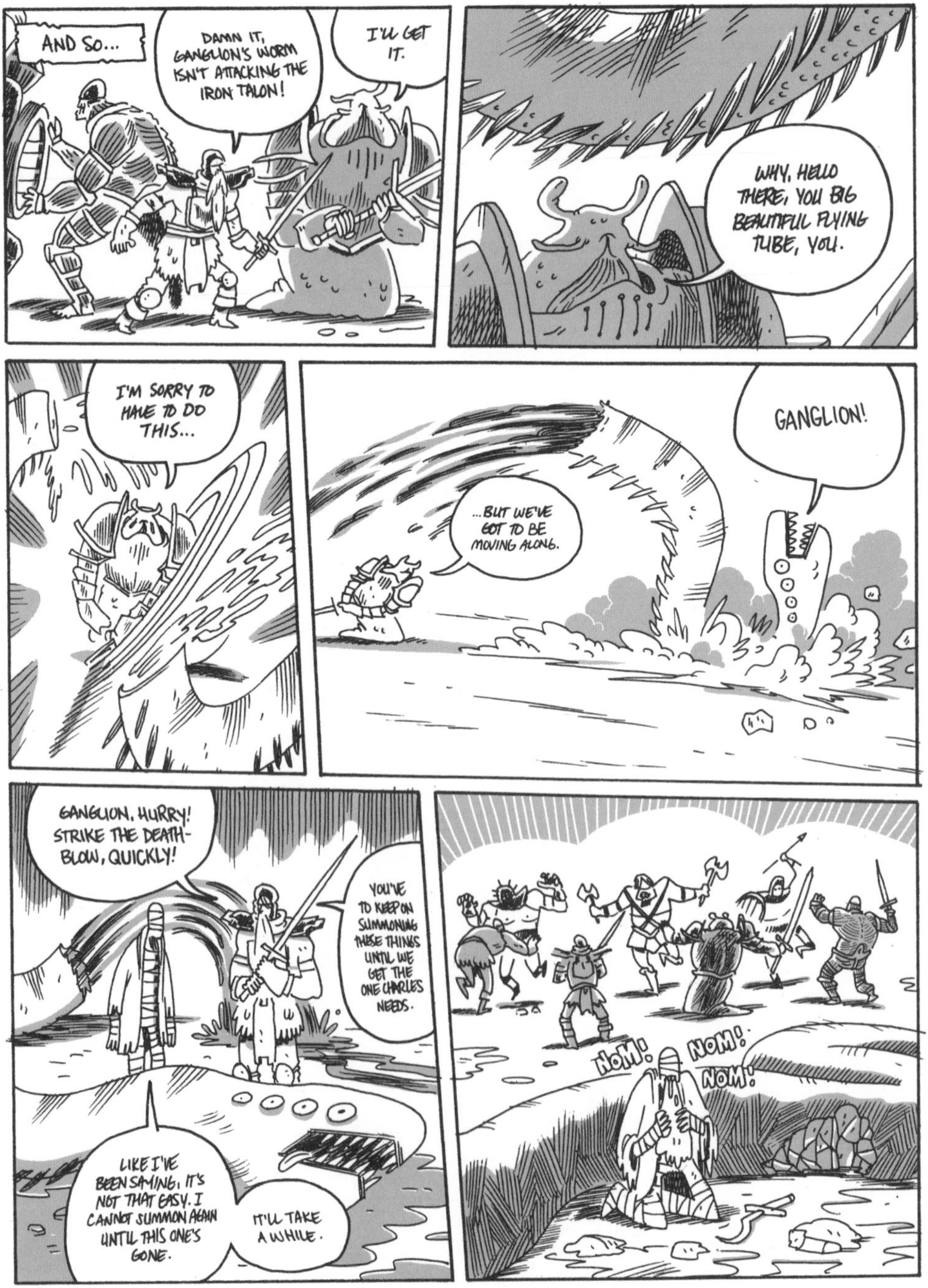
AND SO...
DAMN IT, GANGLION'S WORM ISN'T ATTACKING THE IRON TALON!
I'LL GET IT.
WHY, HELLO THERE, YOU BIG BEAUTIFUL FLYING TUBE, YOU.
I'M SORRY TO HAVE TO DO THIS...
...BUT WE'VE GOT TO BE MOVING ALONG.
GANGLION!
GANGLION, HURRY! STRIKE THE DEATH-BLOW, QUICKLY!
YOU'VE TO KEEP ON SUMMONING THESE THINGS UNTIL WE GET THE ONE CHARLES NEEDS.
LIKE I'VE BEEN SAYING, IT'S NOT THAT EASY. I CANNOT SUMMON AGAIN UNTIL THIS ONE'S GONE.
IT'LL TAKE A WHILE.
NOM! NOM! NOM!

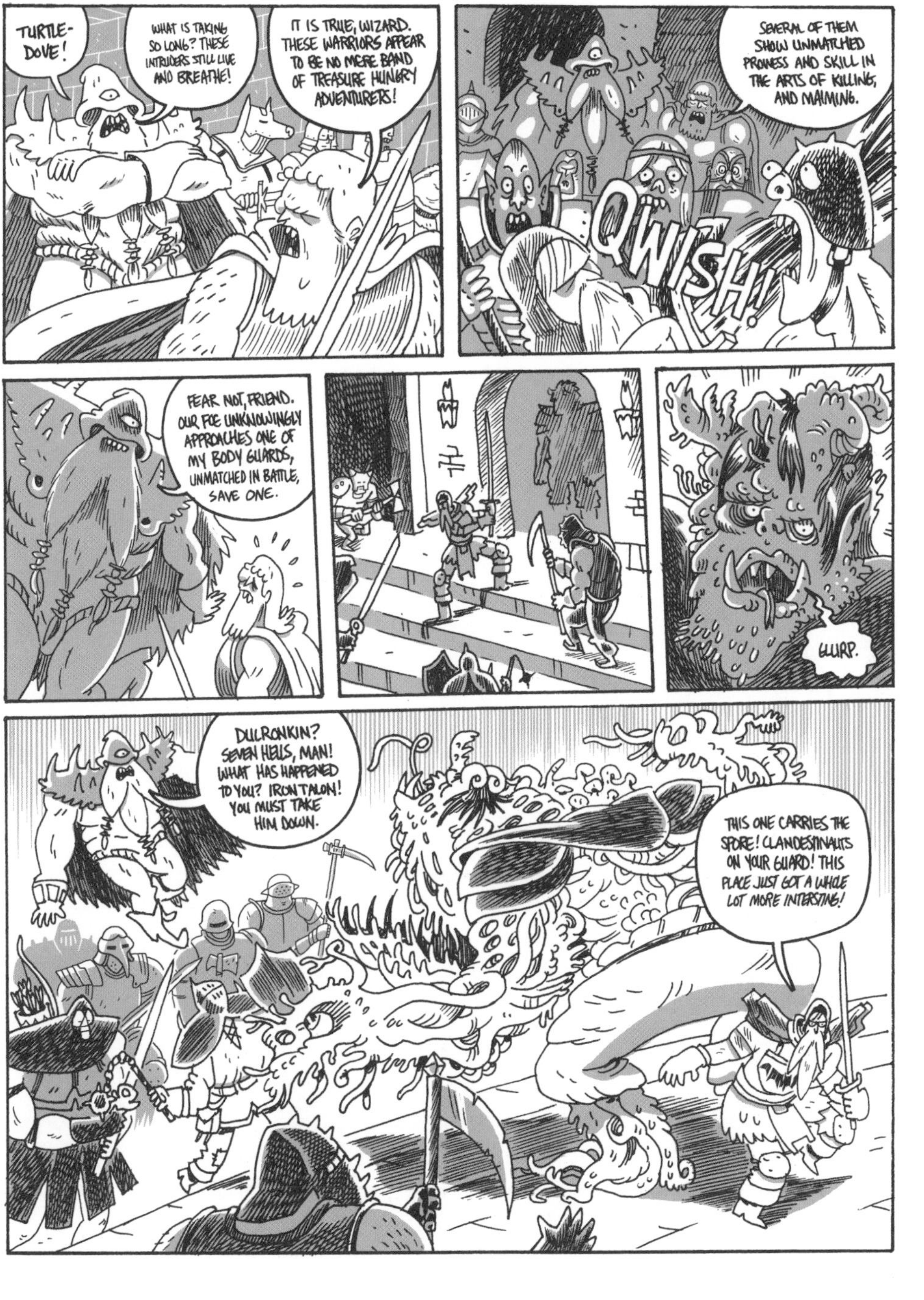
TURTLE-DOVE!
WHAT IS TAKING SO LONG? THESE INTRUDERS STILL LIVE AND BREATHE!
IT IS TRUE, WIZARD. THESE WARRIORS APPEAR TO BE NO MERE BAND OF TREASURE HUNGRY ADVENTURERS!
SEVERAL OF THEM SHOW UNMATCHED PROWESS AND SKILL IN THE ARTS OF KILLING, AND MAIMING.
QWISH!
FEAR NOT, FRIEND. OUR FOE UNKNOWINGLY APPROACHES ONE OF MY BODY GUARDS, UNMATCHED IN BATTLE, SAVE ONE.
GLURP.
DULRONKIN? SEVEN HELLS, MAN! WHAT HAS HAPPENED TO YOU? IRON TALON! YOU MUST TAKE HIM DOWN.
THIS ONE CARRIES THE SPORE! CLANDESTINAUTS ON YOUR GUARD! THIS PLACE JUST GOT A WHOLE LOT MORE INTERSTING!

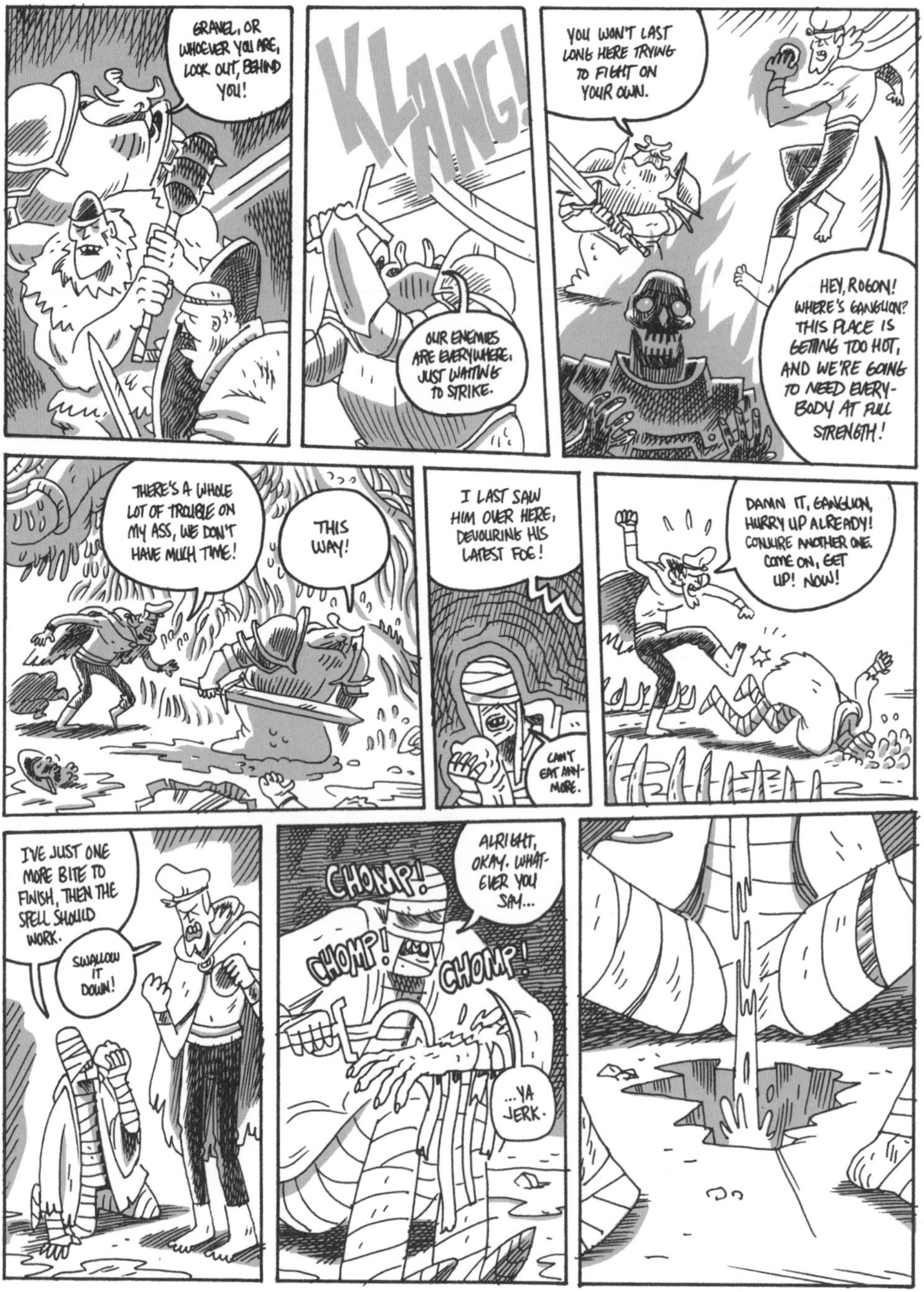
GRAVEL, OR WHOEVER YOU ARE, LOOK OUT, BEHIND YOU!
KLANG!
OUR ENEMIES ARE EVERYWHERE. JUST WAITING TO STRIKE.
YOU WON'T LAST LONG HERE TRYING TO FIGHT ON YOUR OWN.
HEY, ROGON! WHERE'S GANGLION? THIS PLACE IS GETTING TOO HOT, AND WE'RE GOING TO NEED EVERYBODY AT FULL STRENGTH!
THERE'S A WHOLE LOT OF TROUBLE ON MY ASS, WE DON'T HAVE MUCH TIME!
THIS WAY!
I LAST SAW HIM OVER HERE, DEVOURING HIS LATEST FOE!
CAN'T EAT ANYMORE.
DAMN IT, GANGLION, HURRY UP ALREADY! CONJURE ANOTHER ONE. COME ON, GET UP! NOW!
I'VE JUST ONE MORE BITE TO FINISH, THEN THE SPELL SHOULD WORK.
SWALLOW IT DOWN!
ALRIGHT, OKAY. WHATEVER YOU SAY...
CHOMP!
CHOMP!
CHOMP!
...YA JERK.

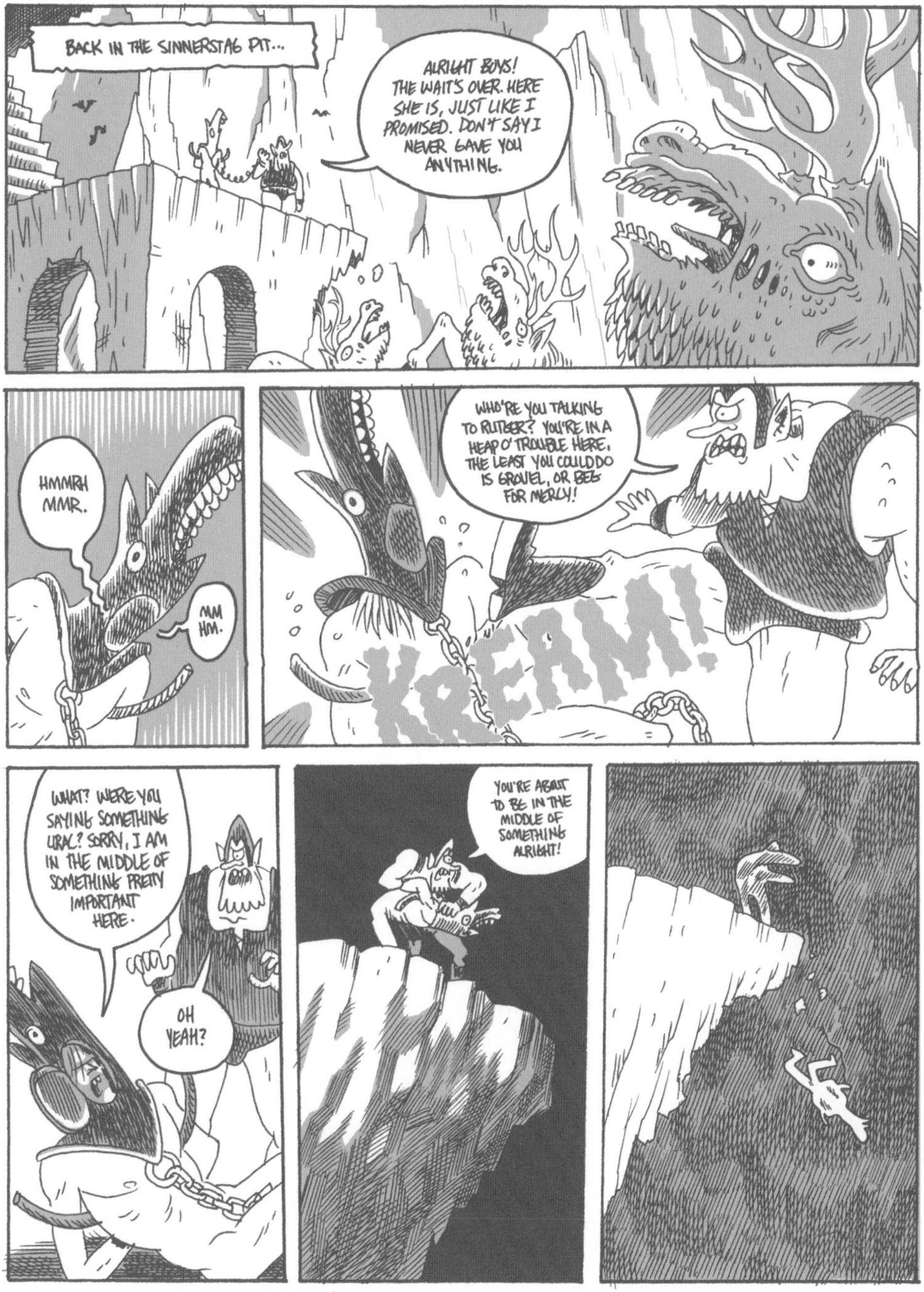
BACK IN THE SINNERSTAG PIT...
ALRIGHT BOYS! THE WAIT'S OVER. HERE SHE IS, JUST LIKE I PROMISED. DON'T SAY I NEVER GAVE YOU ANYTHING.
HMMRH MMR.
MM HM.
WHO'RE YOU TALKING TO RUTGER? YOU'RE IN A HEAP O' TROUBLE HERE. THE LEAST YOU COULD DO IS GROVEL, OR BEG FOR MERCY!
KREAM!
WHAT? WERE YOU SAYING SOMETHING URAC? SORRY, I AM IN THE MIDDLE OF SOMETHING PRETTY IMPORTANT HERE.
OH YEAH?
YOU'RE ABOUT TO BE IN THE MIDDLE OF SOMETHING ALRIGHT!

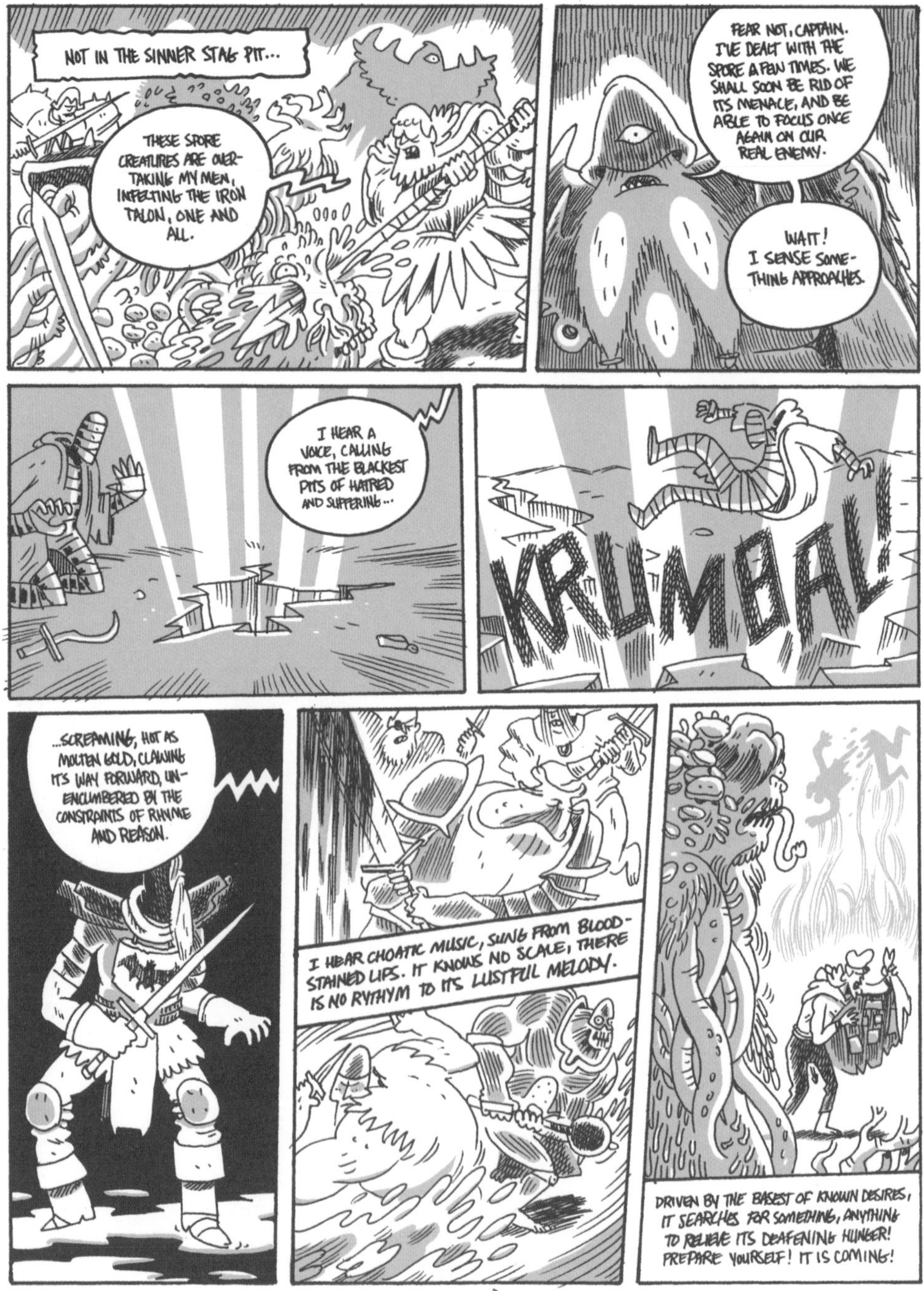
NOT IN THE SINNER STAG PIT...
THESE SPORE CREATURES ARE OVER-TAKING MY MEN, INFECTING THE IRON TALON, ONE AND ALL.
FEAR NOT, CAPTAIN. I'VE DEALT WITH THE SPORE A FEW TIMES. WE SHALL SOON BE RID OF ITS MENACE, AND BE ABLE TO FOCUS ONCE AGAIN ON OUR REAL ENEMY.
WAIT! I SENSE SOME-THING APPROACHES.
I HEAR A VOICE, CALLING FROM THE BLACKEST PITS OF HATRED AND SUFFERING...
KRUMBA!
...SCREAMING, HOT AS MOLTEN GOLD, CLAWING ITS WAY FORWARD, UN-ENCUMBERED BY THE CONSTRAINTS OF RHYME AND REASON.
I HEAR CHOATIC MUSIC, SUNG FROM BLOOD-STAINED LIPS. IT KNOWS NO SCALE, THERE IS NO RYTHYM TO ITS LUSTFUL MELODY.
DRIVEN BY THE BASEST OF KNOWN DESIRES, IT SEARCHES FOR SOMETHING, ANYTHING TO RELIEVE ITS DEAFENING HUNGER! PREPARE YOURSELF! IT IS COMING!

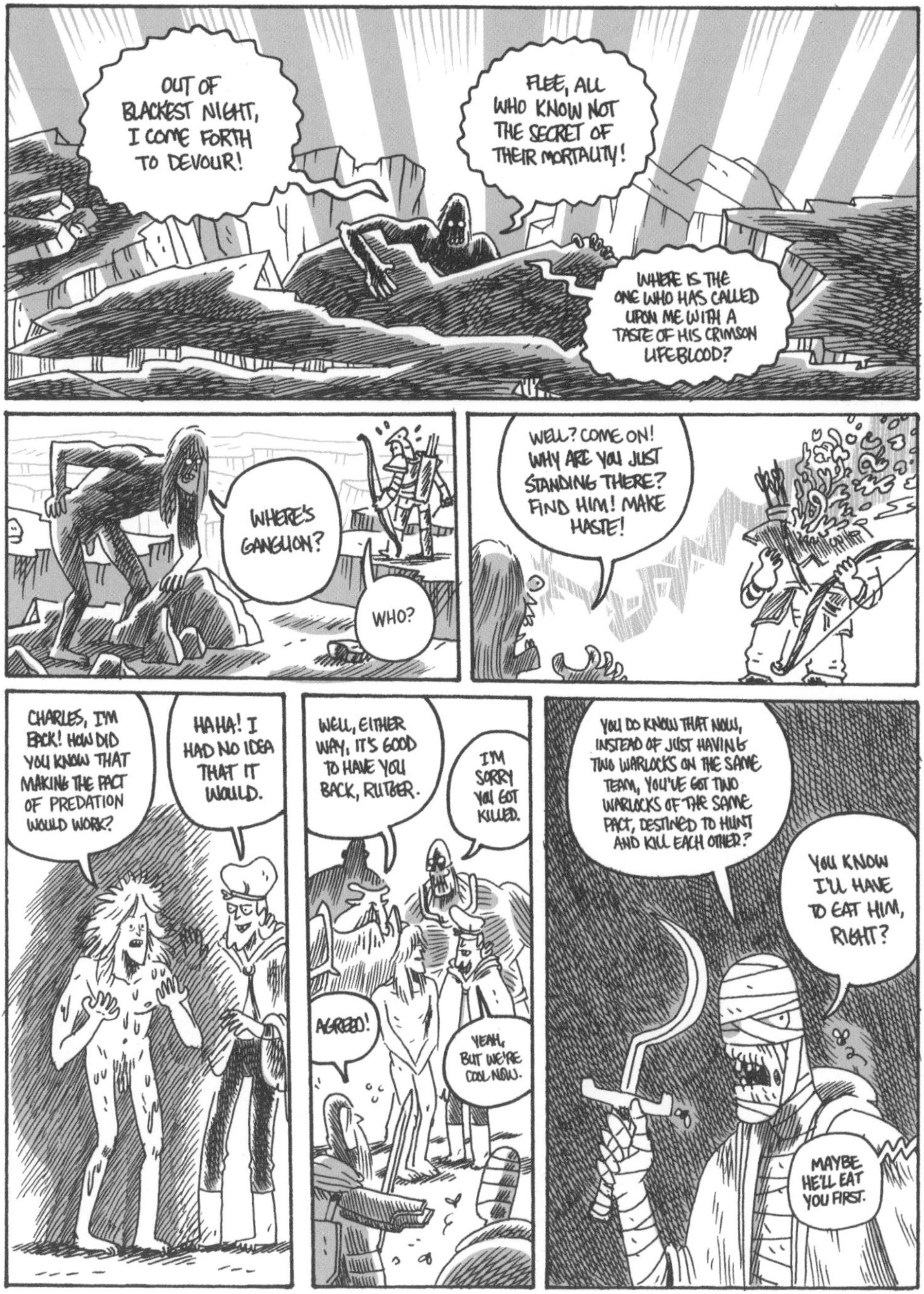
OUT OF BLACKEST NIGHT, I COME FORTH TO DEVOUR!
FLEE, ALL WHO KNOW NOT THE SECRET OF THEIR MORTALITY!
WHERE IS THE ONE WHO HAS CALLED UPON ME WITH A TASTE OF HIS CRIMSON LIFEBLOOD?
WHERE'S GANGLION?
WHO?
WELL? COME ON! WHY ARE YOU JUST STANDING THERE? FIND HIM! MAKE HASTE!
CHARLES, I'M BACK! HOW DID YOU KNOW THAT MAKING THE PACT OF PREDATION WOULD WORK?
HAHA! I HAD NO IDEA THAT IT WOULD.
WELL, EITHER WAY, IT'S GOOD TO HAVE YOU BACK, RUTGER.
I'M SORRY YOU GOT KILLED.
AGREED!
YEAH, BUT WE'RE COOL NOW.
YOU DO KNOW THAT NOW, INSTEAD OF JUST HAVING TWO WARLOCKS ON THE SAME TEAM, YOU'VE GOT TWO WARLOCKS OF THE SAME PACT, DESTINED TO HUNT AND KILL EACH OTHER?
YOU KNOW I'LL HAVE TO EAT HIM, RIGHT?
MAYBE HE'LL EAT YOU FIRST.

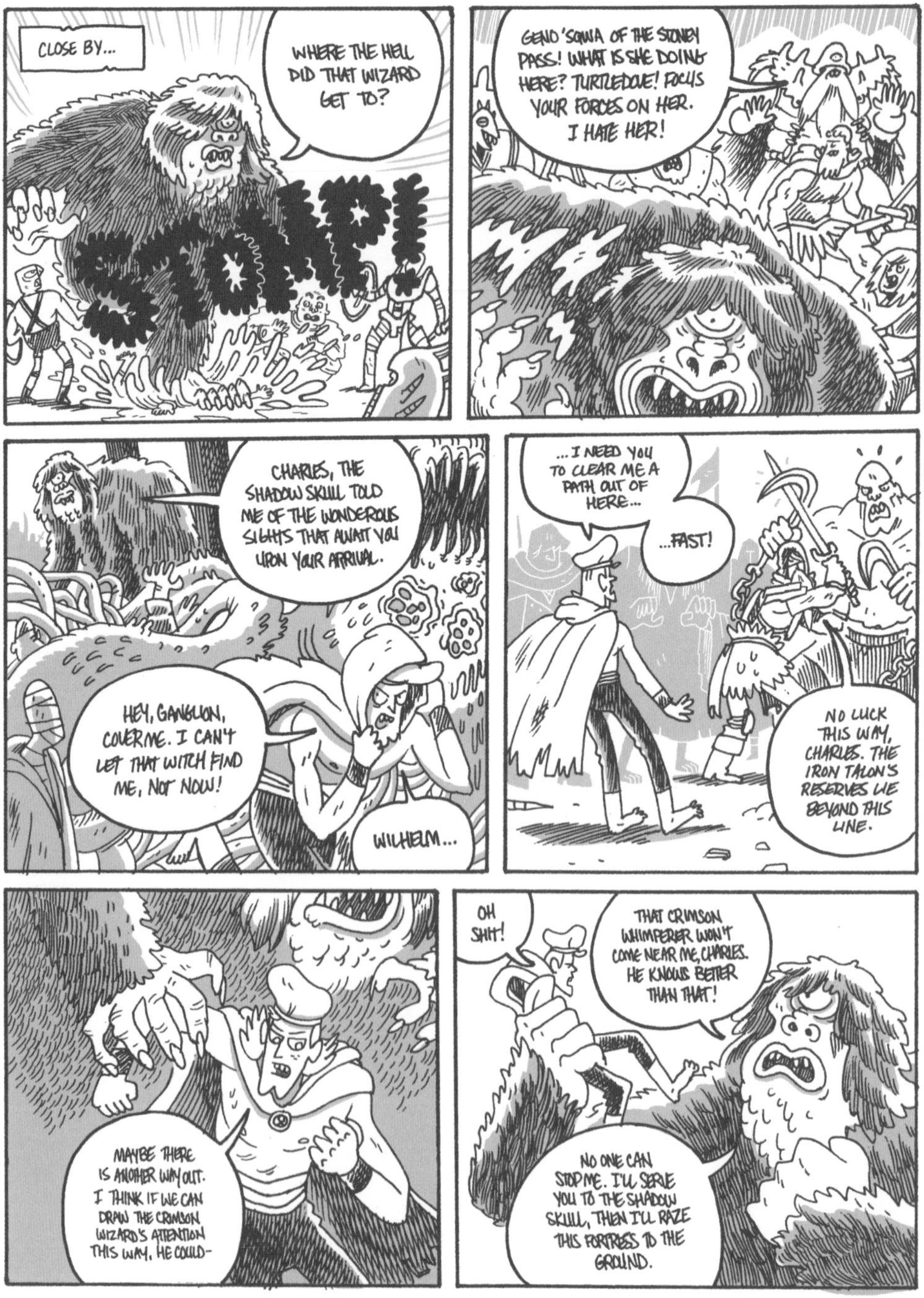
CLOSE BY...
WHERE THE HELL DID THAT WIZARD GET TO?
STOMP!
GENO'SONIA OF THE STONEY PASS! WHAT IS SHE DOING HERE? TURTLEDOVE! FOCUS YOUR FORCES ON HER. I HATE HER!
CHARLES, THE SHADOW SKULL TOLD ME OF THE WONDEROUS SIGHTS THAT AWAIT YOU UPON YOUR ARRIVAL.
HEY, GANGLION, COVER ME. I CAN'T LET THAT WITCH FIND ME, NOT NOW!
WILHELM...
...I NEED YOU TO CLEAR ME A PATH OUT OF HERE...
...FAST!
NO LUCK THIS WAY, CHARLES. THE IRON TALON'S RESERVES LIE BEYOND THIS LINE.
MAYBE THERE IS ANOTHER WAY OUT. I THINK IF WE CAN DRAW THE CRIMSON WIZARD'S ATTENTION THIS WAY, HE COULD-
OH SHIT!
THAT CRIMSON WHIMPERER WON'T COME NEAR ME, CHARLES. HE KNOWS BETTER THAN THAT!
NO ONE CAN STOP ME. I'LL SERVE YOU TO THE SHADOW SKULL, THEN I'LL RAZE THIS FORTRESS TO THE GROUND.

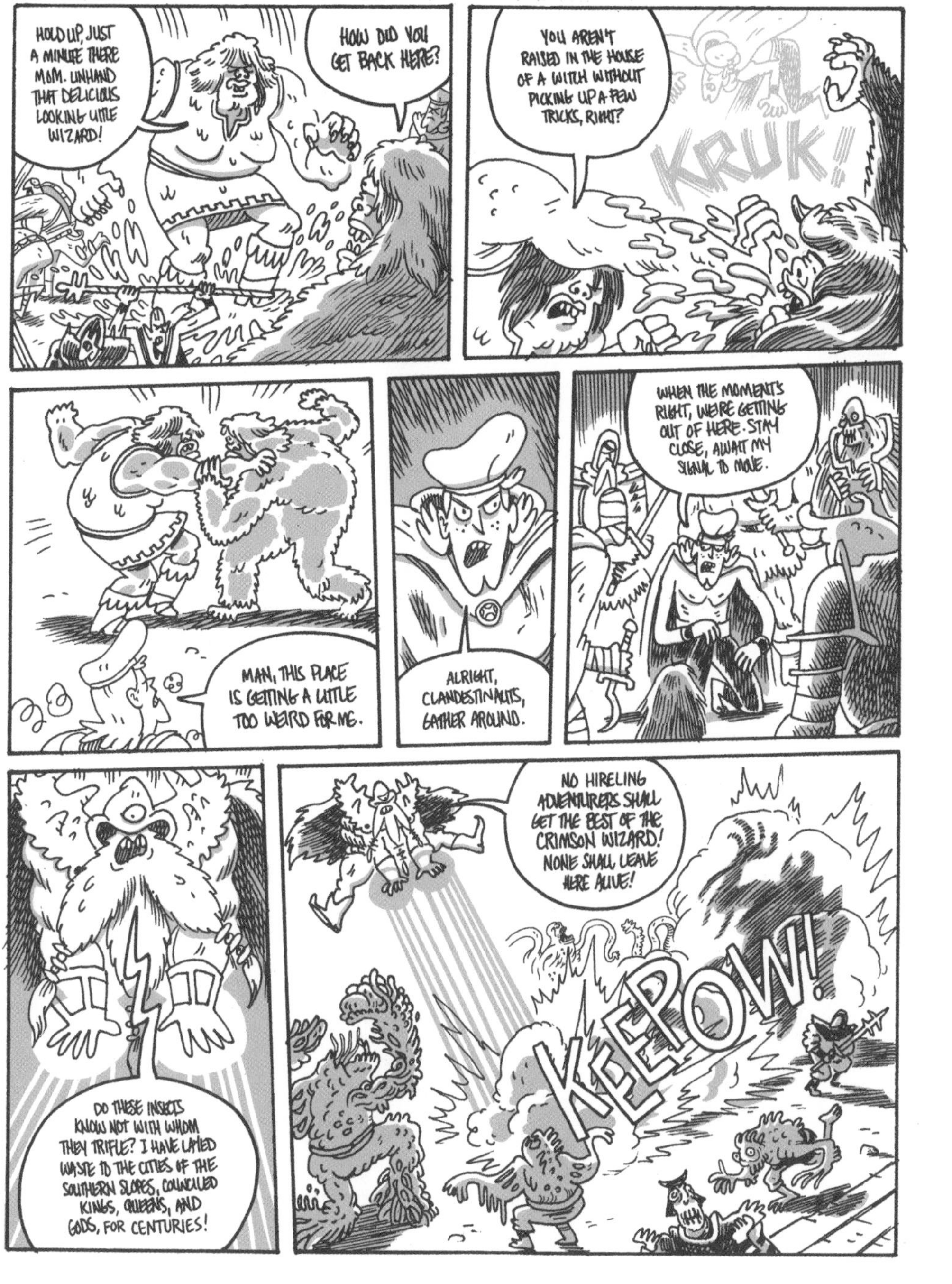
HOLD UP, JUST A MINUTE THERE MOM. UNHAND THAT DELICIOUS LOOKING LITTLE WIZARD!
HOW DID YOU GET BACK HERE?
YOU AREN'T RAISED IN THE HOUSE OF A WITCH WITHOUT PICKING UP A FEW TRICKS, RIGHT?
KRUK!
MAN, THIS PLACE IS GETTING A LITTLE TOO WEIRD FOR ME.
ALRIGHT, CLANDESTINAUTS, GATHER AROUND.
WHEN THE MOMENT'S RIGHT, WE'RE GETTING OUT OF HERE. STAY CLOSE, AWAIT MY SIGNAL TO MOVE.
DO THESE INSECTS KNOW NOT WITH WHOM THEY TRIFLE? I HAVE LAYED WASTE TO THE CITIES OF THE SOUTHERN SLOPES, COUNCILED KINGS, QUEENS, AND GODS, FOR CENTURIES!
NO HIRELING ADVENTURERS SHALL GET THE BEST OF THE CRIMSON WIZARD! NONE SHALL LEAVE HERE ALIVE!
KEEPOW!

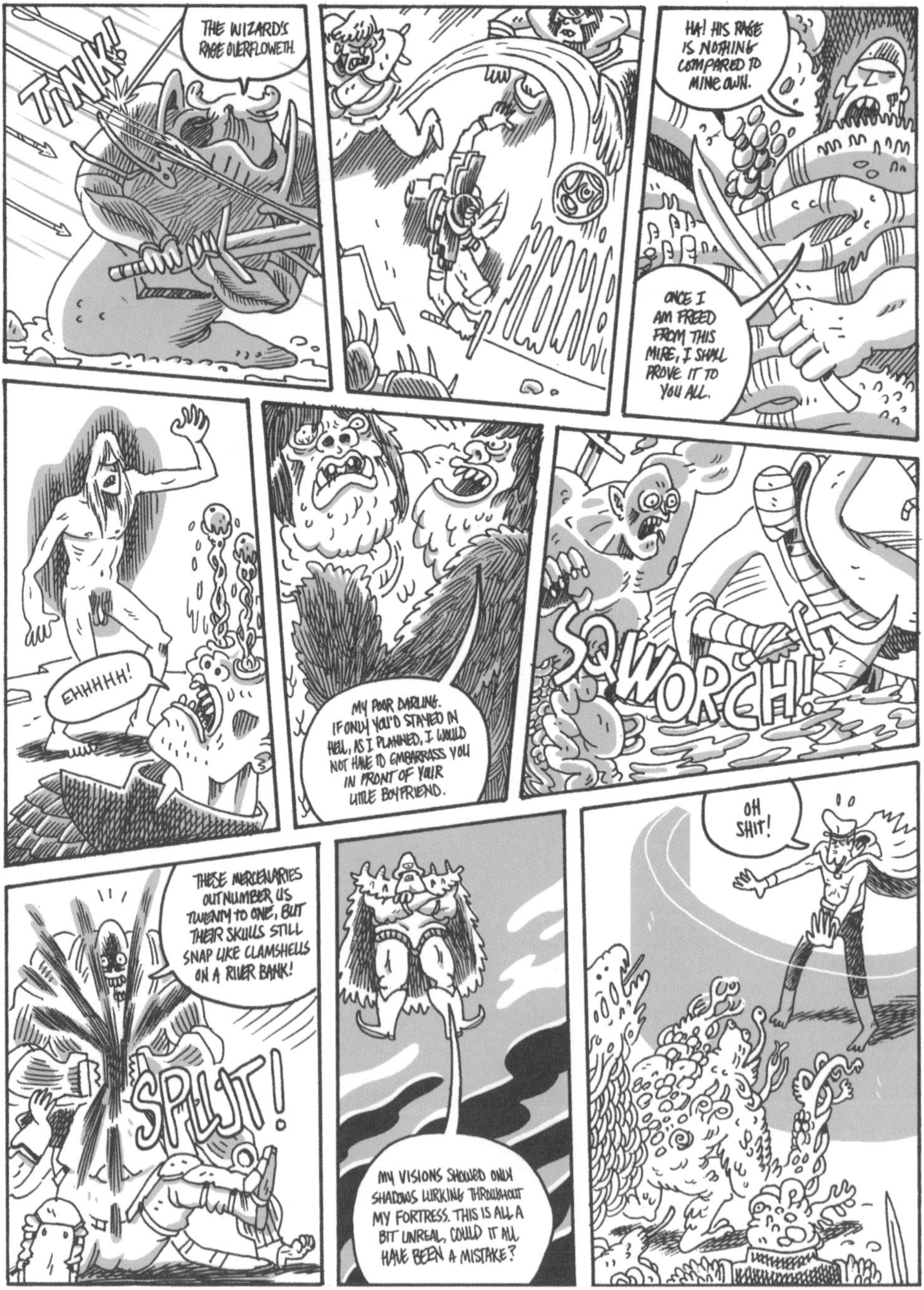

TINK!
THE WIZARD'S RAGE OVERFLOWETH.
HA! HIS RAGE IS NOTHING COMPARED TO MINE OWN.
ONCE I AM FREED FROM THIS MIRE, I SHALL PROVE IT TO YOU ALL.
EHHHHH!
MY POOR DARLING. IF ONLY YOU'D STAYED IN HELL, AS I PLANNED, I WOULD NOT HAVE TO EMBARRASS YOU IN FRONT OF YOUR LITTLE BOYFRIEND.
SQWORCH!
THESE MERCENARIES OUTNUMBER US TWENTY TO ONE, BUT THEIR SKULLS STILL SNAP LIKE CLAMSHELLS ON A RIVER BANK!
SPLIT!
MY VISIONS SHOWED ONLY SHADOWS LURKING THROUGHOUT MY FORTRESS. THIS IS ALL A BIT UNREAL, COULD IT ALL HAVE BEEN A MISTAKE?
OH SHIT!

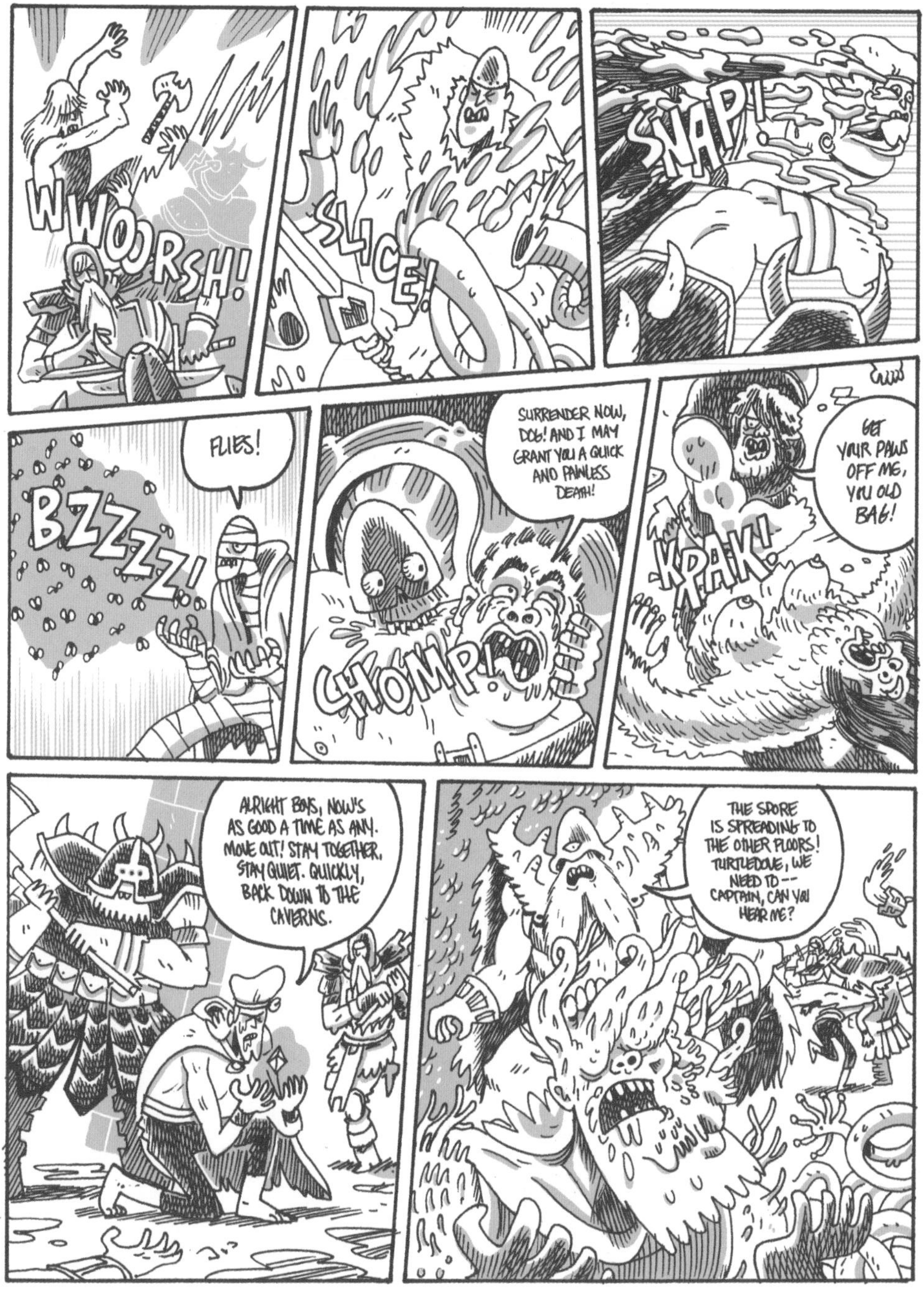
WWOOORSH!
SLICE!
SNAP!
FLIES!
BZZZZZ!
SURRENDER NOW, DOG! AND I MAY GRANT YOU A QUICK AND PAINLESS DEATH!
CHOMP!
GET YOUR PAWS OFF ME, YOU OLD BAG!
KRAK!
ALRIGHT BOYS, NOW'S AS GOOD A TIME AS ANY. MOVE OUT! STAY TOGETHER. STAY QUIET. QUICKLY, BACK DOWN TO THE CAVERNS.
THE SPORE IS SPREADING TO THE OTHER FLOORS! TURTLEDOVE, WE NEED TO-- CAPTAIN, CAN YOU HEAR ME?

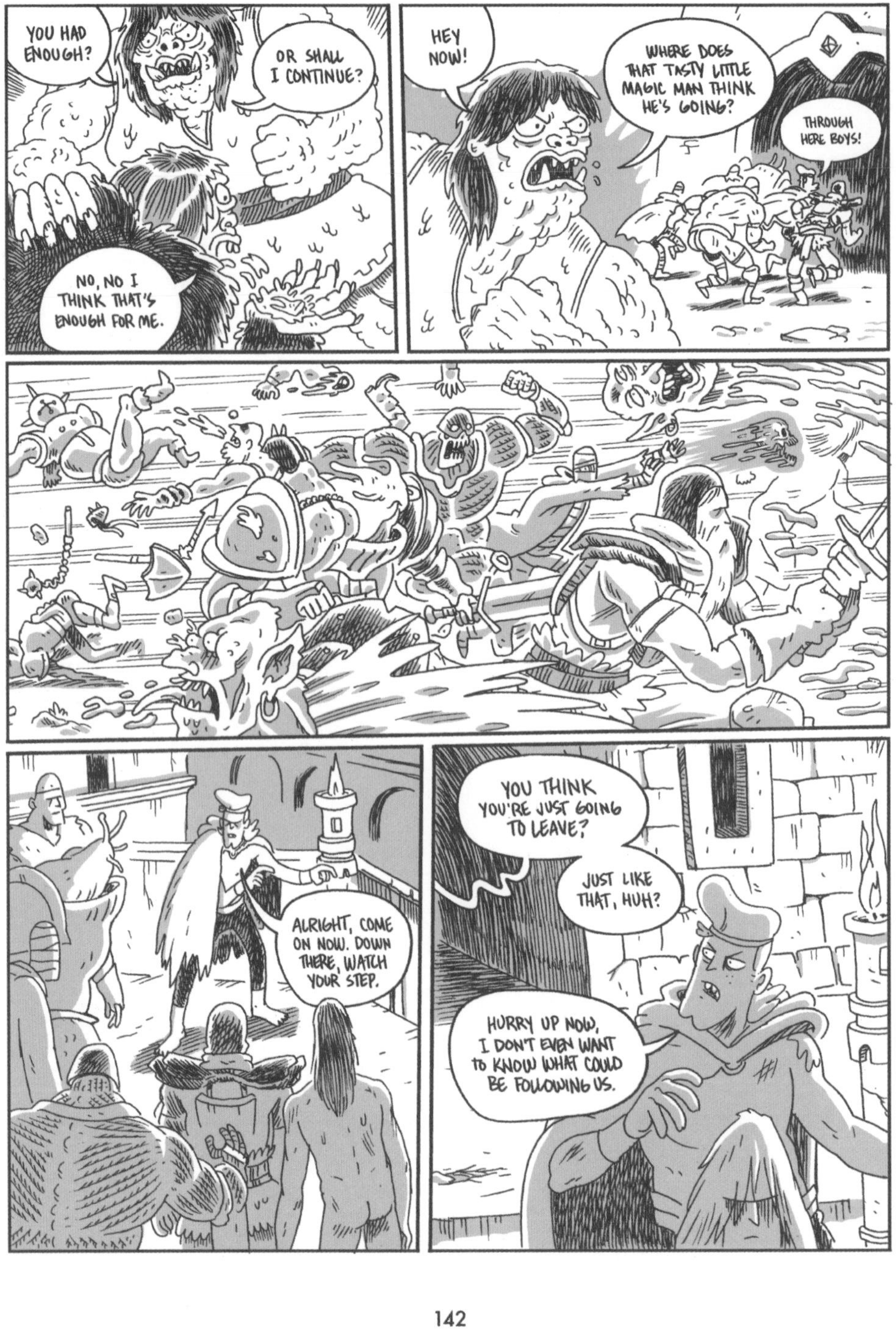
YOU HAD ENOUGH?
OR SHALL I CONTINUE?
NO, NO I THINK THAT'S ENOUGH FOR ME.
HEY NOW!
WHERE DOES THAT TASTY LITTLE MAGIC MAN THINK HE'S GOING?
THROUGH HERE BOYS!
ALRIGHT, COME ON NOW. DOWN THERE, WATCH YOUR STEP.
YOU THINK YOU'RE JUST GOING TO LEAVE?
JUST LIKE THAT, HUH?
HURRY UP NOW, I DON'T EVEN WANT TO KNOW WHAT COULD BE FOLLOWING US.

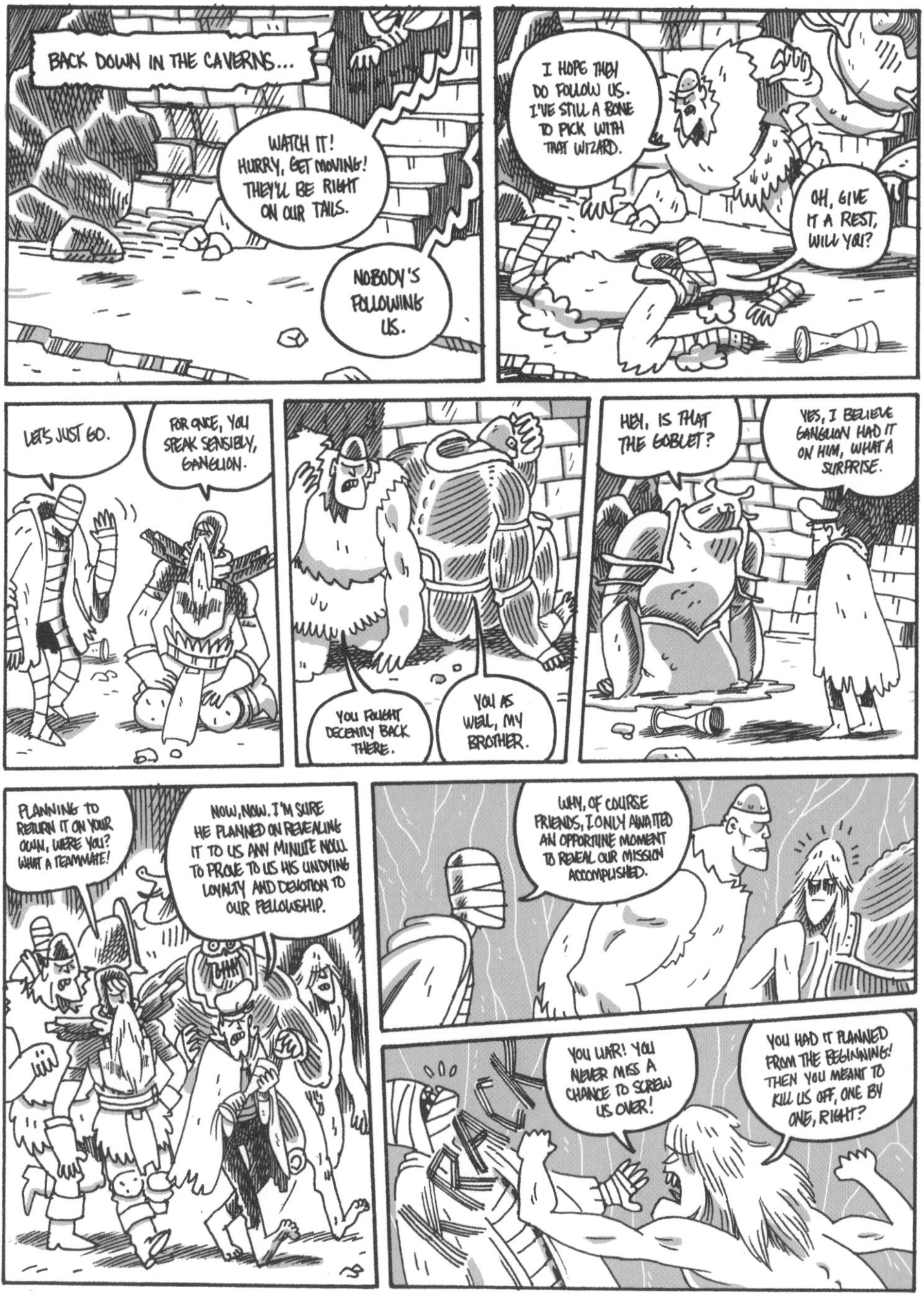
BACK DOWN IN THE CAVERNS...
WATCH IT! HURRY, GET MOVING! THEY'LL BE RIGHT ON OUR TAILS.
NOBODY'S FOLLOWING US.
I HOPE THEY DO FOLLOW US. I'VE STILL A BONE TO PICK WITH THAT WIZARD.
OH, GIVE IT A REST, WILL YOU?
LET'S JUST GO.
FOR ONCE, YOU SPEAK SENSIBLY, GANGLION.
YOU FOUGHT DECENTLY BACK THERE.
YOU AS WELL, MY BROTHER.
HEY, IS THAT THE GOBLET?
YES, I BELIEVE GANGLION HAD IT ON HIM, WHAT A SURPRISE.
PLANNING TO RETURN IT ON YOUR OWN, WERE YOU? WHAT A TEAMMATE!
NOW, NOW. I'M SURE HE PLANNED ON REVEALING IT TO US ANY MINUTE NOW. TO PROVE TO US HIS UNDYING LOYALTY AND DEVOTION TO OUR FELLOWSHIP.
WHY, OF COURSE FRIENDS, I ONLY AWAITED AN OPPORTUNE MOMENT TO REVEAL OUR MISSION ACCOMPLISHED.
YOU LIAR! YOU NEVER MISS A CHANCE TO SCREW US OVER!
YOU HAD IT PLANNED FROM THE BEGINNING! THEN YOU MEANT TO KILL US OFF, ONE BY ONE, RIGHT?

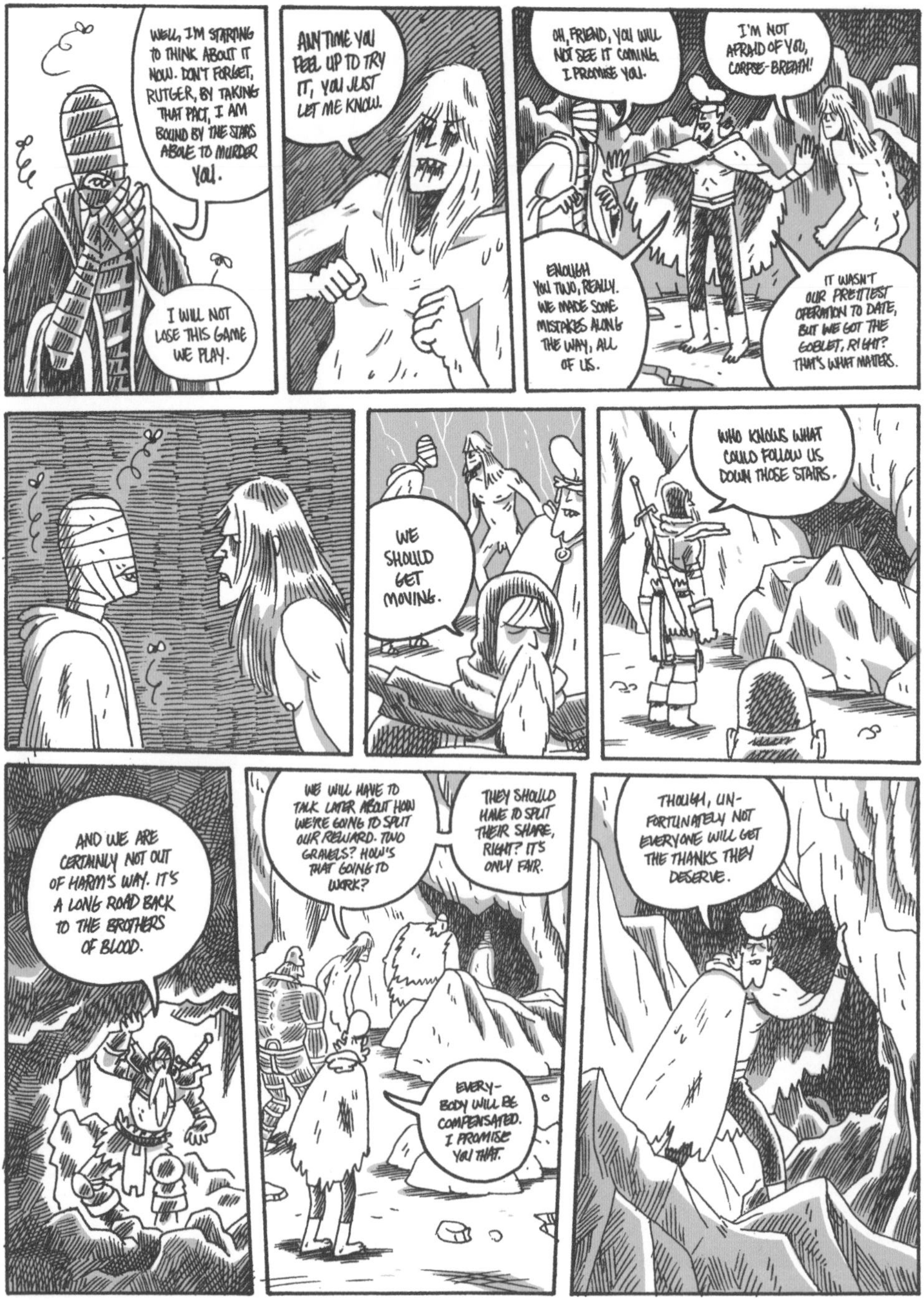
WELL, I'M STARTING TO THINK ABOUT IT NOW. DON'T FORGET, RUTGER, BY TAKING THAT PACT, I AM BOUND BY THE STARS ABOVE TO MURDER YOU.
I WILL NOT LOSE THIS GAME WE PLAY.
ANYTIME YOU FEEL UP TO TRY IT, YOU JUST LET ME KNOW.
OH, FRIEND, YOU WILL NOT SEE IT COMING. I PROMISE YOU.
I'M NOT AFRAID OF YOU, CORPSE-BREATH!
ENOUGH YOU TWO, REALLY. WE MADE SOME MISTAKES ALONG THE WAY, ALL OF US.
IT WASN'T OUR PRETTIEST OPERATION TO DATE, BUT WE GOT THE GOBLET, RIGHT? THAT'S WHAT MATTERS.
WE SHOULD GET MOVING.
WHO KNOWS WHAT COULD FOLLOW US DOWN THOSE STAIRS.
AND WE ARE CERTAINLY NOT OUT OF HARM'S WAY. IT'S A LONG ROAD BACK TO THE BROTHERS OF BLOOD.
WE WILL HAVE TO TALK LATER ABOUT HOW WE'RE GOING TO SPLIT OUR REWARD. TWO GRAVELS? HOW'S THAT GOING TO WORK?
THEY SHOULD HAVE TO SPLIT THEIR SHARE, RIGHT? IT'S ONLY FAIR.
EVERY-BODY WILL BE COMPENSATED. I PROMISE YOU THAT.
THOUGH, UN-FORTUNATELY NOT EVERYONE WILL GET THE THANKS THEY DESERVE.

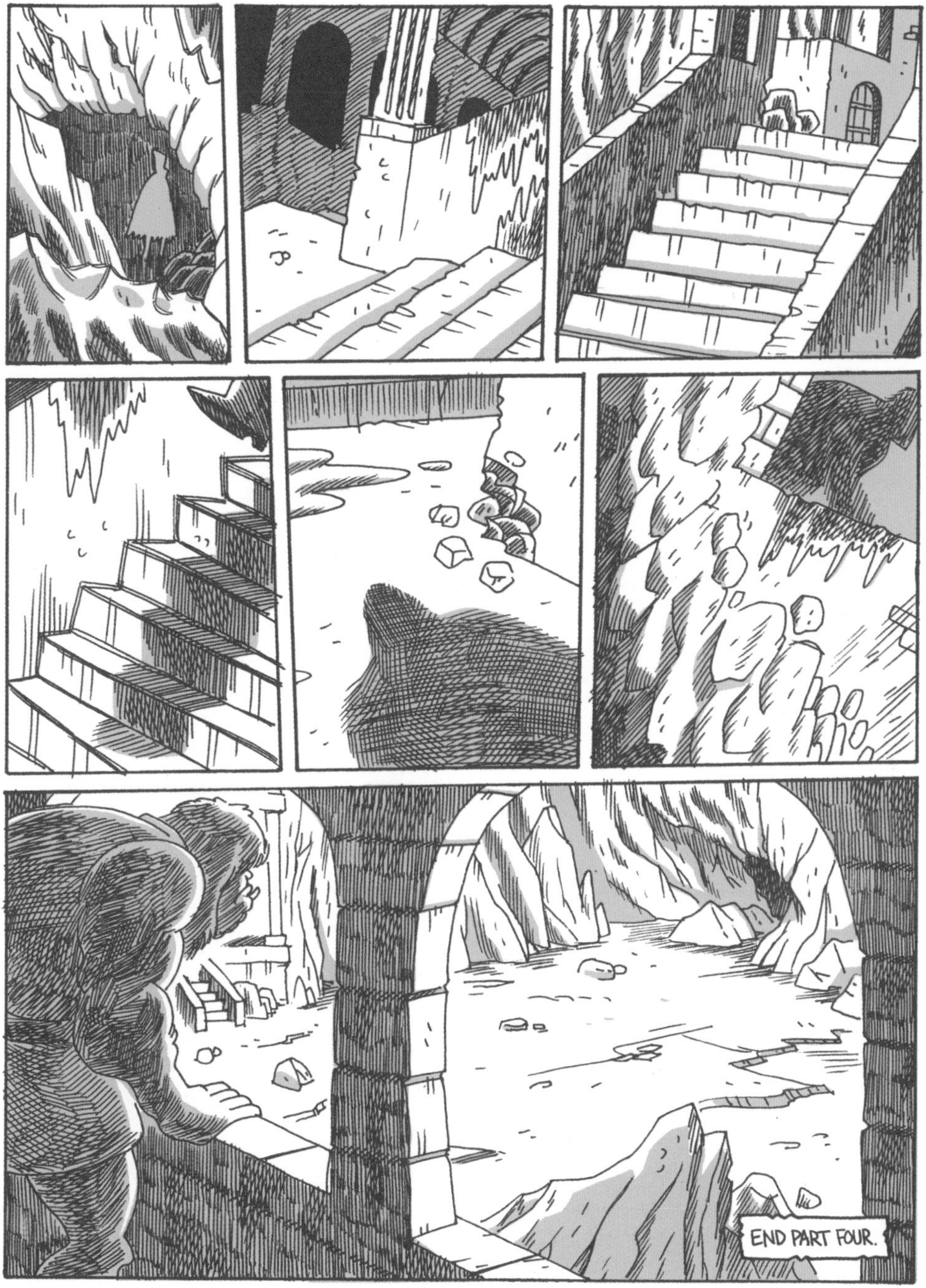
END PART FOUR.

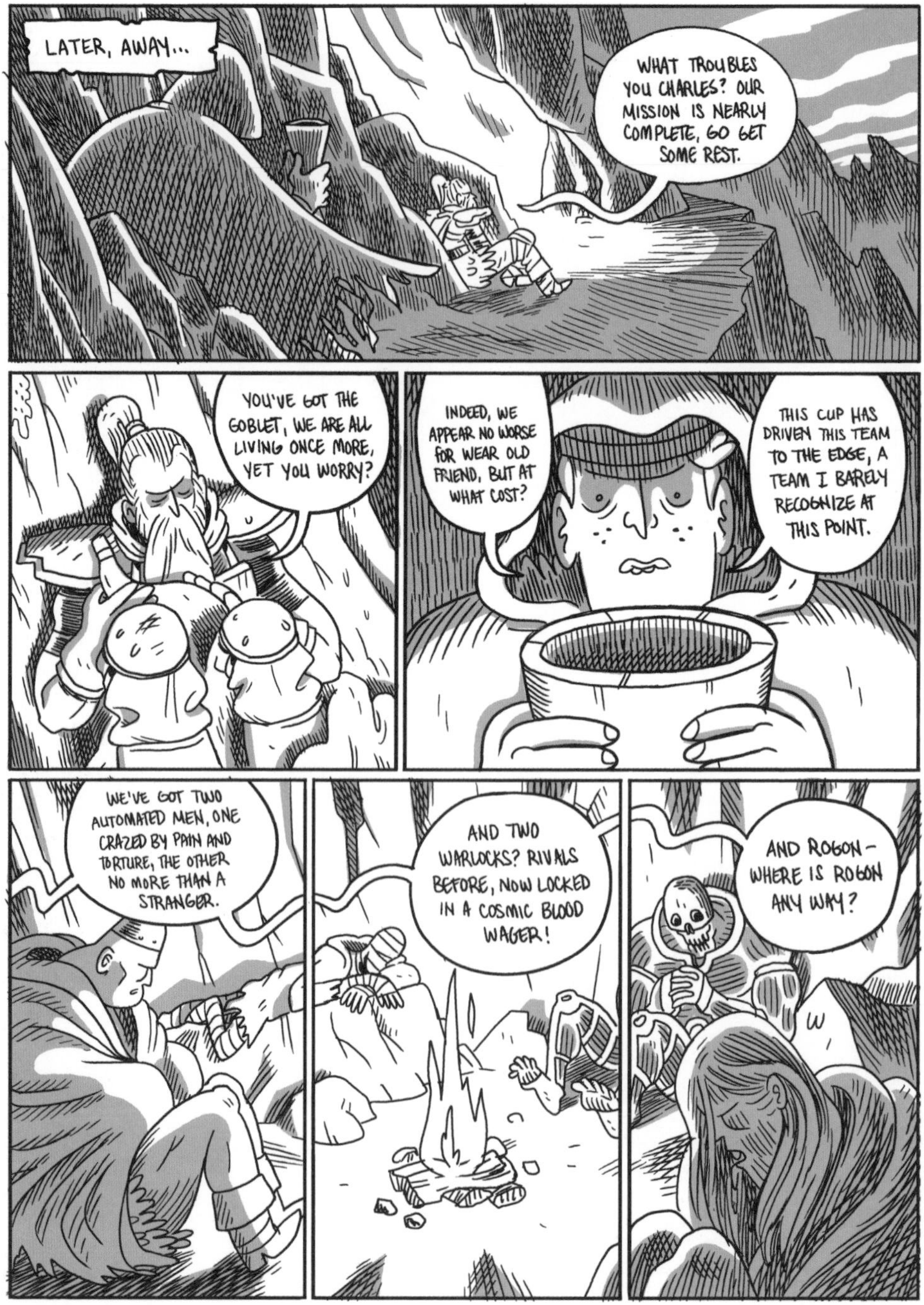
LATER, AWAY...
WHAT TROUBLES YOU CHARLES? OUR MISSION IS NEARLY COMPLETE, GO GET SOME REST.
YOU'VE GOT THE GOBLET, WE ARE ALL LIVING ONCE MORE, YET YOU WORRY?
INDEED, WE APPEAR NO WORSE FOR WEAR OLD FRIEND, BUT AT WHAT COST?
THIS CUP HAS DRIVEN THIS TEAM TO THE EDGE, A TEAM I BARELY RECOGNIZE AT THIS POINT.
WE'VE GOT TWO AUTOMATED MEN, ONE CRAZED BY PAIN AND TORTURE, THE OTHER NO MORE THAN A STRANGER.
AND TWO WARLOCKS? RIVALS BEFORE, NOW LOCKED IN A COSMIC BLOOD WAGER!
AND ROGON- WHERE IS ROGON ANY WAY?

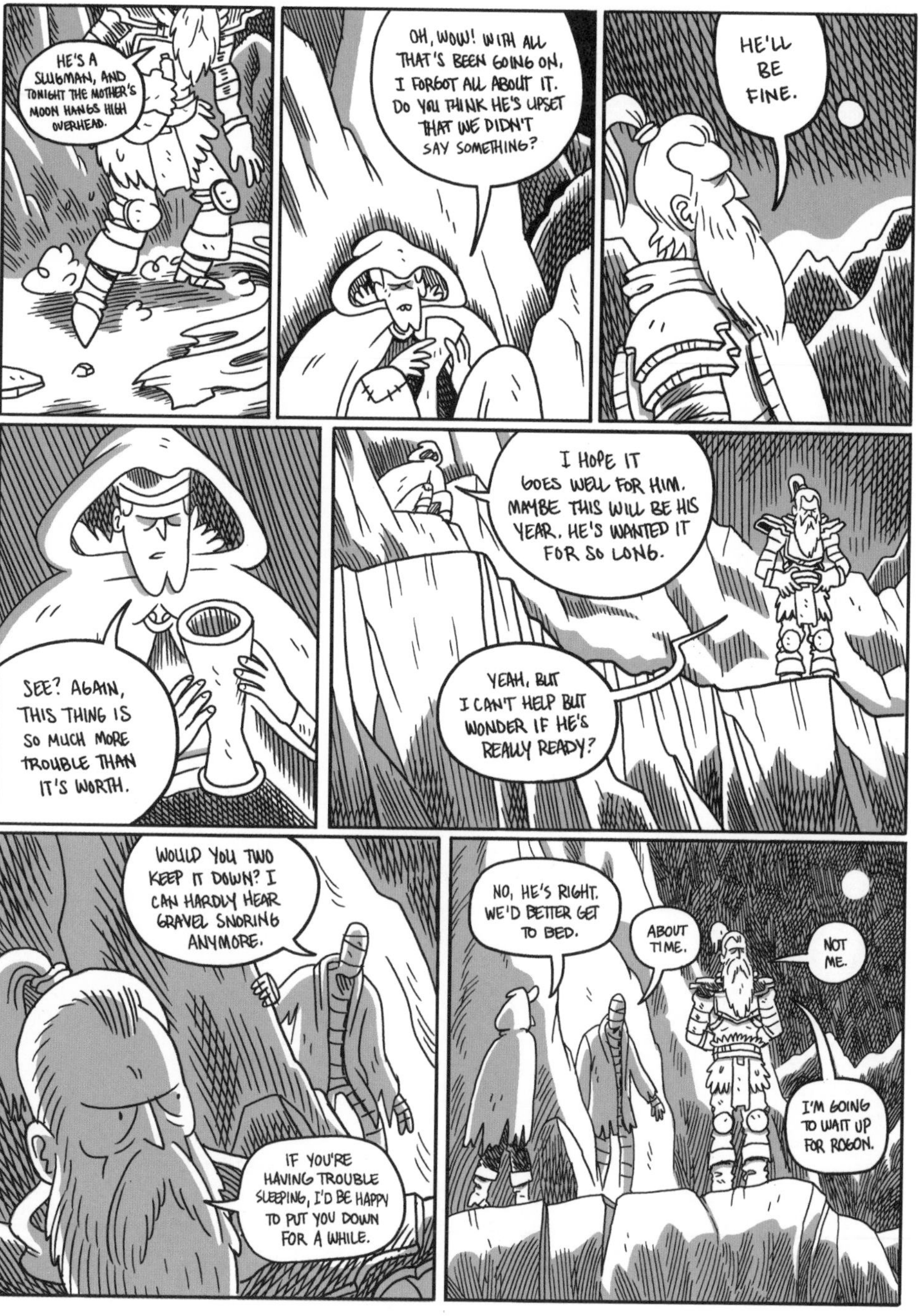
HE'S A SLUGMAN, AND TONIGHT THE MOTHER'S MOON HANGS HIGH OVERHEAD.
OH, WOW! WITH ALL THAT'S BEEN GOING ON, I FORGOT ALL ABOUT IT. DO YOU THINK HE'S UPSET THAT WE DIDN'T SAY SOMETHING?
HE'LL BE FINE.
SEE? AGAIN, THIS THING IS SO MUCH MORE TROUBLE THAN IT'S WORTH.
I HOPE IT GOES WELL FOR HIM. MAYBE THIS WILL BE HIS YEAR. HE'S WANTED IT FOR SO LONG.
YEAH, BUT I CAN'T HELP BUT WONDER IF HE'S REALLY READY?
WOULD YOU TWO KEEP IT DOWN? I CAN HARDLY HEAR GRAVEL SNORING ANYMORE.
IF YOU'RE HAVING TROUBLE SLEEPING, I'D BE HAPPY TO PUT YOU DOWN FOR A WHILE.
NO, HE'S RIGHT. WE'D BETTER GET TO BED.
ABOUT TIME.
NOT ME.
I'M GOING TO WAIT UP FOR ROGON.

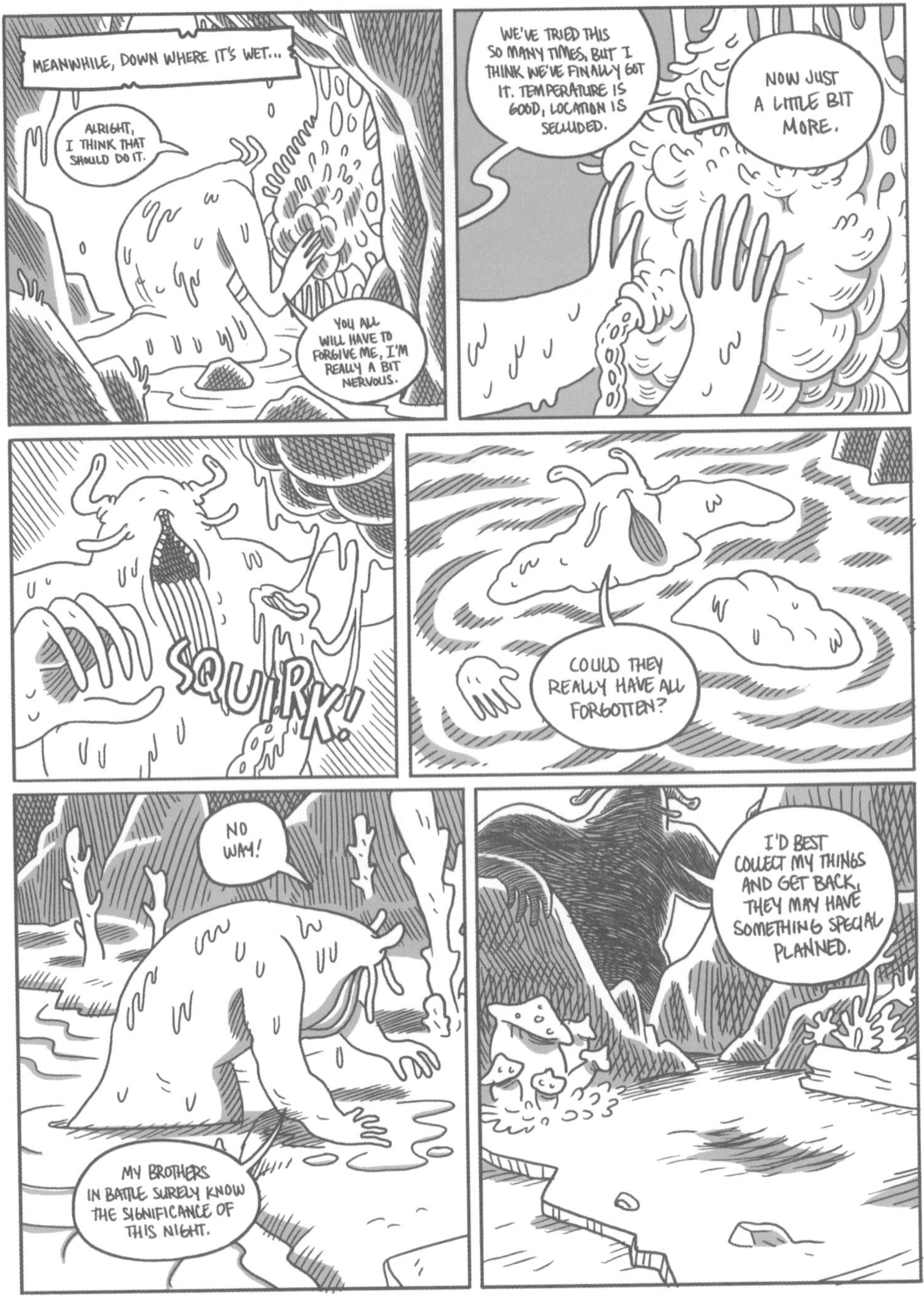
MEANWHILE, DOWN WHERE IT'S WET...
ALRIGHT, I THINK THAT SHOULD DO IT.
YOU ALL WILL HAVE TO FORGIVE ME, I'M REALLY A BIT NERVOUS.
WE'VE TRIED THIS SO MANY TIMES, BUT I THINK WE'VE FINALLY GOT IT. TEMPERATURE IS GOOD, LOCATION IS SECLUDED.
NOW JUST A LITTLE BIT MORE.
SQUIRK!
COULD THEY REALLY HAVE ALL FORGOTTEN?
NO WAY!
MY BROTHERS IN BATTLE SURELY KNOW THE SIGNIFICANCE OF THIS NIGHT.
I'D BEST COLLECT MY THINGS AND GET BACK, THEY MAY HAVE SOMETHING SPECIAL PLANNED.

WHERE THE HELL IS MY ARMOR?

LOOKING FOR YOUR SHELL, SNAIL MAN?

YOU WON'T BE NEEDING IT.

WHAT IN THE WORLD ARE YOU TALKING ABOUT?

MY COMRADES HAVE WAITED WEEKS FOR SUCH A FEAST.

I WILL NOT LET AN OPPORTUNITY LIKE THIS PASS ME BY.

HEY NOW, HOLD ON JUST A MINUTE!

IT'S SAID THAT A HUNGRY ARMY WASTES LITTLE TIME ON THE BATTLEFIELD.

BUT I'LL NOT LET THOSE IDIOTS ON THE WAR COUNCIL STARVE MY PEOPLE TO SUCH A WEAKENED STATE!

HUUUUF!

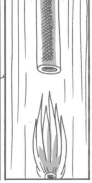

HEY, WAIT!

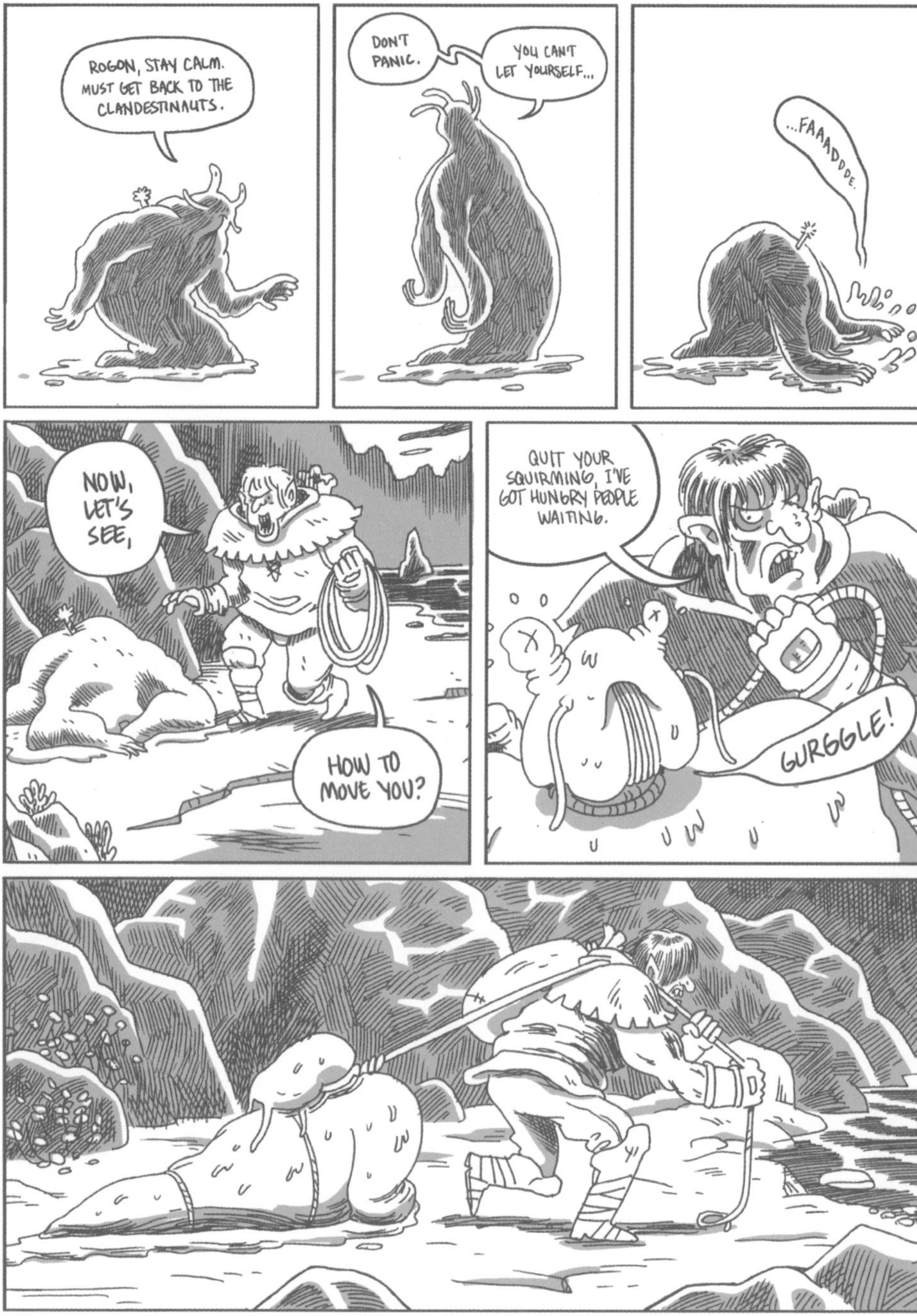
ROGON, STAY CALM. MUST GET BACK TO THE CLANDESTINAUTS.
DON'T PANIC.
YOU CAN'T LET YOURSELF...
...FAAAADDDE.
NOW, LET'S SEE,
HOW TO MOVE YOU?
QUIT YOUR SQUIRMING, I'VE GOT HUNGRY PEOPLE WAITING.
GURGGLE!

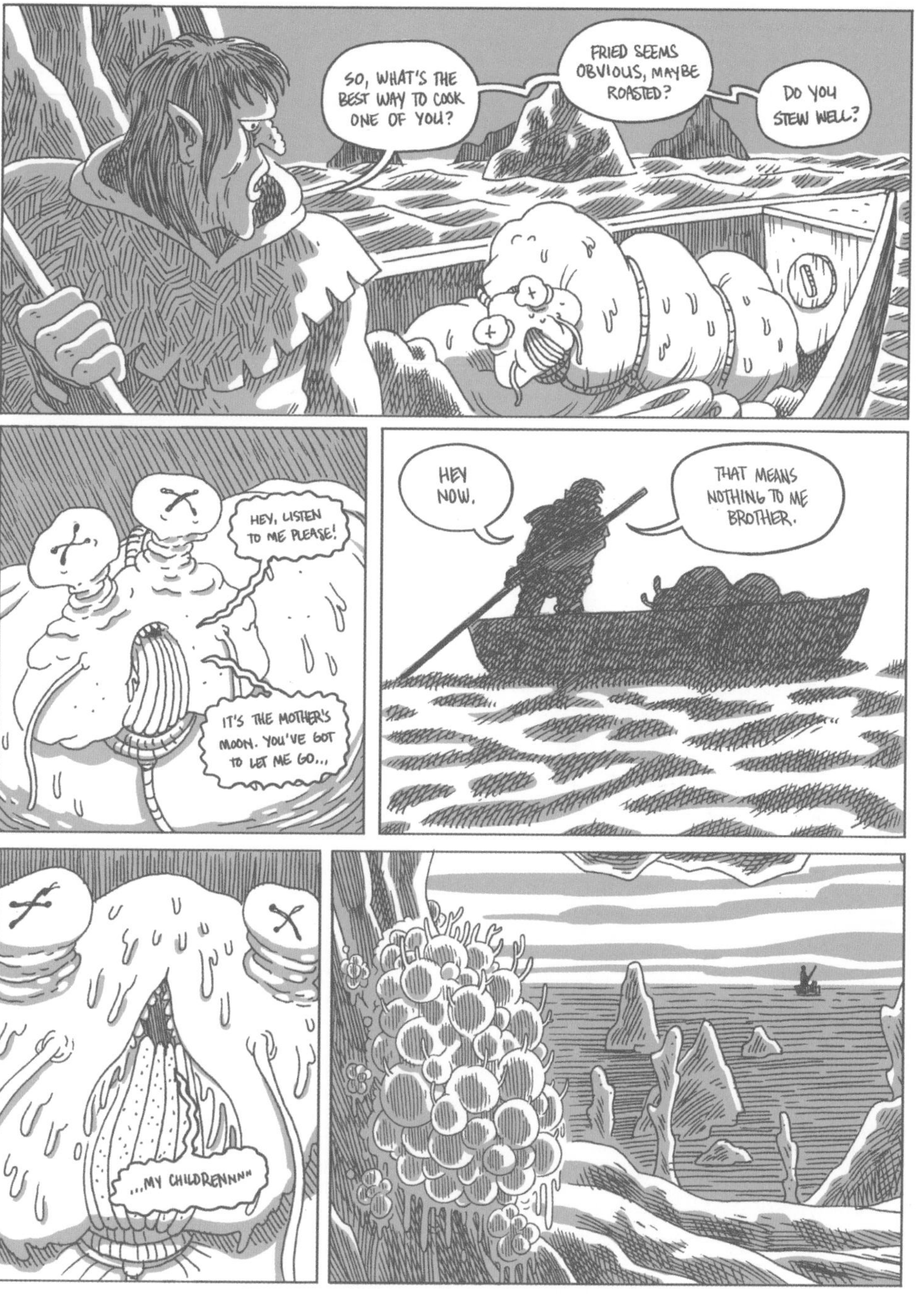
SO, WHAT'S THE BEST WAY TO COOK ONE OF YOU?
FRIED SEEMS OBVIOUS, MAYBE ROASTED?
DO YOU STEW WELL?
HEY, LISTEN TO ME PLEASE!
IT'S THE MOTHER'S MOON. YOU'VE GOT TO LET ME GO...
HEY NOW.
THAT MEANS NOTHING TO ME BROTHER.
...MY CHILDRENNN"

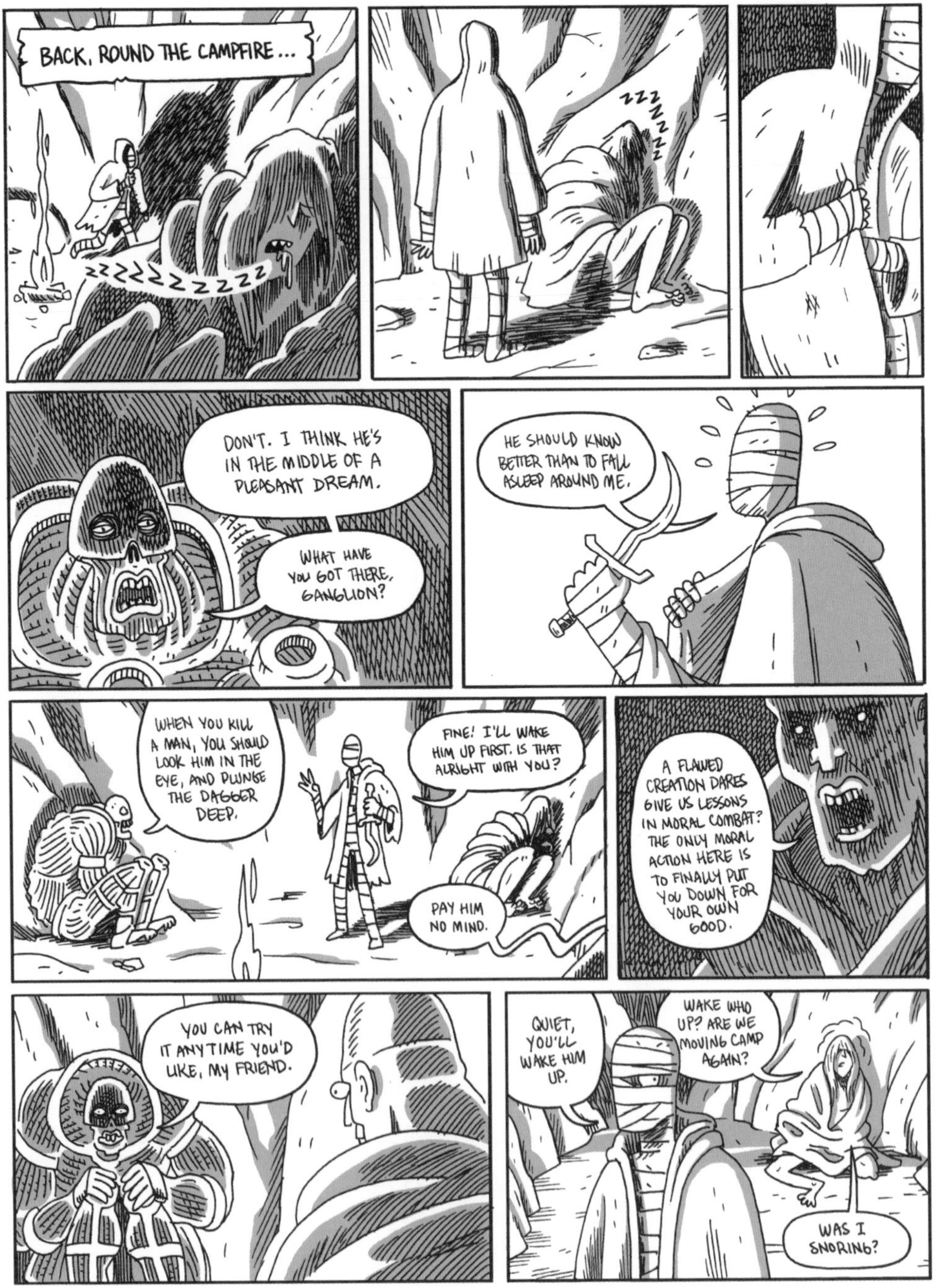
BACK, ROUND THE CAMPFIRE ...
ZZZZZZZZZZZZ
ZZZ
ZZZ
DON'T. I THINK HE'S IN THE MIDDLE OF A PLEASANT DREAM.
WHAT HAVE YOU GOT THERE, GANGLION?
HE SHOULD KNOW BETTER THAN TO FALL ASLEEP AROUND ME.
WHEN YOU KILL A MAN, YOU SHOULD LOOK HIM IN THE EYE, AND PLUNGE THE DAGGER DEEP.
FINE! I'LL WAKE HIM UP FIRST. IS THAT ALRIGHT WITH YOU?
PAY HIM NO MIND.
A FLAWED CREATION DARES GIVE US LESSONS IN MORAL COMBAT? THE ONLY MORAL ACTION HERE IS TO FINALLY PUT YOU DOWN FOR YOUR OWN GOOD.
YOU CAN TRY IT ANYTIME YOU'D LIKE, MY FRIEND.
QUIET, YOU'LL WAKE HIM UP.
WAKE WHO UP? ARE WE MOVING CAMP AGAIN?
WAS I SNORING?

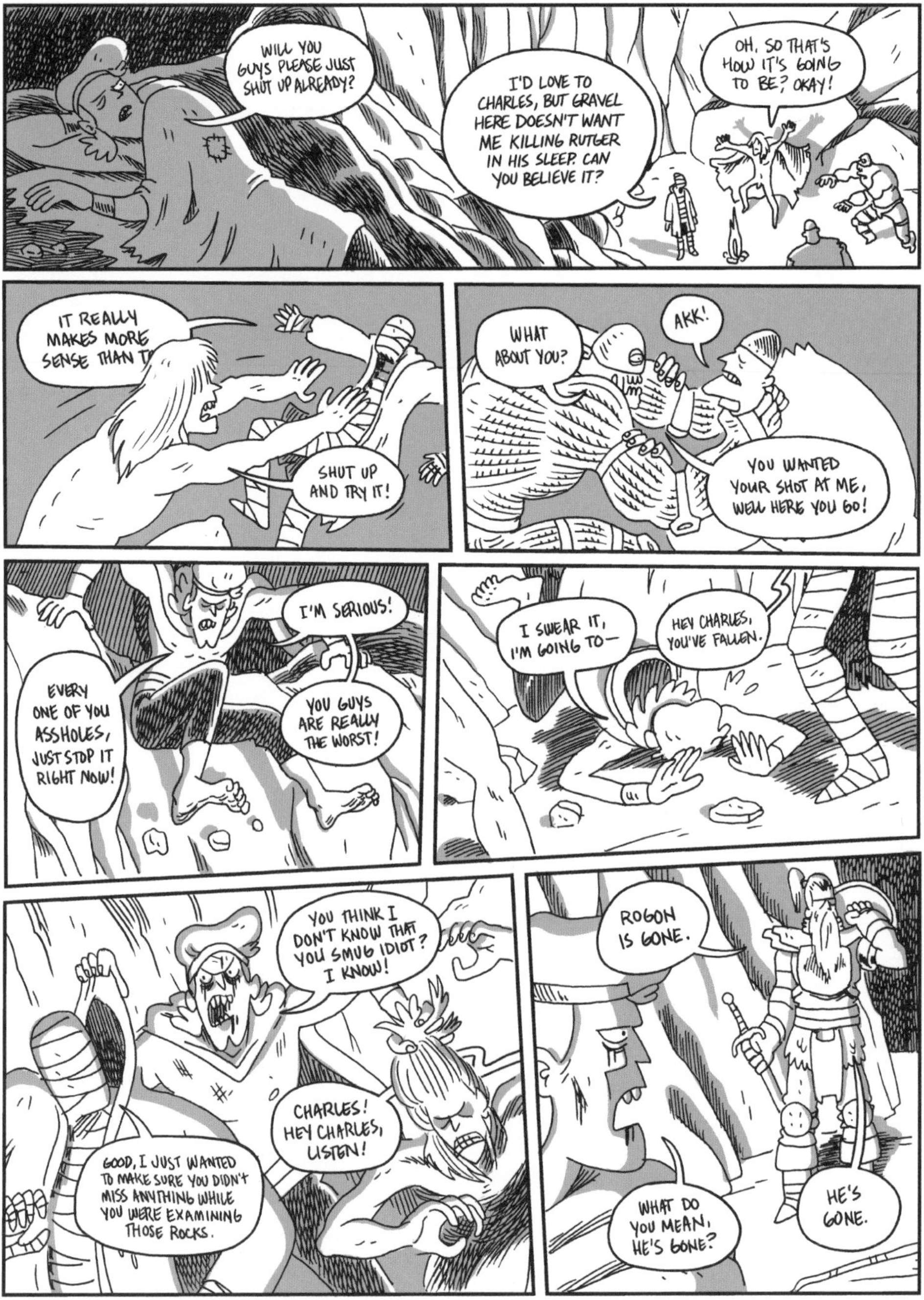
WILL YOU GUYS PLEASE JUST SHUT UP ALREADY?
I'D LOVE TO CHARLES, BUT GRAVEL HERE DOESN'T WANT ME KILLING RUTGER IN HIS SLEEP. CAN YOU BELIEVE IT?
OH, SO THAT'S HOW IT'S GOING TO BE? OKAY!
IT REALLY MAKES MORE SENSE THAN TO
SHUT UP AND TRY IT!
WHAT ABOUT YOU?
AKK!
YOU WANTED YOUR SHOT AT ME, WELL HERE YOU GO!
I'M SERIOUS!
EVERY ONE OF YOU ASSHOLES, JUST STOP IT RIGHT NOW!
YOU GUYS ARE REALLY THE WORST!
I SWEAR IT, I'M GOING TO—
HEY CHARLES, YOU'VE FALLEN.
YOU THINK I DON'T KNOW THAT YOU SMUG IDIOT? I KNOW!
GOOD, I JUST WANTED TO MAKE SURE YOU DIDN'T MISS ANYTHING WHILE YOU WERE EXAMINING THOSE ROCKS.
CHARLES! HEY CHARLES, LISTEN!
ROGON IS GONE.
WHAT DO YOU MEAN, HE'S GONE?
HE'S GONE.

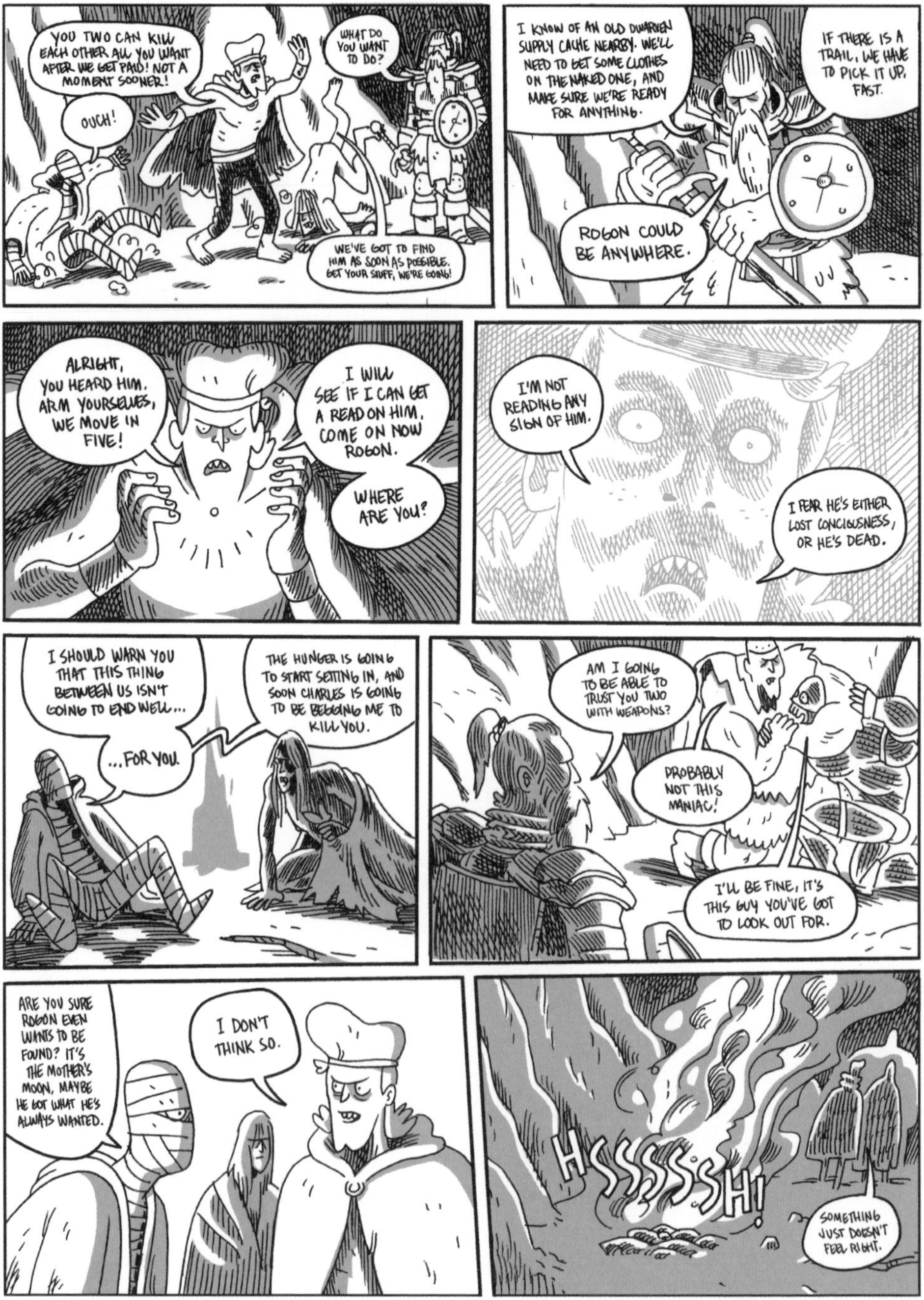

YOU TWO CAN KILL EACH OTHER ALL YOU WANT AFTER WE GET PAID! NOT A MOMENT SOONER!
OUCH!
WHAT DO YOU WANT TO DO?
WE'VE GOT TO FIND HIM AS SOON AS POSSIBLE. GET YOUR STUFF, WE'RE GOING!
I KNOW OF AN OLD DWARVEN SUPPLY CACHE NEARBY. WE'LL NEED TO GET SOME CLOTHES ON THE NAKED ONE, AND MAKE SURE WE'RE READY FOR ANYTHING.
IF THERE IS A TRAIL, WE HAVE TO PICK IT UP, FAST.
ROGON COULD BE ANYWHERE.
ALRIGHT, YOU HEARD HIM. ARM YOURSELVES, WE MOVE IN FIVE!
I WILL SEE IF I CAN GET A READ ON HIM. COME ON NOW ROGON.
WHERE ARE YOU?
I'M NOT READING ANY SIGN OF HIM.
I FEAR HE'S EITHER LOST CONCIOUSNESS, OR HE'S DEAD.
I SHOULD WARN YOU THAT THIS THING BETWEEN US ISN'T GOING TO END WELL...
...FOR YOU.
THE HUNGER IS GOING TO START SETTING IN, AND SOON CHARLES IS GOING TO BE BEGGING ME TO KILL YOU.
AM I GOING TO BE ABLE TO TRUST YOU TWO WITH WEAPONS?
PROBABLY NOT THIS MANIAC!
I'LL BE FINE, IT'S THIS GUY YOU'VE GOT TO LOOK OUT FOR.
ARE YOU SURE ROGON EVEN WANTS TO BE FOUND? IT'S THE MOTHER'S MOON, MAYBE HE GOT WHAT HE'S ALWAYS WANTED.
I DON'T THINK SO.
HSSSSSSH!
SOMETHING JUST DOESN'T FEEL RIGHT.

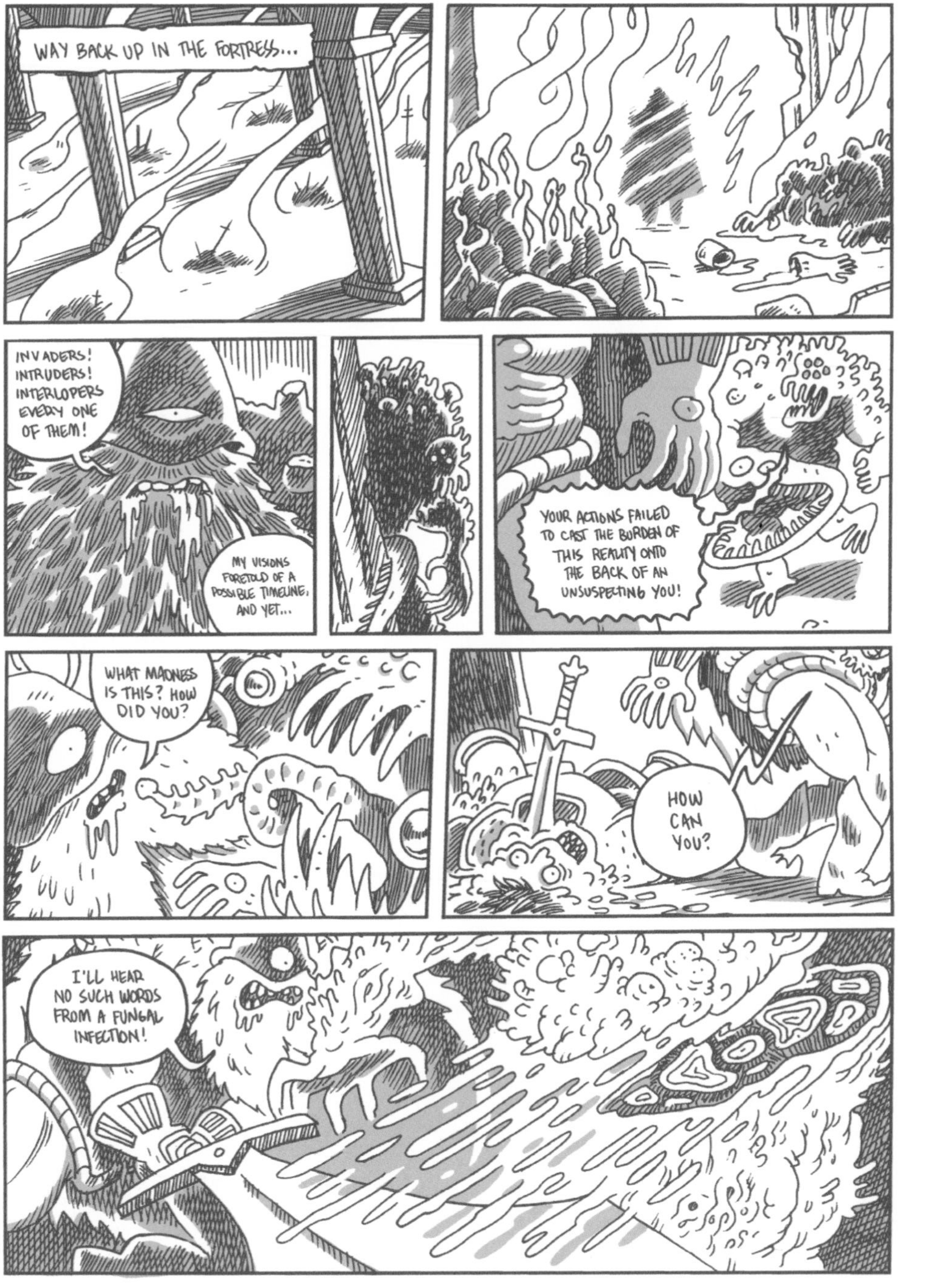
WAY BACK UP IN THE FORTRESS...
INVADERS! INTRUDERS! INTERLOPERS EVERY ONE OF THEM!
MY VISIONS FORETOLD OF A POSSIBLE TIMELINE, AND YET...
YOUR ACTIONS FAILED TO CAST THE BURDEN OF THIS REALITY ONTO THE BACK OF AN UNSUSPECTING YOU!
WHAT MADNESS IS THIS? HOW DID YOU?
HOW CAN YOU?
I'LL HEAR NO SUCH WORDS FROM A FUNGAL INFECTION!

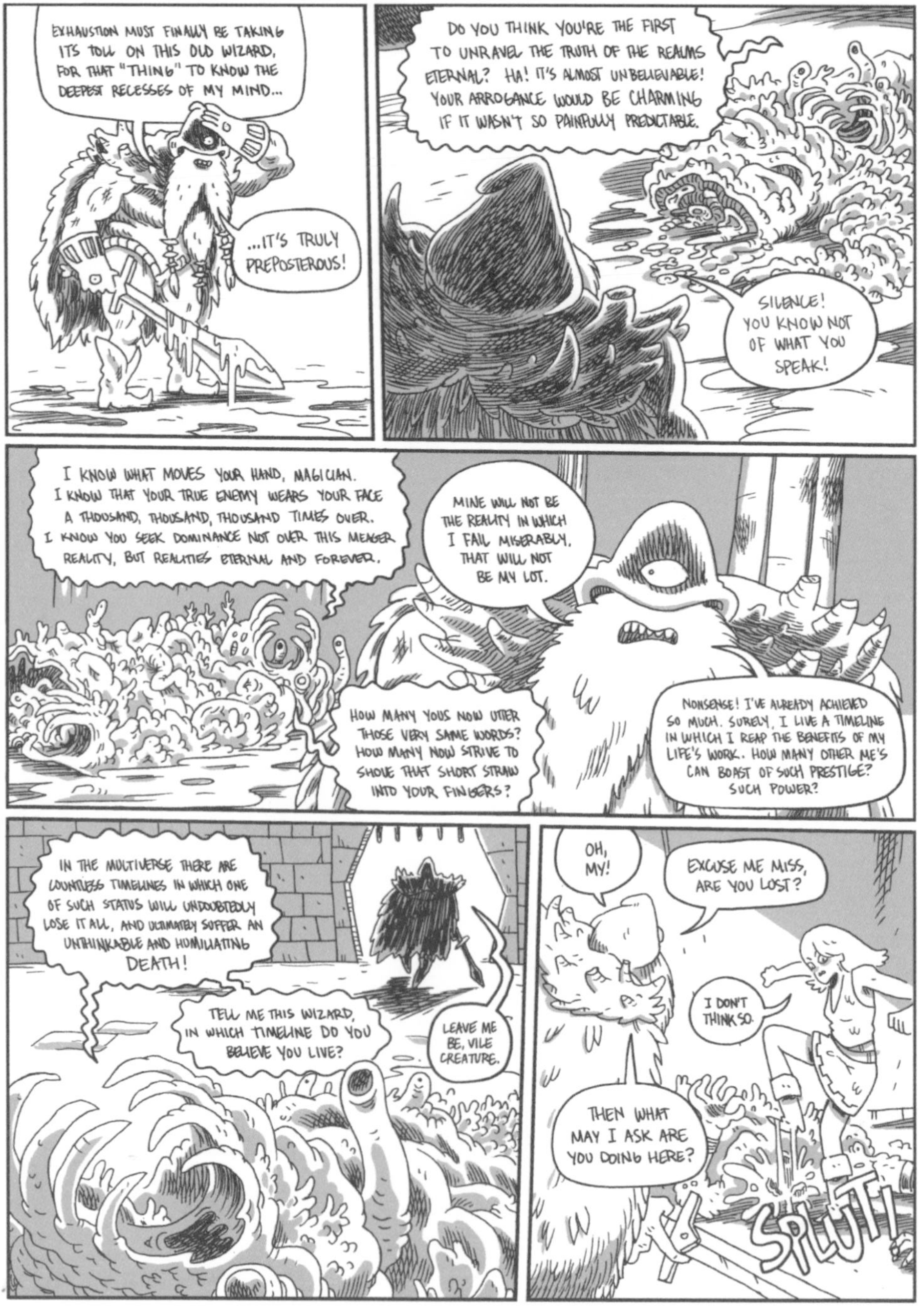
EXHAUSTION MUST FINALLY BE TAKING ITS TOLL ON THIS OLD WIZARD, FOR THAT "THING" TO KNOW THE DEEPEST RECESSES OF MY MIND...
...IT'S TRULY PREPOSTEROUS!
DO YOU THINK YOU'RE THE FIRST TO UNRAVEL THE TRUTH OF THE REALMS ETERNAL? HA! IT'S ALMOST UNBELIEVABLE! YOUR ARROGANCE WOULD BE CHARMING IF IT WASN'T SO PAINFULLY PREDICTABLE.
SILENCE! YOU KNOW NOT OF WHAT YOU SPEAK!
I KNOW WHAT MOVES YOUR HAND, MAGICIAN. I KNOW THAT YOUR TRUE ENEMY WEARS YOUR FACE A THOUSAND, THOUSAND, THOUSAND TIMES OVER. I KNOW YOU SEEK DOMINANCE NOT OVER THIS MEAGER REALITY, BUT REALITIES ETERNAL AND FOREVER.
MINE WILL NOT BE THE REALITY IN WHICH I FAIL MISERABLY. THAT WILL NOT BE MY LOT.
HOW MANY YOUS NOW UTTER THOSE VERY SAME WORDS? HOW MANY NOW STRIVE TO SHOVE THAT SHORT STRAW INTO YOUR FINGERS?
NONSENSE! I'VE ALREADY ACHIEVED SO MUCH. SURELY, I LIVE A TIMELINE IN WHICH I REAP THE BENEFITS OF MY LIFE'S WORK. HOW MANY OTHER ME'S CAN BOAST OF SUCH PRESTIGE? SUCH POWER?
IN THE MULTIVERSE THERE ARE COUNTLESS TIMELINES IN WHICH ONE OF SUCH STATUS WILL UNDOUBTEDLY LOSE IT ALL, AND ULTIMATELY SUFFER AN UNTHINKABLE AND HUMILIATING DEATH!
TELL ME THIS WIZARD, IN WHICH TIMELINE DO YOU BELIEVE YOU LIVE?
LEAVE ME BE, VILE CREATURE.
OH, MY!
EXCUSE ME MISS, ARE YOU LOST?
I DON'T THINK SO.
THEN WHAT MAY I ASK ARE YOU DOING HERE?
SPLUT!

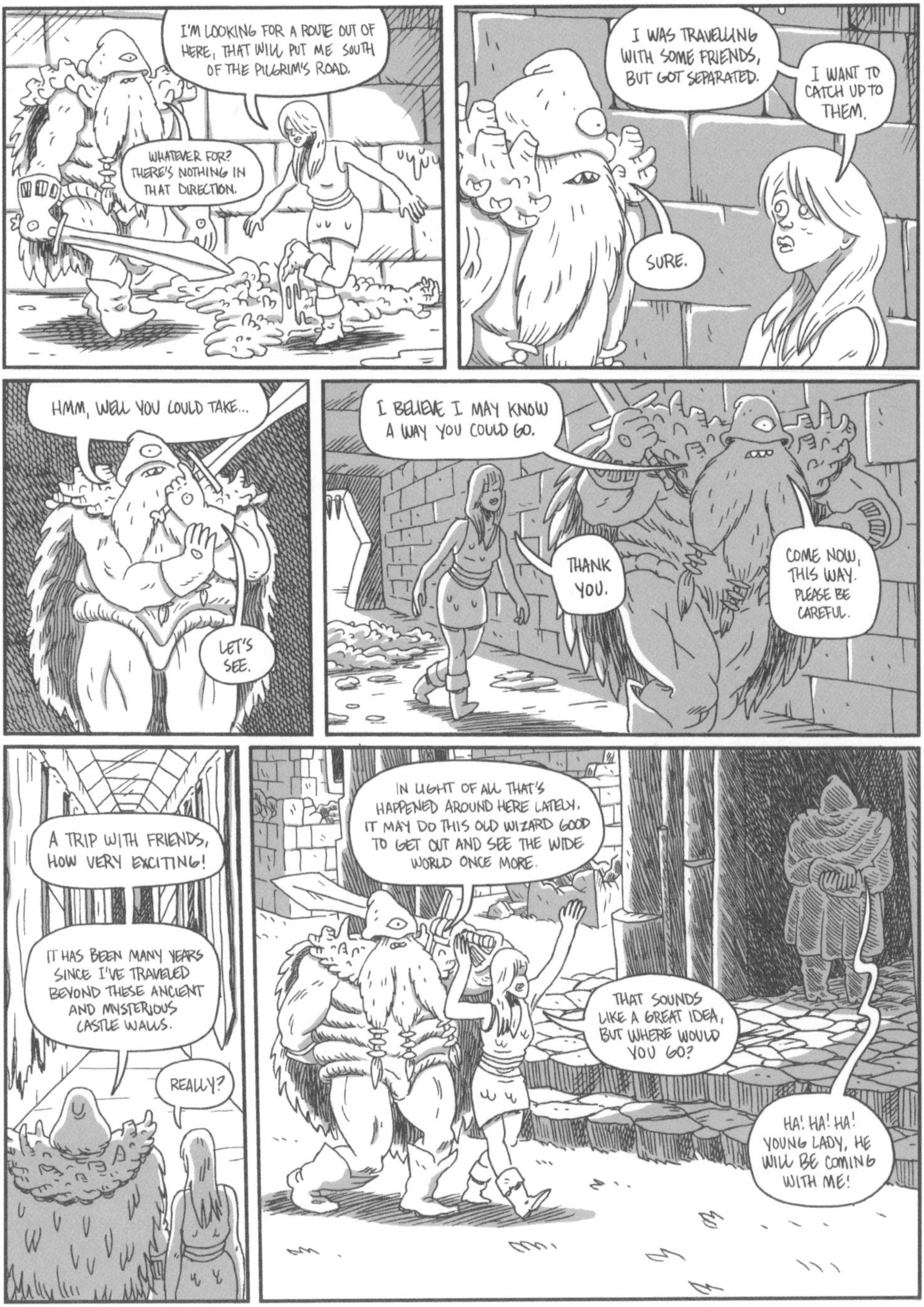
I'M LOOKING FOR A ROUTE OUT OF HERE, THAT WILL PUT ME SOUTH OF THE PILGRIM'S ROAD.
WHATEVER FOR? THERE'S NOTHING IN THAT DIRECTION.
I WAS TRAVELLING WITH SOME FRIENDS, BUT GOT SEPARATED.
I WANT TO CATCH UP TO THEM.
SURE.
HMM, WELL YOU COULD TAKE...
LET'S SEE.
I BELIEVE I MAY KNOW A WAY YOU COULD GO.
THANK YOU.
COME NOW, THIS WAY. PLEASE BE CAREFUL.
A TRIP WITH FRIENDS, HOW VERY EXCITING!
IT HAS BEEN MANY YEARS SINCE I'VE TRAVELED BEYOND THESE ANCIENT AND MYSTERIOUS CASTLE WALLS.
REALLY?
IN LIGHT OF ALL THAT'S HAPPENED AROUND HERE LATELY, IT MAY DO THIS OLD WIZARD GOOD TO GET OUT AND SEE THE WIDE WORLD ONCE MORE.
THAT SOUNDS LIKE A GREAT IDEA, BUT WHERE WOULD YOU GO?
HA! HA! HA! YOUNG LADY, HE WILL BE COMING WITH ME!

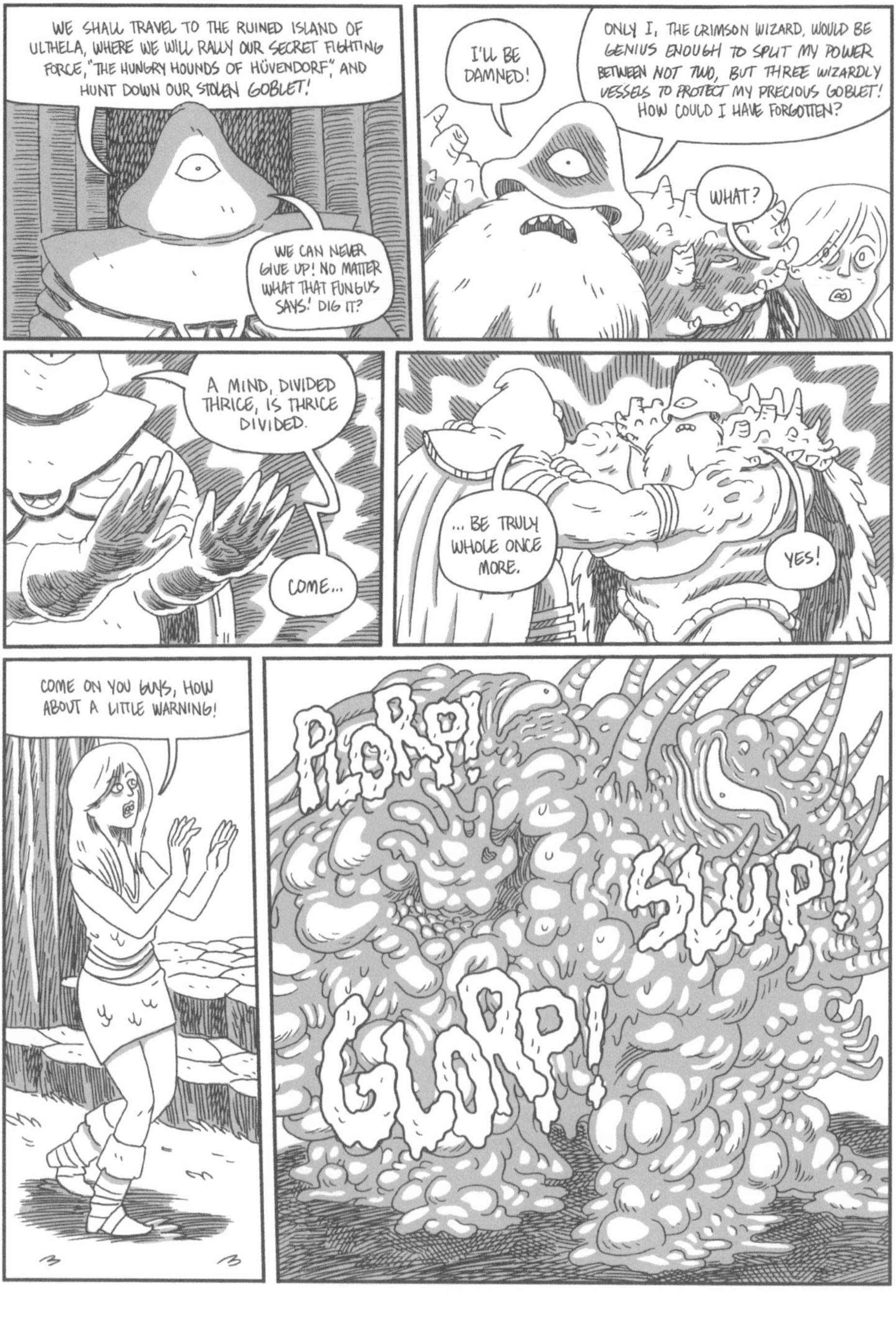
WE SHALL TRAVEL TO THE RUINED ISLAND OF ULTHELA, WHERE WE WILL RALLY OUR SECRET FIGHTING FORCE, "THE HUNGRY HOUNDS OF HÜVENDORF," AND HUNT DOWN OUR STOLEN GOBLET!
WE CAN NEVER GIVE UP! NO MATTER WHAT THAT FUNGUS SAYS! DIG IT?
I'LL BE DAMNED!
ONLY I, THE CRIMSON WIZARD, WOULD BE GENIUS ENOUGH TO SPLIT MY POWER BETWEEN NOT TWO, BUT THREE WIZARDLY VESSELS TO PROTECT MY PRECIOUS GOBLET! HOW COULD I HAVE FORGOTTEN?
WHAT?
A MIND, DIVIDED THRICE, IS THRICE DIVIDED.
COME...
...BE TRULY WHOLE ONCE MORE.
YES!
COME ON YOU GUYS, HOW ABOUT A LITTLE WARNING!
PLORP!
SLUP!
GLORP!

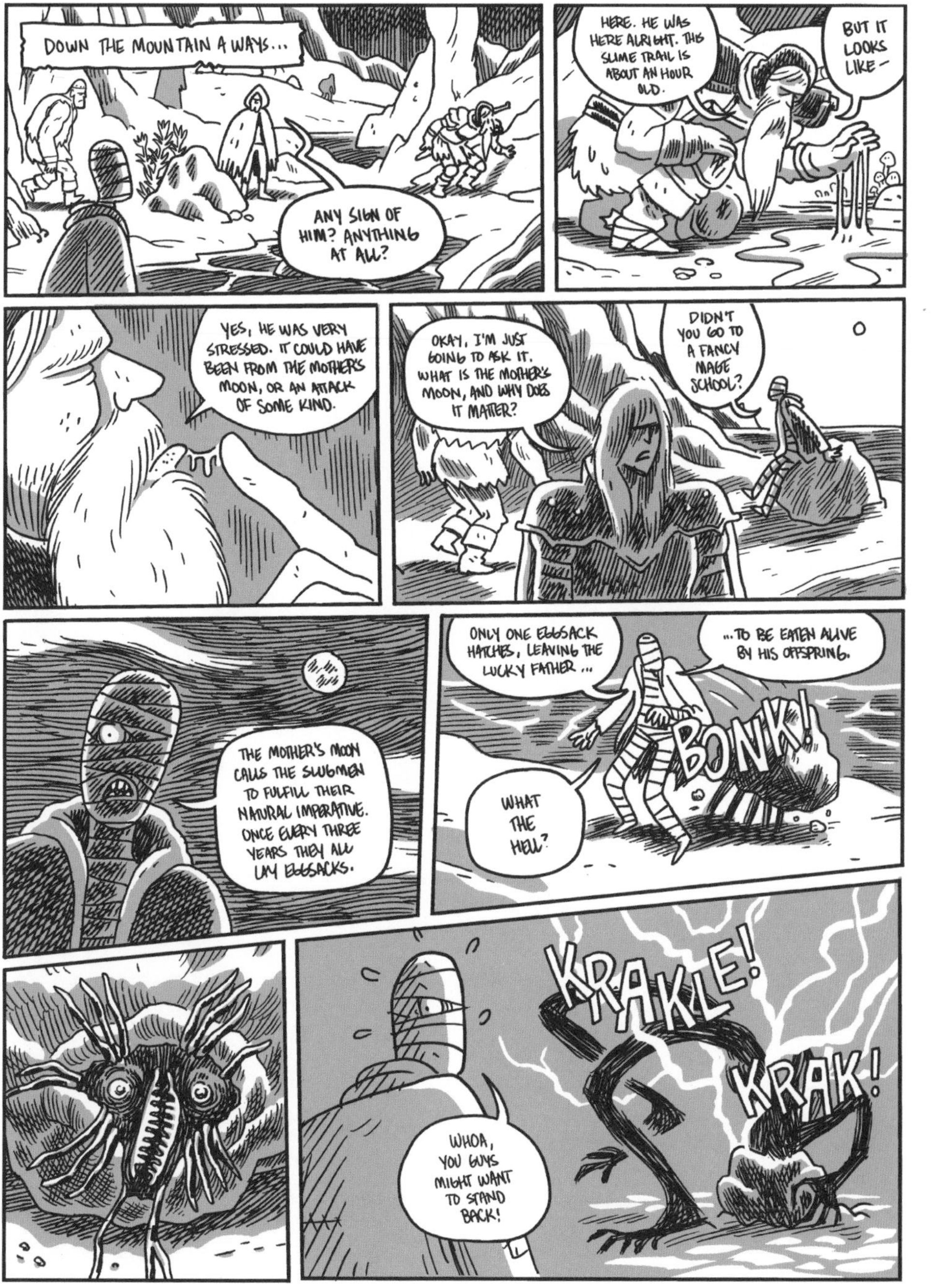
DOWN THE MOUNTAIN A WAYS...
ANY SIGN OF HIM? ANYTHING AT ALL?
HERE. HE WAS HERE ALRIGHT. THIS SLIME TRAIL IS ABOUT AN HOUR OLD.
BUT IT LOOKS LIKE-
YES, HE WAS VERY STRESSED. IT COULD HAVE BEEN FROM THE MOTHER'S MOON, OR AN ATTACK OF SOME KIND.
OKAY, I'M JUST GOING TO ASK IT. WHAT IS THE MOTHER'S MOON, AND WHY DOES IT MATTER?
DIDN'T YOU GO TO A FANCY MAGE SCHOOL?
THE MOTHER'S MOON CALLS THE SLUGMEN TO FULFILL THEIR NATURAL IMPERATIVE. ONCE EVERY THREE YEARS THEY ALL LAY EGGSACKS.
ONLY ONE EGGSACK HATCHES, LEAVING THE LUCKY FATHER...
...TO BE EATEN ALIVE BY HIS OFFSPRING.
BONK!
WHAT THE HELL?
KRAKLE!
KRAK!
WHOA, YOU GUYS MIGHT WANT TO STAND BACK!

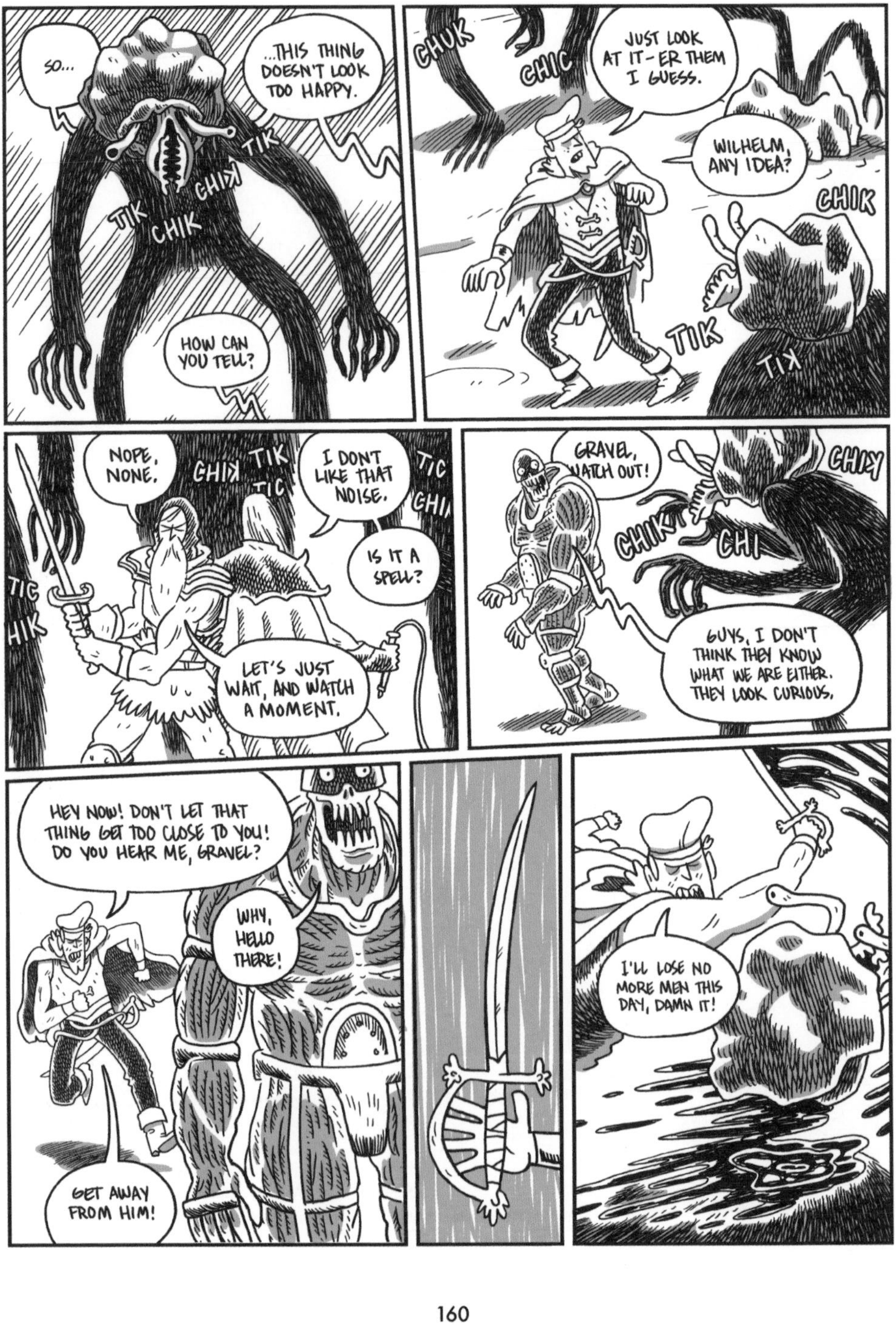
SO...
...THIS THING DOESN'T LOOK TOO HAPPY.
TIK
CHIK
TIK
CHIK
HOW CAN YOU TELL?
CHUK
CHIC
JUST LOOK AT IT- ER THEM I GUESS.
WILHELM, ANY IDEA?
CHIK
TIK
TIK
NOPE, NONE.
CHIK
TIK
I DON'T LIKE THAT NOISE.
IS IT A SPELL?
LET'S JUST WAIT, AND WATCH A MOMENT.
GRAVEL, WATCH OUT!
CHIK
CHIK
CHI
GUYS, I DON'T THINK THEY KNOW WHAT WE ARE EITHER. THEY LOOK CURIOUS.
HEY NOW! DON'T LET THAT THING GET TOO CLOSE TO YOU! DO YOU HEAR ME, GRAVEL?
WHY, HELLO THERE!
GET AWAY FROM HIM!
I'LL LOSE NO MORE MEN THIS DAY, DAMN IT!

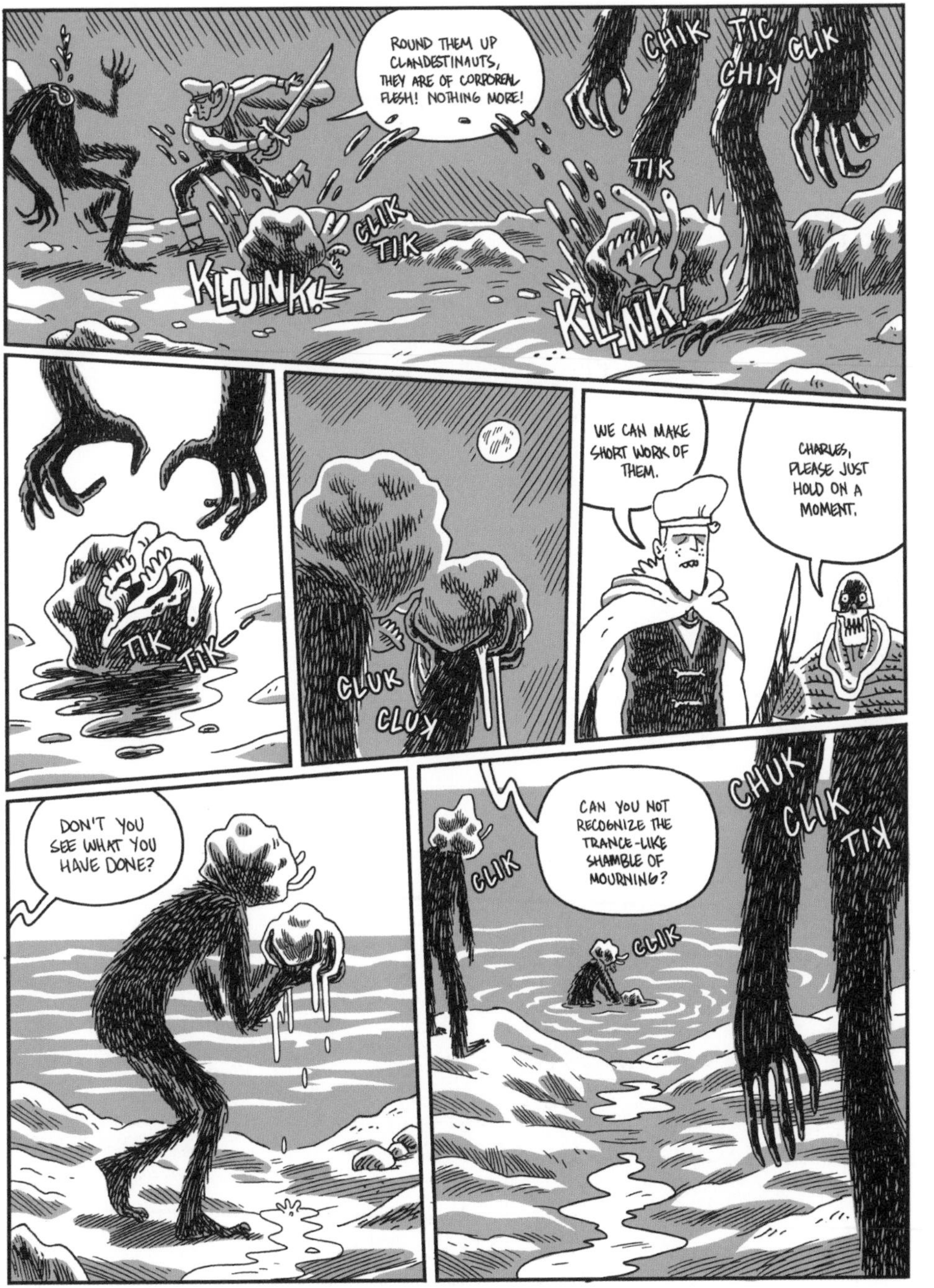
ROUND THEM UP CLANDESTINAUTS, THEY ARE OF CORPOREAL FLESH! NOTHING MORE!
CHIK TIC CHIK CLIK
TIK
CLIK TIK
KLUNK!
KLUNK!
TIK TIK
CLUK CLUK
WE CAN MAKE SHORT WORK OF THEM.
CHARLES, PLEASE JUST HOLD ON A MOMENT.
DON'T YOU SEE WHAT YOU HAVE DONE?
CAN YOU NOT RECOGNIZE THE TRANCE-LIKE SHAMBLE OF MOURNING?
CLIK
CHUK CLIK TIK
CLIK

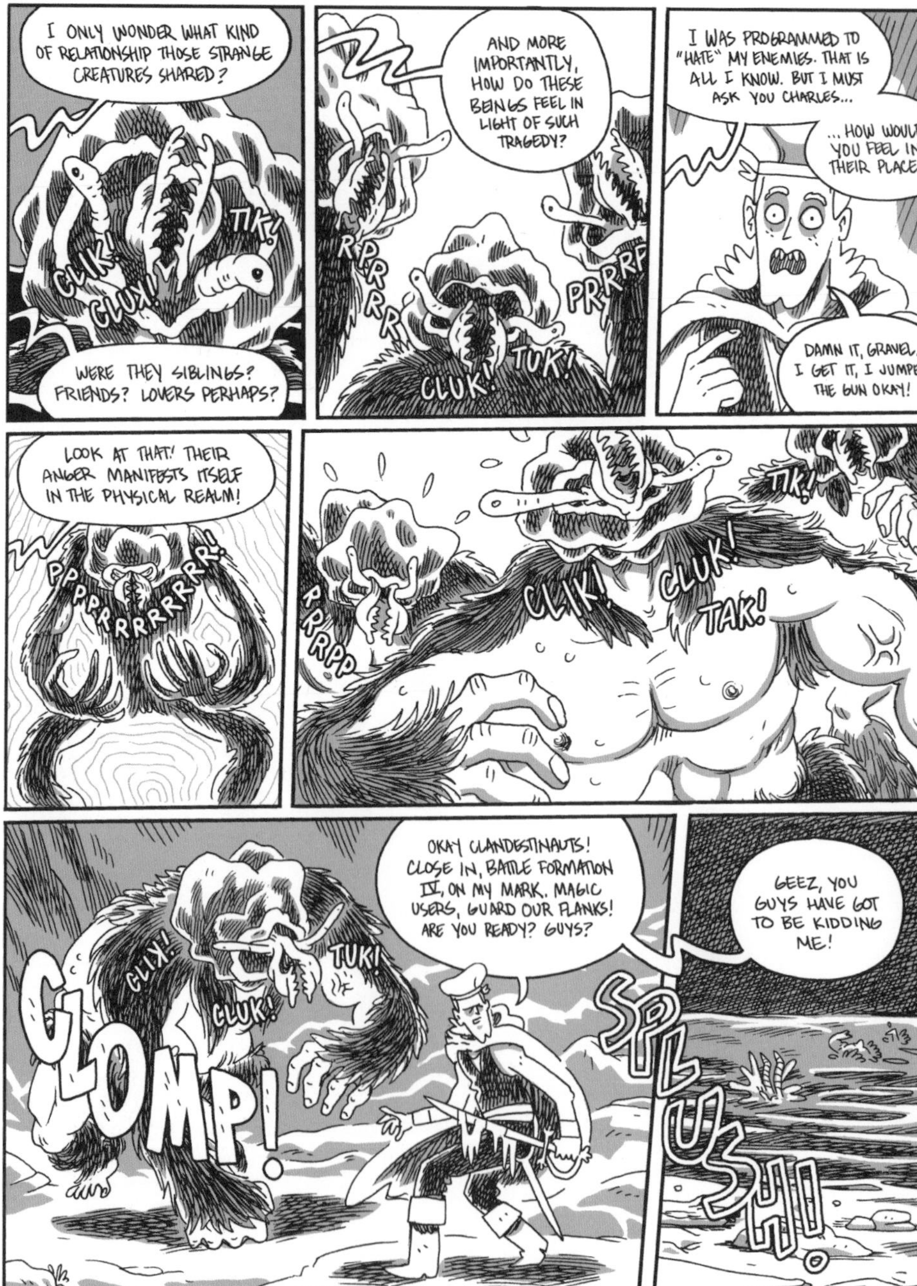
I ONLY WONDER WHAT KIND OF RELATIONSHIP THOSE STRANGE CREATURES SHARED?
TIK!
CLIK!
CLUK!
WERE THEY SIBLINGS? FRIENDS? LOVERS PERHAPS?
AND MORE IMPORTANTLY, HOW DO THESE BEINGS FEEL IN LIGHT OF SUCH TRAGEDY?
RPRRRR
PRRRP
CLUK!
TUK!
I WAS PROGRAMMED TO "HATE" MY ENEMIES. THAT IS ALL I KNOW. BUT I MUST ASK YOU CHARLES...
...HOW WOULD YOU FEEL IN THEIR PLACE?
DAMN IT, GRAVEL. I GET IT, I JUMPED THE GUN OKAY!
LOOK AT THAT! THEIR ANGER MANIFESTS ITSELF IN THE PHYSICAL REALM!
PPPPRRRRRRRRR!
TIK!
CLIK!
CLUK!
TAK!
RRRPP
OKAY CLANDESTINAUTS! CLOSE IN, BATTLE FORMATION IV, ON MY MARK. MAGIC USERS, GUARD OUR FLANKS! ARE YOU READY? GUYS?
CLIK!
TUK!
CLUK!
CLOMP!
SPLUSH!
GEEZ, YOU GUYS HAVE GOT TO BE KIDDING ME!

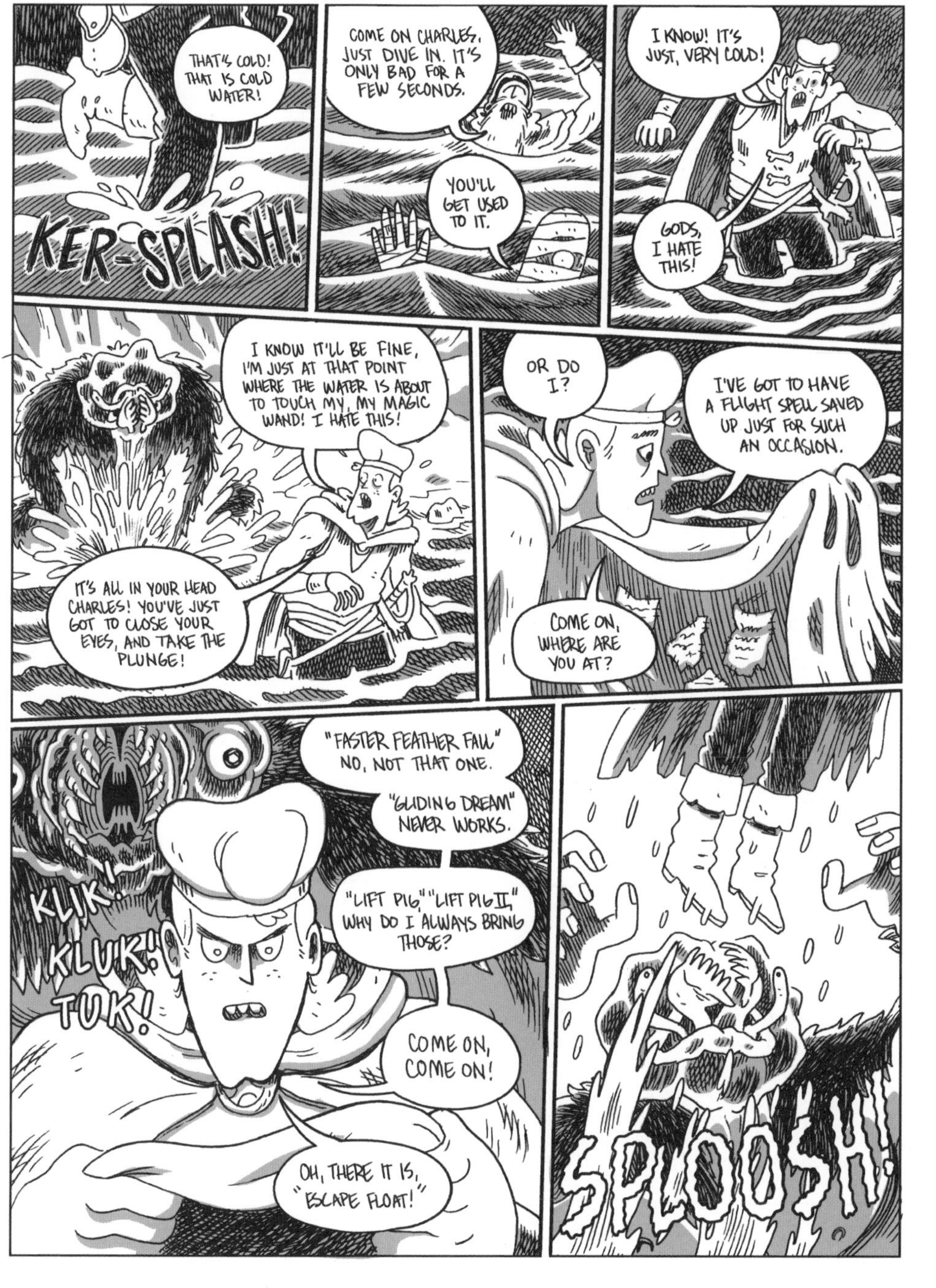
THAT'S COLD! THAT IS COLD WATER!
KER-SPLASH!
COME ON CHARLES. JUST DIVE IN. IT'S ONLY BAD FOR A FEW SECONDS.
YOU'LL GET USED TO IT.
I KNOW! IT'S JUST, VERY COLD!
GODS, I HATE THIS!
I KNOW IT'LL BE FINE, I'M JUST AT THAT POINT WHERE THE WATER IS ABOUT TO TOUCH MY, MY MAGIC WAND! I HATE THIS!
IT'S ALL IN YOUR HEAD CHARLES! YOU'VE JUST GOT TO CLOSE YOUR EYES, AND TAKE THE PLUNGE!
OR DO I?
I'VE GOT TO HAVE A FLIGHT SPELL SAVED UP JUST FOR SUCH AN OCCASION.
COME ON, WHERE ARE YOU AT?
"FASTER FEATHER FALL" NO, NOT THAT ONE.
"GLIDING DREAM" NEVER WORKS.
"LIFT PIG," "LIFT PIG II," WHY DO I ALWAYS BRING THOSE?
KLIK! KLUK! TUK!
COME ON, COME ON!
OH, THERE IT IS, "ESCAPE FLOAT!"
SPLOOSH!

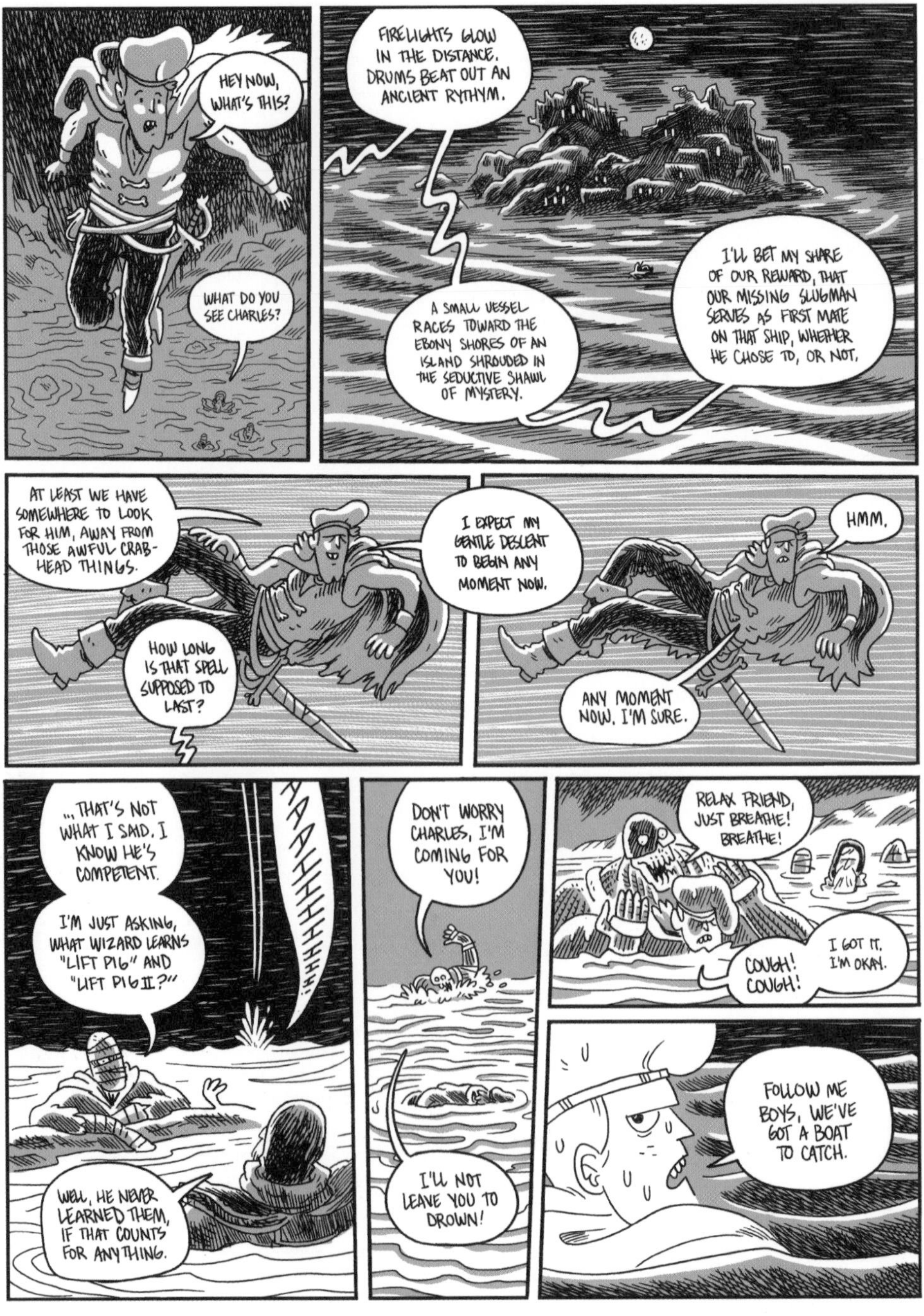
HEY NOW, WHAT'S THIS?
WHAT DO YOU SEE CHARLES?
FIRELIGHTS GLOW IN THE DISTANCE. DRUMS BEAT OUT AN ANCIENT RYTHYM.
A SMALL VESSEL RACES TOWARD THE EBONY SHORES OF AN ISLAND SHROUDED IN THE SEDUCTIVE SHAWL OF MYSTERY.
I'LL BET MY SHARE OF OUR REWARD, THAT OUR MISSING SLUGMAN SERVES AS FIRST MATE ON THAT SHIP, WHETHER HE CHOSE TO, OR NOT.
AT LEAST WE HAVE SOMEWHERE TO LOOK FOR HIM, AWAY FROM THOSE AWFUL CRAB-HEAD THINGS.
HOW LONG IS THAT SPELL SUPPOSED TO LAST?
I EXPECT MY GENTLE DESCENT TO BEGIN ANY MOMENT NOW.
HMM.
ANY MOMENT NOW. I'M SURE.
... THAT'S NOT WHAT I SAID. I KNOW HE'S COMPETENT.
I'M JUST ASKING, WHAT WIZARD LEARNS "LIFT PIG" AND "LIFT PIG II?"
AAAHHHHHHHH!
WELL, HE NEVER LEARNED THEM, IF THAT COUNTS FOR ANYTHING.
DON'T WORRY CHARLES, I'M COMING FOR YOU!
I'LL NOT LEAVE YOU TO DROWN!
RELAX FRIEND, JUST BREATHE! BREATHE!
COUGH! COUGH!
I GOT IT. I'M OKAY.
FOLLOW ME BOYS, WE'VE GOT A BOAT TO CATCH.

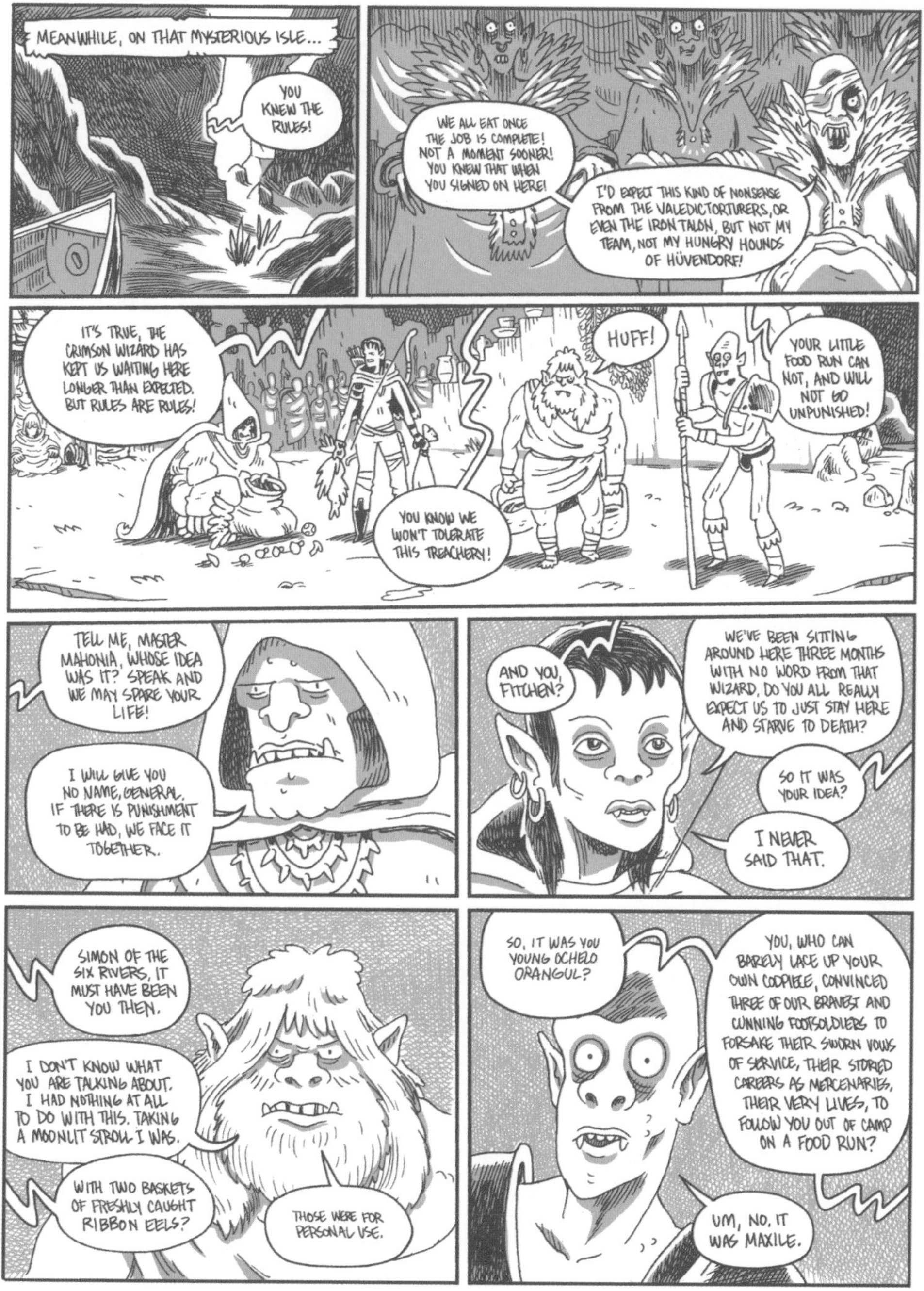
MEANWHILE, ON THAT MYSTERIOUS ISLE...
YOU KNEW THE RULES!
WE ALL EAT ONCE THE JOB IS COMPLETE! NOT A MOMENT SOONER! YOU KNEW THAT WHEN YOU SIGNED ON HERE!
I'D EXPECT THIS KIND OF NONSENSE FROM THE VALEDICTORTURERS, OR EVEN THE IRON TALON, BUT NOT MY TEAM, NOT MY HUNGRY HOUNDS OF HÜVENDORF!
IT'S TRUE, THE CRIMSON WIZARD HAS KEPT US WAITING HERE LONGER THAN EXPECTED. BUT RULES ARE RULES!
HUFF!
YOUR LITTLE FOOD RUN CAN NOT, AND WILL NOT GO UNPUNISHED!
YOU KNOW WE WON'T TOLERATE THIS TREACHERY!
TELL ME, MASTER MAHONIA, WHOSE IDEA WAS IT? SPEAK AND WE MAY SPARE YOUR LIFE!
I WILL GIVE YOU NO NAME, GENERAL. IF THERE IS PUNISHMENT TO BE HAD, WE FACE IT TOGETHER.
AND YOU, FITCHEN?
WE'VE BEEN SITTING AROUND HERE THREE MONTHS WITH NO WORD FROM THAT WIZARD. DO YOU ALL REALLY EXPECT US TO JUST STAY HERE AND STARVE TO DEATH?
SO IT WAS YOUR IDEA?
I NEVER SAID THAT.
SIMON OF THE SIX RIVERS, IT MUST HAVE BEEN YOU THEN.
I DON'T KNOW WHAT YOU ARE TALKING ABOUT. I HAD NOTHING AT ALL TO DO WITH THIS. TAKING A MOONLIT STROLL I WAS.
WITH TWO BASKETS OF FRESHLY CAUGHT RIBBON EELS?
THOSE WERE FOR PERSONAL USE.
SO, IT WAS YOU YOUNG OCHELO ORANGUL?
YOU, WHO CAN BARELY LACE UP YOUR OWN CODPIECE, CONVINCED THREE OF OUR BRAVEST AND CUNNING FOOTSOLDIERS TO FORSAKE THEIR SWORN VOWS OF SERVICE, THEIR STORIED CAREERS AS MERCENARIES, THEIR VERY LIVES, TO FOLLOW YOU OUT OF CAMP ON A FOOD RUN?
UM, NO, IT WAS MAXILE.

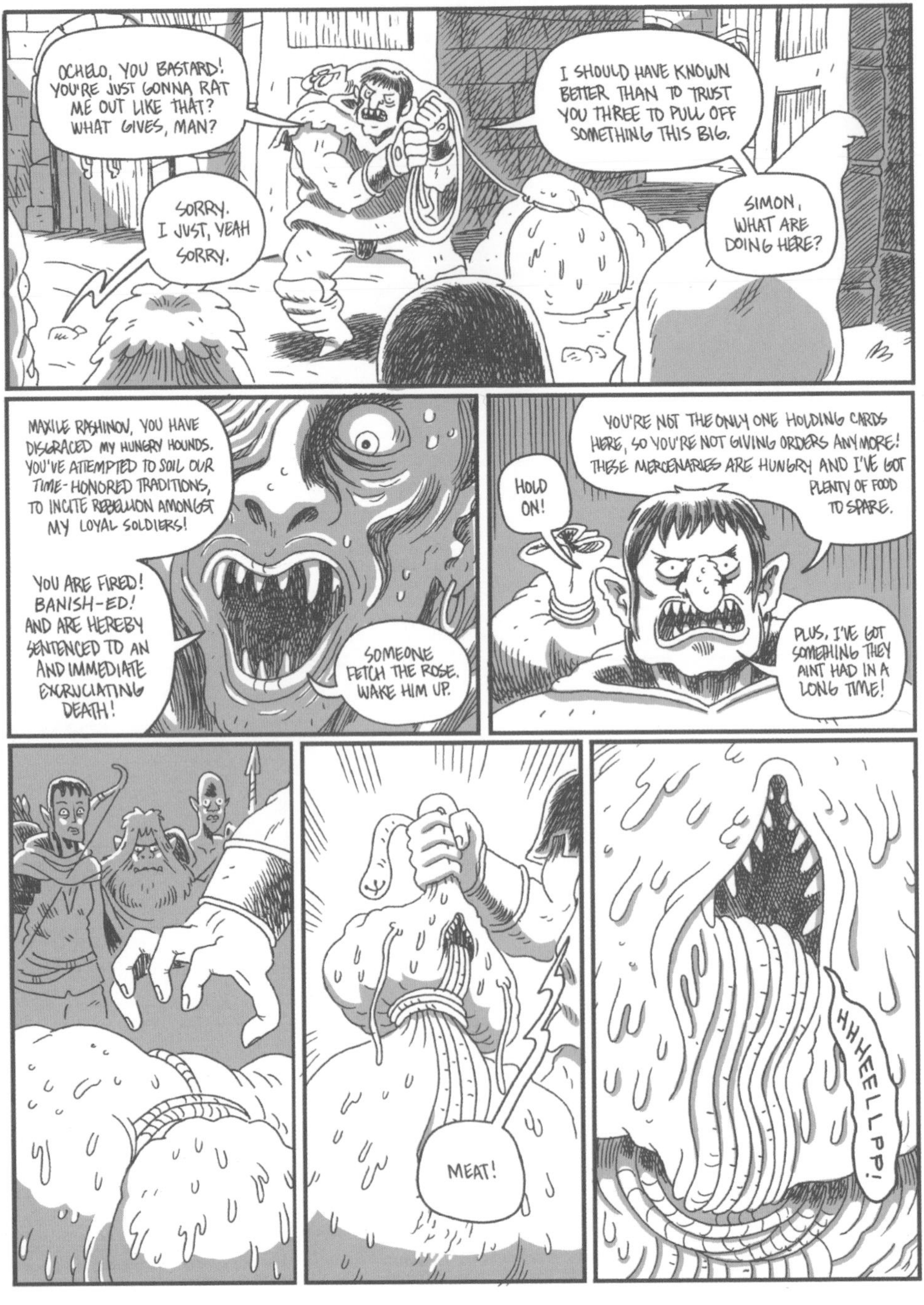
OCHELO, YOU BASTARD! YOU'RE JUST GONNA RAT ME OUT LIKE THAT? WHAT GIVES, MAN?
I SHOULD HAVE KNOWN BETTER THAN TO TRUST YOU THREE TO PULL OFF SOMETHING THIS BIG.
SORRY. I JUST, YEAH SORRY.
SIMON, WHAT ARE DOING HERE?
MAXILE RASHINOV, YOU HAVE DISGRACED MY HUNGRY HOUNDS. YOU'VE ATTEMPTED TO SOIL OUR TIME-HONORED TRADITIONS, TO INCITE REBELLION AMONGST MY LOYAL SOLDIERS!
YOU ARE FIRED! BANISH-ED! AND ARE HEREBY SENTENCED TO AN AND IMMEDIATE EXCRUCIATING DEATH!
SOMEONE FETCH THE ROSE. WAKE HIM UP.
YOU'RE NOT THE ONLY ONE HOLDING CARDS HERE, SO YOU'RE NOT GIVING ORDERS ANYMORE! THESE MERCENARIES ARE HUNGRY AND I'VE GOT PLENTY OF FOOD TO SPARE.
HOLD ON!
PLUS, I'VE GOT SOMETHING THEY AINT HAD IN A LONG TIME!
MEAT!
HHHEELLPP!

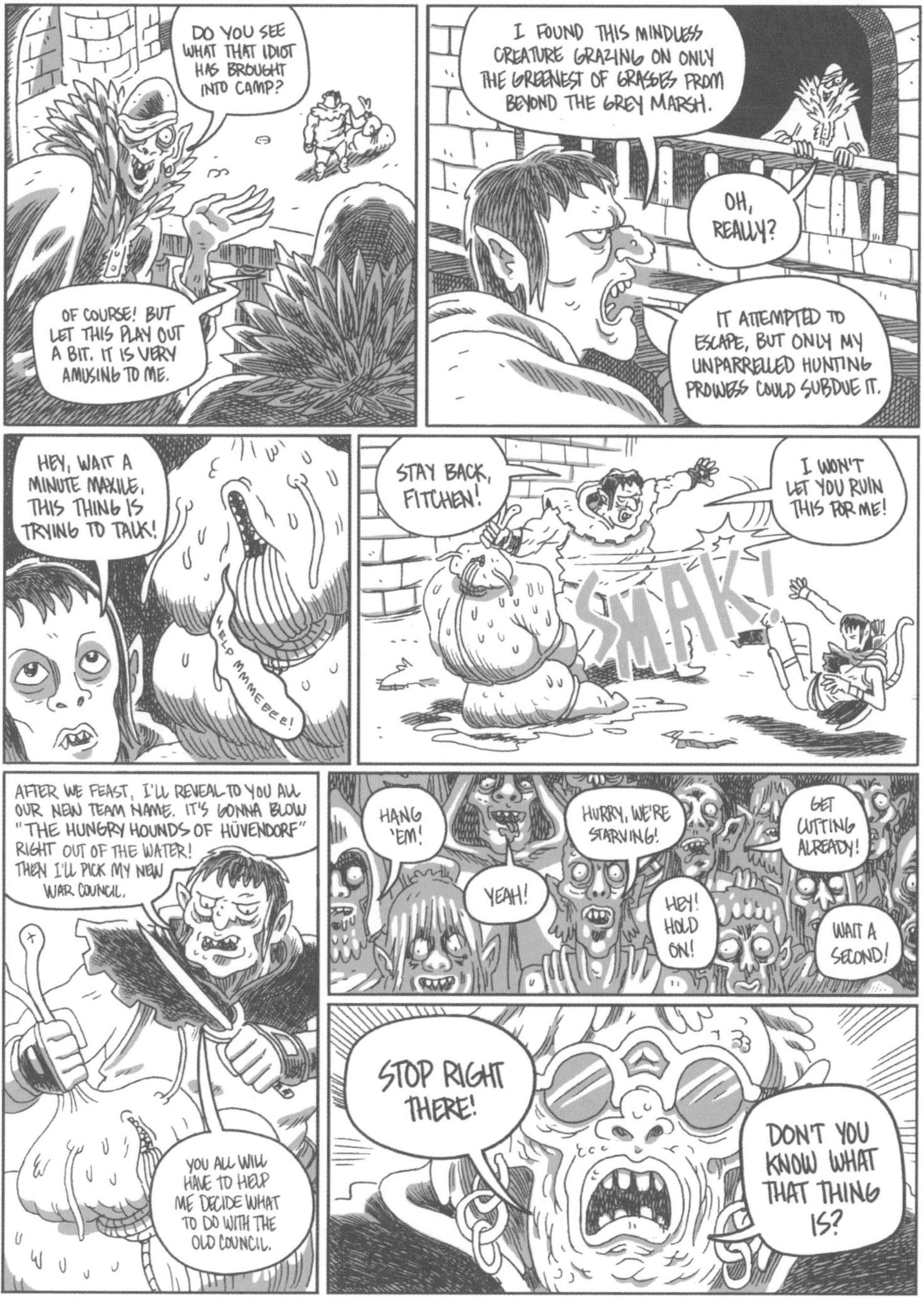
DO YOU SEE WHAT THAT IDIOT HAS BROUGHT INTO CAMP?
OF COURSE! BUT LET THIS PLAY OUT A BIT. IT IS VERY AMUSING TO ME.
I FOUND THIS MINDLESS CREATURE GRAZING ON ONLY THE GREENEST OF GRASSES FROM BEYOND THE GREY MARSH.
OH, REALLY?
IT ATTEMPTED TO ESCAPE, BUT ONLY MY UNPARRELLED HUNTING PROWESS COULD SUBDUE IT.
HEY, WAIT A MINUTE MAXILE, THIS THING IS TRYING TO TALK!
HELP MMMEEEE!
STAY BACK, FITCHEN!
I WON'T LET YOU RUIN THIS FOR ME!
SMAK!
AFTER WE FEAST, I'LL REVEAL TO YOU ALL OUR NEW TEAM NAME. IT'S GONNA BLOW "THE HUNGRY HOUNDS OF HÜVENDORF" RIGHT OUT OF THE WATER! THEN I'LL PICK MY NEW WAR COUNCIL.
YOU ALL WILL HAVE TO HELP ME DECIDE WHAT TO DO WITH THE OLD COUNCIL.
HANG 'EM!
YEAH!
HURRY, WE'RE STARVING!
HEY! HOLD ON!
GET CUTTING ALREADY!
WAIT A SECOND!
STOP RIGHT THERE!
DON'T YOU KNOW WHAT THAT THING IS?

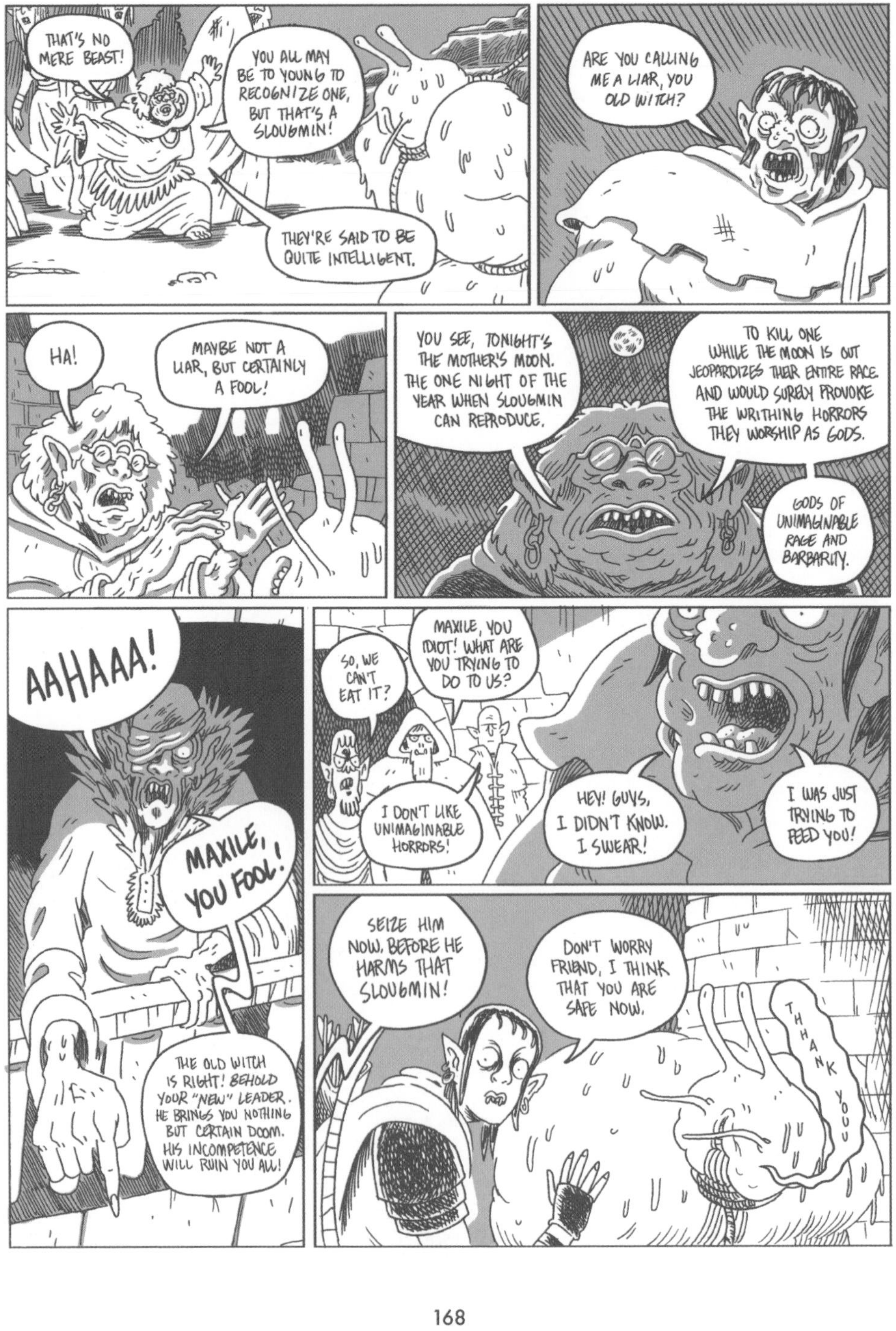
THAT'S NO MERE BEAST!
YOU ALL MAY BE TO YOUNG TO RECOGNIZE ONE, BUT THAT'S A SLOUGMIN!
THEY'RE SAID TO BE QUITE INTELLIGENT.
ARE YOU CALLING ME A LIAR, YOU OLD WITCH?
HA!
MAYBE NOT A LIAR, BUT CERTAINLY A FOOL!
YOU SEE, TONIGHT'S THE MOTHER'S MOON. THE ONE NIGHT OF THE YEAR WHEN SLOUGMIN CAN REPRODUCE.
TO KILL ONE WHILE THE MOON IS OUT JEOPARDIZES THEIR ENTIRE RACE. AND WOULD SURELY PROVOKE THE WRITHING HORRORS THEY WORSHIP AS GODS.
GODS OF UNIMAGINABLE RAGE AND BARBARITY.
AAHAAA!
MAXILE, YOU FOOL!
THE OLD WITCH IS RIGHT! BEHOLD YOUR "NEW" LEADER. HE BRINGS YOU NOTHING BUT CERTAIN DOOM. HIS INCOMPETENCE WILL RUIN YOU ALL!
SO, WE CAN'T EAT IT?
MAXILE, YOU IDIOT! WHAT ARE YOU TRYING TO DO TO US?
I DON'T LIKE UNIMAGINABLE HORRORS!
HEY! GUYS, I DIDN'T KNOW. I SWEAR!
I WAS JUST TRYING TO FEED YOU!
SEIZE HIM NOW, BEFORE HE HARMS THAT SLOUGMIN!
DON'T WORRY FRIEND, I THINK THAT YOU ARE SAFE NOW.
THANK YOUU

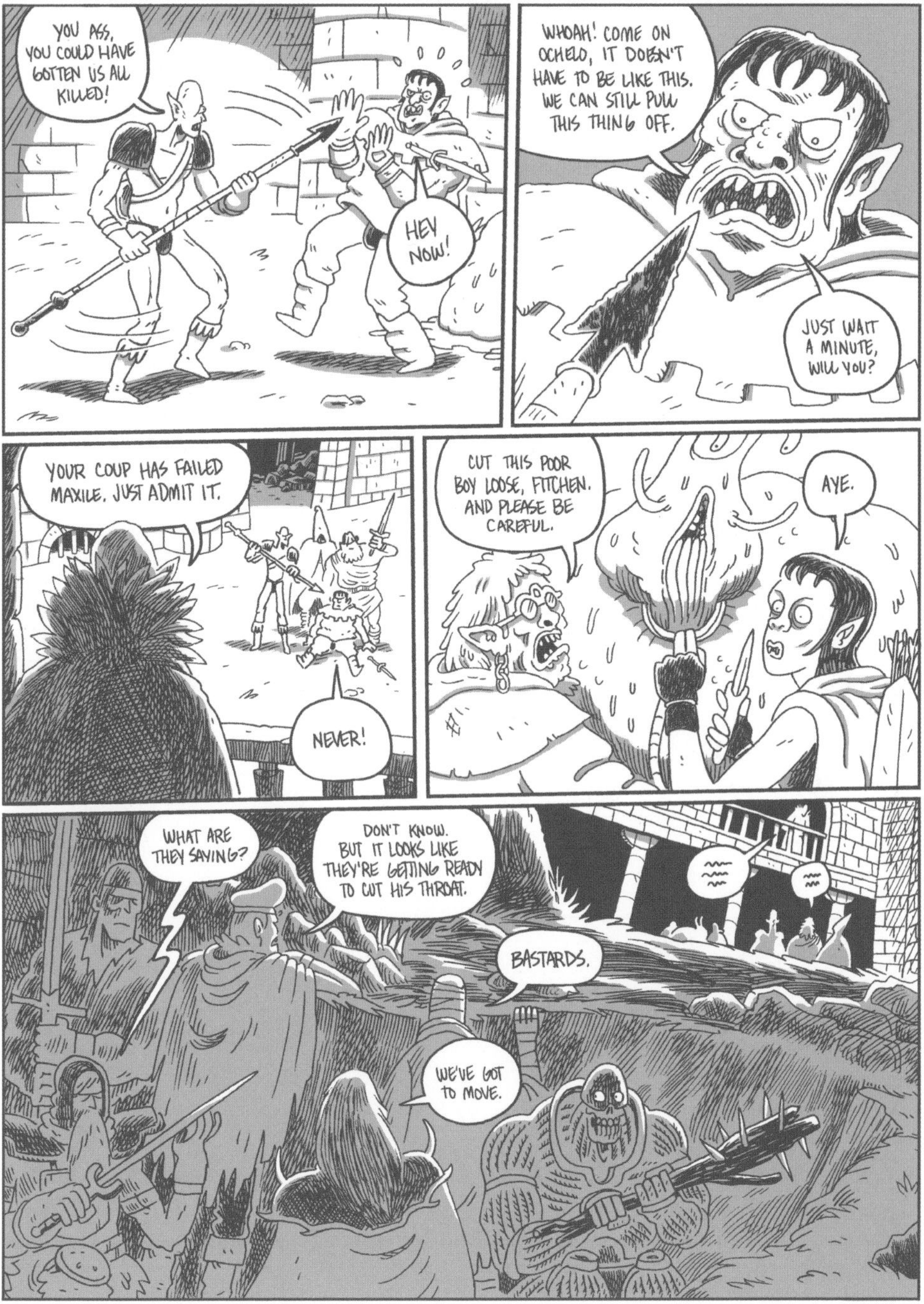
YOU ASS, YOU COULD HAVE GOTTEN US ALL KILLED!
HEY NOW!
WHOAH! COME ON OCHELO, IT DOESN'T HAVE TO BE LIKE THIS. WE CAN STILL PULL THIS THING OFF.
JUST WAIT A MINUTE, WILL YOU?
YOUR COUP HAS FAILED MAXILE. JUST ADMIT IT.
NEVER!
CUT THIS POOR BOY LOOSE, FITCHEN. AND PLEASE BE CAREFUL.
AYE.
WHAT ARE THEY SAYING?
DON'T KNOW. BUT IT LOOKS LIKE THEY'RE GETTING READY TO CUT HIS THROAT.
BASTARDS.
WE'VE GOT TO MOVE.

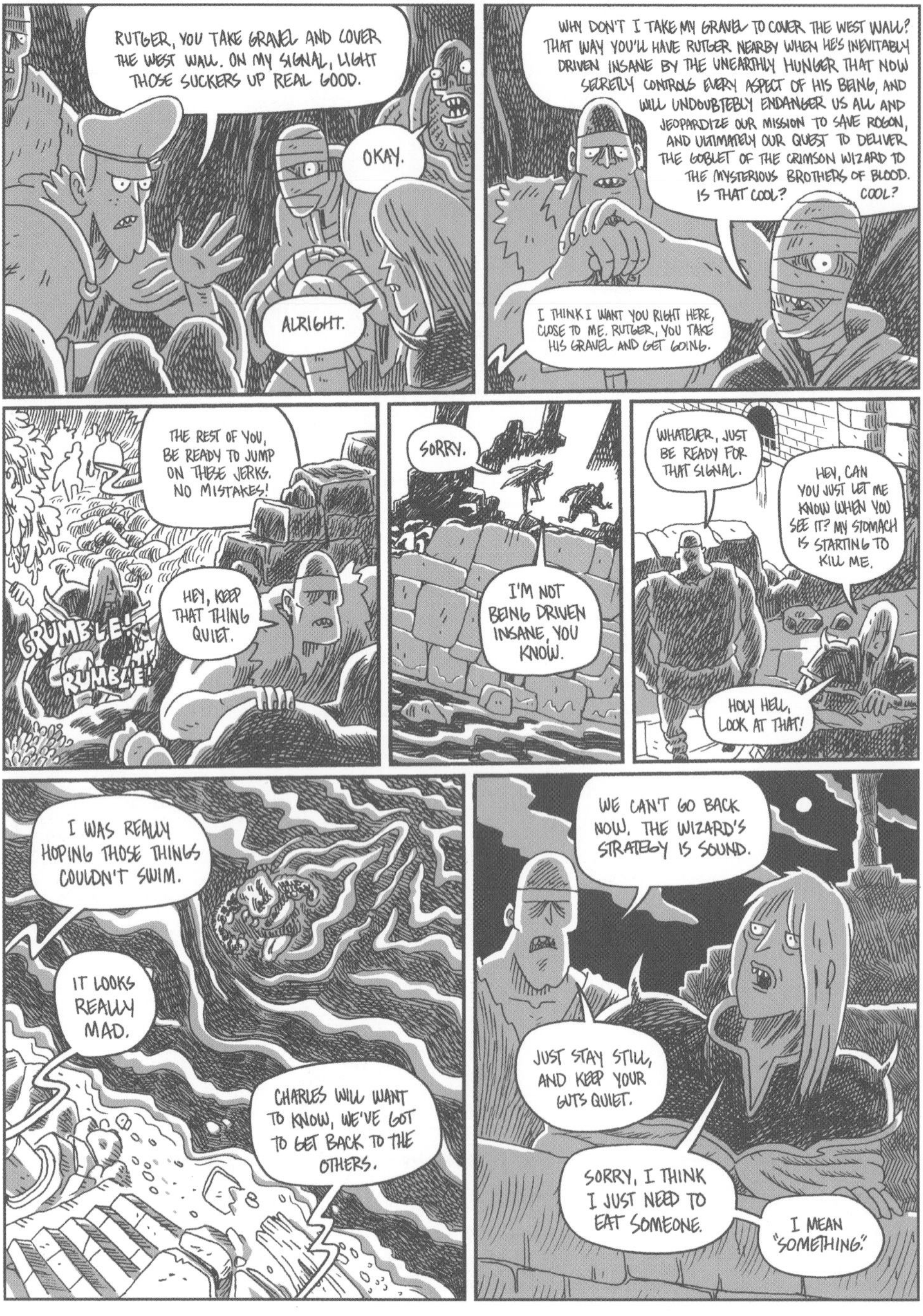
RUTGER, YOU TAKE GRAVEL AND COVER THE WEST WALL. ON MY SIGNAL, LIGHT THOSE SUCKERS UP REAL GOOD.
OKAY.
ALRIGHT.
WHY DON'T I TAKE MY GRAVEL TO COVER THE WEST WALL? THAT WAY YOU'LL HAVE RUTGER NEARBY WHEN HE'S INEVITABLY DRIVEN INSANE BY THE UNEARTHLY HUNGER THAT NOW SECRETLY CONTROLS EVERY ASPECT OF HIS BEING, AND WILL UNDOUBTEBLY ENDANGER US ALL AND JEOPARDIZE OUR MISSION TO SAVE ROGON, AND ULTIMATELY OUR QUEST TO DELIVER THE GOBLET OF THE CRIMSON WIZARD TO THE MYSTERIOUS BROTHERS OF BLOOD. IS THAT COOL? COOL?
I THINK I WANT YOU RIGHT HERE, CLOSE TO ME. RUTGER, YOU TAKE HIS GRAVEL AND GET GOING.
THE REST OF YOU, BE READY TO JUMP ON THESE JERKS. NO MISTAKES!
GRUMBLE! RUMBLE!
HEY, KEEP THAT THING QUIET.
SORRY.
I'M NOT BEING DRIVEN INSANE, YOU KNOW.
WHATEVER, JUST BE READY FOR THAT SIGNAL.
HEY, CAN YOU JUST LET ME KNOW WHEN YOU SEE IT? MY STOMACH IS STARTING TO KILL ME.
HOLY HELL, LOOK AT THAT!
I WAS REALLY HOPING THOSE THINGS COULDN'T SWIM.
IT LOOKS REALLY MAD.
CHARLES WILL WANT TO KNOW, WE'VE GOT TO GET BACK TO THE OTHERS.
WE CAN'T GO BACK NOW. THE WIZARD'S STRATEGY IS SOUND.
JUST STAY STILL, AND KEEP YOUR GUTS QUIET.
SORRY, I THINK I JUST NEED TO EAT SOMEONE.
I MEAN "SOMETHING."

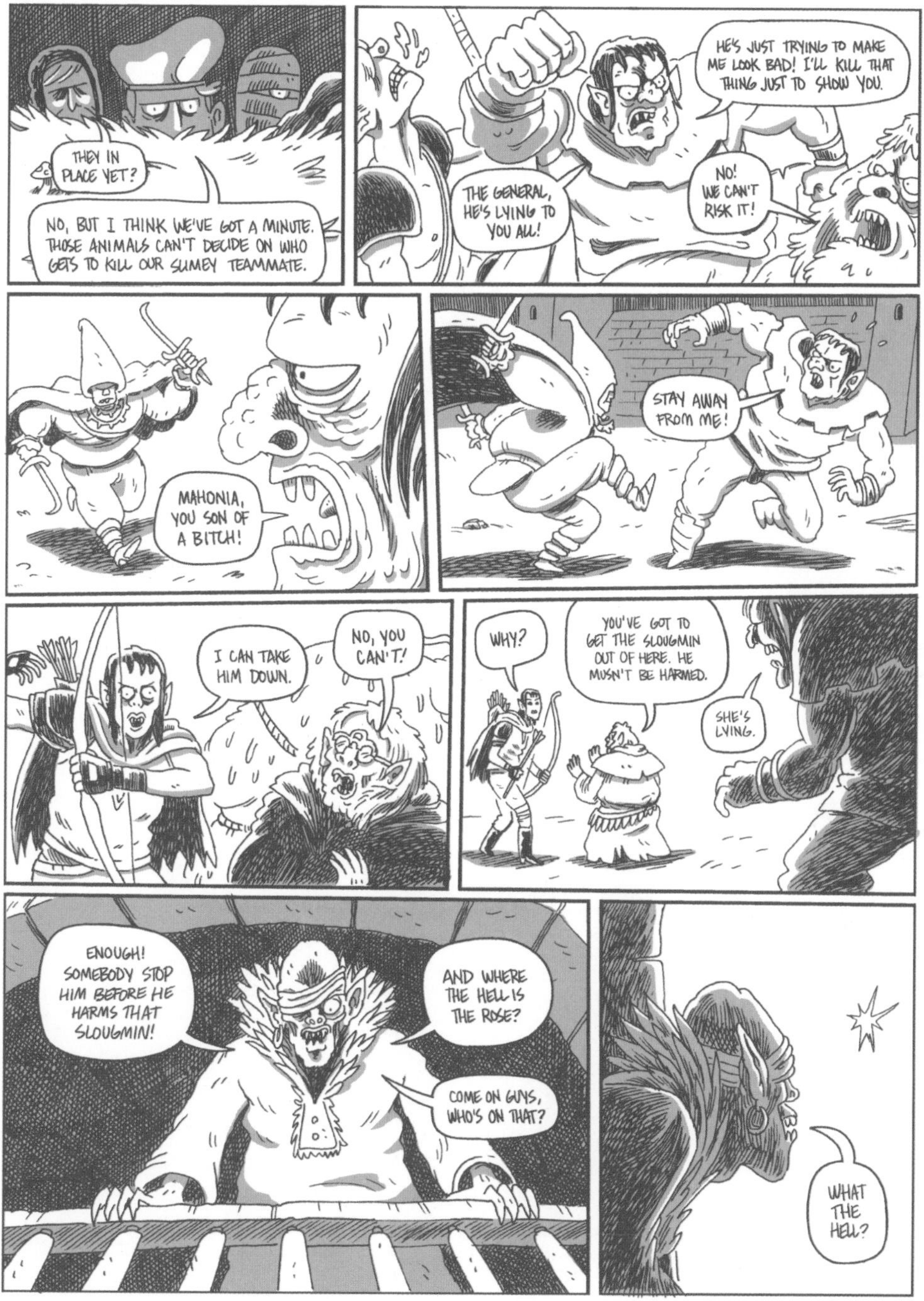
THEY IN PLACE YET?
NO, BUT I THINK WE'VE GOT A MINUTE. THOSE ANIMALS CAN'T DECIDE ON WHO GETS TO KILL OUR SLIMEY TEAMMATE.
HE'S JUST TRYING TO MAKE ME LOOK BAD! I'LL KILL THAT THING JUST TO SHOW YOU.
THE GENERAL, HE'S LYING TO YOU ALL!
NO! WE CAN'T RISK IT!
MAHONIA, YOU SON OF A BITCH!
STAY AWAY FROM ME!
I CAN TAKE HIM DOWN.
NO, YOU CAN'T!
WHY?
YOU'VE GOT TO GET THE SLOUGMIN OUT OF HERE. HE MUSN'T BE HARMED.
SHE'S LYING.
ENOUGH! SOMEBODY STOP HIM BEFORE HE HARMS THAT SLOUGMIN!
AND WHERE THE HELL IS THE ROSE?
COME ON GUYS, WHO'S ON THAT?
WHAT THE HELL?

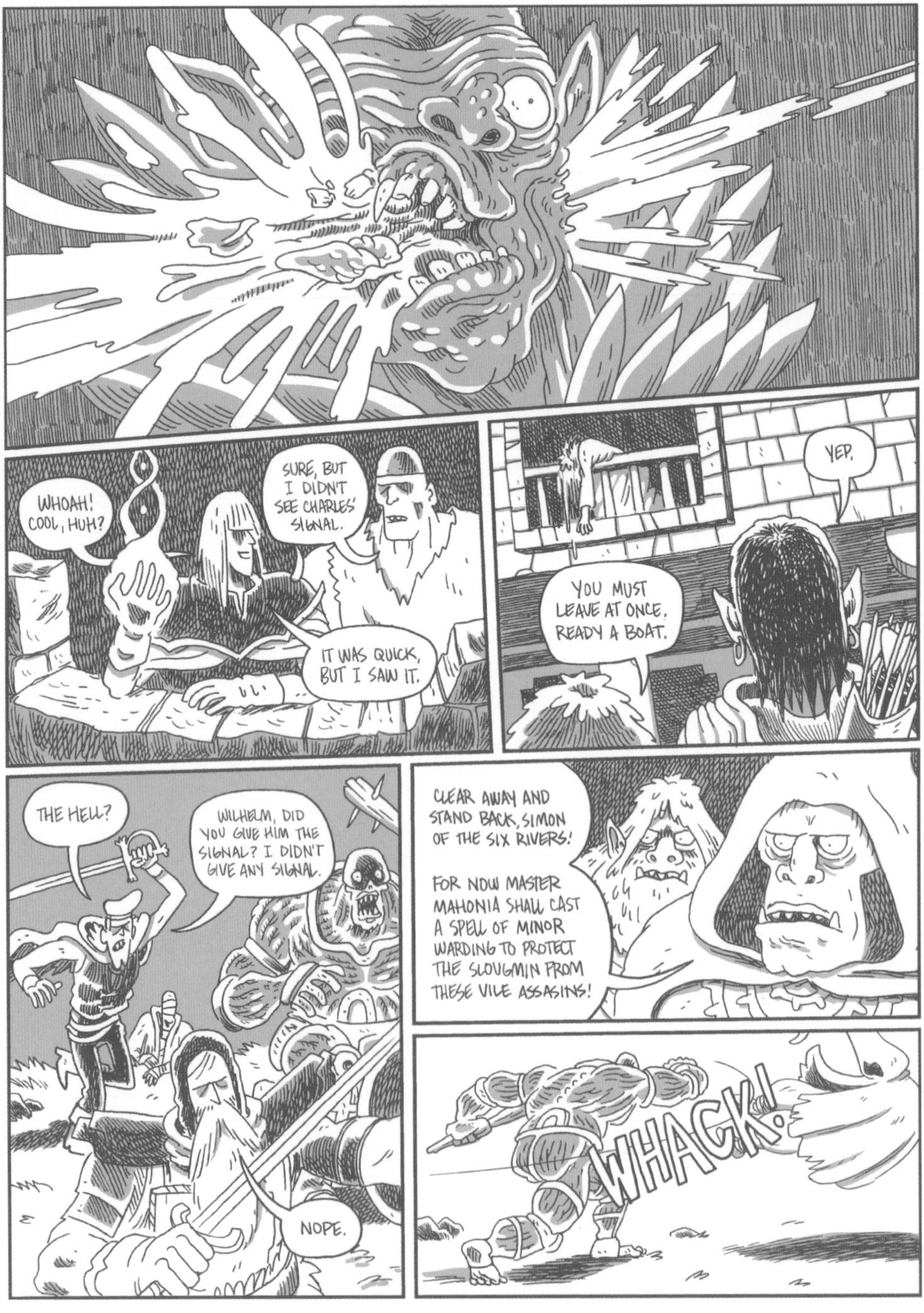
WHOAH! COOL, HUH?
SURE, BUT I DIDN'T SEE CHARLES' SIGNAL.
IT WAS QUICK, BUT I SAW IT.
YEP.
YOU MUST LEAVE AT ONCE, READY A BOAT.
THE HELL?
WILHELM, DID YOU GIVE HIM THE SIGNAL? I DIDN'T GIVE ANY SIGNAL.
NOPE.
CLEAR AWAY AND STAND BACK, SIMON OF THE SIX RIVERS!
FOR NOW MASTER MAHONIA SHALL CAST A SPELL OF MINOR WARDING TO PROTECT THE SLOUGMIN FROM THESE VILE ASSASINS!
WHACK!

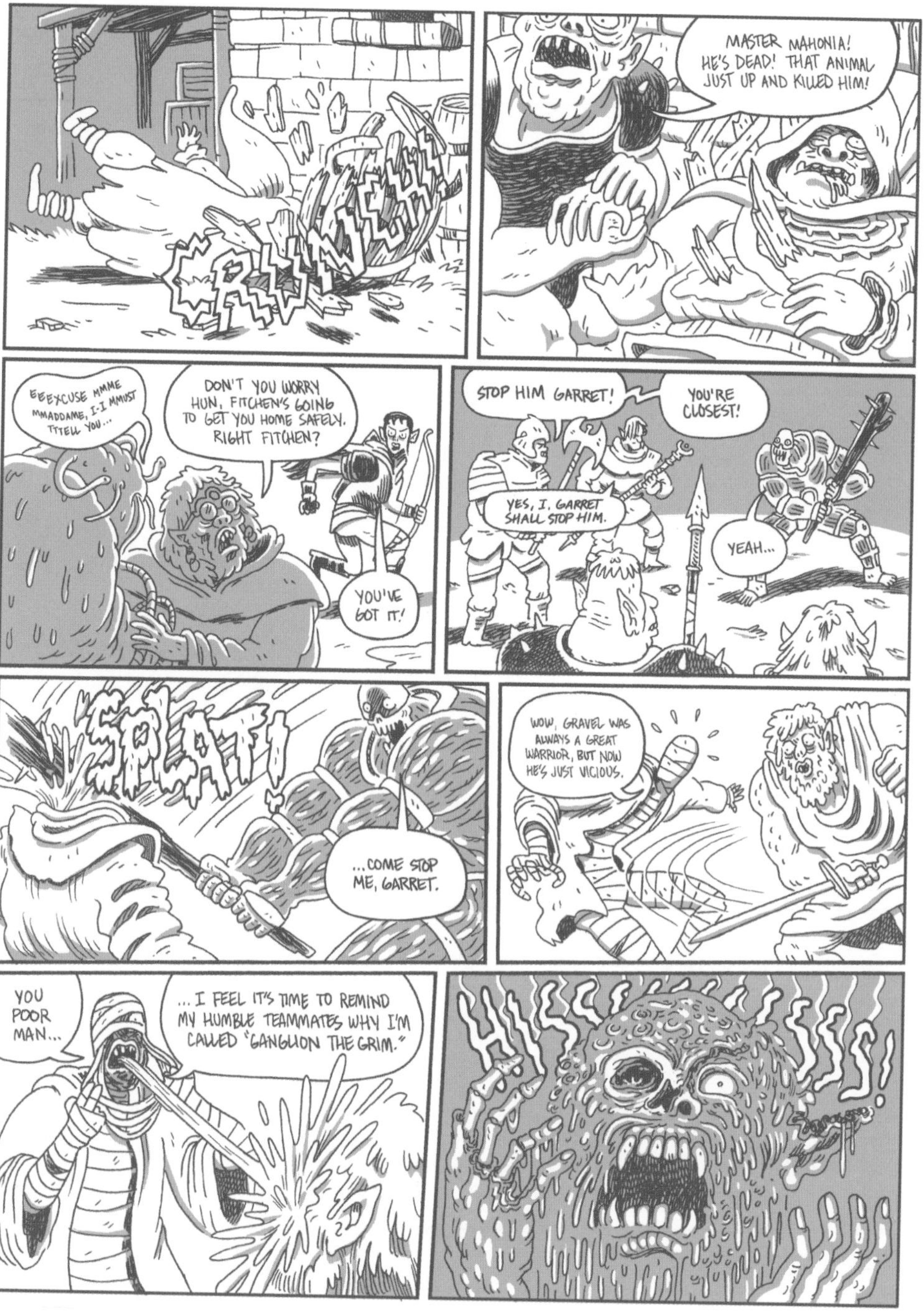
CRUNCH
MASTER MAHONIA! HE'S DEAD! THAT ANIMAL JUST UP AND KILLED HIM!
EEEXCUSE MMME MMADDAME, I-I MMUST TTTELL YOU...
DON'T YOU WORRY HUN, FITCHEN'S GOING TO GET YOU HOME SAFELY. RIGHT FITCHEN?
YOU'VE GOT IT!
STOP HIM GARRET!
YOU'RE CLOSEST!
YES, I, GARRET SHALL STOP HIM.
YEAH...
SPLAT!
...COME STOP ME, GARRET.
WOW, GRAVEL WAS ALWAYS A GREAT WARRIOR, BUT NOW HE'S JUST VICIOUS.
YOU POOR MAN...
...I FEEL IT'S TIME TO REMIND MY HUMBLE TEAMMATES WHY I'M CALLED "GANGLION THE GRIM."
HISSSSSSSSS!

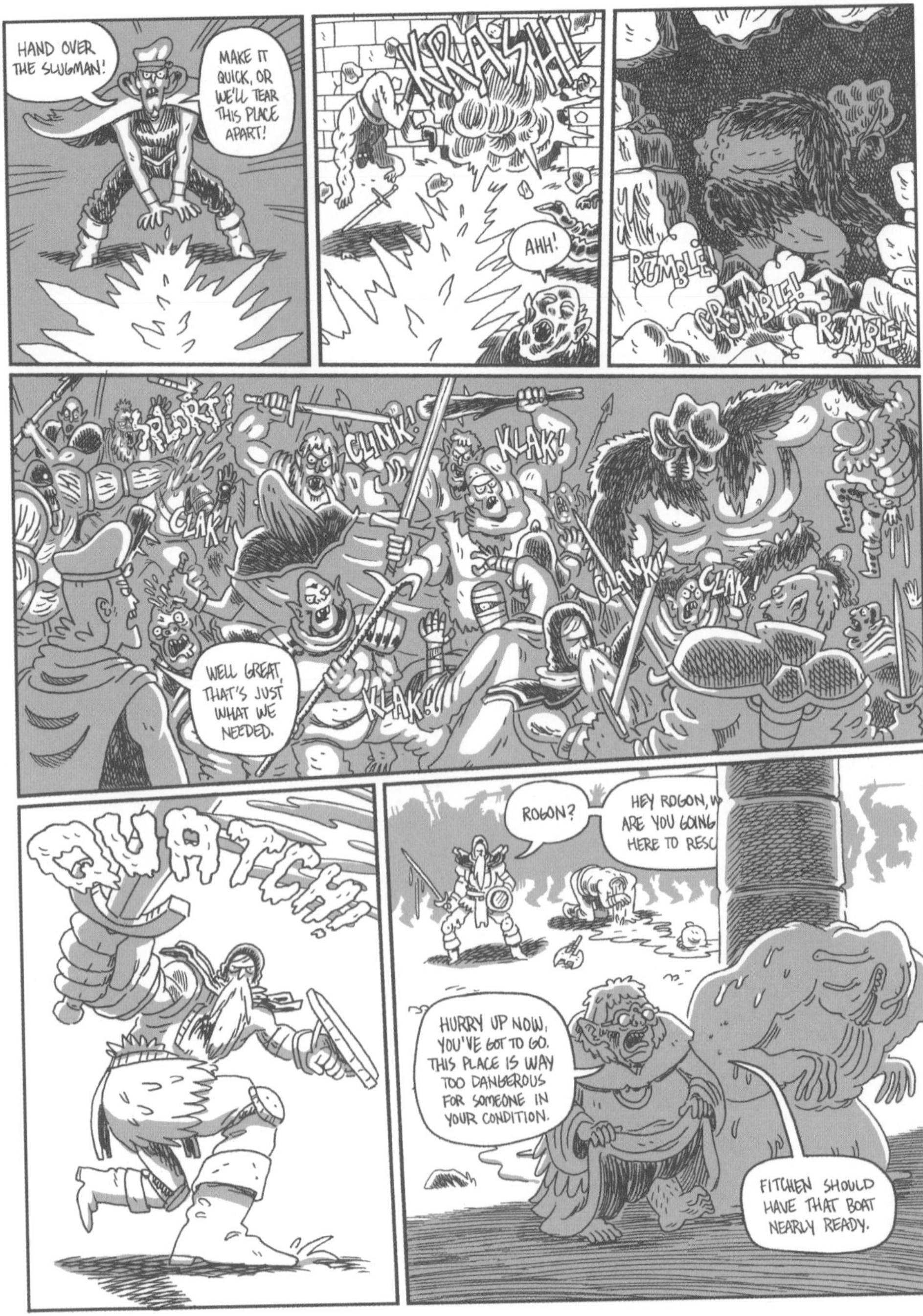
HAND OVER THE SLUGMAN!
MAKE IT QUICK, OR WE'LL TEAR THIS PLACE APART!
KRASH!
AHH!
RUMBLE!
CRUMBLE!
RUMBLE!
SPLORT!
CLINK!
KLAK!
CLAK!
CLANK!
CLAK!
WELL GREAT, THAT'S JUST WHAT WE NEEDED.
KLAK!
QUATCH
ROGON?
HEY ROGON, W
ARE YOU GOING
HERE TO RESC
HURRY UP NOW, YOU'VE GOT TO GO. THIS PLACE IS WAY TOO DANGEROUS FOR SOMEONE IN YOUR CONDITION.
FITCHEN SHOULD HAVE THAT BOAT NEARLY READY.

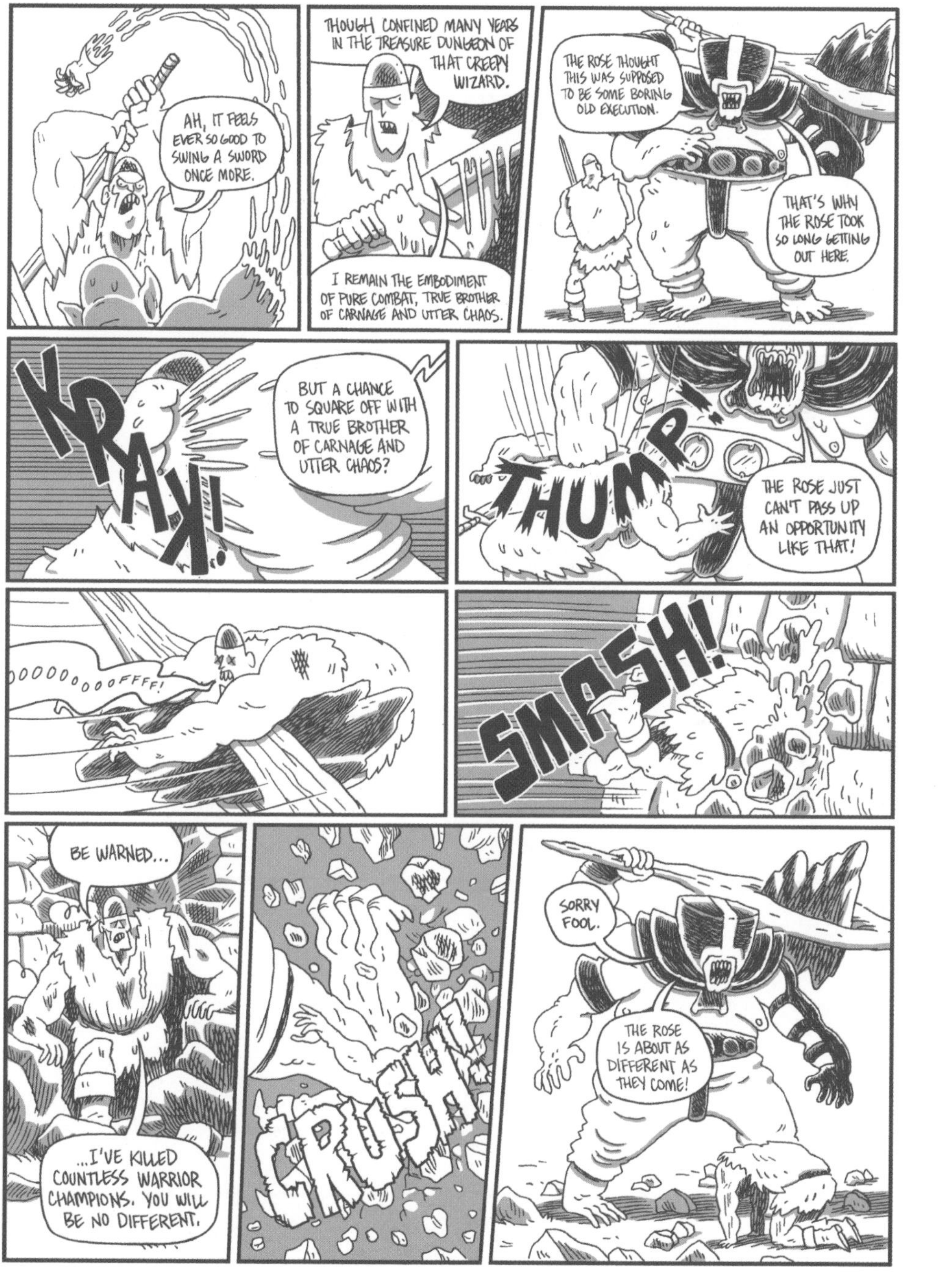
AH, IT FEELS EVER SO GOOD TO SWING A SWORD ONCE MORE.
THOUGH CONFINED MANY YEARS IN THE TREASURE DUNGEON OF THAT CREEPY WIZARD.
I REMAIN THE EMBODIMENT OF PURE COMBAT, TRUE BROTHER OF CARNAGE AND UTTER CHAOS.
THE ROSE THOUGHT THIS WAS SUPPOSED TO BE SOME BORING OLD EXECUTION.
THAT'S WHY THE ROSE TOOK SO LONG GETTING OUT HERE.
KRAK!
BUT A CHANCE TO SQUARE OFF WITH A TRUE BROTHER OF CARNAGE AND UTTER CHAOS?
THUMP!
THE ROSE JUST CAN'T PASS UP AN OPPORTUNITY LIKE THAT!
OOOOOOoooFFFF!
SMASH!
BE WARNED...
...I'VE KILLED COUNTLESS WARRIOR CHAMPIONS. YOU WILL BE NO DIFFERENT.
CRUSH!
SORRY FOOL.
THE ROSE IS ABOUT AS DIFFERENT AS THEY COME!

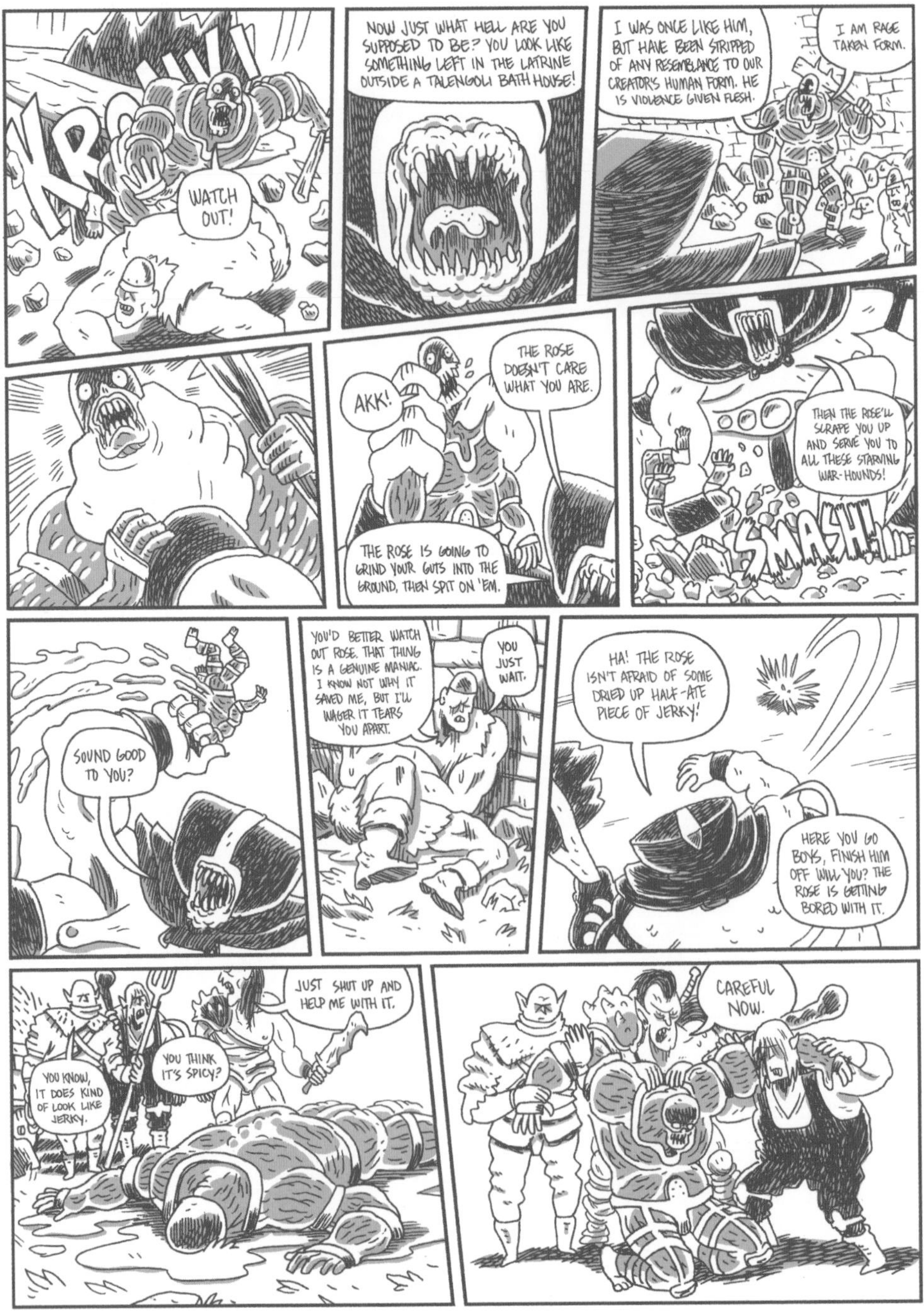
KRAK!
WATCH OUT!
NOW JUST WHAT HELL ARE YOU SUPPOSED TO BE? YOU LOOK LIKE SOMETHING LEFT IN THE LATRINE OUTSIDE A TALENGOLI BATH HOUSE!
I WAS ONCE LIKE HIM, BUT HAVE BEEN STRIPPED OF ANY RESEMBLANCE TO OUR CREATOR'S HUMAN FORM. HE IS VIOLENCE GIVEN FLESH.
I AM RAGE TAKEN FORM.
AKK!
THE ROSE DOESN'T CARE WHAT YOU ARE.
THE ROSE IS GOING TO GRIND YOUR GUTS INTO THE GROUND, THEN SPIT ON 'EM.
THEN THE ROSE'LL SCRAPE YOU UP AND SERVE YOU TO ALL THESE STARVING WAR-HOUNDS!
SMASH!
SOUND GOOD TO YOU?
YOU'D BETTER WATCH OUT ROSE. THAT THING IS A GENUINE MANIAC. I KNOW NOT WHY IT SAVED ME, BUT I'LL WAGER IT TEARS YOU APART.
YOU JUST WAIT.
HA! THE ROSE ISN'T AFRAID OF SOME DRIED UP HALF-ATE PIECE OF JERKY!
HERE YOU GO BOYS, FINISH HIM OFF WILL YOU? THE ROSE IS GETTING BORED WITH IT.
YOU KNOW, IT DOES KIND OF LOOK LIKE JERKY.
YOU THINK IT'S SPICY?
JUST SHUT UP AND HELP ME WITH IT.
CAREFUL NOW.

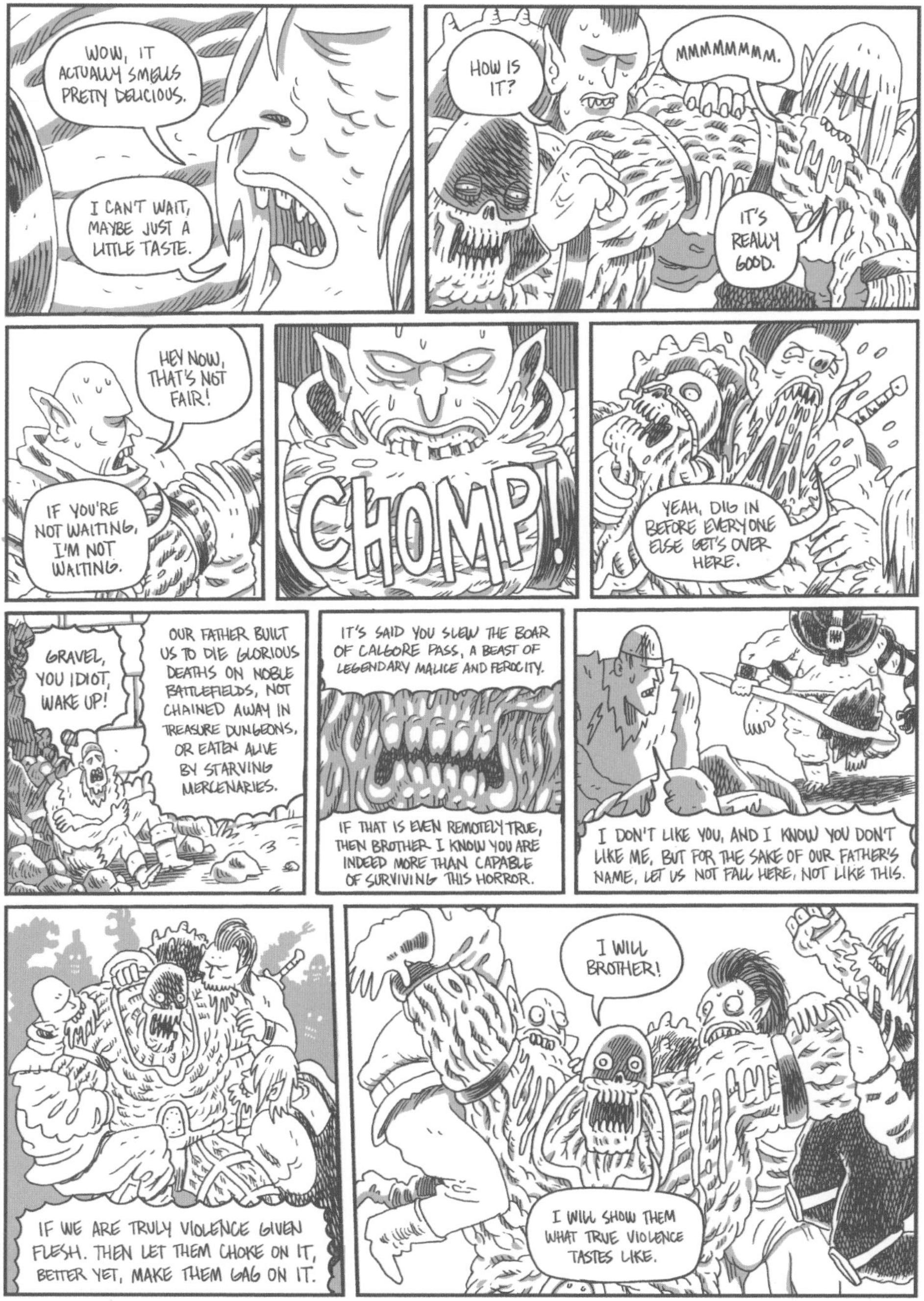
WOW, IT ACTUALLY SMELLS PRETTY DELICIOUS.
I CAN'T WAIT, MAYBE JUST A LITTLE TASTE.
HOW IS IT?
MMMMMMMM.
IT'S REALLY GOOD.
HEY NOW, THAT'S NOT FAIR!
IF YOU'RE NOT WAITING, I'M NOT WAITING.
CHOMP!
YEAH, DIG IN BEFORE EVERYONE ELSE GET'S OVER HERE.
GRAVEL, YOU IDIOT, WAKE UP!
OUR FATHER BUILT US TO DIE GLORIOUS DEATHS ON NOBLE BATTLEFIELDS, NOT CHAINED AWAY IN TREASURE DUNGEONS, OR EATEN ALIVE BY STARVING MERCENARIES.
IT'S SAID YOU SLEW THE BOAR OF CALGORE PASS, A BEAST OF LEGENDARY MALICE AND FEROCITY.
IF THAT IS EVEN REMOTELY TRUE, THEN BROTHER I KNOW YOU ARE INDEED MORE THAN CAPABLE OF SURVIVING THIS HORROR.
I DON'T LIKE YOU, AND I KNOW YOU DON'T LIKE ME, BUT FOR THE SAKE OF OUR FATHER'S NAME, LET US NOT FALL HERE, NOT LIKE THIS.
IF WE ARE TRULY VIOLENCE GIVEN FLESH. THEN LET THEM CHOKE ON IT, BETTER YET, MAKE THEM GAG ON IT.
I WILL BROTHER!
I WILL SHOW THEM WHAT TRUE VIOLENCE TASTES LIKE.

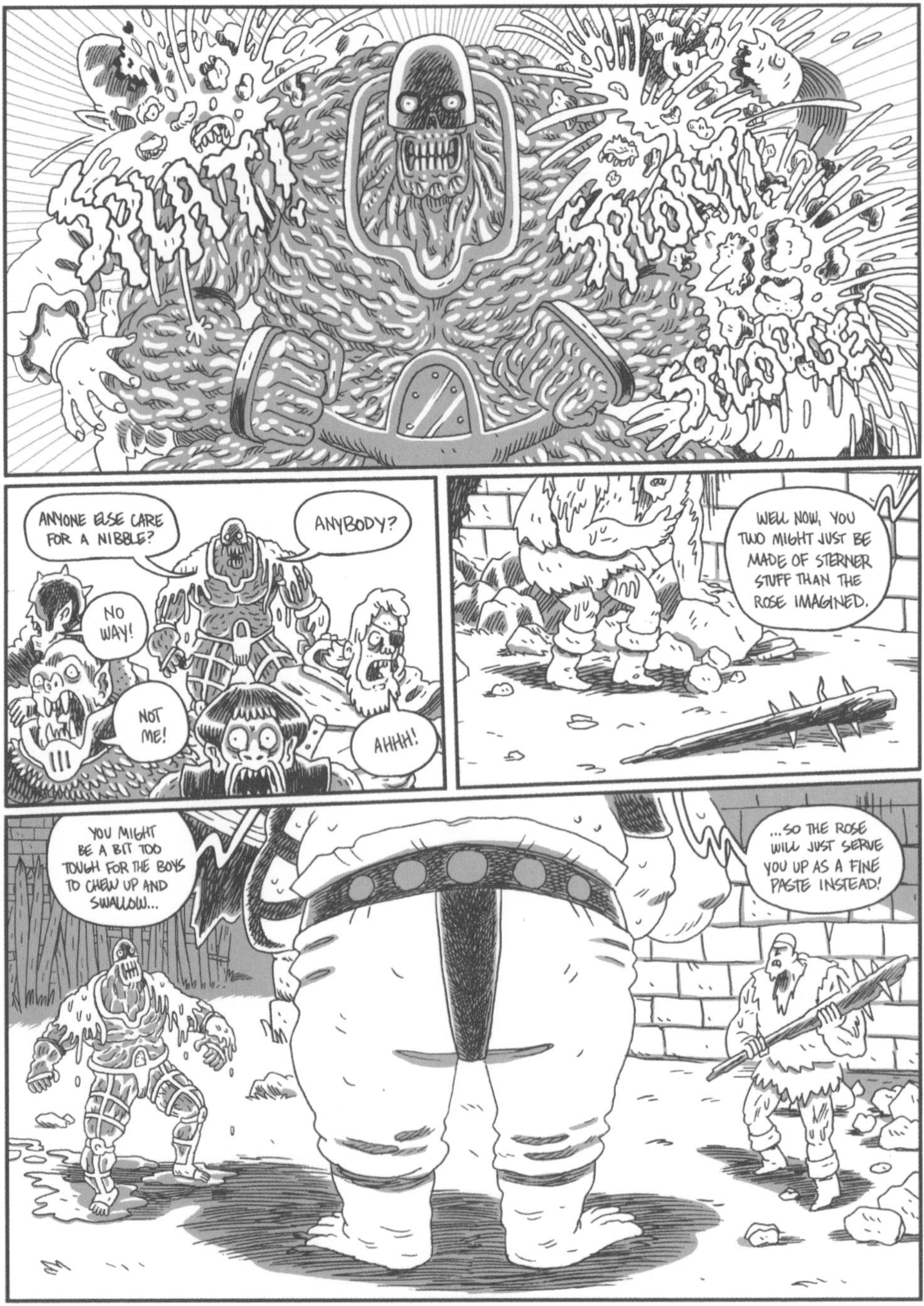
SPLAT!
SPLOOT!
SPLOOGE!
ANYONE ELSE CARE FOR A NIBBLE?
ANYBODY?
NO WAY!
NOT ME!
AHHH!
WELL NOW, YOU TWO MIGHT JUST BE MADE OF STERNER STUFF THAN THE ROSE IMAGINED.
YOU MIGHT BE A BIT TOO TOUGH FOR THE BOYS TO CHEW UP AND SWALLOW...
...SO THE ROSE WILL JUST SERVE YOU UP AS A FINE PASTE INSTEAD!

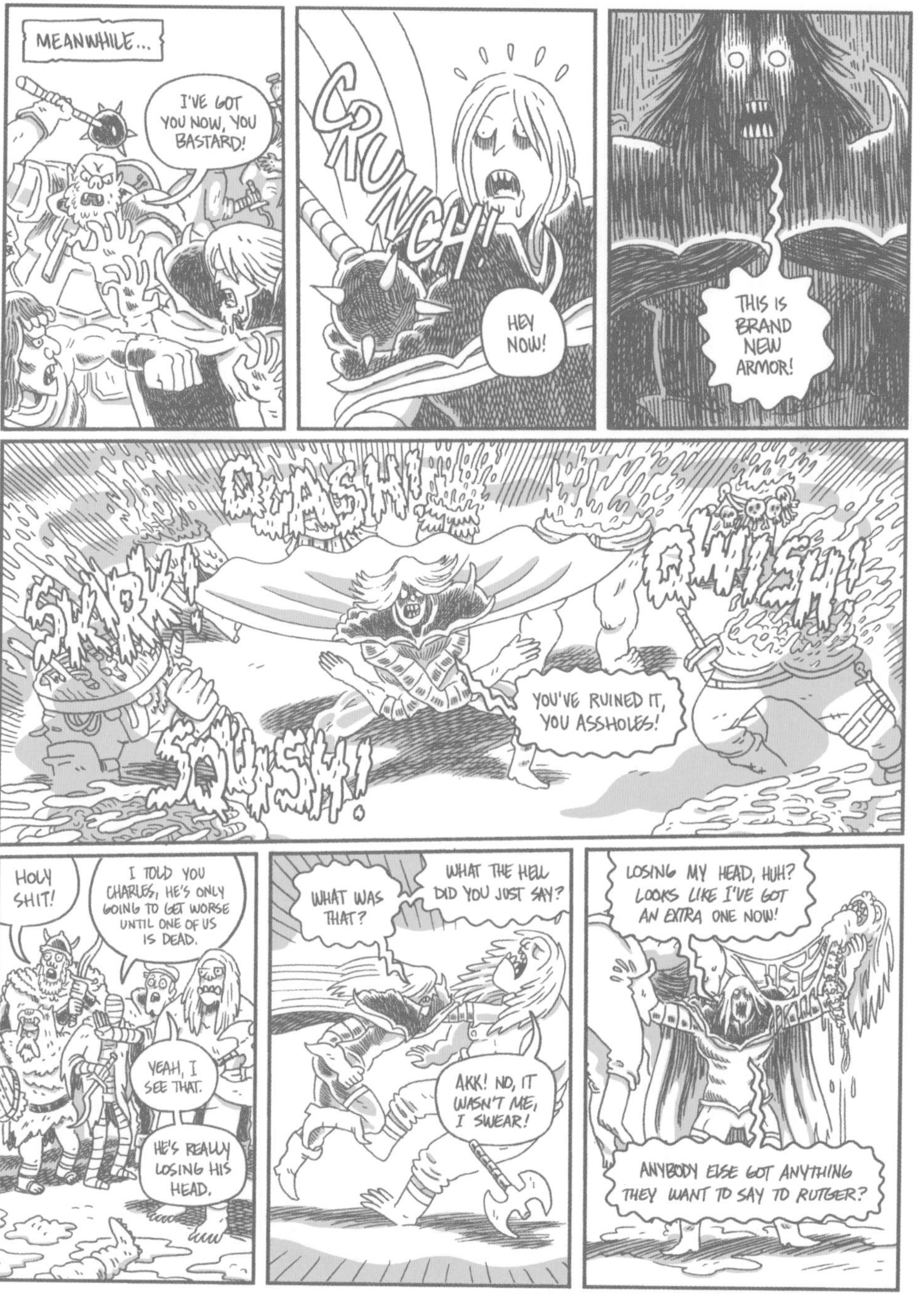
MEANWHILE...
I'VE GOT YOU NOW, YOU BASTARD!
CRUNCH!
HEY NOW!
THIS IS BRAND NEW ARMOR!
CLASH!
SHRK!
QWISH!
YOU'VE RUINED IT, YOU ASSHOLES!
SQUISH!
HOLY SHIT!
I TOLD YOU CHARLES, HE'S ONLY GOING TO GET WORSE UNTIL ONE OF US IS DEAD.
YEAH, I SEE THAT.
HE'S REALLY LOSING HIS HEAD.
WHAT WAS THAT?
WHAT THE HELL DID YOU JUST SAY?
AKK! NO, IT WASN'T ME, I SWEAR!
LOSING MY HEAD, HUH? LOOKS LIKE I'VE GOT AN EXTRA ONE NOW!
ANYBODY ELSE GOT ANYTHING THEY WANT TO SAY TO RUTGER?

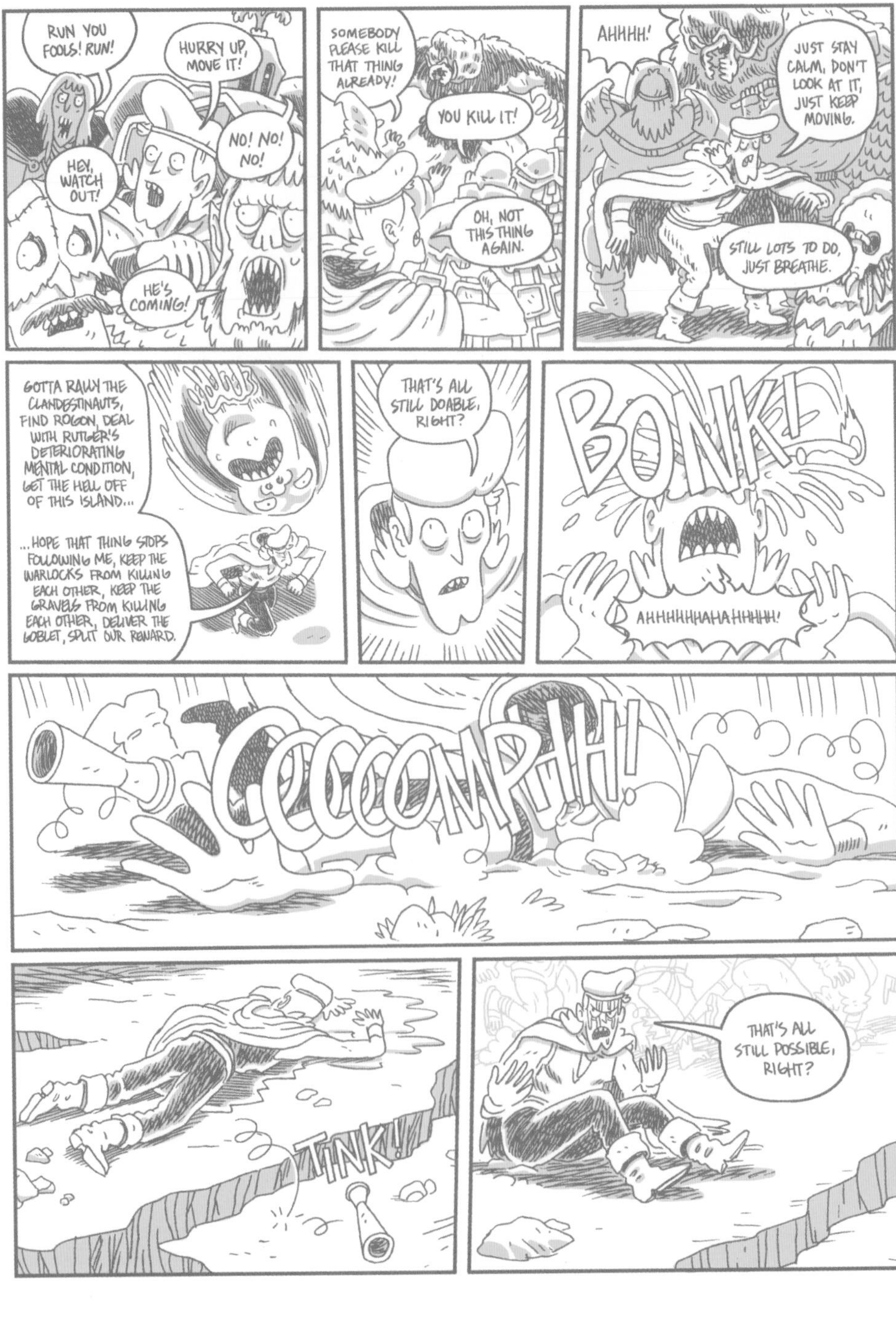
RUN YOU FOOLS! RUN!
HURRY UP, MOVE IT!
HEY, WATCH OUT!
NO! NO! NO!
HE'S COMING!
SOMEBODY PLEASE KILL THAT THING ALREADY!
YOU KILL IT!
OH, NOT THIS THING AGAIN.
AHHHH!
JUST STAY CALM, DON'T LOOK AT IT, JUST KEEP MOVING.
STILL LOTS TO DO, JUST BREATHE.
GOTTA RALLY THE CLANDESTINAUTS, FIND ROGON, DEAL WITH RUTGER'S DETERIORATING MENTAL CONDITION, GET THE HELL OFF OF THIS ISLAND...
...HOPE THAT THING STOPS FOLLOWING ME, KEEP THE WARLOCKS FROM KILLING EACH OTHER, KEEP THE GRAVELS FROM KILLING EACH OTHER, DELIVER THE GOBLET, SPLIT OUR REWARD.
THAT'S ALL STILL DOABLE, RIGHT?
BONK!
AHHHHHHAHAHHHHH!
GOOOOOMPHH!
TINK!
THAT'S ALL STILL POSSIBLE, RIGHT?

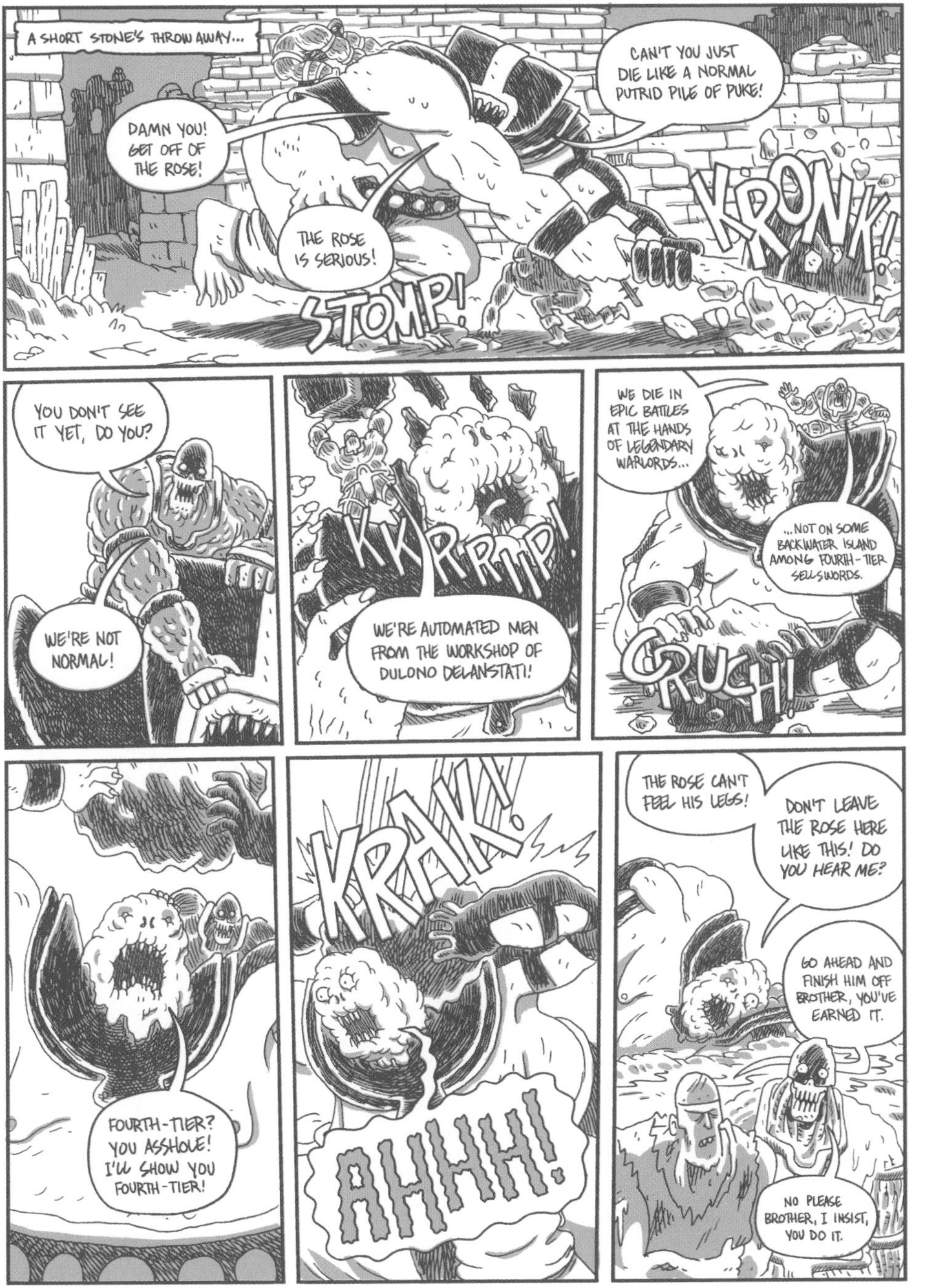
A SHORT STONE'S THROW AWAY...
DAMN YOU! GET OFF OF THE ROSE!
CAN'T YOU JUST DIE LIKE A NORMAL PUTRID PILE OF PUKE!
THE ROSE IS SERIOUS!
STOMP!
KRONK!
YOU DON'T SEE IT YET, DO YOU?
WE'RE NOT NORMAL!
KKRRRIIP!
WE'RE AUTOMATED MEN FROM THE WORKSHOP OF DULONO DELANSTATI!
WE DIE IN EPIC BATTLES AT THE HANDS OF LEGENDARY WARLORDS...
...NOT ON SOME BACKWATER ISLAND AMONG FOURTH-TIER SELLSWORDS.
CRUCH!
FOURTH-TIER? YOU ASSHOLE! I'LL SHOW YOU FOURTH-TIER!
KRAK!
AHHH!
THE ROSE CAN'T FEEL HIS LEGS!
DON'T LEAVE THE ROSE HERE LIKE THIS! DO YOU HEAR ME?
GO AHEAD AND FINISH HIM OFF BROTHER, YOU'VE EARNED IT.
NO PLEASE BROTHER, I INSIST, YOU DO IT.

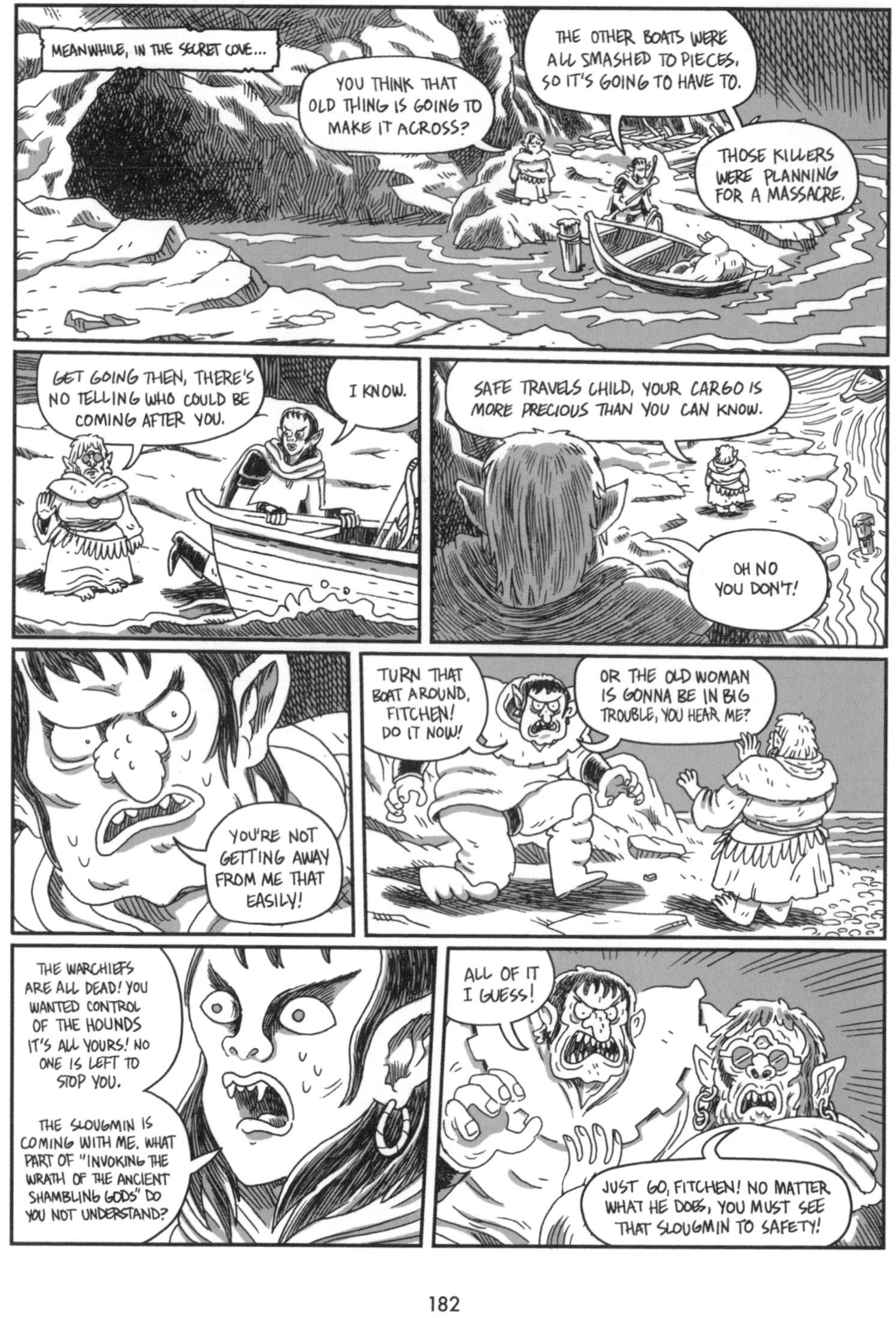
MEANWHILE, IN THE SECRET COVE...
YOU THINK THAT OLD THING IS GOING TO MAKE IT ACROSS?
THE OTHER BOATS WERE ALL SMASHED TO PIECES, SO IT'S GOING TO HAVE TO.
THOSE KILLERS WERE PLANNING FOR A MASSACRE.
GET GOING THEN, THERE'S NO TELLING WHO COULD BE COMING AFTER YOU.
I KNOW.
SAFE TRAVELS CHILD, YOUR CARGO IS MORE PRECIOUS THAN YOU CAN KNOW.
OH NO YOU DON'T!
YOU'RE NOT GETTING AWAY FROM ME THAT EASILY!
TURN THAT BOAT AROUND, FITCHEN! DO IT NOW!
OR THE OLD WOMAN IS GONNA BE IN BIG TROUBLE, YOU HEAR ME?
THE WARCHIEFS ARE ALL DEAD! YOU WANTED CONTROL OF THE HOUNDS IT'S ALL YOURS! NO ONE IS LEFT TO STOP YOU.
THE SLOUGMIN IS COMING WITH ME. WHAT PART OF "INVOKING THE WRATH OF THE ANCIENT SHAMBLING GODS" DO YOU NOT UNDERSTAND?
ALL OF IT I GUESS!
JUST GO, FITCHEN! NO MATTER WHAT HE DOES, YOU MUST SEE THAT SLOUGMIN TO SAFETY!

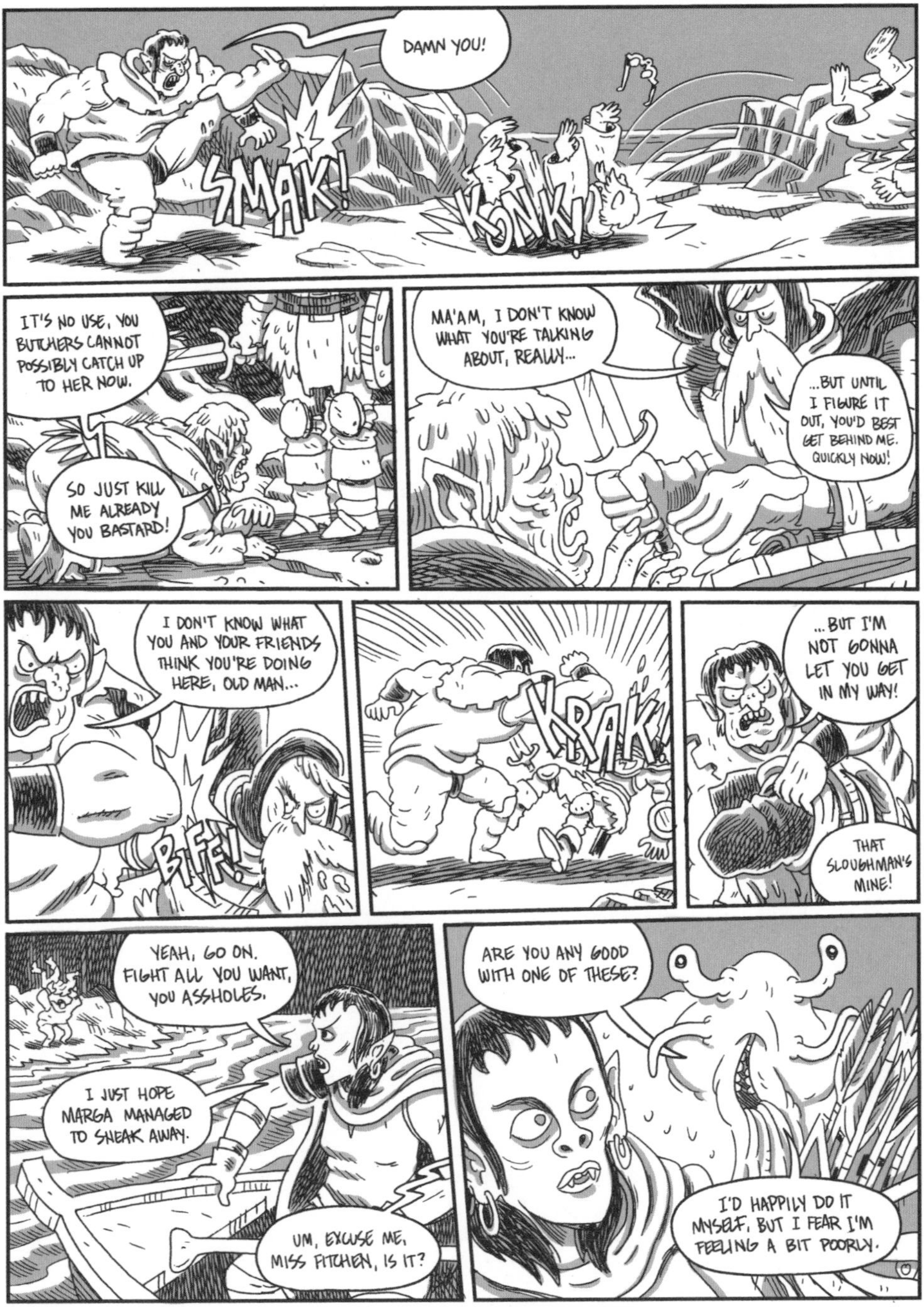
DAMN YOU!
SMAK!
KONK!
IT'S NO USE, YOU BUTCHERS CANNOT POSSIBLY CATCH UP TO HER NOW.
SO JUST KILL ME ALREADY YOU BASTARD!
MA'AM, I DON'T KNOW WHAT YOU'RE TALKING ABOUT, REALLY...
...BUT UNTIL I FIGURE IT OUT, YOU'D BEST GET BEHIND ME. QUICKLY NOW!
I DON'T KNOW WHAT YOU AND YOUR FRIENDS THINK YOU'RE DOING HERE, OLD MAN...
BIFF!
KRAK!
...BUT I'M NOT GONNA LET YOU GET IN MY WAY!
THAT SLOUGHMAN'S MINE!
YEAH, GO ON. FIGHT ALL YOU WANT, YOU ASSHOLES.
I JUST HOPE MARGA MANAGED TO SNEAK AWAY.
UM, EXCUSE ME, MISS FITCHEN, IS IT?
ARE YOU ANY GOOD WITH ONE OF THESE?
I'D HAPPILY DO IT MYSELF, BUT I FEAR I'M FEELING A BIT POORLY.

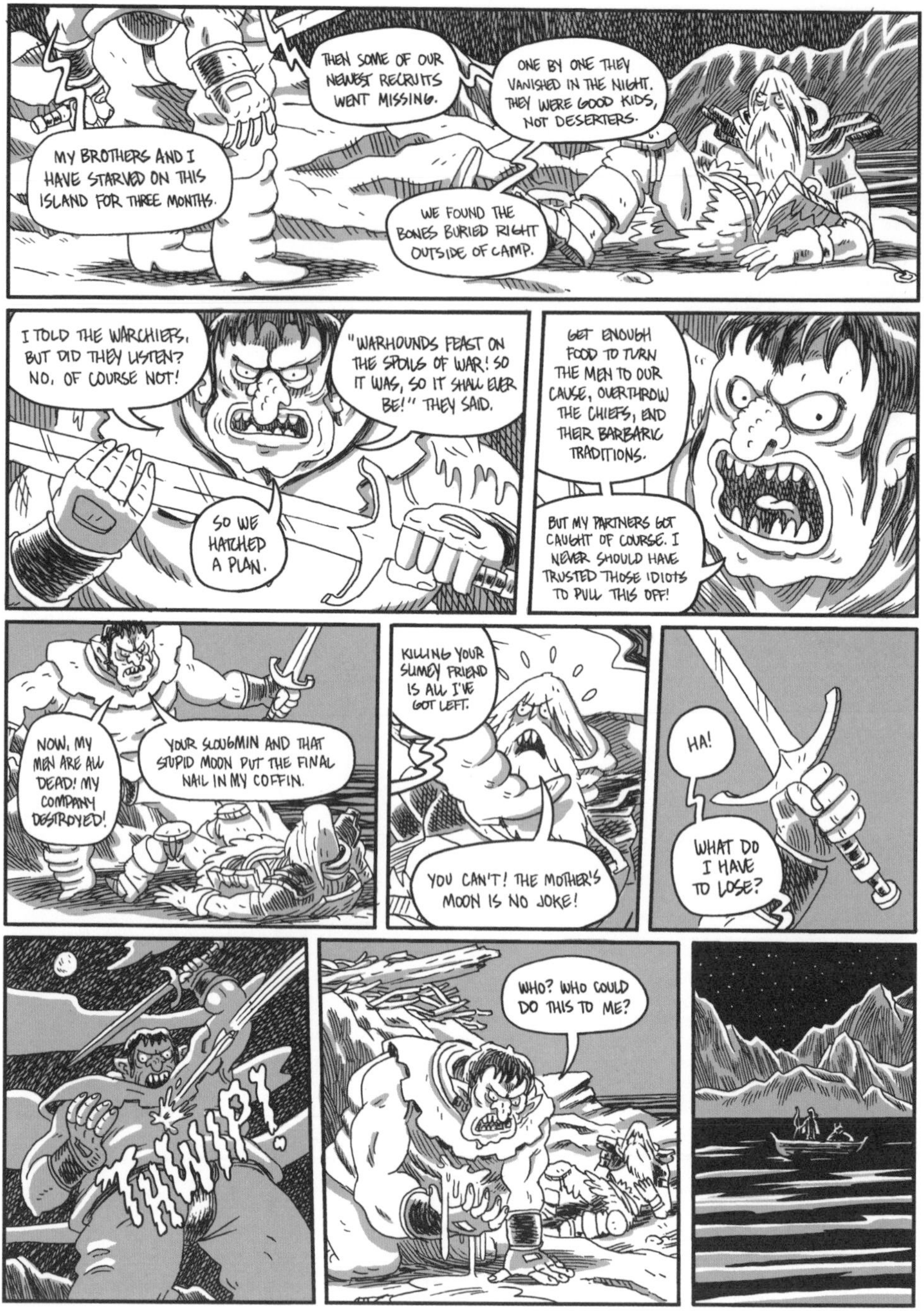
MY BROTHERS AND I HAVE STARVED ON THIS ISLAND FOR THREE MONTHS.
THEN SOME OF OUR NEWEST RECRUITS WENT MISSING.
ONE BY ONE THEY VANISHED IN THE NIGHT. THEY WERE GOOD KIDS, NOT DESERTERS.
WE FOUND THE BONES BURIED RIGHT OUTSIDE OF CAMP.
I TOLD THE WARCHIEFS, BUT DID THEY LISTEN? NO, OF COURSE NOT!
"WARHOUNDS FEAST ON THE SPOILS OF WAR! SO IT WAS, SO IT SHALL EVER BE!" THEY SAID.
SO WE HATCHED A PLAN.
GET ENOUGH FOOD TO TURN THE MEN TO OUR CAUSE, OVERTHROW THE CHIEFS, END THEIR BARBARIC TRADITIONS.
BUT MY PARTNERS GOT CAUGHT OF COURSE. I NEVER SHOULD HAVE TRUSTED THOSE IDIOTS TO PULL THIS OFF!
NOW, MY MEN ARE ALL DEAD! MY COMPANY DESTROYED!
YOUR SLOUGMIN AND THAT STUPID MOON PUT THE FINAL NAIL IN MY COFFIN.
KILLING YOUR SLIMEY FRIEND IS ALL I'VE GOT LEFT.
YOU CAN'T! THE MOTHER'S MOON IS NO JOKE!
HA!
WHAT DO I HAVE TO LOSE?
THWIP!
WHO? WHO COULD DO THIS TO ME?

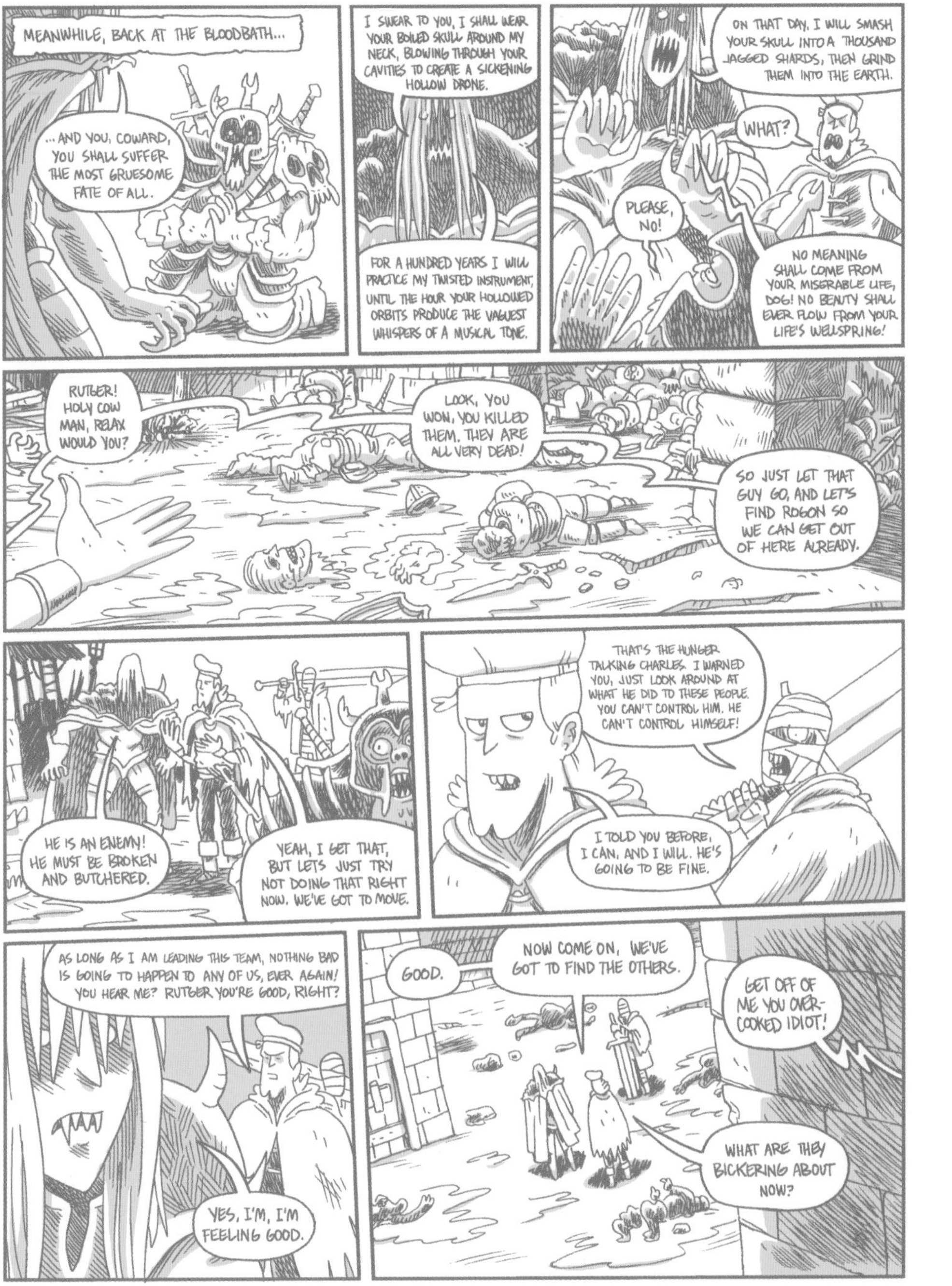
MEANWHILE, BACK AT THE BLOODBATH...
...AND YOU, COWARD, YOU SHALL SUFFER THE MOST GRUESOME FATE OF ALL.
I SWEAR TO YOU, I SHALL WEAR YOUR BOILED SKULL AROUND MY NECK, BLOWING THROUGH YOUR CAVITIES TO CREATE A SICKENING HOLLOW DRONE.
FOR A HUNDRED YEARS I WILL PRACTICE MY TWISTED INSTRUMENT, UNTIL THE HOUR YOUR HOLLOWED ORBITS PRODUCE THE VAGUEST WHISPERS OF A MUSICAL TONE.
ON THAT DAY, I WILL SMASH YOUR SKULL INTO A THOUSAND JAGGED SHARDS, THEN GRIND THEM INTO THE EARTH.
WHAT?
PLEASE, NO!
NO MEANING SHALL COME FROM YOUR MISERABLE LIFE, DOG! NO BEAUTY SHALL EVER FLOW FROM YOUR LIFE'S WELLSPRING!
RUTGER! HOLY COW MAN, RELAX WOULD YOU?
LOOK, YOU WON, YOU KILLED THEM. THEY ARE ALL VERY DEAD!
SO JUST LET THAT GUY GO, AND LET'S FIND ROGON SO WE CAN GET OUT OF HERE ALREADY.
HE IS AN ENEMY! HE MUST BE BROKEN AND BUTCHERED.
YEAH, I GET THAT, BUT LETS JUST TRY NOT DOING THAT RIGHT NOW. WE'VE GOT TO MOVE.
THAT'S THE HUNGER TALKING CHARLES. I WARNED YOU, JUST LOOK AROUND AT WHAT HE DID TO THESE PEOPLE. YOU CAN'T CONTROL HIM. HE CAN'T CONTROL HIMSELF!
I TOLD YOU BEFORE, I CAN, AND I WILL. HE'S GOING TO BE FINE.
AS LONG AS I AM LEADING THIS TEAM, NOTHING BAD IS GOING TO HAPPEN TO ANY OF US, EVER AGAIN! YOU HEAR ME? RUTGER YOU'RE GOOD, RIGHT?
YES, I'M, I'M FEELING GOOD.
GOOD.
NOW COME ON, WE'VE GOT TO FIND THE OTHERS.
GET OFF OF ME YOU OVER-COOKED IDIOT!
WHAT ARE THEY BICKERING ABOUT NOW?

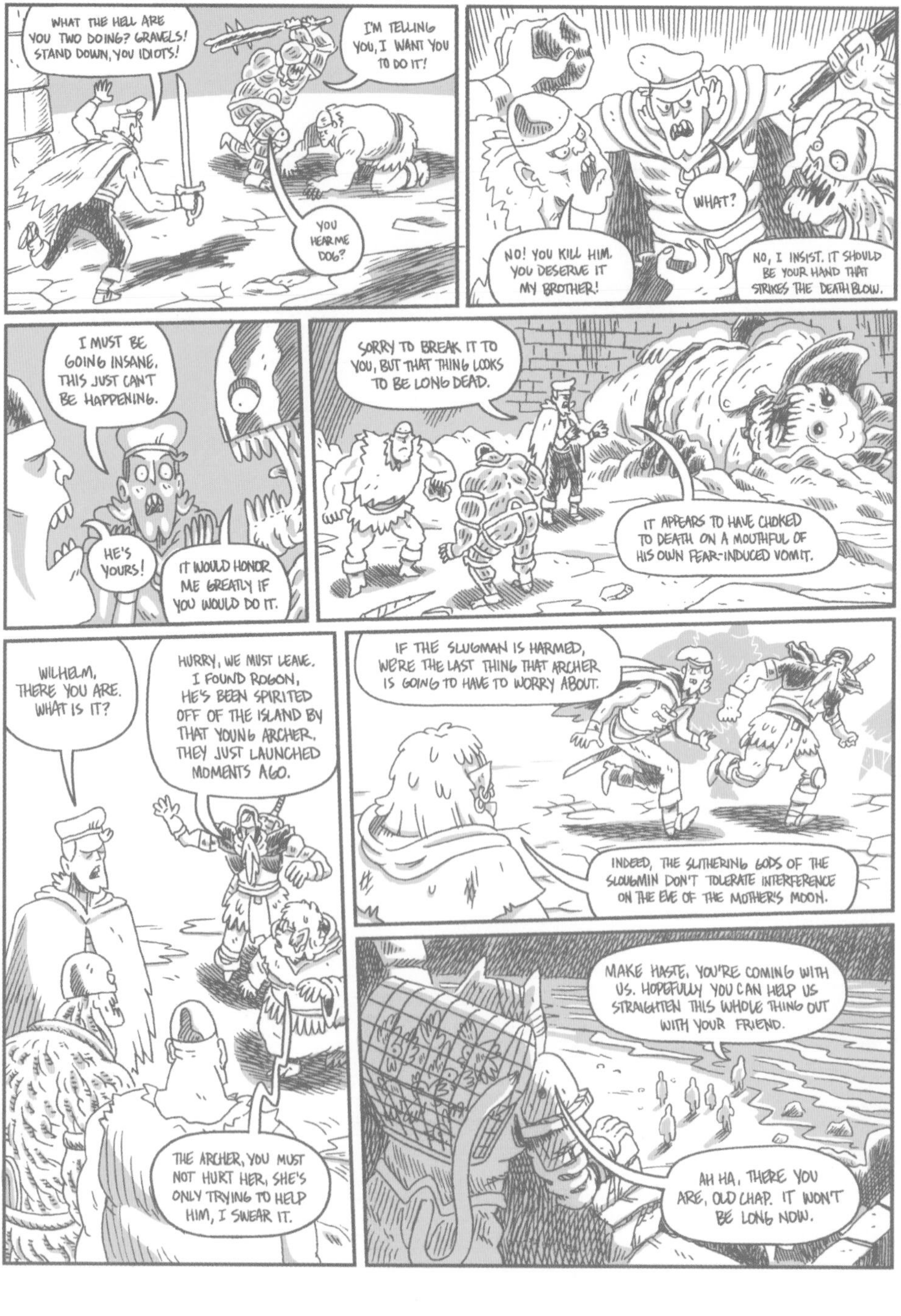
WHAT THE HELL ARE YOU TWO DOING? GRAVELS! STAND DOWN, YOU IDIOTS!
I'M TELLING YOU, I WANT YOU TO DO IT!
YOU HEAR ME DOG?
WHAT?
NO! YOU KILL HIM. YOU DESERVE IT MY BROTHER!
NO, I INSIST. IT SHOULD BE YOUR HAND THAT STRIKES THE DEATH BLOW.
I MUST BE GOING INSANE. THIS JUST CAN'T BE HAPPENING.
HE'S YOURS!
IT WOULD HONOR ME GREATLY IF YOU WOULD DO IT.
SORRY TO BREAK IT TO YOU, BUT THAT THING LOOKS TO BE LONG DEAD.
IT APPEARS TO HAVE CHOKED TO DEATH ON A MOUTHFUL OF HIS OWN FEAR-INDUCED VOMIT.
WILHELM, THERE YOU ARE. WHAT IS IT?
HURRY, WE MUST LEAVE. I FOUND ROGON, HE'S BEEN SPIRITED OFF OF THE ISLAND BY THAT YOUNG ARCHER. THEY JUST LAUNCHED MOMENTS AGO.
THE ARCHER, YOU MUST NOT HURT HER, SHE'S ONLY TRYING TO HELP HIM, I SWEAR IT.
IF THE SLUGMAN IS HARMED, WE'RE THE LAST THING THAT ARCHER IS GOING TO HAVE TO WORRY ABOUT.
INDEED, THE SLITHERING GODS OF THE SLOUGMIN DON'T TOLERATE INTERFERENCE ON THE EVE OF THE MOTHER'S MOON.
MAKE HASTE, YOU'RE COMING WITH US. HOPEFULLY YOU CAN HELP US STRAIGHTEN THIS WHOLE THING OUT WITH YOUR FRIEND.
AH HA, THERE YOU ARE, OLD CHAP. IT WON'T BE LONG NOW.

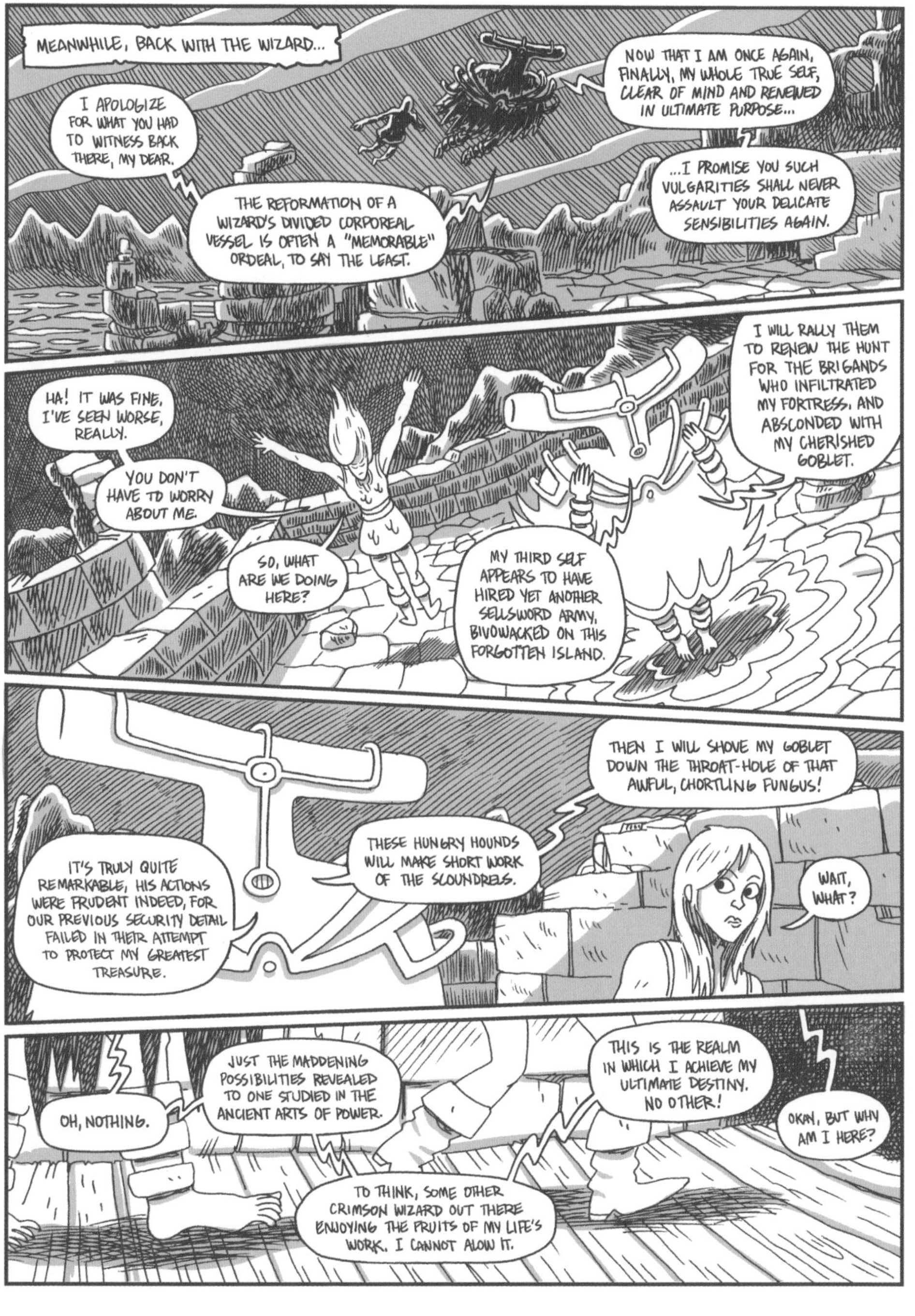
MEANWHILE, BACK WITH THE WIZARD...
I APOLOGIZE FOR WHAT YOU HAD TO WITNESS BACK THERE, MY DEAR.
THE REFORMATION OF A WIZARD'S DIVIDED CORPOREAL VESSEL IS OFTEN A "MEMORABLE" ORDEAL, TO SAY THE LEAST.
NOW THAT I AM ONCE AGAIN, FINALLY, MY WHOLE TRUE SELF, CLEAR OF MIND AND RENEWED IN ULTIMATE PURPOSE...
...I PROMISE YOU SUCH VULGARITIES SHALL NEVER ASSAULT YOUR DELICATE SENSIBILITIES AGAIN.
HA! IT WAS FINE, I'VE SEEN WORSE, REALLY.
YOU DON'T HAVE TO WORRY ABOUT ME.
SO, WHAT ARE WE DOING HERE?
MY THIRD SELF APPEARS TO HAVE HIRED YET ANOTHER SELLSWORD ARMY, BIVOWACKED ON THIS FORGOTTEN ISLAND.
I WILL RALLY THEM TO RENEW THE HUNT FOR THE BRIGANDS WHO INFILTRATED MY FORTRESS, AND ABSCONDED WITH MY CHERISHED GOBLET.
IT'S TRULY QUITE REMARKABLE, HIS ACTIONS WERE PRUDENT INDEED, FOR OUR PREVIOUS SECURITY DETAIL FAILED IN THEIR ATTEMPT TO PROTECT MY GREATEST TREASURE.
THESE HUNGRY HOUNDS WILL MAKE SHORT WORK OF THE SCOUNDRELS.
THEN I WILL SHOVE MY GOBLET DOWN THE THROAT-HOLE OF THAT AWFUL, CHORTLING FUNGUS!
WAIT, WHAT?
OH, NOTHING.
JUST THE MADDENING POSSIBILITIES REVEALED TO ONE STUDIED IN THE ANCIENT ARTS OF POWER.
TO THINK, SOME OTHER CRIMSON WIZARD OUT THERE ENJOYING THE FRUITS OF MY LIFE'S WORK. I CANNOT ALOW IT.
THIS IS THE REALM IN WHICH I ACHIEVE MY ULTIMATE DESTINY. NO OTHER!
OKAY, BUT WHY AM I HERE?

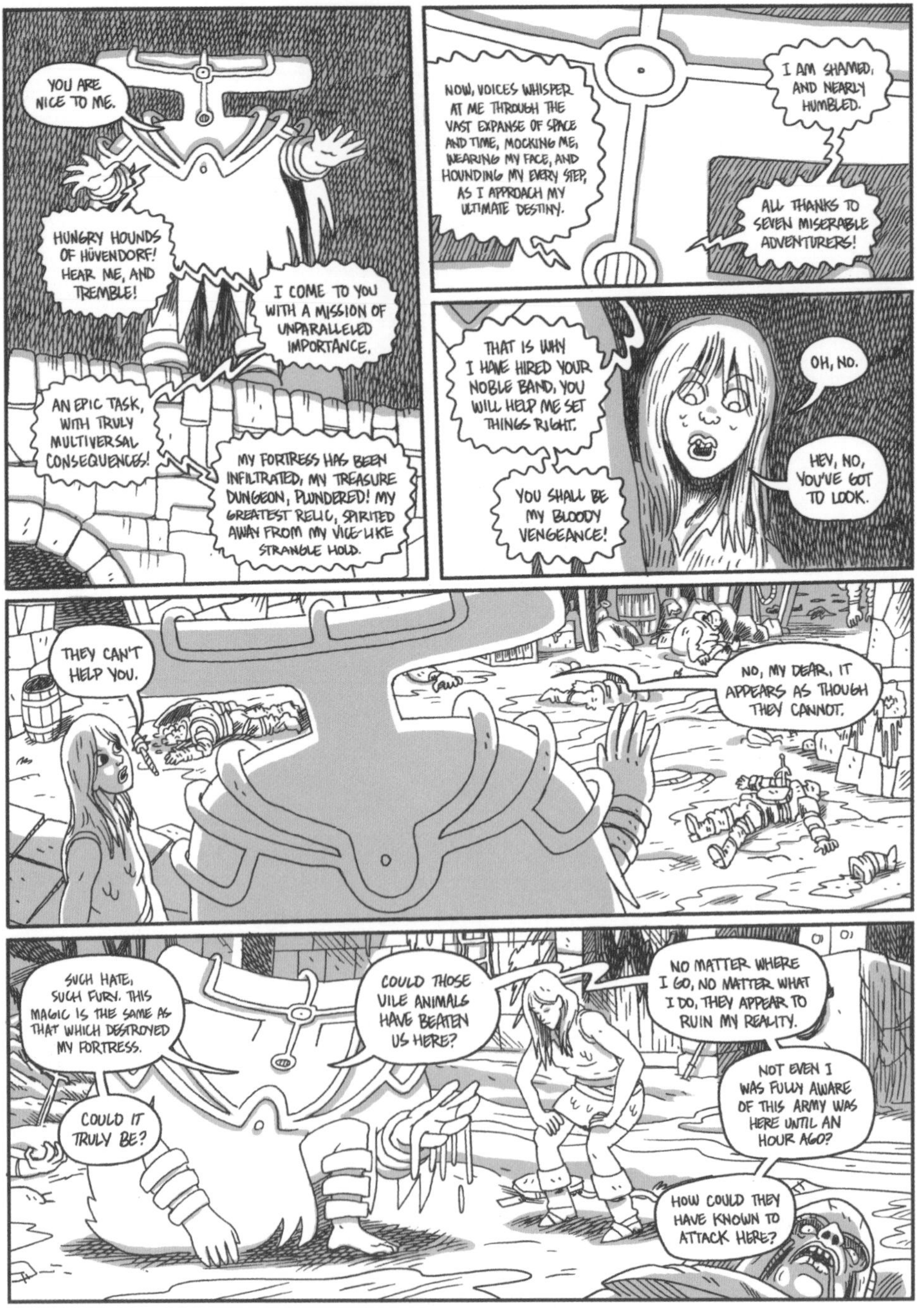
YOU ARE NICE TO ME.
HUNGRY HOUNDS OF HÜVENDORF! HEAR ME, AND TREMBLE!
I COME TO YOU WITH A MISSION OF UNPARALLELED IMPORTANCE.
AN EPIC TASK, WITH TRULY MULTIVERSAL CONSEQUENCES!
MY FORTRESS HAS BEEN INFILTRATED, MY TREASURE DUNGEON, PLUNDERED! MY GREATEST RELIC, SPIRITED AWAY FROM MY VICE-LIKE STRANGLE HOLD.
NOW, VOICES WHISPER AT ME THROUGH THE VAST EXPANSE OF SPACE AND TIME, MOCKING ME, WEARING MY FACE, AND HOUNDING MY EVERY STEP, AS I APPROACH MY ULTIMATE DESTINY.
I AM SHAMED, AND NEARLY HUMBLED.
ALL THANKS TO SEVEN MISERABLE ADVENTURERS!
THAT IS WHY I HAVE HIRED YOUR NOBLE BAND. YOU WILL HELP ME SET THINGS RIGHT.
YOU SHALL BE MY BLOODY VENGEANCE!
OH, NO.
HEY, NO, YOU'VE GOT TO LOOK.
THEY CAN'T HELP YOU.
NO, MY DEAR, IT APPEARS AS THOUGH THEY CANNOT.
SUCH HATE, SUCH FURY. THIS MAGIC IS THE SAME AS THAT WHICH DESTROYED MY FORTRESS.
COULD IT TRULY BE?
COULD THOSE VILE ANIMALS HAVE BEATEN US HERE?
NO MATTER WHERE I GO, NO MATTER WHAT I DO, THEY APPEAR TO RUIN MY REALITY.
NOT EVEN I WAS FULLY AWARE OF THIS ARMY WAS HERE UNTIL AN HOUR AGO?
HOW COULD THEY HAVE KNOWN TO ATTACK HERE?

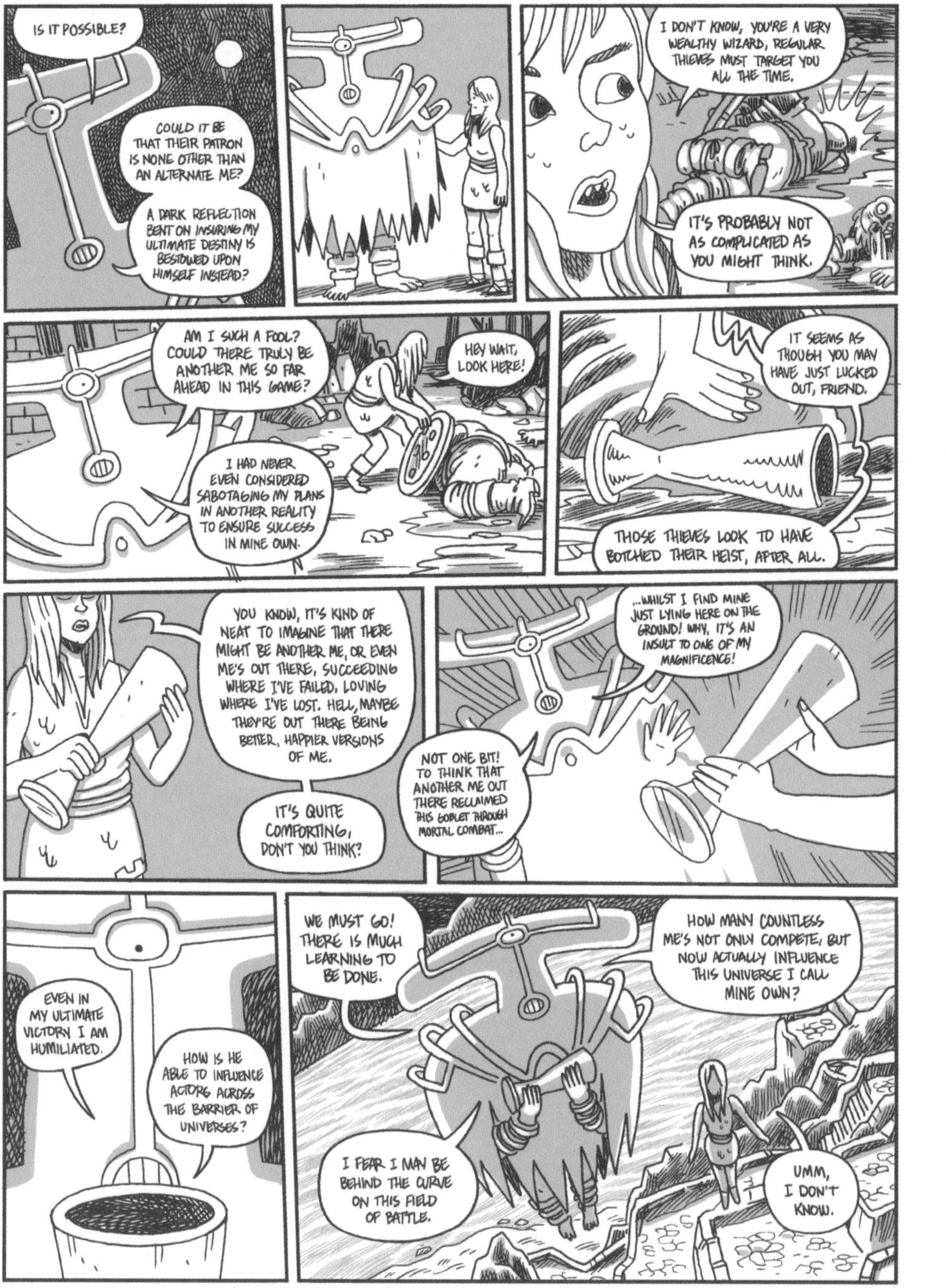

IS IT POSSIBLE?
COULD IT BE THAT THEIR PATRON IS NONE OTHER THAN AN ALTERNATE ME?
A DARK REFLECTION BENT ON INSURING MY ULTIMATE DESTINY IS BESTOWED UPON HIMSELF INSTEAD?
I DON'T KNOW, YOU'RE A VERY WEALTHY WIZARD, REGULAR THIEVES MUST TARGET YOU ALL THE TIME.
IT'S PROBABLY NOT AS COMPLICATED AS YOU MIGHT THINK.
AM I SUCH A FOOL? COULD THERE TRULY BE ANOTHER ME SO FAR AHEAD IN THIS GAME?
I HAD NEVER EVEN CONSIDERED SABOTAGING MY PLANS IN ANOTHER REALITY TO ENSURE SUCCESS IN MINE OWN.
HEY WAIT, LOOK HERE!
IT SEEMS AS THOUGH YOU MAY HAVE JUST LUCKED OUT, FRIEND.
THOSE THIEVES LOOK TO HAVE BOTCHED THEIR HEIST, AFTER ALL.
YOU KNOW, IT'S KIND OF NEAT TO IMAGINE THAT THERE MIGHT BE ANOTHER ME, OR EVEN ME'S OUT THERE, SUCCEEDING WHERE I'VE FAILED, LOVING WHERE I'VE LOST. HELL, MAYBE THEY'RE OUT THERE BEING BETTER, HAPPIER VERSIONS OF ME.
IT'S QUITE COMFORTING, DON'T YOU THINK?
NOT ONE BIT! TO THINK THAT ANOTHER ME OUT THERE RECLAIMED THIS GOBLET THROUGH MORTAL COMBAT...
...WHILST I FIND MINE JUST LYING HERE ON THE GROUND! WHY, IT'S AN INSULT TO ONE OF MY MAGNIFICENCE!
EVEN IN MY ULTIMATE VICTORY I AM HUMILIATED.
HOW IS HE ABLE TO INFLUENCE ACTORS ACROSS THE BARRIER OF UNIVERSES?
WE MUST GO! THERE IS MUCH LEARNING TO BE DONE.
HOW MANY COUNTLESS ME'S NOT ONLY COMPETE, BUT NOW ACTUALLY INFLUENCE THIS UNIVERSE I CALL MINE OWN?
I FEAR I MAY BE BEHIND THE CURVE ON THIS FIELD OF BATTLE.
UMM, I DON'T KNOW.

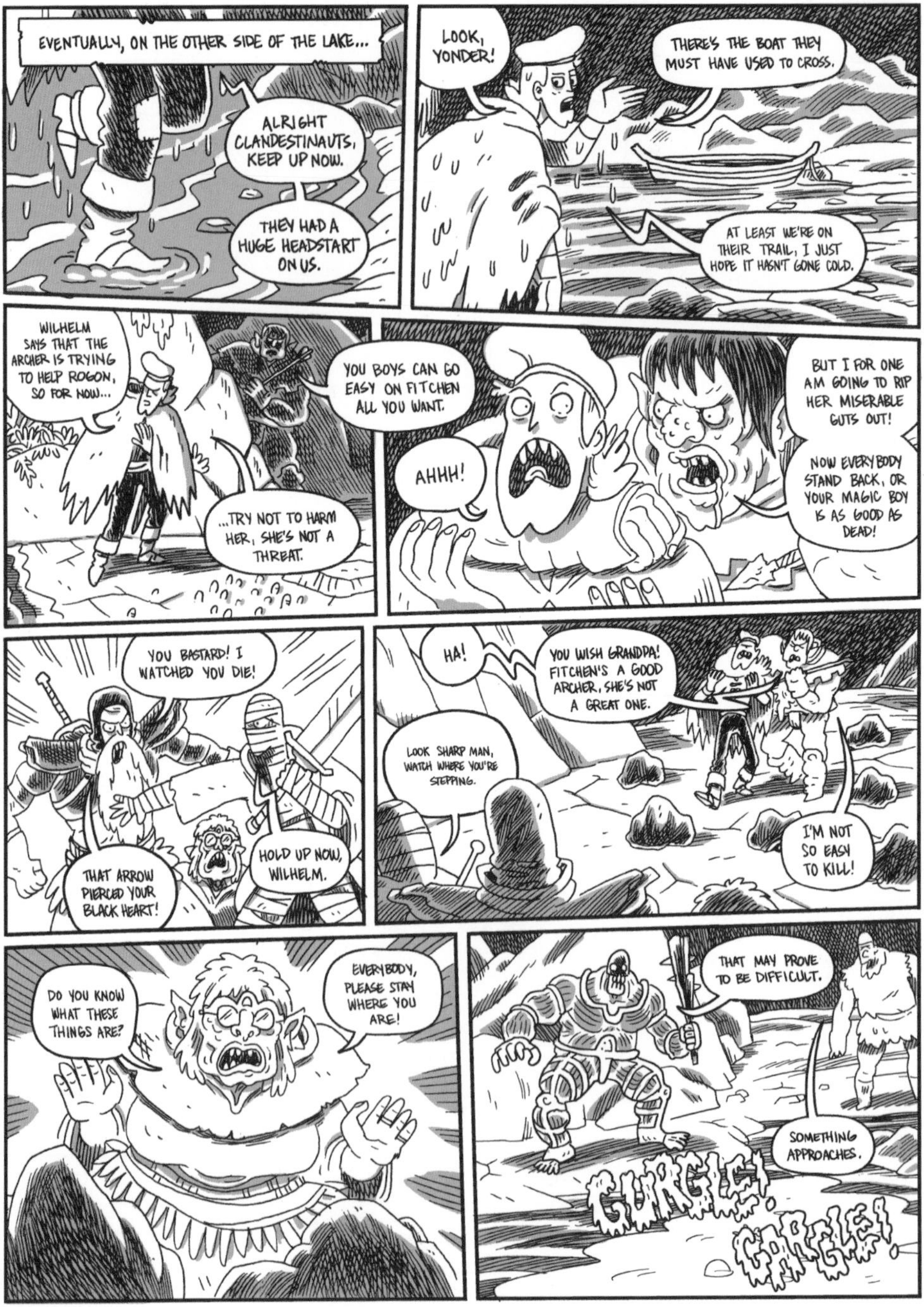

EVENTUALLY, ON THE OTHER SIDE OF THE LAKE...
ALRIGHT CLANDESTINAUTS, KEEP UP NOW.
THEY HAD A HUGE HEADSTART ON US.
LOOK, YONDER!
THERE'S THE BOAT THEY MUST HAVE USED TO CROSS.
AT LEAST WE'RE ON THEIR TRAIL, I JUST HOPE IT HASN'T GONE COLD.
WILHELM SAYS THAT THE ARCHER IS TRYING TO HELP ROGON, SO FOR NOW...
...TRY NOT TO HARM HER, SHE'S NOT A THREAT.
YOU BOYS CAN GO EASY ON FITCHEN ALL YOU WANT.
AHHH!
BUT I FOR ONE AM GOING TO RIP HER MISERABLE GUTS OUT!
NOW EVERYBODY STAND BACK, OR YOUR MAGIC BOY IS AS GOOD AS DEAD!
YOU BASTARD! I WATCHED YOU DIE!
THAT ARROW PIERCED YOUR BLACK HEART!
HOLD UP NOW, WILHELM.
HA!
YOU WISH GRANDPA! FITCHEN'S A GOOD ARCHER, SHE'S NOT A GREAT ONE.
LOOK SHARP MAN, WATCH WHERE YOU'RE STEPPING.
I'M NOT SO EASY TO KILL!
DO YOU KNOW WHAT THESE THINGS ARE?
EVERYBODY, PLEASE STAY WHERE YOU ARE!
THAT MAY PROVE TO BE DIFFICULT.
SOMETHING APPROACHES.
GURGLE! GARGLE!

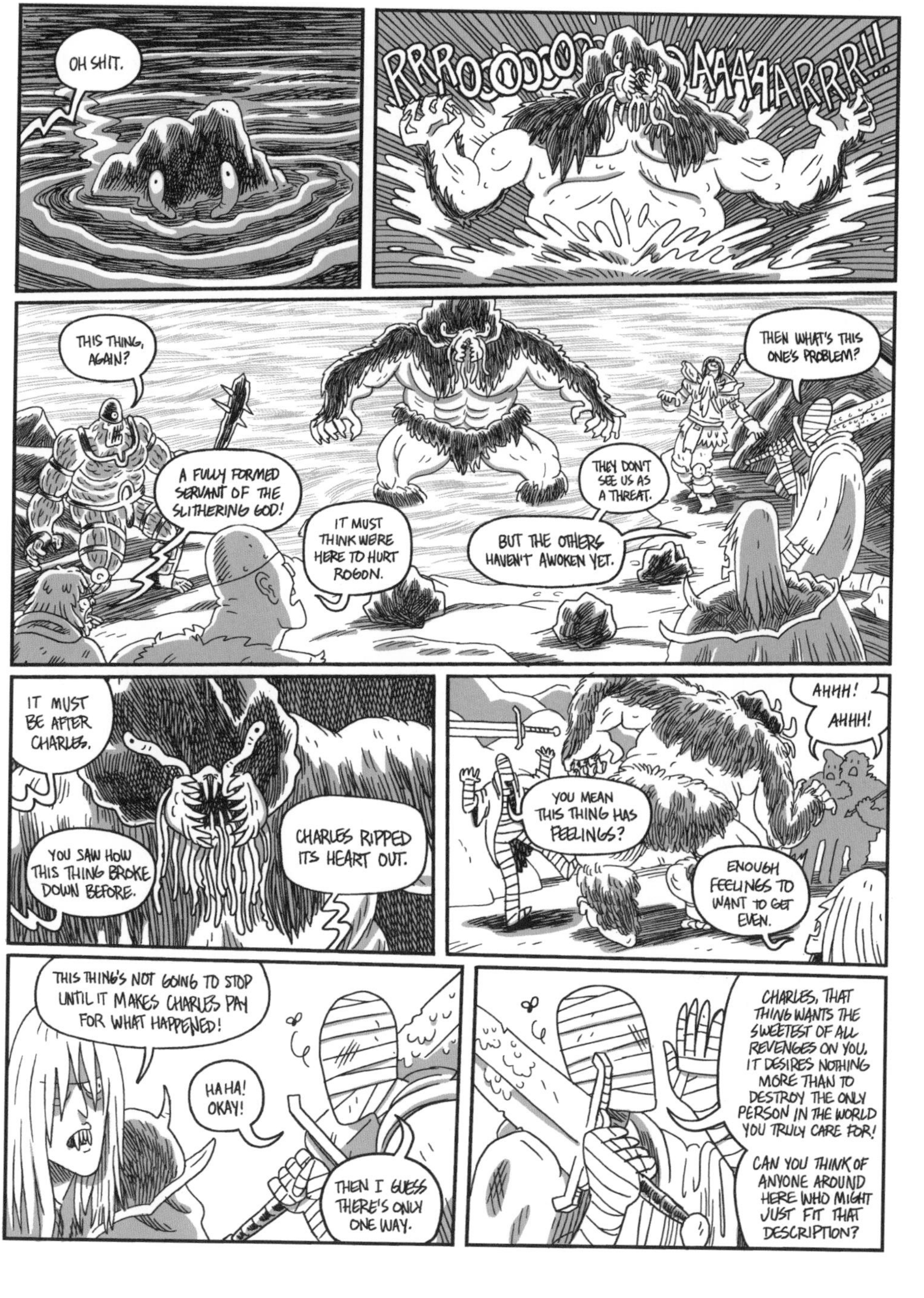
OH SHIT.
RRROOOOOOOOAAAAARRRR!!
THIS THING, AGAIN?
A FULLY FORMED SERVANT OF THE SLITHERING GOD!
IT MUST THINK WE'RE HERE TO HURT ROGON.
THEY DON'T SEE US AS A THREAT.
BUT THE OTHERS HAVEN'T AWOKEN YET.
THEN WHAT'S THIS ONE'S PROBLEM?
IT MUST BE AFTER CHARLES.
YOU SAW HOW THIS THING BROKE DOWN BEFORE.
CHARLES RIPPED ITS HEART OUT.
AHHH!
AHHH!
YOU MEAN THIS THING HAS FEELINGS?
ENOUGH FEELINGS TO WANT TO GET EVEN.
THIS THING'S NOT GOING TO STOP UNTIL IT MAKES CHARLES PAY FOR WHAT HAPPENED!
HA HA! OKAY!
THEN I GUESS THERE'S ONLY ONE WAY.
CHARLES, THAT THING WANTS THE SWEETEST OF ALL REVENGES ON YOU. IT DESIRES NOTHING MORE THAN TO DESTROY THE ONLY PERSON IN THE WORLD YOU TRULY CARE FOR!
CAN YOU THINK OF ANYONE AROUND HERE WHO MIGHT JUST FIT THAT DESCRIPTION?

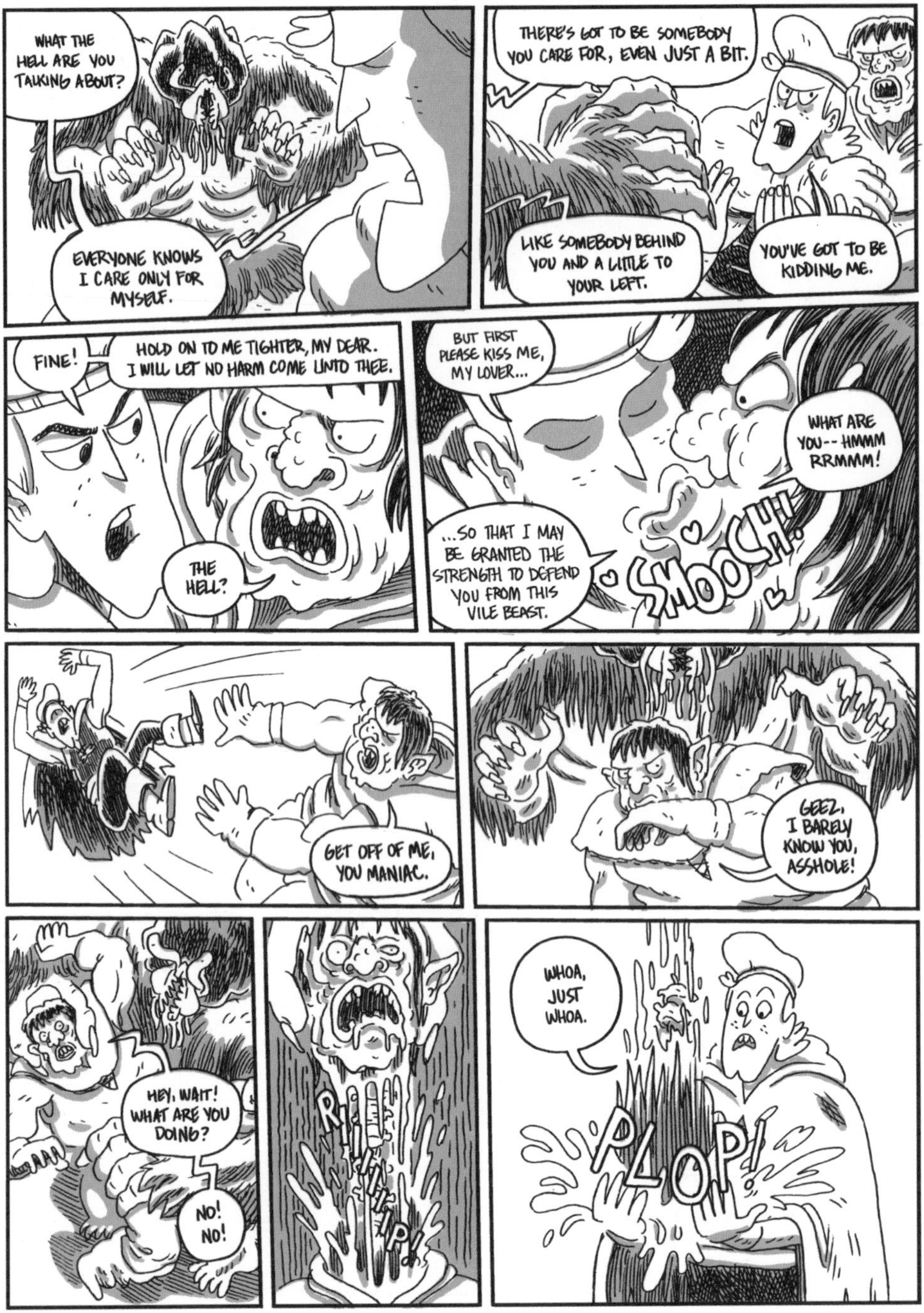
WHAT THE HELL ARE YOU TALKING ABOUT?
EVERYONE KNOWS I CARE ONLY FOR MYSELF.
THERE'S GOT TO BE SOMEBODY YOU CARE FOR, EVEN JUST A BIT.
LIKE SOMEBODY BEHIND YOU AND A LITTLE TO YOUR LEFT.
YOU'VE GOT TO BE KIDDING ME.
FINE!
HOLD ON TO ME TIGHTER, MY DEAR. I WILL LET NO HARM COME UNTO THEE.
THE HELL?
BUT FIRST PLEASE KISS ME, MY LOVER...
...SO THAT I MAY BE GRANTED THE STRENGTH TO DEFEND YOU FROM THIS VILE BEAST.
WHAT ARE YOU--HMMM RRMMM!
SMOOCH!
GET OFF OF ME, YOU MANIAC.
GEEZ, I BARELY KNOW YOU, ASSHOLE!
HEY, WAIT! WHAT ARE YOU DOING?
NO! NO!
RIIIIIIP!
WHOA, JUST WHOA.
PLOP!

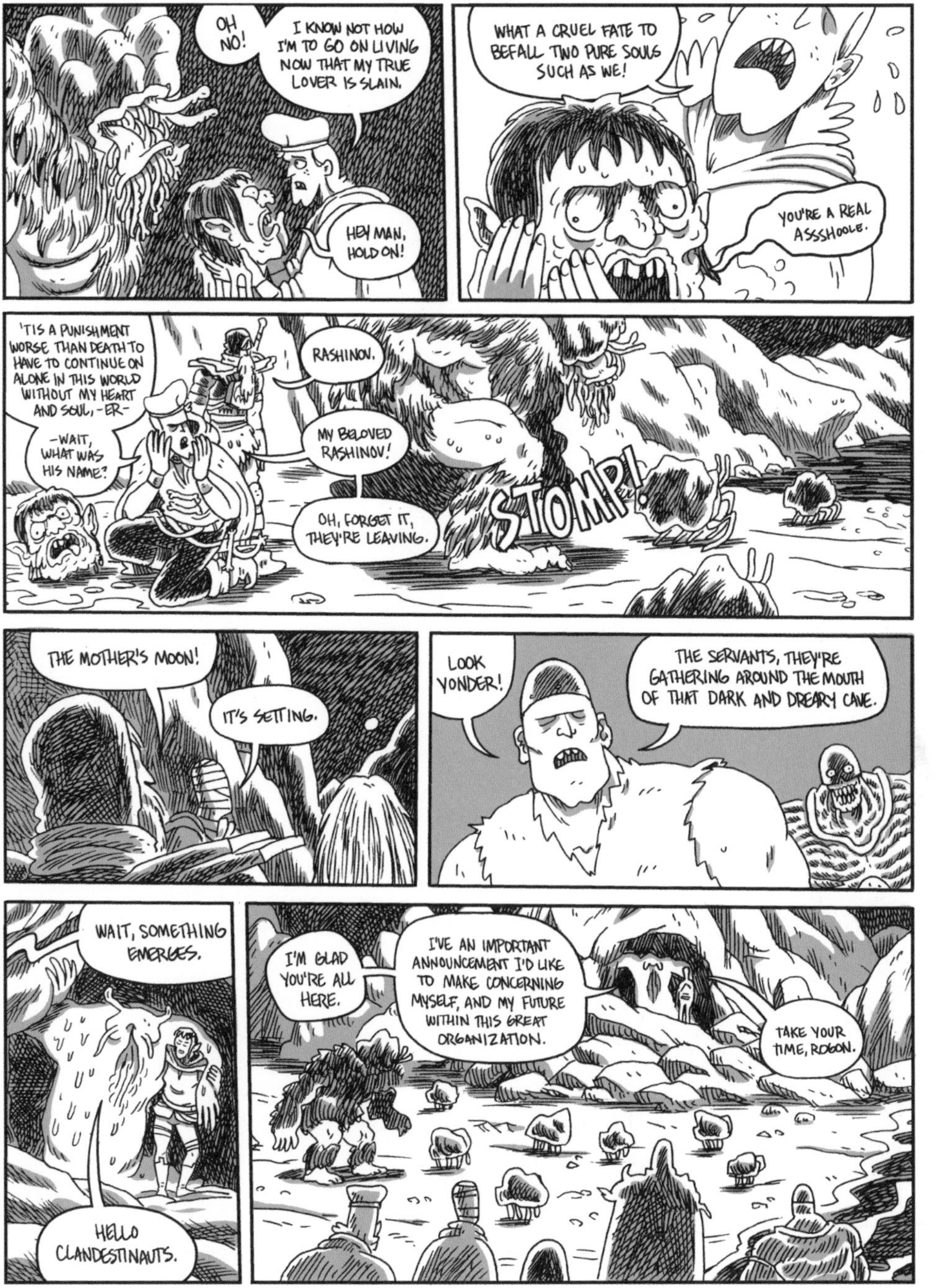
OH NO!
I KNOW NOT HOW I'M TO GO ON LIVING NOW THAT MY TRUE LOVER IS SLAIN.
HEY MAN, HOLD ON!
WHAT A CRUEL FATE TO BEFALL TWO PURE SOULS SUCH AS WE!
YOU'RE A REAL ASSSHOOLE.
'TIS A PUNISHMENT WORSE THAN DEATH TO HAVE TO CONTINUE ON ALONE IN THIS WORLD WITHOUT MY HEART AND SOUL, -ER-
-WAIT, WHAT WAS HIS NAME?
RASHINOV.
MY BELOVED RASHINOV!
OH, FORGET IT, THEY'RE LEAVING.
STOMP!
THE MOTHER'S MOON!
IT'S SETTING.
LOOK YONDER!
THE SERVANTS, THEY'RE GATHERING AROUND THE MOUTH OF THAT DARK AND DREARY CAVE.
WAIT, SOMETHING EMERGES.
HELLO CLANDESTINAUTS.
I'M GLAD YOU'RE ALL HERE.
I'VE AN IMPORTANT ANNOUNCEMENT I'D LIKE TO MAKE CONCERNING MYSELF, AND MY FUTURE WITHIN THIS GREAT ORGANIZATION.
TAKE YOUR TIME, ROGON.

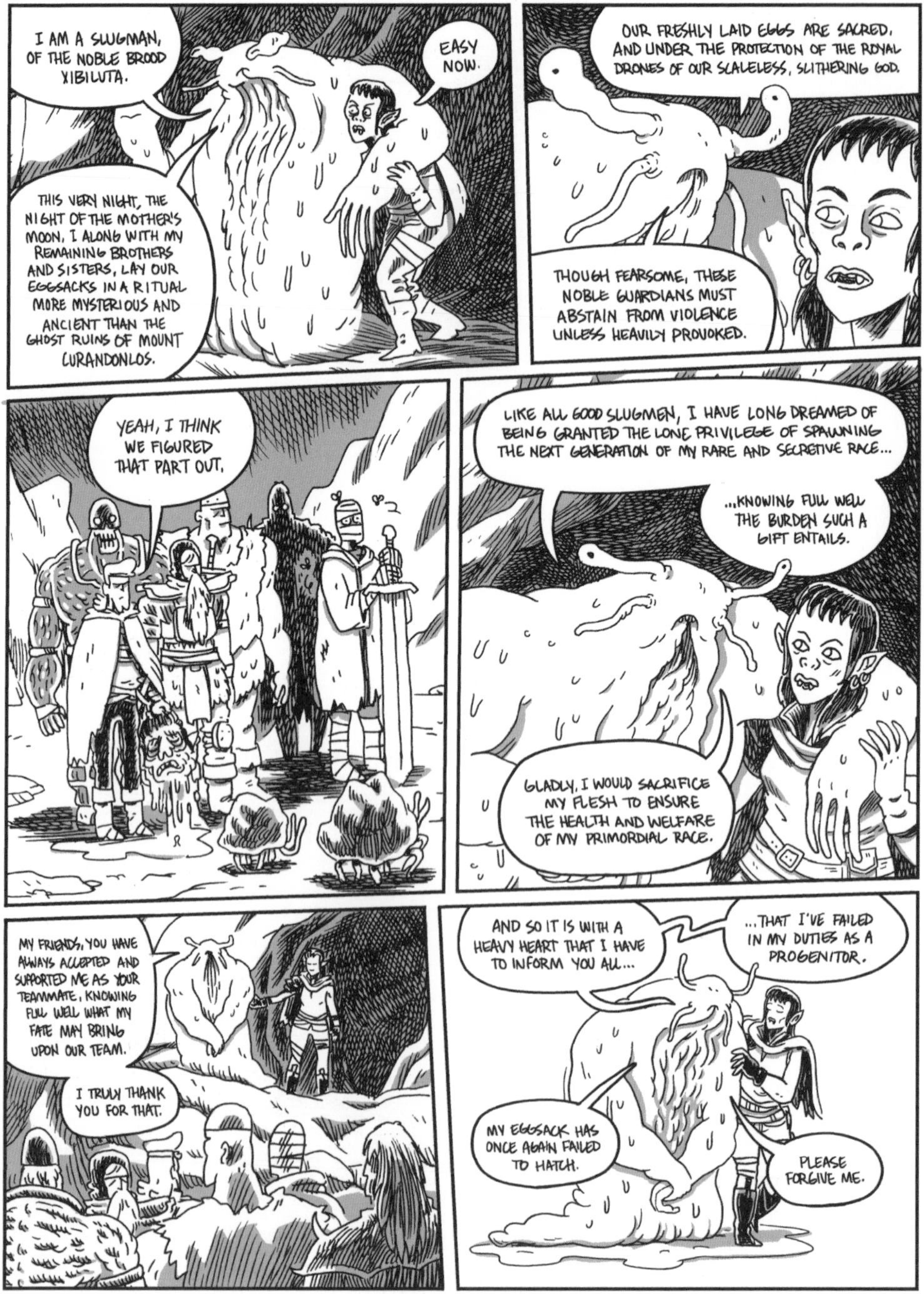
I AM A SLUGMAN, OF THE NOBLE BROOD XIBILUTA.
EASY NOW.
THIS VERY NIGHT, THE NIGHT OF THE MOTHER'S MOON, I ALONG WITH MY REMAINING BROTHERS AND SISTERS, LAY OUR EGGSACKS IN A RITUAL MORE MYSTERIOUS AND ANCIENT THAN THE GHOST RUINS OF MOUNT CURANDONLOS.
OUR FRESHLY LAID EGGS ARE SACRED, AND UNDER THE PROTECTION OF THE ROYAL DRONES OF OUR SCALELESS, SLITHERING GOD.
THOUGH FEARSOME, THESE NOBLE GUARDIANS MUST ABSTAIN FROM VIOLENCE UNLESS HEAVILY PROVOKED.
YEAH, I THINK WE FIGURED THAT PART OUT.
LIKE ALL GOOD SLUGMEN, I HAVE LONG DREAMED OF BEING GRANTED THE LONE PRIVILEGE OF SPAWNING THE NEXT GENERATION OF MY RARE AND SECRETIVE RACE...
...KNOWING FULL WELL THE BURDEN SUCH A GIFT ENTAILS.
GLADLY, I WOULD SACRIFICE MY FLESH TO ENSURE THE HEALTH AND WELFARE OF MY PRIMORDIAL RACE.
MY FRIENDS, YOU HAVE ALWAYS ACCEPTED AND SUPPORTED ME AS YOUR TEAMMATE, KNOWING FULL WELL WHAT MY FATE MAY BRING UPON OUR TEAM.
I TRULY THANK YOU FOR THAT.
AND SO IT IS WITH A HEAVY HEART THAT I HAVE TO INFORM YOU ALL...
...THAT I'VE FAILED IN MY DUTIES AS A PROGENITOR.
MY EGGSACK HAS ONCE AGAIN FAILED TO HATCH.
PLEASE FORGIVE ME.

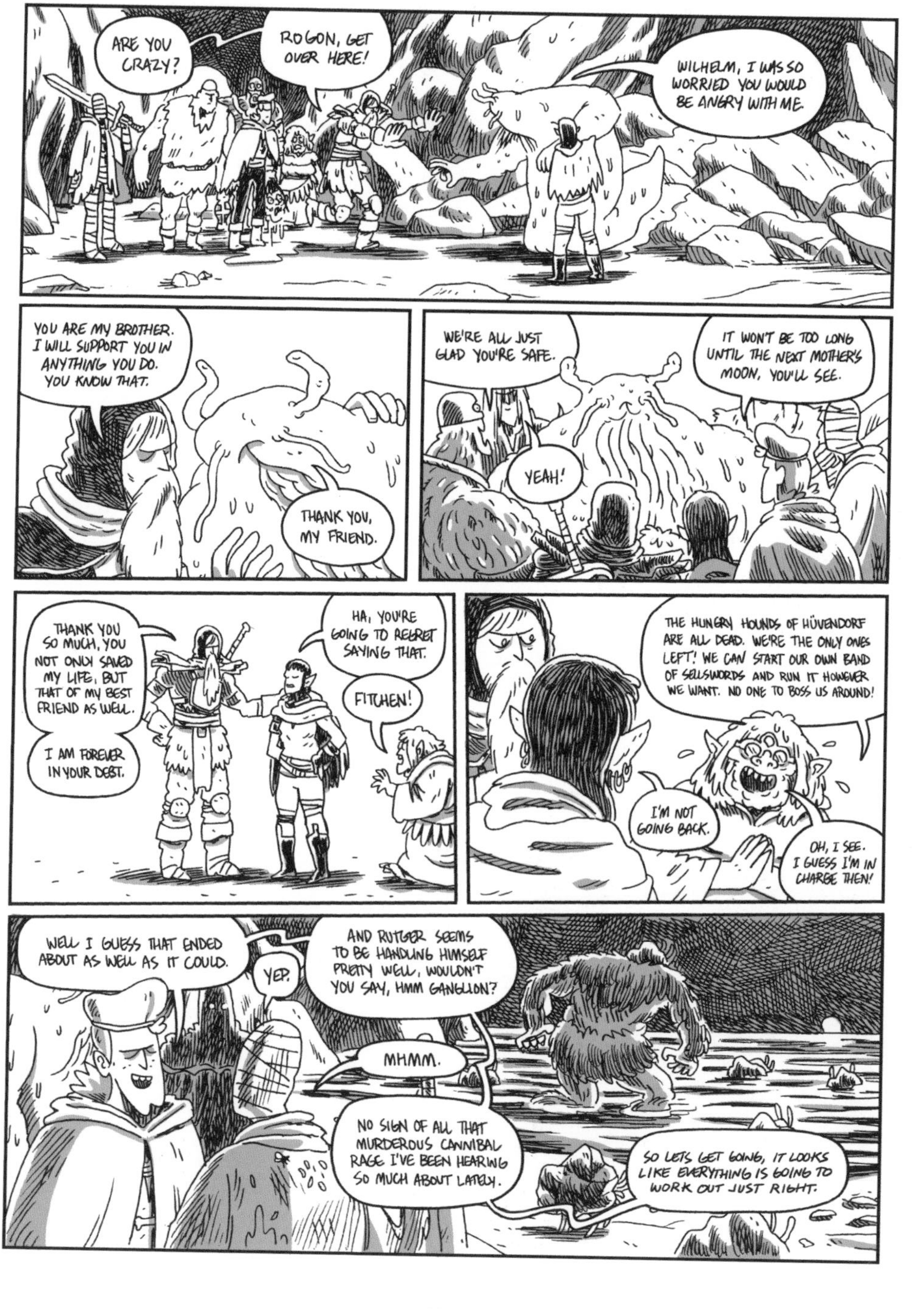
ARE YOU CRAZY?
ROGON, GET OVER HERE!
WILHELM, I WAS SO WORRIED YOU WOULD BE ANGRY WITH ME.
YOU ARE MY BROTHER. I WILL SUPPORT YOU IN ANYTHING YOU DO. YOU KNOW THAT.
THANK YOU, MY FRIEND.
WE'RE ALL JUST GLAD YOU'RE SAFE.
YEAH!
IT WON'T BE TOO LONG UNTIL THE NEXT MOTHER'S MOON, YOU'LL SEE.
THANK YOU SO MUCH, YOU NOT ONLY SAVED MY LIFE, BUT THAT OF MY BEST FRIEND AS WELL.
I AM FOREVER IN YOUR DEBT.
HA, YOU'RE GOING TO REGRET SAYING THAT.
FITCHEN!
THE HUNGRY HOUNDS OF HÜVENDORF ARE ALL DEAD. WE'RE THE ONLY ONES LEFT! WE CAN START OUR OWN BAND OF SELLSWORDS AND RUN IT HOWEVER WE WANT. NO ONE TO BOSS US AROUND!
I'M NOT GOING BACK.
OH, I SEE. I GUESS I'M IN CHARGE THEN!
WELL I GUESS THAT ENDED ABOUT AS WELL AS IT COULD.
YEP.
AND RUTGER SEEMS TO BE HANDLING HIMSELF PRETTY WELL, WOULDN'T YOU SAY, HMM GANGLION?
MHMM.
NO SIGN OF ALL THAT MURDEROUS CANNIBAL RAGE I'VE BEEN HEARING SO MUCH ABOUT LATELY.
SO LETS GET GOING, IT LOOKS LIKE EVERYTHING IS GOING TO WORK OUT JUST RIGHT.

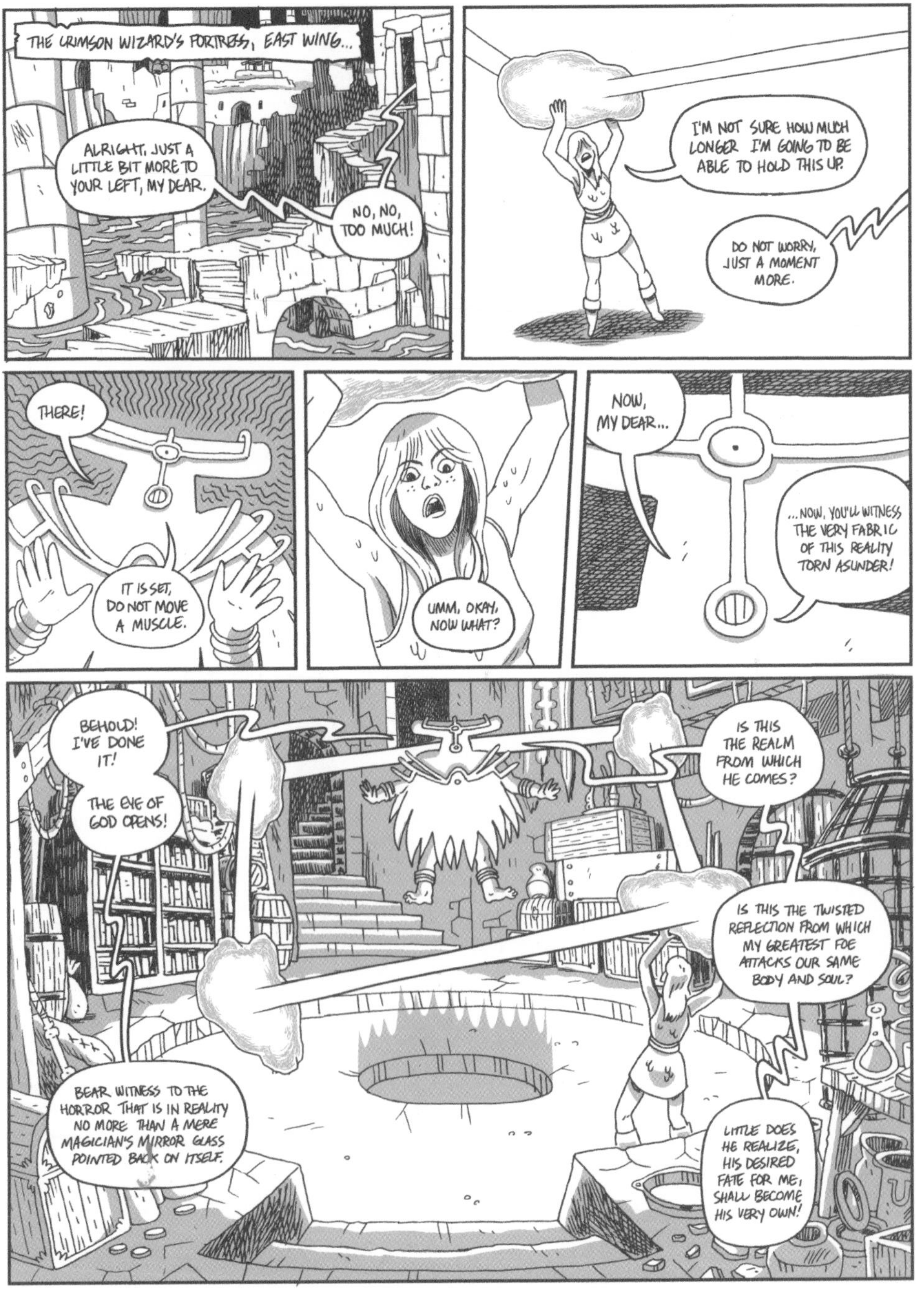

THE CRIMSON WIZARD'S FORTRESS, EAST WING...
ALRIGHT, JUST A LITTLE BIT MORE TO YOUR LEFT, MY DEAR.
NO, NO, TOO MUCH!
I'M NOT SURE HOW MUCH LONGER I'M GOING TO BE ABLE TO HOLD THIS UP.
DO NOT WORRY, JUST A MOMENT MORE.
THERE!
IT IS SET, DO NOT MOVE A MUSCLE.
UMM, OKAY, NOW WHAT?
NOW, MY DEAR...
...NOW, YOU'LL WITNESS THE VERY FABRIC OF THIS REALITY TORN ASUNDER!
BEHOLD! I'VE DONE IT!
THE EYE OF GOD OPENS!
IS THIS THE REALM FROM WHICH HE COMES?
IS THIS THE TWISTED REFLECTION FROM WHICH MY GREATEST FOE ATTACKS OUR SAME BODY AND SOUL?
BEAR WITNESS TO THE HORROR THAT IS IN REALITY NO MORE THAN A MERE MAGICIAN'S MIRROR GLASS POINTED BACK ON ITSELF.
LITTLE DOES HE REALIZE, HIS DESIRED FATE FOR ME, SHALL BECOME HIS VERY OWN!

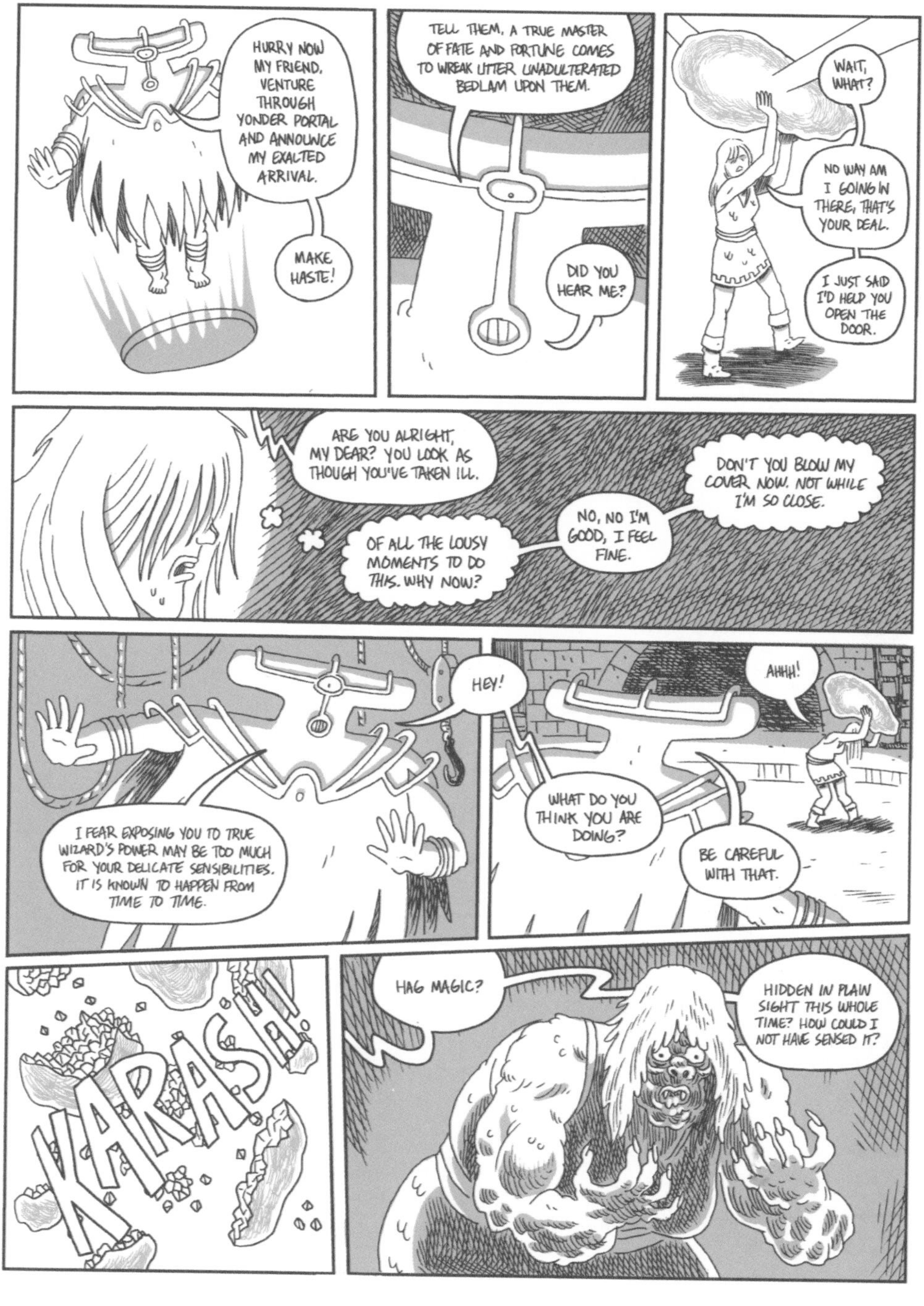
HURRY NOW MY FRIEND, VENTURE THROUGH YONDER PORTAL AND ANNOUNCE MY EXALTED ARRIVAL.
MAKE HASTE!
TELL THEM, A TRUE MASTER OF FATE AND FORTUNE COMES TO WREAK UTTER UNADULTERATED BEDLAM UPON THEM.
DID YOU HEAR ME?
WAIT, WHAT?
NO WAY AM I GOING IN THERE, THAT'S YOUR DEAL.
I JUST SAID I'D HELP YOU OPEN THE DOOR.
ARE YOU ALRIGHT, MY DEAR? YOU LOOK AS THOUGH YOU'VE TAKEN ILL.
OF ALL THE LOUSY MOMENTS TO DO THIS. WHY NOW?
NO, NO I'M GOOD, I FEEL FINE.
DON'T YOU BLOW MY COVER NOW. NOT WHILE I'M SO CLOSE.
HEY!
I FEAR EXPOSING YOU TO TRUE WIZARD'S POWER MAY BE TOO MUCH FOR YOUR DELICATE SENSIBILITIES. IT IS KNOWN TO HAPPEN FROM TIME TO TIME.
AHHH!
WHAT DO YOU THINK YOU ARE DOING?
BE CAREFUL WITH THAT.
KARASH!
HAG MAGIC?
HIDDEN IN PLAIN SIGHT THIS WHOLE TIME? HOW COULD I NOT HAVE SENSED IT?

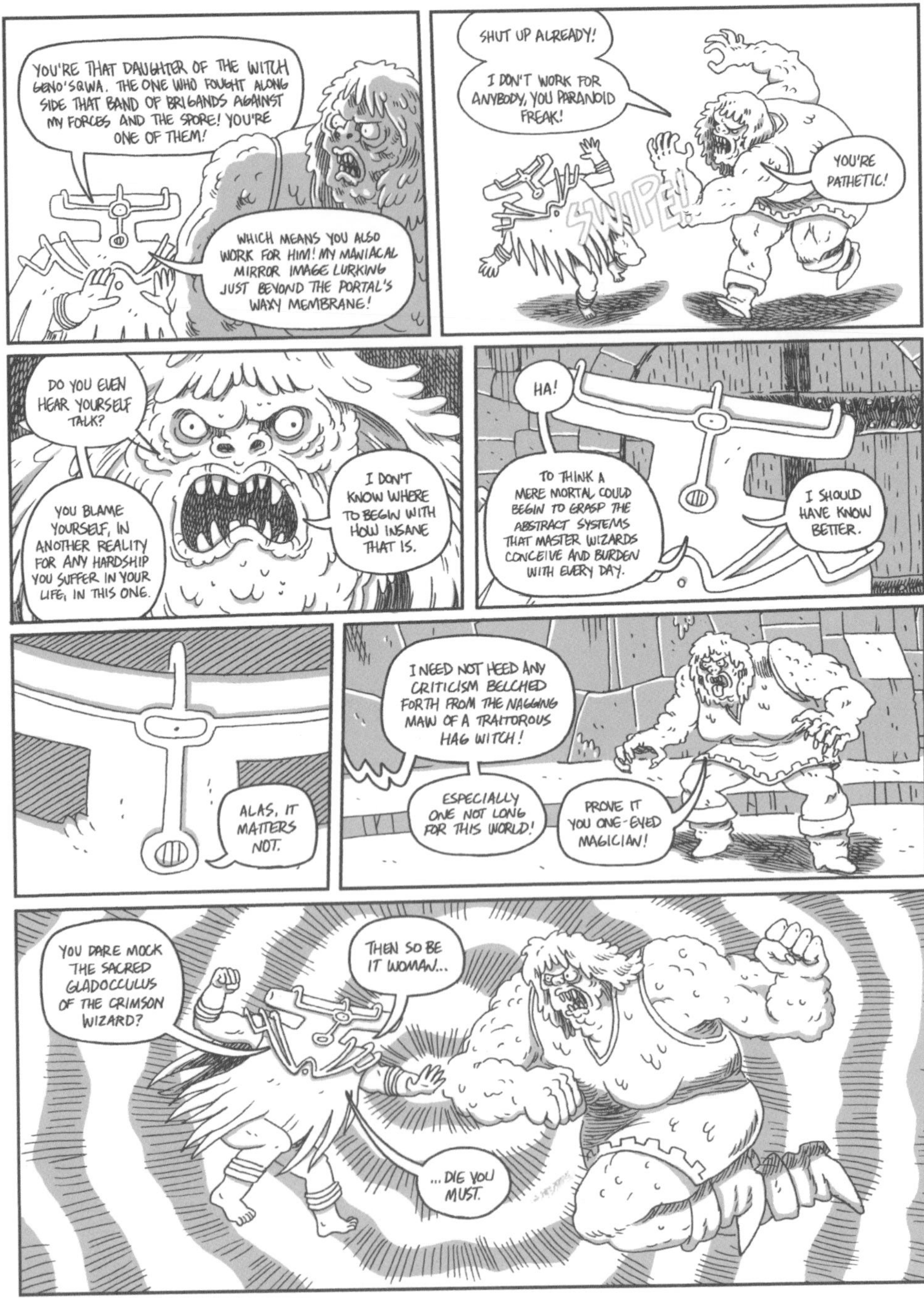
YOU'RE THAT DAUGHTER OF THE WITCH GENO'SQWA. THE ONE WHO FOUGHT ALONG SIDE THAT BAND OF BRIGANDS AGAINST MY FORCES AND THE SPORE! YOU'RE ONE OF THEM!
WHICH MEANS YOU ALSO WORK FOR HIM! MY MANIACAL MIRROR IMAGE LURKING JUST BEYOND THE PORTAL'S WAXY MEMBRANE!
SHUT UP ALREADY!
I DON'T WORK FOR ANYBODY, YOU PARANOID FREAK!
SWIPE!
YOU'RE PATHETIC!
DO YOU EVEN HEAR YOURSELF TALK?
YOU BLAME YOURSELF, IN ANOTHER REALITY FOR ANY HARDSHIP YOU SUFFER IN YOUR LIFE, IN THIS ONE.
I DON'T KNOW WHERE TO BEGIN WITH HOW INSANE THAT IS.
HA!
TO THINK A MERE MORTAL COULD BEGIN TO GRASP THE ABSTRACT SYSTEMS THAT MASTER WIZARDS CONCEIVE AND BURDEN WITH EVERY DAY.
I SHOULD HAVE KNOW BETTER.
ALAS, IT MATTERS NOT.
I NEED NOT HEED ANY CRITICISM BELCHED FORTH FROM THE NAGGING MAW OF A TRAITOROUS HAG WITCH!
ESPECIALLY ONE NOT LONG FOR THIS WORLD!
PROVE IT YOU ONE-EYED MAGICIAN!
YOU DARE MOCK THE SACRED GLADOCCULUS OF THE CRIMSON WIZARD?
THEN SO BE IT WOMAN...
...DIE YOU MUST.

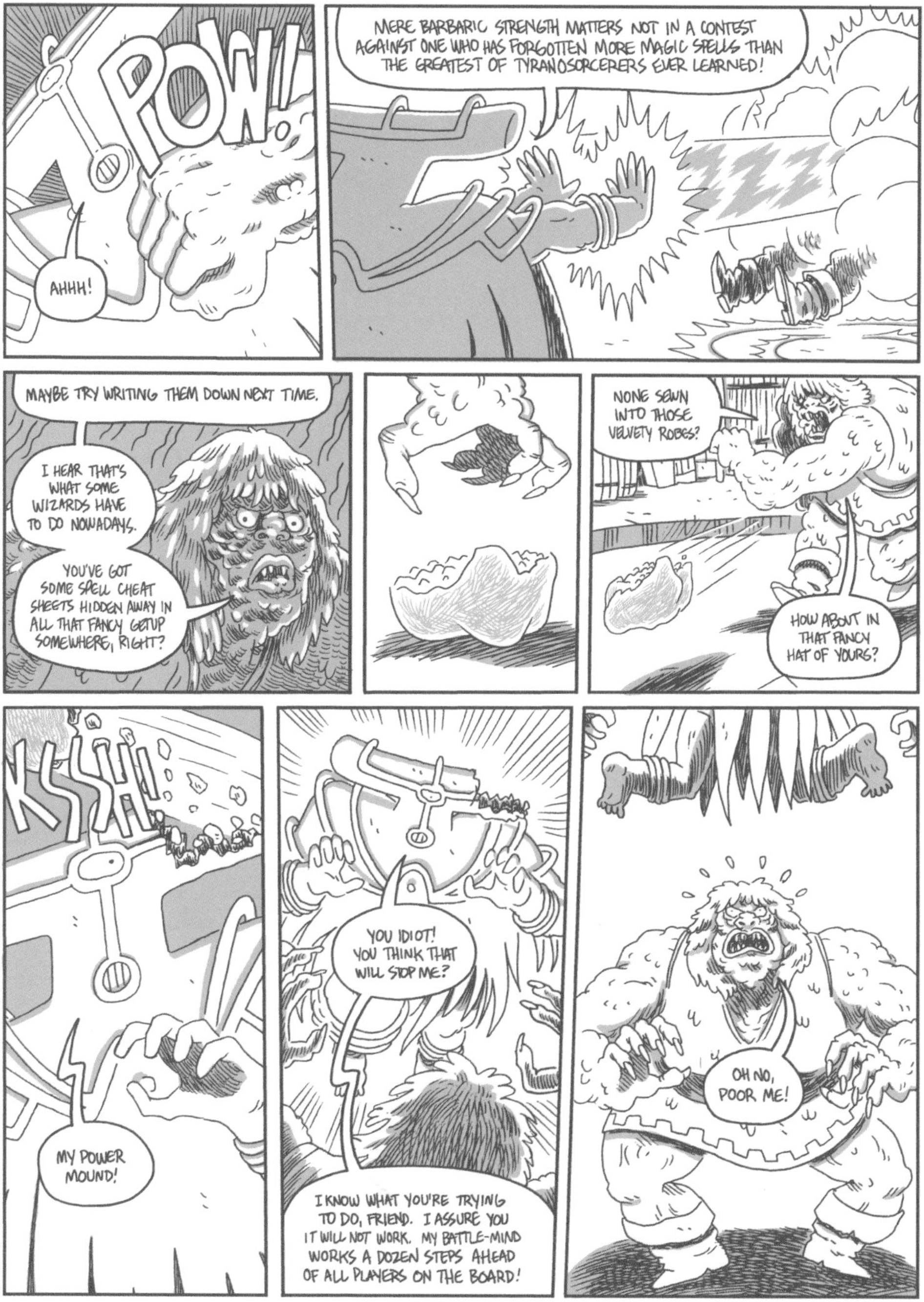
POW!!
AHHH!
MERE BARBARIC STRENGTH MATTERS NOT IN A CONTEST AGAINST ONE WHO HAS FORGOTTEN MORE MAGIC SPELLS THAN THE GREATEST OF TYRANOSORCERERS EVER LEARNED!
MAYBE TRY WRITING THEM DOWN NEXT TIME.
I HEAR THAT'S WHAT SOME WIZARDS HAVE TO DO NOWADAYS.
YOU'VE GOT SOME SPELL CHEAT SHEETS HIDDEN AWAY IN ALL THAT FANCY GETUP SOMEWHERE, RIGHT?
NONE SEWN INTO THOSE VELVETY ROBES?
HOW ABOUT IN THAT FANCY HAT OF YOURS?
KSSH!
MY POWER MOUND!
YOU IDIOT! YOU THINK THAT WILL STOP ME?
I KNOW WHAT YOU'RE TRYING TO DO, FRIEND. I ASSURE YOU IT WILL NOT WORK. MY BATTLE-MIND WORKS A DOZEN STEPS AHEAD OF ALL PLAYERS ON THE BOARD!
OH NO, POOR ME!

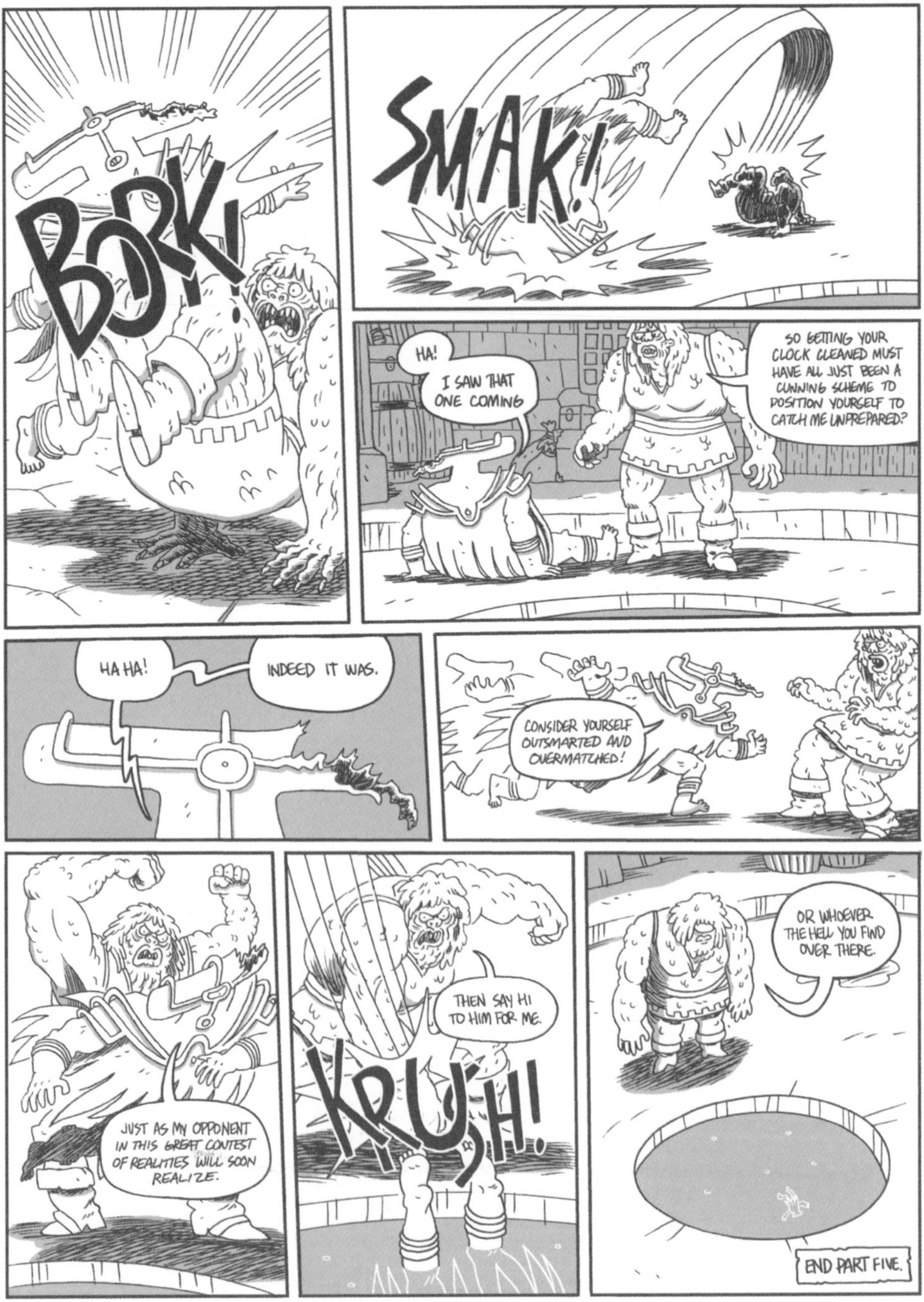
BORK!
SMAK!
HA!
I SAW THAT ONE COMING
SO GETTING YOUR CLOCK CLEANED MUST HAVE ALL JUST BEEN A CUNNING SCHEME TO POSITION YOURSELF TO CATCH ME UNPREPARED?
HA HA!
INDEED IT WAS.
CONSIDER YOURSELF OUTSMARTED AND OVERMATCHED!
JUST AS MY OPPONENT IN THIS GREAT CONTEST OF REALITIES WILL SOON REALIZE.
THEN SAY HI TO HIM FOR ME.
KRUSH!
OR WHOEVER THE HELL YOU FIND OVER THERE.
END PART FIVE.

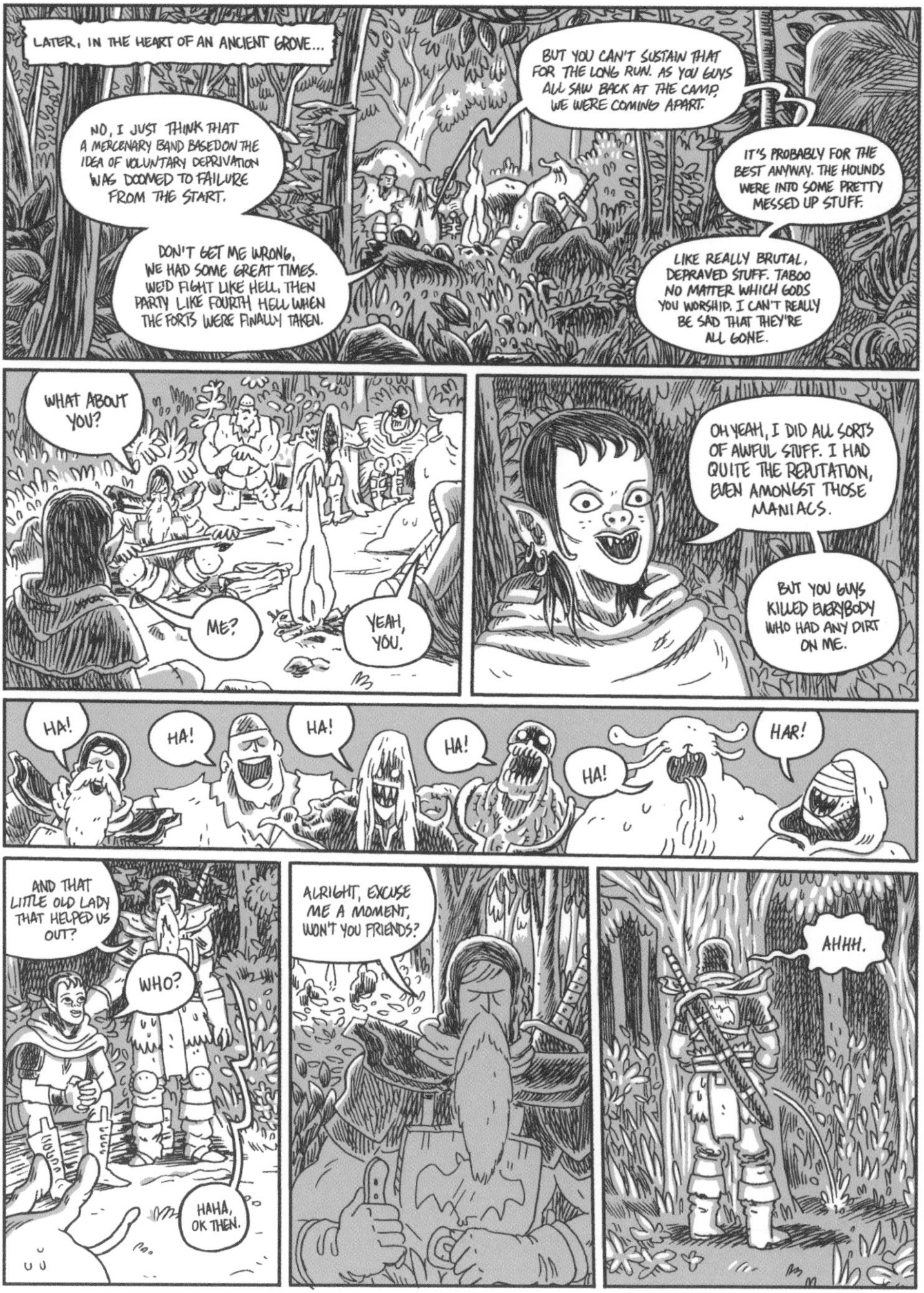
LATER, IN THE HEART OF AN ANCIENT GROVE...
NO, I JUST THINK THAT A MERCENARY BAND BASED ON THE IDEA OF VOLUNTARY DEPRIVATION WAS DOOMED TO FAILURE FROM THE START.
DON'T GET ME WRONG, WE HAD SOME GREAT TIMES. WE'D FIGHT LIKE HELL, THEN PARTY LIKE FOURTH HELL WHEN THE FORTS WERE FINALLY TAKEN.
BUT YOU CAN'T SUSTAIN THAT FOR THE LONG RUN. AS YOU GUYS ALL SAW BACK AT THE CAMP, WE WERE COMING APART.
IT'S PROBABLY FOR THE BEST ANYWAY. THE HOUNDS WERE INTO SOME PRETTY MESSED UP STUFF.
LIKE REALLY BRUTAL, DEPRAVED STUFF. TABOO NO MATTER WHICH GODS YOU WORSHIP. I CAN'T REALLY BE SAD THAT THEY'RE ALL GONE.
WHAT ABOUT YOU?
ME?
YEAH, YOU.
OH YEAH, I DID ALL SORTS OF AWFUL STUFF. I HAD QUITE THE REPUTATION, EVEN AMONGST THOSE MANIACS.
BUT YOU GUYS KILLED EVERYBODY WHO HAD ANY DIRT ON ME.
HA!
HA!
HA!
HA!
HA!
HAR!
AND THAT LITTLE OLD LADY THAT HELPED US OUT?
WHO?
HAHA, OK THEN.
ALRIGHT, EXCUSE ME A MOMENT, WON'T YOU FRIENDS?
AHHH.

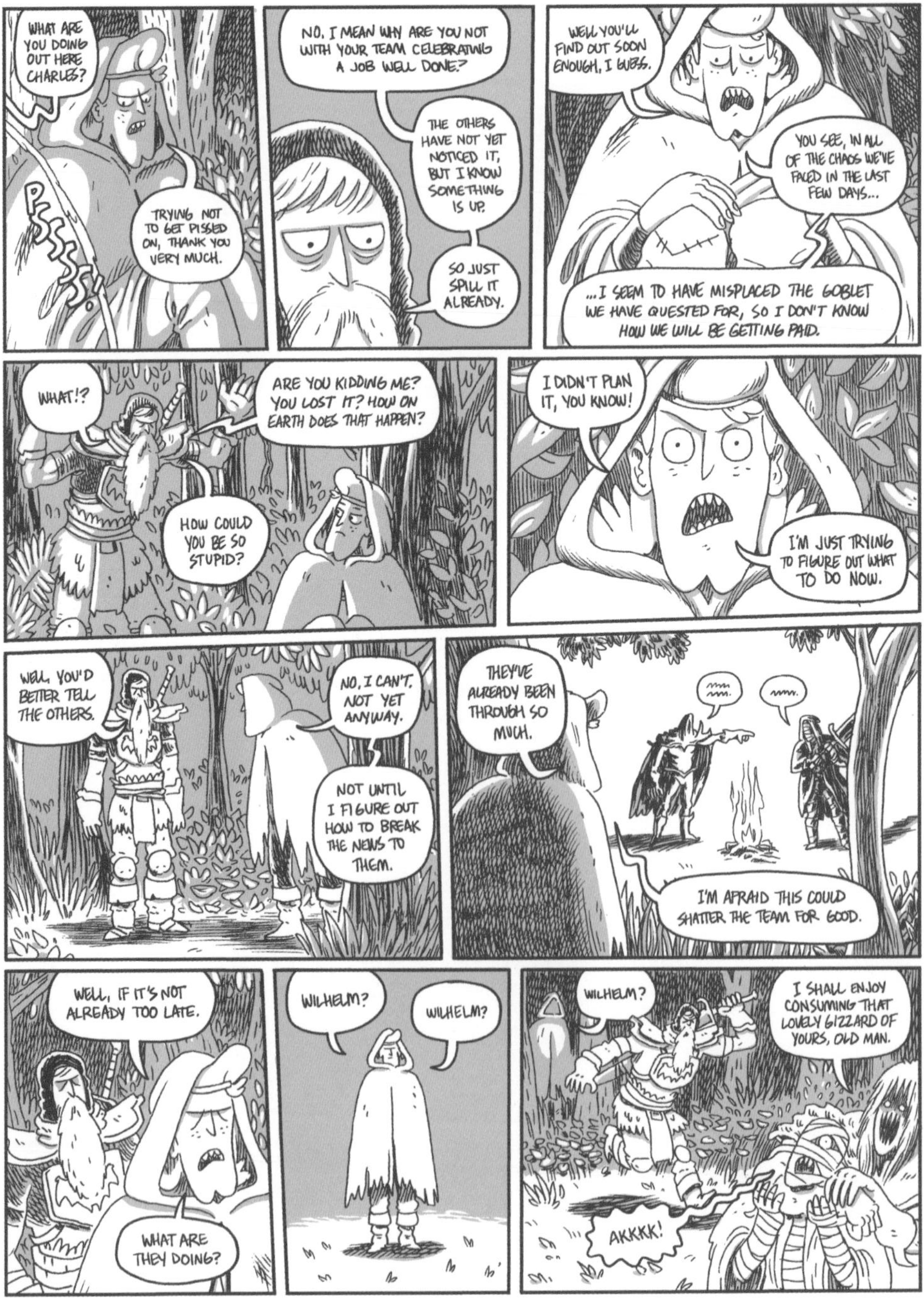
WHAT ARE YOU DOING OUT HERE CHARLES?
PSSSS!
TRYING NOT TO GET PISSED ON, THANK YOU VERY MUCH.
NO, I MEAN WHY ARE YOU NOT WITH YOUR TEAM CELEBRATING A JOB WELL DONE?
THE OTHERS HAVE NOT YET NOTICED IT, BUT I KNOW SOMETHING IS UP.
SO JUST SPILL IT ALREADY.
WELL YOU'LL FIND OUT SOON ENOUGH, I GUESS.
YOU SEE, IN ALL OF THE CHAOS WE'VE FACED IN THE LAST FEW DAYS...
...I SEEM TO HAVE MISPLACED THE GOBLET WE HAVE QUESTED FOR, SO I DON'T KNOW HOW WE WILL BE GETTING PAID.
WHAT!?
ARE YOU KIDDING ME? YOU LOST IT? HOW ON EARTH DOES THAT HAPPEN?
HOW COULD YOU BE SO STUPID?
I DIDN'T PLAN IT, YOU KNOW!
I'M JUST TRYING TO FIGURE OUT WHAT TO DO NOW.
WELL, YOU'D BETTER TELL THE OTHERS.
NO, I CAN'T, NOT YET ANYWAY.
NOT UNTIL I FIGURE OUT HOW TO BREAK THE NEWS TO THEM.
THEY'VE ALREADY BEEN THROUGH SO MUCH.
I'M AFRAID THIS COULD SHATTER THE TEAM FOR GOOD.
WELL, IF IT'S NOT ALREADY TOO LATE.
WHAT ARE THEY DOING?
WILHELM?
WILHELM?
WILHELM?
I SHALL ENJOY CONSUMING THAT LOVELY GIZZARD OF YOURS, OLD MAN.
AKKKK!

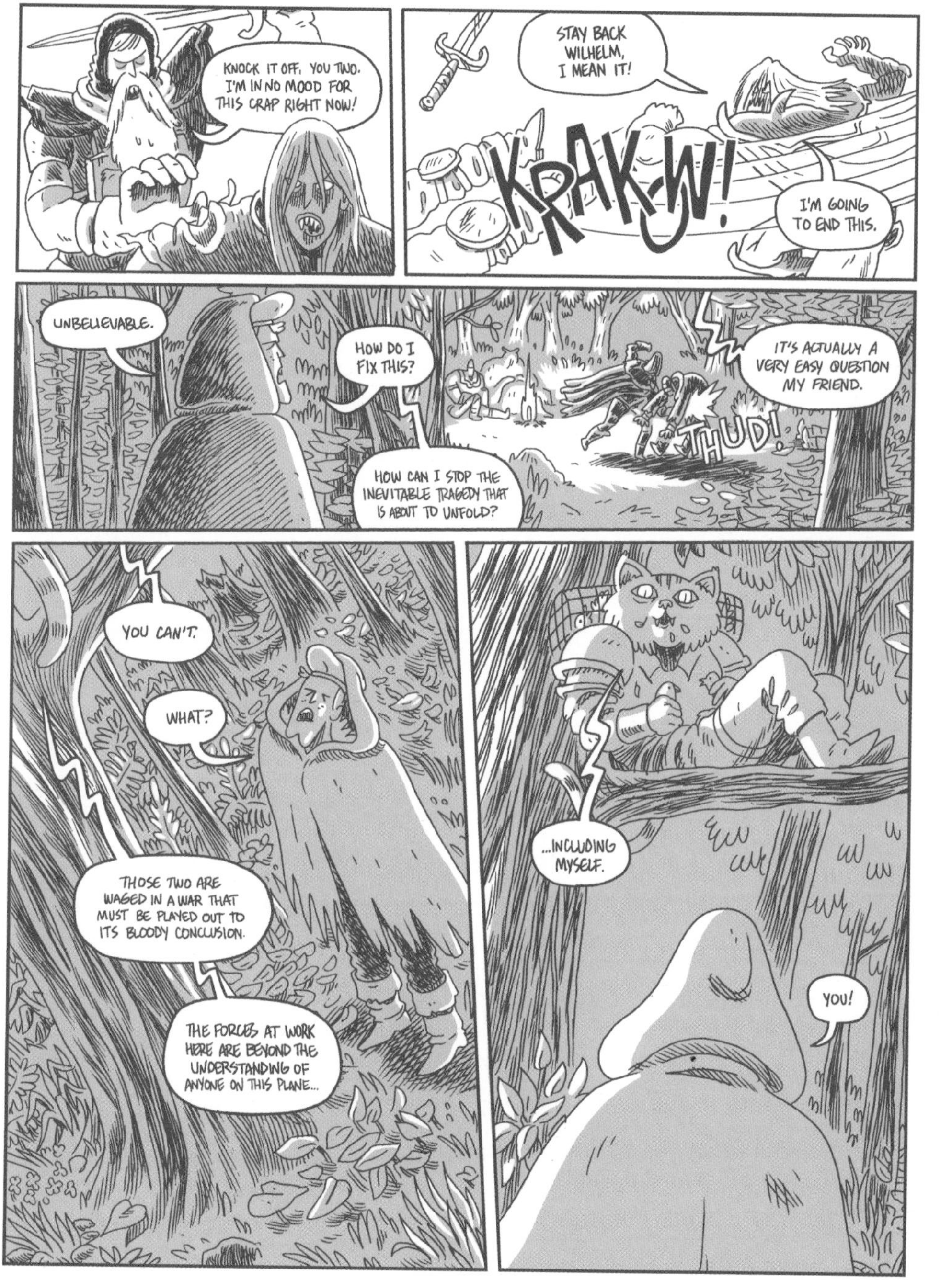
KNOCK IT OFF, YOU TWO. I'M IN NO MOOD FOR THIS CRAP RIGHT NOW!
STAY BACK WILHELM, I MEAN IT!
KRAK-OW!
I'M GOING TO END THIS.
UNBELIEVABLE.
HOW DO I FIX THIS?
HOW CAN I STOP THE INEVITABLE TRAGEDY THAT IS ABOUT TO UNFOLD?
IT'S ACTUALLY A VERY EASY QUESTION MY FRIEND.
THUD!
YOU CAN'T.
WHAT?
THOSE TWO ARE WAGED IN A WAR THAT MUST BE PLAYED OUT TO ITS BLOODY CONCLUSION.
THE FORCES AT WORK HERE ARE BEYOND THE UNDERSTANDING OF ANYONE ON THIS PLANE...
...INCLUDING MYSELF.
YOU!

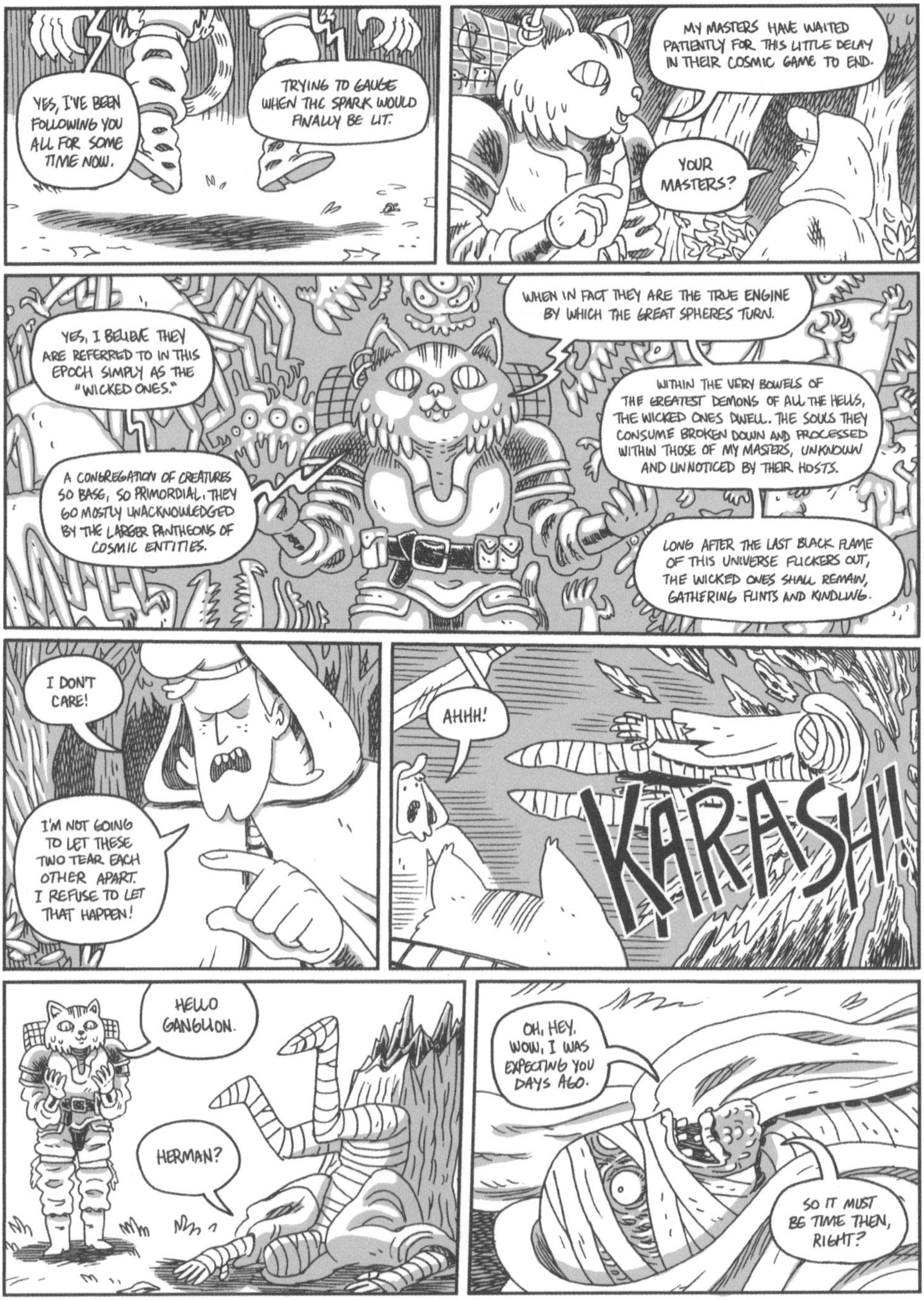

YES, I'VE BEEN FOLLOWING YOU ALL FOR SOME TIME NOW.
TRYING TO GAUGE WHEN THE SPARK WOULD FINALLY BE LIT.
MY MASTERS HAVE WAITED PATIENTLY FOR THIS LITTLE DELAY IN THEIR COSMIC GAME TO END.
YOUR MASTERS?
YES, I BELIEVE THEY ARE REFERRED TO IN THIS EPOCH SIMPLY AS THE "WICKED ONES."
A CONGREGATION OF CREATURES SO BASE, SO PRIMORDIAL, THEY GO MOSTLY UNACKNOWLEDGED BY THE LARGER PANTHEONS OF COSMIC ENTITIES.
WHEN IN FACT THEY ARE THE TRUE ENGINE BY WHICH THE GREAT SPHERES TURN.
WITHIN THE VERY BOWELS OF THE GREATEST DEMONS OF ALL THE HELLS, THE WICKED ONES DWELL. THE SOULS THEY CONSUME BROKEN DOWN AND PROCESSED WITHIN THOSE OF MY MASTERS, UNKNOWN AND UNNOTICED BY THEIR HOSTS.
LONG AFTER THE LAST BLACK FLAME OF THIS UNIVERSE FLICKERS OUT, THE WICKED ONES SHALL REMAIN, GATHERING FLINTS AND KINDLING.
I DON'T CARE!
I'M NOT GOING TO LET THESE TWO TEAR EACH OTHER APART. I REFUSE TO LET THAT HAPPEN!
AHHH!
KARASH!
HELLO GANGLION.
HERMAN?
OH, HEY. WOW, I WAS EXPECTING YOU DAYS AGO.
SO IT MUST BE TIME THEN, RIGHT?

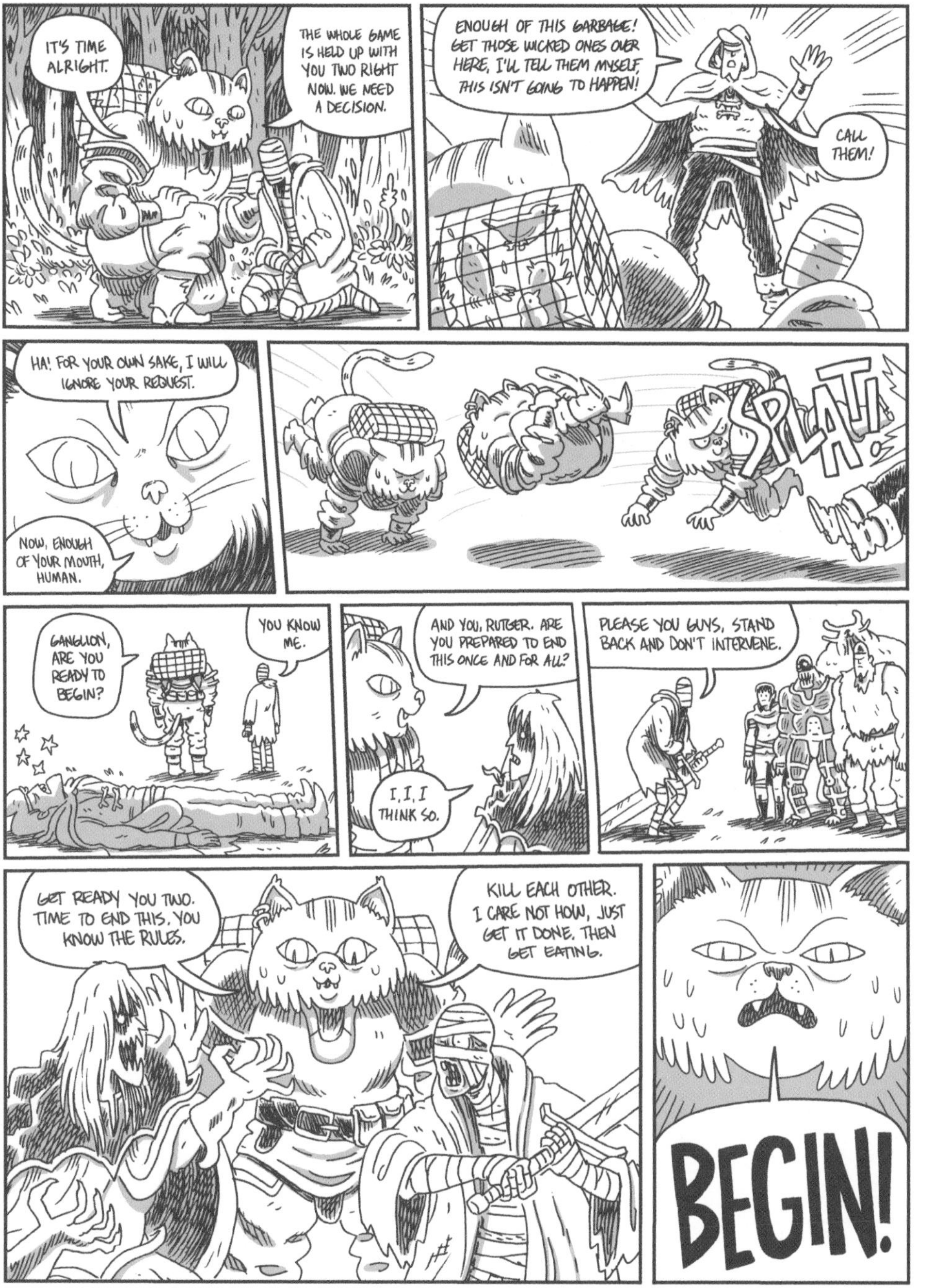

IT'S TIME ALRIGHT.
THE WHOLE GAME IS HELD UP WITH YOU TWO RIGHT NOW. WE NEED A DECISION.
ENOUGH OF THIS GARBAGE! GET THOSE WICKED ONES OVER HERE, I'LL TELL THEM MYSELF, THIS ISN'T GOING TO HAPPEN!
CALL THEM!
HA! FOR YOUR OWN SAKE, I WILL IGNORE YOUR REQUEST.
NOW, ENOUGH OF YOUR MOUTH, HUMAN.
SPLAT!
GANGLION, ARE YOU READY TO BEGIN?
YOU KNOW ME.
AND YOU, RUTGER. ARE YOU PREPARED TO END THIS ONCE AND FOR ALL?
I, I, I THINK SO.
PLEASE YOU GUYS, STAND BACK AND DON'T INTERVENE.
GET READY YOU TWO. TIME TO END THIS. YOU KNOW THE RULES.
KILL EACH OTHER. I CARE NOT HOW, JUST GET IT DONE. THEN GET EATING.
BEGIN!

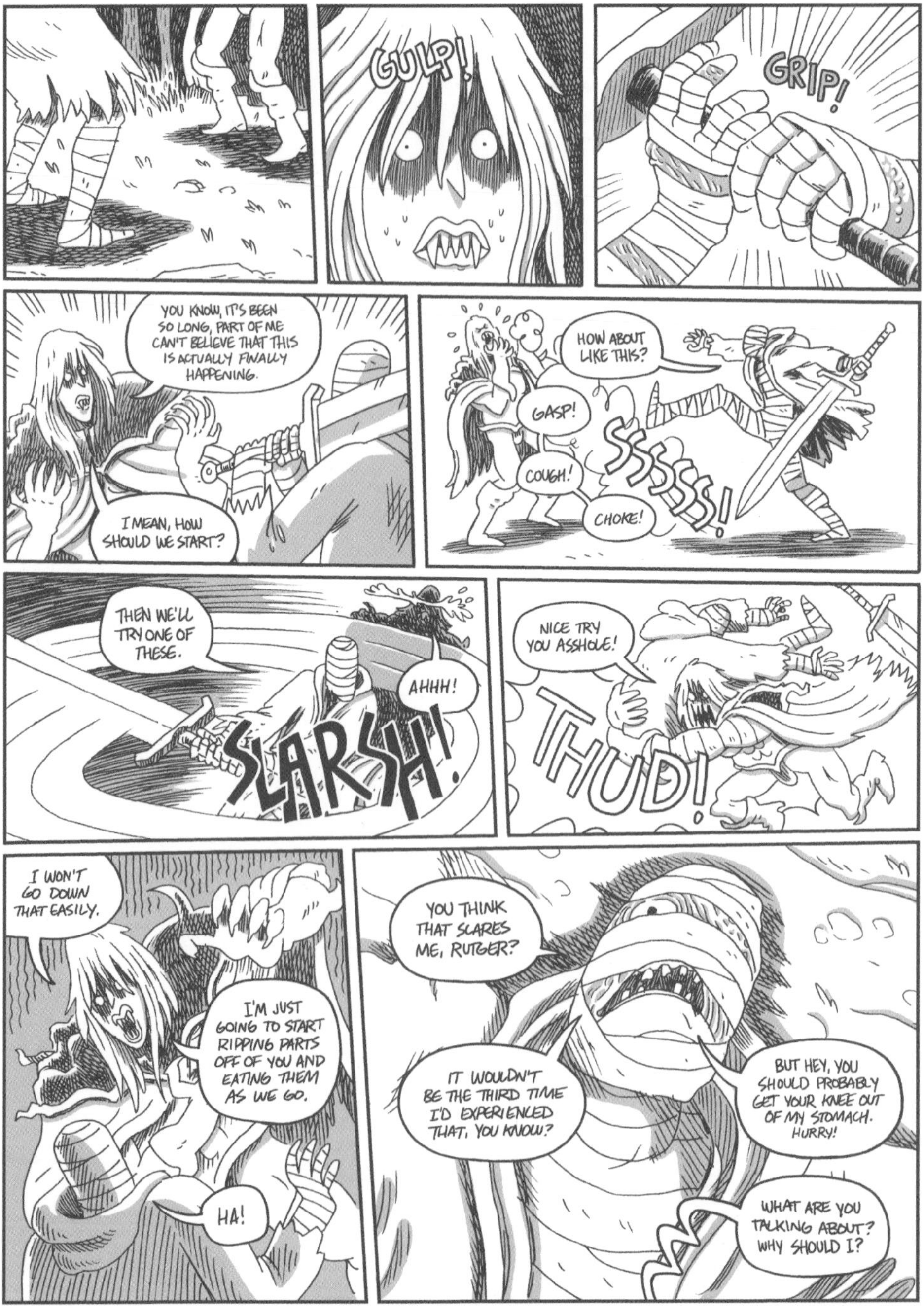
GULP!
GRIP!
YOU KNOW, IT'S BEEN SO LONG, PART OF ME CAN'T BELIEVE THAT THIS IS ACTUALLY FINALLY HAPPENING.
I MEAN, HOW SHOULD WE START?
HOW ABOUT LIKE THIS?
GASP!
COUGH!
CHOKE!
SSSSSS!
THEN WE'LL TRY ONE OF THESE.
AHHH!
SLARSH!
NICE TRY YOU ASSHOLE!
THUD!
I WON'T GO DOWN THAT EASILY.
I'M JUST GOING TO START RIPPING PARTS OFF OF YOU AND EATING THEM AS WE GO.
HA!
YOU THINK THAT SCARES ME, RUTGER?
IT WOULDN'T BE THE THIRD TIME I'D EXPERIENCED THAT, YOU KNOW?
BUT HEY, YOU SHOULD PROBABLY GET YOUR KNEE OUT OF MY STOMACH. HURRY!
WHAT ARE YOU TALKING ABOUT? WHY SHOULD I?

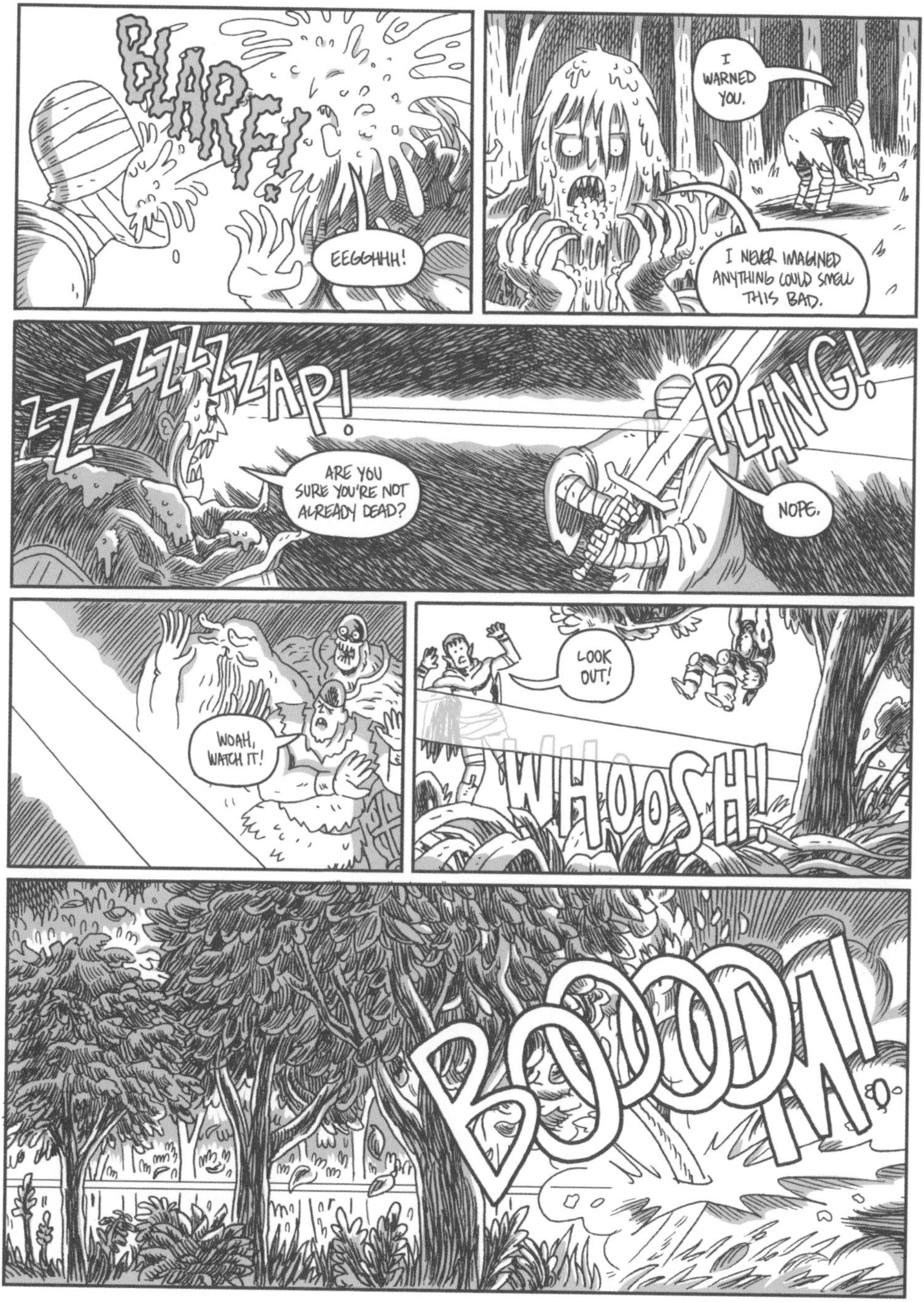
BLARF!
EEGGHHH!
I WARNED YOU.
I NEVER IMAGINED ANYTHING COULD SMELL THIS BAD.
ZZZZZZZZZAP!
ARE YOU SURE YOU'RE NOT ALREADY DEAD?
PLANG!
NOPE.
WOAH, WATCH IT!
LOOK OUT!
WHOOSH!
BOOOOOM!

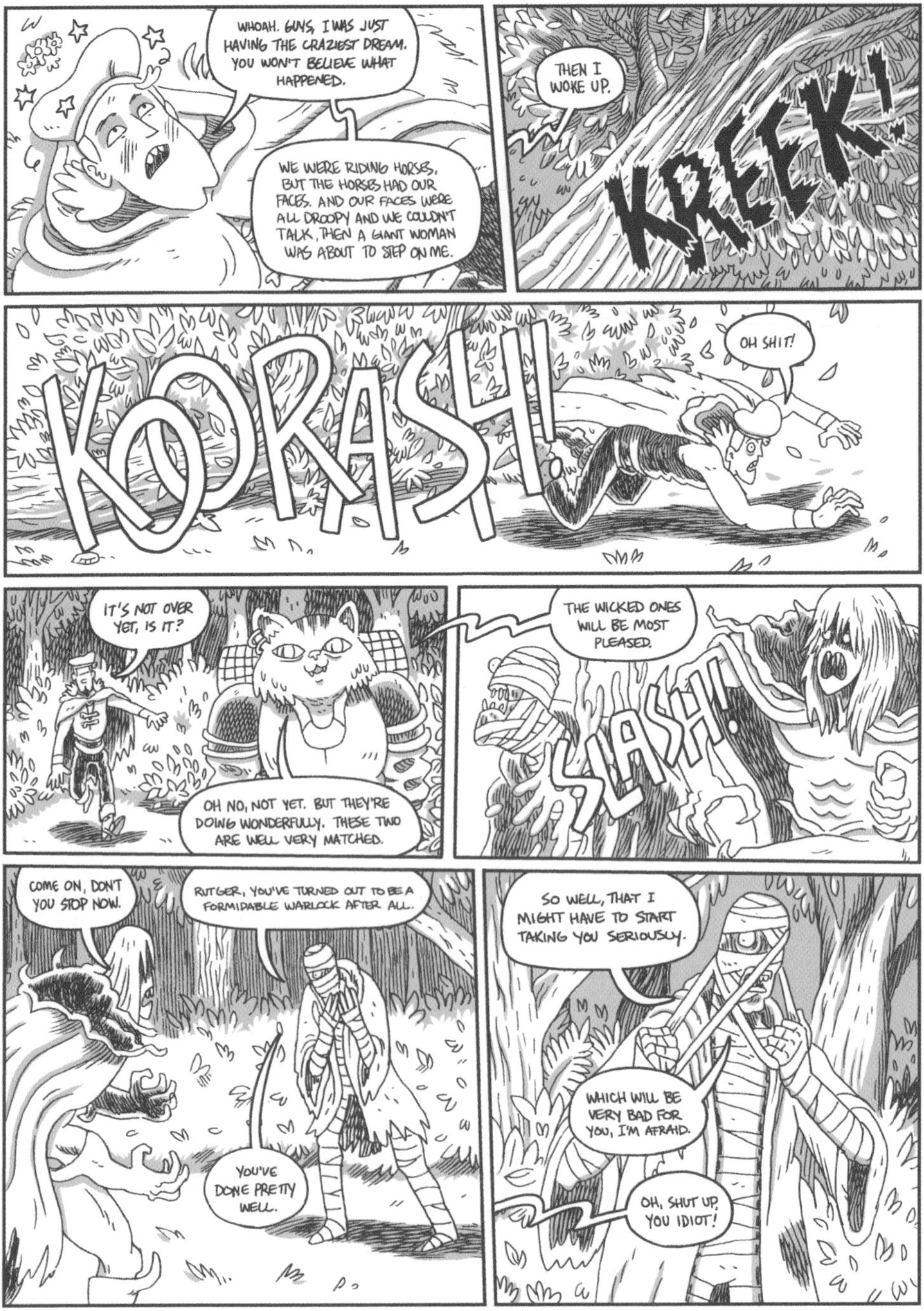

WHOAH. GUYS, I WAS JUST HAVING THE CRAZIEST DREAM. YOU WON'T BELIEVE WHAT HAPPENED.
WE WERE RIDING HORSES, BUT THE HORSES HAD OUR FACES. AND OUR FACES WERE ALL DROOPY AND WE COULDN'T TALK. THEN A GIANT WOMAN WAS ABOUT TO STEP ON ME.
THEN I WOKE UP.
KREEK!
KOORASH!
OH SHIT!
IT'S NOT OVER YET, IS IT?
OH NO, NOT YET. BUT THEY'RE DOING WONDERFULLY. THESE TWO ARE WELL VERY MATCHED.
THE WICKED ONES WILL BE MOST PLEASED.
SLASH!
COME ON, DON'T YOU STOP NOW.
RUTGER, YOU'VE TURNED OUT TO BE A FORMIDABLE WARLOCK AFTER ALL.
YOU'VE DONE PRETTY WELL.
SO WELL, THAT I MIGHT HAVE TO START TAKING YOU SERIOUSLY.
WHICH WILL BE VERY BAD FOR YOU, I'M AFRAID.
OH, SHUT UP, YOU IDIOT!

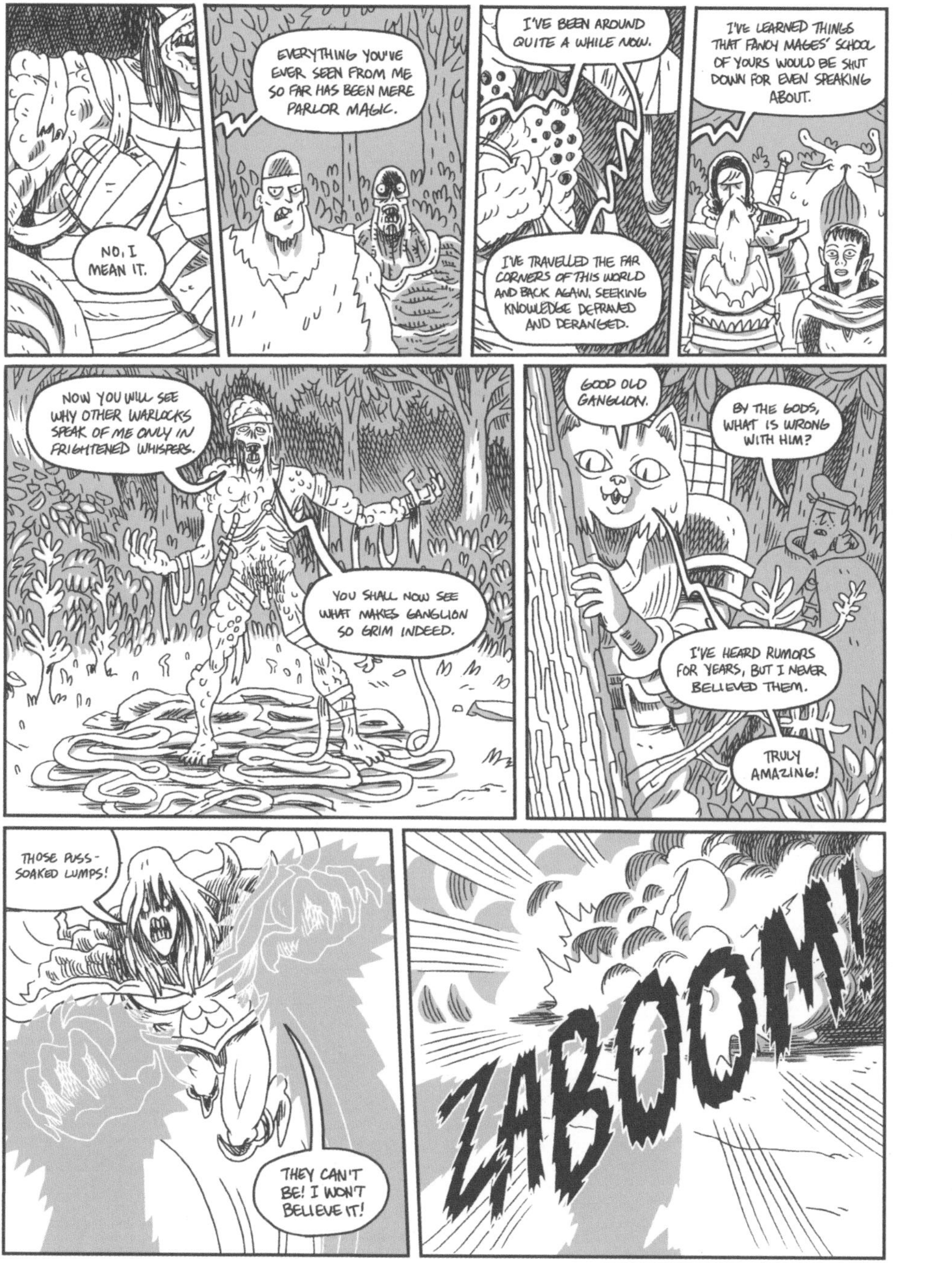
NO, I MEAN IT.
EVERYTHING YOU'VE EVER SEEN FROM ME SO FAR HAS BEEN MERE PARLOR MAGIC.
I'VE BEEN AROUND QUITE A WHILE NOW.
I'VE TRAVELLED THE FAR CORNERS OF THIS WORLD AND BACK AGAIN, SEEKING KNOWLEDGE DEPRAVED AND DERANGED.
I'VE LEARNED THINGS THAT FANCY MAGES' SCHOOL OF YOURS WOULD BE SHUT DOWN FOR EVEN SPEAKING ABOUT.
NOW YOU WILL SEE WHY OTHER WARLOCKS SPEAK OF ME ONLY IN FRIGHTENED WHISPERS.
YOU SHALL NOW SEE WHAT MAKES GANGLION SO GRIM INDEED.
GOOD OLD GANGLION.
BY THE GODS, WHAT IS WRONG WITH HIM?
I'VE HEARD RUMORS FOR YEARS, BUT I NEVER BELIEVED THEM.
TRULY AMAZING!
THOSE PUSS-SOAKED LUMPS!
THEY CAN'T BE! I WON'T BELIEVE IT!
ZABOOM!

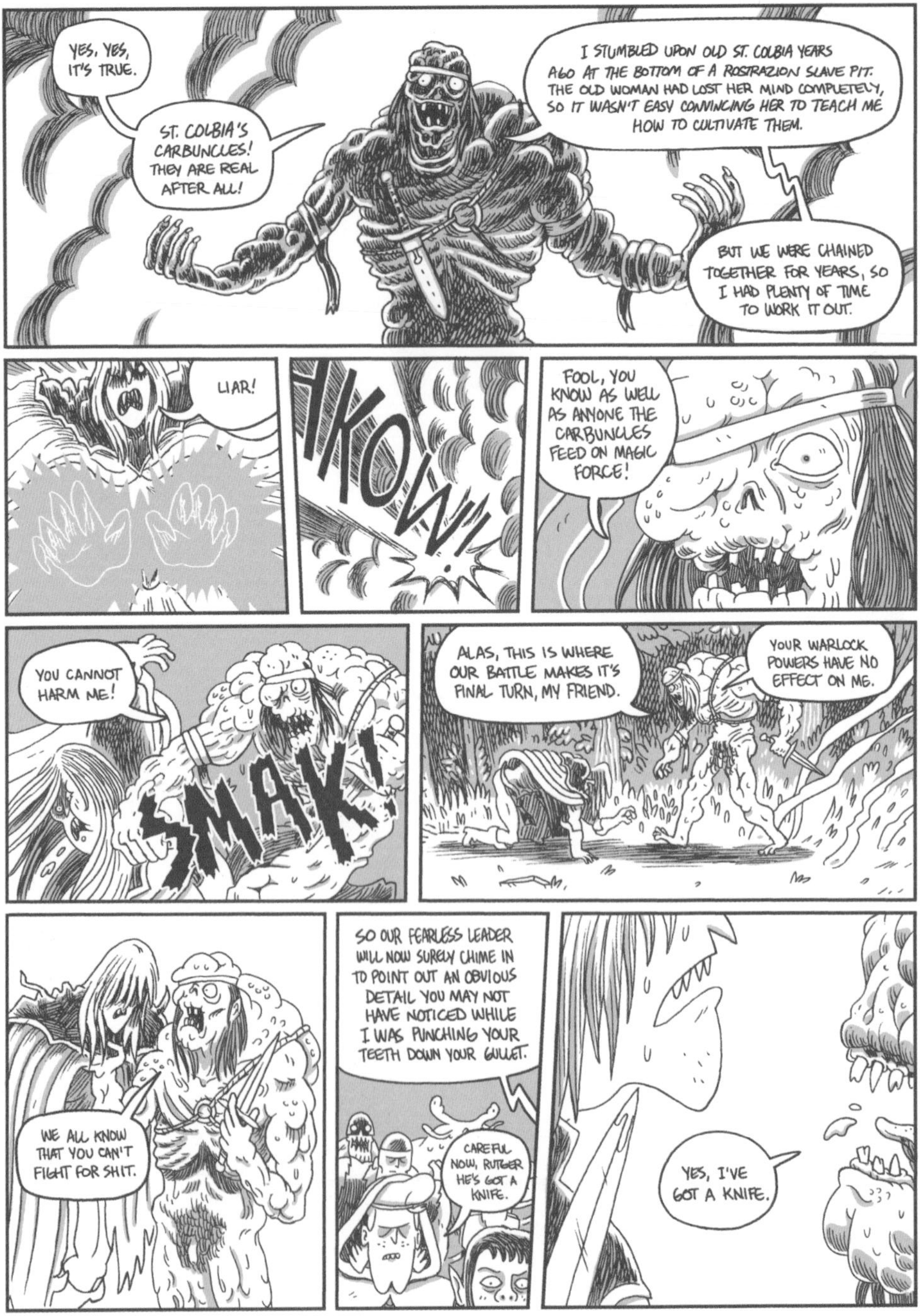
YES, YES, IT'S TRUE.
ST. COLBIA'S CARBUNCLES! THEY ARE REAL AFTER ALL!
I STUMBLED UPON OLD ST. COLBIA YEARS AGO AT THE BOTTOM OF A ROSTRAZION SLAVE PIT. THE OLD WOMAN HAD LOST HER MIND COMPLETELY, SO IT WASN'T EASY CONVINCING HER TO TEACH ME HOW TO CULTIVATE THEM.
BUT WE WERE CHAINED TOGETHER FOR YEARS, SO I HAD PLENTY OF TIME TO WORK IT OUT.
LIAR!
KOW!
FOOL, YOU KNOW AS WELL AS ANYONE THE CARBUNCLES FEED ON MAGIC FORCE!
YOU CANNOT HARM ME!
SMAK!
ALAS, THIS IS WHERE OUR BATTLE MAKES IT'S FINAL TURN, MY FRIEND.
YOUR WARLOCK POWERS HAVE NO EFFECT ON ME.
WE ALL KNOW THAT YOU CAN'T FIGHT FOR SHIT.
SO OUR FEARLESS LEADER WILL NOW SURELY CHIME IN TO POINT OUT AN OBVIOUS DETAIL YOU MAY NOT HAVE NOTICED WHILE I WAS PUNCHING YOUR TEETH DOWN YOUR GULLET.
CAREFUL NOW, RUTGER HE'S GOT A KNIFE.
YES, I'VE GOT A KNIFE.

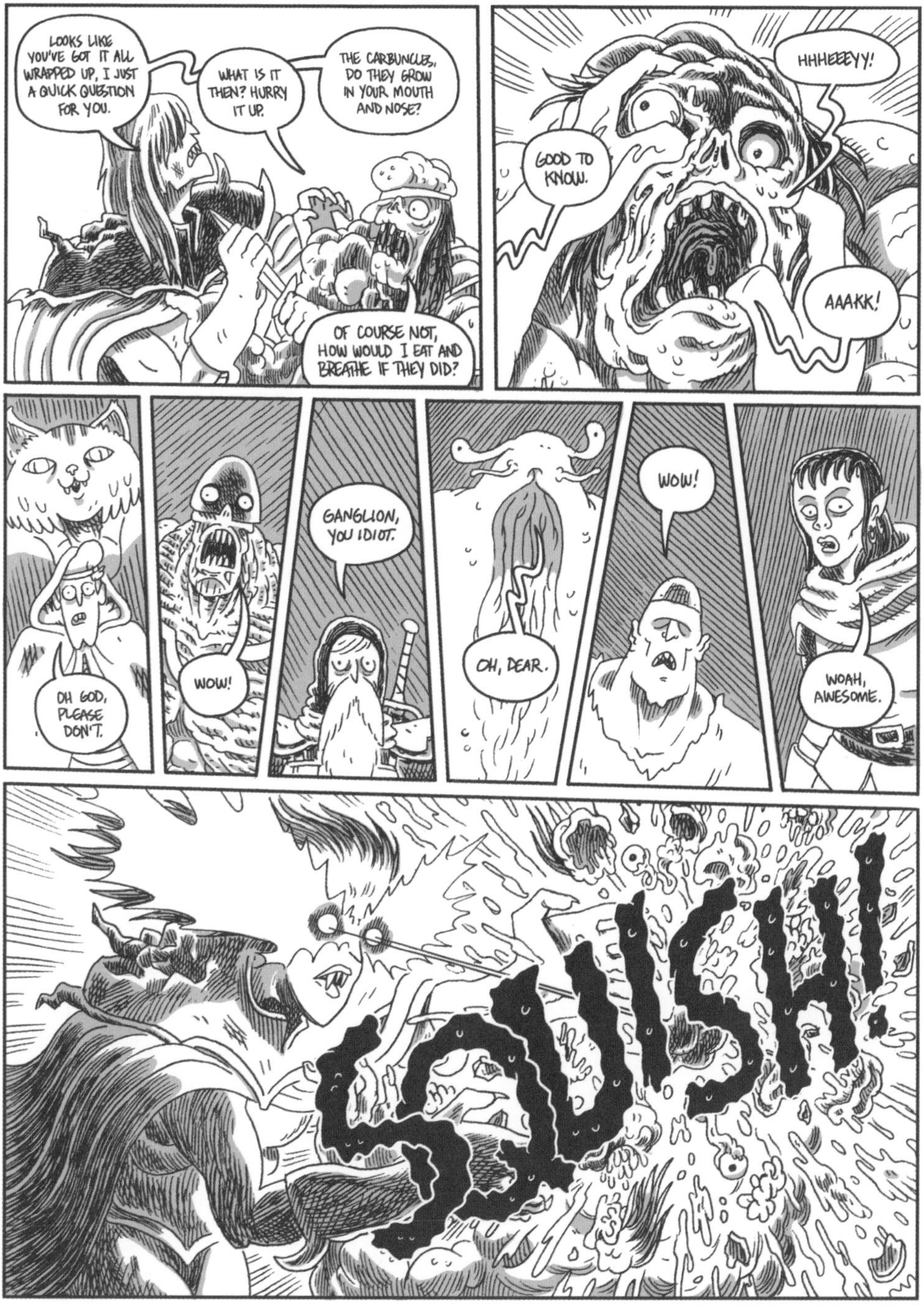
LOOKS LIKE YOU'VE GOT IT ALL WRAPPED UP, I JUST A QUICK QUESTION FOR YOU.
WHAT IS IT THEN? HURRY IT UP.
THE CARBUNCLES, DO THEY GROW IN YOUR MOUTH AND NOSE?
OF COURSE NOT, HOW WOULD I EAT AND BREATHE IF THEY DID?
HHHEEEYY!
GOOD TO KNOW.
AAAKK!
OH GOD, PLEASE DON'T.
WOW!
GANGLION, YOU IDIOT.
OH, DEAR.
WOW!
WOAH, AWESOME.
SQUISH!

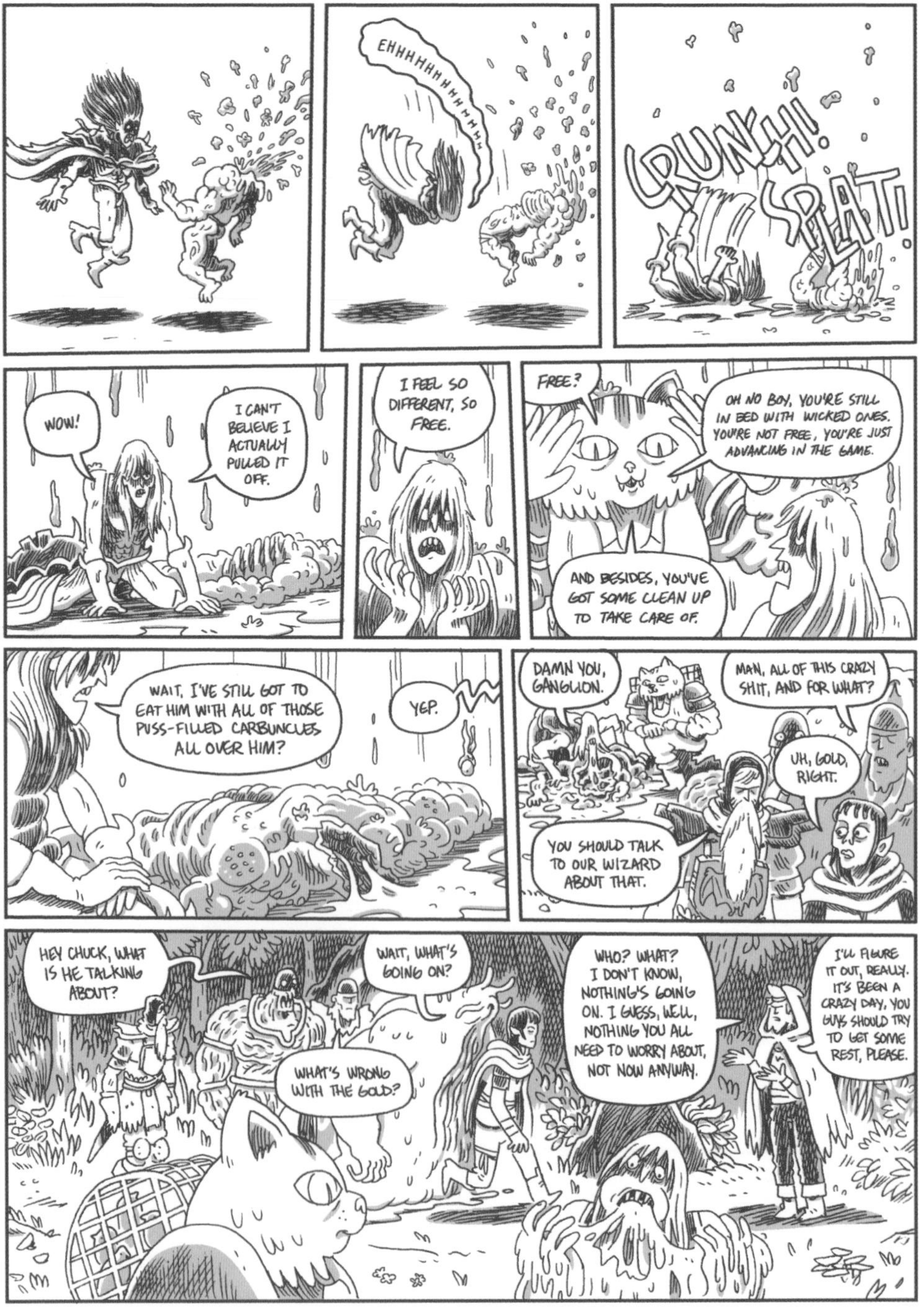
EHHHHHHHHHHHHH
CRUNCH!
SPLAT!
WOW!
I CAN'T BELIEVE I ACTUALLY PULLED IT OFF.
I FEEL SO DIFFERENT, SO FREE.
FREE?
OH NO BOY, YOU'RE STILL IN BED WITH WICKED ONES. YOU'RE NOT FREE, YOU'RE JUST ADVANCING IN THE GAME.
AND BESIDES, YOU'VE GOT SOME CLEAN UP TO TAKE CARE OF.
WAIT, I'VE STILL GOT TO EAT HIM WITH ALL OF THOSE PUSS-FILLED CARBUNCLES ALL OVER HIM?
YEP.
DAMN YOU, GANGLION.
MAN, ALL OF THIS CRAZY SHIT, AND FOR WHAT?
UH, GOLD, RIGHT.
YOU SHOULD TALK TO OUR WIZARD ABOUT THAT.
HEY CHUCK, WHAT IS HE TALKING ABOUT?
WAIT, WHAT'S GOING ON?
WHAT'S WRONG WITH THE GOLD?
WHO? WHAT? I DON'T KNOW, NOTHING'S GOING ON. I GUESS, WELL, NOTHING YOU ALL NEED TO WORRY ABOUT, NOT NOW ANYWAY.
I'LL FIGURE IT OUT, REALLY. IT'S BEEN A CRAZY DAY, YOU GUYS SHOULD TRY TO GET SOME REST, PLEASE.

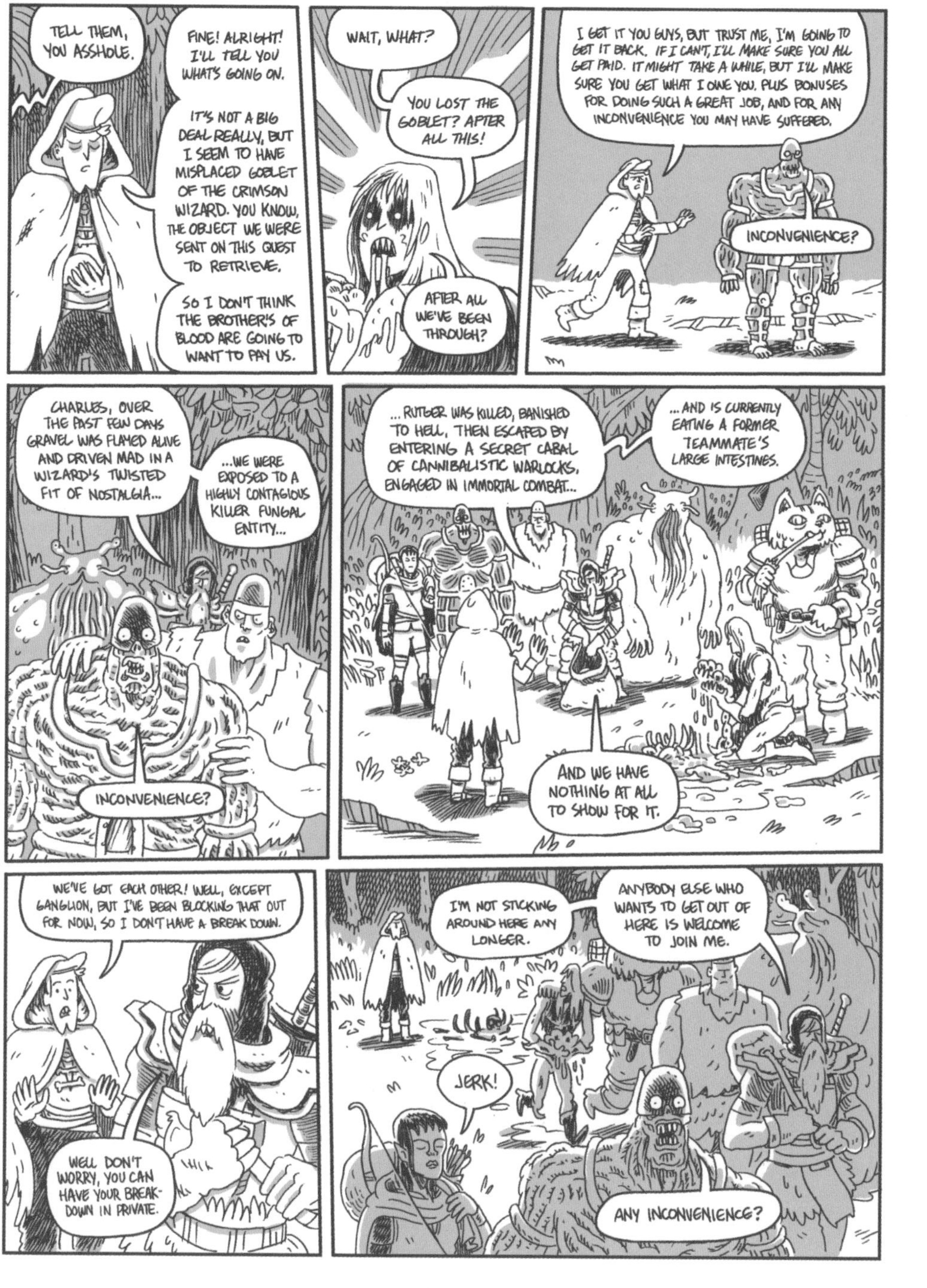

TELL THEM, YOU ASSHOLE.
FINE! ALRIGHT! I'LL TELL YOU WHAT'S GOING ON.
IT'S NOT A BIG DEAL REALLY, BUT I SEEM TO HAVE MISPLACED GOBLET OF THE CRIMSON WIZARD. YOU KNOW, THE OBJECT WE WERE SENT ON THIS QUEST TO RETRIEVE.
SO I DON'T THINK THE BROTHER'S OF BLOOD ARE GOING TO WANT TO PAY US.
WAIT, WHAT?
YOU LOST THE GOBLET? AFTER ALL THIS!
AFTER ALL WE'VE BEEN THROUGH?
I GET IT YOU GUYS, BUT TRUST ME, I'M GOING TO GET IT BACK. IF I CAN'T, I'LL MAKE SURE YOU ALL GET PAID. IT MIGHT TAKE A WHILE, BUT I'LL MAKE SURE YOU GET WHAT I OWE YOU. PLUS BONUSES FOR DOING SUCH A GREAT JOB, AND FOR ANY INCONVENIENCE YOU MAY HAVE SUFFERED.
INCONVENIENCE?
CHARLES, OVER THE PAST FEW DAYS GRAVEL WAS FLAYED ALIVE AND DRIVEN MAD IN A WIZARD'S TWISTED FIT OF NOSTALGIA...
...WE WERE EXPOSED TO A HIGHLY CONTAGIOUS KILLER FUNGAL ENTITY...
INCONVENIENCE?
...RUTGER WAS KILLED, BANISHED TO HELL, THEN ESCAPED BY ENTERING A SECRET CABAL OF CANNIBALISTIC WARLOCKS, ENGAGED IN IMMORTAL COMBAT...
...AND IS CURRENTLY EATING A FORMER TEAMMATE'S LARGE INTESTINES.
AND WE HAVE NOTHING AT ALL TO SHOW FOR IT.
WE'VE GOT EACH OTHER! WELL, EXCEPT GANGLION, BUT I'VE BEEN BLOCKING THAT OUT FOR NOW, SO I DON'T HAVE A BREAK DOWN.
WELL DON'T WORRY, YOU CAN HAVE YOUR BREAK-DOWN IN PRIVATE.
I'M NOT STICKING AROUND HERE ANY LONGER.
ANYBODY ELSE WHO WANTS TO GET OUT OF HERE IS WELCOME TO JOIN ME.
JERK!
ANY INCONVENIENCE?

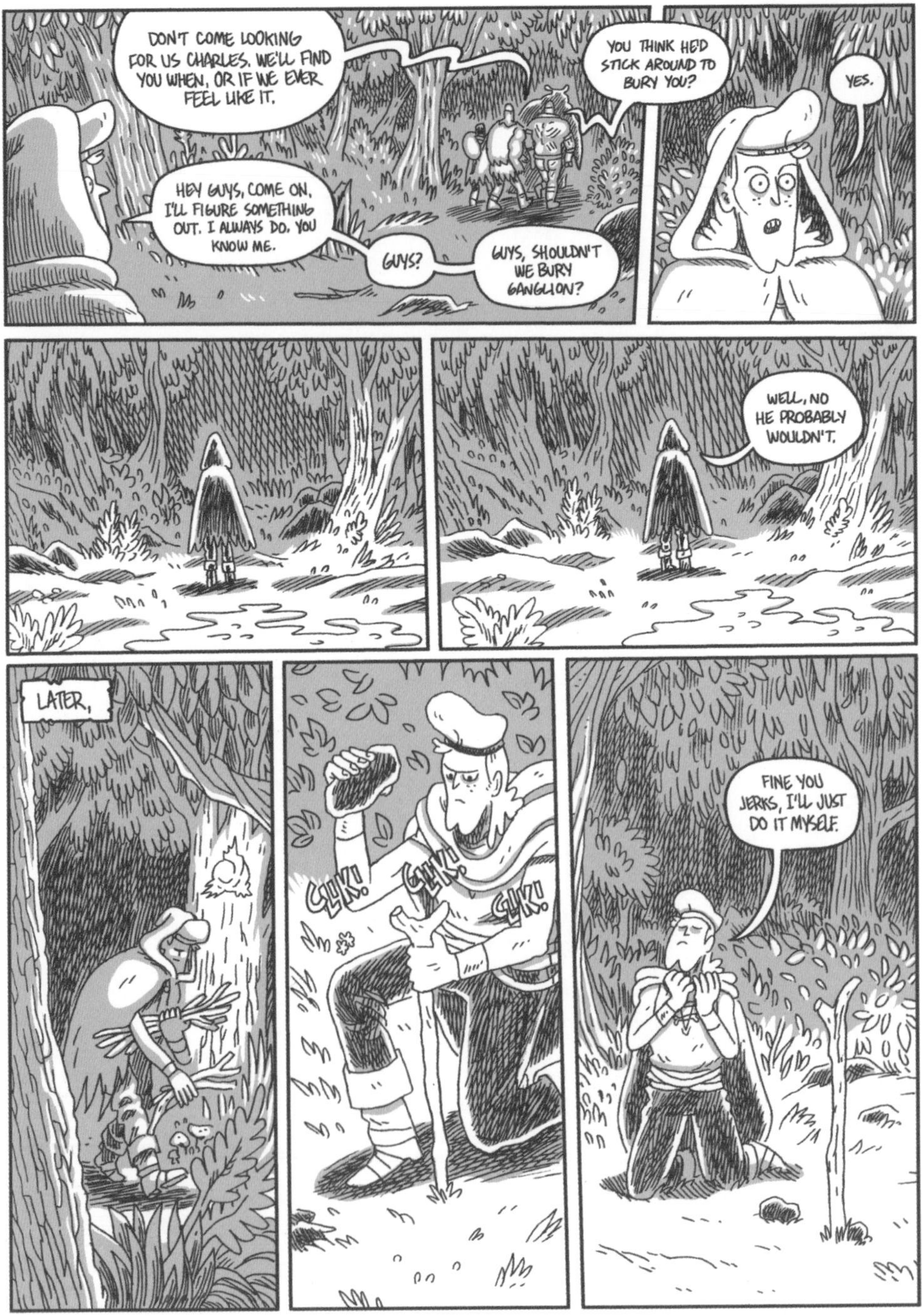
DON'T COME LOOKING FOR US CHARLES. WE'LL FIND YOU WHEN, OR IF WE EVER FEEL LIKE IT.
HEY GUYS, COME ON, I'LL FIGURE SOMETHING OUT. I ALWAYS DO. YOU KNOW ME.
GUYS?
GUYS, SHOULDN'T WE BURY GANGLION?
YOU THINK HE'D STICK AROUND TO BURY YOU?
YES.
WELL, NO HE PROBABLY WOULDN'T.
LATER,
GUK! GUK! GUK!
FINE YOU JERKS, I'LL JUST DO IT MYSELF.

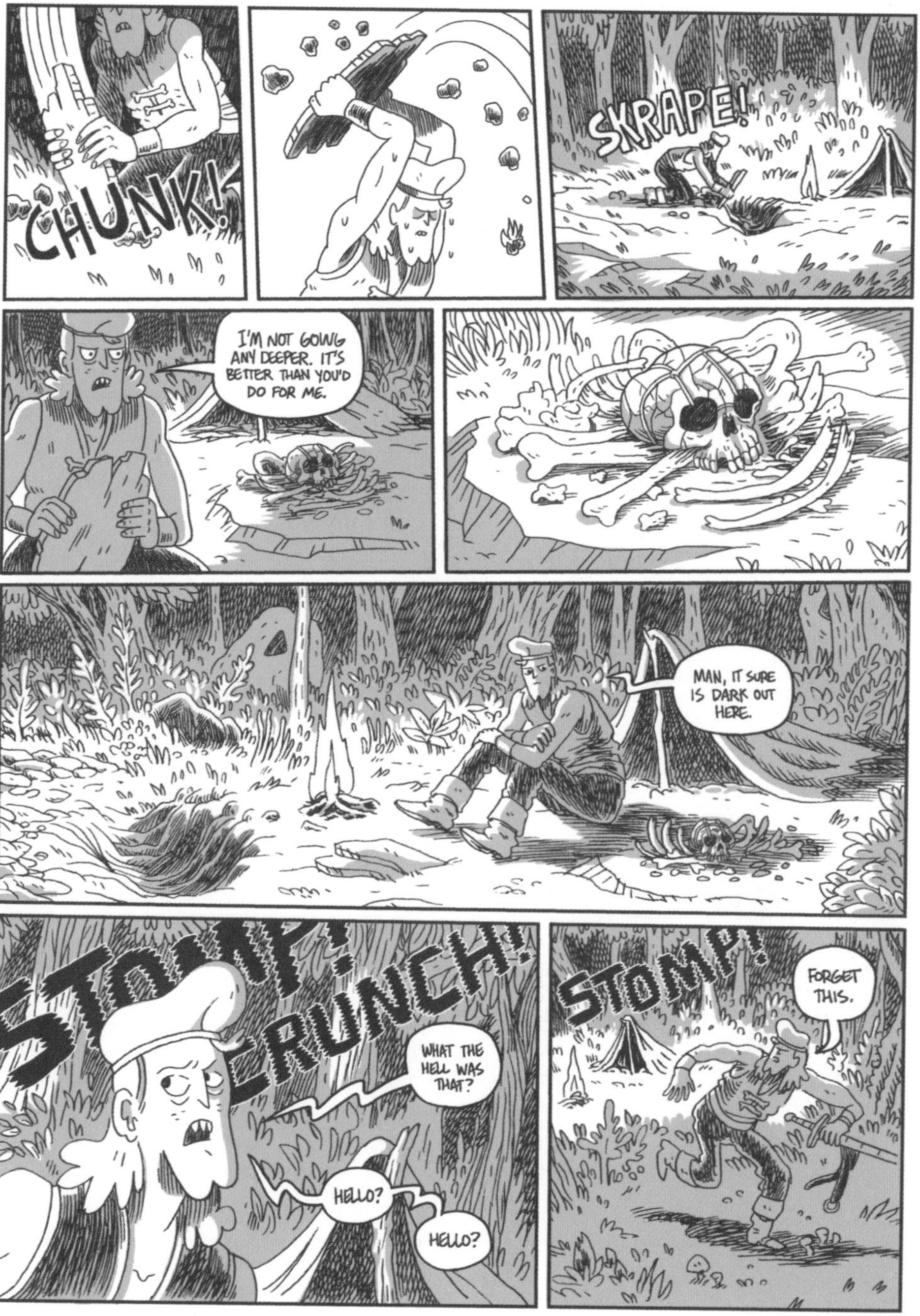
CHUNK!
SKRAPE!
I'M NOT GOING ANY DEEPER. IT'S BETTER THAN YOU'D DO FOR ME.
MAN, IT SURE IS DARK OUT HERE.
STOMP!
CRUNCH!
WHAT THE HELL WAS THAT?
HELLO?
HELLO?
STOMP!
FORGET THIS.

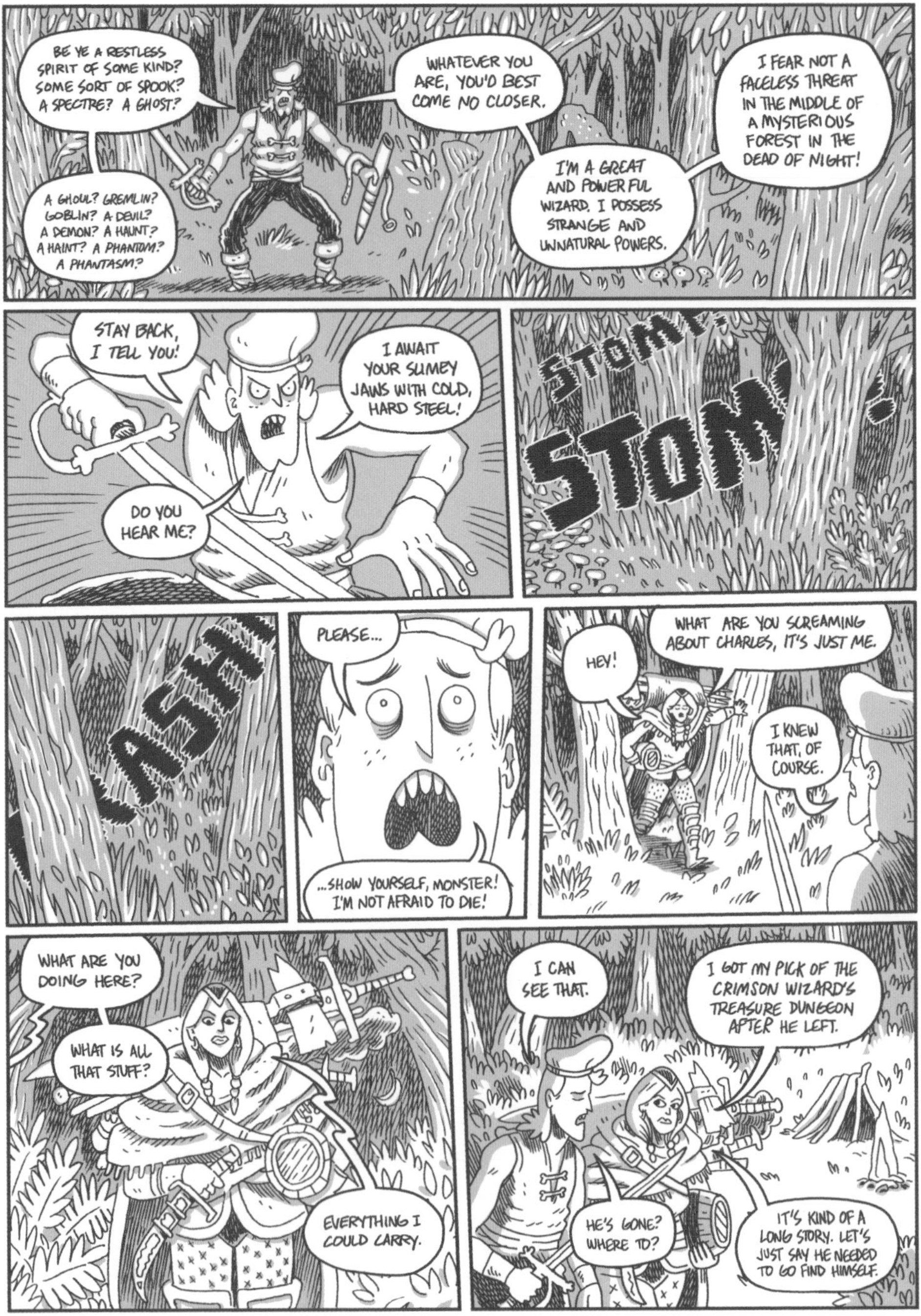
BE YE A RESTLESS SPIRIT OF SOME KIND? SOME SORT OF SPOOK? A SPECTRE? A GHOST?
A GHOUL? GREMLIN? GOBLIN? A DEVIL? A DEMON? A HAUNT? A HAINT? A PHANTOM? A PHANTASM?
WHATEVER YOU ARE, YOU'D BEST COME NO CLOSER.
I'M A GREAT AND POWERFUL WIZARD. I POSSESS STRANGE AND UNNATURAL POWERS.
I FEAR NOT A FACELESS THREAT IN THE MIDDLE OF A MYSTERIOUS FOREST IN THE DEAD OF NIGHT!
STAY BACK, I TELL YOU!
I AWAIT YOUR SLIMEY JAWS WITH COLD, HARD STEEL!
DO YOU HEAR ME?
PLEASE...
...SHOW YOURSELF, MONSTER! I'M NOT AFRAID TO DIE!
HEY!
WHAT ARE YOU SCREAMING ABOUT CHARLES, IT'S JUST ME.
I KNEW THAT, OF COURSE.
WHAT ARE YOU DOING HERE?
WHAT IS ALL THAT STUFF?
EVERYTHING I COULD CARRY.
I CAN SEE THAT.
I GOT MY PICK OF THE CRIMSON WIZARD'S TREASURE DUNGEON AFTER HE LEFT.
HE'S GONE? WHERE TO?
IT'S KIND OF A LONG STORY. LET'S JUST SAY HE NEEDED TO GO FIND HIMSELF.

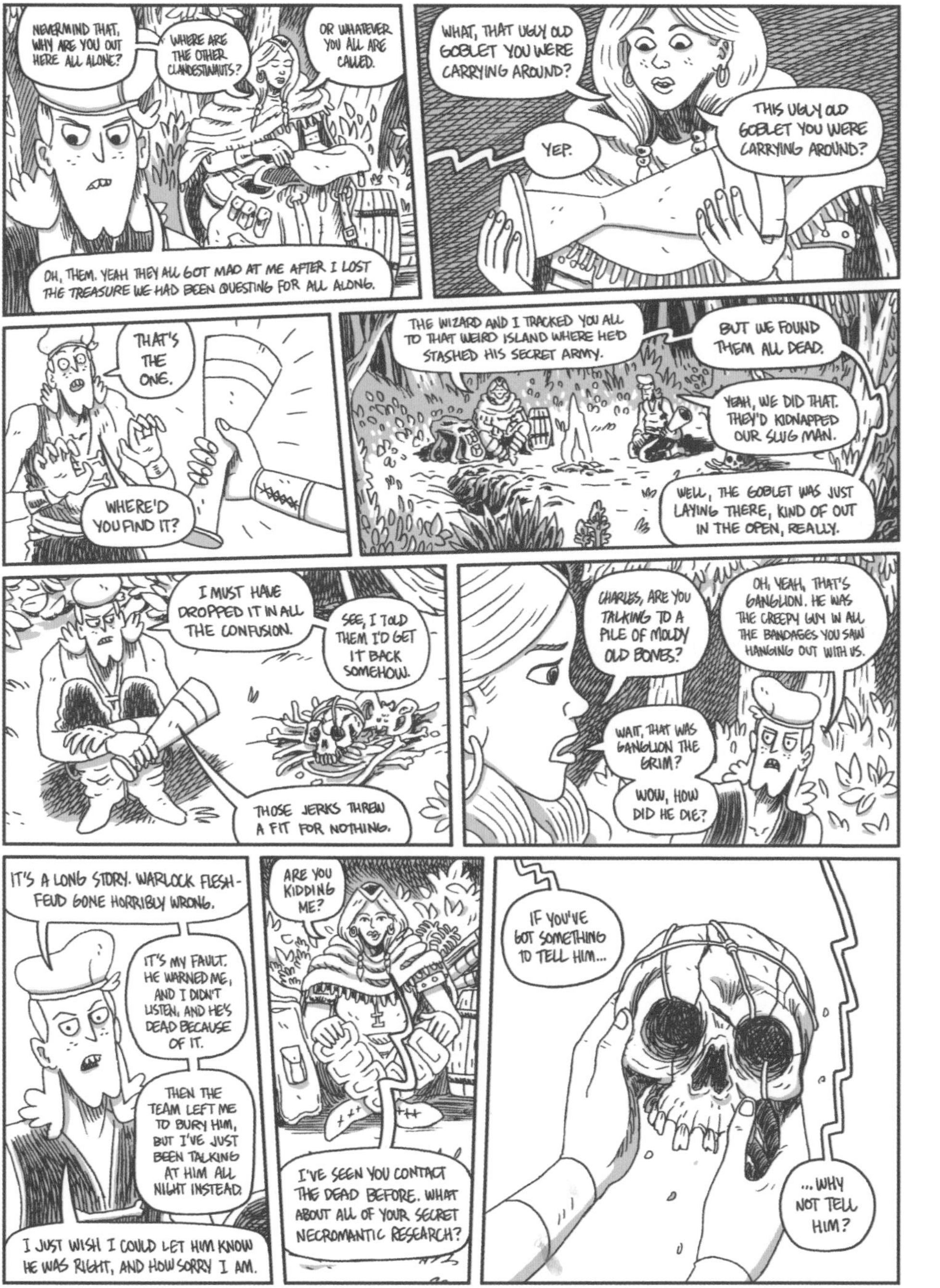
NEVERMIND THAT, WHY ARE YOU OUT HERE ALL ALONE?
WHERE ARE THE OTHER CLANDESTINAUTS?
OR WHATEVER YOU ALL ARE CALLED.
OH, THEM. YEAH THEY ALL GOT MAD AT ME AFTER I LOST THE TREASURE WE HAD BEEN QUESTING FOR ALL ALONG.
WHAT, THAT UGLY OLD GOBLET YOU WERE CARRYING AROUND?
YEP.
THIS UGLY OLD GOBLET YOU WERE CARRYING AROUND?
THAT'S THE ONE.
WHERE'D YOU FIND IT?
THE WIZARD AND I TRACKED YOU ALL TO THAT WEIRD ISLAND WHERE HE'D STASHED HIS SECRET ARMY.
BUT WE FOUND THEM ALL DEAD.
YEAH, WE DID THAT. THEY'D KIDNAPPED OUR SLUG MAN.
WELL, THE GOBLET WAS JUST LAYING THERE, KIND OF OUT IN THE OPEN, REALLY.
I MUST HAVE DROPPED IT IN ALL THE CONFUSION.
SEE, I TOLD THEM I'D GET IT BACK SOMEHOW.
THOSE JERKS THREW A FIT FOR NOTHING.
CHARLES, ARE YOU TALKING TO A PILE OF MOLDY OLD BONES?
OH, YEAH, THAT'S GANGLION. HE WAS THE CREEPY GUY IN ALL THE BANDAGES YOU SAW HANGING OUT WITH US.
WAIT, THAT WAS GANGLION THE GRIM?
WOW, HOW DID HE DIE?
IT'S A LONG STORY. WARLOCK FLESH-FEUD GONE HORRIBLY WRONG.
IT'S MY FAULT. HE WARNED ME, AND I DIDN'T LISTEN, AND HE'S DEAD BECAUSE OF IT.
THEN THE TEAM LEFT ME TO BURY HIM, BUT I'VE JUST BEEN TALKING AT HIM ALL NIGHT INSTEAD.
I JUST WISH I COULD LET HIM KNOW HE WAS RIGHT, AND HOW SORRY I AM.
ARE YOU KIDDING ME?
I'VE SEEN YOU CONTACT THE DEAD BEFORE. WHAT ABOUT ALL OF YOUR SECRET NECROMANTIC RESEARCH?
IF YOU'VE GOT SOMETHING TO TELL HIM...
...WHY NOT TELL HIM?

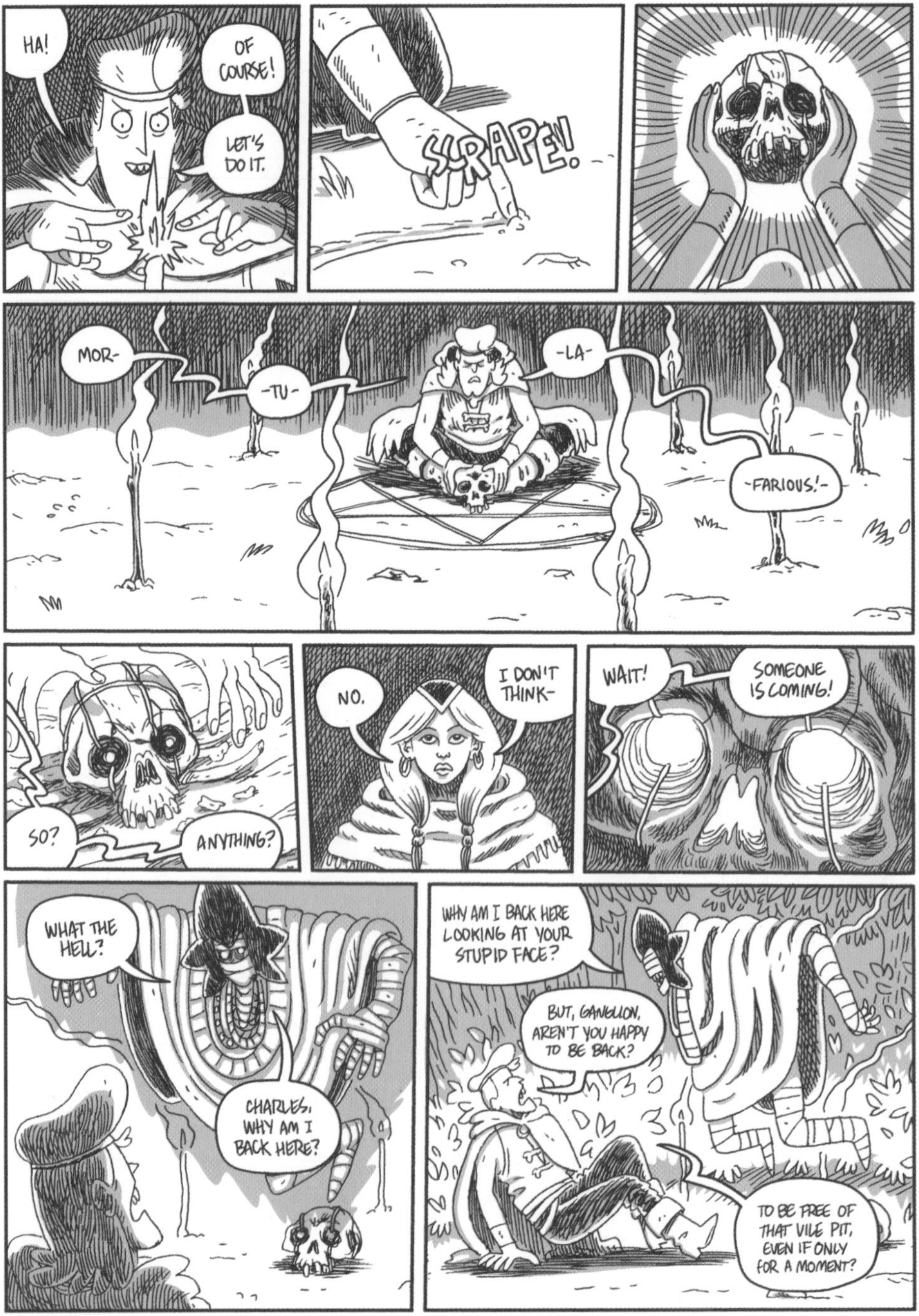
HA!
OF COURSE!
LET'S DO IT.
SCRAPE!
MOR-
-TU-
-LA-
-FARIOUS!-
SO?
ANYTHING?
NO.
I DON'T THINK-
WAIT!
SOMEONE IS COMING!
WHAT THE HELL?
CHARLES, WHY AM I BACK HERE?
WHY AM I BACK HERE LOOKING AT YOUR STUPID FACE?
BUT, GANGLION, AREN'T YOU HAPPY TO BE BACK?
TO BE FREE OF THAT VILE PIT, EVEN IF ONLY FOR A MOMENT?

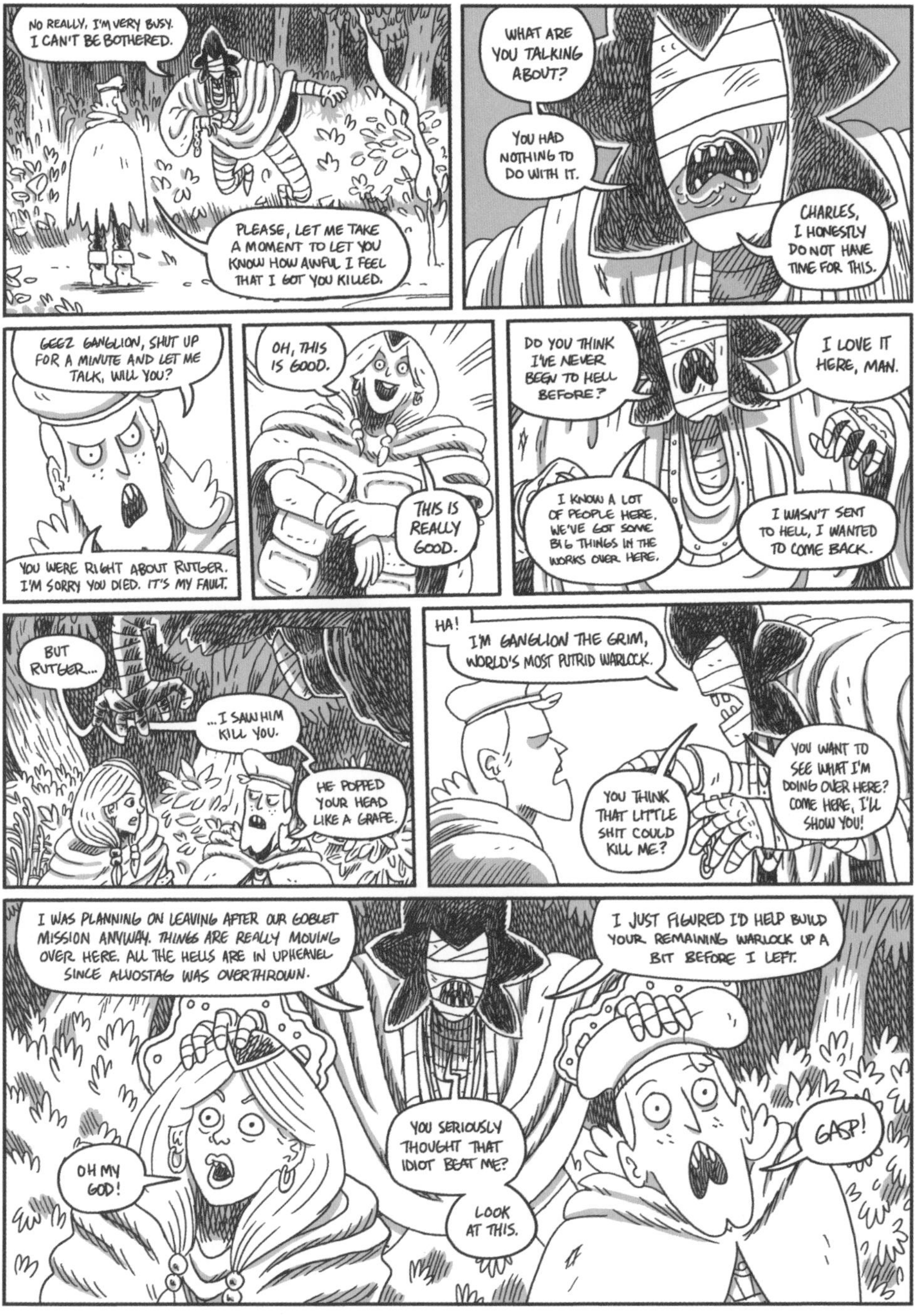
NO REALLY, I'M VERY BUSY. I CAN'T BE BOTHERED.
PLEASE, LET ME TAKE A MOMENT TO LET YOU KNOW HOW AWFUL I FEEL THAT I GOT YOU KILLED.
WHAT ARE YOU TALKING ABOUT?
YOU HAD NOTHING TO DO WITH IT.
CHARLES, I HONESTLY DO NOT HAVE TIME FOR THIS.
GEEZ GANGLION, SHUT UP FOR A MINUTE AND LET ME TALK, WILL YOU?
YOU WERE RIGHT ABOUT RUTGER. I'M SORRY YOU DIED. IT'S MY FAULT.
OH, THIS IS GOOD.
THIS IS REALLY GOOD.
DO YOU THINK I'VE NEVER BEEN TO HELL BEFORE?
I LOVE IT HERE, MAN.
I KNOW A LOT OF PEOPLE HERE. WE'VE GOT SOME BIG THINGS IN THE WORKS OVER HERE.
I WASN'T SENT TO HELL, I WANTED TO COME BACK.
BUT RUTGER...
...I SAW HIM KILL YOU.
HE POPPED YOUR HEAD LIKE A GRAPE.
HA!
I'M GANGLION THE GRIM, WORLD'S MOST PUTRID WARLOCK.
YOU THINK THAT LITTLE SHIT COULD KILL ME?
YOU WANT TO SEE WHAT I'M DOING OVER HERE? COME HERE, I'LL SHOW YOU!
I WAS PLANNING ON LEAVING AFTER OUR GOBLET MISSION ANYWAY. THINGS ARE REALLY MOVING OVER HERE. ALL THE HELLS ARE IN UPHEAVEL SINCE ALVOSTAG WAS OVERTHROWN.
I JUST FIGURED I'D HELP BUILD YOUR REMAINING WARLOCK UP A BIT BEFORE I LEFT.
OH MY GOD!
YOU SERIOUSLY THOUGHT THAT IDIOT BEAT ME?
LOOK AT THIS.
GASP!

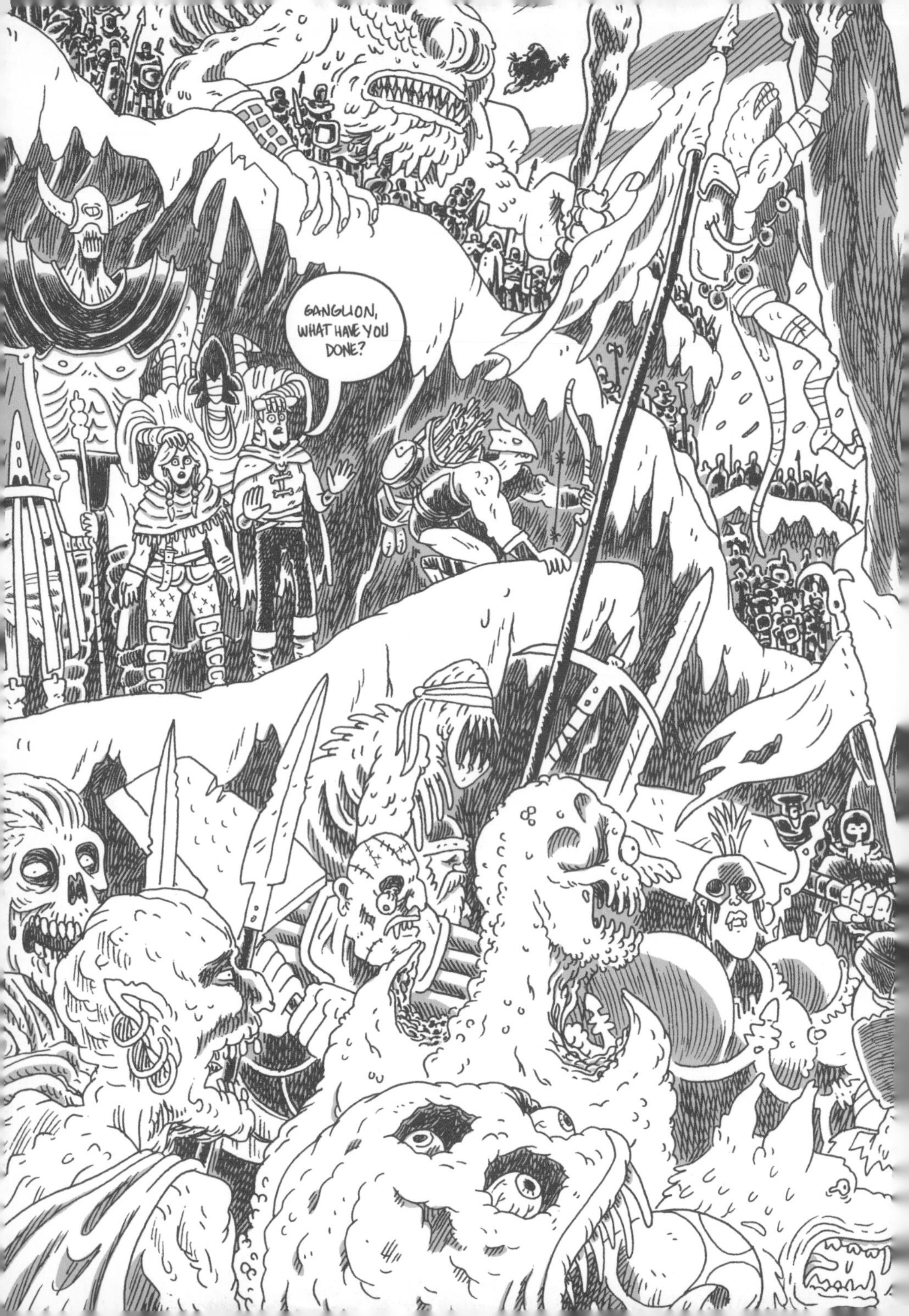
GANGLION, WHAT HAVE YOU DONE?

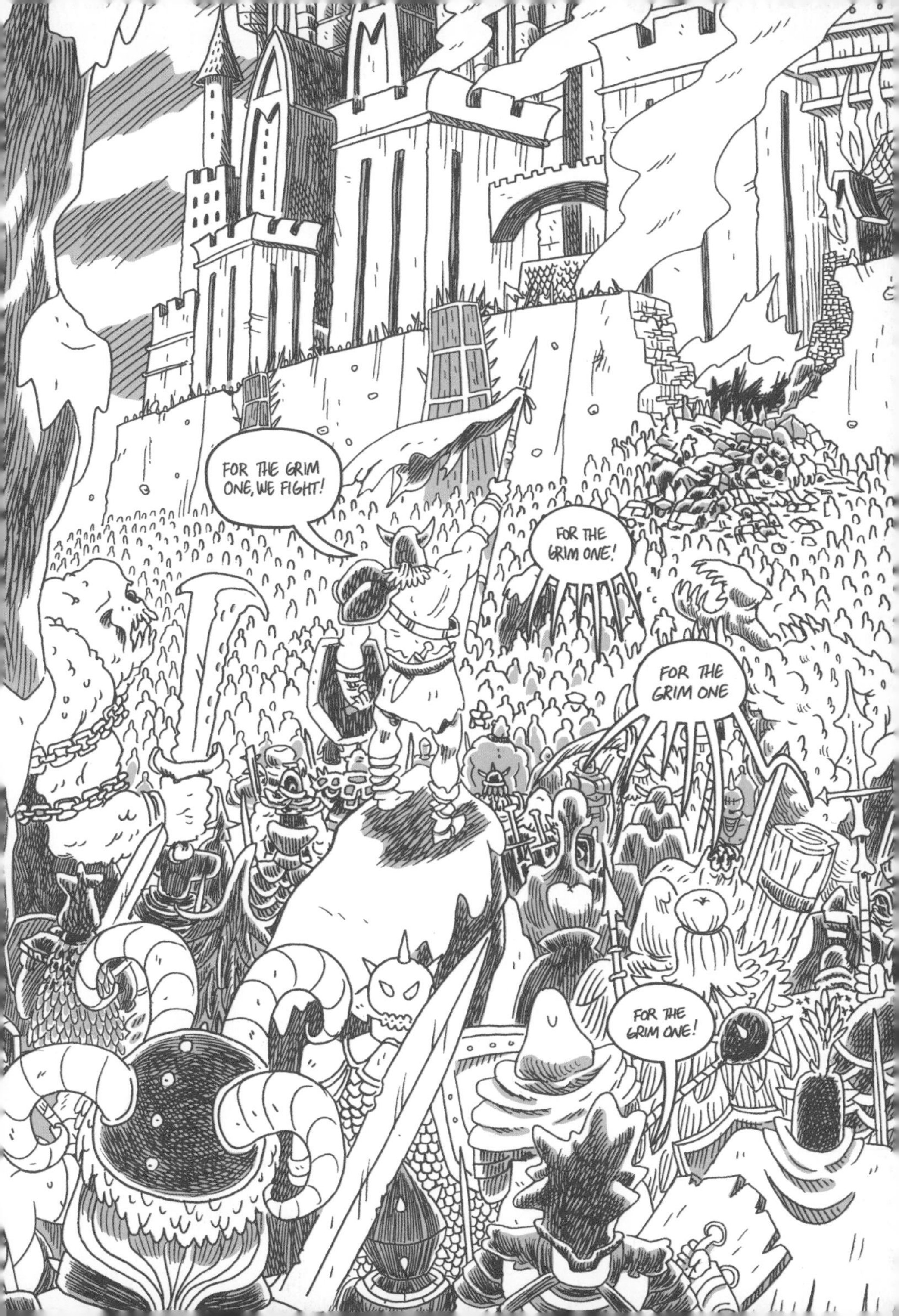
FOR THE GRIM ONE, WE FIGHT!
FOR THE GRIM ONE!
FOR THE GRIM ONE
FOR THE GRIM ONE!

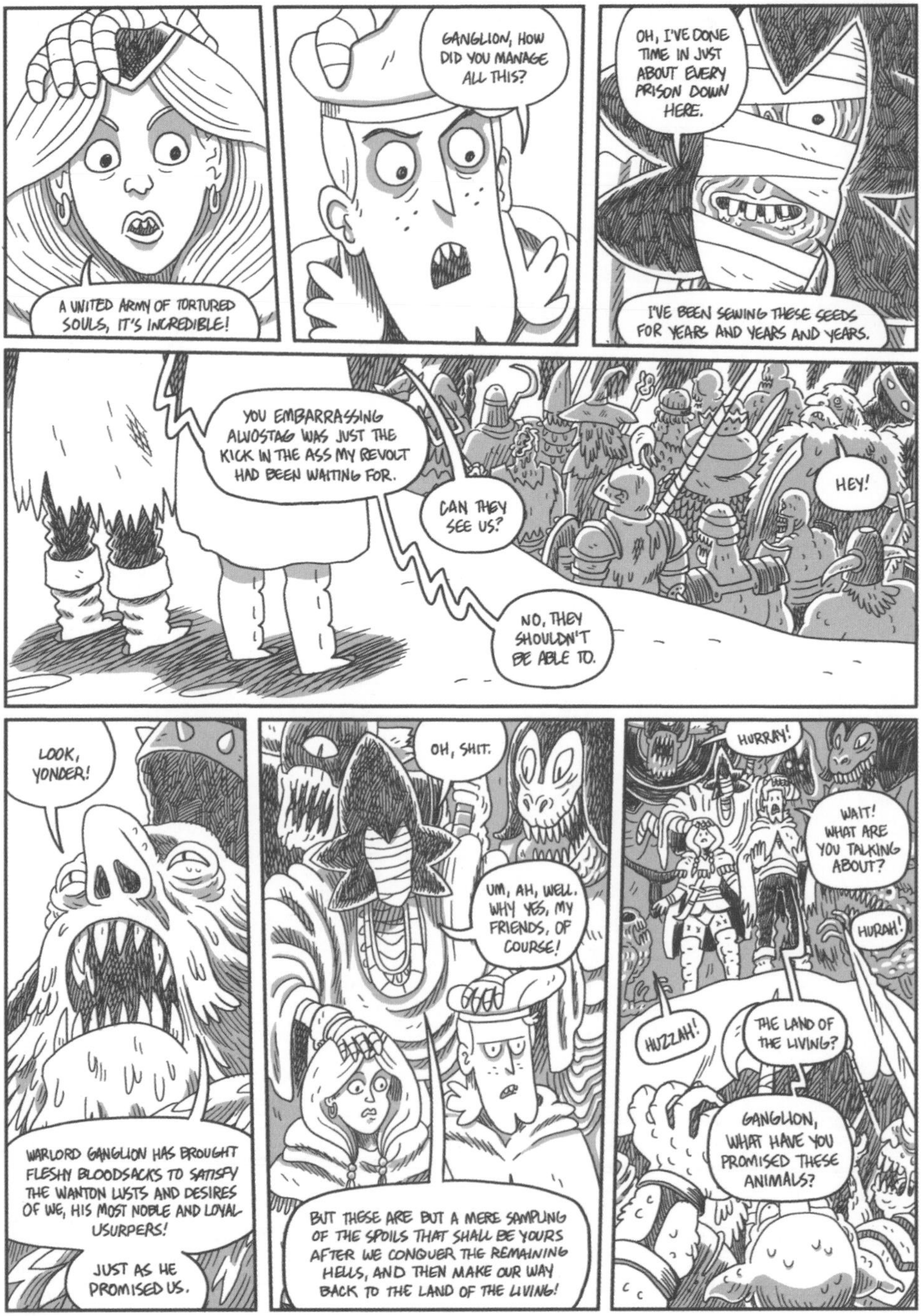
A UNITED ARMY OF TORTURED SOULS, IT'S INCREDIBLE!
GANGLION, HOW DID YOU MANAGE ALL THIS?
OH, I'VE DONE TIME IN JUST ABOUT EVERY PRISON DOWN HERE.
I'VE BEEN SEWING THESE SEEDS FOR YEARS AND YEARS AND YEARS.
YOU EMBARRASSING ALVOSTAG WAS JUST THE KICK IN THE ASS MY REVOLT HAD BEEN WAITING FOR.
CAN THEY SEE US?
HEY!
NO, THEY SHOULDN'T BE ABLE TO.
LOOK, YONDER!
WARLORD GANGLION HAS BROUGHT FLESHY BLOODSACKS TO SATISFY THE WANTON LUSTS AND DESIRES OF WE, HIS MOST NOBLE AND LOYAL USURPERS!
JUST AS HE PROMISED US.
OH, SHIT.
UM, AH, WELL. WHY YES, MY FRIENDS, OF COURSE!
BUT THESE ARE BUT A MERE SAMPLING OF THE SPOILS THAT SHALL BE YOURS AFTER WE CONQUER THE REMAINING HELLS, AND THEN MAKE OUR WAY BACK TO THE LAND OF THE LIVING!
HURRAY!
WAIT! WHAT ARE YOU TALKING ABOUT?
HURAH!
HUZZAH!
THE LAND OF THE LIVING?
GANGLION, WHAT HAVE YOU PROMISED THESE ANIMALS?

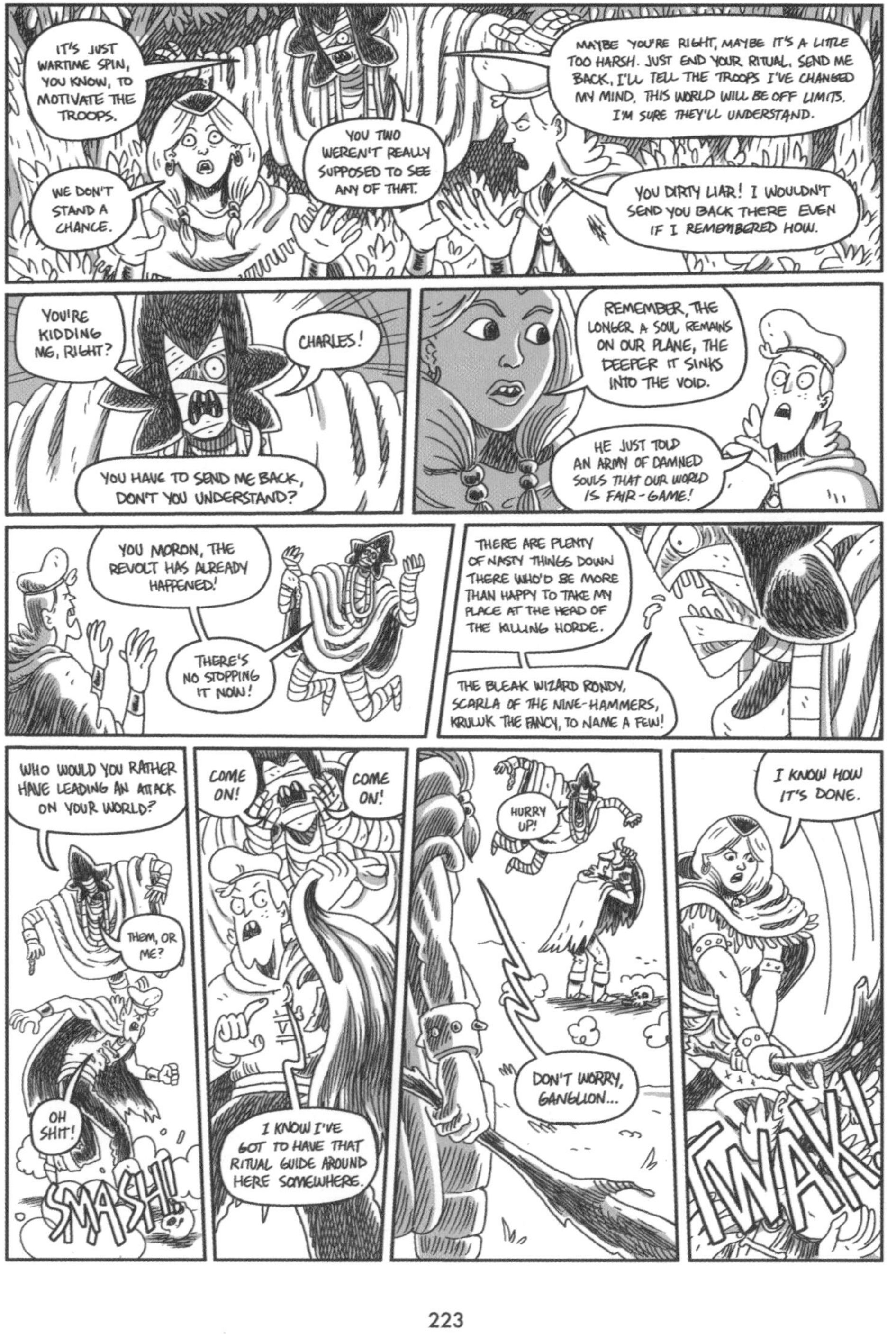
IT'S JUST WARTIME SPIN, YOU KNOW, TO MOTIVATE THE TROOPS.
WE DON'T STAND A CHANCE.
YOU TWO WEREN'T REALLY SUPPOSED TO SEE ANY OF THAT.
MAYBE YOU'RE RIGHT, MAYBE IT'S A LITTLE TOO HARSH. JUST END YOUR RITUAL, SEND ME BACK, I'LL TELL THE TROOPS I'VE CHANGED MY MIND. THIS WORLD WILL BE OFF LIMITS. I'M SURE THEY'LL UNDERSTAND.
YOU DIRTY LIAR! I WOULDN'T SEND YOU BACK THERE EVEN IF I REMEMBERED HOW.
YOU'RE KIDDING ME, RIGHT?
CHARLES!
YOU HAVE TO SEND ME BACK, DON'T YOU UNDERSTAND?
REMEMBER, THE LONGER A SOUL REMAINS ON OUR PLANE, THE DEEPER IT SINKS INTO THE VOID.
HE JUST TOLD AN ARMY OF DAMNED SOULS THAT OUR WORLD IS FAIR-GAME!
YOU MORON, THE REVOLT HAS ALREADY HAPPENED!
THERE'S NO STOPPING IT NOW!
THERE ARE PLENTY OF NASTY THINGS DOWN THERE WHO'D BE MORE THAN HAPPY TO TAKE MY PLACE AT THE HEAD OF THE KILLING HORDE.
THE BLEAK WIZARD RONDY, SCARLA OF THE NINE-HAMMERS, KRULUK THE FANCY, TO NAME A FEW!
WHO WOULD YOU RATHER HAVE LEADING AN ATTACK ON YOUR WORLD?
THEM, OR ME?
OH SHIT!
SMASH!
COME ON!
COME ON!
I KNOW I'VE GOT TO HAVE THAT RITUAL GUIDE AROUND HERE SOMEWHERE.
HURRY UP!
DON'T WORRY, GANGLION...
I KNOW HOW IT'S DONE.
TWAK!

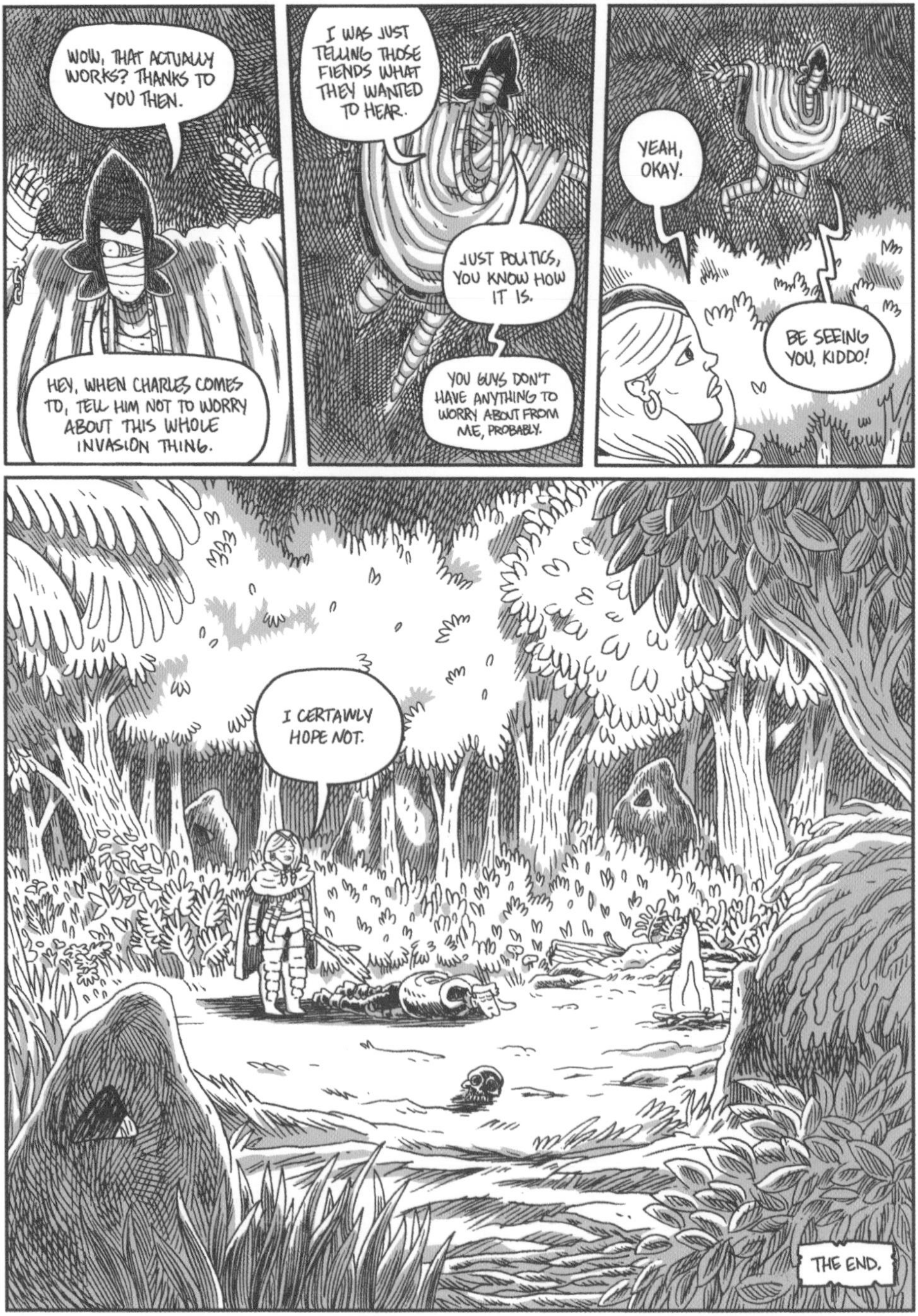
WOW, THAT ACTUALLY WORKS? THANKS TO YOU THEN.
HEY, WHEN CHARLES COMES TO, TELL HIM NOT TO WORRY ABOUT THIS WHOLE INVASION THING.
I WAS JUST TELLING THOSE FIENDS WHAT THEY WANTED TO HEAR.
JUST POLITICS, YOU KNOW HOW IT IS.
YOU GUYS DON'T HAVE ANYTHING TO WORRY ABOUT FROM ME, PROBABLY.
YEAH, OKAY.
BE SEEING YOU, KIDDO!
I CERTAINLY HOPE NOT.
THE END.

I NEED TO THANK TOM AND JORDAN FOR MAKING THIS BOOK POSSIBLE, AND LIZ FOR BEING SO GREAT, AND REWARD A BILLION XP TO THE REAL LIFE CLANDESTINAUTS, BRETT, SCOTT, KELLY, CORY, DONN, AND KATHLEEN FOR HELPING ME BUILD A WORLD THAT WAS SO MUCH FUN TO PLAY IN.

-TIM

TIM SIEVERT IS A CARTOONIST IN MINNEAPOLIS. HIS PUBLISHED WORKS INCLUDE *THAT SALTY AIR*, AND THE CURSE-ED TOME YOU NOW HOLD. DIDN'T KNOW IT WAS CURSED DID YOU? WELL, NOW YOU DO! HE CURRENTLY WORKS IN THE ANIMATION INDUSTRY, AND SPENDS HIS SUMMERS HUNTING BIGFOOT IN THE SOUTHERN UNITED STATES. EXPECT A BOOK ABOUT THOSE ADVENTURES IN THE NEAR FUTURE.

LISTEN, DON'T WORRY TO MUCH ABOUT THAT WHOLE CURSE THING. IT MOSTLY ENTAILS YOU BECOMING MANIACLY OBSESSED WITH VISITING WWW.TIMSIEVERT.COM, PRETTY HARMLESS REALLY.